Routledge Handbook of Fin Technology and Law

Financial technology is rapidly changing and shaping financial services and markets. These changes are considered making the future of finance a digital one.

This Handbook analyses developments in the financial services, products and markets that are being reshaped by technologically driven changes with a view to their policy, regulatory, supervisory and other legal implications. The Handbook aims to illustrate the crucial role the law has to play in tackling the revolutionary developments in the financial sector by offering a framework of legally enforceable principles and values in which such innovations might take place without threatening the acquis of financial markets law and more generally the rule of law and basic human rights.

With contributions from international leading experts, topics will include:

- Policy, High-level Principles, Trends and Perspectives
- Fintech and Lending
- Fintech and Payment Services
- Fintech, Investment and Insurance Services
- Fintech, Financial Inclusion and Sustainable Finance
- Cryptocurrencies and Cryptoassets
- Markets and Trading
- Regtech and Suptech

This Handbook will be of great relevance for practitioners and students alike, and a first reference point for academics researching in the fields of financial markets law.

Iris H-Y Chiu is a professor of Corporate Law and Financial Regulation at University College London (UCL) and Director of the UCL Centre of Ethics and Law, United Kingdom (UK). She is a research fellow of the European Corporate Governance Institute, and most recently, a senior scholar at the European Central Bank's Legal Research Programme.

Gudula Deipenbrock is a professor of Business Law at Hochschule für Technik und Wirtschaft (HTW) Berlin, University of Applied Sciences, Germany, and Associate Research Fellow 2020/2021 at Institute of Advanced Legal Studies (IALS), University of London, United Kingdom (UK).

Routledge Handbook of Financial Technology and Law

Edited by Iris H-Y Chiu and Gudula Deipenbrock

Routledge
Taylor & Francis Group

LONDON AND NEW YORK

First published 2021
by Routledge
2 Park Square, Milton Park, Abingdon, Oxon OX14 4RN

and by Routledge
52 Vanderbilt Avenue, New York, NY 10017

Routledge is an imprint of the Taylor & Francis Group, an informa business

British Library Cataloguing-in-Publication Data
A catalogue record for this book is available from the British Library

Library of Congress Cataloging-in-Publication Data
A catalog record has been requested for this book

ISBN: 978-0-367-34414-6 (hbk)
ISBN: 978-0-367-72655-3 (pbk)
ISBN: 978-0-429-32567-0 (ebk)

Typeset in Galliard
by KnowledgeWorks Global Ltd.

Contents

List of illustrations

Figures

Tables

Acknowledgements

From the many people having supported the production of the Routledge Handbook of Financial Technology and Law (handbook) the editors are grateful, first, to the contributors for sharing their expertise in this handbook and their responsiveness to our requirements in context with its production. The editors are grateful also to Saule T Omarova, Florian Möslein and Emilios Avgouleas for having accepted the invitation to serve on the editorial advisory board for the handbook. Gudula is particularly grateful to her home institution for granting her a research leave in 2019 and to both, the Faculty of Law of the European University Institute in Florence, Italy, and the Institute of European and Comparative Law of the University of Oxford, United Kingdom (UK), for warmly welcoming her as Visiting Fellow/Academic Visitor for time periods in 2019 and offering great opportunities for inspiring discussions on the broader issue of law in the digital age. Gudula is also grateful for her Associate Research Fellowship at IALS, University of London, United Kingdom (UK), granted for the academic years 2018/2019, 2019/2020 and 2020/2021, particularly allowing her to feel part of a wider, international community of legal academics. Iris wishes to thank the Centre for Ethics and Law, UCL, in particular its Advisory Board for supporting her research. The editors also wish to thank the publisher for inviting them to compile this handbook.

Introduction

Advances in financial technology occur at an accelerating pace. They manifest in a profound and an equally rapid transformation of financial services, products and markets. Both incumbent and new actors make use of further advancing financial technologies, new interfaces and markets thereby challenging particularly the way financial products and services have traditionally been intermediated.[1] This affects all three sectors of financial markets: banking, capital markets and insurance. This transformation scenario in financial markets bears the potential of a crisis scenario calling for timely adequate responses by policymakers, legislators, regulators and supervisors worldwide to mitigate the latter by particularly addressing systemic risks, cybersecurity risks, and – more generally – profound risks to the value systems of liberal democratic states, fundamental rights and the rule of law.[2] Financial markets have traditionally spearheaded global, interconnected and flexible business by fostering and using financial innovation and they appear to remain the vanguard also in digital transformation. In this manner, the relevant policy, legislative, regulatory and supervisory responses to financial innovation can be a blueprint for innovation in other sectors.[3] The policy and legal implications of rapidly further evolving financial technology are complex. Research on it has gained considerable momentum challenged particularly by identifying core concepts in the field and defining adequately financial technology or Fintech – the abbreviation widely used in this context – as a prerequisite of any legal-systematic analysis.[4] Originally inspired by the seminal definitional approaches of relevant policy makers such as the Financial Stability Board and the European Commission, the editors developed the idea of the 'Routledge Handbook of Financial Technology and Law' (handbook) however with a focus on the manifold concrete different manifestations of financial technology.

---

1   For an early in-depth discussion on the disruptive potential of Fintech highlighting market themes and changes in legal technology and regulatory implications, in respect of financial product development, financial intermediation interfaces, and/or financial markets and value networks, see, eg, Iris H-Y Chiu, 'Fintech and Disruptive Business Models in Financial Products, Intermediation and Markets – Policy Implications for Financial Regulators' (2016) 21 Journal of Technology Law & Policy 167.
2   See, eg, Gudula Deipenbrock, 'Editorial Introduction of Special Issue: FinTech, InsurTech and the Digital Transformation of Financial Markets – Current Legal and Economic Challenges' (2020) 31 EBLR 1, 1.
3   See, eg, Gudula Deipenbrock, 'Is the Law Ready to Face the Progressing Digital Revolution? – General Policy Issues and Selected Aspects in the Realm of Financial Markets from the International, European Union and German Perspective' (2019) 118 ZVglRWiss 285, 302 et seq.
4   For more information on the definitional approaches and usage of the term Fintech, see Gudula Deipenbrock, 'FinTech – Unbearably Lithe or Reasonably Agile? – A Critical Legal Approach from the German Perspective' (2020) 31 EBLR 3, 3 and 5 et seq.

This introduction hence will abstain from endorsing any one definition of Fintech in order not to prejudice the relevant approaches taken in the chapters compiled in this handbook.

The manifestations of Fintech are diverse and evolve rapidly. Early categorisations of Fintech activities include the realms of (1) payments, clearing and settlement, (2) deposits, lending and capital raising, (3) insurance, (4) investment management and (5) market support.[5] The transformative depth and thrust of innovative financial technology as well as the extent of the disruption caused by its multiple manifestations vary. Already in 2017, the Financial Stability Board observed that innovation in the realm of Fintech is different from preceding changes in financial services as different technologies are tightly integrated in new ways (process innovation), new players might move fast and with agility through the system development life cycle, the scope of innovation in financial services is greater, and the rate of the adoption of such financial services might be quicker.[6] The essence of these observations appear so far to have proved well founded. A constantly accelerating pace and widening scope of financial innovation including high agility of both the relevant players and adopters worldwide call for an equally agile legal, regulatory and supervisory framework for navigating the relevant changing features of financial markets and beyond. Academics and researchers particularly in the realms of information technology, law, ethics and economics have a crucial role to play, here. Their research has to be unbiased by conflicts of interest, committed to the principle of objectivity and fundamental legal and ethical standards. This would prepare a solid ground on which policy makers, legislators, regulators and supervisors can base their policies, laws, relevant approaches and decisions.

Law and regulation have regularly taken a backward-looking approach to reform. In crisis scenarios, focus has primarily been on investigating their causes. Once past events, constellations, structures and conditions have been identified as causal factors, tools are designed aiming at preventing them from occurring anew. In contrast to that, the current digital transformation scenario is in need of a profoundly different approach. The perspective should be future-oriented. Particularly the profound risks linked to technologies such as artificial intelligence and machine learning require that any meaningful analysis and research have to anticipate future scenarios in order to design solutions to prevent worst-case scenarios from happening. Such a forward-looking approach however entails that the current state of the art including the status of development and usage of financial technologies are transparent and well understood. Here, however, lies the crux of the matter. The rapid pace of the digital transformation of financial products, services, players and markets profoundly hampers taking stock. Furthermore, the idiosyncrasies of financial technologies are conducive to opacity rather than transparency of the relevant market activities. Among them are particularly the complexity of financial technologies including the continuously advancing specialism in this field. Agility in the development and application of financial technologies – whether facilitating, improving or replacing customary financial services and products or their intermediation – adds to the problem.

---

5 Financial Stability Board, *Financial Stability Implications from FinTech – Supervisory and Regulatory Issues that Merit Authorities' Attention* (27 June 2017) 8 and 25 et seq.
6 Financial Stability Board, *Financial Stability Implications from FinTech – Supervisory and Regulatory Issues that Merit Authorities' Attention* (27 June 2017) Annex A – Common Drivers of Fintech Innovations, 36.

The multiple manifestations of Fintech also challenge well-established legal and regulatory concepts and taxonomies of financial objects. Cryptocurrencies and cryptoassets vis-à-vis money and assets are examples, here. As to financial technology trends, particularly the further development and use of distributed ledger technology, artificial intelligence and machine learning are expected to play a growing crucial role in the financial sector and beyond. Distributed ledger technology has inter alia facilitated the rise of peer-to-peer-spaces for financial activity thereby challenging traditional institutional models and structures.[7] Furthermore, (exponential) advances in and the use of artificial intelligence and machine learning raise not only legal and regulatory but profound ethical issues apart from those already covered by fundamental human rights. They urgently require a broad societal discussion on how to best contain the real risk of unleashed developments in this field.

Against the backdrop of the above observations, the coverage and scope of any handbook in this realm might only be limited. This is true for the range of topics addressed in the chapters compiled as well as the depth of the analysis provided. Each topic discussed in the chapters selected for the purpose of this handbook appears to lead to a plethora of other new problems. The editors selected those topics for the various chapters that – once compiled – provide a coverage of pivotal up-to-date policy, legal, regulatory and supervisory issues in a rapidly evolving and expanding realm of financial markets. Apart from the challenge of selecting appropriate topics to be covered, the exponentially growing ramifications of and interrelations between financial technologies and the effects on their use in the financial sector made it also difficult to arrange them in a legal-methodologically convincing way. Widely agreed core concepts covering manifestations of Fintech in financial markets law are so far lacking. The editors eventually made the relevant choices, however with the caveat that there might be manifold other ways of compiling a handbook of financial technology and law. This handbook represents the editors' (current) way of doing so. It aims to cover both general policy issues, high-level principles and perspectives as well as concrete relevant policy, legal, regulatory and supervisory implications of various applications of Fintech, in sectoral and cross-sectoral ways.

Overview of the handbook

Part I of the handbook addresses policy issues, high-level principles, trends and perspectives in context with Fintech from the perspective of law and regulation. The subjects of chapters range from legal-methodological challenges in the field of artificial intelligence and machine learning (Deipenbrock), civil law challenges in context with smart contracts (Möslein) to regulatory challenges (Omarova, Ford) while also addressing disintermediation from the view of Law and Economics (Kaja, Martino and Pacces), and systemic risks issues linked to Fintech from an economic perspective (Eickstädt, Horsch). The chapters on regulatory challenges in particular pose queries to policy makers, legislators, regulators

---

7 For more information on pressing issues in context with cryptoasset trading platforms, see, eg, Board of the International Organization of Securities Commissions (OICV-IOSCO), *Issues, Risks and Regulatory Considerations Relating to Crypto-Asset Trading Platforms – Final Report* (FR02/2020, February 2020).

and supervisors, and urge shifts in their mind-sets to better and more effectively respond to innovation.

Parts II to IV of the handbook are grouped according to early categorisations of manifestations of Fintech. They provide dedicated discussions on Fintech in the realm of lending, payment services, investment services and insurance. These innovations challenge established sectors of financial markets. Part II focuses on innovations in lending with a critical account of the recent growth of the Fintech credit industry including the evolution of lending platforms and its implications for financial services (De Pascalis) and a critical discussion of Fintech in consumer credit markets (Aggarwal). Part III discusses Fintech and payment services. The EU Payment Services Regulation and relevant international developments are critically explored, particularly with a view to their impact on the market place (Brener), complemented by a thought-provoking analysis of liability concepts in European financial markets regulation making a convincing case for developing European liability concepts in light of the pivotal regulative objectives of financial stability and client protection (Eidsand Kjørven). Part IV highlights Fintech in the realm of investment and insurance services. Here, robo advice appears to epitomise the Janus-faced character of financial innovation in the realm of investment services. Its benefits and risks for retail investors, as well as its potential as a source of systemic risk require a profound assessment before further adjusting the relevant regulatory environment (Ringe, Ruof). Financial innovation also transforms other important sectors of financial markets such as the insurance sector. Particularly data management and automated decision-making in the insurance business raise manifold legal and regulatory issues such as the 'right to an explanation' to be tackled in order to reap the benefits of the relevant technologies (Manes). The exploration of systemic risk is also taken further in relation to the marriage between Fintech and the strategy of passive investing, in the form of exchange-traded funds (Cullen).

Part V of the handbook addresses the role of Fintech in context with the broader concepts of financial inclusion and sustainable finance including that of disintermediation. In reflecting such overarching themes, Part V connects back to Part I. The chapters discuss Fintech as one element to support achieving the UN Sustainable Development Goals (Buckley, Zetzsche, Arner, Veidt) and address inter alia also in context with the role of Fintech as a driver for financial inclusion the advantages and risks linked to the digital transformation of financial services (Alexander, Karametaxas). In this Part, the role of crowd-sourced finance for small business fund-raising in the EU, as a matter of financial inclusion, is also explored, in particular as to whether the recent regulatory efforts with a view to European crowd-funding would meet policy goals (Macchiavello).

Part VI then turns to cryptocurrencies and cryptoassets. These manifestations of financial innovation also profoundly challenge prominently established legal concepts and regulatory and supervisory approaches. From the multiple issues requiring a thorough legal analysis the chapters compiled here dwell on those exemplifying best the (accelerating) pace, scope and implications of these constantly further developing phenomena. Cryptoassets call for – apart from adequate responses needed in the regulatory context – particularly a thorough analysis of their dogmatic implications from the private law perspective (Allen). Cryptocurrencies have undergone considerable evolution from 'money' to 'asset' (Anderson Schillig), resulting in constituting a new asset class, permanently changing and thereby putting pressure on law and regulation to keep pace (Lee). The specific case of using distributed ledger technology in the realm of sovereign financing and sovereign borrowing in particular provides another interesting example of the legal challenges resulting from such use (Iversen).

Part VII addresses markets and trading. The chapter on high-frequency trading allows particularly insights into how different features of such trading practices might challenge the efficacy of European regulatory efforts (Myklebust). Equally thought-provoking is the analysis of 'trustless' distributed ledgers and custodial services (Solinas).

Part VIII complements the preceding analyses by discussing the phenomena of Regtech and Suptech. A welcome contribution to the evolving (legal) taxonomy in this field is the suggested distinction of three types of Regtech in order also to better explore the benefits and challenges of Regtech including the changing role of supervisors (Colaert). This is complemented by critical observations on the use of Suptech particularly from the institutional perspective (Chirulli). Both chapters show how pivotal the role of regulatory and supervisory authorities is in facilitating, shaping and monitoring the digital transformation of financial markets.

Final remarks

Some final remarks shall conclude this introduction. The chapters are written in a form, which the editors consider suitable for both audience inside and outside academia. This might include advanced students, scholars, policy makers, legislators and legal practitioners including those new to the area as well as those already working in the field. Regulatory and supervisory authorities as well as relevant financial markets players might equally profit from reading the handbook. The authors of chapters include senior figures who have shaped the understanding of Fintech from the legal perspective for quite some time but also younger researchers who have just started to do so. The approaches and views of the authors also reflect the various legal traditions and systems they represent. This makes this handbook attractive particularly to an international audience. The chapters are conceived as stand-alone ones. Any overlap between different chapters might well illustrate the variety of approaches to and views on shared issues.

List of contributors

Editors

Iris H-Y Chiu is a professor of Corporate Law and Financial Regulation at University College London (UCL) and Director of the UCL Centre of Ethics and Law, United Kingdom (UK). She is a research fellow of the European Corporate Governance Institute, and most recently, a senior scholar at the European Central Bank's Legal Research Programme.

Gudula Deipenbrock is a professor of Business Law at Hochschule für Technik und Wirtschaft (HTW) Berlin, University of Applied Sciences, Germany, and Associate Research Fellow 2020/2021 at Institute of Advanced Legal Studies (IALS), University of London, United Kingdom (UK).

Contributors

Nikita Aggarwal is a PhD candidate at the Faculty of Law, University of Oxford, and a research associate at the Oxford Internet Institute's Digital Ethics Lab, United Kingdom (UK).

Kern Alexander holds the Chair for Law and Finance and is a professor of International Financial Law and Banking Regulation, Faculty of Law, University of Zurich, Switzerland.

Jason Grant Allen is a senior research fellow at the Humboldt-Universität Berlin Centre for British Studies, Germany, and holds affiliations at the Cambridge Centre for Alternative Finance, the Queen Mary University London Centre for Commercial Law Studies, both United Kingdom (UK), and the University of Tasmania Faculty of Law, Australia.

Douglas W Arner is the Kerry Holdings Professor in Law and Director of the Asian Institute of International Financial Law at the University of Hong Kong (HKU). He is a senior visiting fellow of Melbourne Law School, University of Melbourne, Australia.

Alan Brener is a teaching fellow at both University College London's Law Faculty and at the Centre for Commercial Law Studies (CCLS), Queen Mary University of London, United Kingdom (UK). He is Deputy Director of the Centre for Ethics and Law at University College London and a council member of The Chartered Institute of Bankers in Scotland.

Ross P Buckley is the KPMG Law and King & Wood Mallesons Professor of Disruptive Innovation and Law, and a Scientia Professor at the University of New South Wales in Sydney, Australia. He chairs the Digital Finance Advisory Panel of the Australian Securities and Investments Commission.

Paola Chirulli is a professor of Administrative Law at Sapienza University of Rome, Italy.

Veerle Colaert holds the Chair for Financial Law at KU Leuven University and is co-director of the KU Leuven Jan Ronse Institute for Company and Financial Law, Belgium. She is the Chair of the Securities and Markets Stakeholders Group (SMSG) advising the European Securities and Markets Authority (ESMA). She is also a member of the Belgian Resolution Authority and a member of the board of directors of the Belgian branch of the European Association for Banking and Financial Law (AEDBF Belgium).

Jay Cullen is a professor of Financial Regulation at the University of York, United Kingdom (UK), and an adjunct research professor at the University of Oslo, Norway.

Gudula Deipenbrock is a professor of Business Law at Hochschule für Technik und Wirtschaft (HTW) Berlin, University of Applied Sciences, Germany, and Associate Research Fellow 2020/2021 at Institute of Advanced Legal Studies (IALS), University of London, United Kingdom (UK).

Francesco De Pascalis is a senior lecturer in Financial Law at Brunel Law School, United Kingdom (UK).

Anja Eickstädt is a research associate at the Chair of Business Administration, esp. Investment and Finance at Technische Universität Bergakademie Freiberg, Germany.

Marte Eidsand Kjørven is a professor in the Department of Private Law at the Faculty of Law, University of Oslo, Norway. She is Vice Chairman of the Oslo Centre for Commercial Law (OSKR), where she also leads the Consumer Law Pillar.

Fatjon Kaja is a lecturer in Law and Economics at the University of Amsterdam and a research associate at the Amsterdam Center for Law and Economics (ACLE), Netherlands.

Cristie Ford is a professor and Associate Dean at the Allard School of Law, University of British Columbia, Vancouver, Canada.

Andreas Horsch holds the Chair of Business Administration, esp. Investment and Finance at Technische Universität Bergakademie Freiberg, Germany.

Astrid Iversen is an associate professor in Law at Inland Norway University of Applied Sciences, Norway.

Xenia Karametaxas is a lecturer in Commercial Law, Faculty of Law, University of Zurich, Switzerland.

Joseph Lee is a senior lecturer in Law at Exeter Law School, United Kingdom (UK).

Eugenia Macchiavello is an assistant professor in Business Law and Banking Law at University of Genoa (Italian licence as an associate professor in Economic Law), Italy.

Paola Manes is a professor of Private Law at University of Bologna, Italy.

Edoardo D Martino is a postdoctoral researcher at the University of Amsterdam and a research associate at the Amsterdam Center for Law and Economics (ACLE), Netherlands.

Florian Möslein is Director of the Institute for Law and Regulation of Digitalisation (www. irdi.institute) and a professor of Law at the Philipps-University Marburg, Germany.

Trude Myklebust is a PhD researcher at the University of Oslo, Norway. She is currently a member of the board of the Norwegian Bank's Guarantee Fund (the Norwegian deposit insurance scheme) and a member of the Council on Ethics for the Norwegian Government Pension Fund Global.

Saule T Omarova is the Beth and Marc Goldberg Professor of Law at Cornell University, United States of America (USA). She is the Director of the Program on the Law and Regulation of Financial Institutions and Markets of Cornell's Jack Clarke Institute for the Study and Practice of Business Law.

Alessio M Pacces is a professor of Law and Finance at the University of Amsterdam and the Director of the Amsterdam Center for Law & Economics (ACLE), Netherlands.

Wolf-Georg Ringe is a professor of Law and Finance and Director of the Institute of Law & Economics at the University of Hamburg, Germany. He is also a visiting professor at the University of Oxford, United Kingdom (UK).

Christopher Ruof is a research associate and PhD candidate at the Institute of Law & Economics, University of Hamburg, Germany.

Michael Anderson Schillig is a professor of Law at King's College London, United Kingdom (UK).

Matteo Solinas is a senior lecturer in Commercial Law at the Law Faculty of Victoria University of Wellington, New Zealand.

Robin Veidt is a research associate at the ADA Chair in Financial Law (Inclusive Finance) of Dirk A Zetzsche at the University of Luxembourg, Luxembourg.

Dirk A Zetzsche is a professor in Law and holds the ADA Chair in Financial Law (Inclusive Finance) at the University of Luxembourg, Luxembourg, as well as a directorship at the Center for Business and Corporate Law at the University of Düsseldorf, Germany. He is a research fellow of and heading the FinTech Working Group of the European Banking Institute.

Part I

Policy, high-level principles, trends and perspectives

Part 1

1 Artificial intelligence and machine learning in the financial sector

Legal-methodological challenges of steering towards a regulatory 'whitebox'

Gudula Deipenbrock

1 Introduction

Artificial Intelligence[1] (AI)[2] and Machine Learning (ML)[3] are ubiquitous phenomena.[4] Their use has powerful implications, however Janus-faced. Amongst the interrelated challenges are particularly the degradation of truth and precision surveillance.[5] Technological advances outpace relevant policies as 'The Global Risks Report 2020' of the World Economic Forum (WEF Risks Report) states,[6] rightly. In addition, technological rivalries render the future geopolitical scenario uncertain.[7] Data are a key aspect in AI techniques.[8] The data race to foster AI has been unleashed for quite some time with both private and public actors at a global scale.[9] Legal frameworks as to personal and

---

1 All following references to items are references to items of this chapter. All following references to sources use the same writing of titles as to capital letters for reasons of stylistic consistency.
2 See the definitional approaches in item 2.1.1 of this chapter.
3 See the definitional approaches in item 2.1.2.
4 With a view to AI, see eg, De Nederlandsche Bank – here Joost van der Burgt, *General Principles for the Use of Artificial Intelligence in the Financial Sector* (2019) 33.
5 Eleonore Pauwels, *The New Geopolitics of Artificial Intelligence* (15 October 2018) <www.weforum.org/agenda/2018/10/artificial-intelligence-ai-new-geopolitics-un> (Call-off date for all hyperlinks, unless stated otherwise: 28 May 2020).
6 See World Economic Forum – here Emilio Granados Franco (lead author) et al – in partnership with Marsh & McLennan and Zurich Insurance Group, *The Global Risks Report 2020* (15th edn, no date) 64 et seq.
7 Compare also eg, World Economic Forum – here Emilio Granados Franco (lead author) et al, *WEF Risks Report* (n 6) 14 et seq.
8 See eg, Ronan Hamon, Henrik Junklewitz and Ignacio Sanchez, *JRC Technical Report – Robustness and Explainability of Artificial Intelligence* (EUR 30040 EN, Publications Office of the European Union 2020) 7.
9 See already Gudula Deipenbrock, 'Is the Law Ready to Face the Progressing Digital Revolution? – General Policy Issues and Selected Aspects in the Realm of Financial Markets from the International, European Union and German Perspective' (2019) 118 ZVglRWiss 285, 293.

non-personal data[10] are crucial, here. The focus has gradually shifted from data governance to AI governance.[11] Policy makers at international, European Union (EU) – here particularly the European Commission (Commission) – and national level have acknowledged the need for more general policies in the context of AI.[12] International initiatives developing governance standards for AI have emerged.[13] Such growing awareness of the urgency of the matter is desirable. But the current disruption of the multinational system fosters fragmentation rather than alignment of the responses to the significant risks.[14] The global challenges of AI development, however, require global governance.[15] At supranational level such as in the EU, one might observe a first move in this direction: the emergence of AI regulation.[16] Legal academia is alert to it. It has started to contribute to the discussion of AI regulation.[17]

These more general observations in mind, the chapter zooms in on the financial sector. In the financial sector,[18] the Financial Stability Board (FSB)[19] has dedicated its report 'Artificial Intelligence and Machine Learning in Financial Services' (FSB Report AI and ML)[20] to the matter quite early. In the FSB's view, the use of AI and ML is spreading rapidly while assessing it remains constantly provisional due to the paucity of (each) current robust data.[21] The pressure for change on actors in the financial sector is huge; their digitalisation strategies might well become a litmus test for whether they serve

10 At EU level, the more general starting point is the Charter of Fundamental Rights of the European Union [2012] OJ EU C 326/391 and more specifically inter alia the following regulations: Regulation (EU) 2016/679 of the European Parliament and of the Council of 27 April 2016 on the protection of natural persons with regard to the processing of personal data and on the free movement of such data, and repealing Directive 95/46/EC (General Data Protection Regulation) [2016] OJ EU L 119/1, and Regulation (EU) 2018/1807 of the European Parliament and of the Council of 14 November 2018 on a framework for the free flow of non-personal data in the European Union [2018] OJ EU L 303/59.

11 See Ronan Hamon, Henrik Junklewitz and Ignacio Sanchez (n 8) 9.

12 See Gudula Deipenbrock, 'FinTech – Unbearably Lithe or Reasonably Agile? – A Critical Legal Approach from the German Perspective' (2020) 31 EBLR 3, 30.

13 For more information on this, see eg, Peter Cihon, *Technical Report – Standards for AI Governance: International Standards to Enable Global Coordination in AI Research & Development* (April 2019).

14 Compare also eg, World Economic Forum – here Emilio Granados Franco (lead author) et al, *WEF Risks Report* (n 6) 64, which calls for multilateral cooperation, here.

15 For more information on this recommending international standards as tools of AI policy, see eg, Peter Cihon (n 13) 7 et seq. and 32.

16 See also eg, Heinz-Uwe Dettling and Stefan Krüger, 'Erste Schritte im Recht der Künstlichen Intelligenz – Entwurf der "Ethik-Leitlinien für eine vertrauenswürdige KI"' (2019) MMR 211, 217.

17 For more information on this, see eg, Thomas Wischmeyer and Timo Rademacher (eds), *Regulating Artificial Intelligence* (Springer 2020). See also Mario Martini, *Blackbox Algorithmus – Grundfragen einer Regulierung Künstlicher Intelligenz* (Springer 2019).

18 If not expressly indicated otherwise, the term financial sector shall include financial services, financial markets and thereby include both FinTech – see the definitional approach in item 2 – firms and incumbent firms as actors.

19 For more information on the FSB as an international body, promoting global financial stability by coordinating the development of regulatory, supervisory and other financial sector policies, and conducting outreach to non-member countries, see FSB <www.fsb.org/work-of-the-fsb>.

20 FSB, *Artificial Intelligence and Machine Learning in Financial Services – Market Developments and Financial Stability Implications* (1 November 2017).

21 FSB, *FSB Report AI and ML* (n 20) 1 and 3.

the good of human beings.[22] The use of AI and ML requires close monitoring.[23] Policy and law makers as well as regulators and supervisors worldwide have to be utmost alert to its disruptive potential. The latter includes fundamental technological risks requiring profound AI safety research and work.[24] Value alignment[25] is discussed, here. The same is true for the control problem.[26] A global, concerted, far-sighted, long-term oriented, responsible and sustainable governance of AI and ML is the urgent law of reason. It shall ensure a regulatory 'whitebox'. The discourse on AI and ML requires rationalisation as observed by experts ranging from moral philosophers[27] to the World Economic Forum in its report 'The New Physics of Financial Services' (WEF New Physics Report)[28] with a view to the financial sector. The chapter aims to contribute to such rationalisation. Focus is on the legal-methodological perspective. It is organised as follows. After this introduction, the chapter discusses selected pivotal legal-methodological challenges to be tackled at the outset of any policy, legal, particularly regulatory and supervisory approach to AI and ML in the financial sector. It seeks to address the following questions. How might AI, ML and related phenomena best be defined? How might one best relate AI and ML to law, methodologically? Is it necessary to put (the policy and legal (-political) approach to) the sector-specific use of AI and ML in the financial sector in context with that to the more general use of AI and ML? What challenges are to be tackled to establish the relevant facts of the case? The chapter then concludes. The strict limitations as to the volume of this chapter require a strict selection of issues discussed. Any reference to relevant sources and (legal) literature is also limited to more exemplary sources.

2 Pivotal legal-methodological challenges – a selection

The chapter begins with exploring the definitional approaches to AI, ML and related phenomena. It then introduces a legal-methodological approach to relating AI and ML to

---

22 For more information on the discussion in the realm of ethics, see eg, Julian Nida-Rümelin and Nathalie Weidenfeld, *Digitaler Humanismus – Eine Ethik für das Zeitalter der Künstlichen Intelligenz* (Piper 2018) 77 et seq.

23 See from the financial stability perspective eg, FSB, *FSB Report AI and ML* (n 20) 1.

24 See in this context also Max Tegmark, 'Let's Aspire to More than Making Ourselves Obsolete' in John Brockman (ed), *Possible Minds – Twenty-Five Ways of Looking at AI* (Penguin Press 2019) 76, 81 et seq., who argues that the controversial position on AI safety research is no longer to advocate for it but to dismiss it.

25 See eg, Tom Griffiths, 'The Artificial Use of Human Beings' in John Brockman (ed), *Possible Minds – Twenty-Five Ways of Looking at AI* (Penguin Press 2019) 125, 128 et seq.

26 See eg, Stuart Russell, *Human Compatible: Artificial Intelligence and the Problem of Control* (Penguin Random House 2019).

27 See eg, Julian Nida-Rümelin, 'Preface' in Julian Nida-Rümelin and Nathalie Weidenfeld, *Digitaler Humanismus – Eine Ethik für das Zeitalter der Künstlichen Intelligenz* (Piper 2018) 9, 11, who argues that there is beyond apocalyptic disaster scenarios and 'technicism-based' hopes of salvation a middle course of maintaining and improving the human living conditions through culturally, socially and politically controlled use of technological means.

28 See World Economic Forum – here R. Jesse McWaters (lead author) et al – prepared in collaboration with Deloitte, *The New Physics of Financial Services – Understanding how Artificial Intelligence is Transforming the Financial Ecosystem* (August 2018) 9, stating that the public discourse on AI in financial services is highly sensationalised, creating an excess of both exuberance and fear. Please see the disclaimer (World Economic Forum – here R. Jesse McWaters (lead author) et al, *WEF New Physics Report*, 1).

law. A discussion on the need to approach AI and ML in the financial sector for legal purposes from a macro perspective follows. Observations on the challenge of establishing the relevant facts of the case[29] and the 'FinTech[30] information mismatch'[31] supplement the preceding analysis.

2.1 *Definitions*

Any legal-systematic approach to AI and ML requires defining it at the outset. The latter is a legal-methodological *conditio sine qua non*.[32] It is the starting point of any AI governance and AI regulation.[33] It is equally important for any empirical study. At EU level, the Commission has paved the way for the former in its 'White Paper on Artificial Intelligence – A European Approach to Excellence and Trust' (Commission White Paper AI).[34] The need to clarify the scope of any such regulatory framework for AI becomes urgent.[35] For the purpose of this chapter, focus is primarily on definitions of relevant policy makers. At international, particularly the G20 states (G20) level, the approach of the FSB[36] is relevant. At EU level, the approach of the Commission is important. The von der Leyen Commission rests on the relevant initiatives of the previous Commission as to AI.[37] Also relevant is the Independent High-Level Expert Group on AI (High-Level Expert Group on AI)[38] set up by the Commission. The same is true for the regulatory and supervisory view of the European Supervisory Authorities (ESAs) – the European Banking Authority (EBA), the European Securities and Markets Authority (ESMA), the European Insurance and Occupational Pensions Authority (EIOPA) and the Joint Committee of the ESAs. At national level, the view of the German Federal Financial Supervisory Authority – the

---

29 For more information on this with further references in context with FinTech, see Gudula Deipenbrock (n 9) 304 et seq., and Gudula Deipenbrock (n 12) 16.

30 The chapter follows the Commission's approach which refers to the FSB defining FinTech as a term used to describe technology-enabled innovation in financial services that could result in new business models, applications, processes or products and could have an associated material effect on financial markets and institutions and how financial services are provided. See Commission, Communication from the Commission to the European Parliament, the Council, the European Central Bank, the European Economic and Social Committee and the Committee of the Regions, *FinTech Action Plan: For a More Competitive and Innovative European Financial Sector* (COM [2018] 109 final, 8 March 2018) 2. For more information on this with further references, see Gudula Deipenbrock (n 12) 5 et seq. and 8.

31 For more information on this with further references in context with FinTech, see Gudula Deipenbrock (n 12) 16.

32 For more information on definitions in context with the digital transformation in financial services and products, see Gudula Deipenbrock (n 12) 5 et seq. See also Expert Group on Regulatory Obstacles to Financial Innovation (ROFIEG), *30 Recommendations on Regulation, Innovation and Finance – Final Report to the European Commission* (December 2019) Recommendation 10, 63 et seq.

33 See also eg, Heinz-Uwe Dettling and Stefan Krüger (n 16) 217.

34 Commission, *White Paper on Artificial Intelligence – A European Approach to Excellence and Trust* (COM [2020] 65 final, 19 February 2020).

35 Commission, *Commission White Paper AI* (n 34) 16.

36 See item 1.

37 Ronan Hamon, Henrik Junklewitz and Ignacio Sanchez (n 8) 6.

38 For more information on this, see Commission <ec.europa.eu/digital-single-market/en/high-level-expert-group-artificial-intelligence>.

Bundesanstalt für Finanzdienstleistungsaufsicht (BaFin)[39] – shall serve as an example. The chapter adds approaches from the international business perspective, here relevant reports published by the World Economic Forum.

2.1.1 *What is artificial intelligence?*

The lack of definitional clarity of the term AI illustrates the so-called AI effect.[40] Multiple definitions of AI exist.[41] At international level, the FSB defines AI as the theory and development of computer systems able to perform tasks that traditionally have required human intelligence.[42] At EU level, the approaches of the Commission and the High-Level Expert Group on AI are relevant. The communication 'Artificial Intelligence for Europe' of the Commission (Commission Communication AI)[43] addresses this issue quite early. The Commission states that AI refers to systems that display intelligent behaviour by analysing their environment and taking actions – with some degree of autonomy – to achieve specific goals, and adds that AI-based systems can be purely software-based, acting in the virtual world, or AI can be embedded in hardware devices, giving examples for both.[44] The High-Level Expert Group on AI explores it in its 'A Definition of AI: Main Capabilities and Disciplines' (HLEG AI Definition),[45] further. It suggests an updated definition with reference to its preceding deliberations: AI systems are software (and possibly also hardware) systems designed by humans – humans design AI systems directly, but they may also use AI techniques to optimise their design – that, given a complex goal, act in the physical or digital dimension by perceiving their environment through data acquisition, interpreting the collected structured or unstructured data, reasoning on the knowledge, or processing the information, derived from this data, and deciding the best action(s) to take to achieve the given goal.[46] The definition proceeds that AI systems can either use symbolic rules or learn a numeric model and they can also adapt their behaviour by analysing how the environment is affected by their previous actions.[47] The definition adds that AI as a scientific discipline includes several approaches and techniques, such as ML (of which deep learning and reinforcement learning are specific examples), machine reasoning (which includes planning, scheduling, knowledge representation and reasoning, search, and optimisation), and robotics (which includes control, perception, sensors and

---

39 For more information on this, see Petra Buck-Heeb, *Kapitalmarktrecht* (10th edn, C.F. Müller 2019) 365 et seq. See also BaFin <www.bafin.de>.
40 World Economic Forum – here R. Jesse McWaters (lead author) et al, *WEF New Physics Report* (n 28) 10.
41 For more information on a critical approach to the German term 'Künstliche Intelligenz' and the term AI with further references, see eg, Maximilian Herberger, '"Künstliche Intelligenz" und Recht' (2018) 71 NJW 2825, 2825 et seq.
42 See FSB, *FSB Report AI and ML* (n 20) 4.
43 Commission, Communication from the Commission to the European Parliament, the European Council, the Council, the European Economic and Social Committee and the Committee of the Regions, *Artificial Intelligence for Europe* (COM [2018] 237 final, 25 April 2018).
44 Commission, *Commission Communication AI* (n 43) 1.
45 High-Level Expert Group on AI, *A definition of AI: Main Capabilities and Disciplines* (8 April 2019). Please see the disclaimer of the document at its beginning stating inter alia that the views expressed reflect those of the High-Level Expert Group on AI and not an official position of the Commission.
46 High-Level Expert Group on AI, *HLEG AI Definition* (n 45) 6.
47 High-Level Expert Group on AI, *HLEG AI Definition* (n 45) 6.

actuators, as well as the integration of all other techniques into cyber-physical systems).[48] The Commission White Paper AI stresses later that in any legal instrument, the definition of AI will need to be sufficiently flexible to accommodate technical progress while being precise enough to provide the necessary legal certainty.[49] For its purpose and further policy initiatives, the Commission White Paper AI aims to clarify the main elements composing AI: data and algorithms.[50] It states that AI can be integrated in hardware and that ML techniques as a subset of AI train algorithms to infer certain patterns based on a set of data in order to determine the actions needed to achieve a given goal and adds that algorithms continue to learn when in use.[51] The Commission White Paper AI adds that while AI-based products can act autonomously by perceiving their environment and without following a pre-determined set of instructions, developers define and constrain largely their 'behaviour' which entails that humans determine and programme the goals which an AI system should optimise for.[52] Particularly the latter explanation appears to stress the factor of human agency. Maintaining the latter is, however, in the author's view an urgent policy concern.

The work of the ESAs also requires defining AI and ML. One example is the 'EBA Report on Big Data and Advanced Analytics' (EBA Big Data Report).[53] The latter adopts for its purpose the definition of AI of the High-Level Expert Group on AI.[54]

At national – here German – level, the study of the BaFin 'Big Data trifft auf künstliche Intelligenz' (BDAI Study)[55] is relevant. It defines AI as a combination of mass data, sufficient computing resources and ML, adding that methods to reproduce general human intelligence – 'strong AI' – are not expected in the foreseeable future.[56]

As to the international business perspective, the WEF New Physics Report suggests that business people use the term AI typically not to depict a particular technical approach or a well-defined school of computer science but a set of capabilities allowing them to run their business in a new way, particularly a suite of technologies, enabled by adaptive predictive power and exhibiting some degree of autonomous learning, that have made dramatic advances in our ability to use machines to automate and enhance pattern detection, foresight, customisation, decision-making, and interaction.[57] Amongst the succeeding reports, the one on 'Transforming Paradigms – A Global AI in Financial Services Survey' – by the World Economic Forum and the Cambridge Centre for Alternative Finance (WEF CCAF

48 High-Level Expert Group on AI, *HLEG AI Definition* (n 45) 6.
49 Commission, *Commission White Paper AI* (n 34) 16.
50 Commission, *Commission White Paper AI* (n 34) 16.
51 Commission, *Commission White Paper AI* (n 34) 16.
52 Commission, *Commission White Paper AI* (n 34) 16.
53 EBA, *EBA Report on Big Data and Advanced Analytics* (EBA/REP/2020/01, January 2020).
54 EBA, *EBA Big Data Report* (n 53) 13 et seq.
55 BaFin, Study, *Big Data trifft auf Künstliche Intelligenz* (15 June 2018). Please see the extensive disclaimer stating inter alia that this study is speculative which should under no circumstances be interpreted as prescript of using any particular technology or business model described therein and that the legal assessments of the study are not intended as a description of the administrative practices within BaFin (BaFin, *BDAI Study*, 2). See also the results of the consultation on the BDAI Study, BaFin – here Jörn Bartels and Thomas Deckers, *Big Data Meets Artificial Intelligence* (Issue 1, 2019) BaFin Perspectives 15.
56 See BaFin, *BDAI Study* (n 55) 7.
57 World Economic Forum – here R. Jesse McWaters (lead author) et al, *WEF New Physics Report* (n 28) 11.

Report)[58] is of interest, here. It is a global empirical study on AI in financial services applied by FinTech firms and incumbents.[59] It refers to the definitional approach of the WEF New Physics Report.[60]

Four more specific AI notions shall supplement the exploration. For the first three AI notions it shall suffice for the purpose of this chapter to solely refer to the approach at EU level, here the High-Level Expert Group on AI: narrow (or weak) AI, general (or strong) AI and blackbox AI.[61] While narrow AI – the currently deployed AI systems are examples of narrow AI – can perform one or few specific tasks that humans can do, general AI is intended to perform most activities that humans can do.[62] Blackbox AI is considered as referring to scenarios where it is not possible to trace back to the reason for certain decisions such as some ML techniques which are accurate but opaque as to understanding the decision-making process.[63]

The fourth AI notion is that of superintelligence. Particularly the FSB refers to it.[64] Superintelligence might be defined as any intellect that greatly exceeds the cognitive performance of humans in virtually all domains of interest.[65] An astonishing increase in intelligence in AI systems which are superior to humans can at least theoretically be considered possible.[66] Technological singularity (Singularität) denotes the point in time in which superintelligence arises.[67] But one has to clarify here: any digital determinism in this context is highly problematic: not digital determinism but technological planning applies meaning that under changing technological, economical, ecological and social conditions technological development can be influenced.[68] The future is open within the laws of nature: one hence uses the plural form 'futures'.[69] Focus shall therefore not be on the timing – when a theoretically conceivable superintelligence might arise – but on its implications.[70]

Also the term Big Data requires to be defined. At international level, the FSB refers to a broad use of the term Big Data describing the storage and analysis of large and/or complicated data sets using a variety of techniques including AI.[71] At EU level, the Commission defines Big Data as referring to large amounts of data produced very quickly by a high

---

58 World Economic Forum and Cambridge Centre for Alternative Finance, University of Cambridge Judge Business School (CCAF) with the support of EY and Invesco, *Transforming Paradigms – A Global AI in Financial Services Survey* (January 2020).
59 World Economic Forum and Cambridge Centre for Alternative Finance, *WEF CCAF Report* (n 58) 11.
60 World Economic Forum and Cambridge Centre for Alternative Finance, *WEF CCAF Report* (n 58) 16.
61 High-Level Expert Group on AI, *HLEG AI Definition* (n 45) 5.
62 High-Level Expert Group on AI, *HLEG AI Definition* (n 45) 5.
63 High-Level Expert Group on AI, *HLEG AI Definition* (n 45) 5.
64 See eg, FSB, *FSB Report AI and ML* (n 20) Annex B, with reference to Nick Bostrom.
65 For more on this with further references, see Nick Bostrom, *Superintelligence – Paths, Dangers, Strategies* (OUP paperback 2016) 26. Singularity (Singularität) and superintelligence (Superintelligenz) are also discussed questions in Klaus Mainzer, *Künstliche Intelligenz – Wann übernehmen die Maschinen?* (2nd edn, Springer 2019) 221 et seq.
66 For more information on this with reference to Nick Bostrom and the examples of speed superintelligence, collective superintelligence and new superintelligence, see Klaus Mainzer (n 65) 221 et seq.
67 See Klaus Mainzer (n 65) 227.
68 For more information on this with further references, see eg, Klaus Mainzer (n 65) 232 et seq.
69 For more information on this with further references, see eg, Klaus Mainzer (n 65) 233.
70 See also the recommendation in context with artificial general intelligence by Max Tegmark (n 24) 80.
71 The FSB refers here to Jonathan Stuart Ward and Adam Barker with further details, see FSB, *FSB Report AI and ML* (n 20) 4.

number of diverse sources.[72] The Commission White Paper AI acknowledges data and algorithms as main elements composing AI.[73] The Commission presents 'A European Strategy for Data' (Commission Data Strategy),[74] in parallel. The High-Level Expert Group on AI does neither define the term Big Data in the HLEG AI Definition and 'Ethics Guidelines for Trustworthy AI' (HLEG AI Ethics Guidelines)[75] nor in its 'Policy and Investment Recommendations for Trustworthy AI' (HLEG AI Policy Recommendations),[76] either. The EBA Big Data Report refers for its purpose to the ESA's tentative definition of Big Data: Big Data refers to large volumes of different types of data, produced at high speed from many and varied sources (eg, the Internet of Things, sensors, social media and financial market data collection), which are processed, often in real time, by IT tools (powerful processors, software and algorithms).[77] At national – here German – level, the BaFin explains Big Data as the availability of large quantities of data and combines the terms of Big Data and AI in the acronym BDAI.[78]

Important in context with any notion of AI is the debate about its potential with a view to emotions and consciousness.[79] This issue is highly problematic.[80] It urgently requires a broad interdisciplinary discourse, but lies outside the scope of this chapter.

2.1.2 *What is machine learning?*

As to the international view, the FSB considers ML a sub-category of AI and defines ML while referring to various sources as a method of designing a sequence of actions to solve a problem, known as algorithms, which optimise automatically through experience and with limited or no human intervention.[81] The FSB proceeds that ML in general deals with (automated) optimisation, prediction, and categorisation, not with causal inference and distinguishes several categories of ML algorithms which vary according to the level of human intervention required in labelling the data.[82] It stresses that ML algorithms are used

---

72 Commission <ec.europa.eu/digital-single-market/en/big-data>.

73 Commission, *Commission White Paper AI* (n 34) 16.

74 Commission, Communication from the Commission to the European Parliament, the Council, the European Economic and Social Committee and the Committee of the Regions, *A European Strategy for Data* (COM [2020] 66 final, 19 February 2020).

75 High-Level Expert Group on AI, *Ethics Guidelines for Trustworthy AI* (8 April 2019). Please see the disclaimer of the document at its beginning stating inter alia that the views expressed reflect those of the High-Level Expert Group on AI and not an official position of the Commission.

76 High-Level Expert Group on AI, *Policy and Investment Recommendations for Trustworthy AI* (26 June 2019). Please see the disclaimer of the document at its beginning stating inter alia that the views expressed reflect those of the High-Level Expert Group on AI and not an official position of the Commission.

77 EBA, *EBA Big Data Report* (n 53) 11, with reference to Joint Committee of the ESAs, *Joint Committee Final Report on Big Data* (JC/2018/04, 15 March 2018).

78 See BaFin, *BDAI Study* (n 55) 7.

79 For more information on this, see the literature listed as further reading and references in Matthias Scheutz, 'Artificial Emotions and Machine Consciousness' in Keith Frankish and William M. Ramsey (eds), *The Cambridge Handbook of Artificial Intelligence* (CUP 2018) 247, 262 et seq.

80 For a critical view on AI research on developing AI systems with humanlike consciousness, see eg, Klaus Mainzer (n 65) 206 et seq.

81 The FSB refers here to Arthur Samuel, Tom Mitchell, Michael Jordan and Tom Mitchell with further details, see FSB, *FSB Report AI and ML* (n 20) 4.

82 See FSB, *FSB Report AI and ML* (n 20) 5.

to identify patterns correlated with other events or patterns, the patterns ML identifies are merely correlations, ML cannot determine causality.[83]

At EU level, the Commission considers ML a type of AI, working by identifying patterns in available data and then applying the knowledge to new data, adding in a footnote, that finding the pattern is itself sometimes the goal of the activity, further explaining the latter.[84] The Commission White Paper AI also explains ML techniques as a subset of AI.[85] The High-Level Expert Group on AI, when exploring AI as a scientific discipline refers to AI techniques and sub-disciplines currently used to build AI systems, and suggests grouping the techniques – apart from robotics as another relevant discipline – into (1) reasoning and decision-making, and (2) learning including inter alia ML (ML techniques are considered as producing a numeric model, that is a mathematical formula, used to compute the decision from the data), neural networks, deep learning and decision trees.[86] The High-Level Expert Group on AI considers supervised learning, unsupervised learning and reinforcement learning the most widespread approaches of ML.[87] As stated above,[88] the EBA adopts the definition of AI of the High-Level Expert Group on AI for the purpose of its EBA Big Data Report and then adds some further deliberations on ML and ML modes.[89]

At national – here German – level, the BaFin explains ML as the term used for enabling computers to learn from data by means of suitable algorithms thereby allowing them to set up a model of their world and solve assigned tasks better.[90] The BaFin proceeds that ML approaches might be characterised on the basis of the learning task (eg, classification, regression, clustering), the data types (special approaches exist as to eg, text, speech or image data) and the algorithms (technical solution of the problem).[91] As to the international business perspective, the WEF CCAF Report refers to the definition of AI in the WEF New Physics Report[92] and considers ML as a technical term for what is essentially an enabling subset of the AI paradigm, thereby making clear that the terms AI and ML cannot be used interchangeably.[93]

2.1.3 *Interim results*

Already defining AI, ML and related phenomena faces profound problems. Notions of AI, ML and Big Data are developed and used in different contexts. They vary considerably. This illustrates both the prevalence as well as the limitations of perspective when approaching AI

---

83 See FSB, *FSB Report AI and ML* (n 20) 6.
84 Commission, *Commission Communication AI* (n 43) 10.
85 Commission, *Commission White Paper AI* (n 34) 16. See item 2.1.1.
86 High-Level Expert Group on AI, *HLEG AI Definition* (n 45) 3.
87 For more information on this, see High-Level Expert Group on AI, *HLEG AI Definition* (n 45) 3 et seq.
88 See item 2.1.1.
89 EBA, *EBA Big Data Report* (n 53) 13 et seq.
90 See BaFin, *BDAI Study* (n 55) 24.
91 See BaFin, *BDAI Study* (n 55) 24 and Appendix, 188 et seq.
92 See item 2.1.1.
93 For more information on this and the use of the term AI as an umbrella term for the suite of technologies investigated in the study, see World Economic Forum and Cambridge Centre for Alternative Finance, *WEF CCAF Report* (n 58) 16 et seq.

(and ML) as they appear to be 'too big to define'.[94] This applies already to the approaches of relevant policy makers selected for the purpose of this chapter. They, however, represent only a minuscule part of the discussion.[95] Any discussion on AI governance and AI regulation at a wider (global) scale has to include further definitional approaches particularly of those players outside the EU with high ambitions in the realm of AI and ML.

Definitional differences are either transparent or not. The latter depends on whether relevant definitions are provided or not. Misunderstandings are pre-programmed. In addition, technologies advance in different (segments of) economies and societies, thereby increasing their complexity, opacity and dynamics. This might become an insurmountable obstacle to a broad consensus on definitions of AI and ML particularly for policy and legal (-political) purposes. The lack of a common language in the realm of FinTech,[96] RegTech and SupTech more generally might also hinder new entrants and the scaling up of FinTech innovation across the EU.[97] The more the discussion on AI governance and AI regulation gains momentum, the more urgent a consensus on definitions of AI and ML becomes. The definitions of the High-Level Expert Group on AI are one important step towards a common understanding of AI and ML. Its intricacies however give a foretaste of the complexity of any ensuing legal or legislative, particularly regulatory and supervisory approach to the matter.[98] At EU level, a further definitional alignment is expected to evolve. One example is the EBA Big Data Report adopting the definition of AI of the High-Level Expert Group on AI.[99] In light of this current fragmentation as to the definitional approaches, the chapter takes the following approach to comply with legal-methodological clarity: any reference to a source implies a reference to its underlying concepts of AI, ML and related phenomena. Apart from such references, the chapter builds on the definitions of AI and ML as proposed by the High-Level Expert Group on AI if not explicitly stated otherwise.

2.2 Legal-methodological approach to relating AI and ML to law

Against the backdrop of the definitional challenges the more fundamental question arises as to how to relate AI and ML to law from a legal-methodological view. Particularly, the following two general perspectives might be distinguished: (1) legal informatics and more currently LegalTech with a focus on the use of AI and ML to optimise processes informed

94 See also John Brockman, 'Introduction: On the Promise and Peril of AI' in John Brockman (ed), *Possible Minds – Twenty-Five Ways of Looking at AI* (Penguin Press 2019) xv, xxv, stating that AI is too big a topic for any one perspective.

95 For more information on the state of the art in the field of AI and important theoretical and philosophical applications of current research, see the contributions by various authors in Keith Frankish and William M. Ramsey (eds), *The Cambridge Handbook of Artificial Intelligence* (CUP 2018). For more information on the various ways of looking at AI, see the contributions by various authors in John Brockman (ed), *Possible Minds – Twenty-Five Ways of Looking at AI* (Penguin Press 2019).

96 For more information on this with further references, see Gudula Deipenbrock (n 12) 5 et seq.

97 See also eg, Expert Group on Regulatory Obstacles to Financial Innovation (n 32) Recommendation 10, 63.

98 For more information with further references on the example of product liability issues in context with the use of AI, see eg, Friedrich Graf von Westphalen, 'Haftungsfragen beim Einsatz Künstlicher Intelligenz in Ergänzung der Produkthaftungs-RL 85/374/EWG' (2019) 40 ZIP 889, 889.

99 EBA, *EBA Big Data Report* (n 53) 13 et seq.

by law, and (2) information technology law with a focus on the legal implications of use cases of AI and ML.[100] In addition to information technology law, also sector-specific rules come into play, depending on the use cases of AI and ML.[101] As to the first perspective, financial institutions might use LegalTech in the realm of (legal) document analysis such as the analysis of commercial credit agreements.[102] Specific forms of information technology-based optimisation of processes informed by law are RegTech[103] and SupTech. RegTech addresses – when employed by regulatory authorities – the use of technology in regulation and SupTech the use of technology in supervision.[104] RegTech addresses – when employed by financial institutions – the use of AI and ML to comply with regulatory requirements such as capital requirements or anti-money laundering rules[105] in the banking sector.[106] As to the second perspective – the legal implications of use cases of AI and ML – those of the sector-specific use of AI and ML such as robo-advice,[107] and algorithmic trading,[108] but also those of further manifestations of FinTech where AI and ML converge with other technologies, particularly blockchain technology,[109] are relevant. Both perspectives might well be employed to further systemise and categorise use cases of AI and ML in the financial sector appropriately from the methodological perspective.

100 See eg, Maximilian Herberger (n 41) 2825, 2825 et seq.
101 For more information with further references on the example of Big Data and related innovative financial technologies at the interface between financial services and information technologies, see eg, Philip Bitter, 'Big Data im Finanz- und Versicherungswesen' in Thomas Hoeren, Ulrich Sieber and Bernd Holznagel (eds), *Handbuch Multimedia-Recht* (48th supp, C.H. Beck, February 2019) paras 1 et seq.
102 For more information on this, see eg, De Nederlandsche Bank – here Joost van der Burgt (n 4) 27.
103 For more information on this with further references, see eg, Jean-Claude Spillmann, '7. Kapitel: RegTech im lokalen und internationalen Aufsichtsrecht' in Ulf Klebeck and Günther Dobrauz-Saldapenna (eds), *Rechtshandbuch Digitale Finanzdienstleistungen* (C.H. Beck 2018) 463.
104 See eg, FSB, *FSB Chair's Letter to G20 Finance Ministers and Central Bank Governors* (18 February 2020).
105 A use of technological solutions helping to improve detection of suspicious transactions and activities in the realm of international and EU anti-money laundering and countering the financing of terrorism however has to comply with international and EU standards in this realm as well as with other EU rules such as those in the realm of data protection and antitrust. See Commission, *Communication from the Commission on an Action Plan for a Comprehensive Union Policy on Preventing Money Laundering and Terrorist Financing* (2020/C 164/06) [2020] OJ EU C 164/21, 25.
106 For more information on this with further references, see eg, Jakob Schemmel, 'Artificial Intelligence and the Financial Markets: Business as Usual?' in Thomas Wischmeyer and Timo Rademacher (eds), *Regulating Artificial Intelligence* (Springer 2020) 255, 260 et seq.
107 See eg, Christoph Kumpan, '§ 15 Interessenwahrung durch Robo-Advisors' in Florian Möslein and Sebastian Omlor (eds), *FinTech-Handbuch* (C.H. Beck 2019) 351. See also eg, Frank Herring, Dennis Kunschke and Elena Bachmann, '"Lizenzleihe" und Robo-Advice' in Dennis Kunschke and Kai A. Schaffelhuber (eds), *FinTech – Grundlagen – Regulierung – Finanzierung – Case Studies* (Erich Schmidt 2018) 95. See also eg, Detmar Loff, '3. Kapitel: Digital Asset Management / Robo-Advice' in Ulf Klebeck and Günther Dobrauz-Saldapenna (eds), *Rechtshandbuch Digitale Finanzdienstleistungen* (C.H. Beck 2018) 193.
108 See eg, Jochen Kindermann, '§ 14 Effektengeschäft: Praktische Anwendungsfragen' in Florian Möslein and Sebastian Omlor (eds), *FinTech-Handbuch* (C.H. Beck 2019) 338, 342 et seq.
109 For more information on this with further references in context with smart contracts, see Florian Möslein, 'Smart Contracts im Zivil- und Handelsrecht' (2019) 183 ZHR 254, 273 et seq.

2.3 *The need for a macro perspective*

The chapter now turns to the question whether it is necessary to put (the policy and legal (-political) approach to) the sector-specific use of AI and ML in the financial sector in context with that to the more general use of AI and ML. Multiple closely interrelated arguments support such an approach from the macro perspective. The chapter introduces the most pivotal ones.

2.3.1 *Artificial intelligence and machine learning are used in multiple sectors and contexts*

The first argument in favour of a macro perspective is that AI and ML are used in multiple sectors and contexts. The High-Level Expert Group on AI, when exploring AI as a scientific discipline, refers to AI techniques and sub-disciplines currently used to build AI systems, and suggests grouping the techniques – apart from robotics as another relevant discipline – into (1) reasoning and decision-making, and (2) learning including inter alia ML (ML techniques are considered as producing a numeric model, that is a mathematical formula, used to compute the decision from the data), neural networks, deep learning and decision trees.[110] Particularly, deep learning has led to remarkable results such as image recognition and natural language processing usable and used also in the financial sector such as automated financial service functions that previously required manual intervention.[111] AI-based systems whether software-based such as search engines, speech and face recognition systems or AI embedded in hardware devices such as advanced robots and Internet of Things applications[112] have already deeply and widely transformed the daily life. Particularly, data links the various sectors and contexts. At EU level, for example, the Commission acknowledges data and algorithms as main elements composing AI.[113] The Commission Data Strategy suggests actions based on four pillars, of which the first one on a cross-sectoral governance framework for data access and use and the fourth one on common European data spaces in strategic sectors and domains of public interest[114] are relevant, here. In the first pillar, the Commission proposes particularly a legislative framework for the governance of common European data spaces, and, as appropriate, a Data Act.[115] In the fourth pillar, the Commission supports the establishment of various common European data spaces including a financial one to stimulate innovation, market transparency, sustainable finance and access to finance for European businesses and a more integrated market through enhanced data sharing.[116] It aims to further detail the common European financial data space in an upcoming Digital Finance Strategy in the third quarter of 2020.[117] Already these policy deliberations at EU level in the realm of data as a main composing element of AI show that use cases of AI and ML arise across sectors and

---

110 High-Level Expert Group on AI, *HLEG AI Definition* (n 45) 3. See item 2.1.2.
111 For more information on this, see FSB, *FSB Report AI and ML* (n 20) 5 et seq.
112 See eg, the definition of AI by the Commission, *Commission Communication AI* (n 43) 1.
113 Commission, *Commission White Paper AI* (n 34) 16. See item 2.1.1.
114 Commission, *Commission Data Strategy* (n 74) 11 et seq. and 21 et seq.
115 Commission, *Commission Data Strategy* (n 74) 12 et seq.
116 Commission, *Commission Data Strategy* (n 74) 21 et seq. and 30 et seq.
117 Commission, *Commission Data Strategy* (n 74) 30 et seq.

contexts and might change sectors and contexts for other ones. Implications and risks of the use of AI and ML in one sector or context might also occur in other sectors or contexts. This might also – amongst other issues – explain the shift towards AI governance and AI regulation[118] more generally.

2.3.2 *Use cases of artificial intelligence and machine learning raise fundamental ethical and legal questions*

Closely connected to the first argument[119] is the second one in support of a macro perspective: use cases of AI and ML raise fundamental ethical[120] and legal questions apart from any sector- and context-specific ones. 'Algorithmisation' and AI are considered one of three (combinations of) main characteristics of the FinTech industry.[121] This is to be put in context with a progressing financialisation[122] of large areas of life. Advanced levels of AI and ML including particularly those in the financial sector touch core values and the very foundation of legal systems. The very foundation of Western democracies are fundamental rights such as the freedom of person including the respect for private life and the protection of personal data and above all human dignity, the inviolable core of all universal values of humankind, guiding principle and objective of any legal response.[123] The need for more general policies in context with AI[124] is reflected in the following initiatives at various levels. At international – here G20 – level, the plea for a human-centred AI and the 'G20 AI Principles' drawn from the OECD recommendation on AI[125] are relevant. At EU level, the Commission has addressed AI in its policies for quite some time.[126] The Commission Communication AI, the Commission's 'Coordinated Plan on Artificial Intelligence' (Commission Coordinated Plan AI)[127] and the Commission's 'Building Trust in Human-Centric Artificial Intelligence' (Commission Building Trust AI)[128] are important, here. In the former, the Commission considers AI as one of the most strategic technologies of the

---

118 Ronan Hamon, Henrik Junklewitz and Ignacio Sanchez (n 8) 9. See item 1.
119 See item 2.3.1.
120 For more information on the ethics of artificial intelligence, see eg, Nick Bostrom and Eliezer Yudkowsky, 'The Ethics of Artificial Intelligence' in Keith Frankish and William M. Ramsey (eds), *The Cambridge Handbook of Artificial Intelligence* (CUP 2018) 316.
121 See Florian Möslein and Sebastian Omlor, '§ 1 Grundlagen' in Florian Möslein and Sebastian Omlor (eds), *FinTech-Handbuch* (C.H. Beck 2019) 1, 3 et seq.
122 The term financialisation is used in a broad sense meaning the growing role of financial motives, financial markets, financial actors and financial institutions in the operation of national and international economies. For more information on this, see Gerald A. Epstein, 'Introduction: Financialization and the World Economy' in Gerald A. Epstein (ed), *Financialization and the World Economy* (Edward Elgar 2006) 3, 3.
123 For more information on this with further references, see Gudula Deipenbrock (n 9) 290 and 296 et seq.
124 See already Gudula Deipenbrock (n 12) 30.
125 G20 Japan 2019 Presidency, *G20 Ministerial Statement on Trade and Digital Economy* (June 2019) 3 et seq. and Annex.
126 See item 2.1.1.
127 Commission, Communication from the Commission to the European Parliament, the European Council, the Council, the European Economic and Social Committee and the Committee of the Regions, *Coordinated Plan on Artificial Intelligence* (COM [2018] 795 final, 7 December 2018).
128 Commission, Communication from the Commission to the European Parliament, the Council, the European Economic and Social Committee and the Committee of the Regions, *Building Trust in Human-Centric Artificial Intelligence* (COM [2019] 168 final, 8 April 2019).

21st century already in 2018.[129] In the latter, it stresses the fundamental values on which
the EU is founded, refers particularly to the EU Charter of Fundamental Rights,[130] the
need for ethics guidelines built on the existing strong regulatory framework and welcomes
the input of the High-Level Expert Group on AI.[131] The Commission addresses AI and its
implications further in its Commission White Paper AI, the Commission Data Strategy and
its 'Report on the Safety and Liability Implications of Artificial Intelligence, the Internet of
Things and Robotics' (Commission AI Safety Report),[132] particularly. The Commission AI
Safety Report highlights new challenges raised by AI particularly in terms of product safety
and liability like connectivity, autonomy, data dependency, opacity, complexity of products
and systems, software updates and more complex safety management and value chains.[133]
Particularly in context with the opacity of systems based on algorithms, the Commission
refers to the requirements for transparency of algorithms, as well as for robustness, accountability, human oversight (when relevant) and unbiased outcomes as proposed in the HLEG
AI Ethics Guidelines.[134] The latter address the ethical implications of AI and ML more
generally stressing inter alia that where democracy, the rule of law and fundamental rights,
underpin AI systems and where such systems continuously improve and defend democratic
culture, innovation and responsible competitiveness can thrive.[135] The HLEG AI Ethics
Guidelines address all AI stakeholders designing, developing, deploying, implementing,
using or being affected by AI, and develop Trustworthy AI as a foundational ambition
requiring it to be lawful,[136] ethical and robust.[137] The HLEG AI Ethics Guidelines make a
plea for human-centricity of AI systems used in the service of humanity and the common
good, and aim to provide guidance for AI applications in general, building a horizontal
foundation to achieve Trustworthy AI, however stressing the context-specificity of AI systems.[138] The HLEG AI Ethics Guidelines address a plethora of issues which cannot be
explored for the purpose of this chapter. Respect for fundamental rights as enshrined in
the legal framework of the EU and international human rights law, within the framework
of democracy and the rule of law is considered the basis for identifying abstract ethical
principles and values which can be operationalised in the context of AI.[139] It is particularly human dignity that provides the foundation of the human-centric approach described
by the HLEG AI Ethics Guidelines.[140] The HLEG AI Ethics Guidelines particularly list
four ethical principles, here, rooted in fundamental rights to be respected in context with
AI systems: (1) respect for human autonomy, (2) prevention of harm, (3) fairness, and

129 Commission, *Commission Communication AI* (n 43) 1.
130 See (n 10).
131 Commission, *Commission Building Trust AI* (n 128) 2 and 9.
132 Commission, Report from the Commission to the European Parliament, the Council and the
    European Economic and Social Committee, *Report on the Safety and Liability Implications of
    Artificial Intelligence, the Internet of Things and Robotics* (COM [2020] 64 final, 19 February 2020).
133 Commission, *Commission AI Safety Report* (n 132) 1 et seq. and 16.
134 Commission, *Commission AI Safety Report* (n 132) 9.
135 See High-Level Expert Group on AI, *HLEG AI Ethics Guidelines* (n 75) 9.
136 The lawfulness of Trustworthy AI is however not dealt with. See High-Level Expert Group on AI,
    HLEG AI Ethics Guidelines (n 75) 2.
137 High-Level Expert Group on AI, *HLEG AI Ethics Guidelines* (n 75) 2 et seq., 4 and 5.
138 High-Level Expert Group on AI, *HLEG AI Ethics Guidelines* (n 75) 4 et seq.
139 High-Level Expert Group on AI, *HLEG AI Ethics Guidelines* (n 75) 9.
140 High-Level Expert Group on AI, *HLEG AI Ethics Guidelines* (n 75) 10.

(4) explicability.[141] They also provide later a non-exhaustive list with examples of critical concerns raised by AI which might already fall within the scope of existing legal requirements, but the latter do not address all ethical concerns arising: (1) identifying and tracking individuals with AI, (2) covert AI systems, (3) AI-enabled citizen scoring in violation of fundamental rights, (4) lethal autonomous weapon systems, and (5) potential longer-term concerns where a risk-based approach suggests that these concerns should be considered in view of possible unknown unknowns and 'black swans'.[142]

The HLEG AI Policy Recommendations entail inter alia recommendations addressing data and infrastructure for AI and a governance and regulatory framework as two of four enablers for Trustworthy AI.[143] The succeeding Commission White Paper AI suggests policy options to enable a trustworthy and secure development of AI in Europe with two building blocks: (1) a policy framework aiming at achieving an 'ecosystem of excellence', and (2) key elements of a future regulatory framework for AI to create an 'ecosystem of trust'.[144] While the former refers particularly to the Commission Communication AI and the Commission Coordinated Plan AI, the latter takes into account particularly the input obtained in the piloting phase of the HLEG AI Ethics Guidelines.[145] In the Commission's view, the existing legislative framework requires to be improved to address the following issues: (1) effective application and enforcement of existing EU and national legislation in view of the opaqueness of AI, (2) limitations of scope of existing EU legislation particularly with a view to stand-alone software, (3) changing functionality of AI systems as existing legislation focuses mainly on safety risks present at the time of placing on the market, (4) uncertainty as to the allocation of responsibilities between different economic operators in the supply chain, and (5) changes to the concept of safety.[146] The Commission favours a European approach thereby tackling the risk of a fragmented single market.[147] The Commission suggests a risk-based approach to regulation to ensure its proportionality.[148] However, the mandatory requirements contained in the new regulatory framework on AI would in principle apply only to those applications identified high-risk in accordance with two cumulative criteria: (1) the AI application is employed in a sector where, given the characteristics of the activities typically undertaken, significant risks can be expected to occur such as in healthcare, transport, energy and parts of the public sector, and (2) the AI application in the sector in question is used in such a manner that significant risks are likely to arise while such assessment of the level of risk could be based on the impact on the affected parties.[149] The Commission White Paper AI refers particularly to the High-Level Expert Group on AI as to the key features of requirements for high-risk AI applications which are training data, data and record-keeping, information to be provided, robustness

---

141 For more information on this with further examples and references, see High-Level Expert Group on AI, *HLEG AI Ethics Guidelines* (n 75) 11 et seq.

142 For more information on this with further examples and references, see High-Level Expert Group on AI, *HLEG AI Ethics Guidelines* (n 75) 33 et seq.

143 High-Level Expert Group on AI, *HLEG AI Policy Recommendations* (n 76) 25 et seq.

144 Commission, *Commission White Paper AI* (n 34) 2 et seq.

145 Commission, *Commission White Paper AI* (n 34) 3, 5 and 9 et seq.

146 Commission, *Commission White Paper AI* (n 34) 14 et seq.

147 Commission, *Commission White Paper AI* (n 34) 15.

148 Commission, *Commission White Paper AI* (n 34) 17.

149 Commission, *Commission White Paper AI* (n 34) 17.

and accuracy, human oversight, and specific requirements for certain particular AI applications, such as those used for purposes of remote biometric identification.[150]

The Commission does not mention the finance sector in the first criterion of a high-risk AI application. In its view, however, there may be also exceptional instances where, due to the risks at stake, the use of AI applications for certain purposes is to be considered as high-risk as such, irrespective of the sector concerned and where the above requirements would still apply.[151] Examples of such exceptions that would always be considered high-risk are in the realm of employment equality the use of AI applications for recruitment processes as well as in situations impacting workers' rights or the use of AI applications for the purpose of remote biometric identification – not to be confused with biometric authentication as a security process relying on the unique biological characteristics of an individual to verify that she/he is who she/he says she/he is – and other intrusive surveillance technologies.[152] Whether such exceptions that would always be considered high-risk might also be identified in the use of AI applications in the financial sector remains to be seen. The Commission White Paper AI also makes clear that the existing EU law inter alia in the realms of consumer protection, unfair commercial practices and data and privacy protection continues to apply in relation to AI, despite any necessary updates to reflect the use of AI.[153] For AI applications that do not qualify as high-risk and are therefore not subject to the above mandatory requirements, the Commission considers the option of a voluntary labelling scheme in addition to the applicable legislation.[154] Institutionally, the Commission favours a European governance structure on AI, here a cooperation framework of national competent authorities with tasks such as advising on standardisation and certification or issuing guidance in context with implementing the legal framework without duplicating or affecting responsibilities of relevant competent authorities under existing EU law in specific sectors or realms such as finance or data and consumer protection.[155] Any further concrete policy and legislative proposals depend particularly on the outcome of the open public consultation on the Commission White Paper AI.[156]

At national level, particularly states have adopted strategies on AI.[157] As to Germany as one example of a Member State of the EU (MS), the national strategy on AI of the German Federal Government also aims at a responsible development and use of AI serving the well-being of people.[158]

The above highlighted work streams at different levels show the various efforts to foster policies in context with AI and particularly AI governance more generally in response to the fundamental ethical and legal issues raised by use cases of AI and ML. Any such efforts mark out the wider 'playing field' of AI and ML and might thereby well impact the relevant

---

150 Commission, *Commission White Paper AI* (n 34) 18.
151 Commission, *Commission White Paper AI* (n 34) 18.
152 Commission, *Commission White Paper AI* (n 34) 18.
153 Commission, *Commission White Paper AI* (n 34) 16.
154 Commission, *Commission White Paper AI* (n 34) 24.
155 Commission, *Commission White Paper AI* (n 34) 24 et seq.
156 Commission, *Commission White Paper AI* (n 34) 25 et seq.
157 For a comparison of various national strategies on AI, see eg, Olaf J. Groth, Mark Nitzberg and Dan Zehr et al, in Konrad-Adenauer-Stiftung e. V. (ed), *Vergleich nationaler Strategien zur Förderung von Künstlicher Intelligenz*, Teil 1 (2018) and Teil 2 (2019).
158 Die Bundesregierung, *KI Nationale Strategie für Künstliche Intelligenz AI Made in Germany* <www.ki-strategie-deutschland.de>.

policy and legal, particularly regulatory and supervisory, responses in the realm of FinTech and vice versa.[159]

2.3.3 *Range of relevant providers and players*

The third argument in favour of a macro perspective addresses the range of relevant providers and players as to use cases of AI and ML in the financial sector. Market players are not only the incumbents, in particular supervised firms such as banks and insurance companies, or comparatively young, technology-oriented providers with specific functions, but also globally active BigTech firms most of which have not been subject to supervision.[160] The report of the FSB 'BigTech in Finance – Market Developments and Potential Financial Stability Implications' (FSB BigTech Report)[161] addresses the issue from the international financial stability perspective. It defines BigTech firms as large companies with established technology platforms.[162] BigTech firms play according to the FSB BigTech Report an increasingly prominent role in the financial system and provide financial services, thereby benefiting from their large existing customer bases including collecting and analysing their customers' data, which allows them to achieve scale rapidly across different business lines including in financial services.[163] The WEF New Physics Report points out that BigTech firms, with immediate-term profitability requirements, are 'betting heavily on AI' demonstrating the belief that AI will improve profitability.[164] As currently BigTech firms see a business imperative to build AI systems of their own, the most powerful and rapidly improving AI systems are controlled by for-profit corporations.[165] The breadth of financial services offered by BigTech firms and their modes of interaction with incumbents vary.[166] The third-party services offered by BigTech firms may also provide access to AI and data analytics capabilities previously unavailable to the wider marketplace.[167] The leveraging of AI capabilities by BigTech firms to enter financial services might well be considered a major competitive threat to FinTech firms as well as incumbents.[168] The ability of BigTech firms to leverage wide-ranging customer data raises additional policy issues as to data ownership, access and portability.[169] In its Commission Data Strategy the Commission also states that it will address particularly the accumulation of vast amounts of data, the use and sharing of it by BigTech firms in context with broader fact-finding on market power of certain

---

159 See also the broader perspective taken by the Expert Group on Regulatory Obstacles to Financial Innovation (n 32) 9 et seq.

160 See eg, BaFin, *BDAI Study* (n 55) 8 and 64.

161 FSB, *BigTech in Finance – Market Developments and Potential Financial Stability Implications* (9 December 2019).

162 See FSB, *FSB BigTech Report* (n 161) 1.

163 For more information on this with a non-exhaustive list of selected BigTech firms, see FSB, *FSB BigTech Report* (n 161) 1.

164 World Economic Forum – here R. Jesse McWaters (lead author) et al, *WEF New Physics Report* (n 28) 8.

165 See eg, W. Daniel Hillis, 'The First Machine Intelligences' in John Brockman (ed), *Possible Minds – Twenty-Five Ways of Looking at AI* (Penguin Press 2019) 170, 176.

166 See FSB, *FSB BigTech Report* (n 161) 1.

167 See FSB, *FSB BigTech Report* (n 161) 1.

168 See also the key findings in World Economic Forum and Cambridge Centre for Alternative Finance, *WEF CCAF Report* (n 58) 13.

169 See FSB, *FSB BigTech Report* (n 161) 2.

platforms and its work on the Digital Services Act package.[170] Hence, a macro perspective is in need to also adequately address the implications and risks resulting from the growing role of BigTech firms in context with use cases of AI and ML in financial services.

2.3.4 *The wide risk scenario*

The fourth argument, also closely linked to the preceding ones in support of a macro perspective, addresses the wide risk scenario. Despite different expert views about the future of AI as to timescales and its forms,[171] AI and ML are expected to have the most revolutionary ramifications on all areas of life.[172] Technologists rather than academics lead AI development; focus is on building real applications for the real world leading to myriad successful use cases across the economy.[173] The FinTech sector might be considered a vanguard with a view to developing sector-specific use cases of AI and ML but also adapting or employing more general use cases of AI and ML.[174] Pivotal key findings of the WEF CCAF Report point in the same direction: (1) AI is expected to turn into an essential business driver across the financial services industry in the short run, (2) the rising importance of AI is accompanied by the increasingly broad adoption of AI across key business functions, (3) risk management is the use domain with the highest current AI implementation rates, followed by the generation of new revenue potential through new AI-enabled products and processes, (4) AI is expected to become a key lever of success for specific financial services sectors, (5) with the race to AI leadership, the technological gap between high and low spenders is widening, and (6) mass AI adoption is expected to exacerbate certain market-wide risks and biases.[175] A complex interchange and interrelation between sector-specific and general use cases of AI and ML impact also the related risks. On the one hand, sector-specific risks of use cases of AI and ML in the financial sector might – due to the nature and structure of risks – also become more general profound risks for other sectors of the economy, the society and life. On the other hand, risks of the more general (cross-sectoral and 'cross-contextual') use cases of AI and ML might also materialise in the financial sector. Particularly major risks such as those related to cyber-security, safety and data protection[176] might manifest sector-specifically as well as across sectors and contexts. Particularly, cyber-security deserves utmost attention.[177] As to the EU level, it is suggested to consider the Commission's initiatives on AI in the more global legal context around cyber-security of digital systems and the initiatives concerning the management of data.[178] As stated above, the Commission AI Safety Report highlights new challenges raised by AI particularly in terms of product safety and liability like connectivity, autonomy, data

170 Commission, *Commission Data Strategy* (n 74) 14.
171 See eg, Nick Bostrom (n 65) 22 et seq.
172 See Gudula Deipenbrock (n 12) 29.
173 World Economic Forum – here R. Jesse McWaters (lead author) et al, *WEF New Physics Report* (n 28) 8.
174 See the examples in FSB, *FSB Report AI and ML* (n 20) 5 et seq. For more information on the finance sector as a vanguard of global, interconnected and flexible business and the role of technology with further references, see Gudula Deipenbrock (n 9) 302 et seq.
175 For more information on this and the survey methodology, see World Economic Forum and Cambridge Centre for Alternative Finance, *WEF CCAF Report* (n 58) 11 et seq. and 21 et seq.
176 Ronan Hamon, Henrik Junklewitz and Ignacio Sanchez (n 8) 1.
177 See eg, Gudula Deipenbrock (n 9) 294.
178 Ronan Hamon, Henrik Junklewitz and Ignacio Sanchez (n 8) 7.

dependency, opacity, complexity of products and systems, software updates and more complex safety management and value chains.[179] Technological risks more generally include inter alia the risk of adverse consequences of technological advances, defined as intended or unintended adverse consequences of technological advances such as AI, geo-engineering and synthetic biology causing human, environmental and economic damage.[180] The at least theoretical possibility of the development of superintelligence[181] appears as the most problematic scenario in this context. As stated above,[182] the fundamental technological risks require profound AI safety research and work.[183] The control problem[184] and the issue of value alignment[185] are discussed, here.

2.3.5 *Interim results*

The selected, closely interrelated arguments above show that it is necessary to put (the policy and legal (-political) approach to) the sector-specific use of AI and ML in the financial sector in context with that to the more general use of AI and ML. The use of AI and ML in multiple sectors and contexts, its far-reaching implications including fundamental ethical and legal issues, the role of BigTech firms in this context, and the wide risk scenario including more general profound risks support taking an approach to the subject-matter from a macro perspective. This also entails that the financial sector is well advised to closely follow the policy and legislative initiatives at various levels including regulatory and supervisory approaches to AI and ML at both sector-specific – here the financial sector – and more general level.

2.4 *The challenge to establish the relevant facts of the case and the 'FinTech information mismatch'*[186]

Tackling the challenge to establish the relevant facts of the case is another legal-methodological *conditio sine qua non* for any legal (-political) analysis and assessment.[187] AI-based systems are used in multiple sectors and contexts including the financial sector.[188] Three specific features of the rapid technological development are relevant in this context. Firstly, different technologies converge. One example is the convergence of blockchain technologies and AI and ML which raises additional novel legal problems.[189] Secondly, AI does not exist in a vacuum, emerging technologies are mutually reinforcing, and

---

179 Commission, *Commission AI Safety Report* (n 132) 1 et seq. and 16. See item 2.3.2.
180 See eg, World Economic Forum – here Emilio Granados Franco (lead author) et al, *WEF Risks Report* (n 6) Figures II, III, IV and Appendix A, 87.
181 See the definition in item 2.1.1. See the reference to Nick Bostrom in FSB, *FSB Report AI and ML* (n 20) Annex B.
182 See item 1.
183 See in this context also Max Tegmark (n 24) 81 et seq.
184 See eg, Stuart Russell (n 26). See item 1.
185 See eg, Tom Griffiths (n 25) 128 et seq. See item 1.
186 For more information on this with further references in context with FinTech, see Gudula Deipenbrock (n 12) 16.
187 For more information on this with further references in context with FinTech, see Gudula Deipenbrock (n 9) 305. See also Gudula Deipenbrock (n 12) 16.
188 See item 2.3.1
189 For more information on this with further references, see Florian Möslein (n 109) 273 et seq.

advancement in any one technology will increase the capabilities of all other technologies interacting with it.[190] Examples are cloud computing providing both the data storage and the processing power necessary to train new AI models, in turn making cloud infrastructure a critical part of organisations, or quantum computing providing advanced and different computation methods which allow AI solving previously incalculable problems.[191] Thirdly, the high-paced and continuously further accelerating technological development including an increasing complexity lacks transparency. The author considers the latter in context with a wider view on FinTech a 'FinTech information mismatch' with (at least) two dimensions: (1) the lack of communication of the relevant information on the structure, design and working of FinTech activities[192] as the more obvious dimension, and (2) the lack of accessibility and comprehensibility of the information shared as the more subtle dimension.[193] Both dimensions are important particularly as to use cases of AI and ML. Different definitional approaches to AI and ML[194] add to the problem. Any legal analysis is confronted with this 'FinTech information mismatch' in the realm of AI and ML. Assessing the facts of the case turns into a profound permanent challenge. How might one tackle or at least mitigate these challenges when setting the scene at the outset of any legal analysis? Firstly, one has to decide on whether focus shall be on use cases of AI and ML primarily or on use cases of AI and ML converging with other technologies. Secondly, one has to critically consider the sources to be consulted to establish the facts of the case. The author suggests that such sources should at least be relevant, produced in compliance with methodological adequacy and represent the current status. As to the requirement of relevance, only those depictions of use cases of AI and ML (in the financial sector) might be chosen which might have (the potential of) regulatory and supervisory implications. This requires, however, only a preliminary and approximate assessment and is not to be confused with the exhaustive legal analysis of whether and how the relevant regulatory and supervisory regime addresses adequately the use cases of AI and ML (in the financial sector) depicted. The requirement of methodological adequacy of the sources entails that the latter are of high quality and unbiased. This includes particularly that appropriate objective research standards are applied. As to the requirement of current status, the depiction of use cases of AI and ML should best include both current and potential future ones. Considering also potential future use cases of AI and ML is owed to the high-paced technological developments requiring utmost agility but also needed as a precaution. Different to the banking and insurance sector, algorithms and large data sets have been used in capital markets, for example in trading, for many years.[195] Focus should be on those potential future use cases which allow grouping them into representative categories of manifestations of AI and ML in the financial sector. Against this backdrop, both studies and reports on relevant, current and future use cases of AI and ML in the realm of academic and other (non-academic) research as well as studies and reports of relevant policy makers, regulators and supervisors

190 World Economic Forum – here R. Jesse McWaters (lead author) et al, *WEF New Physics Report* (n 28) 12.
191 World Economic Forum – here R. Jesse McWaters (lead author) et al, *WEF New Physics Report* (n 28) 12.
192 In context with ML in trading and portfolio management, the FSB observes also a reluctance of relevant markets actors to share proprietary information. See FSB, *FSB Report AI and ML* (n 20) 19.
193 For more information on this with further references, see Gudula Deipenbrock (n 12) 16.
194 See eg, FSB, *FSB Report AI and ML* (n 20) 19, with a view to ML in trading and portfolio management.
195 See eg, BaFin, *BDAI Study* (n 55) 63.

at international, EU and national level might be consulted. As stated above, in the light of the current fragmentation as to the definitional approaches, any reference to these sources has to consider the each underlying concepts of AI, ML and Big Data.[196]

In addition, the various forms of dialogue between financial markets players, policy makers and relevant regulatory and supervisory authorities, particularly innovation hubs, sandboxes[197] or multi-stakeholder forums such as the European AI Alliance including also multi-disciplinary coordination between authorities in the realm of financial regulation and supervision, data protection and competition[198] are key to establishing the relevant facts of the case. The EBA Big Data Report is one example where EBA aims to share knowledge about and enhance understanding of the practical use of Big Data and Advanced Analytics in the banking sector noting the related risks.[199] Hence, utmost agility is in need to keep pace with the developments of use cases of AI and ML generally as well as in the financial sector. Legal-methodologically such agility will require particularly striking a sophisticated balance between (1) identifying general features but also sector- or context- specific details when establishing the facts of the case, and (2) formulating fundamental principles but also sector- or context- specific (detailed) rules when designing adequate policy and legal responses.

3 Conclusion

The legal-methodological challenges to be tackled in preparation of policy and legal (-political), particularly regulatory and supervisory responses to AI and ML in the financial sector are huge. The chapter selects only a few, however pressing ones. Already defining AI and ML faces profound problems. The heterogeneity and intricacies of definitional approaches to AI and ML, the high-paced technological progress and the 'FinTech information mismatch' render any policy and legal approach constantly preliminary. When relating AI and ML to law more fundamentally, both perspectives – the one with a focus on the use of AI and ML to optimise processes informed by law and the one with a focus on legal implications of the use of AI and ML – are conducive to further systemising use cases of AI and ML in financial services. Furthermore, the chapter argues in favour of putting (the policy and legal (-political) approach to) the sector-specific use of AI and ML – here their use in the financial sector – in the wider context of the more general use of AI and ML. Establishing the relevant facts of the case as another legal-methodological *conditio sine qua non* for any legal (-political) analysis is a further fundamental challenge. Utmost agility is in need to keep pace with the relevant (technological) developments. Particularly the 'winner takes all' – logic of the digital economy and the impact of the volume of investment on the speed of innovation and markets share in the realm of AI[200] make tackling the issues of value alignment and the control problem pressing. A global, concerted, far-sighted, long-term oriented, responsible and sustainable governance and regulation of AI and ML is the urgent law of reason. It shall ensure a regulatory 'whitebox'. The latter is the

---

196 See item 2.1.3.
197 For more information on regulatory sandboxes and innovation hubs, see eg, Joint Committee of the ESAs, *Report FinTech: Regulatory Sandboxes and Innovation Hubs* (JC 2018 74, no date).
198 For more information on a relevant recommendation in the realm of FinTech, see Expert Group on Regulatory Obstacles to Financial Innovation (n 32) Recommendation 26, 86 et seq.
199 EBA, *EBA Big Data Report* (n 53) 9.
200 See eg, High-Level Expert Group on AI, *HLEG AI Policy Recommendations* (n 76) 45.

dictate of the moment, of reason and in the face of AI and ML the dictate of humanity for humanity. The financial sector might well become a relevant test case.

Bibliography

Philip Bitter, 'Big Data im Finanz- und Versicherungswesen' in Thomas Hoeren, Ulrich Sieber and Bernd Holznagel (eds), *Handbuch Multimedia-Recht* (48th supp, C.H. Beck, February 2019).

Nick Bostrom, *Superintelligence – Paths, Dangers, Strategies* (OUP paperback 2016).

Nick Bostrom and Eliezer Yudkowsky, 'The Ethics of Artificial Intelligence' in Keith Frankish and William M. Ramsey (eds), *The Cambridge Handbook of Artificial Intelligence* (CUP 2018) 316.

John Brockman, 'Introduction: On the Promise and Peril of AI' in John Brockman (ed), *Possible Minds – Twenty-Five Ways of Looking at AI* (Penguin Press 2019) xv.

John Brockman (ed), *Possible Minds – Twenty-Five Ways of Looking at AI* (Penguin Press 2019).

Petra Buck-Heeb, *Kapitalmarktrecht* (10th edn, C.F. Müller 2019).

Bundesanstalt für Finanzdienstleistungsaufsicht, *Study, Big Data trifft auf Künstliche Intelligenz* (15 June 2018).

Bundesanstalt für Finanzdienstleistungsaufsicht – here Jörn Bartels and Thomas Deckers, *Big Data Meets Artificial Intelligence* (Issue 1, 2019) BaFin Perspectives 15.

Peter Cihon, *Technical Report – Standards for AI Governance: International Standards to Enable Global Coordination in AI Research & Development* (April 2019).

Gudula Deipenbrock, 'Is the Law Ready to Face the Progressing Digital Revolution? – General Policy Issues and Selected Aspects in the Realm of Financial Markets from the International, European Union and German Perspective' (2019) 118 ZVglRWiss 285.

Gudula Deipenbrock, 'FinTech – Unbearably Lithe or Reasonably Agile? – A Critical Legal Approach from the German Perspective' (2020) 31 EBLR 3.

De Nederlandsche Bank – here Joost van der Burgt, *General Principles for the Use of Artificial Intelligence in the Financial Sector* (2019).

Heinz-Uwe Dettling and Stefan Krüger, 'Erste Schritte im Recht der Künstlichen Intelligenz– Entwurf der "Ethik-Leitlinien für eine vertrauenswürdige KI"' (2019) MMR 211.

Die Bundesregierung, *KI Nationale Strategie für Künstliche Intelligenz AI Made in Germany* <www.ki-strategie-deutschland.de>.

Gerald A. Epstein, 'Introduction: Financialization and the World Economy' in Gerald A. Epstein (ed), *Financialization and the World Economy* (Edward Elgar 2006) 3.

European Banking Authority, *EBA Report on Big Data and Advanced Analytics* (EBA/REP/2020/01, January 2020).

European Commission, Communication from the Commission to the European Parliament, the Council, the European Central Bank, the European Economic and Social Committee and the Committee of the Regions, *FinTech Action Plan: For a More Competitive and Innovative European Financial Sector* (COM [2018] 109 final, 8 March 2018).

European Commission, Communication from the Commission to the European Parliament, the European Council, the Council, the European Economic and Social Committee and the Committee of the Regions, *Artificial Intelligence for Europe* (COM [2018] 237 final, 25 April 2018).

European Commission, Communication from the Commission to the European Parliament, the European Council, the Council, the European Economic and Social Committee and the Committee of the Regions, *Coordinated Plan on Artificial Intelligence* (COM [2018] 795 final, 7 December 2018).

European Commission, Communication from the Commission to the European Parliament, the Council, the European Economic and Social Committee and the Committee of the Regions, *Building Trust in Human-Centric Artificial Intelligence* (COM [2019] 168 final, 8 April 2019).

European Commission, *White Paper on Artificial Intelligence – A European Approach to Excellence and Trust* (COM [2020] 65 final, 19 February 2020).

European Commission, Communication from the Commission to the European Parliament, the Council, the European Economic and Social Committee and the Committee of the Regions, *A European Strategy for Data* (COM [2020] 66 final, 19 February 2020).

European Commission, Report from the Commission to the European Parliament, the Council and the European Economic and Social Committee, *Report on the Safety and Liability Implications of Artificial Intelligence, the Internet of Things and Robotics* (COM [2020] 64 final, 19 February 2020).

European Commission, *Communication from the Commission on an Action Plan for a Comprehensive Union Policy on Preventing Money Laundering and Terrorist Financing* (2020/C 164/06) [2020] OJ EU C 164/21.

Expert Group on Regulatory Obstacles to Financial Innovation (ROFIEG), *30 Recommendations on Regulation, Innovation and Finance – Final Report to the European Commission* (December 2019).

Financial Stability Board, *Artificial Intelligence and Machine Learning in Financial Services – Market Developments and Financial Stability Implications* (1 November 2017).

Financial Stability Board, *BigTech in Finance – Market Developments and Potential Financial Stability Implications* (9 December 2019).

Financial Stability Board, *FSB Chair's Letter to G20 Finance Ministers and Central Bank Governors* (18 February 2020).

Keith Frankish and William M. Ramsey (eds), *The Cambridge Handbook of Artificial Intelligence* (CUP 2018).

G20 Japan 2019 Presidency, *G20 Ministerial Statement on Trade and Digital Economy* (June 2019).

Tom Griffiths, 'The Artificial Use of Human Beings' in John Brockman (ed), *Possible Minds – Twenty-Five Ways of Looking at AI* (Penguin Press 2019) 125.

Olaf J. Groth, Mark Nitzberg and Dan Zehr, et al in Konrad-Adenauer-Stiftung e. V. (ed), *Vergleich nationaler Strategien zur Förderung von Künstlicher Intelligenz*, Teil 1 (2018) and Teil 2 (2019).

Ronan Hamon, Henrik Junklewitz and Ignacio Sanchez, *JRC Technical Report – Robustness and Explainability of Artificial Intelligence* (EUR 30040 EN, Publications Office of the European Union 2020).

Maximilian Herberger, '"Künstliche Intelligenz" und Recht' (2018) 71 NJW 2825.

Frank Herring, Dennis Kunschke and Elena Bachmann, '"Lizenzleihe" und Robo-Advice' in Dennis Kunschke and Kai A. Schaffelhuber (eds), *FinTech – Grundlagen – Regulierung – Finanzierung – Case Studies* (Erich Schmidt 2018) 95.

W. Daniel Hillis, 'The First Machine Intelligences' in John Brockman (ed), *Possible Minds – Twenty-Five Ways of Looking at AI* (Penguin Press 2019) 170.

Independent High-Level Expert Group on Artificial Intelligence, *A definition of AI: Main Capabilities and Disciplines* (8 April 2019).

Independent High-Level Expert Group on Artificial Intelligence, *Ethics Guidelines for Trustworthy AI* (8 April 2019).

Independent High-Level Expert Group on Artificial Intelligence, *Policy and Investment Recommendations for Trustworthy AI* (26 June 2019).

Joint Committee of the ESAs, *Joint Committee Final Report on Big Data* (JC/2018/04, 15 March 2018).

Joint Committee of the ESAs, *Report FinTech: Regulatory Sandboxes and Innovation Hubs* (JC 2018 74, no date).

Jochen Kindermann, '§ 14 Effektengeschäft: Praktische Anwendungsfragen' in Florian Möslein and Sebastian Omlor (eds), *FinTech-Handbuch* (C.H. Beck 2019) 338.

Christoph Kumpan, '§ 15 Interessenwahrung durch Robo-Advisors' in Florian Möslein and Sebastian Omlor (eds), *FinTech-Handbuch* (C.H. Beck 2019) 351.

Detmar Loff, '3. Kapitel: Digital Asset Management/Robo-Advice' in Ulf Klebeck and Günther Dobrauz-Saldapenna (eds), *Rechtshandbuch Digitale Finanzdienstleistungen* (C.H. Beck 2018) 193.

Klaus Mainzer, *Künstliche Intelligenz – Wann übernehmen die Maschinen?* (2nd edn, Springer 2019).

Mario Martini, *Blackbox Algorithmus – Grundfragen einer Regulierung Künstlicher Intelligenz* (Springer 2019).

Florian Möslein, 'Smart Contracts im Zivil- und Handelsrecht' (2019) 183 ZHR 254.

Florian Möslein and Sebastian Omlor, '§ 1 Grundlagen' in Florian Möslein and Sebastian Omlor (eds), *FinTech-Handbuch* (C.H. Beck 2019) 1.

Julian Nida-Rümelin, 'Preface' in Julian Nida-Rümelin and Nathalie Weidenfeld, *Digitaler Humanismus – Eine Ethik für das Zeitalter der Künstlichen Intelligenz* (Piper 2018) 9.

Julian Nida-Rümelin and Nathalie Weidenfeld, *Digitaler Humanismus – Eine Ethik für das Zeitalter der Künstlichen Intelligenz* (Piper 2018).

Eleonore Pauwels, *The New Geopolitics of Artificial Intelligence* (15 October 2018) <www.weforum.org/agenda/2018/10/artificial-intelligence-ai-new-geopolitics-un>.

Stuart Russell, *Human Compatible: Artificial Intelligence and the Problem of Control* (Penguin Random House 2019).

Jakob Schemmel, 'Artificial Intelligence and the Financial Markets: Business as Usual?' in Thomas Wischmeyer and Timo Rademacher (eds), *Regulating Artificial Intelligence* (Springer 2020) 255.

Matthias Scheutz, 'Artificial Emotions and Machine Consciousness' in Keith Frankish and William M. Ramsey (eds), *The Cambridge Handbook of Artificial Intelligence* (CUP 2018) 247.

Jean-Claude Spillmann, '7. Kapitel: RegTech im lokalen und internationalen Aufsichtsrecht' in Ulf Klebeck and Günther Dobrauz-Saldapenna (eds), *Rechtshandbuch Digitale Finanzdienstleistungen* (C.H. Beck 2018) 463.

Max Tegmark, 'Let's Aspire to More than Making Ourselves Obsolete' in John Brockman (ed), *Possible Minds – Twenty-Five Ways of Looking at AI* (Penguin Press 2019) 76.

Friedrich Graf von Westphalen, 'Haftungsfragen beim Einsatz Künstlicher Intelligenz in Ergänzung der Produkthaftungs-RL 85/374/EWG' (2019) 40 ZIP 889.

Thomas Wischmeyer and Timo Rademacher (eds), *Regulating Artificial Intelligence* (Springer 2020).

World Economic Forum – here R. Jesse McWaters (lead author) et al – prepared in collaboration with Deloitte, *The New Physics of Financial Services – Understanding how Artificial Intelligence is Transforming the Financial Ecosystem* (August 2018).

World Economic Forum – here Emilio Granados Franco (lead author) et al – in partnership with Marsh & McLennan and Zurich Insurance Group, *The Global Risks Report 2020* (15th edn, no date)

World Economic Forum and Cambridge Centre for Alternative Finance, University of Cambridge Judge Business School (CCAF) with the support of EY and Invesco, *Transforming Paradigms – A Global AI in Financial Services Survey* (January 2020).

2 Smart contracts and civil law challenges

Does legal origins theory apply?

Florian Möslein

1 Technological code and codified law

Blockchain and distributed ledger technologies are widely regarded as regulatory technologies.[1] Their core regulatory devices are so-called smart contracts, that is, self-executing agreements that are usually written in code on the blockchain. When coining this term in the 1990s, Nick Szabo defined a smart contract as 'a computerized transaction protocol that executes the terms of a contract. The general objectives of smart contract design', Szabo went on, 'are to satisfy common contractual conditions (such as payment terms, liens, confidentiality and even enforcement), minimize exceptions, both malicious and accidental and minimize the need for trusted intermediaries. Related economic goals include lowering fraud loss, arbitration and enforcement costs and other transactions costs'.[2] As smart contracts are automatable by computers and enforceable via the tamper-proof execution of software codes, they can perform tasks that have traditionally been assigned to the realm of law. They not only define the rules and penalties around an agreement but also automatically enforce those obligations. The design of smart contracts, therefore, allows for the digital coding of respective legal institutions, and also helps to ensure the automatic enforcement of respective rights and duties.[3] In that sense, smart contracts are a technological expression of contractual terms, and the famous equation 'code is law', coined by Lawrence Lessig in the late 1990s,[4] could also be read as 'code is contract'.

The relationship between smart contracts and contract law, however, is much more subtle. It is currently the subject of intensive academic debate.[5] At least, Lessig's equation does by no means imply that any software-based implementation of contractual rules automatically results in their legal effectiveness.[6] Technological code does not necessarily qualify as legal code, even if it provides rules that serve similar functions. Yet both sets of rules are not necessarily congruent and can lead to different results in substance. Conflicts arise whenever technologically coded rules differ from the applicable legal rules, either in substance or in relation to their enforcement, or whenever both sets of rules, even if their substance

---

1 See, for instance, De Filippi and Hassan (2016) 21.
2 Szabo (1994); see also Szabo (1997).
3 For more details see De Filippi and Wright (2018) 74 et seq; Tur Faúndez (2018) 51–71; see also D Tapscott and A Tapscott (2016) 101–103.
4 Lessig (2000). See also Lessig (1999) 89; Reidenberg (1998).
5 Cf. for instance, DiMatteo, Cannarsa and Poncibò (2019) 3–19; Raskin (2017); see also Möslein (2019d).
6 In a similar vein, Wu (2003) ('*When Code Isn't Law*').

seemingly agrees, are applied in different ways.[7] Legal jurisdictions, therefore, need to define rules that solve these conflicts of laws and codes, either by rules of recognition or by rules subjecting the substance of blockchain-based rules to legal scrutiny.[8] In this respect, different legal systems may well deal differently with smart contracts. Both the extent to which these technological devices are recognised and the level of scrutiny of their substance, are likely to differ from one jurisdiction to another. As a consequence, comparative contract law considerations relating to smart contracts are on the rise.[9]

What is rarely discussed so far, however, is the impact that fundamental differences between contract law systems, namely the divide of civil law and common law, have on the relationship between smart contracts and contract law. Whereas civil law systems codify the core principles in legislative rules and rule-books, which then serve as the primary source of law, common law mainly builds on precedents, that is, judge-made decisions that have previously been decided upon in similar cases.[10] Civil law jurisdictions consist of comprehensive legal codes that formulate general principles at some rather abstract level, and they distinguish between different categories of law, namely substantive rules from procedural rules. Since judges in civil law systems work within frameworks established by comprehensive, codified sets of rules, their decisions are less crucial in shaping the law than in common law systems, which mainly build on precedents. Even if the idea of codes as entirely complete sets of rules remains an illusion,[11] civil law subordinates case law to codified law. However, which effective impact do these conceptual differences have on the relationship between smart contracts and contract law? In accordance with the legal origins theory, developed by La Porta, Lopez-de-Silanes, Shleifer and Vishny, one might assume that these two different legal traditions do not only affect economic outcomes in corporate finance,[12] but also accommodate regulatory technologies such as smart contracts differently. In fact, these authors correlate civil law systems with stricter regulations and less efficient contract enforcement; they claim that these systems place a lower emphasis on private ordering and are, therefore, less easily adaptable to new developments.[13] As a consequence, their claims seem to imply that there may well be a higher demand for smart contracts in civil law systems because of their efficient technological enforcement, but they are less easily accommodated by these systems in comparison to common law jurisdictions which are more innovation-friendly and less heavily regulated. This preliminary thesis requires a thorough discussion, however. The present contribution aims at initiating this debate. With a focus on civil law systems, and on German law in particular, it analyses both the freedom of private parties to subject their mutual relationships to smart contracts, and the specific limitations that restrict this freedom. In accordance with the typical approach of civil law, it thereby starts with the general principle (which in this case, is laid down at constitutional level, sub 2.) and then addresses its more specific ramifications (which is laid down in the German Civil Code – the 'Bürgerliches Gesetzbuch' or BGB – itself, sub 3.).

7 Möslein (2019a) 277.
8 More extensively Möslein (2019a) 278–284.
9 See, for instance, Schurr (2019).
10 In more detail Joseph Dainow (1966); Merryman (1981); Vranken (2015).
11 See, however, Remy (2004) 100: 'C'était in corps, un tout coherent, un système de droit civil prétendant à la completude'.
12 La Porta et al (1998) 1113–1155; La Porta et al (1999) 222–279; La Porta et al (2000) 3–27.
13 Cf. La Porta et al (2008).

2 Smart contracts and freedom of contract

Similar to all other legal systems that underpin market economies, civil law jurisdictions are based on the principles of freedom of contract and private autonomy. Individual economic freedom is exercised by market transactions, and contracts are a key instrument enabling such transactions to be carried out. Contracts thus provide a tool for individuals to exercise their individual freedom, in order to shape their legal relationships according to their own will.[14] As opposed to other civil law systems like France,[15] the German BGB does not, however, explicitly provide for the freedom of contract. Yet private autonomy is deeply rooted in German constitutional law; in particular, Article 2 para 1 of the German Basic Law (Grundgesetz) guarantees every person the right to free development of his personality and thereby also freedom of contract.[16] As a central pillar of individual freedoms in the legal realm, the freedom of contract covers, in particular, the freedom to decide on the conclusion of a contract with a particular contractual partner (freedom of choice), the freedom to decide on its content (freedom of content) and the freedom to conclude agreements without being subject to formal requirements, at least in principle (freedom of form).[17] With specific regard to smart contracts, the question arises whether this principle of private autonomy also extends to their use. With regard to the common definition and the practical applications of smart contracts, two different modes of application need to be distinguished, in order to answer this question.

2.1 *Formation of contracts*

On the one hand, blockchain technology makes it possible to arrange the transaction itself by using smart contracts. Offer and acceptance proceed as computer-assisted transactions.[18] Such a technological arrangement is not necessarily equivalent to the formation of a contract in the legal sense, however. The term 'smart contract' is in fact misleading. Whether such a technological construct qualifies as a contract in the legal sense is by no means a matter of course, but it must be assessed thoroughly from a legal point of view.[19] Blockchain technology, however, allows smart contracts to fulfil functions that are comparable to those of legal contracts. Their technical code can define the services to be exchanged, as well as the conditions under which these services are to be provided.[20] In addition, the smart contract typically ensures that the exchange of those services is effectively carried out. If the program code of the smart contract itself defines the program of obligations of the parties,

---

14 On the basic concept of private autonomy, cf. Flume (1992) § 1, 1.
15 The 'liberté contractuelle' is laid down in Art. 1102 para 1 Code Civil: 'Chacun est libre de contracter ou de ne pas contracter, de choisir son cocontractant et de déterminer le contenu et la forme du contrat dans les limites fixées par la loi'. In more detail, for instance, Malaurie, Aynès and Stoffel-Munck (2018) para 449.
16 In this sense, for instance, many decisions of the German Federal Constitutional Court: BVerfGE 65, 196 (210 et seq) = NJW 1984, 476; BVerfGE 86, 122 (130) = NJW 1992, 2409; BVerfGE 95, 267 (303 et seq) = NJW 1997, 1975. For more details on the constitutional framework, see Möslein (2020) § 145 BGB para 21 et seqs.
17 For more details, see Möslein (2020) § 145 BGB 32 et seqs.
18 Cf. Kaulartz and Heckmann (2016) 621.
19 Similar to Möslein (2019c) 84.
20 In this vein, for instance, De Filippi and Wright (2018) 74.

the 'normative order of the digital'[21] resembles the legal order of the contract without necessarily being congruent with it. Some even refer to digital jurisdictions.[22] Fields of application include, for example, digital autonomous organisations that are based on the Ethereum blockchain and can be joined by acquiring digital tokens.[23] The tokens represent fungible goods and rights of all kinds, including virtual membership rights in those digital autonomous organisations.[24] Their inclusion in blockchain-based smart contracts demonstrates their functional similarity to contracts in the legal sense. The key difference, however, lies in their enforceability; smart contracts are technically enforceable, by means of their software-based code, but they are not necessarily legally enforceable: 'In many ways, smart contracts are no different from today's written agreements [...]. Where traditional legal agreements and smart contracts begin to differ is in the ability of smart contracts to enforce obligations by using autonomous code'.[25]

From a constitutional perspective, this mode of operation primarily relates to two of the fundamental pillars of contractual freedom. By enabling agreements to be concluded without observing formal requirements, the freedom of form also ensures the opportunity for contracting parties to record their contractual agreements in electronic form and, in particular, in the form of software code.[26] Since it also implied that non-linguistic declarations of intent can form the basis of legal contracts,[27] there is nothing to prevent the parties from replacing human language by machine-readable computer protocols, in order to conclude a contract. It is widely recognised that private autonomy also includes the choice of the contractual language.[28] Protocols can also be understood as a kind of contractual language, at least in a broad sense.[29] Sub-constitutional law may well prescribe formal requirements for specific legal transactions with which smart contracts cannot comply (see 3. below). In principle, however, in representing the contractual program of obligations, a smart contract nevertheless enjoys constitutional protection. Even if specific duties are not legally enforceable due to non-compliance with sub-constitutional requirements of form, their technology-based enforcement is not necessarily excluded. At least, Article 2 para 1 of the German Basic Law guarantees the free development of one's personality and thereby not only contractual freedom, but also the freedom to design private transactions in a more comprehensive sense.[30] The constitutional provision, therefore, does not oblige citizens to use legally formal agreements, but allows them to agree on other, non-legal enforcement mechanisms: an 'escape from the legal system' does not necessarily run contrary to Article 2 para 1 of the German Basic Law.[31] Inversely, however, this constitutional

---

21 In similar terms, a conference on '*Normative Orders of the Digital*' took place in July 2017 in the framework of the research cluster on Normative Orders at Goethe University in Frankfurt, cf. <https://www.normativeorders.net/de/veranstaltungen/dokumentation/69-veranstaltungen/5515-normative-orders-of-the-digital>. Access date for all hyperlinks 25 July 2020, unless stated otherwise.
22 See in particular Cuende and Izquierdo (2017) 19; Möslein (2019b) 315.
23 In more detail, for instance Hoppe (2017) 62 et seq.
24 See also with regard to practical implementation, <https://www.ethereum.org/token>.
25 De Filippi and Wright (2018) 74.
26 Cf. Kaulartz (2016) 1028 et seq.
27 See only Möslein (2020) § 145 BGB para 36 et seq.
28 Kaulartz (2016), at 1028 et seq; Börding et al (2017) 139.
29 In more detail Kaulartz and Heckmann (2016) 621 et seq, with further references.
30 In this vein, for instance di Fabio (2019) Art. 2 para 1 German Basic Law para 101.
31 Similar, though with regard to competition law: Jäger (1970) 23.

principle does not coerce the legal system in any way to assist technology-based enforcement in achieving legal validity. The legal system may well reach opposite results, for example where technology-based enforcement which has been carried out despite legal invalidity, is considered an abusive circumvention of the formal requirement in question.

The formation of contracts via smart contracts is also associated with a second pillar of freedom of contracts, namely the freedom to choose a particular contractual partner. At least smart contracts also enable completely unknown persons to enter into contracts with one another, without having to identify and trust one another. Smart contracts make such trust in contractual partners dispensable. Instead, the trust refers exclusively to the reliability of blockchain-based enforcement.[32] In fact, participation in the blockchain usually operates on a pseudonymous basis, because the sender and addressee only need to identify themselves in a digital form.[33] By relying on digital signatures and cryptographic encryption, the technology enables transactions to take place, in which the true identity of both parties needs not to be disclosed.[34] Knowledge of the identity is also less significant for the parties, because smart contracts offer the alternative of technology-based enforcement mechanisms in addition to traditional contract law. This 'second track' of claim enforcement[35] does not require a complete, summonable address of the other party, as opposed to the conventional enforcement of rights through state courts (under German law, cf. § 130 no. 1 of the Code of Civil Procedure, ZPO). Ever since Gerhart Husserl's famous desert example,[36] it has been assumed that the legal order is necessary, because private parties otherwise face the fundamental problem that they cannot enforce their contractual rights, so that the binding force of contracts is not assured.[37] Blockchain technology is capable of overcoming this fundamental problem of trust. From a constitutional perspective, there are no concerns in relation to pseudonymisation, as the freedom to choose a contractual partner also includes the choice of unknown partners. As a dimension of private autonomy, this freedom is rarely discussed, however. This becomes evident, for example, in the realm of the German law of agency, where transactions without knowledge of the other party are considered not to harm the person concerned, provided that such lack of knowledge is of no relevance to the other party.[38] Such knowledge loses relevance, not only in everyday transactions for immediate delivery (the so-called 'buy now, pay now' deals), but also in smart contracts where execution is secured by (blockchain) technology. In a similar vein, German courts have decided that contracts with 'Mr. Still Unknown' via forms on internet websites are admissible, as long as the provider does not explicitly exclude such a possibility and thereby indicates that the identity of the contractual partner is of importance to him.[39] If this is not the case, however, there are no concerns regarding the possibility of entering into contracts with unknown parties. On the contrary, this possibility is, in principle, covered by the

32 De Filippi and Wright (2018) 38 et seq. Accordingly, blockchain technology is regarded as an architecture of trust: Werbach (2018).
33 More extensively Azouvi, Al-Bassam and Meiklejohn (2018).
34 In more detail on pseudonymity: De Filippi and Wright (2018) 38 et seq.
35 Cf. Fries (2018) 87 ('zweite Spur').
36 Husserl (1925) 39; in more detail in relation to that example, for instance: Möslein (2014) 138.
37 In the same vein also the German Constitutional Court, cf. BVerfGE 89, 214 (231 et seq, claiming that, according to its object of regulation, private autonomy is necessarily dependent on state enforcement).
38 See, for example, Wertenbruch (2017) § 28 para 11 et seq (= 329).
39 BGHZ 195, 126, 133 = BGH NJW 2013, 598, 599 et seq (para 20 et seq).

freedom to choose contractual partners. At least, the German Basic Law comprehensively guarantees the freedom to shape legal relationships according to one's own will, and it thus also grants the greatest possible scope for the manner in which this freedom can be exercised, also by means of a smart contract.[40]

2.2 Execution of contracts

On the other hand, smart contracts can simply contribute to the execution of conventionally concluded contracts, in particular, by controlling, monitoring and documenting the promised exchange of services. In this mode, smart contracts serve as a tool for the execution of contracts. The rules of those contracts are formulated in conventional human language and additionally 'translated' into technical code, allowing the software to check independently whether certain agreed preconditions are fulfilled or not, and to automatically provide or block the service promised. For example, leasing contracts can provide for the use of so-called starter interrupt devices. These devices shall ensure the punctual payment of the leasing instalments by means of a software-based code that automatically blocks the starting of a leased car. In this example, the smart contract acts as an enforcement tool of conventional contracts.

This variant of smart contracts concerns contractual freedom in its pillar as freedom of content. If contractual parties are basically free to determine the content of contracts at their own discretion, they can also agree on special forms of (technology-based) enforcement of their claims in the event of a breach of contract. This freedom of content does not only include the substantive-law sphere between the parties. It also includes the entitlement of the parties to determine their legal relationships in accordance with the conflict of laws and thus to subject them to a particular legal system or to withdraw them from it. Last but not least, it also grants them procedural freedom.[41] Private autonomy applies equally to procedural law and gives the parties the opportunity of concluding procedural contracts.[42] Similar to, for example, arbitration agreements, admissible under the fundamental right of contractual freedom under Article 2 of the German Basic Law,[43] private individuals also have the opportunity of submitting disputes to technical enforcement instruments. However, the contractual freedom guaranteed by fundamental law is not unlimited. Sub-constitutional law can restrict it, again similar to arbitration agreements, which are subject to restrictions in terms of content and form by general legal doctrines or by specific rules (cf. especially § 1031 of the Code of Civil Procedure, ZPO).[44] In order to enjoy the protection of contractual freedom, the technical devices in question must in any case have been contractually agreed upon, that is, they must not have been installed secretly by only one contracting party. Accordingly, the German Federal Court of Justice ruled that digital protection measures for software programs, so-called program blocks, are only permissible if

---

40 For a seemingly different position cf. Schwintowski, Klausmann and Kadgien (2018) 1405 (claiming that there is no formation of a contract in addition, because blockchain users remain anonymous).
41 Cf. H Prütting (2005) 708.
42 See the monograph by Wagner (1998).
43 Explicitly in this vein, BAG NJW 1964, 268, 269; similar, for instance, BGH NJW 1976, 852.
44 In more detail, for instance, Münch (2017) § 1029 German Code of Civil Procedure para 16–26b.

the specific circumstances of the individual case allow it and at least an implied contractual agreement exists.[45]

3 Specific challenges of smart contracts

In summary, private parties enjoy freedom of contracts to a large extent, also with regard to smart contracts in a civil law jurisdiction such as Germany. Before considering this conclusion in the context of legal origins theory, however, its specific ramifications require closer examination. In line with the principle-based approach of civil law jurisdictions, this constitutionally guaranteed private autonomy needs to be specified by the sub-constitutional legal rules of the BGB. At least legal transactions are the instrument for the autonomous design of legal relationships.[46] The regulatory framework of legal transactions is laid down in the general section of the BGB. Its rules enable, and at the same time, limit the freedom of the contract, thereby providing the necessary infrastructure for its exercise.[47] Three key questions need to be considered here, namely (1) whether specific formal requirements as laid down in these rules limit the possible uses of smart contracts, (2) in what way and according to which rules are the underlying declarations of intent generated and transmitted and (3) whether the technical set-up of a smart contract constitutes a contract in the legal sense, and if so, how are the rules laid down in the technological code of the smart contract to be interpreted.

3.1 *Formal requirements*

Under German law, the basic principle is freedom of form.[48] In general, contracts can be concluded without observing a specific form. The key provisions of §§ 145 et seq BGB do not provide for any formal requirements for offer and acceptance.[49] For certain legal transactions, however, the law provides for specific formal requirements, be it for the purpose of warning and protection against precipitation, be it (additionally) for purposes of clarification and evidence.[50] The most important forms required by corresponding legal provisions are notarial recording or public authentication in accordance with §§ 128 et seq BGB, the written form and the equivalent electronic form in accordance with §§ 126, 126a BGB and the text form in accordance with § 126b BGB.

---

45 Out of the numerous court decisions, see in particular BGH NJW 1981, 2684, 2685 (claiming that the contractual obligation to actively protect the license program includes the obligation to tolerate appropriate protective measures of the program manufacturer); more extensively, apparently, C Paulus and Matzke (2017) 778 (claiming that admissibility depends on an explicit contractual stipulation).
46 Cf. for instance Bork (2016) para 395 (= 161).
47 In this perspective, for instance Möslein and Riesenhuber (2009) 269: contract law 'is part of a framework or infrastructure for the co-operation of private individuals'.
48 Common law provides similar formal requirements, cf. for instance, with regard to US law: Cardozo Blockchain Project, '*Smart Contracts and Legal Enforceability, Research Report*' (2018) <https://larc.cardozo.yu.edu/cgi/viewcontent.cgi?article=1001&context=blockchain-project-reports>, in particular 9 et seqs.
49 In more detail, for instance Möslein (2020) § 145 BGB para 36.
50 For a more extensive account of these regulatory purposes see, for instance, Musielak (2017) 952.

3.1.1 *Notarial recording and public authentication*

Notarial recording and public authentication are required, for example, for contracts on the acquisition or sale of real estate (§ 311b para 1 BGB) or for the declaration of the subscription of shares, created by a capital increase in limited liability companies (§ 55 para 1 GmbHG). It is obvious that smart contracts as such cannot satisfy this specific form requirement, also because the necessary participation of a third party (the notary or the court) is lacking. At least some of these formal requirements fulfil information, advisory and warning functions. In this case, the possibility of corresponding transactions by smart contracts would appear to be inappropriate, also due to teleological reasons. As a consequence, there is no need to change the law.[51] However, this formal requirement does not mean that smart contracts cannot be used at all with regard to such legal transactions. As an instrument of contract execution, smart contracts may well be used in this respect, provided that only the conclusion of the contract is subject to the formal requirement in question.[52] For purposes of contract formation, however, smart contracts cannot be used in these cases, at least not in a legally effective way.

3.1.2 *Text form*

As opposed to these demanding formal requirements, smart contracts can fulfil the requirement of text form as defined in § 126b BGB. The definition simply requires the submission of a legible declaration, in which the person making the declaration is named on a permanent data carrier. The precondition of readability is generally assumed to be fulfilled if electronic data in standard file formats are used.[53] In particular, encryption is considered not to be an impediment.[54] The cryptographic use of private and public keys, which is typical for blockchain-based smart contracts,[55] therefore, does not conflict with text form. The naming of the party who makes the declaration is technically possible, even in blockchain-based smart contracts and especially in private blockchain networks that are only accessible to authorised users.[56] However, it remains questionable, whether the typical restriction to pseudonyms that results from the use of public keys meets this requirement, because in this case, the digital identities can be clearly traced, but due to the lack of disclosure of actual names, the people behind them are not easily identifiable.[57] However, it will often be possible to identify them at least indirectly, for example, via information from third-party facilities that have been used (such as trading platforms). Such recognisability should be sufficient to fulfil the requirement of § 126b BGB. At least, comparable cases, such as the use of nicknames or function designations, show that the formal standard

---

51 In the same vein Vereinigung der Bayerischen Wirtschaft e. V. (ed), '*Blockchain und Smart Contracts – Recht und Technik im Überblick*' (October 2017) 24 <https://vbw-bayern.de/Redaktion/Frei-zugaengliche-Medien/Abteilungen-GS/Planung-und-Koordination/2017/Downloads/2017-09-12-NH-vbw-Blockchain-und-Smart-Contracts_ChV-Fu%C3%9Fnoten.pdf>.
52 Similar Heckelmann (2018) 507.
53 In this sense, for instance Einsele (2018) § 126b BGB para 4.
54 Cf. Primaczenko and Frohn (2020) § 126b BGB para 11.
55 Extensively De Filippi and Wright (2018) 14–16.
56 On the differences between private and public blockchains, see D Tapscott and A Tapscott (2016) 67 et seq.
57 See references (n 33) et seq.

does not require actual names, but allows the use of pseudonyms.[58] Finally, smart contracts can easily meet the requirement of submitting the declaration on a permanent data carrier, because blockchain-based information can no longer be altered or deleted unilaterally by the parties involved afterwards.[59] Moreover, according to the definition of permanent data carrier in § 126b BGB, digitalised content on storage media also meets the formal requirement.[60]

3.1.3 *Written and electronic form*

Of particular practical importance is the third category of formal requirements, namely the written form. Whether smart contracts fulfil this requirement, however, is disputed. Some claim that the written form cannot be complied with on the blockchain or in smart contracts.[61] Others argue that declarations on the blockchain correspond to an electronic format, which in most cases can replace the written form.[62] While it is certainly true that smart contracts can comply with the electronic form pursuant to § 126a BGB, the scope of this provision is quite narrow and typically not fulfilled. After all, § 126a BGB provides for stricter requirements for personal identifiability than § 126b BGB. According to Regulation (EU) No. 910/2014 on electronic identification and trust services for electronic transactions in the internal market, the condition that the person making the declaration must add his/her name does not exclude the use of pseudonyms,[63] but it at least requires the indication that a pseudonym is used.[64] Moreover, the declaration requires a qualified electronic signature. According to the definition in Art. 3 No. 12 of the Regulation, this signature not only needs to fulfil the requirements for advanced electronic signatures (in particular, unique link to the signatory, identifiability, creation by using trustworthy electronic signature creation data and detectability of subsequent changes, cf. Art. 26 of that Regulation), it also needs to be created by a qualified electronic signature creation device and be based on a qualified certificate for electronic signatures.[65] Whether smart contracts meet these diverse requirements, and whether they are in particular 'capable of identifying the signatory' within the meaning of Art. 26 lit. b) of that Regulation is a question of their specific technical design.

3.2 *Declaration of intent*

If a smart contract shall exclusively be used for the execution of the contract, the contract is to be concluded in the conventional way ('off chain').[66] As a consequence, no specific legal

---

58 In more detail Einsele (2018) § 126b BGB para 7; Primaczenko and Frohn (2020) § 126b BGB para 14.
59 De Filippi and Wright (2018) 35–37.
60 Einsele (2018) § 126b BGB para 6; Primaczenko and Frohn (2020) § 126b BGB para 16.
61 Heckelmann (2018) 507.
62 Vereinigung der Bayerischen Wirtschaft e. V. (n 51) 24.
63 Accordingly, Art. 5 para 2 of the Regulation (EU) No. 910/2014 on electronic identification and trust services for electronic transactions in the internal market and repealing Directive 1999/93/EC [2014] OJ L257/73, provides that 'the use of pseudonyms in electronic transactions shall not be prohibited' by Member States.
64 Cf. Art. 3 no 14, Art. 32 para 1 lit. e) as well as Annex I lit. c) of the Regulation No 910/2014 [2014] OJ L257/73.
65 In more detail, for instance, Roßnagel (2014) 3689.
66 D Paulus and Matzke (2018) 447 et seq.

questions arise in this case. If, on the other hand, a smart contract shall serve as a functional equivalent to a legal contract, several questions arise with regard to the declaration of intent and the formation of the contract. Such smart contracts are not necessarily to be qualified as contracts in the legal sense. They can simply be technical constructs which, due to their rule-based software code, are functionally similar to legal contracts, but do not qualify as such.

3.2.1 *Generation*

Declarations of intent can be transmitted or even generated without or by using technical tools ('electronic declaration of intent').[67] In the second case, a distinction is made between so-called automated and autonomous declarations of intent.[68] All these different sub-forms of declarations also exist in context with smart contracts. In spite of the inherent technological embedding of contract processing, neither the generation nor the transmission of the declaration of intent, has to be necessarily technology-based. On the other hand, such additional use of technology at the stage of contract formation is by no means untypical. The combination of the two key digital technologies, blockchain and artificial intelligence, is rather becoming a technological trend.[69] In future, the initiative to enter into smart contracts will often be based on self-learning algorithms, the decisions of which are not determined by human programming, but are developed independently and without human intervention by recognising patterns in datasets.[70]

The legal problems that autonomous declarations raise can, therefore, also become relevant for smart contracts. This is especially true for the much-debated question of whether declarations that human operators can no longer foresee, can nevertheless be attributed to them as their own declaration, or whether, due to the lack of foreseeability, a kind of partial legal capacity of the autonomous system can be assumed.[71] These questions of autonomous declarations of intent need not be dealt with in greater depth here, because they are a necessary consequence of the use of artificial intelligence, but are not a consequence of smart contracts.[72] (Partially) automated declarations which are generated on the basis of pre-defined rules, are, on the other hand, a widespread, perhaps even typical element of smart contracts.[73] If the occurrence of a certain condition agreed in the contract (eg, timely payment) automatically triggers the issuance of a declaration to effect the transfer of ownership of the object sold, the automated execution of the contract, which is typical for smart contracts, and the automated creation of contracts, interlock closely. From a legal perspective, such an automated generation of declarations is less problematic if the discretion parameters of the technical system are very narrow. If the declaration in question is based on concrete and unambiguous rules, it can easily be attributed to the operator or user of the respective system.[74] Since smart contracts are characterised precisely by the fact that they trigger certain actions depending on digitally verifiable events, the declarations

---

67 In more detail Gomille (2020) § 130 BGB para 33.
68 Extensively in relation to these different perspectives Specht and Herold (2018).
69 See, for instance, Corea (2019) 19 ('*The Convergence of AI and Blockchain*').
70 On such algorithms see Borges (2018) 978; Specht and Herold (2018) 41.
71 In more detail Möslein (2019c) 91.
72 See, however, D Paulus and Matzke (2018) 440–445.
73 Extensively on these different degrees Specht and Herold (2018) 41–43.
74 Cf. Heckelmann (2018) 506; Möslein (2020) § 145 BGB para 71.

they make are typically based on 'mechanical' rules, which provide unambiguous results.[75] The technical systems on which smart contracts are based thus enjoy very little discretion. In general, automated declarations of intent made within the framework of smart contracts can, therefore, be easily attributed to their human users.[76]

3.2.2 *Transmission*

Declarations of intent are not necessarily made by machines, even in the case of block-chain-based transactions and smart contracts. For example, if trading contracts between suppliers and buyers are concluded on blockchain platforms, the underlying decisions are typically not made by machines, but by people. Depending on the technological design, even the transmission of the declaration does not necessarily need to be generated by electronic means. Other forms are illustrated by the often quoted, albeit particularly conventional, example of the vending machine.[77] However, especially in blockchain-based smart contracts, electronic declarations of intent are typical. At least, this technology is characterised by the use of appropriate forms of communication.

Electronic communication of (pre-)contractual declarations does not change the applicability of the conventional contract law rules, but some technology-based particularities must be taken into account. One particular question is whether offering services on the basis of smart contracts qualifies as a binding offer within the meaning of § 145 BGB – or simply invites offers (*invitatio ad offerendum*). In contrast to the presentation of goods in a shop window or on the internet, the provider who offers his services on the basis of smart contracts regularly agrees to the fully automated processing of the contract. The provider thus does not wish to reserve the final decision on the conclusion of the contract, until concrete orders have been received, as is the case with vending machine operators. As a consequence, his implied declaration is to be qualified as a binding offer, albeit under certain conditions, and made public (*ad incertas personas*).[78] In contrast to cases where providers answer e-mails by autoreply,[79] the contract is, therefore, usually concluded at the very moment that the other party makes its declarations. Insofar as questions of the acceptance period arise, the distinction between declarations in presence and in absence is important under German contract law, but also difficult to establish in the case of blockchain-based transactions. Even if the provision on presence includes declarations that are made by 'other technical equipment' (cf. § 147 para 1 sentence 2 BGB), such a qualification requires the opportunity for interactive, simultaneous negotiation.[80] Such an opportunity is usually alien to blockchain-based transactions. On the other hand, German contract law usually requires receiving of the declaration of acceptance, but this requirement will usually be dispensable under § 151 BGB in the case of smart contracts because the offeror, by using the corresponding technological devices, impliedly declares his consent to the automated processing of the contract, and thereby waives that requirement.[81]

---

75 In this vein, from the perspective of data protection: Kaulartz (2016) 1032 et seq.
76 Similar D Paulus and Matzke (2018) 444 et seq.
77 Cf. Raskin (2017) 314.
78 Similar with respect to vending machines: Säcker (2018) Introduction to BGB para 191.
79 Cf. Möslein (2020) § 146 BGB para 32.
80 In more detail Busche (2018) § 147 BGB para 29; Möslein (2020) § 147 BGB para 23.
81 Rather vague insofar D Paulus and Matzke (2018) 447 et seq.

3.3 *Contractual content*

3.3.1 *Consent*

The conclusion of a legal contract requires consent, that is, two declarations of intent which correspond in relation to their contents. In the case of smart contracts, the question is how to determine such an agreement. Some argue that the program code of a smart contract is unable to express declarations of intent.[82] However, since declarations can also be made impliedly, even conduct such as filling up a vehicle or inserting a coin into a machine is regarded as an effective declaration.[83] The same must apply to program codes that explicitly lay down rules and conditions.[84]

Depending on the method of generation, it might seem questionable whether the respective declaration is attributable to the specific human user. The practice that block-chain-based smart contracts typically use standardised sets of rules that are taken from generally accessible databases does not seem problematic in this respect, however.[85] Similar to the use of terms that are drafted by third parties, the use of ready-made sample contracts does not prohibit the attribution of their substantive content to the person that makes the declaration. The fact that declarations are not formulated in human language, but in binary coding does not change their legal qualification either; at least, freedom of contract also includes the free choice of the contractual language. It is solely a question of interpretation – and in the case of pre-formulated contracts also of their validity under the rules of standard contract terms – whether the provisions laid down in the program code legally form part of the contractual agreement.

3.3.2 *Interpretation*

Under German law, the interpretation of contracts requires a comprehensive overall view. Circumstances which lie outside the actual declarations (such as behaviour during the contract negotiations), can be taken into account as an instrument of contract interpretation.[86] As a consequence, the content of the blockchain and the declaration of intent cannot be separated in the case of blockchain-based smart contracts.[87] Conversely, the validity of the legal contract does not necessarily depend on the persistence of the technology-based smart contract.[88] Accordingly, the possibility of so-called forks, in which individual blocks of the blockchain are split up into different ramifications, and the (technically partly provided for) cutting back of individual branches does not call into question the validity of the legal contract. Subsequent circumstances, which occur after the conclusion of a contract, can only influence its interpretation if they allow conclusions regarding the actual will or behaviour at the time of the declaration to be drawn.[89]

---

82 Djazayeri (2016) sub E.I.; in a similar vein D Paulus and Matzke (2018) 448 et seq.
83 In more detail Möslein (2019c) 94.
84 Heckelmann (2018) at 505.
85 Extensively in relation to this practice Kiffer, Levin and Mislove (2018).
86 See, for instance, the decision of BGH NJW 1984, 721, 722.
87 Somewhat misleading, therefore, D Paulus and Matzke (2018) 448 ('*Trennung zwischen Inhalt der Blockchain und Willenserklärung*').
88 In the same vein D Paulus and Matzke (2018) 448; see also Heckelmann (2018) 505 et seq.
89 Cf. for instance BGH NJW 2017, 1887, 1888.

The fact that the contractual agreement and the technical code constitute two different tracks within one and the same declaration[90] becomes important for contractual interpretation, especially if these two tracks differ in content. Methodologically, it is up to interpretation to resolve such contradictions.[91] Since parties regularly conclude a contract for a certain economic purpose, seemingly contradictory provisions are to be interpreted in such a way that the purpose-oriented considerations and ideas behind these provisions (and thus private autonomy) ultimately prevail.[92] In the case of smart contracts, contractual interpretation must not be limited to the technical code or to the clauses formulated in human language. Instead, both layers should be considered as elements of interpretation since they correlate with one another. Even apparently unambiguously coded rules can, therefore, be subject to interpretation.[93] Conversely, the technical code can help to concretise unclear and vague human declarations.

According to §§ 133, 157 BGB, it is decisive how the recipient of the declaration is able to understand the declaration in good faith and with regard to customary practice (the so-called doctrine of the objective horizon of the recipient).[94] The extent to which the coded rules of the smart contract determine the interpretation of the contract, therefore, depends on whether a prudent recipient can understand the meaning of this program code with due care on the basis of all discernible circumstances.[95] Since blockchain-based declarations are usually not addressed to specific addressees, this question has to be answered on an objective basis. The standardisation of this program code, increasingly typical in blockchain-based contractual practice,[96] further reinforces this objective approach. The question relating to which knowledge of rules, that is, which ability is required to understand the respective program code, is, however, a question that cannot be answered in general terms.[97] It rather depends on the respective circumstances. Within the technological industry, the program code is likely to be more relevant for interpretation than for those outside this industry. In the future, the general ability to understand the program code will probably increase as blockchain transactions become more common. The proximity of the parties to technology plays an important role in contractual interpretation.[98] In view of the pseudonymisation and standardisation outlined above, however, such assessment will often face practical limits. In future, the legal practice is likely to address normative expectations of understanding to recipients of declarations, for example, by generally requiring users of blockchain-based smart contracts to be familiar with certain basic knowledge of technical coding; it is possible that users of smart contracts will be expected 'to understand the code'.

---

90 See references (n 35).
91 Busche (2018) § 133 BGB para 52.
92 BGH NJW 1986, 1035; see also Möslein (2020) § 133 BGB para. 9.
93 In general, unambiguity is no longer assumed to exclude the possibility of interpretation, as opposed to the practice under Roman law ('in claris non fit interpretatio'), cf. Möslein (2020) § 133 BGB para 6 et seq.
94 See, for instance, BGHZ 195, 126 para 18 = NJW 2013, 598, 599.
95 More extensively Möslein (2019c) 96 et seq.
96 See reference (n 85).
97 Extensively Lüderitz (1966) 286–299.
98 In general in relation to this assignment as a precondition for interpretation Möslein (2020) § 133 BGB para 36.

4 Conclusion

Smart contracts are self-executing agreements that are usually written in computer code on the blockchain. Smart contracts can perform tasks that have traditionally been assigned to the realm of law. It is still largely unclear how the contract law of jurisdictions worldwide will react to this relatively new phenomenon. While the relationship between smart contracts and contract law is already a subject of intensive academic debate, the impact of the divide of civil law and common law has rarely been discussed to date. Legal origins theory would seem to imply that smart contracts are less easily accommodated by civil law systems than by their common law counterparts. At least, this theory claims that the latter are more innovation-friendly and less heavily regulated.

At this point, the race between these two legal systems in accommodating smart contracts is still too close to call. While the present contribution does not deliver a broad comparative analysis, its focus is on civil law systems and on German law in particular. The contribution analyses both the freedom of private parties to subject their mutual relationships to smart contracts, and the specific limitations that restrict this freedom. It shows that the private autonomy guaranteed by the German Basic Law also guarantees the freedom to use smart contracts, both as an instrument of contract implementation and as a functional contractual equivalent. Specific formal requirements exist but restrict the possibility of using smart contracts in a few cases. With respect to the electronic transmission of declarations, offering services on the basis of smart contracts regularly qualifies as a binding offer, not merely as an *invitatio ad offerendum*. Even if not formulated in a human language, the program code of blockchain-based smart contracts can qualify as a valid declaration. Typically, the declaration consists of both human language and technical code as two different tracks, which can be balanced by contractual interpretation within the framework of a comprehensive overall view. The interpretation must, therefore, not be limited to either the code or to clauses formulated in a human language. The extent to which the coded rules of the smart contract determine the interpretation of the contract, ultimately depends on whether a prudent recipient of the declaration is able to understand the meaning of this program code. All in all, this contribution shows that current German law is, in fact, well prepared to accommodate smart contracts, thereby following a balanced approach as to their legal validity and contractual interpretation. As opposed to what legal origins might seem to imply, civil law systems are, therefore, not necessarily less smart contract-friendly than their common law counterparts.

References

S Azouvi, M Al-Bassam and S Meiklejohn, 'Who Am I? Secure Identity Registration on Distributed Ledgers' in J Garcia-Alfaro et al (eds), *Data Privacy Management, Cryptocurrencies and Blockchain Technology* (Springer 2018).

A Börding et al, 'Neue Herausforderungen der Digitalisierung für das deutsche Zivilrecht' (2017) CR 134.

G Borges, 'Rechtliche Rahmenbedingungen für autonome Systeme' (2018) *NJW* 977.

R Bork, *Allgemeiner Teil des Bürgerlichen Gesetzbuchs* (4th edn, Beck 2016).

J Busche, 'Commentary on § 133 BGB' in F J Säcker et al (eds), *Münchener Kommentar zum Bürgerlichen Gesetzbuch* (8th edn, Beck 2018) Vol 1, § 133.

J Busche, 'Commentary on § 147 BGB' in F J Säcker et al (eds), *Münchener Kommentar zum Bürgerlichen Gesetzbuch* (8th edn, Beck 2018) Vol. 1, § 147.

F Corea, *Applied Artificial Intelligence: Where AI Can Be Used in Business* (Springer 2019).

L Cuende and J Izquierdo, *Aragon Network: A Decentralized Platform for Value Exchange* (White Paper 2017) <https://www.chainwhy.com/upload/default/20180705/49f3850f2702ec6be 0f57780b22feab2.pdf>. accessed date for all hyperlinks 25 July 2020, unless stated otherwise.

J Dainow, 'The Civil Law and the Common Law: Some Points of Comparison' (1966) 15 *Am J Comp L* 419.

P De Filippi and S Hassan, 'Blockchain Technology as a Regulatory Technology: From Code Is Law to Law Is Code' (2016) First Monday <http://firstmonday.org/ojs/index.php/fm/article/view/7113/5657>.

P De Filippi and A Wright, *Blockchain and the Law: The Rule of Code* (Harvard University Press 2018).

U Di Fabio, 'Commentary on Art 2 Para 1 Basic Law' in T Maunz and G Dürig (eds), *Grundgesetz Kommentar* (Beck 2019) Art 2 para 1.

L DiMatteo, M Cannarsa and C Poncibò, 'Smart Contracts and Contract Law' in L DiMatteo, M Cannarsa and C Poncibò (eds), *The Cambridge Handbook of Smart Contracts, Blockchain Technology and Digital Platforms* (Cambridge University Press 2019).

A Djazayeri, 'Rechtliche Herausforderungen durch Smart Contracts' (2016) 12 jurisPR-BKR Anm 1.

D Einsele, 'Commentary on § 126b BGB' in F J Säcker et al (eds), *Münchener Kommentar zum Bürgerlichen Gesetzbuch* (8th edn, Beck 2018) Vol. 1, § 126b.

W Flume, *Allgemeiner Teil des Bürgerlichen Rechts II: Das Rechtsgeschäft* (3rd edn, Springer 1992).

M Fries, 'Smart Contracts: Brauchen schlaue Verträge noch Anwälte?' (2018) AnwBl 86.

C Gomille, 'Commentary on § 130 BGB' in B Gsell et al (eds), *beck-online Großkommentar-BGB* (Beck 2020) § 130 BGB.

M Heckelmann, 'Zulässigkeit und Handhabung von Smart Contracts' (2018) NJW 504.

A Hoppe, 'Blockchain Oracles – Einsatz der Blockchain-Technologie für Offline-Anwendungen' in M Hennemann and A Sattler (eds), *Immaterialgüter und Digitalisierung* (Nomos 2017).

G Husserl, *Rechtskraft und Rechtsgeltung: eine rechtsdogmatische Untersuchung* (Springer 1925).

A Jäger, *Inhalt und Grenzen des Kartellbegriffs in § 1 des Gesetzes gegen Wettbewerbsbeschränkungen* (Carl Heymanns 1970).

M Kaulartz and J Heckmann, 'Smart Contracts – Anwendung der Blockchaintechnologie' (2016) CR 618.

M Kaulartz, 'Rechtliche Grenzen bei der Gestaltung von Smart Contracts' in J Taeger (ed), *Smart World – Smart Law?* (Deutsche Stiftung für Recht und Informatik (DSRI) Conference Proceedings Fall Academy, Oldenburg 2016).

L Kiffer, D Levin and A Mislove, *Analyzing Ethereum's Contract Typology* in 'Proceedings of the ACM Internet Measurement Conference' (Working Paper 2018) <https://mislove.org/publications/Ethereum-IMC.pdf>.

R La Porta et al, 'Law and Finance' (1998) 106 J Polit Econ 1113.

R La Porta et al, 'The Quality of Government' (1999) 15 J L Econ 222.

R La Porta et al, 'Investor Protection and Corporate Governance' (2000) 58 J Financ Econ 3.

R La Porta et al, 'The Economic Consequences of Legal Origins' (2008) 46 J Econ Lit 285.

L Lessig, *Code and Other Laws of Cyberspace* (Basic Books 1999).

L Lessig, 'Code is Law: On Liberty in Cyberspace' (2000) *Harvard Magazine* 1 <https://harvardmagazine.com/2000/01/code-is-law-html>.

A Lüderitz, *Auslegung von Rechtsgeschäften* (Müller 1966).

P Malaurie, L Aynès and P Stoffel-Munck, *Droit des Obligations* (10th edn, LGDJ 2018).

J H Merryman, 'On the Convergence (and Divergence) of the Civil Law and the Common Law' (1981) 17 Stan J Int'l L 357.

F Möslein and K Riesenhuber, 'Contract Governance – A Draft Research Agenda' (2009) 3 ERCL 248.

F Möslein, 'Privatrechtliche Regelsetzung, Governance und Verhaltensökonomik' (2014) Austrian Law J 135.

F Möslein, 'Conflicts of Laws and Codes' in P Hacker et al (eds), *Regulating Blockchain* (Oxford University Press 2019a).

F Möslein, 'Legal Boundaries of Blockchain Technologies' in A de Franceschi and R Schulze (eds), *Digital Revolution – New Challenges for Law: Data Protection, Artificial Intelligence, Smart Products, Blockchain Technology and Virtual Currencies* (Beck, Nomos 2019b).

F Möslein, 'Rechtsgeschäftslehre und Smart Contracts' in T Braegelmann and M Kaulartz (eds), *Rechtshandbuch Smart Contracts* (Beck 2019c).

F Möslein, 'Smart Contracts im Handels- und Wirtschaftsrecht' (2019d) 183 ZHR 254.

F Möslein, 'Commentary on § 133 BGB' in B Gsell et al (eds), *Beck-Online Großkommentar-BGB* (Beck 2020) § 133.

F Möslein, 'Commentary on § 145 BGB' in B Gsell et al (eds), *Beck-Online Großkommentar-BGB* (Beck 2020) § 145.

F Möslein, 'Commentary on § 146 BGB' in B Gsell et al (eds), *Beck-Online Großkommentar-BGB* (Beck 2020) § 146.

F Möslein, 'Commentary on § 147 BGB' in B Gsell et al (eds), *Beck-Online Großkommentar-BGB* (Beck 2020) § 147.

J Münch, 'Commentary on § 1029 German Code of Civil Procedure' in T Rauscher and W Krüger (eds), *Münchener Kommentar zur Zivilprozessordnung mit Gerichtsverfassungsgesetz und Nebengesetzen* (5th edn, Beck 2017) Vol. 3, § 1029.

H-J Musielak, 'Vertragsfreiheit und ihre Grenzen' (2017) JuS 949.

C Paulus and R Matzke, 'Digitalisierung und private Rechtsdurchsetzung' (2017) CR 769.

D Paulus and R Matzke, 'Smart Contracts und das BGB – Viel Lärm um nichts? –' (2018) ZfPW 431.

V Primaczenko and M Frohn, 'Commentary on § 126b BGB' in B Gsell et al (eds), *beck-online Großkommentar-BGB* (Beck 2020) § 126b.

H Prütting, 'Schiedsgerichtsbarkeit und Verfassungsrecht' in B Bachmann et al (eds), *Festschrift for Peter Schlosser* (Mohr Siebeck 2005).

M Raskin, 'The Law and Legality of Smart Contracts' (2017) 1 Geo L Tech Rev 305.

J Reidenberg, 'Lex Informatica: The Formulation of Information Policy Rules through Technology' (1998) 76 Tex Law Rev 553.

P Remy, 'Regards sur le code' in Cour de Cassation et al (eds), *Le Code civil 1804-2004: Livre du Bicentenaire* (Dalloz 2004).

A Roßnagel, 'Neue Regeln für sichere elektronische Transaktionen' (2014) *NJW* 3686.

F J Säcker, 'Introduction to the BGB' in F J Säcker et al (eds), *Münchener Kommentar zum Bürgerlichen Gesetzbuch* (8th edn, Beck 2018) Vol. 1, Einl BGB.

F Schurr, 'Anbahnung, Abschluss und Durchführung von Smart Contracts im Rechtsvergleich' (2019) 118 ZvglRWiss 257.

H-P Schwintowski, N Klausmann and M Kadgien, 'Das Verhältnis von Blockchain-Governance und Gesellschaftsrecht' (2018) NJOZ 1401.

L Specht and S Herold, 'Roboter als Vertragspartner Gedanken zu Vertragsabschlüssen unter Einbeziehung automatisiert und autonom agierender Systeme' (2018) MMR 40.

N Szabo, 'Smart Contracts' (1994) <https://www.fon.hum.uva.nl/rob/Courses/InformationInSpeech/CDROM/Literature/LOTwinterschool2006/szabo.best.vwh.net/smart.contracts.html>.

N Szabo, 'Formalizing and Securing Relationships on Public Networks' (1997) First Monday <http://firstmonday.org/ojs/index.php/fm/article/view/548/469-publisher=First>.

D Tapscott and A Tapscott, *Blockchain Revolution* (Penguin 2016).

C Tur Faúndez, *Smart Contracts – Análisis jurídico* (Reus Editorial 2018).

M Vranken, *Western Legal Traditions: A Comparison of Civil Law and Common Law* (Federation Press 2015).

G Wagner, *Prozessverträge* (Mohr Siebeck 1998).

K Werbach, *The Blockchain and the New Architecture of Trust* (MIT Press 2018).

J Wertenbruch, *BGB Allgemeiner Teil* (4th edn, Beck 2017).

T Wu, 'When Code Isn't Law' (2003) 89 Va L Rev 679.

3 Fintech and the limits of financial regulation

A systemic perspective

Saule T Omarova

1 Introduction

Fintech is the hottest topic in today's finance. An umbrella term for a wide range of recent technological innovations – digital crowdfunding, cryptocurrencies, blockchain or distributed ledger technology (DLT), artificial intelligence and machine learning, 'Big Data' analytics, and so on – fintech is rapidly transforming the methods of delivery and use of financial services.[1] In the mainstream discourse, fintech is seen primarily as a force of market innovation and social progress, a means of making finance both more efficient and more democratic. New technologies offer cheaper and faster access to making payments, borrowing and lending money, managing investments, and keeping financial records – all of it on a single electronic device, without having to go through traditional financial intermediaries.[2] In short, fintech promises to make the presently dysfunctional financial system work much better for the ordinary people.

This rhetoric of transactional efficiency and financial inclusion, however, masks the fundamental normative and political implications of the fintech disruption.[3] Technology is merely a tool that private market actors can use either to advance or to undermine the public's interest in a stable and socially efficient functioning of the financial system. Which path would the unfolding fintech 'revolution' take? And how can we ensure that technological advances, in fact, produce broadly shared public benefits, as opposed to highly concentrated private rents?

To date, the academic and policy discussions of fintech have not produced clear answers to these fundamental questions. In part, this is a reflection of the relative novelty and complexity of fintech as a market phenomenon. In part, however, it is a result of the intellectual framing of the debate, which defines the principal challenge of the fintech era in terms of adapting the existing framework of financial regulation to accommodate specific technological advances in financial markets. The many strands in this debate, accordingly, seek to identify specific 'gaps' in specific regulatory schemes designed for specific financial products or transactions. RegTech, or

---

1 Financial Stability Board, 'Financial Stability Implications from Fintech' (27 June 2017) https://www.fsb.org/2017/06/financial-stability-implications-from-fintech/.

2 See US Department of the Treasury, *Report to President Trump: A Financial System That Creates Economic Opportunities: Nonbank Financials, Fintech, and Innovation* (July 2018) https://home.treasury.gov/sites/default/files/2018-07/A-Financial-System-that-Creates-Economic-Opportunities—Nonbank-Financi....pdf.

3 Saule T Omarova, 'New Tech v. New Deal: Fintech as a Systemic Phenomenon' (2019) 36 Yale Journal on Regulation 735.

'regulatory technology' – a massive move towards relying on technological solutions in the daily supervision and regulation of financial institutions – is often presented as an integral part of this regulatory adjustment strategy.[4]

This chapter seeks to broaden the analytical lens beyond the common preoccupation with the piecemeal revision of specific legal rules that do not map neatly onto fintech developments. It argues that fintech is a fundamentally systemic regulatory challenge, a macro-level force disrupting the currently dominant technocratic paradigm of modern financial regulation. Exploring the key fintech-driven changes in the overall structure and operation of the financial system, the chapter shows how recent technological advances make the financial markets grow ever bigger, move ever faster, and get ever more complex and difficult to manage. These macro-level changes, in turn, exert an insurmountable pressure on the regulatory system built on technocratic principles that strongly favour organisational compartmentalisation, narrow targeting of isolated micro-level phenomena, and normatively neutral decision-making by expert-bureaucrats. From this perspective, the rise of fintech does not merely create discrete regulatory gaps – it threatens to render the entire regulatory system practically ineffectual.

Given these dynamics, a truly effective regulatory response to fintech requires more than simply trying to keep pace with the industry's high-tech campaign to turn finance into a mere application of computer science and Big Data analytics. First and foremost, it necessitates a fundamental shift in our collective understanding of what financial regulation is meant to achieve – and what tools are necessary for these purposes. It requires a deep *normative*, rather than technical or technological, reassessment and re-wiring of the functional definition, structure and operation of today's finance. Ultimately, what fintech is putting on our public policy agenda is a potentially systematic move beyond the traditional confines of technocratic rulemaking and oversight, towards a more explicitly and deliberately *participatory* mode of public action directly within financial markets. In that sense, the rise of fintech presents an inherently political challenge on a systemic scale.

The chapter proceeds as follows. Section 2 describes the key elements of the currently dominant technocratic paradigm of financial regulation. Section 3 identifies and examines five key fintech-driven changes in the structure and dynamics of today's financial system. Section 4 discusses the inherent inability of the existing technocratic regulatory model to accommodate these systemic changes and outlines the core changes in the underlying philosophy of financial regulation necessary in order to meet the fintech challenge. Section 5 concludes.

2 Where we are now: the technocratic paradigm of financial regulation

A sustained inquiry into the systemic meaning and impact of fintech as a regulatory phenomenon must start with an analysis of the defining features of the current system of financial regulation.

---

4 Douglas W Arner, Janos Barberis, Ross P Buckley, 'FinTech, RegTech, and Reconceptualization of Financial Regulation' (2017) 37 Northwestern Journal of International Law and Business 371; Tom Butler, 'Towards a Standards-Based Technology Architecture for RegTech' (2017) 45 Journal of Financial Transformation 49; UNSGSA 'Early Lessons on Regulatory Innovations to Enable Inclusive Fintech: Innovation Offices, Regulatory Sandboxes, and RegTech' (2018).

Despite its many unique characteristics, the US system of financial regulation provides a good reference point for distilling the principal features of the currently dominant paradigm of financial regulation.[5] At the core of this paradigm is the fundamental division of powers and responsibilities between private market participants and the sovereign public acting through various government agencies.[6] Reflecting the essential hybridity of the modern financial system, this arrangement – which I define elsewhere as the New Deal settlement in finance – institutionalises certain politically derived judgments about the optimal balance of private freedom and public control in the financial market.[7] Under its terms, private market actors retain control over substantive decisions on how to *allocate* financial capital to various productive uses – and thus the power to determine the overall volume and structure of financial claims in the system. The public, in turn, bears the primary responsibility for *modulating* credit-money aggregates and maintaining the overall stability of the financial system.[8]

In this arrangement, private market participants are presumed to play the *primary, pro-active, risk-generating* role, while the public is relegated to performing inherently *secondary, reactive, risk-accommodating* functions.[9] This structural primacy of the private side is justified by reference to micro-informational efficiencies: private actors control the allocation of capital because of their putatively superior ability to gather and process vital market information at the micro-level. The government acts primarily as an outside regulator, a largely exogenous force with a limited mandate to influence private market actors' presumptively better-informed decisions on channeling credit and investment flows to specific uses. Accordingly, government regulation serves as the principal mechanism through which the public manages the inevitable moral hazard built into this system. Its primary purpose is to constrain private market participants' ability to generate excessive system-wide risks in pursuit of private profits.[10]

Importantly, however, the underlying public–private dynamics tend to favour the emergence of a particular model of financial sector regulation: a *technocratic* model. For present purposes, this term denotes a cluster of certain core features of regulatory design and philosophy that systematically shape the substance and direction of regulatory action in the financial sector. Identifying these basic features, therefore, helps to expose the internal logic of the existing regulatory process, which makes certain regulatory outcomes more likely than others – and certain regulatory problems inherently more intractable than others.

On the most basic level, the substantive choice of where and how to draw the line between the public and private roles in finance explains an inherently *micro*, rather than *macro*, bias built into the existing regulatory paradigm. Because private market participants, with their

---

5 Saule T Omarova, 'One Step Forward, Two Steps Back? The Institutional Structure of U.S. Financial Services Regulation After the Crisis of 2008' in Robin Hui Huang and Dirk Schoenmaker (eds), *Institutional Structure of Financial Regulation: Theories and International Experiences* (London: Routledge, 2014) 137.

6 See Robert C Hockett and Saule T Omarova, 'The Finance Franchise' (2017) 102 Cornell Law Review 1143.

7 Omarova (n 3) 746–747.

8 Hockett and Omarova (n 6); Omarova (n 3).

9 It is worth noting that this dominant narrative fundamentally mischaracterises the sovereign public's role as the ultimate source of financial flows in modern financial systems. See Hockett and Omarova (n 6); Robert C Hockett and Saule T Omarova 'Public Actors in Private Markets: Toward a Developmental Finance State' (2015) 93 Washington University Law Review 103.

10 Omarova (n 3) 749.

micro-informational advantages and individualised economic incentives, are presumed to be superior decision-makers 'on the ground', their judgments on risks and returns of particular financial transactions and products are generally presumed to be superior to those of the regulators. To the extent that regulators' judgments are driven by generalised public interest considerations rather than by any specific transactional 'efficiencies', however, this normative choice leads to the systematic prioritising of *micro-transactional* factors over *macro-systemic* ones – and of *individual* action over *collective* agency. An implicit assumption here is that, if the former is taken care of, the latter will necessarily follow.[11]

This deeply engrained tenet of the currently dominant regulatory philosophy profoundly affects the structure and operation of today's system of financial regulation.

Structurally, the current system is built on the principle of regulating individual financial firms, licensed and supervised under clearly identified regimes, which is based on the types of products they offer and activities they engage in. The regulatory boundaries among financial institutions (banks, securities broker-dealers, insurers, etc.) and financial products (securities, banking products, insurance, commodity futures, etc.) are drawn in clear categorical terms. An institutional embodiment of this approach is the silo-based regulatory architecture, in which separate government agencies oversee formally separate financial sub-sectors under separate statutory schemes. Within each administrative silo, the relevant regulator operates under a clearly defined set of policy priorities, reflecting the legislative assessment of the core risks posed by the specific regulated entities and activities.[12]

This compartmentalisation has far-reaching implications. Most immediately, it makes formalistic legal categorisation exercises critical for determining substantive regulatory outcomes. Thus, the history of the US financial regulation in recent decades has been marked by the continuing efforts of various regulated entities – including banks, investment banks, fund managers, insurance companies – trying to move into one another's territory by creatively circumventing the definitional product lines.[13] With any novel financial product, the threshold question is always that of its legal and regulatory status as a security, banking product, commodity, insurance contract and so on.

Importantly, regulatory segmentation also sharpens the predominantly micro-transactional focus of regulatory action. Confined within their respective silos, regulatory agencies are structurally conditioned to avoid taking open-ended system-wide actions likely to cross jurisdictional boundaries. There is a strong built-in regulatory preference for the narrow, technically precise targeting of concrete 'market failures' or specifically observed inefficiencies in the operation of a particular market. In effect, financial regulators are incentivised – or even required – to use the minimally invasive tools, precisely tailored to the specific problem at hand. The same factors, moreover, lead them to define regulatory

---

11 Ibid. 747–748.

12 Even in countries with a streamlined bureaucratic structure, different financial products and markets are regulated under substantively and operationally different schemes. Securities regulation, for example, is concerned primarily with protecting investors in capital markets from fraud and overreach by the informationally advantaged issuers of securities and their agents. The principal objective of bank regulation, by contrast, is preservation of systemic stability via ensuring the safety and soundness of individual banking firms. Unlike securities regulation seeking to correct various informational asymmetries in capital markets, bank regulation aims to impose specific conditions on individual banking entities' balance sheet composition and riskiness. These differences are as profound as they are common across jurisdictions.

13 See Saule T Omarova, 'The Quiet Metamorphosis: How Derivatives Changed the "Business of Banking"' (2009) 63 University of Miami Law Review 1041.

problems primarily in the more granular and easily cabined *transactional* terms, as opposed to the more diffused and multi-faceted *structural* ones.

Finally, a strong preference for regulatory solutions based on, and explicitly justified by reference to, the economic theory or empirical data is one of the most salient and familiar manifestations of the technocratic bias built into the existing system of financial regulation. 'Good' financial regulation must reflect not only judgments that are carefully limited and minimally invasive but also facially objective, politically neutral and technically expertised. Even decisions with obvious distributional effects are typically framed in the terms of economic efficiency or necessity. An increasingly specialised bureaucratic expertise – a natural product of the fragmented approach to regulating financial services and licensed service providers – functions as the principal legitimising mechanism in this system. This renders financial regulators inherently uneasy with any potential choices that involve overtly political determinations or require taking aggressive normative stands – another factor that reinforces their preference for micro-level, transaction-oriented regulatory solutions over the macro-level, structural ones.

In sum, today's model of financial regulation systematically prioritises technical expertise over normative commitment and the micro-transactional perspective over the macro-structural one. Its preferred methods of operation involve identifying and isolating discrete micro-level phenomena and decision points, and using minimally invasive technical tools to address specific market inefficiencies. As a technocratic enterprise, financial regulation is apolitical in aspiration and incrementalist in temperament.

This regulatory philosophy, however, is inherently limited in its ability to accommodate and manage the systemic effects of technology-driven financial innovation. These limitations became evident in the run-up to the financial crisis of 2008.[14] But it is the post-crisis rise of fintech that brings the fundamental tension between technocratic regulation and technological change, built into the current finance-regulatory paradigm, into a particularly sharp relief.

3 The impact of fintech on the financial system: five key trends

Fintech is fundamentally changing the way financial services are delivered and transactions are conducted. Today, individuals can transfer money, pay for purchases, borrow and invest – all of it without ever visiting any bank office or speaking with any financial professional. Less visibly, technology is also transforming the broader financial market dynamics. These macro-level changes may be grouped into five closely related but analytically distinct categories.[15]

3.1 *Scale and scope of the financial system*

To begin with, new technology is making today's financial universe bigger, both as a structural matter and in terms of transactional volumes.

---

14 See Cristie Ford, *Innovation and the State: Finance, Regulation, and Justice* (Cambridge: CUP, 2017).
15 For a more detailed analysis of these trends and their impact on the regulatory enterprise, see Saule T Omarova, 'Technology v. Technocracy: Fintech as a Regulatory Challenge' (2020) 6 Journal of Financial Regulation 75.

Increasingly, technology firms are able to offer various financial services, including payments, credit extension, investment advice and unified account management.[16] Smaller fintech firms typically enter particular markets for financial services as a way to commercialise specific technological tools they had developed or adapted to meet perceived customer demand. Big Tech companies, on the other hand, expand into financial services as a way of capitalising on the network effects generated by their non-financial business operations: e-commerce platforms, messaging applications, search engines and so forth.[17]

Fintech innovations are also broadening the menu of financial services and products. As new entrants in a well-established market, fintech companies rely primarily on their ability to keep developing new financial products for customers seeking greater convenience and speed of transacting. This, in turn, prompts incumbent financial institutions either to roll out competing products or to form partnerships with fintech firms and channel new tech-enabled services to their existing customer base.

By creating new, more easily accessible and affordable financial products and services, fintech firms are potentially able to reach out to large swaths of previously under-served population. In fact, financial inclusion is often touted as one of the principal public goods associated with the growth of the fintech sector.[18] Even the traditionally well-served customers are likely to channel more of their money into various new asset classes and tech-enabled trading strategies. In short, fintech innovations operate as a powerful tool of scaling up the financial system by bringing more people – and, more importantly, *more money* – into the ever-growing universe of transactional finance.

3.2 *Speed of financial transactions*

In addition to making the financial system bigger and more diverse, fintech is making it faster, by dramatically increasing the sheer speed of trading in financial markets.

In general, increasing transactional speed and velocity – or *acceleration* of finance – is one of the core mechanisms through which modern financial markets grow and proliferate.[19] Faster trades mean more trading – and, therefore, deeper, more liquid and more informationally efficient markets. To the extent new digital technology and machine learning can make trading faster than ever before, they promise to make financial markets more efficient and more liquid than ever before. Powerful new technical tools allow financial service providers to collect and process increasingly high volumes of data in an increasingly short time. This, in turn, enables them to compress the time required for making business decisions, completing transfers of value or updating transaction records. Big Tech companies, in particular, are well-situated to utilise their access to immense quantities of highly individualised and continuously gathered consumer data for purposes of automating and accelerating – with the help of AI and machine learning – their credit-underwriting, investment advice and other financial services.

16 Jon Frost, Leonardo Gambacorta, Yi Huang, Hyun Song Shin and, Pablo Zbinden, 'BigTech and the Changing Structure of Financial Intermediation' (2019) BIS Working Paper 779.

17 Dirk A Zetzsche, Ross P Buckley, Douglas W Arner and Janos N Barberis, 'From FinTech to TechFin: The Regulatory Challenges of Data-Driven Finance' (2017) EBI Working Paper Series No. 6.

18 Alliance for Financial Inclusion, 'Fintech for Financial Inclusion: A Framework for Digital Financial Transformation' (2018) https://www.afi-global.org/sites/default/files/publications/2018-09/AFI_FinTech_Special%20Report_AW_digital.pdf.

19 Omarova (n 3) 764–765.

The potential for speed-related efficiency gains in the fintech era are especially salient in cross-border payments, clearing and settlement of securities and other financial assets. Currently, most transfers of money and securities across jurisdictional borders are time-consuming and expensive, mainly because they involve multiple banks and other regulated entities complying with multiple legal requirements.[20] Fintech innovations – including, most prominently, DLT – seek to eliminate 'frictions' in this process by enabling real-time asset transfers. In fact, one of the most frequently cited potential benefits of using DLT for payments, clearing and settlement include its ability to reduce complexity in cross-border transactions and improve 'end-to-end processing speed and thus availability of assets and funds'.[21]

3.3 *Techno-centricity of finance*

Furthermore, fintech is fundamentally redefining the nature of financial decision-making by placing computer programming and technical data analysis at the centre of that process.

Thus, in today's tech-driven financial universe, algorithms increasingly replace human judgment. Bitcoin and other cryptocurrencies provide a clear example of this shift. Instead of a traditional central bank, a piece of open-source software determines the aggregate supply of a particular crypto-currency in the economy. A computer program releases new coins into the system, provides the process for verifying and thus legitimising transactions, executes transfers of value and keeps an immutable record of who owns what. Smart contracts take this computerisation of human capacity further by enabling counterparties to encode in a particular program their agreed upon economic and governance rights and obligations.

Crypto enthusiasts view this 'trustless trust' system as a practically and normatively superior alternative to the traditional financial system, in which transacting parties depend on third-party intermediaries, such as banks and broker-dealers. To the extent such intermediaries pursue their own private interests, the argument goes, replacing their discretion with a computer program eliminates potential for abuse of trust by a powerful middleman.[22]

Of course, this argument reflects, at best, a naïve view of the sources and dynamics of power in finance. While computer code does not possess humans' subjective capacity for greed, it is written by humans prone to making mistakes – and, importantly, *for* humans driven by greed and other subjective motives. In this new, tech-driven finance, the ability to determine what exactly the code does, and what it does not do, becomes a source of potentially immense power. This power, moreover, is often hidden from the vast majority of market participants who have no means of evaluating the technical qualities of the algorithm that executes their financial transactions and governs their economic relationships.[23]

20 Committee on Payments and Market Infrastructures (CMPI), 'Distributed Ledger Technology in Payment, Clearing and Settlement' (2017) Bank for International Settlements.
21 Ibid. 1.
22 Kevin Werbach, *The Blockchain and the New Architecture of Trust* (Cambridge, MA: MIT Press, 2018) 95–111.
23 Shaanan Cohney, David Hoffman, Jeremy Sklaroff and David Wishnick, 'Coin-Operated Capitalism' (2019) 119 Columbia Law Review 591.

3.4 *Transparency and governability*

An increasingly central role of algorithms and other technical inputs in structuring and executing financial transactions also makes the financial system potentially less transparent and less governable.

Part of the reason for this is the inherent difficulty of understanding the inner workings of specific computer programs powering specific products and relationships in financial markets. As discussed above, most market participants are simply not equipped to see, let alone understand or manipulate, the precise choices or modelling assumptions behind each particular market outcome. Another part of the reason for this is the increased cus-tomisation of financial products, services, transactions.[24] The use of Big Data, for example, enables financial firms – or Big Tech companies offering financial services – to tailor prices and other terms of their products to individual customers' risk and wealth profile.[25] This is routinely portrayed as a consumer-friendly, efficiency-enhancing application of new tech-nologies. What goes unnoticed, however, is that, in this context, it becomes potentially difficult (if not impossible) to form a meaningful basis for comparing different financial assets' relative value and performance record.

This lack of true comparability fundamentally undermines the efficiency and integrity of financial markets. In the world of infinite atomisation, there is no common basis for market participants to make their autonomous value judgments or to assess the 'fairness' of any particular transactional terms. There is also more space for hidden manipulation of consumer choices and behaviour by the private entities who collect, control and monetise vast swaths of highly individualised data.[26] Thus, ironically, an unprecedented degree of micro-level data availability may result in an equally unprecedented degree of macro-level opacity in financial markets.

Of course, a significantly less transparent financial system is bound to be less predictable and more difficult to control or steer. Identifying and monitoring, in a timely and effective manner, the complex patterns of interconnectedness and channels of contagion across the much bigger, much faster-moving, simultaneously increasingly fragmented and increas-ingly concentrated universe of algorithm-driven finance may be an inherently impossible – rather than strictly resource-dependent – task. This is the essence of what I call the 'gov-ernability' problem that arises from the subtle interplay among these multiple factors and fundamentally alters the context in which both private governance and government reg-ulation of financial markets operate. Without a reliably full and deep insight into complex market dynamics, neither private nor public actors are in a position to manage, guide or

---

24 Cary Coglianese, 'Optimizing Regulation for an Optimizing Economy' (2018) 4 University of Pennsylvania Journal of Law & Public Policy 1, 13 (describing smart regulation as 'regulating just enough and in the right ways').

25 Alberto Cavallo, 'More Amazon Effects: Online Competition and Pricing Behaviors' (10 August 2018) https://kansascityfed.org/~/media/files/publicat/sympos/2018/papersandhandouts/825180810cavallopaper.pdf?la=en; Rana Foroohar, 'Amazon's pricing tactic is a trap for buyers and sellers alike' *Financial Times* (2 September 2018).

26 This new form of market power explains why the problem of tech (or fintech) platform regulation transcends the rigid boundaries of US antitrust laws. Lina Khan, 'The Separation of Platforms and Commerce' (2019) 119 Columbia Law Review 973; Frank Pasquale, 'Privacy, Antitrust and Power' (2013) 20 George Mason Law Review 1009.

even respond effectively to fintech-led transformation.[27] In this sense, the financial system's increasing opacity and complexity are inversely related to its overall governability.

3.5 *Boundary-blurring*

To make things even more complicated, new technology is blurring jurisdictional and market boundaries in potentially unprecedented ways.

Financial innovation often shifts the established legal boundaries among financial products, activities or entities.[28] Fintech, however, presents a challenge to the very concept of spatial and sectoral organisation of financial activities. Digitised financial instruments and transactions exist in cyberspace, which renders geographic borders and power divisions among territorially based sovereign states largely irrelevant.[29] In contrast to the more familiar derivatives and structured products of the pre-fintech era, which were offered and sold to clients by specific financial institutions, many of these new financial instruments and services are delivered via distributed networks. This novel infrastructure fundamentally alters the organisational and transactional patterns that anchor traditional jurisdictional claims.

For example, crypto-assets residing on truly distributed ledgers – or permissionless blockchain networks – are created and tracked by an open-source computer software, downloadable by anyone anywhere in the world. This technical design makes it inherently difficult to determine the exact physical location of the ledger or of the specific 'issuer' of the crypto-asset in question. It also raises conceptually thorny questions about the legally relevant identities of the key elements in the network. Is there a legally cognizable 'entity' that 'issues' Bitcoin and that can be subject to meaningful oversight by any particular state? Who are the intended beneficiaries of regulatory protections, where are they 'located' and which sovereign should have the right to act on their behalf?

Fintech also erodes the legal lines delineating different segments of financial markets. A crypto-token is a fluid, category-defying asset type that creates significant 'gaps' in today's rigidly category-dependent legal and regulatory framework of financial oversight. Not surprisingly, much of the currently ongoing regulatory debate on fintech revolves around the questions of proper legal product, activity and entity classifications that would most closely reflect the functional content and economic substance of new tech-driven financial products and market actors. The regulatory system makes these questions absolutely critical, yet many of them cannot produce fully satisfactory answers.

Even more fundamentally, new technologies blur the legal and economic boundary separating the financial system from the broader commercial markets. Today, it is often difficult to draw clear definitional lines between a financial service and a technology offering, especially from a consumer's perspective. The entry of Big Tech companies into financial services, in particular, reveals the crucial link between the sheer market power these companies yield in purely commercial markets and their potential to emerge as a new breed of

---

27 On the role of systemic complexity as a challenge for financial regulators, see Dan Awrey, 'Complexity, Innovation and the Regulation of Modern Financial Markets' (2012) 2 Harvard Business Law Review 235; Saule T Omarova, 'License to Deal: Mandatory Approval of Complex Financial Products' (2012) 90 Washington University Law Review 64, 68–84.

28 Ford (n 14).

29 Jason Grant Allen and Rosa Maria Lastra, 'Border Problems: Mapping the Third Border' (2020) 83 Modern Law Review 505.

'too big to fail' financial institution. Facebook's plan to launch Libra (later renamed Diem) as the world's leading currency, built on top of the world's most ubiquitous social media platform, illustrates how politically salient these dynamics can be.[30]

4 The impact of fintech on financial regulation: what has to change?

As shown above, the fintech explosion is not merely revolutionising the means of *individual transacting* in financial markets: it also has profound *systemic* implications. Adopting an explicitly systemic perspective on fintech, in turn, reveals how the ongoing tech-driven changes in the financial market increasingly exert pressure on the existing system of financial regulation – and thus necessitate a fundamental revisiting of the regulatory philosophy underlying it.[31]

4.1 *Why the technocratic regulatory paradigm is no longer adequate*

Taken as a whole, the five tech-driven systemic shifts, discussed above, both magnify the existing and create new demands on financial regulators.

On the most basic level, the rapidly growing size of the financial system means a potentially dramatic expansion in the scale and scope of the regulatory oversight zone. Increasing the regulatory perimeter to include a wide variety of tech firms presents both quantitative and qualitative challenges for the agencies set up along the familiar 'functional' lines to license and regulate banks, securities firms, insurers, fund managers and other traditional financial service providers. New entrants in financial markets often lack the requisite resources or even appreciation for their new regulatory compliance duties. The growing spectrum of financial services offered by fintech firms and incumbent financial institutions striving to compete with them also presents regulatory problems. For example, selling a greater number of finance-related apps and other products to a greater number of individuals, who may not be able to verify the quality or veracity of the information provided to them, dramatically heightens the specter of potentially abusive, deceptive or fraudulent market conduct.

By enabling fully or nearly frictionless trading, new technology also unlocks potentially unprecedented opportunities for massive growth in financial asset speculation.[32] The superfast and low-cost trade processing directly incentivises speculative trading, compresses the timeframe for trading decisions, and allows trading signals travel through the market in near-real time. As a result, a system built on instantaneous trading in digital assets is inherently more volatile and prone to more violent cycles than a system with built-in transactional frictions. These dynamics magnify the systemic role of, and amplify the pressure on, central banks and other public instrumentalities charged with ensuring financial stability. The financial system's increased vulnerability to sudden – potentially instantaneous – asset price fluctuations requires a public market-making entity that is fully capable of taking instantaneous and decisive countercyclical action on a truly market-wide scale. In simple

---

30 Saule Omarova and Graham Steele, 'There's a Lot We Still Don't Know About Libra' *New York Times* (4 November 2019).
31 For an in-depth examination of the issues discussed below, see Omarova (n 15).
32 Omarova (n 3).

terms, hyper-fast and hyper-expansive financial markets demand a hyper-fast and hyper-ca-
pacious public actor backing them up.[33]

In the fintech era, however, financial regulators and supervisors are increasingly forced
to operate outside of their professional zone of comfort. To detect and counteract potential risks to systemic stability, or to protect consumers from abusive and unfair practices,
financial regulators will need to understand, isolate and target the limitations and vulnerabilities of various computer programs and complex technical choices built into them. The
increasingly techno-centric nature of financial markets and practices decreases the practical
efficacy of the traditional bureaucratic expertise. To regulate tech-powered finance, technocrats have to become, or give way to, technologists.

The relentless boundary-blurring impact of fintech also disrupts the core technocratic
principle of regulatory compartmentalisation. In the current regulatory system, key jurisdictional and substantive regulatory lines are drawn among the principal categories of
financial product – securities, commodities, banking products, insurance contracts – tying
their economic substance to their legal form. By contrast, new technological tools allow
reducing tradable financial assets to a *pure token form*. By creating a seamlessly unified
transactional space for trading an infinite variety of substantively different economic claims
in a universally recognised digital form, fintech potentially renders the current approach to
financial regulation outdated as a matter of *principle*, rather than *degree*.[34]

The *de facto* cross-pollination of financial and commercial markets – and private firms
operating in them – raises particularly salient concerns in this respect. Thus, the heightened
potential for cross-sectoral concentration of market power in the hands of a few dominant
Big Tech companies makes it impossible to ignore that financial regulators' domain is also
extending far beyond the traditional confines of the financial market.[35] To protect the financial system's stability and integrity in the fintech era, financial regulators must continuously
monitor developments in other sectors of the economy. They also must learn to incorporate
a much more explicit and broader economy-wide view into their decision-making.

Even a brief recitation of these challenges makes it clear that the rapid tech-driven transformation of finance requires a corresponding surge in the legal and institutional capacity
of financial regulators overseeing it. Simply to keep up with market developments and to
enforce the rules of the game under constantly changing conditions requires significantly
greater human, technological and economic resources than those currently available to
most regulatory agencies. This part of the fintech challenge is widely acknowledged.[36]

It is equally important, however, to acknowledge that financial regulators also need
more extensive and flexible legal tools and administrative powers that would enable them
to address emerging systemic problems and cross-sectoral interdependencies in a timely

33 For in-depth discussions of what this type of a capacious public instrumentality might look like, see
   Hockett and Omarova (n 6); Hockett and Omarova (n 9).
34 Although derivatives and other complex financial instruments of the pre-fintech era exhibited the same
   tendency towards virtualisation of economic substance, the institutional context in which they were
   traded was qualitatively different from today's crypto-markets. Omarova (n 3). Even so, the high degree
   of adaptability of derivative contracts to substantively different economic transactions rendered these
   instruments notoriously difficult to regulate. Omarova (n 13).
35 See generally Financial Stability Board, 'Big Tech in Finance: Market Developments and Potential
   Financial Stability Implications' (2019), https://www.fsb.org/2019/12/bigtech-in-finance-market-
   developments-and-potential-financial-stability-implications/.
36 See Arner, Barberis and Buckley (n 4); Zetzsche et al (n 17).

and effective manner. In the borderless and hyper-fast world of tech-powered finance, the value and riskiness of individual firms' assets and liabilities increasingly directly depend on the systemic, market-wide dynamics. By rendering the reliance on clearly drawn legal and administrative lines largely ineffectual in practice, fintech has created an urgent need for significantly broadening – and potentially qualitatively redefining – financial regulators' substantive and jurisdictional mandates.

Mandates, however, do not exist in a vacuum: they reflect important normative choices and political decisions. In other words, they reflect fundamental value judgments on the part of the polity. At present, the entire edifice of financial regulation continues to rest on a particular political settlement that explicitly limits the sovereign public's role in finance to providing critical infrastructural support for private markets' otherwise uninhibited operation.[37] The technocratic model of financial regulation is both a direct product of and a principal tool of implementing this nearly century-old arrangement. As private innovation continues to push financial markets beyond the technocrats' capacity to deliver the expected level of oversight, it increasingly calls into question the practical efficacy and social desirability of the technocratic regulatory model – and the political settlement underlying it.

In this sense, fintech poses a truly paradigmatic, or philosophical, regulatory challenge. Yet, to date, there has been little public or academic discussion of what this big-picture challenge involves.

4.2 *Bringing normativity back in: towards a new regulatory philosophy*

So far, the limited efforts to articulate the essence of fintech as a systemic regulatory challenge have proceeded mainly under an aspirational heading of 'smart' financial regulation.[38] In the pre-2008 era, 'smart' regulation was a popular metaphor for a wide range of market-friendly, minimally intrusive and often outright deregulatory strategies of the kind that enabled the unchecked growth of complex derivatives and other structured products.[39] Having disappeared from the academic and policy discourse in the wake of the crisis, the notion of 'smart' regulation is undergoing resurgence in the context of today's fintech debate. As applied to fintech, 'smart' regulation is re-emerging as a marker of politically neutral, surgically precise targeting of specific known tech-driven risks, while at the same time explicitly pre-committing to promoting innovation.[40] While cognizant of – and often explicitly concerned with – various forms of systemic risk, proponents of 'smart' regulation generally strive to offer narrowly tailored and individually customised legal rules for specific fintech products and activities. By equating regulatory

---

37 Omarova (n 3); Hockett and Omarova (n 6).
38 In this chapter, I use 'smart regulation' as an umbrella term referring to a broad range of fundamentally similar approaches to fintech regulation. Specific labels used for these various approaches may include 'principles-based', 'risk-based', 'flexible', 'tailored', 'responsive' regulation and so forth. For present purposes, the key is not to enumerate all of these variations on the same theme but to highlight the core elements they have in common.
39 Ford (n 14).
40 Thus, 'smart regulation' is often described as a sequenced set of 'proportionate' regulatory responses to identified fintech-driven risks, which explicitly aim to promote financial innovation. See eg, Dirk A Zetzsche, Ross P Buckley, Douglas W Arner and Janos Nathan Barberis, 'Regulating a Revolution: From Regulatory Sandboxes to Smart Regulation' (2017) 23 Fordham Journal of Corporate & Financial Law 31.

efficacy with technical micro-optimisation, 'smart' regulation effectively supplies a normative blueprint for adapting an old technocratic paradigm to the demands on new tech-driven finance, an ideal mode of 'regulating just enough and in the right way'.[41]

A closely related strand in this debate focuses on RegTech.[42] Unlike the familiar notion of 'smart' regulation, RegTech is a new term of art that denotes a trend towards 'the automation and streamlining of regulatory processes', including digitised data collection and compliance monitoring.[43] By utilising the latest technological tools, RegTech promises to lower both the administrative costs of overseeing an increasingly fast and complex financial system and the industry's private costs of complying with applicable regulations.[44]

Without a doubt, adoption of new tools for purposes of simplifying and facilitating production, collection and processing of regulatory data is both a reasonable and socially desirable response to technological progress. At the same time, however, it is important not to overstate the benefits of RegTech as an efficiency-enhancing regulatory strategy. Excessive reliance on computer software by financial regulators and supervisors may lead to socially undesirable outcomes. In addition to increasing potential cybersecurity and other operational risks, this trend threatens to undermine the critically important ability of financial regulators and supervisors to conduct dynamic and flexible *qualitative* assessments of quantitative performance metrics in the overall context of individual firms' and the broader market's operation.[45]

This potential loss of embedded flexibility is especially dangerous given the heightened salience of the regulators' ability to keep a keen eye on the wide range of hyper-fluid systemic factors that shape, often non-transparently, individual market actors' behaviour in the hyper-fast and techno-centric financial universe. In the worst-case scenario, an overoptimistic embrace of RegTech can significantly dilute the present capacity of the technocratic regulatory model to generate substantively valuable micro-level information.[46] On a deeper level, a widespread belief in the superiority of technological management of financial markets and activities may effectively preclude the emergence of an alternative regulatory paradigm.[47]

The search for a new, more effective philosophy of fintech regulation has to move beyond the limits of today's discourse on RegTech, 'smart' regulation and other efforts to rejuvenate the old technocratic model. A fintech-ready regulatory philosophy should seek to

---

41 Coglianese (n 24) 13.

42 For purposes of this discussion, RegTech refers to the government's use of new technologies for regulatory and supervisory purposes; it does not include private firms' use of technology for purposes of regulatory compliance.

43 Arner, Barberis and Buckley (n 4) 376.

44 Arner, Barberis and Buckley (n 4); Zetzsche et al (n 40); UNSGSA (n 4).

45 Whether or not an algorithm is better at detecting troublesome signs than a human bank examiner, for instance, depends on the myriad of specific technical choices embedded in its operation. Preventing, catching and correcting potential errors encoded in the program would require either an exceptionally high level of technical expertise on the part of financial regulators or an equally exceptional level of knowledge of finance and its regulation on the part of software engineers and programmers.

46 It is, of course, impossible to define in the abstract the optimal balance between human judgment and data-led automation in the process of financial supervision. The point here is merely to highlight the danger of allowing the latter to supplant rather than supplement the former, either intentionally or inadvertently.

47 For a recent book-length discussion of the interaction between 'technological management' and traditional regulation aiming to shape human conduct, see Roger Brownsword, *Law, Technology and Society: Re-Imagining the Regulatory Environment* (Abingdon and New York: Routledge, 2019).

conform not to the internal dictates of an outdated paradigm but to the practical demands and realities of technological change.

To this end, it is critical to overcome the fundamentally *micro-transactional,* as opposed to *macro-structural,* focus of the traditional technocratic regulatory model. The pervasive micro-level bias, built into the existing regulatory paradigm, explains the persistent conceptual framing of today's policy debate in terms of specific transactional 'efficiencies' associated with specific technologies. This is the case even where the discussion on its face is prompted by, or focused on, fintech's potential to create or exacerbate certain forms of systemic risk in financial markets. Such an inherently fragmented, technology-by-technology approach inhibits financial regulators' ability to identify and understand the key structural trends that make fintech a systemic regulatory challenge.[48]

More broadly, an explicitly macro-systemic approach to fintech enables us to see and appreciate a potentially decisive shift in the underlying *public–private* balance of power in finance.[49] If left unaddressed, this shift threatens to put the sovereign public in an untenable position of having to back up and stabilise a rapidly expanding, diverse and non-transparent financial system, in which speculation is frictionless and market power is fluid to an unprecedented degree. Micro-optimising, technology-focused regulatory approaches are not directly responsive to this fundamental disruption at the core of the system.

The growing imbalance of the sovereign public's and private market actors' relative powers and competencies in the financial sphere also heightens the significance of *normative,* as opposed to *technical,* factors in guiding regulatory strategy in the fintech era. In contrast to the increasingly popular rhetoric of 'smart' regulation, a truly effective systemic response to the fintech challenge should explicitly recognise the primacy of normative judgment over purely technological tools in determining specific regulatory choices.

This is a critically important point that, despite its apparent simplicity, often gets lost in the current policy discourse. Reintroducing normativity as the key input in the regulatory process requires more than an acknowledgement of standard systemic stability concerns that the financial crisis of 2008 made impossible to ignore. On a more fundamental level, it requires an explicit recognition that financial regulation nearly always involves difficult trade-offs and politically salient choices.[50] The supposed normative neutrality of technocratic regulation merely operates to obscure the substance and practical effects of these tradeoffs and choices. The seductive rhetoric of objectively 'smart' approach to technological innovation, for example, may effectively disguise regulatory passivity and acquiescence. It may also create a false hope of finding 'win-win' solutions to specific problems,

---

48 The increasingly popular 'fintech sandbox' strategy exemplifies how this micro-transactional conceptual framing translates into regulatory practice. A typical regulatory 'sandbox' is explicitly geared towards controlled live-testing of individual fintech products offered by individual firms under individually tailored (and significantly relaxed) regulatory conditions. See Hilary J Allen, 'Regulatory Sandboxes' (2019) 87 George Washington Law Review 579; UNSGSA (n 4). For a critical assessment of the 'regulatory sandbox' response to the distinctly systemic challenges posed by fintech, see Saule T Omarova, 'Dealing with Disruption: Emerging Approaches to Fintech Regulation' (2020) 61 Washington University Journal of Law & Policy 25.

49 For an in-depth analysis of specific mechanisms and manifestations of this shift, see Omarova (n 3).

50 For a discussion of some of these trade-offs in modern finance, see Saule T Omarova, 'Ethical Finance as a Systemic Challenge: Risk, Culture, and Structure (2018) 27 Cornell Journal of Law and Public Policy 797.

conveniently redefined as a matter of optimally aligning micro-level private incentives with the macro-level public interest.[51]

Of course, such a perfect public–private incentive alignment is rarely attainable in practice. Simply acknowledging this basic reality, however, necessitates a clear articulation of the core principles that should guide policy-makers' and regulators' choices. It requires a principled basis for making social value judgments.

In the context of today's tech-driven finance, this means, first and foremost, that the 'innovativeness' of newly created financial products should not be reduced or evaluated by reference to their purely technical, or micro-level, transactional aspects – such as, for example, the use of DLT or digital tokens to eliminate specific 'frictions' in a particular setting. This standard technocratic approach produces only a superficial understanding of what a particular market 'innovation' signifies from the viewpoint of transacting counterparties. By contrast, the social value of individual innovations in financial markets should be determined on *normative* grounds, by reference to their *macro-level* impact. Importantly, this macro-level analysis must encompass new technologies' impact not only on the financial system but also on the broader non-financial, or 'real', economy.[52]

In this framing, the decisional basis is easy to define, at least in principle. Thus, a well-functioning – or 'good' – financial system continuously allocates capital to productive non-financial enterprise. A malfunctioning – or 'bad' – financial system continuously misallocates capital to unproductive financial speculation, thus undermining the real economy's capacity for long-term growth and development.[53] It follows, therefore, that the task of evaluating and regulating financial innovation from a systemic perspective requires explicit prioritising of the potential macro-level benefits (or losses) over private counterparties' micro-level transactional gains. That a particular technology helps to optimise certain forms of interaction in financial markets is merely the starting point in the inquiry. Ultimately, the key factor in this process should be the degree to which any particular tech-powered financial product is likely to improve the flow of capital from the financial system to the productive enterprise in the real economy.[54]

An explicit normative commitment to promoting innovation *in the public interest* lays the necessary foundation on which to build a qualitatively new model of fintech – or, more broadly, financial – regulation. This new regulatory model would bear three principal characteristics.

First, in direct contrast to the increasingly outdated technocratic paradigm, it would empower financial regulators to take a fundamentally *proactive* – as opposed to presently reactive – approach to technological developments. Second, it would explicitly prioritise *structural* – as opposed to transactional – regulatory measures and solutions to emerging problems and imbalances in the financial system. Finally, and perhaps most importantly, this shift in the underlying philosophy of financial regulation would open much-needed

---

51 This is not to say that the rhetoric of 'smart' regulation invariably reflects or deliberately channels an anti-regulatory ideology or intent. On the contrary, the point here is to highlight the implicit framing effects of adopting this particular conceptual vocabulary, even in the absence of any political agenda or subjective intent to undermine public oversight of finance.

52 Saule T Omarova, 'What Kind of Finance Should There Be?' (2020), 83 Law & Contemporary Problems 195.

53 Ibid.; Robert C Hockett and Saule T Omarova, 'Private Wealth and Public Goods: A Case for a National Investment Authority' (2018) 43 Journal of Corporation Law 437.

54 Omarova (n 52).

policy space for developing new – and restoring old – tools of direct *public participation* in financial markets.[55] Adding more proactively participatory tools to the existing arsenal of financial regulation and supervision is a critical part of an effective systemic response to fintech disruption discussed in this chapter. Only by acting directly within the frictionless and borderless digital finance can the sovereign public successfully 'keep up' with tech-driven changes in the structure and operation of financial markets – and maintain these markets' stability.

These three defining elements of a comprehensive new strategy of fintech regulation – its fundamentally proactive posture, emphasis on structural solutions and creative use of market participation mechanisms – are key to redefining the public–private balance of power in modern finance. In this sense, they form the building blocks of a *post-technocratic* regulatory philosophy as an indispensable guide in our search for concrete solutions to system-level frictions caused by the continuing growth of fintech.[56]

5 Conclusion

This chapter examines fintech as a systemic challenge to the continuing efficacy of the currently dominant technocratic model of financial regulation. New financial technologies are dramatically increasing the scale and scope of the financial system, making it move at humanly imperceptible speed, putting computer programs at the centre of financial decision-making, rendering financial markets less transparent and more complex and blurring traditional jurisdictional boundaries. In this algorithm-driven financial universe, it is increasingly difficult to isolate and target in a controlled manner specific product types, entities, functions or effects – and presume that a desired system-wide result will follow, naturally and unavoidably. It is no longer possible to sustain the illusory ideal of a normatively neutral regulatory process seamlessly translating various micro-transactional efficiencies into macro-systemic stability. Boosting financial regulators' technological capabilities, lowering entry barriers for presumptively 'innovative' fintech offerings, rewriting legal rules in machine-programmable language, and similar measures currently on the fintech regulatory agenda do not, and are not designed to, address this underlying conflict between an old-era regulatory paradigm and the new-era market realities.

Effectively meeting systemic challenges posed by fintech requires deeper and more comprehensive rethinking of the fundamental goals and tools of financial regulation – a complex and demanding undertaking well beyond the scope of this chapter. The crucial first step towards this goal, however, is to reassert the primacy of *normative* over purely technical factors in organising, managing and regulating today's increasingly technology-dependent finance. Accordingly, this chapter outlines a few normative principles at the core of the new, fintech-ready regulatory philosophy. Explicitly articulating and further operationalising these normative principles would significantly broaden the scope of public policy choices and tools. It would provide a solid normative basis for developing more assertive and proactive macro-level (as opposed to micro-level), structural (as opposed to

---

55 For detailed analyses of the existing experience with, and potential future design of, certain key tools of direct public participation in financial markets, see Omarova (n 15); Hockett and Omarova (n 53); Hockett and Omarova (n 9).

56 For a discussion of what some of these concrete regulatory measures may look like, see Omarova (n 15).

transactional) and comprehensive (as opposed to piecemeal) tools of, and approaches to, regulating fintech – or finance, more generally.

Bibliography

Hilary J Allen, 'Regulatory Sandboxes' (2019) 87 George Washington Law Review 579.

Jason Grant Allen and Rosa Maria Lastra, 'Border Problems: Mapping the Third Border' (2020) 83 Modern Law Review 505.

Alliance for Fin. Inclusion (AFI) (2018) 'Fintech for Financial Inclusion: A Framework for Digital Financial Transformation' https://www.afi-global.org/sites/default/files/publications/2018-09/AFI_FinTech_Special%20Report_AW_digital.pdf.

Douglas W Arner, Janos Barberis and Ross P Buckley, 'FinTech, RegTech, and Reconceptualization of Financial Regulation' (2017) 37 Northwestern Journal of International Law and Business 371.

Dan Awrey, 'Complexity, Innovation and the Regulation of Modern Financial Markets' (2012) 2 Harvard Business Law Review 235.

BIS Committee on Payments and Market Infrastructures (CMPI) (2017) 'Distributed Ledger Technology in Payment, Clearing and Settlement' https://www.bis.org/cpmi/publ/d157.pdf.

Roger Brownsword, *Law, Technology and Society: Re-Imagining the Regulatory Environment* (Abingdon and New York: Routledge, 2019).

Tom Butler, 'Towards a Standards-Based Technology Architecture for RegTech' (2017) 45 Journal of Financial Transformation 49.

Alberto Cavallo (2018) 'More Amazon Effects: Online Competition and Pricing Behaviors' https://kansascityfed.org/˜/media/files/publicat/sympos/2018/papersandhandouts/825180810cavallopaper.pdf?la=en.

Cary Coglianese, 'Optimizing Regulation for an Optimizing Economy' (2018) 4 University of Pennsylvania Journal of Law and Public Policy 1.

Shaanan Cohney et al (2019) 'Coin-Operated Capitalism' 119 Columbia Law Review 591.

Financial Stability Board (FSB) (2017) Financial Stability Implications from Fintech.

Financial Stability Board (FSB) (2019) Big Tech in Finance: Market Developments and Potential Financial Stability Implications.

Cristie Ford (2017) *Innovation and the State: Finance, Regulation, and Justice* (New York: Cambridge University Press).

Rana Foroohar (2018) 'Amazon's Pricing Tactic Is a Trap for Buyers and Sellers Alike' *FT.com* (2 September 2018).

Jon Frost et al (2019) 'BigTech and the Changing Structure of Financial Intermediation' BIS Working Paper 779, https://www.bis.org/publ/work779.htm.

Robert C Hockett and Saule T Omarova, 'Public Actors in Private Markets: Toward a Developmental Finance State' (2015) 93 Washington University Law Review 103.

Robert C Hockett and Saule T Omarova, 'The Finance Franchise' (2017) 102 Cornell Law Review 1143.

Robert C Hockett and Saule T Omarova, 'Private Wealth and Public Goods: A Case for a National Investment Authority' (2018) 43 Journal of Corporation Law 437.

Lina Khan, 'The Separation of Platforms and Commerce' (2019) 119 Columbia Law Review 973.

Saule T Omarova, 'The Quiet Metamorphosis: How Derivatives Changed the "Business of Banking"' (2009) 63 University of Miami Law Review 1041.

Saule T Omarova, 'License to Deal: Mandatory Approval of Complex Financial Products' (2012) 90 Washington University Law Review 64.

Saule T Omarova, 'One Step Forward, Two Steps Back? The Institutional Structure of U.S. Financial Services Regulation After the Crisis of 2008' in Robin Hui Huang, Dirk Schoenmaker (eds), *Institutional Structure of Financial Regulation: Theories and International Experiences* (London: Routledge 2014) 137–165.

Saule T Omarova, 'Ethical Finance as a Systemic Challenge: Risk, Culture, and Structure' (2018) 27 Cornell Journal of Law and Public Policy 797.

Saule T Omarova, 'New Tech v. New Deal: Fintech as a Systemic Phenomenon' (2019) 36 Yale Journal on Regulation 735.

Saule T Omarova, 'What Kind of Finance Should There Be?' (2020a) 83 Law and Contemporary Problems 25.

Saule T Omarova, 'Technology v. Technocracy: Fintech as a Regulatory Challenge' (2020b) 6 Journal of Financial Regulation 75.

Saule T Omarova, 'Dealing with Disruption: Emerging Approaches to Fintech Regulation' (2020c) 61 Washington University Journal of Law & Policy 25.

Saule T Omarova and Graham Steele (2019) 'There's a Lot We Still Don't Know About Libra' *New York Times* (4 November 2019) https://www.nytimes.com/2019/11/04/opinion/facebook-libra-cryptocurrency.html?searchResultPosition=1.

Frank Pasquale, 'Privacy, Antitrust and Power' (2013) 20 George Mason Law Review 1009.

UNSGSA (2018) 'Early Lessons on Regulatory Innovations to Enable Inclusive Fintech: Innovation Offices, Regulatory Sandboxes, and RegTech'.

US Department of the Treasury (2018) *Report to President Trump: A Financial System That Creates Economic Opportunities: Nonbank Financials, Fintech, and Innovation*, https://home.treasury.gov/sites/default/files/2018-07/A-Financial-System-that-Creates-Economic-Opportunities—Nonbank-Financi….pdf.

Kevin Werbach, *The Blockchain and the New Architecture of Trust* (Cambridge, MA: MIT Press, 2018).

Dirk A Zetzsche et al (2017a) 'From FinTech to TechFin: The Regulatory Challenges of Data-Driven Finance' EBI Working Paper Series No. 6, https://papers.ssrn.com/sol3/papers.cfm?abstract_id=2959925.

Dirk A Zetzsche et al (2017b) 'Regulating a Revolution: From Regulatory Sandboxes to Smart Regulation' 23 Fordham Journal of Corporate & Financial Law 31.

4 A regulatory roadmap for financial innovation

Cristie Ford

1 Challenging times

It is hard to imagine that there has been another time, or industry, in which regulators have been faced with a more challenging task than financial regulators face now, with respect to fintech. How do we 'future proof' ourselves, our regulations, this book?

Private sector innovation is tricky for regulators at the best of times. Whether we are speaking of cryptocurrencies, biotechnology, the platformisation of the economy or any number of other phenomena, the trajectory that innovation takes is unpredictable. It evolves in unexpected directions. Today's hot new technology may be tomorrow's dead letter. New technologies, new players and new effects seemingly emerge from nowhere, carrying unexpected and sometimes hard-to-recognise new risks with them. Regulators can be caught flat-footed, focusing on the wrong things as their assumptions and their jurisdiction prove to be out of sync with actual facts on the ground.

Moreover, financial innovation is especially tricky. Intangible products are essentially concepts, not physical objects. This makes them exceptionally fast-moving, mutable and almost infinitely variable. They also actually alter markets when they enter them, in ways that can be difficult to predict. Fintech – whether developed by venture capital-funded non-bank startups, or by global financial institutions with substantial resources and multijurisdictional options, or by global 'Bigtech' companies like Amazon or Facebook or Ant Financial – often crosses the increasingly arbitrary-looking regulatory boundaries that we drew in an earlier era around 'banking', or 'finance'. And fintech is evolving at such a pace that it is difficult even for experts in the field to keep up.

Responding to this challenge demands that regulators reorient their perspectives, to locate innovation at the center of their regulatory models. Regulators and scholars must come to terms with the extraordinary fluidity and contingency in which they are forced to operate. Rather than heroically trying to nail down clear boundaries and guidelines for fintech, which would be akin to trying to wallpaper over a moving object, regulators must recognise their and their systems' profound vulnerability to change, and then build regulatory responses that can manage it. This is not the same thing as simply celebrating private sector innovation through mechanisms such as the regulator-sponsored 'sandbox', and it is not the same thing as deregulation. Instead, it requires recognising that *private sector innovation is actually the single most profound challenge that regulators must confront*. Their first question in any decision-making environment should be, 'how is private sector innovation, in this case fintech, undermining my assumptions, changing relationships, denaturing products and markets, and seeping around regulatory definitions and boundaries, right now?'

2 What, about fintech, is genuinely new?

Fintech is sometimes described as the digitisation of the financial industry. It is the application of information technology, internet communications capacity, increased computing speed and programming capacity and sometimes 'big data' to traditional financial institutional functions, in areas as wide-ranging as corporate finance (eg, peer-to-peer lending and crowdfunding), personal finance and financial management, financial data analytics and investing (eg, algorithmic trading, index funds, robo-advising), mediums of exchange and record-keeping (eg, cryptocurrency, distributed ledger technology) and mobile payments and e-commerce. Fintech initiatives are developing new business models, products and services, thereby targeting traditional business models – particularly banking models – and the institutions that rely on them. For its proponents, fintech is promising because it stands to lower the barriers to entry to these sectors and to reduce costs within them, making banking more inclusive and efficient, including for those in the Global South. The decentralisation, de-institutionalisation and destabilisation that we have seen operating in other areas where technology has disrupted a sector are also present here, as, more recently, is the orientation towards making the consumer experience as frictionless as possible.

How should financial regulators approach fintech? Are there, for example, useful parallels between fintech and the financial engineering rage that preceded the financial crisis that reached its peak in 2008? Can we learn from that hard experience? In a broad sense, the answer is yes: both are examples of private sector innovation that fundamentally challenges existing regulatory structures. In its specifics, however, the answer may be no: financial engineering was about the creation of new financial products, which operated with an unexpected degree of interconnectedness and systemic significance, and thus posed underappreciated new risks. Certainly, those same concerns exist with respect to some fintech too – consider, especially, value tokens that are embedded into distributed ledger technology, as Ethereum and Bitcoin are embedded in their blockchains.

However, fintech also potentially undermines financial regulatory concepts in an additional, novel way. Much fintech comes down to the application of disintermediating and disruptive tech tools and business processes to finance, and this is new. The institutional structures and categorising assumptions that regulators have relied on, and that have shaped and defined the fundamental businesses of banking (deposits and lending), securities (investment and investment advising, and efficient capital allocation) and insurance (risk spreading), can no longer be taken for granted. Financial engineering before the financial crisis also undermined the traditional institution-oriented distinctions between banking, securities and insurance. This much we have seen before. However, fintech has the potential to generate entirely new ways of engaging with consumers, which burst the bounds of financial regulation entirely. Moreover, the techno-optimists that are building fintech products do not necessarily take as a given the idea that the financial markets are complex and should not be cavalierly 'disrupted'; that a reliable financial system requires intermediaries; that prudential regulation need be imposed on financial institutions; that there are natural boundaries around the 'business of banking'; or that the concept of a 'security' is internally coherent or even useful, in a digital world.

Fintech also implicates other areas of regulation in a way that pre-crisis financial engineering did not to the same degree. Certainly, the financial crisis taught us about the unexpected interplay between, for example, capital adequacy rules and US federal

bankruptcy provisions, among other relationships. We understand clearly now that financial products and markets do not operate in silos. However, fintech could have even
broader implications. If adopted at scale, cryptocurrencies could actually limit sovereigns' ability to make and implement monetary policy. Even after having been scaled
down following regulatory concerns, a complicated new product with the potential to
be applied at scale, such as Facebook's Libra cryptocurrency (and its Colibra Novi digital
wallet), could have effects on areas as disparate as monetary policy, money laundering,
privacy, data ownership and security and securities regulation. Seemingly lightweight
online consumer financial products, which help with personal finance tasks like budgeting, managing student loan payments or facilitating credit card transactions for small
businesses (consider Revolut, Robinhood, Square and others), may in fact manage to capture profitable e-commerce functions. In the United States, through novel agreements
with small state banks to provide the back-end depository and credit functions that support e-commerce, those lightweight 'apps' could become key money-movers within the
economy, in the way that banks traditionally have been, without necessarily impinging on
what American federal regulators would consider to be the regulated 'business of banking'. (Some, like Square and Varo, obtained FDIC licenses themselves in 2020.) Clayton
Christensen's well-known description of the 'disruptive innovator', who starts with low-
value marginal business lines and then incrementally creeps up the value chain and ultimately overthrows Goliath incumbents, may be instructive when it comes to these kinds
of players.[1] Piecemeal regulatory responses miss that larger context. On the other end of
the institutional continuum, global financial institutions, which sit on a treasure trove of
data about their depositors, consumers and investors, could be poised to be significant
players in an informational market which raises significant concerns about privacy, surveillance and even human dignity. These are not problems that financial regulators have
typically had to confront.

Getting one's arms around this kind of challenge requires more robust and effective
data-gathering and analytical capacities than many financial regulators have, even now,
more than a decade after the financial crisis. It also requires that regulators recognise that
they are dealing with genuinely epistemological questions on a daily basis; that is, they are
continually confronted with the awkward fact that they do not know what they do not
know. Fortunately, as uncomfortable as this may be, at least this recognition means that
regulators are oriented towards the most difficult challenge they face.

In spite of the magnitude of this challenge, it is not insurmountable. What regulators need to do is to put financial innovation at the very center of their thinking – to
systematically and continually inquire, as a first order question, into how fintech innovation is reshaping its environment, challenging regulatory jurisdiction and undermining assumptions. This is not to displace regulators' traditional responsibilities to, for
example, ensure banks' safety and soundness, to protect investors and consumers or to
foster fair and efficient capital markets. Rather, this innovation-ready orientation is the
lens through which these regulatory responsibilities should be seen, in order to make
regulation effective.

The sections below outline a roadmap through which regulators can begin to grapple
with fintech, as a particularly challenging form of private sector innovation. It offers a

---

1 See generally Clayton M Christensen, *The Innovator's Dilemma: When New Technologies Cause Great
  Firms to Fail* (Boston: Harvard Business School Press, 1997).

systematic way of thinking about how innovation could be transforming their industries, and how they might respond.[2] It is based on four basic questions, each of which is discussed further below:

- What does the regulator know about the fintech that is emerging in its sector, and how does it know it? What does it not know?
- How is regulation structured with regard to fintech, and what flows from these structural choices?
- What mechanisms are in place within the regulator to make it adaptable, resilient and capable of learning through monitoring and experience?
- What strategic choices are available to the regulator in thinking about how to frame and interpret a particular fintech innovation?

3 What does the regulator know and how does it know it? What does it not know?

Regulators and regulatory scholars are not, generally, experts in how innovation develops. Even innovative private actors – who may focus considerable energy on fostering an innovative corporate culture, or creating a novel product – are not generally experts in how private sector innovation operates at a larger scale, thereby influencing the economy and altering social behaviour. And yet, understanding some of the basics of how innovation moves as a phenomenon is an essential starting point for regulators, who are continually required to retrofit their structures, institutions and interpretations in order to recognise and adapt to new innovation-related challenges. For this we must turn to organisational sociologists, financial geographers and other relatively unfamiliar disciplines. Below is some of what they can tell us.[3]

3.1 *Networks and nodes*

Innovation scholars will tell us that innovation is a social, not an individual, phenomenon. It clusters in particular locations, within which particular actors emerge as 'nodes' within a network. Scholars have mapped networks of institutional relationships with a view to understanding how risk and contagion spread. New computer modelling has demonstrated how networks can be based on institutional connections, products, and markets. A network approach is newly being applied to financial regulation.[4] What is sometimes missed, however, is the degree to which networks for the transmission and diffusion of ideas and innovation can be, in consequential ways, intensely interpersonal, contingent and *social*.

Whether or not their innovations are the best innovations, nodes are especially influential in transmitting ideas. This is both because they are connected to a greater proportion of the other actors in the network, and because simply being recognised as a node generates a level of social capital that causes other actors to accord their ideas greater respect and

---

2 The roadmap is based on Chapter 9 of Cristie Ford, *Innovation and the State: Finance, Regulation, and Justice* (New York: Cambridge University Press, 2017).

3 For more, see *supra* Cristie Ford, Chapters 6–8.

4 See eg, Luca Enriques, 'Network-Sensitive Financial Regulation' (2020) 45 J Corp L 351–398.

gravitas – to question less, and to accept on faith more. This was the case in the financial crisis, for example, when buyers as far away from high finance as northern Norwegian municipalities purchased complex financial products like CDOs from financial institutions on Wall Street and in the City of London. As financial geographer Roger Lee notes,

> At that distance, decisions appear to have been made on the 'reputations' of offering banks, the claimed superior innovativeness of Anglo-American markets and the rumour-mill of actions taken by competing banks in other jurisdictions. Whereas institutions involved in currency trading have had to develop rigorous checks [...] on a 24/7/365 basis, this type of discipline was apparently not applied to participation in exotic products.[5]

Regulators should therefore ask themselves, with a view to understanding innovation and its diffusion: what do both the institutional and social fintech networks look like, in my jurisdiction and beyond? Where are the nodes? Crucially, financial innovation is salient even when it is not officially labelled 'fintech' by, for example, a government-sponsored sandbox or an investor. Fintech is also operating across the classic institutional divisions of banking, securities and insurance. It is operating across jurisdictions. It is developing organically, with more energy directed towards some areas of finance – e-commerce Application Programming Interfaces (better known as APIs), cross-border remittances, distributed ledger technology. Fintech is also bursting the bounds of financial regulation altogether, as when it deploys financial institutions' deep data sources to, for example, kick off AI-fueled new ventures. Regulators must make decisions about what kind of fintech to concentrate on, and at what scale. A regulator approaching a fintech problem must make some clear choices about who its regulated community is, and then must map the relevant network's typology and determine where the institutional and social nodes are. This information will help identify how the most disruptive phenomena will develop and diffuse, allowing the regulator to concentrate its efforts in a risk-based regulatory fashion.

That said, one analytical starting point is geography: a great deal of fintech activity takes place in London, New York, Silicon Valley and Singapore. (To repeat, whether the geographic approach is optimal for any particular regulatory strategy is something that the regulator in question must decide, not just assume.) Fintech in London and Singapore in particular is supported by official 'sandboxes', within which fintech innovators can experiment, unfettered by the usual regulatory restrictions, with new ideas. These are potential fonts of innovation and insight. Regulators should also not overlook the expanding set of private 'fintech sandboxes' offered by venture capital-funded non-profits, management consultants, self-regulatory organisations and others. If they are succeeding, many of these sandboxes should be generating innovative networks. An especially active sandbox like the one operated by the United Kingdom's Financial Conduct Authority is likely generating multiple interlocking networks. The sandboxes themselves, including the leading private actors operating within them, are likely to be network nodes. The ideas they test out within a fintech sandbox are likely to have effects – including potentially subtle or indirect ones – that could pop up in unexpected places.

---

5   Roger Lee et al, 'The Remit of Financial Geography – Before and After the crisis' (2009) 9 J Econ Geog 723–747.

Venture capital funds (and their new competitors, corporate venture capital funds – a form of venture capital where the corporate funds of large public companies like Intel, GlaxoSmithKline, Citigroup and GE are directly invested in external private companies in their sectors) are also potential nodes. These investors could be sector-specific nodes, and others could be more geographically localised nodes. Regulators will want to work out whether these VCs and CVCs can be leverage points to manage information flow or regulatory compliance from the fintechs in which they invest. Potentially, given appropriate incentives, some of them could even potentially serve as what Neil Gunningham and his coauthors have described as 'regulatory intermediaries'.[6] These are private parties (or insurers, industry associations or others similarly situated) that have the necessary relationships and their own endogenous reasons to want to ensure that the smaller parties with whom they interact, in this case fintech startups, comply with regulation. If investors are not operating as nodes for whatever reason, are there other potential nodes, or can other (perhaps government-sponsored) nodes be established?

Innovation scholarship indicates that focusing on network nodes can do disproportionate work in gathering information, and in influencing non-node actors as well. Put another way, it better reflects the risk, including systemic risk, that those actors present as a function of their nodal position. If sufficiently granular, well-calibrated network-sensitive regulation can be put in place, it can help alleviate potential concerns about arbitrage by, or disproportionate impact upon those nodes.[7] The approach is not infallible, since innovation is unpredictable. In a world of unlimited resources, regulators could be engaging in sweeping environmental scans across all areas where potentially influential fintech innovations may arise. Yet real-life regulators faced with resource constraints would do well to concentrate their resources towards network nodes, because of the disproportionate influence that those nodes are likely to have. Understanding the fintech networks that are operating will also allow regulators to better predict and track potential fintech diffusions, which are also important. By closely tracking the kinds of innovations that are occurring and diffusing from the nodes in particular, a resource-constrained real-life regulator will be in a relatively good position to recognise the innovations that are more likely to have broad influence.

3.2 *Who is innovating?*

In addition to understanding innovators' positions within a network, regulators should pay attention to those innovators' characteristics. Who, exactly, are the main fintech innovators in this space? What do regulators know about them, and how do they know it?

For example, large incumbent financial institutions will be players in fintech, and the particular way in which they engage with it will be a function of who they, organisationally and historically, are. In general, innovation scholarship tells us that their innovations are more likely to reflect the incumbent's own worldview, if that is not too grand a word, and its understanding of its business and its industry. The story of Xerox's Palo Alto Research Center (PARC) is probably familiar to many, as an example of an incumbent being hobbled by internal hierarchy and a narrow understanding of its own business. By the late 1970s, researchers

---

6 Neil Gunningham and Darren Sinclair, *Leaders and Laggards: Next-Generation Environmental Regulation* (Sheffield: Greenleaf, 2002).

7 See *supra* note 4.

at PARC had developed several new technologies including a personal computer, email, a graphic user interface (with pull-down menus and icons), and an improved computer mouse. Xerox failed to capitalise on any of these advances, in part simply because it understood itself as a printing-on-paper business that would be threatened by the arrival of a paperless office. PARC may be an extreme example, and one from which other incumbents have learned, but the inevitable conceptual torque imposed by an existing business does not ever entirely go away. (Some large financial institutions, notably in London, try to get around the limitations of their legacy culture by creating their own spinoff fintech 'startups'.)

Incumbents are also more likely to be influenced by long familiarity with the rules that govern their industries, and to have ongoing institutional and interpersonal relationships with their regulators and with other key players. These are valuable assets. At the same time, this embeddedness in the existing order suggests that incumbents are perhaps less likely to be profoundly, epistemologically disruptive. Incumbents also generally possess substantial resources and, in many cases, have the market power to absorb or destroy newcomers. It seems that even startups that operate in an incumbent-dominated ecosystem are more likely to try to 'change the system from within': this is a commonly remarked upon difference between Silicon Alley fintechs in New York, who (stereotypically) want to work with and sell to existing big banks, and Silicon Valley fintechs, who (stereotypically) want to eliminate them.

Neither incumbent players nor their regulators are necessarily in an ideal position to register the significance of other, more disruptive, genuinely 'outsider' innovators in their space. In fintech, these are many. In the United States, with its fractured regulatory structure, multiple fast-growing companies in the personal finance and e-commerce spaces are shattering the atom of the traditional banking function, and seizing some client-facing aspects of financial intermediation, all without being subject to banking (or much other) regulation. Does the relevant financial regulator know who these players are, how they operate, and what drives their innovations? Does it have a strategy for identifying new ones as they emerge? How does the regulator gather such information? Are its information-gathering resources appropriate and effective? (Particular regulatory structures and their implications are discussed in the next section, below.)

In fintech, the third and potentially most destabilising set of players are American Bigtech companies such as Facebook, Amazon, Apple and Google (as well as enormous Chinese companies like Tencent, which operates WeChat; and Alibaba Group, which operates Ant Financial/Alipay). Large financial institutions regularly identify Bigtechs, not small fintech startups, as their most significant potential competitors. Like the proverbial iceberg, most of the work that Bigtechs do is outside any financial regulator's jurisdiction. Yet, the influence and resources that fuel Bigtechs also influence their salience and potential for success inside the financial regulator's jurisdictional bubble.[8] Their connection to the purchasing, searching, and other online behaviour that consumers already engage in is an asset. Financial regulators should not assume that innovations such as Alipay, Google Pay and the like will be the end of those Bigtechs' desires to operate in the financial arena. These companies' priorities and worldviews will govern their behaviour; understanding those priorities and worldviews will therefore be important to

---

8 Bank for International Settlements Annual Economic Report, 'Big Tech in Finance: Opportunities and Risks' (*BIS*, 23 June 2019) <https://www.bis.org/publ/arpdf/ar2019e3.pdf> accessed 10 March 2020.

regulators as they seek to understand what is happening to traditional financial business models. Regulators may need significant new resources to track the Bigtechs' movements within regulated space.

One of the large priorities for regulators is identifying gaps in their knowledge, and limits to their sources of information. For example, if the regulator is getting most of its information from people with whom it has a relationship, meaning the larger incumbent players, it may be missing the important effects of fintech startups nibbling at the edges of those incumbents' businesses. Operating based on information from incumbents also potentially discounts concerns about actors that seem to be of a very different nature, like a Bigtech company, which does not 'look' like a familiar financial institution. Regulators should be conscious of the limits of their own vision. As well, they should scrutinise their own processes. For example, is information flow within a regulatory organisation hierarchical and centralised, or do its institutional structures allow information to flow from more junior staffers, or those who were hired for their unique expertise, and whose perspectives may not be so constrained by familiarity and history?

3.3 *What are the innovations?*

In addition to asking who is innovating, regulators should ask *what* they know about potentially innovative products in their spaces: cross-border remittances and e-commerce APIs, for example, are different even while both are retail customer-facing. As of this writing, there is a great deal of fintech activity taking place around payment processing, an area that will have implications for banking, money laundering, e-commerce, and potentially antitrust regulation. Are regulators equipped to consider the potential impact of this innovation in these areas? How do regulators plan to learn about the next 'big thing' in fintech? (Regulatory sandboxes, as a strategy for obtaining good information about new developments, are among the regulatory structures discussed in the next section, below.)

3.4 *What is the context?*

Background environmental factors influence the nature and trajectory of innovative products. Knowledge about industry context and market matters. For example, is there in this area of fintech development, as there is in finance, a strong first mover advantage? In the run up to the financial crisis, this caused the pace of innovation to accelerate. Combined with a deep market thirst for any product that could generate a better-than-average return, it produced scores of 'innovative' financial products that did little to actually perfect markets or generate actual value.

What contexts operate in fintech? Do so-called network effects ('I'm on this social media platform because everyone else is on this social media platform') incentivise particular fintech platforms to scale up as quickly as possible? Or, is there a volume of unbanked and underbanked individuals who can constitute a new market for more accessible fintech products? Are there (rent-seeking) intermediaries whose work can easily be replicated or circumvented, in the way that index funds are reducing employment opportunities for stock-pickers? Lawyers, real estate agents, mortgage lenders and others similarly situated may fall into this category for some fintechs' purposes. Are traditional financial institutions operating in a mature market where there is little room for growth, thereby prompting moves into new business lines? (This may be the case among the Big Four banks in Australia, which are moving aggressively into other areas of technology where their deep data banks can be an asset.) Are any of the players involved in fintech focusing their efforts on owning the platform on which other actors' financial transactions must take place?[9]

The fintech market will be different in different jurisdictional and business environments. It is also different on the consumer-facing side, and the logistical back-end – where there are significant prizes to be gained in providing systems and interfaces between players. It is different at the retail level, and at the wholesale level. Each of these unique environments needs to be understood if regulators wish to be able to recognise, and ideally anticipate, the ways in which fintech innovation could proceed.

4 Regulatory structure and implications

Regulatory design matters. Whether a regulatory regime operates on, for example, an *ex ante* compliance-oriented model or an *ex post* enforcement-oriented model will influence its engagement with industry in myriad ways. Whether it is principles-based and risk-oriented, whether it anticipates a cooperative relationship with most industry players, whether it is disclosure-oriented or tightly prescriptive, whether and how it relies on thresholds and licensing mechanisms – all of these considerations will affect how regulation operates within its space. In thinking about a private sector innovation-related challenge like fintech, however, two aspects of regulatory design are especially relevant: the boundaries of regulatory jurisdiction, and the assumptions that are built into the regulatory regime.

4.1 *Regulatory boundaries*

The jurisdictional boundaries of a particular regulator mean that it only has authority over a particular region and subject matter. Influences from outside its regulatory boundaries can have a considerable effect within them, even while those outside forces are not amenable to the regulator's control. In the United States, the dual banking system and the fractured regulatory environment cause problems for visibility and responsiveness, which ought to demand a more coordinated set of responses. In fintech globally, cooperative efforts across jurisdictions, like the Global Financial Innovation Network (GFIN), can help to mitigate this challenge. But even if all of this were in place, there are deeper, cognitive and epistemological, challenges associated with boundaries that a fintech-oriented regulator should be aware of.

Regulatory boundaries quite literally affect what a regulator can see, and not see. Every regulator operates from a particular set of assumptions, and with a particular 'focal object' in mind.[10] Regulatory jurisdiction is established with those focal objects in mind so that, for example, securities regulation operates most cleanly when it is dealing with the straightforward corporate share for which it was initially designed. Its application to other kinds of financial instruments, such as derivatives or crypto tokens, operates by analogy to that central, focal object. (Consider the way in which the United States Securities and

---

9 Lina M Khan, 'Amazon's Antitrust Paradox' (2017) 126 Yale L J 710–805.
10 See Boaventura de Sousa Santos, 'Law: A Map of Misreading. Toward a Post-Modern Conception of Law' (1987) 14 JL & Soc'y 279–302.

Exchange Commission (SEC) asserted jurisdiction over digital assets distributed through an Initial Coin Offering, based – reasonably – on Supreme Court caselaw from the 1940s, which described the nature of a particular kind of security called an 'investment contract'.[11]) However, the further away from its archetypal product we stray, the more difficult it is for securities regulation to 'see' the new object clearly, and to understand how to apply its provisions appropriately.

Thriving on the boundaries of different regulatory zones may be products that seem to be neither fish nor fowl, and therefore that raise challenges around comprehensibility and regulatability. Importantly, these products may be perfectly 'legible' to the market, and could grow in use and significance, even while they remain illegible to the regulatory structures that should be overseeing them. Swaps were in this liminal place once. Even as the market for interest rate and foreign exchange swaps exploded in the United States, those swaps remained virtually unregulated for years because the relevant regulators, the US SEC and the US Commodity Futures Trading Commission, could not easily slot them into the pre-existing regulatory categories of security, future or loan.[12] Which other fintech products could be seeping between regulatory categories in this way?

Going further, fintech, almost by definition, straddles the realms of financial and non-financial business. The banking-commercial separation doctrine, which operates in the United States and other jurisdictions (though not in the United Kingdom or Australia), imposes a cognitive limitation. The fact that Bigtech companies are not regulated as banks or financial institutions means that we may not appreciate how much essentially financial business they are actually doing. It also arguably imposes a sense of complacency, about the possibility that even federally chartered American banks could be engaging in commercial activity, which is belied by the facts.[13]

On the other side of the coin, the limited scope of financial regulation makes it difficult to see financial institutions' businesses as implicating other, non-financial regulatory concerns. That is, financial regulators tend not to think a great deal about privacy policy, or about whether individuals' data ought to be an asset that financial institutions can exploit for their own gain. Again, this is especially the case in jurisdictions where the banking-commercial separation doctrine is in place. In jurisdictions where it is not – in the European Union, the United Kingdom and Australia – banks are now subject to some data-oriented requirements. In those jurisdictions, 'open banking' initiatives require all institutions that offer payment accounts to make their data accessible to regulated third-party providers, at their customers' request. Fostering competition and innovation in the financial services market is a central goal. The European Commission has recently tabled a proposal requiring Bigtech firms to open up their data to smaller rivals as well, with a view to reducing barriers to entry for new players.

However, in general, the normative framework around data is still somewhat underdeveloped: regardless of whether they share their data with other companies, should individuals be able to prevent financial institutions or Bigtechs from using their data for those

---

11 US Securities and Exchange Commission, 'Framework for "Investment Contact" Analysis of Digital Assets' (*US Securities and Exchange Commission,* 3 April 2019) <https://www.sec.gov/corpfin/framework-investment-contract-analysis-digital-assets> accessed 10 March 2020.

12 Russell J Funk and Daniel Hirschman, 'Derivatives and Deregulation: Financial Innovation and the Demise of Glass-Steagall' (2014) 59 Admin Sci Q 669–704.

13 United States, Office of the Comptroller of the Currency, *Controller's Licensing Manual: Subsidiaries and Equity Investments* (Washington, 2019).

companies' profit, either without permission or generally? Going deeper, is individual control over their own data, as contemplated under Open Banking and related initiatives, going to be adequate to control the associated risks to individuals? Or, should more proactive and protective regulatory arrangements be put in place? Are we confident that effectively downloading the responsibility for making decisions about personal data use to members of the public is likely to protect those members of the public? Securities regulation continues to operate in this way: it presumes that information disclosure to ostensibly rational self-interested individual investors will protect those investors and create efficient markets. Even if we accept that this works in the securities regulatory space, we should not assume that it will work in the online service provision space, which is replete with boilerplate contracts and consumers' time-constrained, click-through behaviour. It may instead be time for a comprehensive reconsideration of both financial regulation, and personal data privacy regulation, in a way that better protects the dignity and the interests of us imperfectly rational and inevitably time-constrained human beings.

4.2 *Regulatory assumptions*

Just as no analytical regime can operate without boundaries and priorities, no analytical regime can operate without assumptions. They are inevitable and necessary. However, like boundaries and focal objects, regulatory assumptions can also affect what we see, and do not see.

In the run-up to the financial crisis, regulators made a series of assumptions about the new products on offer at the time, which proved to be misplaced. With respect to commercial paper, for example, regulators assumed that the market would self-regulate because no one would purchase commercial paper unless it was supported by indicia of soundness. Poor-quality commercial paper would be effectively unsellable, and therefore not something that regulators needed to be concerned about. Regulators also assumed that financial institutions would operate in their own rational self-interest, and would not invest in poorly understood markets or products at such vast and unsafe levels that they risked destroying the entire international financial system. All of these assumptions were, of course, wrong. Much of financial regulation – especially securities regulation, but also prudential regulation – still rests on assumptions about transparency and rational self-interest, derived from economics, that we now know to be imperfect. As Elinor Ostrom observed in the context of common property regimes, when a particular concept – in her account, this concept was the famous 'prisoner's dilemma' – is the hammer that one has at hand, then everything starts to look like a nail.[14] In fact, as she empirically demonstrated, the prisoner's dilemma is not nearly so inevitable as game theory might have us believe. Regulatory assumptions are framing devices, and as such are very powerful.

Regulatory assumptions play a particularly prominent role in genuinely new contexts, where a regulator cannot rely on past experience, or analogy to comparable examples, to make sense of unfamiliar phenomena. Especially in those contexts, regulators will want to be alive to the assumptions underlying their regulatory regimes, and to the inevitable limits of those assumptions. A financial regulator trying to navigate through the stormy waters of rapid and heterogeneous fintech generation will want to regularly check that its

---

14 Elinor Ostrom, *Governing the Commons: The Evolution of Institutions for Collective Action* (New York: Cambridge University Press, 1990).

assumptions remain sound. It should check, in particular, that it is not overly swayed by self-serving industry perspectives, or by a sense that innovation will, somehow, inevitably turn out to be socially beneficial. Each of these assumptions was present among key regulators in the run-up to the financial crisis, and the result was that regulators functionally ceded the field to industry actors, with profoundly damaging effects on the global financial system. Are regulators making similar assumptions about fintech?

Regulators should articulate in advance – before, for example, establishing a regulatory fintech sandbox – what exactly they believe to be in the public interest. Moreover, to be clear, people working in well-established financial regulators are not likely to share that many background convictions with private sector innovators coming out of a coding, 'tech' environment. This does not automatically delegitimate the regulatory perspective. Fintech innovators may not, for example, agree that it is in the public interest that chartered, traditional banks exist; that sovereign control over monetary policy is a good thing; that there may be reasons to shield individuals from unfettered market forces; or that regulation (by imperfect human regulators operating within imperfect human structures) brings more benefits than it does costs. Even more than in other contexts, regulators should not place too much faith in the possibility of what Julia Black once called the 'regulatory Utopia', within which capable and responsible firms share with regulators the goal of optimising all of efficiency, competition and *effective public regulation*.[15] Clear thinking about one's own assumptions, and clear and unromantic communication about others', will be crucial.

4.3 *Reflexivity: if you build it, they will come*[16]

Years ago, sociologist Donald McKenzie argued that financial modelling was 'an engine, not a camera' – meaning that models and assumptions that seemed to be merely descriptive were in fact influencing the markets for the things they were describing. He explained how a mathematical formula, the Black-Scholes option-pricing model, established a better basis for calculating the premium of an option, and thereby its present value. When it was incorporated into financial modelling, however, the Black-Scholes formula produced more than just an apparent improvement in pricing certainty. It gave options markets credibility and legitimacy. It actually transformed how people *saw* derivatives markets, from something akin to gambling, to a far more legitimate-seeming, even noble, method for allocating risk and perfecting markets.[17] In terms of its potential to be an 'engine', the same is at least as true of regulation.

Financial systems and markets are constructed, not naturally occurring. A reflexive relationship exists between regulatory structure and the corresponding creation of particular markets, the flourishing of particular products, and the creation of particular risks. In the run-up to the financial crisis, for example, the capital adequacy rules that were imposed on global financial institutions allowed the largest ones to use their own proprietary risk modelling software to determine how much capital they needed to keep on hand. This delegation of, essentially, regulatory judgment helped to produce internal systems that severely

---

15 Julia Black, 'Forms and Paradoxes of Principles-Based Regulation' (2008) 3 Cap Mark L J 425–430.

16 With apologies to the film *Field of Dreams,* produced by Phil Alden Robinson (Universal, 1989).

17 Donald MacKenzie, *An Engine, Not a Camera: How Financial Models Shape Markets* (Cambridge: MIT Press, 2006).

under-estimated risk and the need for capital. Moreover, within those capital adequacy rules, the fact that certain assets, notably home mortgages, were considered to be 'safe' for risk-weighting and capital reserve purposes provoked a massive rush by financial institutions into those assets, without any independent assessment of their actual safety.

Regulation changes behaviour, and it provokes innovation in both intentional and unintentional, ultimately prosocial and ultimately malign, ways. With regard to fintech, we should recognise that government-sponsored fintech sandboxes are intentionally innovation-fostering. If well designed, we should expect that they would produce *more* private sector fintech innovation. As potentially positive as this may be, it will also increase the burden on regulators to deal with that innovation.

So: does the presence of a fintech sandbox, which is designed to accelerate fintech innovation, also exacerbate the legibility and data problems that regulators face when it comes to genuinely new products and services? The answer will very likely come down to whether the sandbox has been designed in a way that forces fintech players to provide regulators with excellent, ongoing access to top quality, fine-grained, real-time information. It is also necessary that regulators have their own considerable and suitable material and human resources, and a considerable degree of independent-mindedness, to ensure that the regulator is able to keep up with that innovation and the disruption it produces. Regulators should not imagine that sandbox structures require them to be less inquisitive, less well-resourced or less independent-minded than more traditional regulatory rules and categories. On the contrary, sandboxes require more of each of these assets. There is hardly a more challenging regulatory task than trying to imagine how to apply a set of normative commitments and regulatory goals to entirely new kinds of business, in real time.

5 Can the regulator learn and adapt? What resources are in place to do that?

In the Welfare State era of top-down, detail-oriented, prescriptive regulatory regimes, drafting legislation and its associated regulations tended to be the most difficult part. Once drafted, compliance and enforcement personnel had clear marching orders, and the task was far simpler.

This is no longer the case. The speed and complexity that characterise financial markets, and changes in the financial sector, cannot be responded to in such a static manner. International competition for global financial business also provides a clear incentive for regulators to develop flexible, context-sensitive, 'optimised' regulatory structures that impose the least possible regulatory burden on financial industry actors. In this environment, drafting general principles-based legislation and delegating decision-making authority (including to private actors) is actually the easier part. The far harder part is ensuring that such a flexible regime is nevertheless robust and meaningful; that is, that there is the back-end capacity needed to gather and digest information, to track and evaluate changes, and to learn from experience. This work can be tedious and it is never-ending, but it is indispensable. It requires tenacity, commitment and resources. In case after case in financial regulation, it is at this implementation stage that efforts fall short.

Implementing innovation-ready regulation in a meaningful way can be difficult for a few different reasons. We can underestimate the resources required, or provide the wrong kind of resources, or resourcing can dry up over time – something that is especially possible during times when things seem to be going well. We can become complacent as markets rise, or as fintech innovations seem to deliver benefits. Regulatory judgment can be swayed by self-interested industry framing of issues, or even simply by the social and emotional appeal of being pro-innovation, forward-looking, plugged-in. We can fall back on heuristics, assumptions and default rules, for the sake of clarity and comfort, and those shortcuts can lead us astray.

With respect to fintech and other fast-moving environments, humans' cognitive limitations also play a role. As a species, along with the other pitfalls above, it turns out that we do not like uncertainty that much, and we are liable to underplay it. We are also not terribly good at registering or responding to change. This includes human-generated change. We are especially poor at registering incremental change, which by its nature never trips an alarm. Fintechs' incursion into the traditional business of banking may be an innovation of this variety. On the other hand, after a high salience disaster has occurred, we suffer from hindsight bias and tend to overreact, over-blame and behave reductively. One can imagine such a reaction in the event that a popular fintech product were to collapse and harm members of the public. We can also be heavily influenced by the hierarchy and strategic priorities of the organisations in which we operate. When it comes to fintech in particular, regulators should also recognise the interjurisdictional competitiveness that may be pushing them towards overeager acceptance of, and perhaps inadequate scepticism about new products. Pretending that these factors are not operating is not helpful. What is helpful is to develop mechanisms, including analytical roadmaps and better data, to compensate for the cognitive limitations and institutional pressures that are operating.

The question of how regulation should engage with fintech is not one that can be answered at one point in time, and so resolved. Regulators must continually gather data and roll it back into their own learning and analysis. Relevant data would include not only information gathered from within a government-sponsored fintech sandbox, if one is in place in the jurisdiction, but also from the broader environment. Regulators must ask themselves, continually, whether they still know who the main fintech actors in their space are, whether their assumptions still hold true, what might be happening beyond the borders of their vision and so on. This requires a substantially different frame of mind, and different training, than that which most financial regulators held across most of the last century. It also requires courage, independence and the ability to try to imagine how to apply regulation's underlying normative commitments and its goals to continually new contexts.

6 Strategic choices

Financial regulators are not passive actors when it comes to private sector financial innovation. While they are subject to a degree to political will, they are still the creators of worlds. Careful thinking on their parts about regulatory priorities and regulatory design can be profoundly influential.

A regulator will want to decide where its key challenges, in relation to recognising and tracking fintech, lie. Different regulatory challenges provoke different regulatory responses. For example, in trying to answer the questions above (who is innovating, what the innovations and context are, etc.), the regulator may decide that one of its main challenges is that it does not have sufficient data about a particular fast-moving fintech innovation. It could then consider regulatory responses designed to slow innovation down and force information upward. Licensing and permitting regimes, including for access to a government-sponsored fintech sandbox, are one such technique. Alternatively, the regulator may decide that a key challenge is tracking incremental innovation around fintech, where change across time may prove to be consequential even if each incremental innovation is not. In that case, an appropriate response may be to improve its information-gathering capacity and to establish benchmarks for safety, investor protection and other regulatory goals that it can track across time. If the challenge is identifying fintech innovations at or outside its jurisdictional boundaries, a regulator could choose to engage with other regulators in adjacent spaces, and to map out the unregulated or under-regulated areas. Quite a bit can be accomplished under regulatory authority, through regulatory design choices, even when political will or attention is somewhat lacking.

These are subjective choices, which require judgment and expertise. Regulators across jurisdictions are already making many of these choices. This chapter seeks to help support those efforts, by making explicit the main questions that a regulator should ask when trying to regulate fintech. Approaching questions of regulatory design and regulatory priorities in a more systematic and intentional way, with the understanding that private sector innovation is the key challenge that regulators confront today, has the potential to produce more comprehensive and better regulatory outcomes.

Financial regulation matters. Regulation is at the operational front line when it comes to breathing life into our most cherished social commitments. Seemingly mundane regulatory decisions implicate questions of fairness, equality and justice, and thus directly influence peoples' lives and prospects. We see their effects in our politics, and our communities. Financial regulation in particular can be the site of some of the most pernicious effects of power and domination. In its best forms, however, it can also be the site of broadly distributed, almost democratic, opportunities for human flourishing. Fintech presents that potential as well as those risks, and financial regulators are uniquely positioned to manage and help direct it for the benefit of us all.

Bibliography

Bank for International Settlements Annual Economic Report, 'Big Tech in Finance: Opportunities and Risks' (23 June 2019). Bank for International Settlements <https://www.bis.org/publ/arpdf/ar2019e3.pdf> accessed 10 March 2020.

J Black, 'Forms and Paradoxes of Principles-Based Regulation' (2008) 3 Cap Mark L J 425–430.

C M Christensen, *The Innovator's Dilemma: When New Technologies Cause Great Firms to Fail* (Boston: Harvard Business School Press, 1997).

Santos B De Sousa, 'Law: a Map of Misreading. Toward a Post-Modern Conception of Law' (1987) 14 JL & Soc'y 279–302.

Luca Enriques, Alessandro Romano and Thom Wetzer, 'Network-Sensitive Financial Regulation' (2020) 45 J Corp L 351–397.

R J Funk and D Hirschman, 'Derivatives and Deregulation: Financial Innovation and the Demise of Glass-Steagall' (2014) 59 Admin Sci Q 669–704.

N Gunningham and D Sinclair, *Leaders and Laggards: Next-Generation Environmental Regulation* (Sheffield: Greenleaf, 2002).

L M Khan, 'Amazon's Antitrust Paradox' (2017) 126 Yale L J 710–805.

Lee et al, 'The Remit of Financial Geography — Before and After the Crisis' (2009) 9 J Econ Geog 723–747.

D MacKenzie, *An Engine, Not a Camera: How Financial Models Shape Markets* (Cambridge: MIT Press, 2006).

E Ostrom, *Governing the Commons: The Evolution of Institutions for Collective Action* (New York: Cambridge University Press, 1990).

P A Robinson, 'Field of Dreams (1989)' (2004) DVD. Universal.

United States, Office of the Comptroller of the Currency, *Controller's Licensing Manual: Subsidiaries and Equity Investments* (Washington, 2019).

US Securities and Exchange Commission, 'Framework for "Investment Contact" Analysis of Digital Assets' *US Securities and Exchange Commission,* (3 April 2019) <https://www.sec.gov/corpfin/framework-investment-contract-analysis-digital-assets> accessed 10 March 2020.

5 FinTech and the law and economics of disintermediation

Fatjon Kaja, Edoardo D Martino, and Alessio M Pacces[1]

1 Financial technology and disintermediation

Are banks dead? Or are the reports greatly exaggerated? Boyd and Gertler's title article has managed to stay coherent after a quarter of a century, pushing one to rethink the dimensions of the banking industry and its future.[2] Boyd and Gertler's dismissal of the growing consensus according to which disruptive financial innovation, such as securitisation, was about to erase the need of banks as financial intermediaries was novel and unorthodox, but time shows us that they were right; the reports were greatly exaggerated, as the banking industry exhibited resilience and adaptiveness to technological developments.[3]

History does not repeat itself, though we cannot help but note some similarities with the current fever for FinTech and financial applications of the blockchain technology. However, the two waves of innovations differ in scale and in scope. In fact, the current technological step forward is arguably bigger, and its target is financial intermediation as a whole.

This chapter will discuss the wave of technologically enabled disintermediation of financial services, which is broadly referred to as FinTech. We take a law and economics approach, consisting of two questions. First, what market failures does FinTech involve? Second, how can FinTech regulation cope with such market failures?[4]

Financial intermediation refers to a heterogeneous set of financial services that facilitate the efficient allocation of funds and are carried out through professional intermediaries. Financial intermediation is costly. Despite financial and technological innovation this cost has remained relatively constant over the past 130 years.[5] A broad distinction can be drawn between bank and non-bank intermediation. Banks perform Qualitative Asset Transformation (QAT) via the balance sheets, turning their short-term, liquid and safe liabilities into long-term, illiquid and risky assets.[6] Non-bank financial intermediaries provide

---

1 Although this chapter is entirely the result of joint work, Sections 2 and 3 should be attributed to Edoardo Martino. We thank Balázs Bodó, Iris Chiu, Gudula Deipenbrock and Luca Enriques for valuable input and feedback. All errors are our own.
2 John H Boyd and Mark Gertler, 'Are Banks Dead? Or Are the Reports Greatly Exaggerated?' (National Bureau of Economic Research 1995).
3 This adaptiveness had costs attached to it. See Gary Gorton and Andrew Metrick, 'Securitized Banking and the Run on Repo' (2012) 104 Journal of Financial Economics 425.
4 Alessio M Pacces, 'A Law and Economics Perspective on Normative Analysis' in Sanne Taekema et al. (eds), *Facts and Norms in Law* (Edward Elgar Publishing, 2016) 171.
5 Thomas Philippon, 'Has the US Finance Industry Become Less Efficient? On the Theory and Measurement of Financial Intermediation' (2015) 105 American Economic Review 1408.
6 Sudipto Bhattacharya and Anjan V Thakor, 'Contemporary Banking Theory' (1993) 3 Journal of Financial Intermediation 2.

a variety of services to facilitate participation in financial markets, matching sellers and buyers without transforming their claims.[7]

FinTech can be defined as the use of information technology to provide financial services alternative to those that financial intermediaries offer.[8] Huge technological developments have created the possibility to provide services that were not even imaginable until a few years ago: from digital wallets for payment (eg, PayPal), to cryptocurrencies (eg, Bitcoin), to investment advice through automated algorithms (eg, 'Robo-advice') and many more.

Information technology can achieve significant efficiency improvements compared to traditional financial intermediation. First, it can reduce transaction costs, making financial exchange more efficient. Think, for instance, of faster and cheaper money transfers via digital wallets and lower operating costs of Peer-to-Peer (hereinafter 'P2P') and Peer-to-Business (hereinafter 'P2B') lending platforms compared to bank loans. Second, information technology can reduce information asymmetries, exploiting the growing computation powers and the amount of available data, for instance in the case of Big-Data automated credit scores.[9] Third, information technology can provide some liquidity advantages, notably by improving the efficiency of the payment system and the transmission of monetary policy.[10]

This chapter focuses on the risks associated with disintermediating finance via FinTechs. Financial intermediaries are regulated because the industry is particularly prone to market failures.[11] Disintermediation potentially challenges this regulation.

Financial regulation pursues two goals in general: (1) financial stability and (2) investor protection.[12] On the one hand, regulation deals with the negative externalities that the instability of financial institutions, banks in particular, cause. Qualitative Asset Transformation, while fostering lending and thus economic development, makes banks inherently fragile and exposed to runs on short-term, money-like debt.[13] Moreover, banks are leveraged and interconnected institutions, so that the failure of one can trigger contagion and generate large adverse consequence for the whole financial system and the real economy, as the failure of Lehman Brothers in 2008 exemplified.[14] On the other hand, investor protection regulation addresses problems of asymmetric information between investors, intermediaries

---

7   Franklin Allen and Anthony M Santomero, 'What Do Financial Intermediaries Do?' (2001) 25 Journal of Banking & Finance 271.
8   Anjan V Thakor, 'Fintech and Banking: What Do We Know?' (2020) 41 Journal of Financial Intermediation 100833, 1.
9   One of the main reasons for the existence of financial intermediaries is to cope with the information asymmetry problem, where perspective lenders cannot reliably distinguish good from bad borrowers. See, Richard Brealey, Hayne E Leland and David H Pyle, 'Informational Asymmetries, Financial Structure, and Financial Intermediation' (1977) 32 The Journal of Finance 371. Another issue related to intermediaries and information asymmetry relates to relationship banking and its benefits. See Arnoud W A Boot and Anjan V Thakor, 'Can Relationship Banking Survive Competition?' (2000) 55 The Journal of Finance 679. These aspects will be better detailed in Section 2.
10   The net contribution of FinTechs to liquidity is unclear, as many technological applications (eg, cryptocurrencies) seem to dramatically increase volatility.
11   See Markus Konrad Brunnermeier and others, *The Fundamental Principles of Financial Regulation* (ICMB, Internat Center for Monetary and Banking Studies 2009) Vol 11.
12   John Armour and others, *Principles of Financial Regulation* (Oxford University Press 2016) Ch 3.
13   Douglas W Diamond and Philip H Dybvig, 'Bank Runs, Deposit Insurance, and Liquidity' (1983) 91 Journal of Political Economy 401.
14   For a functional overview of the main cornerstones of financial regulation, see Brunnermeier and others (n 11).

and borrowers which in many cases means between unsophisticated and professional market participants. If investors fear that their funds are not safe and that there is potential for fraud, then they will avoid investing in the first place.[15]

Therefore, the first law and economics question addressed in this chapter is: will technology-enabled financial innovations generate market failures or worsen existing ones? Without the ambition to answer this question conclusively, this chapter focuses on two types of intermediation, one related to banks and the other to investment services. FinTech promises to increase competition for both banks and investment firms. More competition is usually welcomed as it fosters innovation, improves quality and reduces prices. However, in the financial industry, more competition may undermine financial stability and investor protection.[16] This can happen both directly through FinTechs, and indirectly through the adjustments incumbent intermediaries implement to maintain their competitive edge. This brings to the second law and economics question: is the current regulatory framework efficient?

This chapter will articulate the theoretical framework to answer these questions, highlighting the role financial regulation plays and making recommendations on the legal tools and strategies to determine the optimal level of disintermediation. The scope of the analysis is particularly broad. Therefore, we do not strive to be exhaustive. This chapter will only lay down the analytical foundations to discuss different FinTechs and their regulatory implications.

This chapter is structured as follows: Section 2 discusses disintermediation of banking services. It highlights the crucial features of banking intermediation and focuses on two distinct cases of disintermediation: P2P Lending and cryptocurrencies. Section 3 discusses disintermediation of investment services and focuses on the opportunities and challenges of disintermediating non-banking services. Section 4 presents the law and economics analysis in two parts: first, the market failures of FinTechs and second, a regularity strategy towards FinTechs. Section 5 concludes.

2 Disintermediation of banking

2.1 *What banks do and why is it special?*

Banks are known to be a special type of firm. As like any financial intermediary, banks collect funds from economic units with a surplus, typically households, and allocate these funds to economic units with funding needs.[17] Yet, differently from any other intermediaries, banks perform this task following a special business model.

Banks are highly leveraged institutions whose funding comes predominantly from short-term liabilities, such as demand deposits. On the other side of the balance sheet, commercial

---

15 For a comprehensive introduction, see Armour and others (n 12) Ch 5.
16 Notably, the UK Financial Conduct Authority has promotion of competition in the financial sector as an additional goal to the aforementioned ones. Whether these objectives are compatible and how to strike the appropriate balance between them remains an open question. Stephen Dickinson, David Humphry, Paolo Siciliani, Michael Straughan and Paul A Grout, 'The Prudential Regulation Authority's Secondary Competition Objective' (2015) *Bank of England Quarterly Bulletin*, Q4.
17 Allen and Santomero (n 7) 273.

banks' assets mainly consist of long-terms loans and other illiquid assets.[18] Banks perform Qualitative Asset Transformation (QAT), which is to say, they turn liquid, short-term and safe claims into illiquid, long-term and risky assets.[19] This characteristic makes banks inherently fragile, prone to runs and panics because assets cannot be liquidated quickly enough to honour the short-term liabilities at once.[20]

The long-lasting success of banks depends on their unique ability to perform QAT.[21] In a world without banks, lenders and borrowers would meet in the marketplace. Information on the creditworthiness of borrowers is unknown to prospective lenders. Private, more accurate, information can be produced at a cost through screening and monitoring the perspective borrowers. Many lenders are unwilling to bear the cost of monitoring, so they decide to delegate it to economic actors that are willing to invest in such activities.[22] In this view, banks act as delegated monitors on behalf of depositors, who entrust the bank with their money, and in return the bank promises to lend only to creditworthy borrowers.[23]

Therefore, bank intermediation solves a problem of information asymmetry as many other intermediaries can do.[24] But, performing asset transformation makes banking especially valuable for borrowers and lenders (depositors), as both categories get the type of financial contract that suit them best. Crucially, banks lend long against short-term deposits but also against a fraction of equity so to limit risk-taking incentives; equity operates both as a curb on the size of banking and to counter moral hazard.[25]

On the asset side of the balance sheet, banks engage in costly monitoring, gaining private information on their borrowers. The information becomes even more valuable in case of repeated interaction, the so-called 'relationship banking'. The cost of monitoring decreases over time and the long-term relationship provides the bank with flexibility to adjust the terms to the ever-evolving situation.[26] Competition and innovation have progressively driven banks away from pure relational lending towards a more transaction-based

---

18 Financial innovations that happened over the past decades incentivized banks to move from relational to transactional banking. See Boot and Thakor (n 8) 681. Nonetheless, this does not alter much the basic representation of banks as firms performing transformations activities. On this, see Armour and others (n 12) Ch 13.

19 Bhattacharya and Thakor (n 6) 15.

20 Hyun Song Shin, 'Reflections on Northern Rock: The Bank Run That Heralded the Global Financial Crisis' (2009) 23 Journal of Economic Perspectives 101.

21 For a thorough overview, see Gary Gorton and Andrew Winton, 'Financial Intermediation', *Handbook of the Economics of Finance* (Elsevier 2003) Vol 1, 437–461.

22 Douglas W Diamond, 'Financial Intermediation and Delegated Monitoring' (1984) 51 The Review of Economic Studies 393.

23 Ibid. Diamond also shows that in equilibrium, delegated monitoring represents a commitment device to solve the problem of 'monitoring the monitor'. This way, banks disincentive depositors to simultaneously withdraw their money, triggering a run. This latter aspect is modelled in Diamond and Dybvig (n 13).

24 See Section 3.

25 In this context, moral hazard means the incentives to take on more risks than socially efficient, expecting that someone else bears the downside of the risk. See, Jihad Dagher and others, *Benefits and Costs of Bank Capital* (IMF Staff, International Monetary Fund 2016).

26 Joseph G Haubrich, 'Financial Intermediation: Delegated Monitoring and Long-Term Relationships' (1989) 13 Journal of Banking & Finance 9; Arnoud W A Boot, Stuart I Greenbaum and Anjan V Thakor, 'Reputation and Discretion in Financial Contracting' (1993) The American Economic Review 1165. On the hold-up problems that may suggest having multiple banking relationships or to resort to the market, see Xavier Freixas, 'Deconstructing Relationship Banking' (2005) 29 Investigaciones Económicas 3.

banking. Handling portfolio risk through monitoring is costly and financial innovations, such as securitisation, made market solution cheaper at the expense of financial stability.[27] Section 2.2 discusses whether technology-enabled solutions can exacerbate this problem.

On the liability side of the balance sheet, banks offer their depositors safety and liquidity. Modern finance treats these concepts separately, but they are related.[28] Safety implies liquidity: if tomorrow's value of an asset is known with certainty, one could sell it today for a given amount of cash (market liquidity). Otherwise, one could borrow the same amount of cash using the asset as collateral (funding liquidity).[29] Liquidity is valuable to the extent that there is uncertainty and economic agents want to retain the option to liquidate their assets before maturity. Deposits are as liquid as money because these are funds repayable on demand: depositors can withdraw the face value of their claim anytime.[30] Banks are unique providers of such safe and liquid assets. However, other institutions may too issue liabilities carrying the promise to convert into a given amount of cash on demand.[31] These institutions are called shadow banks.[32] Because shadow banking is not fundamentally different from banking and does not depend on technology, this chapter will only discuss it to the extent that FinTech relates to it.

In the aftermath of the global financial crisis, research showed that investors have a preference for safe assets beyond what the theory on portfolio diversification can explain.[33] Another reason why bank deposits and other short-term liabilities are able to satisfy the increasing demand for safety is the regulatory safety net.[34] First, deposit guarantee schemes cover demand deposits, making depositors insensitive to the bank's riskiness. Moreover, banks have access to the liquidity central banks as lenders of last resort (LOLR) offer. Finally, banks traditionally benefit from the implicit government guarantee on their solvency in the event of a systemic crisis, although regulation has recently tried to limit the extent of this guarantee. The last two features apply to shadow banking too.

Liquidity and safety make bank liabilities a suitable medium for exchange, a key aspect of monetary policy transmission and one of the pillars of the payment system.[35] Section 2.3 discusses the attempt of FinTechs to provide such service in a different way, particularly by way of cryptocurrencies.

---

27 Hyun Song Shin, 'Securitisation and Financial Stability' (2009) 119 The Economic Journal 309.
28 Armour and others (n 12) Ch 13.
29 Markus K Brunnermeier, 'Deciphering the Liquidity and Credit Crunch 2007–2008' (2009) 23 Journal of Economic Perspectives 77.
30 Similarly, Pistor defines liquidity as the ability to sell any asset at will. See Katharina Pistor, 'A Legal Theory of Finance' (2013) 41 Journal of Comparative Economics 315, 316.
31 The question, however, is whether the promise is credible. As Minsky puts it, 'everyone can create money; the problem is to get it accepted'. See Hyman P Minsky, *Stabilizing an Unstable Economy* (New Haven: Yale UP, 1986) 225.
32 Hossein Nabilou and Alessio M Pacces, 'The Law and Economics of Shadow Banking' in Iris Chiu and Ian MacNeil (eds), *Research Handbook on Shadow Banking* (Edward Elgar Publishing 2018) 7.
33 Gary Gorton, Stefan Lewellen and Andrew Metrick, 'The Safe-Asset Share' (2012) 102 American Economic Review 101, 105. The safety-premium has been estimated in 27 basis points, meaning that investors are willing to accept lower returns for an increase in safety. See Arvind Krishnamurthy and Annette Vissing-Jorgensen, 'The Aggregate Demand for Treasury Debt' (2012) 120 Journal of Political Economy 233, 259.
34 See Gorton, Lewellen and Metrick (n 33) 102.
35 Jeffrey M Lacker, 'Clearing, Settlement and Monetary Policy' (1997) 40 Journal of Monetary Economics 347.

2.2 *Disintermediating lending*

The most prominent example of technologically enabled financial services, alternative to bank lending, is P2P lending. The idea behind P2P lending is to provide a platform where lenders and borrowers are matched without an intermediating bank.[36] As will be further discussed in Section 4, FinTech and financial disintermediation are very heterogeneous concepts that do not necessarily involve blockchain technology. P2P lending represents a paradigmatic example in this sense. In fact, the first P2P lending platforms started to gain traction in the aftermath of the global financial crisis, when trust in traditional banks was at its lowest point.[37]

P2P lending does not amount to a full disintermediation of lending. Rather, it uses technology to gain and process information substituting 'heavy' bank intermediation with a 'light' platform intermediation. Prospective borrowers apply for a loan to the platform, which screens the creditworthiness of borrowers and assigns them a 'loan grade' according to the project's riskiness. The investors (lenders) bid on the projects and then the platform pools together the bids and originates the loan.

As opposed to banking intermediation, the platform itself does not invest in the loan and the platform does not issue any debt: the whole amount of the loan is a direct investment of the lenders. Therefore, there is no QAT and no possibility of withdrawal. The investors' capital is locked in the project and its safety only depends on the probability of default of the borrower.

A P2P lending platform is not, however, a veil matching lenders and borrowers, but a corporation acting as an agent of both. To illustrate this point, it is interesting to analyse the compensation scheme of the platform. Platform compensation is fee-based.[38] First, the platform charges a fee for loan origination, and typically a fee for late repayments. Moreover, they earn a percentage of borrower repayments (usually 1%) in the form of a service fee.[39] P2P lending platforms are, therefore, profit-maximising entities, not just computer codes. As they take discretionary decisions that can be opaque, for instance by setting up the algorithm to screen the loan applications, trust of borrowers and investors is of essence.

P2P lending is a form of bank disintermediation that can achieve efficiency gains in terms of operating costs of a loan.[40] To properly assess these efficiency gains, one should also consider the possible costs in terms of financial stability concerns. As mentioned before, P2P platforms do not perform asset transformation activities themselves, so they seem not to pose direct financial stability concerns. Yet, there may be more subtle, indirect effects.

First, the fact that systemic risk will not materialise at the platform level does not imply that P2P lending does not contribute to build up systemic risk. In fact, there is evidence

---

36 Thakor (n 8) 3.
37 Jefferson Duarte, Stephan Siegel and Lance Young, 'Trust and Credit: The Role of Appearance in Peer-to-Peer Lending' (2012) 25 The Review of Financial Studies 2455.
38 This confirms in a sense the trend of financial intermediaries of shifting from interest rate-based earnings to fee-based earnings, from relational banking to transactional financial intermediation. See Allen and Santomero (n 7) 291.
39 Thakor (n 8) 4.
40 The operating cost of Lending Club, a leading P2P platform in the US, have been estimated in 2.70%, as opposed to 7% at banks. See Welltrado, 'Global Blockchain-Backed Loans Marketplace ICO' (2018) 7 <https://icotop.io/wp-content/uploads/2018/05/Welltrado-Whitepaper.pdf> accessed 01 December 2020.

that many lenders investing in these loans are highly leveraged themselves.[41] Moreover, the fee-based compensation scheme of the platforms generates incentives to over-lend, originating riskier and riskier loans.[42] Therefore, if the P2P lending market scales up, massive defaults due to an abrupt shock can trigger contagion potentially outside of any supervisory scrutiny.

Second, the increased competitive pressure on banks may induce those to engage more and more in transactional activities to save costs, abandoning more and more relationship banking. In this regard, one can note a certain parallelism with the reaction of banks to securitisation two decades ago.

Finally, if banks will acquire FinTechs, partner with them or set up their own platforms, the two threats to financial stability highlighted above may be magnified.[43]

2.3 *Disintermediating money and payment*

We now turn to discussing how FinTech can disintermediate the services provided by bank to depositors, namely safety, liquidity and payments. Cryptocurrencies are the most paradigmatic example.[44] Cryptocurrencies aim to disrupt the centralised system of money and payments. Ideally, the blockchain technology should provide a completely decentralised and trustless system replacing the current system characterised by licensed intermediaries and trusted central gatekeepers, such as central banks that have a legal monopoly to issue fiat money.

In its simplest description, the blockchain is a chronological database of transactions recorded in a network of computers. Some participants to the network (miners) verify the validity of the transaction, and whether ownership of cryptocurrency is actually transferred, through solving complex mathematical problems that ensure there is no double spending.[45] This decentralised method of verification allegedly makes intermediaries, such as banks, unnecessary to carry out transactions.

We contend that, at this technological stage, a completely decentralised and trustless system is far from being achieved, if it is ever possible. We offer three main reasons to support our claim. Firstly, cryptocurrencies are exchanged on the blockchain, but are stored in digital wallets. Moreover, digital platforms, such as Coinbase, usually support such transactions. Hacking the blockchain is extremely difficult and costly to an extent that it was deemed impossible.[46] Even assuming that the blockchain cannot be corrupted, hacking

---

41 Thakor (n 8) 4.

42 Viral Acharya and Hassan Naqvi, 'The Seeds of a Crisis: A Theory of Bank Liquidity and Risk Taking over the Business Cycle' (2012) 106 Journal of Financial Economics 349.

43 Arnoud W A Boot, Jeroen E Ligterink and Jens K Martin, 'Understanding Fintech and Private Equity' 12.

44 Even though not the only one, especially in the area of payments. Think for instance of all digital wallet services, like PayPal, that do not necessarily work with the blockchain.

45 Aaron Wright and Primavera De Filippi, 'Decentralized Blockchain Technology and the Rise of Lex Cryptographia' (2015) Available at SSRN 2580664.

46 But see the problem of the '51% attack', where a member of the network that owns more than the half of the blockchain can double spend. See <https://www.technologyreview.com/2019/02/19/239592/once-hailed-as-unhackable-blockchains-are-now-getting-hacked/> accessed 31 May 2020.

digital wallets and platforms is much easier.[47] Therefore, who uses cryptocurrencies might blindly rely on the blockchain to trade them, but still needs to trust the ecosystem's intermediaries to store them.

Secondly, parties may want to condition the transaction in the blockchain to future, uncertain contingencies. In this case, parties can code the obligation they intend to undertake in 'if-then' type digital statements, creating a self-executing contract, a so-called smart contract.[48] In this case, parties need to trust the coder.[49] The coder can be a third party, acting as an agent of the contracting parties, or one of the contracting parties. Either way, coding contractual obligations is an opaque mechanism that a party may be unable to understand. Opacity can only be accepted if the counterparty or the agent is trusted.

Thirdly, cryptocurrencies cannot fully replace fiat money. First of all, there are transactions that cannot be settled via cryptocurrency, for instance all the transactions between private parties and the governments, which require legal tender. Relatedly, the majority of the sellers still do not accept cryptocurrencies as means of payment. The fact that states have a monopoly on fiat money affects the ability of disintermediate banks via the blockchain.

Cryptocurrencies could be converted into fiat money, but that requires intermediaries. Moreover, because cryptocurrencies work on a decentralised basis and are not backed by any central authority, their conversion rate is highly volatile. The first reported purchase made using Bitcoin is a good example. In 2010, a man in Florida bought two pizzas worth 25 dollars for 10.000 bitcoins. In December 2017, the same amount was exchanged for almost 200 million dollars; at the end of May 2020 those were still worth more than 95 million dollars.[50]

Traditionally, money is been defined according to three functions it performs in the economy: medium of exchange, store of value and unit of account.[51] Arguably, given the current state of technology, cryptocurrencies perform none of these functions.[52] In this respect, Facebook's proposed Libra project is a little different. The cryptocurrencies issued in the Libra ecosystem would be pegged to a basket of main currencies to avoid volatility and increase public confidence in the coins.[53] Here comes the importance of state monopoly on fiat money. The monetary authorities in the US and the EU have credibly threatened to subject the Libra project to financial regulation as dealing in currency-denominated assets requires a banking or an investment services licence, which is easy to enforce. On

---

47 Famously, in 2014 hackers attached Mt. Gox, a bitcoin exchange, and stole 850000 bitcoins worth 14 billion $. See 5 things to know about Mt. Gox crisis, The Wall Street Journal, 25 February 2014, <https://blogs.wsj.com/briefly/2014/02/25/5-things-about-mt-goxs-crisis/?mg=prod/accounts-wsj> accessed 06 June 2020.

48 Smart Contract Alliance, 'Smart Contract: Is the Law Ready?' (2018) 10.

49 RC Merton, 'Solving Global Challenges Using Finance Science: Past and Future', *Proceedings of the China International Conference in Finance*. Tianjin, China. July (2018) 12.

50 See Bitcoin Pizza Day: Celebrating the $80 Million Pizza Order, <https://www.investopedia.com/news/bitcoin-pizza-day-celebrating-20-million-pizza-order/> accessed 31 May 2020.

51 William Stanley Jevons, *Money and the Mechanism of Exchange* (D Appleton 1876) Vol 17.

52 Thakor (n 8) 10.

53 The Libra Association is backed by Facebook. At this point it is not clear which kind of cryptocurrencies will be issued. The initial project aimed at backing Libra with a basket of multiple currencies but latterly it seems that Libra wants to offer stable coins, each of those backed by a single State currency. See <https://www.cnbc.com/2020/04/16/facebooks-libra-plans-new-crypto-offering-backed-by-just-one-currency.html> accessed 31 May 2020.

these grounds, the project has been put on hold: Facebook is currently considering downsizing Libra to a digital wallet.[54]

Finally, several central banks are experimenting with digital currencies.[55] This is a way to exploit the promise of the blockchain in terms of management of money supply and efficiency of settlements, while maintaining the role of central banks as gatekeeper of money and monetary policy. Libra and government-controlled digital currencies could scale up in the coming years. Nevertheless, these projects hardly imply disintermediation of money and payments, as governments are either directly involved or require intermediaries to have a licence in order to convert digital into traditional currencies. Rather, these projects change the way money and payments are intermediated, exploiting the blockchain.

3 Disintermediation of investment services

3.1 *Investment firms: problem solvers and problem makers*

Banks are not the only financial intermediaries pursuing the efficient allocation of financial resources. Several investment firms intermediate investment in financial markets too. For instance, underwriters intermediate public offerings between the issuers and the investors; mutual funds invest in the financial market the investing public's savings according to predetermined strategies; brokers-dealers intermediate between investors and a stock exchange. This section scrutinises how FinTech firms can disintermediate the services offered by financial firms other than banks and what the promises and the perils of such disintermediation are.

To understand disintermediation of financial services, it is important to understand first why investment firms exist in the first place, which are the problems they solve, and what are the market failures associated with them.

In the standard economic model of resource allocation, non-bank financial intermediaries play no role.[56] However, the vast majority of investors are not involved in financial transactions and do not understand increasingly complex financial markets.[57] Therefore, intermediaries acting in the financial markets reduce the 'participation costs' of financial transactions for non-professional investors.[58] These services come at a cost, usually a fee that intermediaries charge to their clients. Interestingly, empirical evidence shows that the unit cost of financial intermediation has been rather stable in the last 130 years, despite technological innovations improving efficiency. This suggests that rent extraction by financial intermediaries increased overtime.[59] This observation leads us to the market failures in investment services provision. First, there is significant asymmetric information between investment firms and investors. This depends on the participation services investment firms

---

54 See <https://justmoney.org/k-pistor-the-case-for-free-money-a-real-libra/> accessed 29 June 2020.
55 Stijn Claessens and others, 'Fintech Credit Markets Around the World: Size, Drivers and Policy Issues' (2018) BIS Quarterly Review September.
56 John Geanakoplos, 'Arrow–Debreu Model of General Equilibrium', *The New Palgrave: A Dictionary of Economics* (1987) 116.
57 Alessio M Pacces, 'Financial Intermediation in the Securities Markets Law and Economics of Conduct of Business Regulation' (2000) 20 International Review of Law and Economics 479, 481.
58 Franklin Allen and Anthony M Santomero, 'The Theory of Financial Intermediation' (1997) 21 Journal of Banking & Finance 1461, 1462.
59 Philippon (n 5).

provide. As a consequence of information asymmetry, the quality of the services offered by intermediaries remains unknown to customers, creating an adverse selection problem.[60]

In theory, the market could self-correct the asymmetric information problem if the uninvolved investors could follow the signals that informed, marginal investors produce.[61] In this setting, providers of investment services would compete for the marginal investors and this would in turn protect the uninformed. Yet, the marginal consumer argument seems not to hold true for financial services. Most financial services are experience goods that both marginal and uninvolved investors purchase infrequently. This fact prevents marginal investors from quickly learning all the quality aspects of the services purchased and engaging in comparison shopping.[62]

Cognitive biases worsen the market failures that asymmetric information generates. Behavioural finance reveals that investors, especially the unsophisticated ones, suffer from a variety of cognitive biases in their decision-making.[63] Financial firms exploit cognitive biases in financial decisions through the adoption of marketing and contractual strategies that appeal to those biases.[64] This provides a further reason why marginal, informed investors cannot protect the inframarginal, uninformed ones. Marginal investors can identify aggressive marketing, opt out of harsh terms, and contract for better terms. Firms have incentives to cross-subsidise the better terms offered to marginal investors by introducing non-salient, harsh terms in the packages offered to unsophisticated investors.[65]

Financial advice could seemingly ameliorate market failure, but that's illusory. One would expect financial advisors to remedy the information asymmetry, providing even unsophisticated investors with guidance on which financial service or product to choose in a rational way. However, investors face the same asymmetry of information when they choose a financial advisor. Moreover, investors have no way of determining whether the performance of their investment depends on the quality of the financial advice or on the investment risks. This is to say, financial advice is a credence good and the quality of credence goods cannot be ascertained, not even after a process of repeated purchase.[66] This leaves considerable room for financial advisors to extract rents from unsophisticated investors, colluding with other financial firms with which they share financial ties, customers and network.[67]

The aforementioned arguments support regulatory intervention in financial markets.[68] These also represent a suitable benchmark to assess the promises and perils of technology-enabled disintermediation: can FinTech cope with the market failures discussed above? Or is FinTech making the matter worse?

60 David T Llewellyn, 'Regulation of Retail Investment Services' (1995) 15 Economic Affairs 12.
61 Louis L Wilde and Alan Schwartz, 'Equilibrium Comparison Shopping' (1979) 46 The Review of Economic Studies 543.
62 Pacces (n 57) 483.
63 See, for instance, Shlomo Benartzi and Richard Thaler, 'Heuristics and Biases in Retirement Savings Behavior' (2007) 21 Journal of Economic Perspectives 81.
64 Xavier Gabaix and David Laibson, 'Shrouded Attributes, Consumer Myopia, and Information Suppression in Competitive Markets' (2006) 121 The Quarterly Journal of Economics 505.
65 Armour and others (n 12) 215.
66 Pacces (n 57) 483.
67 Armour and others (n 12) 217.
68 Ibid., 218.

3.2 *Disintermediating financial services*

Technologically enabled financial services can potentially improve the allocation of financial resources.[69] At the same time, they also pose considerable challenges. This section discusses both issues.

As mentioned, there is a severe asymmetric information between investors and providers of financial services. This allows financial intermediaries to exploit investors by way of conflicts of interest. FinTechs can ameliorate this situation setting up arm's length transactions between investors and issuers, which allegedly avoid conflicts of interests. Crowdfunding platforms are a case in point.[70] Such platforms offer entrepreneurs, primarily start-ups, an alternative access to finance allowing the 'crowd' to directly provide capital in typically small amounts. The challenge is that crowdfunding doesn't address the issue of investor protection. Small, unsophisticated investors have a limited capacity to assess the potential of a business, especially if it is a start-up. Moreover, their decision to join the crowd might be based on behavioural biases and herding behaviour.[71]

Another paradigmatic example of technology-enabled financial service is Robo-advice. It consists in algorithmic-based financial advice with minimal or no human interaction. Early empirical evidence shows that Robo-advice increases return on investment and reduces volatility.[72] Yet, unsophisticated investors have limited capacity to determine whether the advice fits their preferences.[73] Likewise, consumers usually are not in the position to appreciate the soundness of the algorithm on which the advice is based, no matter how transparent such algorithm is.

Based on these examples, it is possible to identify a few pros and cons of FinTech in financial services. FinTech opens up great opportunities for entrepreneurs to access cheap finance and for investors to participate in a wide variety of financial transactions at a reasonably low cost. Moreover, algorithmic-based financial services and the use of Big Data can decrease the asymmetric information inherent to financial services. However, considerable challenges for investor protection remain. Algorithms do not solve the old investor protection issues but rather bring new issues of investor protection. They may obscure the same exploitative tendencies financial intermediaries have and are more difficult to monitor for deficits in investor protection. As discussed before, platforms and algorithms cannot be merely considered veils between lenders and borrowers. Platforms are profit-maximising corporations. Their conflicts of interests may be hidden in the way algorithms are programmed. As in the case of P2P lending, FinTechs provide investment services based on fees. Therefore, they have an interest to induce investors to trade and invest, exploiting their behavioural biases. Moreover, traditional financial institutions are increasingly

---

69 The efficient allocation of resources represents, in its essence, the ultimate goal of financial markets.

70 Guido Ferrarini and Eugenia Machiavello, 'FinTech and Alternative Finance in the CMU' in Danny Busch, Emilios Avgouleas and Guido Ferrarini (eds), *Capital Markets Union in Europe* (Oxford, UK: Oxford University Press 2018) 208.

71 John Armour and Luca Enriques, 'The Promise and Perils of Crowdfunding: Between Corporate Finance and Consumer Contracts' (2018) 81 The Modern Law Review 51, 53.

72 Francesco D'Acunto, Nagpurnanand Prabhala and Alberto G Rossi, 'The Promises and Pitfalls of Robo-Advising' (2019) 32 The Review of Financial Studies 1983.

73 Wolf-Georg Ringe and Christopher Ruof, 'A Regulatory Sandbox for Robo Advice' (University of Hamburg, Institute of Law and Economics 2018).

acquiring FinTechs, which results in more conflicts of interest depending on the provision of multiple activities.[74]

As a final note, the 'wisdom of the crowd' is attracting considerable attention among the proponents of financial disintermediation. According to the narrative, experts acting as intermediaries pursue their own interests at the expense of the crowd, whereas information technology allows the crowd to choose wisely without the need of self-interested intermediaries.[75] Information technology is thought to improve the quality of the noisy public signals about investment opportunities, which used to call for intermediaries to improve financial information.[76] However, anecdotal evidence suggests that crowds are not always wise.[77] On the contrary, herding behaviour is a serious threat for investors that may fund suboptimal projects or be victim of fraudulent arrangements.[78] Interestingly, FinTechs are sorting out ways to elicit the crowd's wisdom, for instance making more salient to uninformed investors the behaviours of better informed ones.[79]

4 A law and economics approach to FinTech

4.1 *FinTech and market failure*

FinTech has a large potential to improve the efficiency of financial markets by disintermediating banking and non-banking services. However, this potential comes with the risk of exacerbating market failures because the regulations applicable to traditional financial intermediaries are not always neatly applicable to FinTech. In this section, we look at market failures more closely, discussing how regulation can cope with them.

The law and economics problem is twofold. First, banking and non-banking services result in different market failures. As mentioned, the main goal of banking regulation is to cope with the externalities stemming from financial instability, whereas the regulation of investment services is mainly concerned with protecting investors from the consequences of asymmetric information. Second, there is the issue of enforcement. Some FinTechs operate on the blockchain. Because the blockchain supports smart contracts, which are self-executing, blockchain-based FinTechs are harder to subject to regulation, which in turn affects the ability of governments to correct market failure.

QAT is a defining feature of banking.[80] This transformation makes banking fragile because they are exposed to runs. For this reason, virtually anywhere in the world, banking requires a licence. Licensing triggers prudential regulation of banks and gives them access to the safety net, both of which aim to promote financial stability.[81] Licensing, however, also shields banks from competition. FinTechs challenge banks' monopoly to the extent

---

74 Luigi Zingales, 'The Future of Securities Regulation' (2009) 47 Journal of Accounting Research 391.

75 James Surowiecki, 'The Wisdom of Crowds: Why the Many Are Smarter than the Few and How Collective Wisdom Shapes Business' (2004) 296 Economies, Societies and Nations.

76 Raghuram Rajan and Andrew Winton, 'Covenants and Collateral as Incentives to Monitor' (1995) 50 The Journal of Finance 1113.

77 The best example of this might be the dotcom bubble of the early 2000s.

78 Abhijit V Banerjee, 'A Simple Model of Herd Behavior' (1992) 107 The Quarterly Journal of Economics 797.

79 For more detailed consideration on this point, see Armour and Enriques (n 71) 79.

80 See Section 2.

81 Alessio M Pacces and Dirk Heremans, 'Regulation of Banking and Financial Markets' in Alessio M Pacces and Roger J Van den Berg (eds), *Encyclopedia of Law and Economics* (Edward Elgar Publishing 2012) Vol 9, 558.

that they provide banking services without a licence. As the previous discussion reveals, it is difficult for FinTechs to provide core banking services such as, on the one hand, relationship lending and, on the other, repayable funds functioning as safe assets.

For instance, P2P lending does not involve core banking. Although some jurisdictions regard it as banking,[82] P2P platforms do not take any position or risk in the loan concluded between the investors and the borrowers, and most importantly, do not promise liquidity on demand. Thus, P2P lending competes with banks on the extension of credit, but not on the provision of safe assets. Like other forms of crowdfunding, P2P lending raises concerns for investor protection but not for financial stability, as platforms do not issue liabilities, loans are illiquid and the scale of P2P lending is still small.[83] However, the threat to financial stability might be *indirect*. P2P platforms potentially undermine the value of a banking licence and prompt banks to take more risk to the extent that P2P attracts better loans. Whether this is going to be the case is theoretically unclear as P2P platforms may be no match for bank's trust in long-term credit relationships and banks increasingly acquire P2P platforms for arm's length credit. Only time will tell whether P2P lending can grow as big as to make traditional banking riskier.

Cryptocurrencies are potentially more troublesome. In principle, they provide means of payment and of investment. As far as the payment function is concerned, cryptocurrencies exploit the efficiency of digital wallets and other technological innovations. Going a step further, they offer an alternative to fiat money. It is questionable whether cryptocurrencies can replace money. Private money creation is not the problem, as banks routinely engage in this, subject to regulation, and shadow banking does that too, trying to end-run regulation.[84] Private money undermines financial stability to the extent that its safe assets status comes into question during a financial crisis.

However, private money needs the option to convert into fiat money to be credible.[85] Convertibility makes banking and shadow banking dangerous. Because cryptocurrencies lack convertibility into fiat money, their ability to disintermediate banking is limited. Cryptocurrencies are extremely volatile as they are not backed by a financial institution or a pool of assets that could confer upon them liquidity and safety. Libra – the only attempt to overcome this limitation so far – has been effectively opposed by the monetary authorities. The lesson from this is twofold. First, money creation is too important for financial stability to be left out of the regulatory perimeter. On this perspective, central banks are increasingly considering issuing fiat money in digital form.[86] Second, the effective way to stop FinTechs from creating a parallel monetary system is to deny access to (ie, conversion into) fiat money in the absence of a banking or non-banking services licence. This point has more far-reaching consequences than financial stability.

Regarded as investment, cryptocurrencies are paradigmatic of the investment services dimension of FinTech. As discussed, this includes crowdfunding (both equity and P2P lending) and Robo-advice, among others. All of these services share an important characteristic, which make them prone to market failure: they allow particularly (but not exclusively) retail investors to invest their savings at a negligible entry cost. It is

---

82 These include, eg, Italy, France and Germany. See Ferrarini and Machiavello (n 70) 217.
83 Thakor (n 8) 3.
84 Nabilou and Pacces (n 32), 28.
85 Perry Mehrling, *The New Lombard Street: How the Fed Became the Dealer of Last Resort* (Princeton University Press 2010).
86 Thakor (n 8) 10.

very easy to invest in cryptocurrencies, and in general low-key access to investment services is one of the competitive advantages of FinTech. This potentially exacerbates the market failures stemming from asymmetric information, such as unsuitable investment choice, vulnerability to aggressive marketing and exposure to conflicts of interest.[87] Because financial services are experience goods infrequently purchased, or even credence goods, it may take some time (or some high-profile scandals) before FinTech undermines investor confidence in financial markets. Regulation should try to correct market failures before then.

4.2 *How to regulate FinTech?*

FinTech regulation faces two hurdles. First, technology-enabled financial services exploit some regulatory vacuum in order to offer alternative services competitively. Their competitive advantage could vanish were they simply subject to the same regulations as traditional financial services. This leads to the second challenge. In order to escape the threat of regulation, some FinTechs offer services through smart contracts.[88] Because smart contracts are self-executing on the blockchain, financial regulators may be unaware of the services offered in this fashion. To stay under the regulatory radar, transactions must be settled in cryptocurrencies.

The first problem is a classic policy problem in the face of (financial) innovation. There is always a tension between the efficiency advantages of more competition in financial services and other market failures. Optimal regulation depends on context. Such a nuanced discussion of FinTech is beyond the scope of this chapter. It is worth noting, however, that regulation should functionally address market failures. For instance, the strategy for FinTechs to avoid regulation in the EU has been to avoid dealing with 'financial instruments' or otherwise falling into the scope of application of the MiFID.[89] This is a sensible strategy because the MiFID, as securities regulation in general, triggers massive compliance obligations which are overly burdensome for lightly organised FinTechs. Nevertheless, bespoke regimes of disclosure, conduct of business rules, and conflict of interest should be able to commit FinTechs to investor protection without undermining their competitive advantage.[90] Regulatory sandboxes and mentoring arrangements with licensed intermediaries are two promising strategies to design such regimes.[91]

The second challenge is admittedly harder. It seems difficult to regulate what you cannot see, such as 'smart' investment contracts that are fully designed and executed on the blockchain. These smart contracts 'can be described as computer programs that trigger certain prespecified actions (such as sending a certain amount of tokens to a specific address

---

87 See Section 3.1.

88 See eg, <https://defiprime.com> accessed 29 June 2020.

89 Directive 2014/65/EU of the European Parliament and of the Council of 15 May 2014 on markets in financial instruments and amending Directive 2002/92/EC and Directive 2011/61/EU [2015] *OJ L 173/ 349*. For more details on this argument, see Ferrarini and Machiavello (n 70) 218–219.

90 Guido Ferrarini and Eugenia Machiavello, 'Investment-Based Crowdfunding: Is MiFID II Enough', in Danny Busch and Guido Ferrarini (eds), *Regulation of the EU Financial Markets: MiFID II and MiFIR* (Oxford: OUP 2017) 659.

91 Ringe and Rouf (n 73). See also Luca Enriques and W Georg Ringe, 'Bank-Fintech Partnerships, Outsourcing Arrangements and the Case for a Mentorship Regime' (2020) European Corporate Governance Institute – Law Working Paper No. 527/2020.

in the network) if the conditions set out in the code are met'.[92] As the execution of smart contracts doesn't require cooperation from the legal system, regulation cannot prevent it from happening unless smart contracts are illegal and the legal system can enforce their prohibition. And yet, the blockchain is not only a source of strength for such contracts, but also a limitation. Smart contracts cannot enforce actions outside the blockchain.[93] A crucial action in the provision of financial services is the exchange of financial resources on specified dates or contingencies. On the blockchain, only the transfer of cryptocurrencies is self-enforcing.

FinTechs operating on the blockchain might be less difficult to regulate than it looks. The reason is similar to the argument, made above, that FinTechs are not a big threat for financial stability so long as they cannot operate as shadow banks, that is, so long as they cannot credibly promise the conversion of cryptocurrencies into fiat money. In order for such promises to be credible, FinTechs should own a sufficiently large amount of safe assets to support convertibility. However, governments control these assets either because they produce them, as public debt or fiat money, or because they can (not necessarily do) regulate the financial institutions and the contracts creating new safe assets.[94]

On the one hand, a promise to convert cryptocurrencies into euro, dollars or assets denominated in one of these currencies requires the cooperation of the legal system to be enforceable, if only because FinTechs must own such assets via licensed intermediaries. On the other hand, investors need fiat money to pay for goods and services that cannot be purchased in cryptocurrencies and to settle transactions with the government. Therefore, to make blockchain-operated financial services emerge from darkness, financial regulation could restrict the conversion of cryptocurrencies into fiat money. This approach could address the quick emerge of stablecoins, of which Libra is just one example, tackling directly the attempt to decrease a cryptocurrency's volatility by pegging it to assets denominated in fiat money.

We leave the discussion on how exactly to design a regulatory strategy focusing on the convertibility of cryptocurrencies for another day. However, it is important to note that it requires licensed intermediaries to operate as gatekeepers, denying convertibility to the FinTechs that do not comply with financial regulation. This isn't trivial. It is not sufficient to focus on banks, because cryptocurrencies could also be converted via the shadow banking system. Shadow banking still needs liquidity and liquidity ultimately means trading securities, which also requires a licence. Nevertheless, it may be impossible for regulation to control access to every safe asset that could work as means of payment. The same problem applies to illegal markets. Still, reserving the conversion of cryptocurrencies to licensed intermediaries could be a first step towards attracting blockchain-based FinTechs to the regulatory perimeter.

5 Conclusion

In this chapter, we have analysed the economics of FinTech and the case for its regulation depending on market failure. Based on the theory of financial regulation and its relationship

---

92 Jens Frankenreiter, 'The Limits of Smart Contracts' (2019) 1 Journal of Institutional and Theoretical Economics (JITE), published Online First February 4.

93 Ibid.

94 Nabilou and Pacces (n 32), 40.

with FinTech, we distinguish between technology-enabled services that work outside and inside the blockchain. For the former, the crucial regulatory trade-off is between efficiency gains from innovation and regulatory arbitrage. For the latter, our analysis suggests that regulating the convertibility of cryptocurrencies into fiat money is a promising strategy not only to safeguard financial stability, but also to attract financial services to the regulatory perimeter, whenever it is efficient to do so.

Bibliography

V Acharya and H Naqvi, 'The Seeds of a Crisis: A Theory of Bank Liquidity and Risk Taking Over the Business Cycle' (2012) 106 Journal of Financial Economics 349.

F Allen and A M Santomero, 'The Theory of Financial Intermediation' (1997) 21 Journal of Banking & Finance 1461.

F Allen and A M Santomero, 'What Do Financial Intermediaries Do? (2001) 25 Journal of Banking & Finance 271.

J Armour, *Principles of Financial Regulation* (Oxford University Press 2016).

J Armour and L Enriques, 'The Promise and Perils of Crowdfunding: Between Corporate Finance and Consumer Contracts' (2018) 81 The Modern Law Review 51.

A V Banerjee, 'A Simple Model of Herd Behavior' (1992) 107 The Quarterly Journal of Economics 797.

S Benartzi and R Thaler, 'Heuristics and Biases in Retirement Savings Behavior' (2007) 21 Journal of Economic Perspectives 81.

S Bhattacharya and A V Thakor, 'Contemporary Banking Theory' (1993) 3 Journal of Financial Intermediation 2.

A W A Boot, S I Greenbaum and A V Thakor, 'Reputation and Discretion in Financial Contracting' (1993) The American Economic Review 1165.

A W A Boot, J E Ligterink and Martin J K, 'Understanding Fintech and Private Equity' (Amsterdam Center for Corporate Finance 2018).

A W A Boot and A V Thakor, 'Can Relationship Banking Survive Competition? (2000) 55 The Journal of Finance 679.

J H Boyd and M Gertler, 'Are Banks Dead? Or Are the Reports Greatly Exaggerated?' (National Bureau of Economic Research 1995).

R Brealey, H E Leland and D H Pyle, 'Informational Asymmetries, Financial Structure, and Financial Intermediation' (1977) 32 The Journal of Finance 371.

M K Brunnermeier, 'Deciphering the Liquidity and Credit Crunch 2007-2008' (2009) 23 Journal of Economic Perspectives 77.

M K Brunnermeier, A Crocket, C Goodhart, A D Persaud and H Shin, *The Fundamental Principles of Financial Regulation* (ICMB, International Center for Monetary and Banking Studies 2009) Vol 11.

S Claessens, J Frost, G Turner and F Zhu, 'Fintech Credit Markets Around the World: Size, Drivers and Policy Issues' (2018) BIS Quarterly Review September 1.

F D'Acunto, N Prabhala and A G Rossi, 'The Promises and Pitfalls of Robo-Advising' (2019) 32 The Review of Financial Studies 1983.

J Dagher, *Benefits and Costs of Bank Capital* (IMF Staff, International Monetary Fund 2016).

D W Diamond, 'Financial Intermediation and Delegated Monitoring' (1984) 51 The Review of Economic Studies 393.

D W Diamond and P H Dybvig, 'Bank Runs, Deposit Insurance, and Liquidity' (1983) 91 Journal of Political Economy 401.

S Dickinson and D Humphry, P Siciliani and M Straughan, 'The Prudential Regulation Authority's Secondary Competition Objective' (2015) Bank of England Quarterly Bulletin Q4.

J Duarte, S Siegel and L Young, 'Trust and Credit: The Role of Appearance in Peer-to-Peer Lending' (2012) 25 The Review of Financial Studies 2455.

L Enriques and W G Ringe, 'Bank-Fintech Partnerships, Outsourcing Arrangements and the Case for a Mentorship Regime', European Corporate Governance Institute – Law Working Paper No. 527/2020 (2020) Available at SSRN 3625578.

G Ferrarini and E Machiavello, 'Investment-Based Crowdfunding: Is MiFID II Enough' in D Busch and G Ferrarini (eds), *Regulation of the EU Financial Markets: MiFID II and MiFIR* (Oxford: OUP, 2017) 659.

G Ferrarini and E Machiavello, 'FinTech and Alternative Finance in the CMU' in D Busch, E Avgouleas and G Ferrarini (eds), *Capital Markets Union in Europe* (UK: Oxford University Press Oxford, 2018) 208.

Financial Stability Board, 'Key Attributes of Effective Resolution Regimes for Financial Institutions' (2011) <https://www.fsb.org/wp-content/uploads/r_141015.pdf> accessed 01 December 2020.

J Frankenreiter, 'The Limits of Smart Contracts' (2019) 1 J Inst Theor Econ (JITE), published Online First February.

X Freixas, 'Deconstructing Relationship Banking' (2005) 29 Investigaciones Económicas 3.

X Gabaix and D Laibson, 'Shrouded Attributes, Consumer Myopia, and Information Suppression in Competitive Markets' (2006) 121 The Quarterly Journal of Economics 505.

J Geanakoplos, 'Arrow–Debreu Model of General Equilibrium' (1987) The New Palgrave: A Dictionary of Economics 116.

G Gorton, S Lewellen and A Metrick, 'The Safe-Asset Share' (2012) 102 American Economic Review 101.

G Gorton and A Metrick, 'Securitized Banking and the Run on Repo' (2012) 104 Journal of Financial Economics 425.

G Gorton and A Winton, 'Financial Intermediation', in G Constantinides, R M Stulz and M Harris (eds) *Handbook of the Economics of Finance* (Elsevier 2003) Vol 1.

J G Haubrich, 'Financial Intermediation: Delegated Monitoring and Long-Term Relationships' (1989) 13 Journal of Banking & Finance 9.

W S Jevons, *Money and the Mechanism of Exchange* (D Appleton 1876) Vol 17.

A Krishnamurthy and A Vissing-Jorgensen, 'The Aggregate Demand for Treasury Debt' (2012) 120 Journal of Political Economy 233.

J M Lacker, 'Clearing, Settlement and Monetary Policy' (1997) 40 Journal of Monetary Economics 347.

D T Llewellyn, 'Regulation of Retail Investment Services' (1995) 15 Economic Affairs 12.

P Mehrling, *The New Lombard Street: How the Fed Became the Dealer of Last Resort* (Princeton University Press 2010).

R C Merton, 'Solving Global Challenges Using Finance Science: Past and Future', *Proceedings of the China International Conference in Finance*. Tianjin, China. July (2018).

H P Minsky, *Stabilizing an Unstable Economy* (New Haven: Yale UP, 1986).

H Nabilou and A M Pacces, 'The Law and Economics of Shadow Banking' in I H-Y Chiu and I G MacNeil (eds), *Research Handbook on Shadow Banking* (Edward Elgar Publishing 2018) 7.

A M Pacces, 'Financial Intermediation in the Securities Markets Law and Economics of Conduct of Business Regulation' (2000) 20 International Review of Law and Economics 479.

A M Pacces, 'A Law and Economics Perspective on Normative Analysis' in Sanne Taekema et al (eds), *Facts and Norms in Law* (Edward Elgar Publishing 2016) 171.

A M Pacces and D Heremans, 'Regulation of Banking and Financial Markets' in A M Pacces and R J Van den Berg (eds), *Encyclopedia of Law and Economics* (Edward Elgar Publishing 2012) Vol 9.

T Philippon, 'Has the US Finance Industry Become Less Efficient? On the Theory and Measurement of Financial Intermediation' (2015) 105 American Economic Review 1408.

K Pistor, 'A Legal Theory of Finance' (2013) 41 Journal of Comparative Economics 315.

R Rajan and A Winton, 'Covenants and Collateral as Incentives to Monitor' (1995) 50 The Journal of Finance 1113.

W-G Ringe and C Ruof, *A Regulatory Sandbox for Robo Advice* (University of Hamburg, Institute of Law and Economics 2018).

H S Shin, 'Reflections on Northern Rock: The Bank Run That Heralded the Global Financial Crisis' (2009) 23 Journal of Economic Perspectives 101.

H S Shin, 'Securitisation and Financial Stability' (2009) 119 The Economic Journal 309.

Smart Contract Alliance, 'Smart Contract: Is the Law Ready?' (2018) <https://digitalchamber.s3.amazonaws.com/Smart-Contracts-Whitepaper-WEB.pdf> accessed 01 December 2020.

J Surowiecki, 'The Wisdom of Crowds: Why the Many Are Smarter Than the Few and How Collective Wisdom Shapes Business' (2004) 296 Economies, Societies and Nations 5.

A V Thakor, 'Fintech and Banking: What Do We Know?' (2019) Journal of Financial Intermediation 100833.

Welltrado, Global Blockchain-Backed Loans Marketplace ICO (2018) <https://icotop.io/wp-content/uploads/2018/05/Welltrado-Whitepaper.pdf> accessed 01 December 2020.

L L Wilde and A Schwartz, 'Equilibrium Comparison Shopping' (1979) 46 The Review of Economic Studies 543.

A Wright and P De Filippi, 'Decentralized Blockchain Technology and the Rise of Lex Cryptographia' (2015) Available at SSRN 2580664.

L Zingales, 'The Future of Securities Regulation' (2009) 47 Journal of Accounting Research 391.

6 Financial technologies and systemic risk

Some general economic observations

Anja Eickstädt and Andreas Horsch

1 Introduction

This chapter is dedicated to exploring the links between financial technology and systemic risk. Thus, it connects two phenomena that, technically speaking, are not inventions of the 21st century, but have become the centre of attention recently. More specifically, the crises that have dominated the financial markets since 2007[1] have led to the present focus on financial technology and systemic risk.

Leading to the creation of new organisations and rules, financial technology and systemic risk play each already a relevant part in the ever-ongoing institutional change.[2] Linking them might lead to additional institutional change. This primer explores potential linkages in both directions, that is, the potential of fintechs affecting systemic risk as well as systemic risk affecting fintechs. For this purpose, we proceed as follows: Section 2 discusses the evolution of the terms and contents of financial technology and systemic risk critically. Thereafter, Section 3 connects both concepts as described above, focusing on the extent to which fintechs are exposed to systemic risk and to which they can be a source of it. With particular regard to the latter, Section 4 addresses the problem of fintech regulation. Section 5 concludes.

2 Financial technology and systematic risk: old wine in new bottles?

2.1 *From financial technologies to fintech*

Addressing financial technology and systemic risk involves a particular understanding of both terms. Today, the most common understanding of *financial technology* refers to financial industry start-ups whose business model is offering specific financial services digitally: these innovative entrepreneurs and their *organisations* are thus called 'fintechs'.[3]

---

1 Of the numerous works on the financial crises since 2007, see the recent compilation of Robert Z Aliber and Gylfi Zoega (eds), *The 2008 Global Financial Crisis in Retrospect – Causes of the Crisis and National Regulatory Responses* (Palgrave Macmillan 2019). See also James R Barth and George G Kaufman (eds), *The First Great Financial Crisis of the 21st Century: A Retrospective* (Now Publishers 2016).

2 Most seminal on institutional change and also the distinction between rules and organisations are the contributions of Nobel laureate Douglass C North, see eg, Douglass C North, *Institutions, Institutional Change and Economic Performance* (Cambridge University Press 1990); Douglass C North, *Understanding the Process of Economic Change* (Princeton University Press 2005).

3 See European Commission, *FinTech Action Plan: For a More Competitive and Innovative European Financial Sector* Brussels (8 March 2018) COM(2018) 109 final 1, 2.

Although fintechs are a long way from taking over the financial system, they have become fierce competitors of traditional financial intermediaries. One of the most prominent examples showing the importance of fintech is the inclusion of the fintech *Wirecard* in the central German stock market index in September 2018 and the concurrent removal of traditional universal bank *Commerzbank* from the DAX.[4]

Despite the extensive use of the term, there is no consensus on a definition of 'fintech' so far.[5] As fintechs are start-ups competitors that follow a resolutely technology-based approach to offer selected financial services in innovative ways,[6] they are process innovators according to Schumpeter.[7] Rather than suggesting another definition, the chapter considers actual types of fintechs and their potential links to systemic risk. As they focus on particular products or processes, there are more types of fintechs than of traditional banks. One general systematisation[8] distinguishes as follows:

- *Payment Services Providers* not only making financial transfers or transactions faster (real-time transactions), cheaper and smoother (eg, not depending on opening hours or conditions of a stationary bank), primarily resulting from its underlying new technologies, but also providing payment alternatives in the form of virtual currencies.
- *Wealth Managers* offering asset management services of different added value from everyday information provision (robo-advice) to automated financial portfolio management, that is, buying and selling securities on behalf of the customer.
- *Lenders* helping capital seekers to find providers of capital, usually among private households contributing to (SME) corporate finance (P2B lending), or private finance (P2P lending). The larger the financing transaction's volume, the more the group of households involved resembles a 'crowd', turning the transaction into crowdfunding as well.

---

4 See eg, Olaf Storbeck, 'Commerzbank to Be Replaced by Wirecard in Dax Index' *Financial Times* (London, 5 September 2018).
5 On the 'desperate need for a common understanding of the word FinTech', see Patrick Schueffel, 'Taming the Beast: A Scientific Definition of Fintech' (2016) 4(4) Journal of Innovation Management 32, 33. See also Annette Mackenzie, 'The FinTech Revolution' (2015) 26(3) London Business School Review 50, 50. From a legal point of view, see Gudula Deipenbrock, 'FinTech: Unbearably Lithe or Reasonably Agile? A Critical Legal Approach from the German Perspective' (2020) 31(1) European Business Law Review 3, 5–8.
6 See, among others, Mark Carney, *The Promise of FinTech – Something New Under the Sun?* Speech at the Deutsche Bundesbank G20 Conference on Digitising Finance, Financial Inclusion and Financial Literacy (25 January 2017), later adopted by the Financial Stability Board (FSB), *Financial Stability Implications from FinTech – Supervisory and Regulatory Issues that Merit Authorities' Attention* (27 June 2017) 1, 1, and the Basel Committee on Banking Supervision (BCBS), *Sound Practices: Implications of Fintech Developments for Banks and Bank Supervisors* (Bank for International Settlements (BIS) February 2018) 1, 8; see also European Commission (n 3) 1, 2.
7 See Joseph A Schumpeter, *Business Cycles – A Theoretical, Historical, and Statistical Analysis of the Capitalist Process* (McGraw-Hill 1923) 87; Joseph A Schumpeter, 'The Creative Response in Economic History' (1947) 7(2) The Journal of Economic History 149, 151.
8 See eg, In Lee and Yong Jae Shin, 'Fintech: Ecosystem, Business Models, Investment Decisions, and Challenges' (2018) 61(1) Business Horizons 35, 38–40. Common denominator of all fintech types is the use of new technologies or technical infrastructures like cloud computing, artificial intelligence applications, the blockchain, and distributed ledger technologies as well as hereupon based cryptocurrencies or smart contracts. Elaborating these technologies in a legal context, see Deipenbrock (n 5) 3, 20–30.

- *Capital Market Agents* specialised in traditional investment banking areas, such as capital market research, foreign exchange or (securities) trading. In doing so, they provide information and further help connect market participants using new technology, particularly mobile devices.
- *Insurers* ('*insurtechs*') collecting customer data more dynamically and accurately than traditional insurance companies because their technical infrastructure allows them to connect to personal devices and homes of clients ('Big Data') and consequently to cover almost every area of an individual's life around the clock for purposes of risk calculation.[9]
- *Regulatory Technologies* ('*regtechs*') encompass two different fintech-related phenomena. First, regtechs represent fintech firms that provide software solutions for capturing and checking whether specific key figures of a regulated entity meet present and future regulatory requirements (almost) in real-time. Second, regtechs could also be seen as the underlying technology, computer programs, algorithms and interfaces, used by regulators for the supervision of regulated companies ('suptechs'[10]). Those technologies recognise, comprehend and exchange data more efficiently so that regulators can quickly assess whether firms adhere to the regulatory framework or if interventions are needed.[11]

Fintech firms could also be grouped according to their size and interconnectedness. Apart from the fintech prototype of rather small start-ups described above, so-called '*bigtech*' or '*supertech*' firms have evolved. The latter are large technology companies providing financial services or technological infrastructure directly to a vast number of private and corporate clients. At the same time, they employ a massive number of (primarily technical) well-experienced employees and offer self-developed software solutions, giving these firms the chance to grow exceptionally fast.[12]

The focus of fintechs on (digital) technologies constitutes their distinguishing feature and the most significant competitive advantage over traditional bank intermediaries. Most fintechs do not strive for a full bank licence that would permit them to offer the complete service portfolio of 'full banks'. They instead prefer to serve niche markets with just a few selected but innovative financial services.[13] This business model might also be partly a result of the fact that since the financial crises starting in 2008, their offline counterparts (banks) have seen a wave of crisis-driven (re-)regulation that significantly increased their regulatory burden (ie, transaction cost), making them retreat from some business fields, and thus

---

9 See Anjan V Thakor, 'Fintech and Banking: What Do We Know?' (January 2020) 41 Journal of Financial Intermediation 100833.

10 Abbreviation for supervisory technologies, mainly used for supervisory purposes, see Simone di Castri and others, *The Suptech Generations* Financial Stability Institute (FSI) Insights on policy implementation No 19 (BIS October 2019).

11 Following the second definition, see eg, Dong Yang and Min Li, 'Evolutionary Approaches and the Construction of Technology-Driven Regulations' (2018) 54(14) Emerging Markets Finance & Trade 3256, 3257; Hedwige Nuyens, 'How Disruptive Are FinTech and Digital for Banks and Regulators?' (2019) 12(3) Journal of Risk Management in Financial Institutions 217, 219.

12 See, in particular, BCBS, *Sound Practices* (n 6) 1, 15; FSB, *FinTech and Market Structure in Financial Services: Market Developments and Potential Financial Stability Implications* (14 February 2019) 1, 21; Nuyens (n 11) 217, 221.

13 See Lee and Shin (n 8) 35, 37.

opening gaps which fintechs were happy to fill.[14] However, this raises the question in how far fintechs could – in particular by their insolvency – destabilise the financial system – or be hit by financial instability.

2.2 *From system protection to systemic risk*

Since the early days of banking, the stability of the financial system has been an issue, although banking crises only were a rarity until the 20th century.[15] The importance of financial stability is rooted in two fundamental factors:

- Size: The financial system is a crucial element of any economy, and its potential to cause massive damage to the (growth of the) economy in case of failure is extraordinarily high.[16]
- Probability: The probability of such enormous damage is increased as financial systems – unlike other parts of the economy – are particularly vulnerable due to the domino effect (financial contagion) connecting the system's components, that is, financial institutions.[17]

Systemic risk is closely related to the second objective, as it means the destabilisation of the financial system as a whole – which could be caused by a chain reaction set in motion by the failure of just one financial institution – and would thus be relevant for the systems' stability. So, what exactly is systemic risk? In the wake of the 2007/2008 financial crisis, systemic risk became a hotly debated topic amongst academics, politicians, regulators and industry. However, no generally accepted definition has emerged yet. Instead, the coexistence of dozens of definitions[18] has led several scholars to the conclusion that systemic risk

---

14 Greg Buchak and others, 'Fintech, Regulatory Arbitrage, and the Rise of Shadow Banks' (2018) 130(3) Journal of Financial Economics 453, 453 et seqq.

15 Extensively, see the works of Charles P Kindleberger (1910–2003), in particular, Robert Z Aliber and Charles P Kindleberger, *Manias, Panics, and Crashes: A History of Financial Crises* (Palgrave Macmillan 2015). For a brief retrospective on financial crises, see Franklin Allen and Douglas Gale, *Understanding Financial Crises* (Oxford University Press 2007) 2–5.

16 Ground-breaking empirical contributions have been those of Robert G King and Ross Levine, see eg, Robert G King and Ross Levine, 'Finance and Growth: Schumpeter Might Be Right' (1993) 108(3) Quarterly Journal of Economics 717, 717 et seqq.; Robert G King and Ross Levine, 'Financial Intermediation and Economic Development' in Colin Mayer and Xavier Vives (eds), *Capital Markets and Financial Intermediation* (Cambridge University Press 1993) 156; retrospectively, see also Xavier Freixas, Luc Laeven and José-Luis Peydró, *Systemic Risk, Crises, and Macroprudential Regulation* (Cambridge University Press 2015) 49, with further references.

17 See Douglas W Diamond and Philip H Dybvig, 'Bank Runs, Deposit Insurance, and Liquidity' (1983) 91(3) Journal of Political Economy 401, 401 et seqq. Extensively on financial contagion, see the eponymous paper of Franklin Allen and Douglas Gale, 'Financial Contagion' (2000) 108(1) Journal of Political Economy 1, 1 et seqq., also their book chapter on contagion in Allen and Gale, Understanding Financial Crises (n 15) 260–295.

18 For an early yet extensive overview, see Olivier de Bandt and Philipp Hartmann, 'Systemic Risk: A Survey' (November 2000) European Central Bank (ECB) Working Paper No 35 1, 1 et seqq. For a more recent synopsis, see Sylvain Benoit and others, 'Where the Risks Lie: A Survey on Systemic Risk' (2017) 21(1) Review of Finance 109, 109 et seqq.

can be referred to as a phenomenon that is difficult to define, though easy to recognise once it occurs.[19]

At the most basic level, systemic risk can be defined as the danger that a trigger, either a general external ('macro') shock or the internal malfunctioning of one ('micro-')component of a system, leads to the malfunctioning of the system as a whole. Following a general approach – that considers a system's importance – systemic risk belongs to systems 'on which society depends – health, transport, environment, telecommunications, etc.'.[20] Although systemic risk can occur in several (economic) surroundings, it is predominantly discussed in a financial market context. A specific trigger event, especially the failure of one financial institution, can destabilise the financial system as a whole, finally leading to spillovers into the rest of the economy.[21] As this scenario has become a main rationale of the (re-)regulation of financial intermediaries such as banks,[22] the term predominantly refers to new *rules* in a financial system.

The lack of a generally accepted definition might well be explained by the (relative) novelty of the discussion. It was mainly from 1985 onwards that economic papers addressing systemic risk concerning financial markets were published. They might be classified as follows:

1   Papers dealing with the systemic risk of the global financial market caused by the defaults of sovereign debtors.[23] This way of thinking was obvious, since crises in the global financial system manifested in the form of sharp currency devaluations or financial distress of sovereign debtors, showing their potential to affect a large number of market participants negatively.

2   Papers issued by organisations of the United States (US) Federal Reserve System, which discussed systemic risk concerning payments systems, including implicit definitions, for example, of systemic risk as 'the interdependence of participants in a payment

---

19   Leading to comparisons going as far as that to the monster of Loch Ness, see George Sheldon and Martin Maurer, 'Interbank Lending and Systemic Risk: An Empirical Analysis for Switzerland' (1998) 134(IV) Swiss Journal of Economics and Statistics 685, 685. Referring to this comparison, see also Paweł Smaga, 'The Concept of Systemic Risk' (2014) Systemic Risk Centre (SRC), The London School of Economics and Political Science Special Paper No 5 1, 3. On systemic risk as a 'hard-to-define-but-you-know-it-when-you-see-it concept', see Benoit and others (n 18) 109, 109 et seqq.

20   OECD, *Emerging Risks in the 21st Century – An Agenda for Action* (OECD Publications Service 2003) 1, 9, also 33. In this extensive report, the OECD considers 'Five categories of such risks [...]: natural disasters, industrial accidents, infectious diseases, terrorism, and food safety [, but] does not deal with systemic risks to markets, notably to financial markets, although some aspects of financial systems are considered in the analysis'.

21   On systemic risk in general, see Marcel Prokopczuk, *Essays on Systemic Risk* (PhD thesis, University of Mannheim 2009) 1–4. Applying a financial system focus, see the early contribution of E Philip Davis, *Debt, Financial Fragility, and Systemic Risk* (Clarendon Press 1992) 117–118. See also Steven L Schwarcz, 'Systemic Risk' (2008) 97(1) Georgetown Law Review 193, 196–198; Freixas, Laeven and Peydró (n 16) 13, 18.

22   See de Bandt and Hartmann (n 18) 1, 10.

23   See, extensively, William R Cline, *International Debt: Systemic Risk and Policy Response* (Institute for International Economics 1984); for a summary of his approach, see also William R Cline, 'International Debt: From Crisis to Recovery?' (1985) 75(2) The American Economic Review (Papers and Proceedings) 185, 185 et seqq.

system and the resulting vulnerability of many banks directly or indirectly to a single counterparty's failure to settle'.[24]

3 Contributions spurred by the stock market crash of mid-October 1987, which caused numerous market participants to withdraw from the stock market first and from other markets – that is, for debt contracts, or clearing/settlement – after that, sending shock waves through the financial system, thus causing systemic risk.[25]

Consequently, particularly the second group of contributions on systemic risk of the financial system was motivated by financial technology, at that time represented by electronic payment systems/electronic funds transfers, which started to replace traditional payment techniques, namely cash and cheques. In particular, the new option of daylight overdrafts led to the consideration of 'payments system risk',[26] which was deemed to have the potential to turn into a systemic risk in relation to the financial system as a whole.[27]

3 The interrelation of fintechs and systemic risk

3.1 *Systemic risk affecting fintechs*

When interrelating fintechs and systemic risk, one might take two different perspectives. On the one hand, the systemic risk could affect the existence and stability of fintech companies. On the other hand, these start-up innovators could affect the stability of the financial system as a whole, meaning that fintechs cause (or reduce) systemic risk. Because of the relative newness of fintech's evolution, both effects have not yet been fully identified.[28]

As their business models are closely related to those of banks, (exogenous and endogenous) systemic risks could affect fintechs, which have been observed before with traditional intermediaries,[29] possibly however to a different extent:

---

24 Edward J Stevens, 'Risk in Large-Dollar Transfer Systems' (Fall 1984) 20(4) FRB of Cleveland Economic Review 2, 8.

25 For more information on a thorough review of the crisis and recommendations for future regulation, see US President's Working Group on Financial Markets, *Interim Report of The Working Group on Financial Markets – Submitted to the President of the US* (US Government Printing Office 1988) 1–3.

26 See, extensively, David D VanHoose and Gordon H Sellon Jr., 'Daylight Overdrafts, Payments, System Risk, and Public Policy' (September/October 1989) 74 FRB of Kansas City Economic Review 9, 17–21. See also Terrence M Belton and others, 'Daylight Overdrafts and Payments System Risk' (November 1987) 73 Federal Reserve Bulletin 839, 839 et seqq.

27 See R Alton Gilbert, 'Payments System Risk: What Is It and What Will Happen If We Try to Reduce It?' (1989) 71(1) FRB of St. Louis Review 3, 4: 'Systemic risk refers to the risk that the failure of one bank will cause one or more other banks to fail. One way that this could happen is through participation in CHIPS'. See also Gerald R Faulhaber, Almarin Phillips and Anthony M Santomero, 'Payment Risk, Network Risk, and the Role of the Fed' in David B Humphrey (ed), *The US Payment System: Efficiency, Risk and the Role of the Federal Reserve* (Kluwer 1990) 197–213.

28 From a regulatory point of view, see eg, FSB, *Financial Stability Implications from FinTech* (n 6) 1, 7. See also the scientific contributions of Gregor Dorfleitner and others, *FinTech-Markt in Deutschland* (Bundesfinanzministerium 2016) 1, 87; Dong He and others, 'FinTech and Financial Services: Initial Considerations' (2017) IMF Staff Discussion Note 1, 15; Ioannis Anagnostopoulos, 'Fintech and Regtech: Impact on Regulators and Banks' (2018) 100(C) Journal of Economics and Business 7, 22.

29 For a general overview, see, for instance, FSB, *Financial Stability Implications from FinTech* (n 6) 1, 17 et seqq.

1   As the core competitive advantage of fintech firms is their strength to detect innovative business models to adapt to continually and profit out of fast-paced, dynamic market conditions,[30] their ability to cope with and immediately react to external system-wide shocks flexibly might be higher than that of traditional banks.

2   Fintechs lack main channels of financial contagion: deposits and loans. Apart from that, their vulnerability depends on their specific business model. For example, payment-servicing fintechs would suffer from a slowdown of the financial system because the numbers and volumes of financial transfers would decrease.

On the contrary, fintechs could be less resilient to systemic risk than banks, because they lack a well-diversified portfolio as well as a sufficient loss-absorbing capital basis. The latter could be a consequence of lighter regulatory treatment but also of youth, which prevented the procuring and reserving of profits. As systemic risks in most cases lead to (extended) periods of economic weakening of the performance of firms or even industries, fintech start-ups do not possess the robustness or the capital reserves required to survive[31] severe crises. Moreover, most fintechs suffer from poorly scalable business concepts (within a niche market), making it hard to address new customer groups during crisis processes or afterwards.[32] Additionally, the demand for fintech services could decrease more seriously than the demand for bank services, as customers withdraw from new, less-established suppliers more easily than from established ones, which they rather perceive as a safe haven, particularly in times of crises. Therefore, it can be expected that fintechs are hit more severely by systemic risks and financial instabilities than their broadly positioned traditional counterparts. Even if they conquered the storm, the usual processes of crisis-driven (re-)regulation would increase the danger of indebtedness or illiquidity, as their business model would no longer be compatible with the adjusted regulatory framework, making it lose its previous competitive advantage of flexibility and adaptability.[33] Consequently, market developments reveal that fintechs increasingly tend to cooperate or merge into/with banks,[34] benefiting from the bank's stronger resilience.

By nature, systemic risk endangers any part of the system, and thereby fintechs. Nevertheless, one might only learn in the next systemic crisis, whether banks or fintechs are more vulnerable when exposed to systemic risk – until then, this must remain an educated guess.

---

30 See Dorfleitner and others (n 28) 1, 1.

31 See ibid., 1, 88, as well as William Magnuson, 'Financial Regulation in the Bitcoin Era' (2018) 23(2) Stanford Journal of Law Business & Finance 159, 186–187.

32 See Christopher Schmitz, Jan-Erik Behrens and Dmytro Shevchenko, 'Germany FinTech Landscape, Fintech Beyond Borders: Cross-Border Fintech Activity' (November 2018) Ernst & Young Assurance Tax Transactions Advisory Study <http://docplayer.net/146952404-Germany-fintech-landscape.html> 1, 11. Call-off date for all hyperlinks, unless stated otherwise: 12 March 2020. Apart from that, a reason for failure could also be seen in the lacking of investors that they might find in well-established banks or other traditional financial institutions, see ibid., 1, 18.

33 See Nuyens (n 11) 217, 219.

34 See Bundesanstalt für Finanzdienstleistungsaufsicht (BaFin), *BaFin Journal November 2019* (2019) 1, 35.

3.2 *Fintechs affecting systemic risk*

In general, system stability is supported by the diversification, but endangered by the con-centration of financial supply. More precisely, in the context of fintech phenomena, the systemic risk might result from the market approach of at least some fintechs, which do not aim to substitute particular financial intermediaries, like one bank crowding out a compet-ing bank. Instead, they claim to replace whole parts of the financial system, that is, all the banks, or all the current types of currencies. The closer they get to these disruptive goals, the more essential they become for the financial system (leading to the very extreme of becoming systematically important). If, for example, every financial market participant uses fintech X – and no longer one of the numerous traditional banks – for money transfers, a breaking down of this monopolist X would stop money transfer worldwide, leading to massive system instability.[35] Referring to the fintech categories introduced above, their system-related importance can be described as follows:

- First, there is a potential probability of triggering systemic risks through fintechs cov-ering the sector of payment services. Specifically, some fintech firms offer to settle pay-ments through or making investments in digital (crypto) currencies that exist parallel to the 'off-line ones'. The central issue is not that they are provided electronically, as even a digital Euro is considered.[36] Still, they are missing a physical equivalent, which is why they can be hardly attached a value. Consequently, cryptocurrencies can rein-force the creation of (price) bubbles and herding effects resulting from being highly overestimated and hyped by investors. With this alone being a potential systemic risk affecting financial stability,[37] the rise of digital currencies might lead to parallel finan-cial systems or markets (analogous to shadow banking), with those fintech branches being more prone to corruption and fraud.[38] Danger to systemic stability caused by payment service providers grows with their market share, and thus becomes worst for a *big- or supertech.*
- As to fintech in the realm of *wealth management*, potential systemic risks could most likely arise from *robo-advisors*. Their potential to influence or even harm financial sta-bility stems from using similar algorithms recommending or running the same invest-ment strategies for related customer information, leading to the potential threat of herding.[39] As technologies and algorithms represent seminal resources and competitive advantages of companies, their potential to harm financial stability cannot be gauged

---

35 While still far from being monopolists, selected fintechs have gained remarkable market shares already. Apple Pay settles about 75% of contactless payments in the United States. At the same time, Alipay and WeChat account for probably even a higher quota on the Chinese market, see Yang and Li (n 11) 3256, 3259–3260.

36 See eg, Thomas Mayer, 'A Digital Euro to Compete with Libra' (2019) 16(1) The Economists' Voice 1.

37 See eg, Thomas Theobald and Silke Tober, *IMK Finanzmarktstabilitätsreport 2017/2018* (February 2018) Institut für Makroökonomie und Konjunkturforschung (IMK) Report 134 1, 3, 22 et seqq.; Galyna Azarenkova and others, 'The Influence of Financial Technologies on the Global Financial System Stability' (2018) 15(4) Investment Management and Financial Innovations 229, 232 et seqq.

38 For potential negative (but also positive) impacts of (appropriately regulated) cryptocurrencies on finan-cial stability, see eg, Claus Dierksmeier and Peter Seele, 'Cryptocurrencies and Business Ethics' (2018) 152(1) Journal of Business Ethics 1, 1 et seqq.

39 See Depository Trust & Clearing Corporation (DTCC), *Fintech and Financial Stability* (October 2017) 1, 10.

fully without insights about programming and source codes (of as many robo-advisors as possible). This technology-based problem becomes even more severe for big players whose market shares enable them to influence the market through their decisions. New trading strategies such as social trading (ie, copying successful trades of other market participants, for example, significant robo-advisors like *Wealthfront*)[40] aggravate the problem of one-sided investment decision making. Consequently, the probability of system-wide incidents caused by similar technologies, similar strategies, and the same behaviour becomes relevant.

- For fintechs in the realm of *lending*, an oversupply of P2P loans can be observed.[41] While this increased access to and supply of financial services might appear desirable concerning (credit portfolio) diversification, the extra comfortable and fast provision of loans might mainly attract debtors of weak solvency (*adverse selection*). This phenomenon is aggravated by the complexity of incomplete regulation of fintechs as well as by the nature of the services they offer. Moreover, the lack of transparency within the fintech market could lead to debtors' difficult-to-trace concatenations. In contrast to banks, those structures might lead to chain reactions if it comes to (massive) loan defaults within a specific fintech segment in generating systemic risks (potential threat of *lump risks*).[42]

- From an economic point of view, fintechs acting as *capital market agents, insurtechs* and *regtechs* show no recognisable negative implications for systemic risk and financial stability, which is why these fintech types will not be considered further.

In addition to specific threats of specific types, some natural features of the general business model of fintechs could harm financial stability. By their very nature, fintechs are particularly exposed to technological risk, that is, malfunctioning, misusing or manipulation of technological infrastructures caused by external events (hacking and other cybercrime) or internal processes (ab initio programming errors in the code itself, or errors caused by posterior data entry mistakes).[43] One feature that makes these risks particularly problematic is the legal question of attribution of liability.[44]

Additionally, technical risks are triggered by the centralisation of and dependency on only a few (data) providers, for example, oligopolistic cloud providers or money transfer

---

40 See FSB, *Financial Stability Implications from FinTech* (n 6) 1, 20.

41 More precisely on the 'P2P lending platform-boom', see Ning Zhang and Wuyu Wang, 'Research on Balance Strategy of Supervision and Incentive of P2P Lending Platform' (2019) 55(13) Emerging Markets Finance and Trade 3039, 3039.

42 See FSB, *Financial Stability Implications from FinTech* (n 6) 1, 19.

43 See Ross P Buckley and others, 'The Dark Side of Digital Financial Transformation: The New Risks of FinTech and the Rise of TechRisk' (2019) European Banking Institute (EBI) Working Paper 2019/54 1, 11 et seqq.

44 See Penny Crosman, 'Are Fintechs a Systemic Risk?' (2018) 183(173) American Banker 1, 1. Trust in fintechs also suffers from alleged or proven (fraudulent) misbehaviour of some companies, as recently shown by the accounting forgery scandal of former flagship-fintech Wirecard, see Dan McCrum, 'Wirecard: The Rise and Fall of a German Tech Icon' *Financial Times* (London, 25 June 2020), as well as by some virtual currency (especially Bitcoin) and trading providers/platforms. See eg, Daniel Liebau and Patrick Schueffel, 'Cryptocurrencies & Initial Coin Offerings: Are They Scams? – An Empirical Study' (2019) 2(1) Journal of the British Blockchain Association 1.

institutions.[45] Cyber-monoculture arising from oligopolistic market structures in the area of technology usage further contributes to technological risks. The same is true for the still-evolving digital technology, which makes fintechs use the same algorithms, computer programs and technical infrastructures.[46] Disruptions or failures in the functioning of these technologies consequently affect a high number of fintechs at the same time, leading to a breakdown of the whole financial system in the worst case (*contagion effect*). Altogether, this means that even in the absence of monopolists, business models (and low capital reserves) of even a multitude of fintechs are so similar that a shock would hit them and fail 'as one'.

Finally, the phenomenon of 'erosion or even crisis of trust'[47] comes into play: the average customer is still more sceptical about fintechs than about traditional financial intermediaries, as the former have no proven track record, making them less predictable and credible. Thus, customers are prone to react more nervously in the wake of a fintech than in the wake of a bank crisis. In consequence, negative news or even failure of one single fintech could prove extraordinarily contagious, as customers withdraw from other fintechs without making a difference. So, even if the real (technical or economic) homogeneity of this part of the financial system is limited, the *assumed homogeneity* of fintechs could 'maximize the probability of the entire system collapsing'[48] analogously. While the persistence of different fintechs will weaken this homogeneity assumption, it could also support different ways of contagion. The longer fintechs exist and the more they are able to connect to other financial intermediaries, be it traditional ones or other fintechs (inter-fintech cooperation),[49] this might drive probability and the extent of damages. The growing complexity of the system will make it hard or even impossible to identify, prevent and control every single security gap or gateway for hackers within the whole fintech system.[50] Sceptics might feel even more confident because of current negative examples of lacking reputation and technical vulnerabilities[51] of some fintech companies. Thus, potential (cyber)security risks do not always have to go back to the fintech provider itself, but to its affiliates/contract partners whenever they provide interfaces or are a part of the provision of services in any other way.[52] Particular problems arise in the case of *supertechs* or *bigtechs*. By their very nature, these competitors are too large to be ignored by others.

45 See Crosman (n 44) 1, 1. Even if new technologies are known for their ability to decentralise and diversify, see eg, FSB, *Financial Stability Implications from FinTech* (n 6) 1, 16 et seqq., they suffer from dependence on the (technical) functionality of a few key interfaces and providers.
46 See Buckley and others (n 43) 1, 15.
47 Ibid., 1, 9.
48 Andrew G Haldane and Robert M May, 'Systemic Risk in Banking Ecosystems' (2011) 469 Nature 351, 351.
49 See eg, DTCC (n 39) 1, 9.
50 See, more precisely, Buckley and others (n 43) 1, 9 et seqq.
51 Besides the spectacular Wirecard insolvency of June 2020, see, for instance, the failed ICO (virtual IPO) of fintech Envion AG causing 37,000 investors still waiting for the repayment of their deposits, eg, Nathaniel Popper, 'In the World of Cryptocurrency, Even Good Projects Can Go Bad' *New York Times* (New York, 31 May 2018); or critical operational incidents and security gaps within fintech N26, see Tobias Buck and Olaf Storbeck, 'German Fintech N26 Appeases Regulators as It Eyes Future IPO' *Financial Times* (London, 14 August 2019).
52 Current examples of such security failures resulting from business partnerships are Google Pay and PayPal: Due to security gaps at PayPal, hackers were able to take over customer accounts, see David Z Morris, 'Researchers Say They Found a Hole in PayPal's Security. PayPal Says It's No Big Deal' *Fortune* (New York, 5 March 2020).

To what extent *fintechs, big- or supertechs* can harm financial stability depends on how the markets (competitors) react. According to the Financial Stability Board (FSB), two basic patterns of reaction can be distinguished[53]:

1   Cooperation or even merger of fintech with traditional bank intermediaries: in this case, two scenarios are possible. Firstly, the fintech's failure will be cushioned by the – probably higher liquidity and capital reserves of – the established intermediary. Secondly, if the latter is too weakened itself, the fintech's failure could spread to the banking industry even more quickly.
2   Competition with traditional bank intermediaries: avoiding cooperation, fintechs try to fight ordinary suppliers economically. Whereas this could lead to reduced profits, higher risk exposure, and finally, forced market exits of weaker parties of both, fintechs and banks, and a destabilised financial system, new competitors also spur the entrepreneurial activities of established ones, possibly leading them to higher profits, capital and resilience.

Currently, the first pattern seems to prevail, but stand-alone fintechs still exist, some of them of comparable size. Concerning their risk exposure and potential role in the financial system, the case of systemically important entities must be addressed. Consequently, the next section deals with the possible regulatory classification of fintechs and its regulatory consequences in preventing system risks in favour of system protection.

4 Regulatory consequences

4.1 *General regulation of fintechs*

Rule-makers and regulators have been criticised for being focused on a single financial institution while at the same time neglecting the risk of system-wide instability.[54] Against this backdrop, a system-wide perspective is applied to alternative financial intermediaries, too. In doing so, it should be kept in mind that the rise of fintechs is at least partly due to current banking regulations, as new competitors now could profit from, and base their business model on, regulatory arbitrage.[55] Although markets saw numerous bank insolvencies, and economists assembled a good amount of knowledge regarding bank insolvencies and their effects on the financial system, much remains unknown, the unexpected has to be expected. This uncertainty is even more real for fintechs, as theory and practice just started to collect information.

As modern (information) technology allows for low-cost production (and low-cost communication of competitive advantages) of financial services, fintechs could turn into a magnet for the customers they focus on. The more customers they attract, the more people would be affected by the failure of a fintech, revealing a trade-off between individual rationality (saving transaction cost) and collective damage (increased cost of regulation or

53 See FSB, *FinTech and Market Structure in Financial Services* (n 12) 1, 17 et seqq.
54 See, extensively, Freixas, Laeven and Peydró (n 16) 251–289, 329–365.
55 See Buchak and others (n 14) 453 et seqq. For instance, in the case of crowdlending, see also Deirdre M Ahern, 'Regulatory Arbitrage in a FinTech World: Devising an Optimal EU Regulatory Response to Crowdlending' (1 March 2018) EBI Working Paper Series No 24 1, 1 et seqq.

failure). This potential threat becomes even more realistic as fintechs start to offer wider ranges of services to integrate clients in any respect of their personal needs and data in a fintech ecosystem. The more a fintech expands its services portfolio, the more it might benefit from total risk reduction, but the more it would become bank-like, too. Once defined as a bank, a fintech would be subject to bank regulation, because if an institution '"quacks like a bank, and swims like a bank", then it should be subject to the rules pertaining to the structure and operation of being a bank'.[56] Relevant rules as to the scope of application like the ones of the German Kreditwesengesetz (KWG) enable regulators to distinguish between bank-fintechs and nonbank-fintechs. While the former would become subject to normal banking regulation, the latter would not.

At the same time, the urgency of general fintech regulation seems limited from an economic point of view: The regulation of financial intermediaries is justified by (1) customer protection and (2) system protection. Consequently, the first question addresses the protection-worthiness of fintech customers. Looking at banking or insurance regulation reveals that their regulation is motivated by the protection of only some customers: private household depositors and insured/third parties. People who have a de facto *creditor* position against a financial intermediary, face specific *credit risk* without being able to assess and manage it properly and could be ruined if this credit risk hits. In comparison, fintechs show no significant indebtedness to private households. Consequently, depositor protection seems a smaller issue.

Considering macro shocks, fintechs show a homogeneous exposure to technology risk/cybercrime. However, the diversity of their business models makes fintechs less vulnerable to external or macro shocks in general. However, even if fintech-specific risks can be identified, this would not justify regulation automatically. As most industries show industry-specific exposures to particular risk categories, these risks are usually handled by the management acting on behalf of shareholders and further stakeholders of the company. Instead, proper regulation requires (1) a particular market failure, which governmental regulation promises to alleviate or even eliminate (2a) effectively and (2b) efficiently.[57] So far, substantial evidence is still pending for regulating the fintech industry.

Even if the requisite proof could be obtained, any regulatory approach will suffer from two core problems:

1   The heterogeneity of fintech types and business models makes the development of perfectly fitting rules using the approach 'one size fits all' difficult. Identifying and addressing all kinds of risks – including systemic risk resulting from fintechs – might be impossible for regulators due to the dynamic business landscape of fintechs and the rapid technological progress.
2   For regulating fintechs, regulators need legal and (financial) economic as well as technical and programming skills.[58]

56 John Hill, *Fintech and the Remaking of Financial Institutions* (Academic Press 2018) 286.
57 See Andreas Horsch, 'Regulating SIFIs in the European Union: A Primer from an Economic Point of View' in Mads Andenas and Gudula Deipenbrock (eds), *Regulating and Supervising European Financial Markets* (Springer International 2016) 393–420, 401.
58 See Magnuson (n 31) 159, 187–189.

Despite these economic considerations, fintech regulation has already been put in place. Concentrating on the risks of the underlying technology or assets of fintech business models,[59] regulators have recently paid more attention to make the use of technology within financial services more secure and resistant to cybersecurity issues.[60] In the EU, the principle of technology neutrality applies, meaning that financial markets regulation is required to regulate activities and not technology.[61] Consequently, early fintech regulation concentrates on (1) measures directly regulating their activities (eg, payment servicers); (2) rules that focus on the market participants' use of new technologies (eg, cloud computing) when it comes to providing financial products and (3) measures promoting the delivery of digital services more particularly, that is, the establishment of innovation hubs, sandboxes or accelerators for giving fintechs the possibility of testing their services in the surrounding of (sometimes facilitated testing) market conditions and under the supervision of regulators, competitors and (technical and economic) experts.[62]

Researchers aim to assess the effectiveness of these regulatory measures.[63] Regarding their potential advantageousness in identifying and reducing fintech-related systemic risks, the third group of measures might be the most reasonable. Within regulatory sandboxes and comparably innovation-friendly surroundings, fintechs and regulators are in constant dialogue, the former providing information about their business models, underlying technologies and algorithms to enter these specific testing hubs.[64] More insight and knowledge about internal processes of fintechs and their technologies make it easier to identify for example, similarities of algorithms and therefore prevent the systemic risk arising from equal and unbiased investment recommendations of robo-advisors. Moreover, the data obtained and evaluated can be applied to fintechs not participating in the sandbox, but exhibiting comparable business ideas and technologies. Based hereupon, fintech-related systemic risk could be detected, while the approaches towards activities and technologies could be used to set targeted standards or rules.

Furthermore, to strengthen fintechs' institutional stability, internal risk management systems and processes could be supplemented by special reserves or instruments complementing or covering their specific risk positions (eg, loss-absorbing buffers, insurance contracts[65] or hedges to mitigate technical risks). These standards could be considered

---

59 See Fernando Restoy, *Regulating Fintech: What Is Going on, and Where Are the Challenges?* (BIS Speech 16 October 2019) 1, 3 et seqq.

60 For instance, in the context of the blockchain technology the state of Arizona has established a specific blockchain law, see Dirk A Zetzsche, Ross P Buckley and Douglas W Arner, 'The Distributed Liability of Distributed Ledgers: Legal Risks of Blockchain' (2017) EBI Working Paper Series No 14 1, 19 et seqq.

61 In the context of robo-advice, see FSB, *Financial Stability Implications from FinTech* (n 6) 1, 27. Generally, see Restoy (n 59) 1, 3.

62 For an overview of potential fintech-related policy measures, see Restoy (n 59) 1, 1 et seqq.

63 See eg, European Supervisory Authorities (ESAs), *Report: FinTech: Regulatory Sandboxes and Innovation Hubs* (7 January 2019); European Banking Authority (EBA), *Report on Regulatory Perimeter, Regulatory Status and Authorisation Approaches in Relation to FinTech Activities* (18 July 2019); Péter Fáykiss and others, 'Regulatory Tools to Encourage FinTech Innovations: The Innovation Hub and Regulatory Sandbox in International Practice' (2018) 17(2) Financial and Economic Review 43, 43 et seqq.

64 See eg, Hilary Allen, 'Regulatory Sandboxes' (2019) 87(3) The George Washington Law Review 579, 580 et seqq.

65 For example, cyber risk insurances, see Lawrence D Bodin and others, 'Cybersecurity Insurance and Risk-Sharing' (2018) 37(6) Journal of Accounting and Public Policy 527, 527 et seqq.

for fintechs as well as for banks cooperating with them as they become more exposed to technology and cybersecurity risks.

Basically, regulators should aim to improve the provision and exchange of information between regulators and fintechs and their technical and networking surrounding quantitatively and qualitatively. For avoiding the emergence of systemic risks, topics such as cybersecurity and data protection law, the clarification of competences[66] and responsibilities and optimal standard-setting and enforcing processes on a national and European level are compulsory to avoid regulatory arbitrage.

For that purpose, general test scenarios could be used to check whether technologies reveal technical vulnerabilities.[67] Therefore, back testing and stress tests for new technologies used by fintechs, should be as compulsory as the current regulatory stress testing of banks. Test scenarios might also be a proper way to assess the effects which endogenous or exogenous adverse shocks will have on several fintech types. Moreover, these proceedings might help identify which capital reserves appear sufficient for each fintech business model without overregulating them. In the long run, these tests would help collect data on fintechs, which could be used to design even better regulatory frameworks.

In addition to these qualitative or disclosure instruments, quantitative minimum (capital) requirements could be applied to these new market actors. In their entirety, these regulatory measures could improve the problem of lack of trust in new technologies and fintechs in general as they would be legally obliged to maintain additional reserves. If fintechs also comply with fulfilling capital requirements for banks or even apply for a bank licence, their reputation and reliability would increase further. The same effect could be achieved by providing more information about their business models and technologies for getting an official label or rating that the applied technologies are secure and hard to hack. In the end, minimum capital standards, supervisory review processes, market discipline, compulsory guaranty funds or any other institution must be benchmarked against effectiveness and efficiency. The same holds for the responsible supervisory body: should it be bank regulators, other regulators already at work or a new organisation? To answer these questions, further research is needed.

4.2 *Special regulation of fintechs*

While the previous section considered a general regulation of (all the) fintechs, this final section takes a different view. It discusses in how far particular fintechs could represent a unique (systemic) risk and thus should be subject to special regulation. Further pursuing the reasoning outlined above, fintechs that qualify as banks or other financial intermediaries in a first step must be scrutinised if they could be more than just another financial institution but a systemically important financial institution. In particular, bigtechs and supertechs could qualify as 'Systematically Important FinTechs' (SIFT(ech)). Together, this leads to four possible regulatory categories of fintechs to be considered:

---

66 See Magnuson (n 31) 159, 188–189.
67 This could be done in the surrounding of regulatory sandboxes or general periodic tests. On the modelling of regulatory sandboxes, see Wolf-Georg Ringe and Christopher Ruof, 'Keeping Up with Innovation: Designing a European Sandbox for Fintech' (2019) European Capital Market Institute (ECMI) Commentary No 58 1, 4 et seqq. On a more global level, see Financial Conduct Authority (FCA), *Global Financial Innovation Network Consultation* (August 2018) 1, 12.

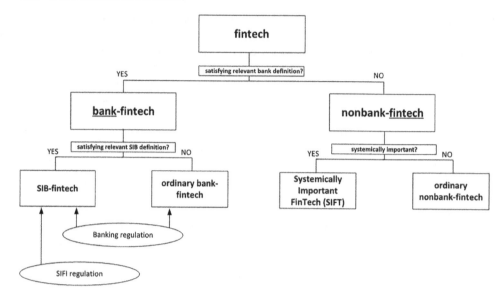

Figure 6.1 Regulatory categories of fintech.

Source: Authors' own illustration.

Whereas bank-fintechs (left part of figure 6.1) are already subject to regulatory regimes, nonbank-fintechs (right part of figure 6.1) do not fall within the banking regulation scope. Instead, specific regulation has to be considered for the latter, with SIFT regulation raising additional questions. Whether any institution is capable of destabilising the financial system or not remains unknown until the supposed trigger event happens. In the meantime, systemic importance cannot be more than an educated guess.

This problem has already been discussed for Systemically Important Financial Institutions (SIFIs). Two concepts have been suggested here: model-based approaches of economic theory and criteria-based approaches of regulators, both showing severe limitations. While the model-based ones suffer from complexity and lack of data, criteria-based ones always suffer from the simplicity and lack of theoretical basis.[68] As the data problem must be even more serious for fintechs, model-based approaches will remain infeasible for years. So, for the time being, criteria-based approaches would be the second-best alternative. The current catalogue used for the identification of Systemically Important Banks (SIBs) (lower left part of figure 6.1) could serve as a starting point. The respective Basel approach[69] uses the following five categories (supplemented by multiple indicators identified by the Basel Committee to assess the main categories)[70]:

1   Cross-jurisdictional activity (eg, according to cross-jurisdictional claims and liabilities)
2   Size (eg, according to total exposures as defined by regulatory concepts like Basel III's leverage ratio)

68   See Horsch (n 57) 393, 404–409.
69   See BCBS, *Global Systemically Important Banks: Revised Assessment Methodology and the Higher Loss Absorbency Requirement* (BIS July 2018) 1, 3–6.
70   See, more precisely, ibid., 1, 5 et seqq.

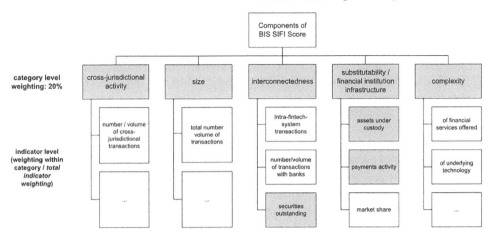

Figure 6.2 Sample for an indicator-based identification of SIFTs.

Source: Authors' own illustration.

3 Interconnectedness (as, for example, represented by intra-financial system assets, intra-financial system liabilities and securities outstanding)
4 Substitutability/financial institution infrastructure (as indicated by, eg, assets under custody, payments activity and underwritten transactions in debt and equity markets)
5 Complexity (with, eg, the notional amount of over-the-counter (OTC) derivatives, Level 3 assets[71] and trading and available-for-sale securities as respective indicators)

These categories – in particular the first and the third one – appear reasonable and applicable in a fintech context, too. Others than these main categories (eg, the criteria of complexity) are less applicable as the respective indicators are not perfectly fitting and have to be adapted or expanded. Therefore, for example, new indicators such as the complexity of supplied financial services and products as well as of technologies, processes and algorithms used by the fintech concerned could be introduced. Consequently, a new catalogue of indicators should be elaborated. Figure 6.2 above makes a suggestion, with the shaded components taken from Basel's SIB approach.

Once a catalogue of main categories and indicators has been agreed upon, it could help distinguish ordinary (nonbank-)fintechs from SIFTs (lower right part of figure 6.1). The latter would then – in a second step – need to be regulated adequately. Continuing the SIB-parallel, would, for example, mean that they keep an additional 'SIFT capital buffer'. Whether extra quantitative, qualitative or other regulations should be preferred depends on their effectiveness and efficiency. The discussion of regulatory alternatives, however, must be left to future research. Against this backdrop, one might conclude:

71 Level 3 assets represent financial assets and liabilities usually hard to value which is why banks are allowed to use internal models for their valuation, see BCBS, 'The Interplay of Accounting and Regulation and Its Impact on Bank Behaviour: Literature Review' (January 2015) Working Paper No 28 1, 6 (footnote 9).

- If a fintech neither is nor will potentially become systemically important, there is hardly a justification for regulating it to sustain financial stability. However, this does not preclude any regulation required to ensure investor/customer/depositor protection.
- If a fintech is or might potentially become systemically important, regulating it appears justified on the grounds of sustaining financial stability. The question of how to regulate it remains a different issue.

5 Conclusion

Financial technology, as well as systemic risk, require proper, internationally agreed definitions from a 21st-century point of view. The chapter aimed to contribute to such definitions, but was focused on identifying characteristic risk exposures and various connections between fintechs and systemic risk. The respective findings finally led to the question of regulating modern fintechs to protect the financial system's stability. To mitigate their potential of contributing to systemic risk, regulation has to be flexible and dynamic. As the continually changing business models, technologies and contract partners of fintechs are hard to include in the regulatory framework ex-ante, the latter has to be adjusted ex-post, but with minimal regulatory lagging, whenever new fintech types surface.

Finally, the question remains: will the emergence of fintechs decrease or increase the systemic risk of traditional financial intermediaries? A decrease appears likely if fintechs take over risky business areas and leave low-risk areas to traditional banks. If they turn out to be superior managers of these areas, not only the banks rid of these activities, but the system as a whole would benefit. An increase appears likely if fintechs take over low-risk business areas and leave the risky ones to traditional banks. The same applies if the emergence of fintechs, in general, incentivises bank managers to turn to riskier strategies to fight the new competitors. Consequently, future research should address the systemic risk contribution of fintechs and banks alike.

Bibliography

D M Ahern, 'Regulatory Arbitrage in a FinTech World: Devising an Optimal EU Regulatory Response to Crowdlending' (1 March 2018) EBI Working Paper Series 2018 No 24.

R Z Aliber and C P Kindleberger, *Manias, Panics and Crashes: A History of Financial Crises* (7th edn, Palgrave Macmillan 2015).

R Z Aliber and G Zoega (eds), *The 2008 Global Financial Crisis in Retrospect – Causes of the Crisis and National Regulatory Responses* (Palgrave Macmillan 2019).

F Allen and D Gale, 'Financial Contagion' (2000) 108(1) Journal of Political Economy 1–33.

F Allen and D Gale, *Understanding Financial Crises* (Oxford University Press 2007).

H Allen, 'Regulatory Sandboxes' (2019) 87(3) The George Washington Law Review 579–645.

I Anagnostopoulos, 'Fintech and Regtech: Impact on Regulators and Banks' (2018) 100(C) Journal of Economics and Business 7–25.

G Azarenkova, I Shkodina, B Samorodov, M Babenko and I Onishchenko, 'The Influence of Financial Technologies on the Global Financial System Stability' (2018) 15(4) Investment Management and Financial Innovations 229–238.

J R Barth and G G Kaufman (eds), *The First Great Financial Crisis of the 21st Century: A Retrospective* (Now Publishers 2016).

Basel Committee on Banking Supervision (BCBS), 'The Interplay of Accounting and Regulation and Its Impact on Bank Behaviour: Literature Review' (BIS January 2015) Working Paper No 28.

Basel Committee on Banking Supervision (BCBS), *Sound Practices: Implications of Fintech Developments for Banks and Bank Supervisors* (BIS February 2018).

Basel Committee on Banking Supervision (BCBS), *Global Systemically Important Banks: Revised Assessment Methodology and the Higher Loss Absorbency Requirement* (BIS July 2018).

T M Belton, M D Gelfand, D B Humphrey and J C Marquard, 'Daylight Overdrafts and Payments System Risk' (November 1987) 73 Federal Reserve Bulletin 839–852.

S Benoit, J E Colliard, C Hurlin and C Pérignon, 'Where the Risks Lie: A Survey on Systemic Risk' (2017) 21(1) Review of Finance 109–152.

L D Bodin, L A Gordon, M P Loeb and A Wang, 'Cybersecurity Insurance and Risk-Sharing' (2018) 37(6) Journal of Accounting and Public Policy 527–544.

G Buchak, G Matvos, T Piskorski and A Seru, 'Fintech, Regulatory Arbitrage, and the Rise of Shadow Banks' (2018) 130(3) Journal of Financial Economics 453–483.

T Buck and O Storbeck, 'German Fintech N26 Appeases Regulators as It Eyes Future IPO' *Financial Times* (London, 14 August 2019).

R P Buckley, D W Arner, D A Zetzsche and E Selga, 'The Dark Side of Digital Financial Transformation: The New Risks of FinTech and the Rise of TechRisk' (2019) EBI Working Paper 2019/54.

Bundesanstalt für Finanzdienstleistungsaufsicht (BaFin), *BaFin Journal November 2019* (2019).

M Carney, *The Promise of FinTech – Something New under the Sun?* Speech at the Deutsche Bundesbank G20 Conference on Digitising Finance, Financial Inclusion and Financial Literacy, Wiesbaden (25 January 2017).

W R Cline, *International Debt: Systemic Risk and Policy Response* (Institute for International Economics 1984).

W R Cline, 'International Debt: From Crisis to Recovery?' (1985) 75(2) The American Economic Review (Papers and Proceedings) 185–190.

P Crosman, 'Are Fintechs a Systemic Risk?' (2018) 183(173) American Banker 1–1.

E P Davis, *Debt, Financial Fragility, and Systemic Risk* (Clarendon Press 1992).

O de Bandt and P Hartmann, 'Systemic Risk: A Survey' (November 2000) ECB Working Paper No 35.

G Deipenbrock, 'FinTech: Unbearably Lithe or Reasonably Agile? – A Critical Legal Approach from the German Perspective' (2020) 31(1) European Business Law Review 3–32.

Depository Trust & Clearing Corporation (DTCC), 'Fintech and Financial Stability – Exploring How Technological Innovations Could Impact the Safety & Security of Global Markets' (October 2017) DTCC White Paper.

S di Castri, S Hohl, A Kulenkampff and J Prenio, *The Suptech Generations* FSI Insights on policy implementation No 19 (BIS October 2019).

D W Diamond and P H Dybvig, 'Bank Runs, Deposit Insurance, and Liquidity' (1983) 91(3) Journal of Political Economy 401–419.

C Dierksmeier and P Seele, 'Cryptocurrencies and Business Ethics' (2018) 152(1) Journal of Business Ethics 1–14.

G Dorfleitner, L Hornuf, M Schmitt and M Weber, *FinTech-Markt in Deutschland* (Bundesfinanzministerium 2016).

European Banking Authority (EBA), *Report on Regulatory Perimeter, Regulatory Status and Authorisation Approaches in Relation to FinTech Activities* (18 July 2019) EBA Report.

European Commission, *FinTech Action Plan: For a More Competitive and Innovative European Financial Sector* Brussels (8 March 2018) COM(2018) 109 final.

European Supervisory Authorities (ESAs), *Report: FinTech: Regulatory Sandboxes and Innovation Hubs* (7 January 2019) ESAs Joint Report.

G R Faulhaber, A Phillips and A M Santomero, 'Payment Risk, Network Risk, and the Role of the Fed' in D B Humphrey (ed), *The U.S. Payment System: Efficiency, Risk and the Role of the Federal Reserve* 197–213 (Kluwer Academic Publishers 1990).

P Fáykiss, D Papp, P Sajtos and Á Törös, 'Regulatory Tools to Encourage FinTech Innovations: The Innovation Hub and Regulatory Sandbox in International Practice' (2018) 17(2) Financial and Economic Review 43–67.

Financial Conduct Authority (FCA), *Global Financial Innovation Network (GFIN) Consultation Document* (August 2018) GFIN Consultation Document.

Financial Stability Board (FSB), *Financial Stability Implications from FinTech – Supervisory and Regulatory Issues that Merit Authorities' Attention* (27 June 2017) FSB Report.

Financial Stability Board (FSB), *FinTech and Market Structure in Financial Services: Market Developments and Potential Financial Stability Implications* (14 February 2019) FSB Report.

X Freixas, L Laeven and J-L Peydró, *Systemic Risk, Crises, and Macroprudential Regulation* (The MIT Press 2015).

R A Gilbert, 'Payments System Risk: What Is It and What Will Happen If We Try to Reduce It?' (1989) 71(1) FRB of St. Louis Review 3–17.

A G Haldane and M M Robert, 'Systemic Risk in Banking Ecosystems' (2011) 469 Nature 351–355.

D He, R Leckow, V Haksar, T Mancini-Griffoli, N Jenkinson, M Kashima, T Khiaonarong, C Rochon and H Tourpe, 'FinTech and Financial Services: Initial Considerations' (2017) IMF Staff Discussion Note.

J Hill, *Fintech and the Remaking of Financial Institutions* (Academic Press 2018).

A Horsch, 'Regulating SIFIs in the European Union: A Primer from an Economic Point of View' in M Andenas and G Deipenbrock (eds), *Regulating and Supervising European Financial Markets* 393–420 (Springer International 2016).

R G King and R Levine, 'Finance and Growth: Schumpeter Might Be Right' (1993) 108(3) The Quarterly Journal of Economics 717–737.

R G King and R Levine, 'Financial Intermediation and Economic Development' in C Mayer and X Vives (eds), *Capital Markets and Financial Intermediation* 156–189 (Cambridge University Press 1995).

I Lee and Y J Shin, 'Fintech: Ecosystem, Business Models, Investment Decisions, and Challenges' (2018) 61(1) Business Horizons 35–46.

D Liebau and P Schueffel, 'Cryptocurrencies & Initial Coin Offerings: Are They Scams? – An Empirical Study' (2019) 2(1) Journal of the British Blockchain Association 1–7.

A Mackenzie, 'The FinTech Revolution' (2015) 26(3) London Business School Review 50–54.

W Magnuson, 'Financial Regulation in the Bitcoin Era' (2018) 23(2) Stanford Journal of Law, Business & Finance 159–209.

T Mayer, 'A Digital Euro to Compete With Libra' (2019) 16(1) The Economists' Voice 1–7.

D McCrum, 'Wirecard: The Rise and Fall of a German Tech Icon' *Financial Times* (London, 25 June 2020).

D Z Morris, 'Researchers Say They Found a Hole in PayPal's Security. PayPal Says It's No Big Deal' *Fortune* (New York, 5 March 2020).

D C North, *Institutions, Institutional Change and Economic Performance* (Cambridge University Press 1990).

D C North, *Understanding the Process of Economic Change* (Princeton University Press 2005).

H Nuyens, 'How Disruptive Are FinTech and Digital for Banks and Regulators?' (2019) 12(3) Journal of Risk Management in Financial Institutions 217–222.

Organisation for Economic Co-operation and Development (OECD), *Emerging Risks in the 21st Century – An Agenda for Action* (OECD Publications Service 2003).

N Popper, 'In the World of Cryptocurrency, Even Good Projects Can Go Bad' *The New York Times* (New York, 31 May 2018).

M Prokopczuk, *Essays on Systemic Risk* (PhD thesis, University of Mannheim 2009).

F Restoy, *Regulating Fintech: What Is Going on, and Where Are the Challenges?* BIS Speech at ASBA-BID-FELABAN XVI Banking Public-Private Sector Regional Policy Dialogue 'Challenges and Opportunities in the New Financial Ecosystem', Washington D.C. (16 October 2019).

W-G Ringe and C Ruof, 'Keeping up with Innovation: Designing a European Sandbox for Fintech' (January 2019) European Capital Market Institute (ECMI) Commentary No 58.

C Schmitz, J-E Behrens and D Shevchenko, 'Germany FinTech Landscape. FinTech Beyond Borders: Cross-border FinTech Activity' (November 2018) Ernst & Young Assurance Tax Transactions Advisory Study.

P Schueffel, 'Taming the Beast: A Scientific Definition of Fintech' (2016) 4(4) Journal of Innovation Management 32–54.

J A Schumpeter, *Business Cycles – A Theoretical, Historical, and Statistical Analysis of the Capitalist Process* (McGraw-Hill 1923) Vol. 1 of 2.

J A Schumpeter, 'The Creative Response in Economic History' (1947) 7(2) The Journal of Economic History 149–159.

S L Schwarcz, 'Systemic Risk' (2008) 97(1) Georgetown Law Review 193–249.

G Sheldon and M Maurer, 'Interbank Lending and Systemic Risk: An Empirical Analysis for Switzerland' (1998) 134(IV) Swiss Journal of Economics and Statistics 685–704.

P Smaga, 'The Concept of Systemic Risk' (2014) Systemic Risk Centre (SRC) The London School of Economics and Political Science Special Paper No 5.

E J Stevens, 'Risk in Large-Dollar Transfer Systems' (Fall 1984) 20(4) FRB of Cleveland Economic Review 2–16.

O Storbeck, 'Commerzbank to Be Replaced by Wirecard in Dax Index' *Financial Times* (London, 5 September 2018).

A V Thakor, 'Fintech and Banking: What Do We Know?' (January 2020) 41 Journal of Financial Intermediation 100833.

The Working Group on Financial Markets, *Interim Report of The Working Group on Financial Markets* (US Government Printing Office 1988).

T Theobald and S Tober, *IMK Finanzmarktstabilitätsreport 2017/2018* (February 2018) Institut für Makroökonomie und Konjunkturforschung (IMK) Report 134.

D D VanHoose and G H Sellon Jr., 'Daylight Overdrafts, Payments, System Risk, and Public Policy' (September/October 1989) 74 FRB of Kansas City Economic Review 9–29.

D Yang and M Li, 'Evolutionary Approaches and the Construction of Technology-Driven Regulations' (2018) 54(14) Emerging Markets Finance and Trade 3256–3271.

D A Zetzsche, R P Buckley and D W Arner, 'The Distributed Liability of Distributed Ledgers: Legal Risks of Blockchain' (2017) EBI Working Paper Series No 14.

N Zhang and W Wang, 'Research on Balance Strategy of Supervision and Incentive of P2P Lending Platform' (2019) 55(1) Emerging Markets Finance and Trade 1–19.

Part II
Fintech and lending

7 FinTech credit firms

Prospects and uncertainties

Francesco De Pascalis

1 Introduction

The financial services industry has undergone major developments over the past decade. There are several reasons for these changes. First, the wave of regulatory reforms triggered by the 2007–2009 financial crisis significantly affected the structure and business operations of banks and other financial institutions. Second, advances in technology allowed the flourishing of technology-driven financial services providers in addition to traditional participants. Particularly in the post-crisis period, the meaningfulness of the technology trend can be perceived through the introduction and use of names such as blockchain, cryptocurrency, crowdfunding, robo-advice, chatbots, etc., which constitute the nomenclature of the so-called FinTech industry.[1] Scholars, practitioners, regulators and policymakers acknowledge the definition of FinTech provided by the Financial Stability Board (FSB), as a blend between the words finance and technology, to underline how the use of technology in the financial world ensues innovative business models, applications, processes and products: in other words, a new financial ecosystem.[2] A significant feature of this ecosystem is the presence of firms that through critical technological innovations aim at evolving the financial services industry into a newer, more accessible and diversified landscape. Inevitably, this process poses the FinTech firms in stark contrast with banks and other (traditional) financial services providers so that the inter-relationship between FinTech firms (the challengers) and financial institutions (the incumbents) is hotly debated within the FinTech literature, underpinned by questions on the extent to which challengers have the potential to disrupt incumbents or coexist with them.[3]

This chapter addresses the advent of crowdfunding as a new financing tool originated from and spurred through advances in technologies in the financial services industry. As an internet-based financing tool, crowdfunding has undergone impressive growth and sustained scholarly attention.[4] The specific focus of this contribution is on FinTech credit, one of the most promising sectors in the crowdfunding market. Put

I would like to thank the editors for their comments on an early draft of this chapter. All errors and omissions remain the author's.

1 J Dermine, 'Digital Disruption and Bank Lending' (2017) 2 European Economy, Banks, Regulation and the Real Sector 63.
2 Financial Stability Board (FSB), 'Financial Stability Implications from FinTech, Supervisory and Regulatory Issues that Merit Authorities' Attention' (2017) 7 <https://www.fsb.org/wp-content/uploads/R270617.pdf> accessed 24 June 2019.
3 S Chishti and J Barberis, *The FinTech Book. The Financial Technology Handbook for Investors, Entrepreneurs and Visionaries* (Wiley 2016).
4 D Cumming and L Hornuf (eds), *The Economics of Crowdfunding. Startups, Portals and Investor Behavior* (Palgrave Macmillan 2018).

simply, FinTech credit refers to the provision of credit via web-based platforms.[5] Since its inception, web-based lending has been identified as a valuable alternative finance tool vis-à-vis commercial bank lending. Indeed, via the platforms, borrowers can find lenders matching their financial needs without a financial institution acting as a middleman. Consequently, the relationship between FinTech credit and commercial banks has been addressed in terms of financial disintermediation versus financial intermediation.[6] Nonetheless, the growth and evolution of some crowd-lending platforms prompted some scholars to identify a re-intermediation trend within the FinTech credit segment.[7] This chapter appraises the significance of the platforms' disintermediation and re-intermediation trends by taking stock of the evolution of some of the major online lending platforms. On this account, we point out that FinTech credit firms leverage their re-intermediation to act as chameleonic players within the mainstream area. This is evidenced by those platforms exploring how their own innovation fits with the innovation brought by other FinTech players to create hybrid structures. Against this backdrop, we discuss the potentiality of the FinTech credit sector but also stress its challenges to coexist with other financial intermediaries within the same domain.

The rest of this chapter is organised as follows. Section 2 sets the scene by briefly reviewing the current understanding of crowdfunding. This helps contextualise FinTech credit as a type of crowdfunding. Section 3 addresses the specificities of FinTech credit. Specifically, this part provides a picture of the FinTech credit market as highly stratified due to the involvement of different players as borrowers and lenders, whose financial interests and interactions pave the way for various subcategories of FinTech credit. Section 4 discusses the characteristics of online lending platforms as disintermediated and re-intermediated players. In so doing, this section ponders the meaningfulness of platform re-intermediation by critically reviewing the terminology used by the Peer-to-Peer (P2P) literature to foresee its impact (eg, 'eliminating or substituting' traditional financial intermediaries, 'blurring into mainstream'). Section 5 offers further thoughts. Taking a cue from the current Covid-19 pandemic and the struggle of some UK online lending platforms, we reflect on the challenges ahead for the FinTech credit sector to gain distinctiveness in the financial services industry as valid credit providers. Drawing on the previous parts, Section 6 brings the chapter to a conclusion.

2 Obtaining funds from the crowd

The most recent scholarly works explain FinTech credit as part of the broad crowdfunding world. Given this relationship, any discussion of FinTech credit needs to be premised on the analysis of crowdfunding. Recent studies propose general definitions

---

5 S Claessens et al, 'FinTech Credit Markets Around the World: Size, Drivers and Policy Issues' (2018) BIS Quarterly Review 30 <https://www.bis.org/publ/qtrpdf/r_qt1809e.pdf> accessed 28 June 2019.

6 See, for example, A Sciarrone Alibrandi et al, *Marketplace Lending. Verso Nuove Forme di Intermediazione Finanziaria?* (2019) 5 Quaderni FinTech, Consob <http://www.consob.it/documents/46180/46181/FinTech_5.pdf/a92a97f0-7d0e-43de-9fcd-4acfd97199f2> accessed 08 August 2019.

7 T Balyuk and S Davidenko, 'Reintermediation in FinTech: Evidence from Online Lending' (2018) Michael J Brennan Irish Finance Working Paper Series Research Paper No. 18-17 <https://papers.ssrn.com/sol3/papers.cfm?abstract_id=3189236> accessed 03 September 2019.

of crowdfunding, which then evolved into sophisticated characterisations because of the various business models that have been identified meanwhile.[8] For this reason, some authors argue that general definitions are unhelpful to discern the complexity of the phenomenon.[9] In reality, they are useful to identify its precursors, evolution and stratification into diversified business models, as well as the forces behind its emergence as a dynamic field of research within the FinTech world. Accordingly, crowdfunding can be defined as seeking (and perhaps obtaining) funds from the public through internet-based platforms. The first component of this definition (fundraising from the public) makes crowdfunding an ancient practice. Baumgardner et al qualify microfinance as the forerunner of the modern crowdfunding by referring, among others, to the Irish campaign to raise funds from the public and lend small amounts of money to poor tradesmen in the 1700s.[10] The second element (online platforms) suggests that today the fundraising purpose is facilitated and attained via technology. Internet-based platforms are key to understanding the development of modern crowdfunding. To begin with, the internet revolution that happened in the early 2000s permits us to establish a link between crowdfunding and crowdsourcing. This is another important aspect for understanding the phenomenon in question. Online crowdsourcing emerged through the creation of Web 2.0, which enabled wide networks of people to interact in a faster and more decentralised way for performing certain activities.[11] Specifically, Brabham stresses that, within a myriad of definitions of crowdsourcing, it is possible to identify its distinctive characteristics by combining the following elements: organisation, community, online environment and mutual benefit.[12] The word 'organisation' is used in relation to anyone (individual, company, or non-profit organisation) proposing the voluntary undertaking of a task. The receivers of the proposal are the community, or crowd, which is expected to bring their knowledge, skills and experience to the task. The interaction between the organisation and the crowd takes place through an online environment, which facilitates the co-existence and co-creative efforts of both parties.[13] The outcome is of mutual benefit. The crowdsourcer will utilise what the crowd has contributed, while the crowd may receive social recognition or skill-improvement advantages depending on the type, characteristics, aims and complexity of the task.[14]

---

8 See P Bellaflame et al, 'Crowdfunding: Tapping the Right Crowd' (2014) 29(5) Journal of Business Venturing 585 <https://perso.uclouvain.be/paul.belleflamme/papers/JBV2013.pdf> accessed 12 September 2019.

9 E R Mollick, 'The Dynamics of Crowdfunding: An Exploratory Study' (2014) 29(1) Journal of Business Venturing 1 <https://www.sciencedirect.com/science/article/pii/S088390261300058X> accessed 16 September 2019.

10 T Baumgardner et al, 'Crowdfunding as a Fast Expanding Market for the Creation of Capital and Shared Value' (2017) 59(1) Thunderbird International Business Review 115 <https://onlinelibrary. wiley.com/doi/abs/10.1002/tie.21766> accessed 16 September 2019. The crowdfunding literature also cites other examples; donations for Mozart's and Beethoven's concerts or funds raised for the Statue of Liberty are the main historical examples cited by the crowdfunding literature. See, for instance, N Scholz, *The Relevance of Crowdfunding* (Springer Gabler 2015).

11 D C Brabham, *Crowdsourcing* (Massachusetts Institute of Technology 2013).

12 Ibid.

13 Ibid.

14 Ibid.

The literature considers crowdfunding as the monetary variant of crowdsourcing to the extent that the crowd is exploited to bridge a funding need.[15] Like in crowdsourcing, online technology is instrumental in bringing together people for different purposes. However, the essence and distinctive characteristic of crowdfunding is that the platform is the means for facilitating the matching between those in deficit and those in surplus of funds. The platform is the catalyst of borrowers such as consumers, small and medium-sized enterprises (SMEs) and individuals who donate, lend or invest their money into projects or entrepreneurial ideas.[16] This explains the view of crowdfunding as an umbrella term including different sub-types in accordance with the characteristics of the involved actors.

While there are some attempts at providing all-inclusive definitions,[17] it is more useful to consolidate the understanding of crowdfunding by acknowledging the convergence of the crowdfunding literature on the identification of two macro-models, namely non-return financial models and return financial models. The first category consists of sub-species such as donation, reward or pre-selling crowdfunding. Under this model, the return is non-financial, ranging from nothing to a product or service. For instance, the donation model best represents the 'nothing in return' philosophy as it relies on the sense of altruism of the crowd, which ultimately gives funds for a noble purpose, such as cancer research.[18] The reward model provides for a return for the crowd, which is always symbolic and never proportionate to the amount of funds that the caller seeks.[19] Finally, the pre-selling model is tied to the fund-seeker's promise to deliver a product, prototype or service proportionate to the amount of funds they received.[20] Conversely, in the financial-return crowdfunding models, an investment is made with the expectation to gain a financial advantage. There are two categories falling into this model: crowdlending, in which loans are granted at a fixed interest rate; and the equity-based crowdfunding model, in which investors fund start-up or small businesses in return for equity.[21] In general, the crowd is often referred to as the backer of the financial needs of the fundraiser. Such a nomenclature becomes more specific in connection with the identified models and related sub-categories. For instance, backers are donors under the donation model, lenders in crowdlending or investors in equity-based crowdfunding.[22] This demonstrates the heterogeneity of the crowdfunding world, in which several understandings and different lines of investigation are possible in connection with the variety of purposes this mechanism can satisfy.

15 Space-tec Capital Partners, 'Crowdfunding Innovative Ventures in Europe. The Financial Ecosystem and Regulatory Landscape' (2014) A Study Prepared for the European Commission DG Communications Networks, Content & Technology <https://ec.europa.eu/digital-single-market/en/news/crowdfunding-innovative-ventures-europe-financial-ecosystem-and-regulatory-landscape-smart> accessed 22 September 2019.
16 Bellaflame et al (n 8) 585.
17 See, for instance, T Lambert and A Schwienbacker, 'An empirical Analysis of Crowdfunding' (2010) Louvain-la-Neuvwe, Louvain School of Management, Catholic University of Louvain: 'an open call [...] for the provision of financial resources either in form of donation or in exchange for some form of reward and/or voting rights in order to support initiatives for specific purposes' <https://kunnskapsverket.org/litteraturdatabase/publikasjon/empirical-analysis-crowdfunding> accessed 04 October 2019.
18 Cumming and Hornuf (n 4) 4.
19 Ibid.
20 Ibid.
21 Ibid.
22 Ibid.

3 The FinTech credit world

Under the crowdfunding umbrella, the phrase 'FinTech credit' refers to lending-based crowdfunding projects, in which interest rates are offered in addition to and in return for the sums borrowed for a specific project, idea or need. Kiva, an international non-profit organisation founded in San Francisco in 2005, is regarded as a pioneer in FinTech credit. By serving borrowers in developing countries across five continents and with an average of $2.5 million in loans each week, Kiva is among the most important actors within the FinTech credit world.[23] Unquestionably, advances in technology played a fundamental role in the rise of Kiva and other major pioneer lending platforms, such as Zopa in the United Kingdom (UK) and Lending Club in the United States (US).[24] However, the 2007–2009 financial crisis is another driver behind the proliferation of lending-based platforms. Notable episodes of bank failures in the US and Europe during the crisis time[25] and the consequent implementation of regulations imposing new capital requirements and conduct rules for financial institutions increased a situation of funding gap, in which access to finance for individuals and SMEs became more difficult.[26] The funding gap triggered a search for return through alternative vehicles vis-à-vis the traditional channels represented by banks and other financial institutions.[27] This climate is among the driving forces of the FinTech industry. Particularly, with regard to FinTech credit, it represents the possibility for individuals, groups and SMEs to obtain funds for their ventures through online processes.

Before going into greater analysis and discussing any related implications, some preliminary considerations are necessary. As a crowdfunding category, FinTech credit, in turn, incorporates its own sub-categories. This may create confusion, if only because the qualifications given to some sub-species are often used interchangeably. To begin with, the phrase 'FinTech credit' is used to identify the practice of obtaining loans through web-based platforms and thus to distinguish this practice from other return and non-return financial crowdfunding practices. Nonetheless, the literature also applies other terminologies to discuss the same practice. For instance, 'crowd-lending' or 'debt-based crowdfunding' are also used to connote the activities that involve borrowers and lenders via internet. Furthermore, 'peer-to-peer lending' (P2P) was used during the early stage of the rise of the phenomenon to emphasise how the relationship between borrowers and lenders was mediated through the platform without the traditional middlemen (banks and other financial institutions).[28] Now, some authors emphasise how P2P

23 See www.kiva.org accessed 18 October 2019.
24 Financial Stability Board and Committee on the Global Financial System (FSB/CGFS), 'FinTech Credit. Market Structure, Business Models and Financial Stability Implications' (2017) 3 <https://www.fsb.org/wp-content/uploads/CGFS-FSB-Report-on-FinTech-Credit.pdf> accessed 23 October 2019.
25 Q Li, 'What Causes Bank Failures during the Recent Economic Recession?' (2013) 28 Honors Projects <http://digitalcommons.iwu.edu/busadmin_honproj/28> accessed 20 October 2019.
26 E Kirby and S Worner, 'Crowdfunding: An Infant Industry Growing Fast' (2014) Staff Working Paper of the IOSCO Research Department <https://www.iosco.org/research/pdf/swp/Crowd-funding-An-Infant-Industry-Growing-Fast.pdf> accessed 23 October 2019.
27 Ibid.
28 G Borello, 'Analisi Economica dei Lending Marketplace' in A Sciarrone Alibrandi et al (eds), *Marketplace Lending. Verso Nuove Forme di Intermediazione Finanziaria?* (2019) 5 Quaderni FinTech, Consob <http://www.consob.it/documents/46180/46181/FinTech_5.pdf/a92a97f0-7d0e-43de-9fcd-4acfd97199f2> accessed 04 November 2019.

lending captures the consumer nature of both lenders and borrowers so that 'consumer-to-consumer' lending (C2C) is synonymous to P2P.[29] This gives evidence of the breadth of the FinTech credit phenomenon and, hence, the necessity of identifying and mapping its sub-species based on the characteristics of the lending platform users. Indeed, 'peer-to-business lending' (P2B) refers to funding sought by SMEs. Within this context, by dictating who can borrow and lend, national legislation widens the nomenclature. In France, for example, only institutional investors can lend to SMEs. In this respect, P2B is described as 'business-to-business lending' (B2B).[30] On the other hand, the UK brings forward examples of 'consumer-to-business lending' (C2B) and 'business-to-consumer lending' (B2C).[31] In all these contexts, the online platform is central for meeting the demand and supply of funds. This also generates further classifications, as other scholars refer to the FinTech credit platforms as 'lending marketplaces' and 'marketplace lending' as an alternative word for discussing the FinTech credit phenomenon.[32] Consequently, FinTech credit is a complex, highly stratified area within the broad crowdfunding world. The market segments that FinTech credit reaches (consumers, business, etc.) and the way they interact with each other through the online platforms testify to the constant evolution of the phenomenon, and the reasons why many classifications are used. Using most of them as equivalent may generate confusion and, above all, may be incorrect as the FinTech credit sub-species have their own specific (and different) characteristics.

Within this contribution, 'FinTech credit' is the preferred word versus other denominations of the same phenomenon. First, it denotes the belonging of this practice to the broad FinTech industry, in which the provision of financial services is informed by the use of sophisticated, innovative technology. Second, it has a wide scope because, as stressed by the FSB, it covers 'all credit activities' mediated through web-based platforms.[33] This paves the way for the identification of various sub-species and their specific characteristics, thus stimulating research and analysis.

4 Characteristics and evolution

4.1 *Disintermediation trends*

The global crowdfunding market (GCM) has grown exponentially since its establishment in the early 2000s. Recent figures predict that the GCM is likely to be valued at 28.8 billion USD by 2025.[34] Within the GCM, FinTech credit has come to prominence since the launch of the first lending platforms in the UK and the US between 2005 and 2006. China is also among the largest FinTech credit markets worldwide.[35] Compared to these

---

29 Ibid.
30 E Macchiavello, 'Analisi Comparata delle Principali Normative Speciali Europee in Materia di Marketplace Lending' in A Sciarrone Alibrandi et al (eds), *Marketplace Lending. Verso Nuove Forme di Intermediazione Finanziaria?* (2019) 5 Quaderni FinTech, Consob <http://www.consob.it/documents/46180/46181/FinTech_5.pdf/a92a97f0-7d0e-43de-9fcd-4acfd97199f2> accessed 04 November 2019.
31 Ibid.
32 A Sciarrone Alibrandi et al (n 6) 13.
33 FSB/CGFS (n 24) 2.
34 See CISION PR Newswire <https://www.prnewswire.com/in/news-releases/the-global-crowdfunding-market-wasvalued-at-10-2-billion-us-in-2018-and-is-expected-to-reach-28-8-billion-us-with-a-cagr-of-16-by-2025-valuates-reports-888819175.html> accessed 06 November 2020.
35 FSB/CGFS (n 24) 6.

three major markets, the European FinTech credit market is still small and fragmented but set to grow in the future. Currently, Germany, France, the Netherlands, Spain and Italy are ranked as the top five European countries for alternative finance.[36] Among them, Germany, France and the Netherlands boast the highest volumes of FinTech credit transactions, though in different sectors. France, for instance, lags behind Germany as to P2P consumer lending, while the Netherlands leads in P2P business lending.[37] After a peak between 2013 and 2016, some studies pinpoint a decrease in credit volumes across the global FinTech credit market.[38] Nonetheless, the sector continues to raise strong interest among academics, professionals and policymakers. Since their creation, online-based platforms have been analysed in terms of financial disintermediation vis-à-vis bank-based financial intermediation. In general, financial disintermediation refers to the possibility of cutting the middleman; that is, a financial institution (a bank) that stands between those in surplus and deficit of capital.[39]

In the context of FinTech credit, disintermediation depends on several reasons. First, online lending firms appear to have a technological advantage vis-à-vis traditional financial intermediaries. They collect an amount of customer information and data that is higher than traditional lenders by relying, among other tools, on Big Data analytics.[40] Technology allows the platforms to process information rapidly and therefore to match borrowers and lenders quickly.[41] Banks also rely on digital techniques, but they are not as advanced as the platforms' techniques.[42] Second, unlike banks, FinTech credit firms do not need to maintain branch network and existing IT systems, as access to their services only takes place through web-based platforms. Accordingly, online lending appears to offer advantages in terms of costs along with service rapidity. Third, crowd-lending reaches those market segments that traditional financial intermediaries are reticent to serve. Borrowers relying on web-based lending range from consumers to SMEs, which traditional financial intermediaries would consider ineligible for loans because they are under-collateralised and have a poor credit history.[43] For this reason, online lending platforms are regarded as alternative tools to bridge a funding gap vis-à-vis mainstream financial channels. Fourth, consequent to the regulatory and supervisory reforms that followed the 2007–2009 financial crisis, banks and other financial institutions are subject to stronger liquidity and capital requirements, as well as data reporting requirements relating to their business models and balance

36 T Ziegler et al, 'Expanding Horizons. The 3rd European Alternative Finance Industry Report' (2018) Cambridge Centre for Alternative Finance <https://www.jbs.cam.ac.uk/fileadmin/user_upload/research/centres/alternative-finance/downloads/2018-02-ccaf-exp-horizons.pdf> accessed 20 November 2019.
37 Ibid.
38 Claessens et al (n 5) 34.
39 See K Alexander, *Principles of Banking Regulation* (Cambridge University Press 2019).
40 Claessens et al (n 5) 31.
41 'From start to finish, the process usually takes no more than 5 working days for you to receive the money' see Zopa <https://helpcentre.zopa.com/en/articles/3514282-how-quickly-could-i-get-the-money> accessed 10 December 2019.
42 See B Van Liebergen, 'Machine Learning: A Revolution in Risk Management Compliance?' 45 Journal of Financial Transformation 65 <https://www.iif.com/portals/0/Files/private/32370132_van_liebergen_-_machine_learning_in_compliance_risk_management.pdf> accessed 10 December 2019.
43 G Leboeuf and A Schienwaker, 'Crowdfunding as a New Financing Tool' in D Cumming and L Hornuf (eds), *The Economics of Crowdfunding. Startups, Portals and Investor Behavior* (Palgrave Macmillan 2018).

sheets.[44] FinTech credit firms, instead, are regarded as market players operating outside these regulatory constraints. Furthermore, unlike banks, they do not take deposits and would not perform other activities which are typical of traditional financial intermediaries.[45] In particular, the absence of credit risk responsibilities is another interesting platform feature vis-à-vis traditional financial intermediaries, which is finally reflected in the business models through which some US and UK portals operate. For instance, under the client segregated account model, crowd-lenders take on the credit risk due to their contractual relationship with the crowd-borrowers. The platform facilitates the matching of borrowers and lenders, and coordinates the inflow and outflow of money, loan servicing, and debt collection, but is not part of their contractual relationship and thus has no credit risk responsibility. Indeed, funds go into a 'legally segregated account' held by a third intermediary.[46] The notary model follows the same pattern. The only difference is that the loan is originated by a bank. In short, the platform acts as an agent matching crowd-borrowers' funding requests with crowd-lenders' funding offers. Once the funding offers reach the amount needed by the borrowers, a partnering bank originates the loan. The platform, in turn, will issue notes to the lenders to the value of their respective contributions. Once again, the portal is not responsible in the event of borrower default.[47] Clearly, under disintermediation, FinTech credit firms are infrastructures for facilitating a contractual relationship between borrowers and lenders. They only provide services that are essential to this end.

4.2 Re-intermediation trends

Disintermediation, however, is not the unique distinctive characteristic of online lending platforms. Over the past years, some major platforms went through a dramatic growth process by increasing their portfolio services. The FinTech credit literature describes this process as the platform re-intermediation trend. Back in 2010, Hildebrand et al analysed online lending platforms as contexts in which there are no financial intermediaries.[48] Specifically, to question the extent to which responsible lending can be ensured despite the lack of financial intermediaries, they examined the US platform Prosper as a venue in which 'lenders can give their money directly to borrowers without the intermediation of a financial institution'.[49] Very recently, Bayluk and Davidenko reviewed the evolution of the same platform between 2005 and 2013. They identified a disintermediated period between

44 Van Liebergen (n 42) 64.
45 See C Bertsch and C-J Rosenvinge, 'FinTech Credit: Online Lending Platforms in Sweden and Beyond' (2019) 2 Sveriges Riksbank Economic Review 45 <https://www.riksbank.se/globalassets/media/rapporter/pov/artiklar/engelska/2019/191010/2019_2-fintech-credit-online-lending-platforms-in-sweden-and-beyond.pdf> accessed 20 December 2019, highlighting that the majority of online lending platforms engage mainly in credit risk analysis and asset transformation.
46 UK platforms such as Zopa, Funding Circle and RateSetter operate under the Client Segregated Account model.
47 US platforms such LendingClub and Prosper, as well as European platforms such as the German Auxmoney, operate under the notary model. This model is popular in those jurisdictions where only licensed financial institutions can originate credit.
48 T Hildebrand et al, 'Skin in the Game: Evidence from the Online Social Lending Market' (2010) Duke University <https://www.semanticscholar.org/paper/Skin-in-the-Game-%3A-Evidence-from-the-Online-Social-Hildebrand-Puri/0b378d977fa993362cce35147b7e55d64bd1d680> accessed 07 February 2020.
49 Bayluk and Davidenko (n 7) 9.

2005 and 2010, in which the platform was simply facilitating direct transactions between borrowers and lenders, and its evolution to re-intermediation between 2011 and 2013, in which the platform started playing a significant intermediary role within the P2P loan market through the increase and consolidation of services such as loan screening, pricing and evaluation, pooling funds, loan auto-allocation, and risk management services.[50]

This trend also has implications for their business models. The FSB emphasises the rise of other models in which platforms operate as credit manufacturers. For instance, in the guarantee-return model, the portal guarantees the lenders' credit and interest.[51] Under this model, the platform takes direct responsibility for borrowers' default.[52] Likewise, under the balance sheet model the platforms are involved in credit origination and keep risks on their balance sheet.[53] The re-intermediation trend denotes a significant active role of the firms so that they are no longer mere meeting points for their users.[54] This can be seen, among others, in the degree of control some of the largest UK FinTech credit firms exercise on the selection and choice of the investors' deals. In essence, some platforms play an active role in spreading the lenders' capital across a variety of borrowers, while others allow lenders to choose their investment. For instance, RateSetter's investors can decide to lend at the variable interest rate sets by the platform ('Going Rate') or at the rate they will set ('Your Rate'). Then, the platform automatically matches lending demands and offers.[55] The platform retains, therefore, a key role in the selection of deals. On the other hand, Assetz Capital strikes a balance. The lenders' capital is split into micro loans. However, investors can choose between accounts which automatically invest money across a variety of loans (auto-allocation) or accounts in which investors select their own loan.[56] Zopa has instead a stronger auto-allocation approach. The lenders' capital is sliced and diced. Based on the lenders' risk appetite, the platform automatically assigns each portion to borrowers having different ranks of creditworthiness. Finally, each borrower receives no more than one percent of the capital invested by the lenders.[57]

The more the FinTech credit firms are active between borrowers and lenders through the provision of sophisticated services, the more they emerge as middlemen within the financial services industry.

4.3 *Issues and significance*

Re-intermediation trends feature the continued growth of the FinTech credit sector since its establishment. As such, they have generated discussions as to the potential of platforms to eliminate or substitute traditional financial intermediaries. This perspective foretells a disruptive, somehow revolutionary, impact of FinTech credit firms on the financial

50 Ibid.
51 FSB/CGFS (n 24) 14.
52 Ibid.
53 Ibid.
54 See Oxera, 'The Economics of Peer-to-Peer Lending' (2016) <https://www.oxera.com/wp-content/uploads/2018/03/The-economics-of-P2P-lending_30Sep_.pdf-1.aspx.pdf > accessed 28 May 2020.
55 RateSetter, 'Investor Terms' (2020) <https://www.ratesetter.com/siteassets/media/legal/01-2020-investor-terms-1.pdf> accessed 28 May 2020.
56 Assetz Capital, <https://www.assetzcapital.co.uk/invest/our-accounts> accessed 30 May 2020.
57 Zopa, < https://www.zopa.com/invest> accessed 30 May 2020.

ecosystem.[58] On the other hand, re-intermediation is regarded as the platform metamorphosis process, to the extent that they start operating like financial intermediaries. As a result, the degree of affinity of online lenders to banks or other financial intermediaries should be questioned.[59] Both arguments are relevant and worthy of a critical review.

4.3.1 *Elimination versus substitution*

The first argument (elimination versus substitution) focuses on the relationship between FinTech credit firms and banks. As mentioned earlier, the 2007–2009 financial crisis undermined trust in the banking sector. In addition, the sector is regarded as vulnerable to disruption because of the flourishing of new firms providing the same services. The FinTech industry brings a new generation of technology-driven challengers posing the so-called unbundling risk to incumbent banks. In other words, FinTech firms, specialised in the provision of selected services, may become 'the best of breed providers in certain areas' and thus dismantle an established business model under which banks work as one-stop shops for a variety of financial services.[60] The unbundling risk is only a prediction in the aftermath of the rise and growth of the FinTech industry, but it is far from being a consolidated trend. It is nevertheless a thought-provoking argument to the extent that some authors foresee possible outcomes for the banking industry. Against the backdrop of a battle between incumbent banks and FinTech entrants for winning or retaining the customer relationship and customer data, the Basel Committee on Banking Supervision (BCBS) highlights the following scenarios: the challengers will acquire the management of the customer relationship, and banks will be relegated to providing commoditised banking services to the former (operational processes, risk management, etc.); or they will entirely take over banks in customer financial transactions (the 'disintermediated bank scenario').[61] In between, there is another scenario in which banks and FinTech companies compete for owning the financial customer relationship (the 'distributed bank scenario').[62] This last scenario should not be conceived exclusively as an upfront battle between challengers and incumbents, but also as an opportunity for synergies between the banks and the FinTech companies for best serving their customers.

By way of referring these scenarios to the relationship between FinTech credit and bank lending, the first two raise scepticism. At present, the FinTech credit market still represents a tiny proportion of the overall credit across jurisdictions despite a significant growth.[63] Therefore, arguing in favour of a potential for eliminating the traditional financial intermediaries sounds like a stretch. Besides, banks are essential within some business models, such as the notary model. Indeed, the synergy between the online lending platforms and

---

58 Basel Committee on Banking Supervision (BCBS), 'Sound Practices. Implications of FinTech Developments for Banks and Bank Supervisors' (2018) <https://www.bis.org/bcbs/publ/d431.pdf> accessed 04 December 2019.

59 J Ford, 'Peer-to-peer Lenders are Blurring into Mainstream Banks' (2016) *Financial Times* <https://www.ft.com/content/236e43f6-ba1e-11e6-8b45-b8b81dd5d080> accessed 31 May 2020.

60 A Glas and M Truszel, 'Current Trends in Financial Technology' in S Chishti and J Barberis (eds), *The FinTech Book. The Financial Technology Handbook for Investors, Entrepreneurs and Visionaries* (Wiley 2016).

61 BCBS (n 58) 16–20.

62 Ibid.

63 FSB/CFGS (n 24) 6.

banks justifies the peculiarities of this model: *all personal loans originated through the platform are made by WebBank*.[64] The two words 'originated' and 'made' are emblematic of the fact that the technological lender needs the traditional lender to service its own customers.

'Substituting', instead, appears to be a more appropriate interpretation of the relationship between the platforms and banks. In the first place, a substitution role of the platforms refers to their being alternative to traditional financial intermediaries. As mentioned above, this is an important feature of FinTech credit, as it provides funding opportunities for those borrower segments banks are usually reticent to serve. Consequently, substitution may infer replacing the traditional lender. Nevertheless, 'replacing' sounds too reductive in that the possibility for online lending platforms to reach bank-underserved borrowers may be the basis for establishing some forms of cooperation between FinTech credit firms and banks. The recent partnership between Funding Circle and UK Santander may provide an interesting example. This partnership is based on a mutual referral arrangement, according to which the bank will refer to the platform small business customers looking for a loan, while Funding Circle will signal to Santander those borrowers seeking specific bank services that the platform cannot offer.[65] The alliance between the Spanish bank Liberbank and the French crowd-lending platform 'October' in 2018 demonstrates a similar relationship. The bank brings customers and infrastructures, while the platform contributes the agility and speed of its own technology, through which they can give a 'rating in one minute and financing in one week'.[66]

Through this lens, 'substitution' needs to be extensively interpreted to refer to positive associations between FinTech credit firms and banks to the extent that they complement each other. This appears to be a realistic picture of how technological lending coexists with bank lending in the same domain.

4.3.2 *Blurring into mainstream*

The second argument considers the possible overlapping between FinTech credit firms and other business models once they begin operating like middlemen. Indeed, the loan auto-allocation mechanisms we mentioned previously resemble the characteristics and operations of collective investment schemes (CIS). CIS similarities can also be seen in the development of provision funds by platforms such as RateSetter and Assetz Capital, through which small fractions of the loan fees paid by the borrowers are channelled into a fund to automatically reimburse lenders in the event of borrowers' failure to repay.[67] In this case, credit risk pooling is involved and, once again, the question is raised as to the extent to which FinTech credit replicates asset management. These issues have been widely discussed in the UK, where the Financial Conduct Authority (FCA) also pointed out close similarities to the banking business due to the increased engagement of FinTech credit firms with maturity

64 Prosper, 'Borrower Registration Agreement and Limited Power of Attorney' (2019) <https://www.prosper.com/plp/borrower-registration-agreement/> accessed 10 January 2020.

65 Funding Circle, 'Funding Circle & Santander Announce Partnership to Support Thousands of UK Businesses' (2014) <https://www.fundingcircle.com/blog/2014/06/funding-circle-santander-announce-partnership-support-thousands-uk-businesses/> accessed 20 January 2020.

66 October, 'Four Trends Driving the European FinTech Sector in 2019' (2019) <https://october.eu/4-trends-driving-the-european-fintech-sector-in-2019/> accessed 30 January 2020.

67 See, for instance, RateSetter, 'Provision Fund Policy' (2020) <https://www.ratesetter.com/siteassets/media/fca/12-2019-provision-fund-policy.pdf> accessed 05 May 2020.

transformation services and credit risk management functions.[68] Through this lens, re-intermediation trends are paradigmatic of the controversy surrounding online lending platforms. In practice, the provision of other intermediaries' core services makes a platform re-intermediation a process of duplication rather than a metamorphosis towards a new intermediary. This interpretation can justify the concerns highlighted by the FinTech credit literature in terms of regulatory arbitrage, financial stability, and consumer protection risks, and thus the need to set out a proper regulatory perimeter around a sector whose players come in different sizes and shapes, from disintermediated to re-intermediated actors. In this regard, some authors argue that banking regulation, portfolio manager regulation, payment service regulation, or securities regulation could be relevant for FinTech credit in accordance with the services on which the online portals focus, while others stress that the similitudes with other models only exist at first glance, but finally substantial differences remain.[69] Although these issues are beyond the scope of the present analysis, they have sparked a lively debate on the identity of re-intermediated online lending platforms.

Nevertheless, it is also worth analysing the re-intermediation trends from another angle, as a process originating new structures by way of building on and integrating other business models: in other words, not as a mere process for being categorised like traditional players but as the springboard for continued evolution. In this respect, there are some relevant examples. In 2018, Funding Circle made its debut on the London Stock Exchange as a publicly traded company. This was a significant event within the FinTech credit world as the firm was the first P2P platform to access the Main Market.[70] Other marketplace lenders pursued different but equally noteworthy strategies. In fact, Zopa launched its banking brand in the same year and ultimately obtained its full banking licence in 2020. Zopa bank is expected to match 'the way that high street banks are regulated'.[71] A full banking licence is strategic for giving customers access to other products, but it is emphasised that this is a different bank as a hybrid P2P and digital bank.[72] In view of this, re-intermediation trends represent the platform capacity to increase their portfolio services and, at the same time, their ductility to evolve into structures blending the philosophies and technologies of different areas. This shows how the FinTech world is a fertile ground for challengers, in which they can build on each other's innovation.[73] Overall, operating like other financial intermediaries does not represent the end but the beginning of

---

68 Financial Conduct Authority (FCA), 'Interim Feedback to the Call for Input to the Post-implementation Review of the FCA's Crowdfunding Rules' (2016) <https://www.fca.org.uk/publications/feedback-statements/fs16-13-interim-feedback-post-implementation-review-crowdfunding-rules> accessed 15 March 2020.
69 Ibid.
70 J Archer, 'Funding Circle joins London Stock Exchange with Valuation of £1.5bn' (2018) *The Telegraph* <https://www.telegraph.co.uk/technology/2018/09/28/funding-circle-goes-public-london-15bn-market-cap/> accessed 28 February 2020.
71 T O'Neill, *Zopa's Launching a Bank* (2018) Zopa Blog <https://blog.zopa.com/2018/12/04/zopas-launching-bank/> accessed 25 February 2020.
72 Ibid.
73 Further examples can be cited in this respect: the talks between Metro Bank and RateSetter to acquire the latter. This would give Metro Bank a 'ready-made platform through which [Metro] could drive potentially quite profitable growth', see L Harley-McKeown, 'Metro Bank share price plunges as it enters exclusive talks with RateSetter' (2020) *Express* <https://www.express.co.uk/finance/city/1296062/metro-bank-share-price-merger-talks-ratesetter> accessed 15 June 2020; or the fact that a Singapore-based cryptocurrency exchange is launching a P2P lending feature, see F Erazo, 'Singapore-Based TomoChain Launches P2P Lending Feature' (2020) *Cointelegraph* <https://cointelegraph.com/news/singapore-based-tomochain-launches-p2p-lending-feature> accessed 06 May 2020.

a metamorphosis process through which FinTech credit firms set greater objectives within the financial services industry.

5 Charting the course

Over a decade, FinTech credit firms have been able to position themselves as alternatives to traditional financial intermediaries. However, there are important differences between being regarded as alternatives and being recognised as valid alternatives. While the former implies awareness of the existence of the platforms, the latter implies gaining distinctiveness in the financial services industry. FinTech credit firms have moved through the first stage, but they have still much to demonstrate for being considered a valid alternative to the mainstream. In this regard, some reflections can be made in connection with the global economic downturn caused by the Covid-19 pandemic.

Lockdown measures applied worldwide have been severely disrupting the global supply chain and creating urgent cash needs across industries. Amid the present turmoil, online lending platforms have been dealing with extraordinary requests from lenders to sell their loans, as they fear a huge wave of borrowers' defaults. As a result, some of the largest P2P platforms responded by cutting their interest pay-outs or suspending their secondary market operations temporarily.[74] Their actions exhibit the peculiarities and risks of P2P lending, where investors are constrained by the terms of the loan. This means that, unlike bank savings account, the platforms do not provide for instant access to the lent money. Should investors claim repayment before the loan maturity, they have no other option but to sell their loans to secondary markets.[75] Consequently, investors not only bear the risk of individual loan default but also liquidity risk in the event they are unable to exit their loans in secondary markets.[76] Finally, their capital is not protected in the event of platform failure. For instance, P2P investments offered by UK platforms are not covered by the Financial Services Compensation Scheme, which protects customers of failed financial institutions up to £85.000.[77] These risks are not a discovery. They have always been known as inherent to the P2P sector. Nonetheless, the Covid-19 crisis has the effect of making them tangible and overshadowing the portals' reputation as ideal venues for obtaining rapid investments through cutting-edge technology. The majority of the largest lending platforms were launched after the 2007–2009 financial crisis and, as mentioned above, built their success within a bank anticlimactic context. They did not experience that crisis. Now, like any other business, they are affected by a health crisis and its global recession scenarios. Sustainability should be the platforms' flagship in pandemic times. They need to demonstrate that they are resilient infrastructures, with viable policies to keep lending and support investors' returns. Therefore, their ability to

---

74 K Gaw, 'Funding Circle Suspends Secondary Market' (*Peer2Peer Finance News,* 9 April 2020) <https://www.p2pfinancenews.co.uk/2020/04/09/funding-circle-suspends-secondary-market/> accessed 23 April 2020.

75 R Lacey, 'What Next for P2P? We Investigate the Coronavirus Impact on P2P Lenders and Borrowers' (2020) *Moneywise* <https://www.moneywise.co.uk/investing/what-next-peer-peer-we-investigate-coronavirus-impact-p2p-lenders-borrowers> accessed 25 April 2020.

76 See Financial Conduct Authority (FCA), 'Call for Inputs for the Post-implementation Review of the FCA's Crowdfunding Rules' (2016) <https://www.fca.org.uk/publications/calls-input/post-implementation-review-fca-crowdfunding-rules> accessed 25 April 2020.

77 Ibid.

withstand the impact of the present pandemic will be crucial for their distinctiveness in the financial services industry.

Ability to continue lending during these times also stimulates discussion regarding the extent to which online lending platforms have a *de facto* possibility of playing a central role as a valuable port of call for the businesses' credit needs. Some thought-provoking implications arise from the UK, where the government adopted a package of measures to support SMEs experiencing cashflow problems following the coronavirus lockdown. For example, under the Coronavirus Business Interruption Loan Scheme (CBILS), lenders can invest up to £5 million via the lending institutions partnering with the British Business Bank (a government-owned business development bank).[78] Within this context, an interesting comparison could be made between a bank-based CBILS and a FinTech credit-based CBILS, if only because banks have been so far criticised for being quite slow at lending under this scheme.[79] Through their technology, web-based platforms could show efficiency and possibly capture all those SMEs which are eligible for the CBILS but finally not served by high street banks. However, a FinTech credit-based CBILS remains mostly untested because the CBILS scheme suggests an exclusionary ethos towards lending portals. Specifically, the CBILS temporarily replaces the Enterprise Finance Guarantee Programme (EFG), which guarantees loans from £1.000 to £1.2 million. The EFG scheme excluded P2P platforms from the circle of accredited lenders as 'their differing structures and diverse sources of funding make them unsuitable for EFG'.[80] The CBILS, instead, is open about the inclusion of the platforms as lending partners only where they 'provide credit to the underlying borrowers' or act as 'lenders of record'.[81] The CBILS accreditation process has mainly involved high street banks and FinTech banks as lending partners. Among FinTech credit firms, only Funding Circle, Assetz Capital, LendingCrowd and ThinCats have so far obtained accreditation, while others have been lobbying for inclusion.[82] On the other side of the Atlantic, the situation is not dissimilar, with some US lending platforms pushing for involvement in the Small Business Association's Paycheck Protection Program. This gives evidence of the long way the portals must go to consolidate their reputation as valid alternatives to traditional financial intermediaries. The exclusion under the EFG is absolute and denotes distrust towards the FinTech credit sector. On the other hand, the CBILS conditions seem to hint that the more the platforms hold the reins (as credit manufacturers) of the borrower–lender relationship, the more opportunities they have to join the circle.

In either case, it is significant that these limitations apply despite the UK FinTech credit sector having been fully regulated since 2014. Prior to the pandemic outbreak,

---

78 British Business Bank (BBB), 'Coronavirus Business Interruption Loan Scheme (CBILS) An Opportunity for Lending Institutions to Partner with the British Business Bank' (2020) <https://www.british-business-bank.co.uk/wp-content/uploads/2020/04/RFP-CBILS-Clean-07.04.20.pdf> accessed 25 April 2020.

79 A Carrick, 'Banks Blasted Over Disappointingly Slow Pace as Coronavirus Loans Hit £5.5bn' (2020) <https://www.cityam.com/banks-blasted-over-disappointingly-slow-pace-of-lending-as-coronavirus-loans-hit-5-5bn/> accessed 16 May 2020.

80 BBB, 'Enterprise Finance Guarantee. An Opportunity for Lending Institutions to Partner with the British Business Bank' (2019) <https://www.british-business-bank.co.uk/wp-content/uploads/2019/04/190401-EFG-Request-for-Proposal-Final.pdf> accessed 01 December 2020.

81 BBB (n 78) 18.

82 See BBB list of accredited lenders <https://www.british-business-bank.co.uk/ourpartners/coronavirus-business-interruption-loan-scheme-cbils-2/current-accredited-lenders-and-partners/> accessed 26 May 2020.

the FCA even finalised new rules to enhance standards and consumer protection in the sector following some episodes of fraud and poor business practices.[83] UK online lending platforms argue that being under the regulatory purview entails the right to be treated on equal footing with banks, including access to the same liquidity schemes provided by the government to support the banking system during this pandemic.[84] This means that they regard themselves as established actors with proven credentials in the financial services industry. Regulators, instead, through a specific regulatory framework appear to draw a line between non-bank and bank lending sectors, with the former regarded as still young and untested.[85] It is submitted that, because of the CBILS closed circle of accredited lenders, the platforms' technology could be outsourced by the accredited lenders, thus relegating the FinTech credit firms to the role of mere credit distributors for the (lender of record) banks.[86] This would be the worst-case scenario, which makes lending platforms coexist with banks under a subordinated role. Furthermore, it must be noted how those FinTech credit firms that have obtained the CBILS accreditation have either temporarily or permanently paused their lending for retail investors as, under the CBILS scheme, only institutional investors like banks and pension funds can back loans to support Covid-19 disrupted businesses. Simply put, CBILS loans will be only funded by (accredited) FinTech credit firms in combination with institutional investors. Retail investors are excluded. Against this backdrop, some argue that the FinTech credit sector will be moving away from the P2P model it launched (in which retail investors make loans to businesses and individuals) to develop into a model only open to institutional capital.[87] These are speculations driven by the uncertainty fuelled by the Covid-19 pandemic. In any case, the pandemic crisis and the UK context brings to attention how the online lending platforms' characteristic of serving those market segments which are unserved by the rest of the system means little against the regulator and policy-maker scepticism. This environment also appears to diminish the meaningfulness of the re-intermediation process as previously analysed through the lens of assimilation to traditional financial intermediaries or gateway for further innovation. As a result, FinTech credit firms would neither blur into the mainstream to the extent of being like banks or other intermediaries, nor is their innovation sufficient to give them the status of 'valid' credit providers. They need therefore to build a culture of trust around them while growing. The way they endure the present crisis and the role they can play will steer much of the future debate on the P2P sector.

83 Financial Conduct Authority (FCA), 'Loan-based ('Peer-to-peer') and Investment-based Crowdfunding Platforms: Feedback to CP18/20 and Final Rules' (2019) PS19/14 <https://www.fca.org.uk/publication/policy/ps19-14.pdf> accessed 26 May 2020.
84 M Darbyshire, 'P2P Platforms Seek "Urgent" UK government Help to Keep Lending' (2020) *Financial Times* <https://www.ft.com/content/6633f55e-6d27-11ea-89df-41bea055720b> accessed 26 May 2020.
85 FCA (n 76) 7.
86 N Megaw, 'Pandemic Hands Fintech Lenders a Chance to Prove Their Worth' (2020) *Financial Times* <https://www.ft.com/content/dcdd3016-797f-4d02-9d54-95a5b10cc2cd> accessed 26 May 2020.
87 M Darbyshire and N Megaw, 'Peer-to-peer Lenders Forced to Abandon Retail Roots' (2020) *Financial Times* <https://www.ft.com/content/b26ecf08-fd2f-4c7f-93ce-f6d55888da83> accessed 21 June 2020.

6 Concluding remarks

Crowdfunding is a broad phenomenon that encompasses non-financial return models and financial-return models. FinTech credit presents very interesting peculiarities as a financial-return model, characterised by a high level of heterogeneity because of the interaction between multiple users, from consumers to businesses. Their interaction has originated various sub-categories of crowd-lending so that 'FinTech credit' may be also regarded as a catch-all phrase including different structures, depending on the characteristics and needs of the involved actors. The emergence of some online lending portals as credit manufacturers has raised attention on FinTech credit as an area characterised by disintermediation and re-intermediation trends. Whereas the former relates to the classic peer-to-peer models in which the platforms are the agent for facilitating the matching between borrowers and lenders, the latter implies a stronger role of the platforms as middlemen, which finally assimilates them to traditional financial intermediaries. Such trends stimulate discussion in terms of the relationship with banks and other financial institutions. The necessary role of banks in some business models makes traditional financial intermediaries complementary to the platform's services, while some forms of synergies or partnership resulting in customer signposting lead to mutual cooperation between challengers and incumbents. This 'living together' scenario is an answer to the question that the crowdfunding literature has always posed as to the potential of the FinTech industry to disrupt traditional financial services: no threats are posed presently. However, this cannot be regarded as a definitive answer. The evolutionary path of some FinTech credit firms demonstrates how their re-intermediation is the launch pad for exploring and instituting more sophisticated solutions in which different, technology-based business models blend. The extent to which this process is disruptive vis-à-vis traditional bank lending remains to be seen. In fact, the FinTech credit sector is a universe where actors come in different shapes and sizes. Overall, online lending platforms coexist with traditional financial intermediaries within the same domain, but they have still many challenges ahead for the endorsement of their business model as the valid alternative to the traditional mainstream. The current Covid-19 crisis offers elements to test, for the first time, the platform strength in difficult times. The pandemic marks the end of the platform golden age meant as the period in which, after the 2007–2009 financial crisis, they could flourish and show themselves as the alternative to banks. Now, they are experiencing global crisis times, and much of the trust they can retain from their customers depends on their capacity to meet their needs. Moreover, the Covid-19 pandemic makes us question the extent to which the innovation that the online lending platforms bring is synonymous with power within the financial services industry. The UK example, where very few platforms have obtained the CBILS accreditation, manifests the contraposition between the FinTech credit firms' view as prominent actors within the financial services industry and the regulator view of FinTech credit as a sector that has yet to be known. Consequently, defining FinTech credit firms as the new financial intermediaries has multiple meanings. It represents the enthusiasm through which the rise of the platforms was waived by scholars and practitioners, with all the ensuing discussion on their possibility of eliminating or substituting traditional financial intermediaries. It also describes the platforms' view of themselves as bringers of innovation that gives them the right to feature prominently and on equal footing with other intermediaries. Finally, being new simply means being young and, thus, with numerous tests to pass. All these meanings are relevant to digest the present and future of the FinTech credit sector.

Bibliography

K Alexander, *Principles of Banking Regulation* (Cambridge University Press 2019).

J Archer, 'Funding Circle joins London Stock Exchange with Valuation of £1.5bn' (2018) *The Telegraph* <https://www.telegraph.co.uk/technology/2018/09/28/funding-circle-goes-public-london-15bn-market-cap/> accessed 28 February 2020.

T Balyuk and S Davidenko, 'Reintermediation in FinTech: Evidence from Online Lending' (2018) Michael J Brennan Irish Finance Working Paper Series Research Paper No. 18-17 <https://papers.ssrn.com/sol3/papers.cfm?abstract_id=3189236> accessed 03 September 2019.

G Barba Navaretti et al, 'FinTech and Banks: Friends or Foes?' (2017) 3 European Economy Banks, Regulation, and the Real Sector 2, 9 <https://european-economy.eu/book/fintech-and-banks-friends-or-foes/> accessed 28 February 2020.

T Baumgardner et al, 'Crowdfunding as a Fast Expanding Market for the Creation of Capital and Shared Value' (2017) 59(1) Thunderbird International Business Review 115 <https://onlinelibrary.wiley.com/doi/abs/10.1002/tie.21766> accessed 16 September 2019.

Basel Committee on Banking Supervision (BCBS), 'Sound Practices. Implications of FinTech Developments for Banks and Bank Supervisors' (2018) <https://www.bis.org/bcbs/publ/d431.pdf> accessed 04 December 2019.

P Bellaflame et al, 'Crowdfunding: Tapping the Right Crowd' (2014) 29(5) Journal of Business Venturing 585 <https://perso.uclouvain.be/paul.belleflamme/papers/JBV2013.pdf> accessed 12 September 2019.

C Bertsch and C-J Rosenvinge, 'FinTech Credit: Online Lending Platforms in Sweden and Beyond' (2019) 2 Sveriges Riksbank Economic Review <https://www.riksbank.se/globalassets/media/rapporter/pov/artiklar/engelska/2019/191010/2019_2-fintech-credit-online-lending-platforms-in-sweden-and-beyond.pdf> accessed 20 December 2019.

G Borello, 'Analisi Economica dei Lending Marketplace' in A Sciarrone Alibrandi et al (eds), *Marketplace Lending. Verso Nuove Forme di Intermediazione Finanziaria?* (2019) 5 Quaderni FinTech, Consob <http://www.consob.it/documents/46180/46181/FinTech_5.pdf/a92a97f0-7d0e-43de-9fcd-4acfd97199f2> accessed 04 November 2019.

D C Brabham, *Crowdsourcing* (Massachusetts Institute of Technology 2013).

British Business Bank, 'Enterprise Finance Guarantee. An Opportunity for Lending Institutions to Partner with the British Business Bank' (2019) <https://www.british-business-bank.co.uk/wp-content/uploads/2019/04/190401-EFG-Request-for-Proposal-Final.pdf> accessed 10 May 2020.

British Business Bank, 'Coronavirus Business Interruption Loan Scheme (CBILS) An Opportunity for Lending Institutions to Partner with the British Business Bank' (2020) <https://www.british-business-bank.co.uk/wp-content/uploads/2020/04/RFP-CBILS-Clean-07.04.20.pdf> accessed 25 April 2020.

CISION PR Newswire <https://www.prnewswire.com/in/news-releases/the-global-crowdfunding-market-wasvalued-at-10-2-billion-us-in-2018-and-is-expected-to-reach-28-8-billion-us-with-a-cagr-of-16-by-2025-valuates-reports-888819175.html> accessed 06 November 2020.

S Chishti and J Barberis, *The FinTech Book. The Financial Technology Handbook for Investors, Entrepreneurs and Visionaries* (Wiley 2016).

S Claessens et al, 'FinTech Credit Markets Around the World: Size, Drivers and Policy Issues' (2018) *BIS Quarterly Review* <https://www.bis.org/publ/qtrpdf/r_qt1809e.pdf> accessed 28 June 2019.

D Cumming and L Hornuf (eds) *The Economics of Crowdfunding. Startups, Portals and Investors Behaviours* (Palgrave Macmillan 2018).

M Darbyshire, 'P2P Platforms Seek "Urgent" UK government Help to Keep Lending' (2020) *Financial Times* <https://www.ft.com/content/6633f55e-6d27-11ea-89df-41bea055720b> accessed 26 May 2020.

M Darbyshire and N Megaw, 'Peer-to-peer Lenders Forced to Abandon Retail Roots' (2020) *Financial Times* <https://www.ft.com/content/b26ecf08-fd2f-4c7f-93ce-f6d55888da83> accessed 21 June 2020.

J Dermine, 'Digital Disruption and Bank Lending' (2017) 2 European Economy, Banks, Regulation and the Real Sector 63.

G Ferrarini, 'Regulating FinTech: Crowdfunding and Beyond' (2017) 3(2) European Economy Banks, Regulation, and the Real Sector 9 <https://european-economy.eu/book/fintech-and-banks-friends-or-foes/> accessed 28 February 2020.

Financial Conduct Authority, 'Call for Inputs for the Post-implementation Review of the FCA's Crowdfunding Rules' (2016) <https://www.fca.org.uk/publications/calls-input/post-implementation-review-fca-crowdfunding-rules> accessed 25 April 2020.

Financial Conduct Authority, 'Loan-based ('peer-to-peer') and Investment-based Crowdfunding Platforms: Feedback to CP18/20 and Final Rules' (2019) PS19/14 <https://www.fca.org.uk/publication/policy/ps19-14.pdf> accessed 26 May 2020.

Financial Stability Board (FSB), 'Financial Stability Implications from FinTech, Supervisory and Regulatory Issues that Merit Authorities' Attention' (2017) <https://www.fsb.org/wp-content/uploads/R270617.pdf> accessed 24 June 2019.

Financial Stability Board and Committee on the Global Financial System (FSB/CGFS), 'FinTech Credit. Market Structure, Business Models and Financial Stability Implications' (2017) 3 <https://www.fsb.org/wp-content/uploads/CGFS-FSB-Report-on-FinTech-Credit.pdf≥ accessed 23 October 2019.

J Ford, 'Peer-to-peer Lenders are Blurring into Mainstream Banks' (2016) *Financial Times* <https://www.ft.com/content/236e43f6-ba1e-11e6-8b45-b8b81dd5d080> accessed 31 May 2020.

Funding Circle, 'Funding Circle & Santander Announce Partnership to Support Thousands of UK Businesses' (2014) <https://www.fundingcircle.com/blog/2014/06/funding-circle-santander-announce-partnership-support-thousands-uk-businesses/> accessed 20 January 2020.

K Gaw, 'Funding Circle Suspends Secondary Market' (*Peer2Peer Finance News,* 9 April 2020) <https://www.p2pfinancenews.co.uk/2020/04/09/funding-circle-suspends-secondary-market/> accessed 23 April 2020.

A Glas and M Truszel, 'Current Trends in Financial Technology' in S Chishti and J Barberis (eds), *The FinTech Book. The Financial Technology Handbook for Investors, Entrepreneurs and Visionaries* (Wiley 2016).

E Kirby and S Worner, 'Crowd-funding: An Infant Industry Growing Fast' (2014) Staff Working Paper of the IOSCO Research Department <https://www.iosco.org/research/pdf/swp/Crowd-funding-An-Infant-Industry-Growing-Fast.pdf> accessed 23 October 2019.

L Harley-McKeown, 'Metro Bank Share Price Plunges as It Enters Exclusive Talks with RateSetter' (2020) *Express* < https://www.express.co.uk/finance/city/1296062/metro-bank-share-price-merger-talks-ratesetter> accessed 15 June 2020.

T Hildebrand et al, 'Skin in the Game: Evidence from the Online Social Lending Market' (2010) Duke University <https://www.semanticscholar.org/paper/Skin-in-the-Game-%3A-Evidence-from-the-Online-Social-Hildebrand-Puri/0b378d977fa993362cce35147b7e55d64bd1d680> accessed 07 February 2020.

T Lambert and A Schwienbacker, 'An Empirical Analysis of Crowdfunding' (2010) Louvain-la-Neuvwe, Louvain School of Management, Catholic University of Louvain, <https://kunnskapsverket.org/litteraturdatabase/publikasjon/empirical-analysis-crowdfunding> accessed 04 October 2019.

G Leboeuf and A Schienwaker, 'Crowdfunding as a New Financing Tool' in D Cumming and L Hornuf (eds), *The Economics of Crowdfunding. Startups, Portals and Investor Behavior* (Palgrave Macmillan 2018).

Q Li, 'What Causes Bank Failures during the Recent Economic Recession?' (2013) 28 Honors Projects <http://digitalcommons.iwu.edu/busadmin_honproj/28> accessed 20 October 2019.

E Macchiavello, 'Analisi Comparata delle Principali Normative Speciali Europee in Materia di Marketplace Lending' in A Sciarrone Alibrandi et al (eds), *Marketplace Lending. Verso Nuove Forme di Intermediazione Finanziaria?* (2019) 5 Quaderni FinTech, Consob <http://www.consob.it/documents/46180/46181/FinTech_5.pdf/a92a97f0-7d0e-43de-9fcd-4acfd97199f2> accessed 04 November 2019.

E Macchiavello and A Sciarrone Alibrandi, 'L'inquadramento Giuridico delle Attività Svolte dai Lending Marketplace. Linee di Fondo' in A Sciarrone Alibrandi et al (eds), *Marketplace Lending. Verso Nuove Forme di Intermediazione Finanziaria?* (2019) 5 Quaderni FinTech, Consob <http://www.consob.it/documents/46180/46181/FinTech_5.pdf/a92a97f0-7d0e-43de-9fcd-4acfd97199f2> accessed 20 February 2020.

E R Mollick, 'The Dynamics of Crowdfunding: An Exploratory Study' (2014) 29(1) Journal of Business Venturing 1 <https://www.sciencedirect.com/science/article/pii/S088390261300058X> accessed 16 September 2019.

October, 'Four Trends Driving the European FinTech Sector in 2019' (2019) <https://october.eu/4-trends-driving-the-european-fintech-sector-in-2019/> accessed 30 January 2020.

T O'Neill, *Zopa's Launching a Bank* (2018) Zopa Blog <https://blog.zopa.com/2018/12/04/zopas-launching-bank/> accessed 25 February 2020.

Oxera, 'The Economics of Peer-to-Peer Lending' (2016) < https://www.oxera.com/wp-content/uploads/2018/03/The-economics-of-P2P-lending_30Sep_.pdf-1.aspx.pdf > accessed 28 May 2020.

Prosper, 'Borrower Registration Agreement and Limited Power of Attorney' (2019) <https://www.prosper.com/plp/borrower-registration-agreement/> accessed 10 January 2020.

RateSetter, 'Investor Terms' (2020) < https://www.ratesetter.com/siteassets/media/legal/01-2020-investor-terms-1.pdf> accessed 28 May 2020.

RateSetter, 'Provision Fund Policy' (2020) <https://www.ratesetter.com/siteassets/media/fca/12-2019-provision-fund-policy.pdf> accessed 05 May 2020.

N Scholz, *The Relevance of Crowdfunding* (Springer Gabler 2015).

Space-tec Capital Partners, 'Crowdfunding Innovative Ventures in Europe. The Financial Ecosystem and Regulatory Landscape' (2014) A Study Prepared for the European Commission DG Communications Networks, Content & Technology <https://ec.europa.eu/digital-single-market/en/news/crowdfunding-innovative-ventures-europe-financial-ecosystem-and-regulatory-landscape-smart> accessed 22 September 2019.

B Van Liebergen, 'Machine Learning: A Revolution in Risk Management Compliance?' 45 Journal of Financial Transformation 65 <https://www.iif.com/portals/0/Files/private/32370132_van_liebergen_-_machine_learning_in_compliance_risk_management.pdf> accessed 10 December 2019.

T Ziegler et al, 'Expanding Horizons. The 3rd European Alternative Finance industry Report' (2018) Cambridge Centre for Alternative Finance <https://www.jbs.cam.ac.uk/fileadmin/user_upload/research/centres/alternative-finance/downloads/2018-02-ccaf-exp-horizons.pdf> accessed 20 November 2019.

Zopa's Principles' <https://www.zopa.com/principles> accessed 20 December 2019.

8 Fintech credit and consumer financial protection

Nikita Aggarwal

1 Introduction

The current era in fintech is characterised by three, key sociotechnical trends: digitisation, disintermediation and datafication. *Digitisation* describes the shift from analog to digital technology; from physical to electronic, 'from atoms to bits'.[1] This trend has been in motion for several decades, however has accelerated significantly since the early 2000s, with the wider diffusion of the Internet, mobile and cloud computing. The second key trend, *disintermediation*, refers to the dislocation of traditional financial intermediaries – such as banks, insurance companies and central clearing counterparties – by technology-led, 'peer-to-peer' (P2P) platforms, including more recently Big Tech companies such as Apple and Amazon.[2] This trend is part of the broader P2P or 'sharing economy', in which digital, market-based platforms/apps have disintermediated incumbents in many sectors, including transportation (eg, the ride-sharing app Uber) and hospitality (eg, the house-sharing app Airbnb).

Disintermediation has been driven both by the aforementioned advances in digital and networked technology, as well as by changes in the macroeconomic and regulatory environment. In particular, the tightening of credit standards by many banks following the 2008 global financial crisis created an opportunity for (then un-regulated) startups to develop innovative financial products, such as P2P loans, to reach underserved consumers.[3] However, as discussed further in Section 2, P2P platforms and marketplace lenders have over time come to take on greater responsibility in the credit evaluation process. To that extent, they represent a degree of *re*-intermediation of consumer credit markets.[4]

The third key trend, *datafication*, describes the increasing reliance on data and data-driven computational methods such as machine learning (ML) in financial decision-making. The volume of available (personal) data has increased exponentially as society has become increasingly networked, digitised and 'datafied', as well as due to improvements in

---

1 N Negroponte, *Being Digital* (Alfred A. Knopf 1995).
2 Y Yadav and C Brummer, 'Fintech and the Innovation Trilemma' (2019) 107(2) Georgetown Law Journal 235, 275-278.
3 D W Arner, J N Barberis and R P Buckley, 'The Evolution of Fintech: A New Post-Crisis Paradigm?'(2015) University of Hong Kong Faculty of Law Research Paper No. 2015/047; G Buchak, G Matsos and A Seru, 'Fintech, Regulatory Arbitrage and the Rise of Shadow Banks' (2018) <http://www.nber.org/papers/w23288> accessed 01 June 2020.
4 T Balyuk and S Davydenko, 'Reintermediation in Fintech: Evidence from Online Lending' (2019) <http://dx.doi.org/10.2139/ssrn.3189236> accessed 01 June 2020.

computing power, the tools and infrastructure needed to capture and process these data, and theoretical advances in ML methods, particularly since the mid-2000s.[5]

These three trends are transforming financial markets, and consumer credit markets are no exception. This chapter examines the digitisation, disintermediation and datafication of consumer credit – a phenomenon referred to as 'fintech credit'. Following an overview of the fintech credit ecosystem, the chapter examines the potential opportunities and risks of fintech credit for consumer credit markets, and considers how regulation should best respond to these risks, focusing on the challenges for consumer protection regulation. Although the chapter focuses on the UK, the analysis will also be relevant for other jurisdictions in which fintech credit is present.

2 What is fintech credit?

Fintech credit represents a small but rapidly growing share of the consumer credit market, both in the UK and globally.[6] In order to map the contours of the fintech credit ecosystem, this section examines three archetypes of fintech credit, each of which embody the broader fintech trends of digitisation, disintermediation (reintermediation) and datafication. These are: (i) **Zopa**, the P2P lending platform; (ii) **Monzo**, the digital challenger bank and (iii) **Apple Card,** the digital credit card from Apple and Goldman Sachs. These examples are selected to exemplify the range of entities, business models and regulatory arrangements in the current fintech credit ecosystem. In particular, fintech credit encompasses both non-bank platforms – such as Zopa[7] and Apple – as well as traditional banks. The latter includes both newly established 'challenger' banks, such as Monzo, as well as banking behemoths, such as Goldman Sachs.

As such, this section paints a nuanced picture of fintech credit as more than simply (non-bank) P2P lending or 'credit activity facilitated by electronic platforms'.[8] Indeed, the general trend of datafication, digitisation and disintermediation in consumer credit markets is blurring the boundary between 'fintech' and 'traditional' consumer credit. To the extent that most credit providers are turning to data-driven, digital technology, all credit is or soon will be fintech credit.

- *Zopa*
  Established in 2005, Zopa is the original P2P lending platform, facilitating P2P loans and investments between lenders (retail and institutional investors) and borrowers. It is a digital lender, accessible only through the Zopa website or mobile app. Zopa

---

5 The phenomenon of analysing large and complex datasets is also commonly called 'Big Data'. See V Mayer-Schönberger and K Cukier, *Big Data: A Revolution That Will Transform How We Live, Work and Think* (John Murray 2013).

6 CGFS and FSB, 'FinTech Credit: Market Structure, Business Models and Financial Stability Implications' (2017) <https://bit.ly/2W6yGF5> accessed 01 June 2020; S Claessens et al, 'Fintech Credit Markets Around the World: Size, Drivers and Policy Issues' (2018) <https://www.bis.org/publ/qtrpdf/r_qt1809e.htm> accessed 01 June 2020.

7 This section focuses only on Zopa as a P2P platform. Zopa is in the process of receiving a full banking licence, authorised by the PRA, pursuant to which it will offer traditional (FSCS-protected) personal savings accounts, credit cards and bank loans alongside its original P2P loans and investment products (see https://blog.zopa.com/2018/12/04/weve-received-banking-licence-happens-next/).

8 CGFS and FSB (n 6).

does not retain any risk on its balance sheet for P2P loans,[9] and P2P loans and investments are *not* protected by the Financial Services Compensation Scheme (FSCS), the UK government deposit insurance and investor compensation scheme. It is licensed and regulated by the UK Financial Conduct Authority (FCA) in its capacity as a P2P platform, and derives its income from commissions and fees, rather than interest rate spreads.[10]

Zopa's business and regulatory model, as with other P2P lending platforms, has evolved since its inception. In particular, the influx of institutional investors (banks, insurance companies, etc.) means that Zopa is no longer 'peer-to-peer' in the strictest sense of the term (hence the popularity of the alternative term 'marketplace lending').[11] Furthermore, the greater role played by these platforms in the credit evaluation and pricing process (as compared to the original auction mechanism)[12] makes them more akin to intermediaries than markets or trading venues for matching credit supply and demand. In this way, they represent a *re*intermediation of the consumer credit markets that they once disintermediated.[13] As examined further in Section 4, the regulatory obligations incumbent on Zopa and other P2P platforms have also increased since their inception, although they still benefit from significantly lower operating and regulatory costs (eg, due to lower capital and liquidity requirements) than traditional lenders.

Zopa leverages digital technology, large volumes of 'alternative' consumer data and sophisticated data-analytic techniques such as ML to match lenders and borrowers and to automate and streamline the credit underwriting process.[14] Alternative data used by Zopa and other fintech lenders include both *non-credit,* financial data (eg, rental and mobile phone payment data), as well as *non-credit, non-financial* data, such as social media activity ('liking' posts, clicks and time-per-view), health fitness activity data – even data on how consumers interact with the lender's website.[15] Indeed, non-bank, fintech credit providers such as Zopa are the pioneers of 'algorithmic credit scoring', using alternative data and ML to improve the accuracy of creditworthiness assessment.[16] Zopa also uses predictive data analytics and behavioural insights to personalise credit and improve personal financial management, for instance by setting up a repayment schedule that better matches the borrower's expenditure patterns and affordability, as well as automating debt repayments.

9 On different business models for platform lending, see ibid., 11–17.
10 C Odinet, 'Consumer Bitcredit and Fintech Lending' (2018) 69(781) Alabama Law Review 100, 108.
11 B Zhang et al, 'The 5th UK Alternative Finance Industry Report' (2018) <https://bit.ly/3dl9ekV> accessed 01 June 2020, 17ff.
12 Oxera, 'The Economics of Peer-to-peer Lending' (2016) <https://www.oxera.com/wp-content/uploads/2018/03/The-economics-of-P2P-lending_30Sep_.pdf-1.aspx.pdf> accessed 01 June 2020, 25–26.
13 T Balyuk and S Davydenko (n 4).
14 T O'Neill, 'The Birth of Predictor – Machine Learning at Zopa' (2016) <https://blog.zopa.com/2016/10/21/the-birth-of-predictor/> accessed 01 June 2020.
15 T Berg et al, 'On the Rise of FinTechs – Credit Scoring Using Digital Footprints' (2019) Michael J. Brennan Irish Finance Working Paper Series Research Paper No. 18-12 <https://ssrn.com/abstract=3163781> accessed 01 June 2020.
16 M A Bruckner, 'The Promise and Perils of Algorithmic Lenders' Use of Big Data' (2018) 93(1) Chicago-Kent Law Review 3; N Aggarwal, 'The Norms of Algorithmic Credit Scoring' (2020) <https://papers.ssrn.com/sol3/papers.cfm?abstract_id=3569083> accessed 01 June 2020. For an accessible explanation of how ML is used to build an algorithmic credit scoring model, see M Hurley and J Adebayo, 'Credit Scoring in the Era of Big Data' (2016) 18 Yale Journal of Law and Technology 148, 168–183.

- *Monzo*

  Established in 2012, Monzo is part of a wave of recently licensed 'challenger' banks, or 'neobanks', in the UK. Similar to Zopa, it is a digital, 'app-only' bank – it has no physical branches, and customers interact entirely via the Monzo website and mobile app. Monzo also takes a highly data-driven approach to consumer finance. The main factor that distinguishes Monzo from the first generation of (P2P) fintech lenders is that it is a fully licensed, deposit-taking bank, authorised by the PRA and protected by the FSCS. As such, Monzo and other challenger banks do not set out to disintermediate consumer finance in the manner of P2P lending, so much as compete with less tech-savvy incumbent banks through a leaner, more digital and data-driven business model.

  In particular, the use of digital and data-driven technology enables Monzo to offer lower-cost, more convenient and more personalised credit to consumers compared to mainstream banks.[17] This includes instant access to credit upon approval and lower fees (eg, zero debit card transaction and prepayment fees). Similar to Zopa, it leverages behavioural insights, alternative data and ML to improve consumer creditworthiness assessment and identity verification processes, as well as to assist borrowers with personal financial management. Examples of the latter include personalised prompts and notifications to help the borrower save and/or avoid defaulting on their debts; automated savings and bill management (including bill 'pots' and 'roundups'); and instant payment and bill-splitting functions.

  The use of digital, data-driven technology also supports enhanced security features, such as location-based security and more accurate detection and mitigation of suspicious account activity, as well as more efficient account management. For example, a customer can freeze their account immediately and directly through their phone app if they lose their card. This contrasts with the notoriously blunt and cumbersome fraud processes of traditional banks.

  Like many other digital challenger banks, Monzo targets younger, so-called 'millenial' borrowers. In addition to its digital and app-only platform, this target market is reflected in the bank's credit product range, which is limited to small, unsecured loans and arranged overdrafts (it does not offer mortgages, or other secured loans). Most customers use Monzo as a second account; however, this trend may be shifting – in part, no doubt, due to incentives such as early salary payment.[18] Another salient feature is Monzo's marketplace or 'financial hub' for non-credit consumer services – such as travel insurance and bill switching.[19] In this regard, Monzo is part of a broader trend towards 'platform banking' and newer forms of cross-selling by financial institutions.[20]

---

17 To compete with challenger banks such as Monzo, traditional banks have launched their own (consumer-facing) digital banks, although not always successfully eg, Bó (closed) and Mettle by RBS/Natwest Group (see <https://www.cnbc.com/2020/05/01/rbs-drops-bo-its-attempt-to-rival-monzo-and-revolut-why-it-failed.html>).

18 Monzo, 'Monzo Limited Annual Report and Group Financial Statements' (2019) <https://monzo.com/static/docs/annual-report-2019.pdf> accessed 01 June 2020, 10.

19 See <https://monzo.com/blog/2019/01/29/2019-features>.

20 Deloitte, 'Platform Banking as a New Business Model' (2019) <https://www2.deloitte.com/us/en/pages/financial-services/articles/platform-banking-as-a-new-business-model.html> accessed 01 June 2020.

- *Apple Card*

  Launched in 2019, the Apple Card is a consumer credit card offered by Apple and issued by Goldman Sachs, using the Mastercard payment platform.[21] The Apple Card is a digital-first card, accessible through the iPhone mobile payment wallet (Apple Wallet/Apple Pay). It leverages large volumes of consumer data – particularly data collected from the cardholder's iPhone and other iOS devices – and ML techniques to provide real-time transaction information and personalised advice to help cardholders with financial planning and budgeting. Other salient features include daily cash-back on purchases made using the card and significantly lower fees than traditional credit cards.

  Apple also distinguishes itself through enhanced security and privacy for customers, through the use of encryption/tokenisation, biometric customer authentication and federated ML technologies. As a result, customer data (included credit card numbers) are not shared with Apple nor can they be 'tied back to' the customer.[22] Although the Apple Card is currently not available in the UK, once launched it would likely fall under the regulatory oversight of the FCA and PRA (with respect to the provision of consumer credit by the issuing bank), and the Payment Systems Regulator (PSR) (with respect to the Mastercard payment system). However, due to encryption/tokenisation, Apple Pay and Wallet *per se* appear to fall outside the scope of EU payment services regulation, for example, as a payment initiation service provider (see further Section 4).[23]

  The key novelties of the Apple Card, and thus its relevance in helping us to map the contours of the fintech credit ecosystem, are that, unlike other digital credit cards, it is: (i) offered by a (Big) Tech company; (ii) in partnership with a large, mainstream bank. As such, the Apple Card represents a new form of disruption and disintermediation of consumer credit markets, this time by large established tech companies rather than smaller tech startups (in the tradition of Monzo and Zopa). At the same time, by partnering with traditional incumbent banks, it represents a different form of *re*-intermediation in consumer credit markets.

  This 'TechFin' phenomenon – Big Tech companies entering financial services – is not limited to Apple.[24] Amazon, Google and Alibaba (Ant Financial), amongst other tech companies, are all expanding their financial service offerings, particularly in consumer credit. For example, Amazon has partnered with Synchrony Bank in the United

---

21 At the time of writing, the Apple Card is only available in the United States, however is expected to launch in due course in the UK (see <https://www.apple.com/newsroom/2019/08/apple-card-launches-today-for-all-us-customers/>). Apple also offers interest free instalment credit to assist consumers with the purchase of Apple products (in the UK, this form of consumer financing is provided through Barclays and Paypal: see <https://www.apple.com/uk/shop/browse/financing>).

22 See <https://www.apple.com/uk/apple-pay/>.

23 See FCA Handbook PERG 5.13 Q25B ('In our view, the provider of a service that transmits a payer's card details, along with a payment order, to the payer's payment service provider, **but does not come into possession of personalised security credentials**, is not carrying out a payment initiation service', emphasis added) <https://www.handbook.fca.org.uk/handbook/PERG/15/?view=chapter> and PERG 5 Annex 3, paragraph j <https://www.handbook.fca.org.uk/handbook/PERG/15/Annex3.html> accessed 01 June 2020.

24 D Zetsche et al, 'From FinTech to Techfin: The Regulatory Challenges of Data-Driven Finance' (2017) University of Hong Kong Faculty of Law Research Paper No. 2017/007 <https://papers.ssrn.com/sol3/papers.cfm?abstract_id=2959925> accessed 01 June 2020.

States to offer store credit cards to customers, as well as a secured credit card for unbanked and underbanked customers. Amazon also offers customers a visa credit card issued by Chase Bank.[25] Similarly, Uber offers a consumer credit card in partnership with Barclays Bank.[26]

From the perspective of Big Tech companies, offering branded credit and other financial services is a way of bringing more consumers into their ecosystem, as well as locking-in existing customers. This amplifies network effects and provides access to more data about consumers – in particular, financial transaction data, which are used to train and improve the accuracy of their ML models. In turn, this allows for more accurate prediction of consumers' preferences, *inter alia*, to sell targeted ads and products.[27] Furthermore, partnering with existing banks enables Big Tech companies to gain a share of the lucrative financial services market without incurring start-up and regulatory compliance costs themselves.

From the perspective of incumbent banks like Goldman Sachs, partnering with Big Tech allows them to tap into the latter's superior sales and distribution channels, due to a large and captive customer base, more and better-quality customer data and more advanced and efficient technology – without incurring the costs of replacing their own legacy infrastructure.[28] This is particularly important for smaller, community banks that don't have the resources to invest in sophisticated technology. Indeed, incumbent banks are not only partnering with large tech companies but also smaller fintech (credit) startups.

In this regard, there are various models of bank–fintech partnership. Some banks refer borrowers to fintech credit providers; the latter in turn promote the bank's services to their customer base. Other banks lend directly through fintech startups; for example, Metro Bank and Starling Bank (UK challenger banks) both lend via Zopa's P2P platform. Furthermore, P2P loans are increasingly being securitised and sold to institutional investors.[29] Other examples of partnership between 'old and new' include incumbent lenders investing in fintech (credit) startups – for example, BBVA was an early investor in Atom Bank, another UK challenger bank – and conversely, fintech startups acquiring banks.[30]

Of course, partnership is not the only TechFin model. Several tech companies, such as Alibaba's Ant Financial in China, and Kakao Bank in Korea, offer consumer credit directly.

25 See <https://www.cbinsights.com/research/report/amazon-across-financial-services-fintech/>.
26 See <https://www.uber.com/newsroom/introducing-uber-money/>.
27 BIS, 'Big Tech in Finance: Opportunities and Risks' (2019) <https://www.bis.org/publ/arpdf/ar2019e3.pdf> accessed 01 June 2020.
28 See <https://www.economist.com/finance-and-economics/2019/11/21/big-tech-takes-aim-at-the-low-profit-retail-banking-industry> accessed 01 June 2020.
29 C Odinet, 'Securitizing Digital Debts' (2020) 52 Arizona State Law Journal 505. See also <https://blog.zopa.com/2019/12/09/new-securitisation-of-zopa-loans-receives-first-ever-aaa-rating-for-p2p-loans-globally/>.
30 For example, Lending Club's recent acquisition of Radius Bank (US) <https://radiusbank.com/lendingclub-announces-acquisition-of-radius-bank/>.

3 Opportunities and risks of fintech credit[31]

Fintech credit presents both opportunities as well as risks for consumer credit markets. On the one hand, it offers to increase efficiency and distributional fairness. In particular, the use of digital technology and data-driven techniques such as ML offers to reduce the cost and time it takes to acquire relevant information about borrowers, both to process their credit applications *ex ante*, as well to monitor their behaviour *ex post,* thereby mitigating allocative inefficiency in consumer credit markets due to informational asymmetry and adverse selection or moral hazard effects.[32]

Notably, the use of data-driven, algorithmic credit scoring enables fintech lenders to more accurately assess the creditworthiness (credit risk and affordability)[33] of borrowers and price credit, in turn improving access to credit for borrowers who are penalised by a lack of data relevant to their creditworthiness (so-called 'thin file' or 'no file' borrowers).[34] Furthermore, the reduction in transaction costs due to the use of digital technology and automation enables fintech lenders to extend smaller value loans that are too expensive for traditional lenders to underwrite, as well as to reach consumers for whom access to credit is restricted by their remote location (eg, a lack of bank branches) or the inconvenience of lengthy credit approval processes at traditional lenders.[35]

Likewise, data-driven digital technologies offer to generate efficiencies in other parts of the credit process, such as borrower identity verification and monitoring of fraud and money laundering, as well as by improving consumer financial literacy and personal debt management. For example, the automated saving and debt pay down features offered by many fintech credit apps can help to overcome some of the more common behavioural biases that undermine personal financial management by consumers.

Big Tech companies like Apple are particularly well-positioned to capture these efficiency gains. Notably, by combining newly acquired financial transaction data with their existing

---

31 Portions of the discussion in the following sections are adapted from N Aggarwal 'Machine Learning, Big Data and the Regulation of Consumer Credit Markets: The Case of Algorithmic Credit Scoring' in N Aggarwal et al (eds), *Autonomous Systems and the Law* (Beck 2019); and N Aggarwal (n 16).

32 J Stiglitz and A Weiss, 'Credit Rationing in Markets with Imperfect Information' (1981) 71(3) The American Economic Review 393; J Stiglitz and A Weiss, 'Asymmetric Information in Credit Markets and its Implications for Macro-Economics' (1992) 44(4) Oxford Economic Papers 694.

33 FCA Handbook, Consumer Credit Sourcebook ('CONC') sections 5.2A (Creditworthiness assessment) and 5.5A (Creditworthiness assessment: P2P agreements). For empirical evidence demonstrating greater predictive accuracy due to algorithmic credit scoring, see: A Fuster et al, 'Predictably Unequal? The Effects of Machine Learning on Credit Markets' (2020) <http://dx.doi.org/10.2139/ssrn.3072038> accessed 01 June 2020; J Jagtiani and C Lemieux, 'The Roles of Alternative Data and Machine Learning in Fintech Lending: Evidence from the Lending Club Platform' (2018) Federal Reserve Bank of Philadelphia Working Paper No. 18-15 <https://ssrn.com/abstract=3178461> accessed 01 June 2020.

34 On thin-file borrowers and financial inclusion due to algorithmic credit scoring, see Experian, '5.8m Are Credit Invisible, and 2.5m Are Excluded from Finance by Inaccurate Data. How Data and Analytics Can Include All' (2019) <https://bit.ly/38AS9QQ> accessed 01 June 2020; J Jagtiani and C Lemieux, 'Do Fintech Lenders Penetrate Areas That Are Underserved by Traditional Banks' (2018) <https://ssrn.com/abstract=3178459> accessed 01 June 2020; T Berg et al (n 15).

35 J Jagtiani, L Lambie-Hanson and T Lambie-Hanson, 'Fintech Lending and Mortgage Credit Access' (2019) <https://doi.org/10.21799/frbp.wp.2019.47> accessed 01 June 2020 (showing that fintech lenders have been effective in expanding mortgage access in non-metropolitan areas in the United States); M Petersen and R Rajan, 'Does Distance Still Matter? The Information Revolution in Small Business Lending' (2002) LVII(6) The Journal of Finance 2533.

troves of consumer data, and well-trained ML models, they are able to predict consumer preferences and behaviour with even greater precision than other data-driven lenders. This could lead to more accurate screening of borrowers, credit allocation and pricing and more effective credit monitoring and enforcement.[36] Furthermore, by integrating credit and other financial services into the everyday technology used by consumers – notably, personal smartphones – Techfins such as Apple stand to significantly increase the ease and convenience of credit for consumers.

More personalised, accurate and efficient credit processes and improved access to credit also stand to enhance distributional fairness in consumer credit markets, given that the borrowers typically excluded from mainstream credit markets (thin-files as well as those living in non-metropolitan areas) are more likely to come from low-income, less educated and ethnic minority backgrounds.[37] Furthermore, fintech credit could enhance distributional fairness by reducing unlawful discrimination by lenders.[38] Notably, by substituting and supporting (human) loan officers with data-driven, algorithmic credit scores, the scope for discrimination – for example, due to the sexist or racist preferences of a loan officer – could decrease. More generally, greater competition in consumer credit markets due to the entry of fintech lenders stands to increase efficiency and reduce discrimination in lending.[39]

However, it is important not to overstate the potential efficiency and fairness gains due to fintech credit. *Inter alia*, the potential to improve distributional fairness and allocative efficiency through better access to credit, particularly for the most marginalised consumers, depends on *how* fintech lenders use their newly acquired data insights. Indeed, rather than improving access to credit for higher-risk borrowers (that is, borrowers whose perceived creditworthiness is improved by the use of tools such as algorithmic credit scoring, yet nonetheless remain high risk), fintech lenders may instead use their data-driven insights to 'skim the most creditworthy segment of the market for themselves',[40] or improve access to credit for *low-risk* borrowers, whilst only substituting (high-cost) bank credit for high-risk borrowers.[41]

---

36 J Frost et al, 'BigTech and the Changing Structure of Financial Intermediation' (2019) BIS Working Papers no. 779 <https://www.bis.org/publ/work779.pdf> accessed 01 June 2020; H Hau et al, 'How FinTech Enters China's Credit Market' (2019) 109 AEA Papers and Proceedings 60–64 <https://www.aeaweb.org/articles?id=10.1257/pandp.20191012> accessed 01 June 2020 (finding more accurate creditworthiness assessment by Big Tech SME credit providers).

37 Runnymede Trust, 'Financial Exclusion and Ethnicity – An Agenda for Research and Policy Action' (2008) <https://www.runnymedetrust.org/uploads/publications/pdfs/FinancialInclusion-2008.pdf> accessed 01 June 2020 (observing that the majority of the financially excluded in the UK come from the most deprived areas); J Y Campbell et al, 'Consumer Financial Protection' (2011) 25(1) Journal of Economic Perspectives 91.

38 S Deku, A Kara and P Molyneux, 'Access to Consumer Credit in the UK' (2016) 22(10) European Journal of Finance 941–964 (finding evidence of discrimination in consumer credit against non-White households in the UK).

39 R Bartlett et al, 'Consumer Lending Discrimination in the Fintech Era' (2019) NBER Working Paper No. 25943 <https://www.nber.org/papers/w25943> accessed 01 June 2020 (demonstrating reduction in discrimination in the US mortgage market due to competition from fintech lenders).

40 J Jagtiani, L Lambie-Hanson and T Lambie-Hanson (n 35), 3. See also S Freedman and G Jin, 'Learning by Doing with Asymmetric Information: Evidence from Prosper.com' (2011) <http://www.nber.org/papers/w16855> accessed 01 June 2020 (finding that over time, the P2P lender Prosper excluded subprime borrowers and evolved towards the population served by traditional credit markets).

41 J Cornaggia, B Wolfe and W Yoo, 'Crowding Out Banks: Credit Substitution by Peer-To-Peer Lending' (2018) <http://dx.doi.org/10.2139/ssrn.3000593> accessed 01 June 2020.

Likewise, rather than passing on cost savings to consumers[42] and supporting personal financial management, fintech lenders could instead use their data-driven insights about borrowers to (more effectively) exploit the latter's cognitive and behavioural biases, through less desirable forms of price discrimination, targeted marketing and cross-selling of unfavourable (financial) products.[43] The risk of inefficient price discrimination and exploitative or anti-competitive cross-selling is especially pronounced in the case of Techfins such as Apple, given their superior access to consumer data and influence over consumers' everyday lives, as well as their extensive ecosystem of consumer services and products.

Not only is this type of rent-seeking inefficient, it also raises distributional fairness concerns as it is more likely to harm less well-off and less-educated individuals (additionally skewed by race and age) who, experiencing greater financial desperation and with lower levels of financial literacy, are more susceptible to such exploitation.[44] In addition, bias and inaccuracy in the data used to develop ML models, and inadequate model testing, could create new avenues for distributional unfairness and inefficiency. For example, if in a training dataset the successful credit applicants are overwhelmingly White and male (due either to historical discrimination in lending, or data bias due to poor sampling and data pre-processing), the ML model could learn to associate Whiteness or maleness – or proxies for these variables, such as income, credit history or post/zip code – with good creditworthiness. Deploying these models without rigorously testing results thus risks reinforcing and perpetuating these biases and historic patterns of unlawful discrimination.[45]

Furthermore, the greater opacity and complexity of certain 'black-box' ML techniques used by fintech lenders for credit risk modelling (such as deep neural nets) could impede model interpretability and frustrate efforts to detect unlawful discrimination.[46] A related fairness concern is that high-risk borrowers who were previously receiving implicit insurance through a lack of, or hidden, information could be harmed by improved observability of their (negative) characteristics due to data-driven lending. Although more accurate price differentiation in this way may be considered an efficient outcome, it is likely to have regressive distributional effects – as corroborated by recent empirical studies in the US mortgage

---

42 T Philippon, 'The FinTech Opportunity' (2016) <https://www.nber.org/papers/w22476> accessed 01 June 2020, 3–6.
43 O Bar-Gill, 'Algorithmic Price Discrimination: When Demand Is a Function of Both Preferences and (Mis)Perceptions' (2019) 86(3) The University of Chicago Law Review 217. On consumer exploitation in data-driven markets generally, see R Calo, 'Digital Market Manipulation' (2014) 82 George Washington Law Review 995; G Wagner and H Eidenmüller, 'Down by Algorithms? Siphoning Rents, Exploiting Biases and Shaping Preferences – The Dark Side of Personalized Transactions' (2019) 86 University of Chicago Law Review 581.
44 J Armour et al, *Principles of Financial Regulation* (OUP 2016), 222–223; FCA, 'Price Discrimination in Financial Services. How Should We Deal with Questions of Fairness?' (2018) <https://bit.ly/2W783jl> accessed 01 June 2020.
45 C O'Neil, *Weapons of Math Destruction: How Big Data Increases Inequality and Threatens Democracy* (Random House 2016); S Barocas and A Selbst, 'Big Data's Disparate Impact' (2016) 104 Calif L. Rev. 671; d boyd and K Crawford, 'Six Provocations for Big Data' (2011) <https://ssrn.com/abstract=1926431> accessed 01 June 2020; J Kleinberg et al, 'Human Decisions and Machine Predictions' (2018) 133(1) The Quarterly Journal of Economics 237–293.
46 Y LeCun, Y Bengio and G Hinton, 'Deep Learning' (2015) 251 Nature 436. However, this is an active area of research with various methods being developed to 'explain' ML model outputs. See, eg, P Bracke et al, 'Machine Learning Explainability in Finance: An Application to Default Risk Analysis' (2019) Bank of England Staff Working Paper No. 816 <https://bit.ly/2TyIk0d> accessed 01 June 2020.

lending context.[47] Likewise, the trend towards data-driven lending could incentivise lenders and other firms to *over-invest* in gathering private information, in a way that is socially wasteful.[48]

At the macro level, the impact of fintech credit on the overall volume of household debt and the rate of credit expansion in the economy needs close monitoring. Certainly, there are ominous parallels between the use of alternative data for algorithmic credit scoring and securitisation of fintech loans, and the circumstances that foreshadowed the 2008 global financial crisis. It also remains to be seen whether improvements in predictive accuracy and lower customer default rates observed by fintech credit providers simply reflect the relatively benign macroeconomic environment since 2008 in which ML fintech credit models have been trained.[49] A prolonged period of low interest rates has also attracted investment in (high-risk) fintech loans from investors searching for yield. As such, the economic fallout from the Covid-19 pandemic is certain to test the strength of fintech business models.[50]

As consumer lending becomes more dependent on digital and data-driven technology – and third-party technology vendors – the scope for inefficiency in financial markets due to (systemic) technological failure also increases.[51] The entry of Big Tech in consumer credit markets raises further macro risks from anti-competitive practices, particularly due to the exploitation of market power and network effects, as well as regulatory arbitrage through shadow banking activities, as examined further in Section 4.[52]

Finally, fintech credit presents a significant and growing threat to consumer privacy – and thus consumer autonomy – due to its dependence on (personal) data.[53] The datafication of consumer lending increases the risk of both 'objective' and 'subjective' privacy harm to consumers. Objective harms arise, for example, where consumers' data are hacked and used to coerce them, *inter alia* through identity theft.[54] Subjective privacy harms include the chilling effects on consumers of ubiquitous data collection and surveillance.[55] The knowledge that all data is credit data constrains consumers' ability to act freely given that *any* of their (digital) behaviour can now impact their credit prospects.

Moreover, highly data-driven consumer lending could undermine consumers' autonomy by reducing their ability to understand and control how data relating to them are used to

---

47 R Bartlett et al (n 39); A Fuster et al (n 33). On the distinction between price differentiation and price discrimination, see O Bar-Gill (n 43).

48 J Hirshleifer, 'The Private and Social Value of Information and the Reward to Inventive Activity' (1971) 61(4) AER 561–574.

49 J Danielsson, R Macrae and A Uthemann, 'Artificial Intelligence and Systemic Risk' (2019) <http://dx.doi.org/10.2139/ssrn.3410948> accessed 01 June 2020.

50 Zopa announced a tightening of its lending policy in the wake of Covid-19 <https://www.zopa.com/coronavirus-and-my-investment>.

51 A Acquisti, 'The Economics and Behavioural Economics of Privacy' in Lane et al (eds), *Privacy, Big Data, and the Public Good: Frameworks for Engagement* (Cambridge University Press 2014), 83–84.

52 BIS (n 27).

53 On privacy as autonomy, see J E Cohen, 'What is Privacy For' (2013) 126 Harv. L. Rev. 1904; J Cheney-Lippold, *We Are Data: Algorithms and the Making of Our Digital Selves* (New York University Press 2017); L Floridi, 'The Informational Nature of Personal Identity' (2011) 21(4) Minds and Machines 549–566.

54 US Federal Trade Commission, 'Equifax to Pay $575 Million as Part of Settlement with FTC, CFPB, and States Related to 2017 Data Breach' (2019) <https://bit.ly/3aMZxKe> accessed 01 June 2020.

55 P Swire, 'Financial Privacy and the Theory of High-Tech Government Surveillance' (1999) 77 WASH. U. L. Q. 461, 473–475. On the subjective-objective dichotomy see R Calo, 'The Boundaries of Privacy Harm' (2011) Indiana Law Journal 86.

shape their (financial) identities. Notably, the inferences drawn from alternative data are often unintuitive, making it difficult for consumers to know what behaviour is likely to impact credit decisions relating to them. For example, it is relatively straightforward for consumers to understand that a good credit history is positively associated with creditworthiness. In contrast, the association between social media activity data – 'likes' and posts, or the size and composition of one's social network – and creditworthiness is a lot less intuitive.[56]

It might be argued that the cost to consumers' autonomy of having less control over how data relating to them are used is outweighed by the apparent gain in autonomy due to improved access to credit – particularly for thin-file and no-file consumers – and better personal financial management. However, these apparent short-term gains in autonomy cannot easily be offset against the systemic, longer-term harms to autonomy due to fintech credit. That is, consumers' future autonomy could be jeopardised by the datafication of consumer (financial) markets if what emerges is a 'surveillance society' in which all of their activities are monitored and measured, and opaque predictions based on their data are increasingly used to influence and shape their identities.[57] The entry of Big Tech in consumer lending makes these concerns especially pronounced, given the unique access that these companies have to data and behavioural insights about their 'users'.

4 Regulating fintech credit

Fintech credit thus presents itself as a double-edged sword. On the one hand, it offers the opportunity to increase efficiency and fairness in consumer credit markets, *inter alia* by reducing unlawful discrimination and improving personal financial management and access to credit, particularly for marginalised and vulnerable consumers. On the other hand, it could generate *in*efficiency and *un*fairness, *inter alia* due to the exploitation of vulnerable consumers, and give rise to new avenues for unlawful discrimination. Furthermore, fintech credit presents a critical threat to consumers' privacy and autonomy, due to its dependence on consumer data and predictive analytics. This section focuses on the *consumer protection* risks due to fintech credit, particularly for consumer privacy, and examines both private, market-based mechanisms as well as public regulatory mechanisms that could help mitigate these risks.

Thus, with respect to market-based solutions, the use of privacy-enhancing technologies such as ad and cookie blockers, or third-party anonymising tools (such as the tor browser or Google Chrome's 'incognito' mode) could help to reduce the risks to consumers' privacy.[58] In some cases, privacy-enhancing measures have become the market default. For example, operating systems such as Apple iOS (including Apple Pay) and messaging applications such

---

56 See further U.S. Bureau for Consumer Financial Protection, 'Request for Information Regarding Use of Alternative Data and Modeling Techniques in the Credit Process' (2017) 82 FR 11183 <https://bit.ly/2IMH7NK> accessed 01 June 2020, 17–18; S Wachter and B Mittelstadt, 'A Right to Reasonable Inferences: Re-Thinking Data Protection Law in the Age of Big Data and AI' (2019) 2 Columbia Business Law Review 494; N Aggarwal, 'Big Data and the Obsolescence of Consumer Credit Reports' (2019) < https://www.law.ox.ac.uk/business-law-blog/blog/2019/07/big-data-and-obsolescence-consumer-credit-reports > accessed 01 June 2020.

57 F A Pasquale, *The Black Box Society: The Secret Algorithms That Control Money and Information* (Harvard University Press 2015); S Zuboff, *The Age of Surveillance Capitalism* (Profile Books 2019).

58 See <https://www.torproject.org/>.

as WhatsApp use end-to-end encryption by default. Likewise, emerging blockchain-based platforms such as the Bloom 'credit chain' enable consumers to better manage their financial identity; third-party virtual financial assistants help to 'de-bias' consumers and mitigate exploitation of consumer ignorance by unscrupulous lenders.[59]

However, whilst consumer-helping solutions such as these clearly have a role to play, their potential effectiveness is constrained by the large asymmetries of knowledge and power between lenders and borrowers,[60] behavioural weaknesses of consumers (including financial and technological illiteracy) and, in the context of consumer privacy, the negative externalities of data processing that prevent most consumers from understanding the value of, and therefore adopting, these solutions in the first place. In particular, the future-oriented, uncertain and intangible nature of many privacy/autonomy harms – a data hack or identity theft that may not happen, 'invisible' digital manipulation – means that consumers easily discount their severity, *inter alia* due to optimism and present biases.[61]

Consumers typically do not fully understand nor internalise potential future uses of their data, and therefore potential privacy harms – certainly not at the point of 'consenting' to hand over their data. Moreover, consumers do not internalise the undesirable social costs to the privacy and autonomy of *other* consumers due to secondary and tertiary uses of their data – the negative externalities of data processing.[62] The inadequacy of purely market-based solutions thus calls for a strong collective, regulatory response to protect consumers, particularly consumer privacy. The rest of this section examines the existing consumer credit and data protection regulatory frameworks that govern datafied consumer credit markets in the UK, and considers some of the ways in which these frameworks could be strengthened to better respond to the consumer protection risks due to fintech credit, with a focus on consumer privacy.

The obvious starting point in this respect is the financial conduct regime overseen by the Financial Conduct Authority (FCA), a key objective of which is to protect consumers.[63] This regime variously governs each of the fintech credit archetypes described in Section 2. As a general matter, the principles and conduct-based approach of this regime gives the FCA flexibility to respond dynamically to the consumer protection risks arising from the use of new and fast evolving technologies by market participants. *Inter alia*, the principles that firms must 'treat customers fairly', act with 'due care, skill and diligence' and ensure that product marketing is 'clear, fair and not misleading', provide a broad legal basis for regulators to respond to potential exploitation and discrimination against consumers through the use of new, data-driven technologies, and for firms to design appropriate systems and controls in order to achieve the outcomes enshrined in these principles.[64]

---

59 See <https://bloom.co/>.
60 E Posner and R M Hynes, 'The Law and Economics of Consumer Finance' (2001) John M. Olin Program in Law and Economics Working Paper No. 117 <https://ssrn.com/abstract=261109> accessed 01 June 2020.
61 A Acquisti, 'The Economics of Personal Data and the Economics of Privacy' (2010) <https://bit.ly/32JAaX6> accessed 01 June 2020, 25ff.
62 O Ben-Shahar, 'Data Pollution' (2019) 11 Journal of Legal Analysis 104–159; A Acquisti (ibid.), 27; S Barocas and H Nissenbaum, 'Big Data's End Run Around Anonymity and Consent' in Lane et al (eds) *Privacy, Big Data, and the Public Good: Frameworks for Engagement* (Cambridge University Press 2014), 44–75.
63 Financial Services and Markets Act 2000, Section 1C.
64 FCA Handbook, PRIN 2.1.

Recent amendments to this regime directed at P2P lending platforms and payment services firms stand to strengthen consumer protection. In particular, these amendments seek to ensure that retail investors on P2P platforms benefit from the same level of protection through risk disclosure as other retail investors. P2P platforms are also now subject to conduct rules relating to consumer creditworthiness assessment and marketing, as well as the Senior Managers and Certification Regime.[65] In addition, the FCA's increasing emphasis on using behavioural insights and data-driven tools, including ML, to supervise market participants could help to improve detection of and enforcement against harmful behavior, thus supporting consumer protection.[66]

To further strengthen consumer protection under this regime, and to reduce the scope for regulatory arbitrage, non-bank fintech credit firms should be required to put in place stronger governance and oversight arrangements relating to the use of ML credit risk models. *Inter alia*, this should include requirements for data quality verification, as well as continuous model feedback testing, cross-validation and auditing to mitigate overfitting and algorithmic bias risks.[67] Whilst banks are already subject to credit risk and stress testing model validation requirements under the Basel framework, non-bank P2P lending platforms and other fintech lenders are not. Furthermore, careful consideration needs to be given to the regulation of Techfins, such as Apple, as they advance into consumer credit markets, in order to mitigate gaps in consumer financial protection. As discussed earlier, Apple Pay/Wallet *per se* appears to fall outside the financial regulatory perimeter (although it is subject to cross-sectoral data protection and consumer law, *inter alia*).

In addition to the FCA regime, governmental debt advisory and financial literacy programs, for example as provided by the UK Money and Pensions Service, offer a useful mechanism for educating and empowering consumers, and thereby protecting them from harm due to exploitation by (fintech) credit providers.[68] Likewise, the FCA's consumer helpline and the Financial Ombudsman Service offer important avenues for consumer redress. However, whilst these mechanisms certainly have a role to play, their effectiveness is constrained by the behavioural weaknesses of consumers, and the steep informational asymmetry in datafied consumer credit markets discussed earlier, which impede consumers from seeking redress or acting on advice.[69]

---

65 See FCA, 'PS18/19: Assessing Creditworthiness in Consumer Credit – Feedback on CP 17/27 and Final Rules and Guidance' (2018) <https://www.fca.org.uk/publication/policy/ps18-19.pdf>; FCA, 'PS19/14: Loan-based ('peer-to-peer') and Investment-based Crowdfunding Platforms: Feedback to CP18/20 and Final Rules' (2019) <https://bit.ly/2SmeSei>.

66 S Hunt, 'From Maps to Apps: The Power of Machine Learning and Artificial Intelligence for Regulators' (2017) <https://fca.org.uk/publication/documents/from-maps-to-apps.pdf> accessed 01 June 2020; J Proudman, 'Supervisor-centred Automation – the Role of Human-centred Automation in Judgement-centred Prudential Supervision' (2020) <https://bit.ly/2W8xn6S> accessed 01 June 2020.

67 C Sandvig et al, 'Auditing Algorithms: Research Methods for Detecting Discrimination on Internet Platforms' (2014) <https://bit.ly/1tGotry> accessed 01 June 2020; J Kroll et al, 'Accountable Algorithms' (2017) 165 U. Pa. L. Rev. 633.

68 See <https://singlefinancialguidancebody.org.uk/>.

69 HM Treasury, 'Review of the Money Advice Service' (2015) <https://www.gov.uk/government/publications/review-of-the-money-advice-service> accessed 01 June 2020; D Kingsford-Smith and O Dixon, 'The Consumer Interest and the Financial Markets' in N Moloney, E Ferran and J Payne (eds) *The Oxford Handbook of Financial Regulation* (OUP 2015), 707–710.

Cross-sectoral data protection regulation under the GDPR provides an additional avenue for protecting consumers from the harms due to fintech credit, particularly privacy harms.[70] This regime, which is overseen in the UK by the Information Commissioner's Office (ICO), establishes obligations for data controllers and processors, rights for data subjects, and regulatory enforcement powers with respect to the processing of personal data. However, the effectiveness of this regime in protecting consumers is similarly limited by the structural and behavioural impediments in datafied consumer credit markets, as highlighted above.

In particular, the effectiveness of informational and contractual rights under the GDPR – such as the rights to data portability and explanation of automated decisions, and the requirement for consumers to provide their 'informed consent' to data processing – is constrained by the asymmetry of knowledge and power between borrowers and lenders, negative externalities to data sharing and behavioural weaknesses of consumers.[71] As such, strengthening these private, rights-based mechanisms – for example, through more detailed disclosure of 'alternative data' used by fintech lenders, or more detailed explanation of algorithmic credit decisions – is unlikely to sufficiently increase the protection of consumer privacy.

Rather, there is a more fundamental imperative to substantively restrict the scope and scale of consumer data processing, including but not only in the context of fintech credit. There are various ways of advancing this goal. One approach is simply to prohibit the further processing of certain types of personal data – such as relationship and health data – outside of their 'native' contexts, for example, for consumer credit decisions. Commodifying these types of sensitive and personal data through practices such as algorithmic credit scoring may be especially detrimental to consumers' identity and dignity and furthermore would undermine the contextual integrity of the data.[72] Indeed, the GDPR partly embodies this perspective through the stricter regime for processing certain types of 'sensitive' personal data, such as health data.[73]

In addition, or alternatively, the burden of proof for processing consumer data should be raised, through more granular obligations for firms to prove the necessity and proportionality of such processing. This stricter legal basis for data processing should be implemented at both the cross-sectoral level, in data protection law, as well as sectorally, in consumer credit law. *Inter alia*, (fintech) credit firms could be required to demonstrate *ex ante*, and as part of stricter ongoing model validation and data quality verification obligations (as highlighted above), that the proposed processing of personal data makes a sufficiently significant improvement to predictive accuracy, for example in the assessment of consumer creditworthiness, in order to be justified. Consideration should also be given to requiring lenders to adopt technical measures that could better

---

70 Regulation (EU) 2016/679 OJ L 119/1, incorporated into UK law by the Data Protection Act 2018.
71 The same structural factors could limit the effectiveness of customer/consumer-led data sharing mechanisms – notably, data portability under the GDPR and Open Banking under PSD2 – in encouraging competition in financial services. See further <https://www.openbanking.org.uk/>.
72 On the commodification objection, see M J Sandel, *What Money Can't Buy: The Moral Limits of Markets* (Penguin 2012). On contextual integrity see H Nissenbaum, 'Privacy as Contextual Integrity' (2004) 79 Wash. L. Rev. 119.
73 GDPR, Art. 9.

protect consumers' privacy, such as the use of synthetic data and the anonymization of consumer data using (more robust) techniques such as differential privacy.[74]

These stricter obligations for personal data processing should be part of an overall strengthening of oversight and *enforcement* of the data processing obligations of fintech credit firms. This includes stricter enforcement of the existing data protection principles (such as 'purpose limitation' and 'data minimisation'),[75] as well as the obligations of data processors to carry out 'data protection impact assessments' and implement 'data protection by design and default'. Key to better oversight and enforcement is developing more effective regulatory guidance for fintech credit firms with respect to the implementation of their data protection obligations. Although the ICO has produced generic data protection guidance, there is very limited sector-specific guidance in the (consumer) financial context, for example, guiding firms on how to implement data-protection-by-design.[76]

As such, the data protection gap in fintech credit markets can partly be filled through more tailored data protection guidance for (fintech) credit firms. Ideally, this guidance should be produced jointly by the FCA and ICO. More fundamentally, better enforcement of data protection obligations and the protection of fintech consumers from privacy harms, requires the FCA to assume a greater role in overseeing and enforcing data protection in consumer financial markets. Indeed, the datafication and digitalisation of consumer credit markets due to fintech credit makes protecting consumer privacy increasingly important to the overarching goal of 'consumer financial protection'. This suggests that the FCA's consumer protection mandate needs to be interpreted more broadly, to include not only efficiency and fairness norms (the *status quo*)[77] but also privacy norms.[78]

Furthermore, the context-specific nature of privacy norms and normative trade-offs (eg, determining what are reasonable and proportionate uses of personal data for credit decisions) advocates in favour of treating consumer privacy as a sector-specific objective of consumer finance regulation. At the same time, however, the interconnectedness of different data processing and consumption contexts – a credit consumer is also a social media user, and personal data could legitimately be shared between these contexts – means that cross-sectoral data protection regulation will continue to play an important role in safeguarding the privacy and autonomy of credit consumers.

At the institutional level, regulating fintech credit thus requires both increased oversight by the FCA, as well as enhanced coordination between data protection and financial sector regulators (in the UK, the ICO and FCA), in particular to ensure a common vision on the scope and form of data protection in consumer finance.[79] Likewise, the progress of Big Tech into consumer credit markets calls for stronger regulatory cooperation and coordination between data protection, competition and financial regulatory authorities,

---

74 C Dwork et al, 'Calibrating Noise to Sensitivity in Private Data Analysis', in S Halevi and T Rabin (eds) *Theory of Cryptography: Third Theory of Cryptography Conference* (Springer 2006); M Kearns and A Roth, *The Ethical Algorithm* (OUP 2020), 22–47.

75 Art. 5(1) GDPR (data protection principles).

76 For example, see ICO ' Guidance on AI and Data Protection' <https://bit.ly/2VOZIzf>.

77 See further V Mak, 'Financial Services and Consumer Protection' in C Twigg-Flesner (ed) *Research Handbook on EU Consumer and Contract Law* (Edward Elgar 2016); J Y Campbell (n 37); O Bar-Gill and E Warren, 'Making Credit Safer' (2008) 157 University of Pennsylvania Law Review 1.

78 Financial Services and Markets Act 2000, s. 1C (the FCA's consumer protection objective).

79 The FCA and ICO have recently updated their joint MoU (see <https://bit.ly/2WeC3br>).

in order to minimise the risks of regulatory arbitrage between sectors – for instance, where Big Tech companies such as Apple (Pay) fall outside the financial regulatory perimeter – as well as internationally, given the pan-global presence and operations of many of these companies.

Bibliography

A Acquisti, 'The Economics of Personal Data and the Economics of Privacy' (2010) <https://bit.ly/32JAaX6> accessed 01 June 2020.

A Acquisti, 'The Economics and Behavioural Economics of Privacy' in Lane et al (eds) *Privacy, Big Data, and the Public Good: Frameworks for Engagement* (Cambridge University Press 2014).

N Aggarwal, 'Machine Learning, Big Data and the Regulation of Consumer Credit Markets: The Case of Algorithmic Credit Scoring' in N Aggarwal et al (eds) *Autonomous Systems and the Law* (Beck 2019).

N Aggarwal, 'Big Data and the Obsolescence of Consumer Credit Reports' (2019) <https://www.law.ox.ac.uk/business-law-blog/blog/2019/07/big-data-and-obsolescence-consumer-credit-reports> accessed 01 June 2020.

N Aggarwal, 'The Norms of Algorithmic Credit Scoring' (2020) <https://papers.ssrn.com/sol3/papers.cfm?abstract_id=3569083> accessed 01 June 2020.

J Armour et al, *Principles of Financial Regulation* (OUP 2016).

D W Arner, J N Barberis and R P Buckley, 'The Evolution of Fintech: A New Post-Crisis Paradigm?' (2015) University of Hong Kong Faculty of Law Research Paper No. 2015/047.

T Balyuk and S Davydenko, 'Reintermediation in Fintech: Evidence from Online Lending' (2019) <http://dx.doi.org/10.2139/ssrn.3189236> accessed 01 June 2020.

O Bar-Gill, 'Algorithmic Price Discrimination: When Demand Is a Function of Both Preferences and (Mis)Perceptions' (2019) 86(3) The University of Chicago Law Review 217.

O Bar-Gill and E Warren, 'Making Credit Safer' (2008) 157 University of Pennsylvania Law Review 1.

S Barocas and H Nissenbaum, 'Big Data's End Run Around Anonymity and Consent' in Lane et al (eds) *Privacy, Big Data, and the Public Good: Frameworks for Engagement* (Cambridge University Press 2014).

S Barocas and A Selbst, 'Big Data's Disparate Impact' (2016) 104 California Law Review 671.

R Bartlett et al, 'Consumer Lending Discrimination in the Fintech Era' (2019) NBER Working Paper No. 25943 <https://www.nber.org/papers/w25943> accessed 01 June 2020.

O Ben-Shahar, 'Data Pollution' (2019) 11 Journal of Legal Analysis 104.

T Berg et al, 'On the Rise of FinTechs – Credit Scoring Using Digital Footprints' (2019) Michael J. Brennan Irish Finance Working Paper Series Research Paper No. 18-12 <https://ssrn.com/abstract=3163781> accessed 01 June 2020.

BIS, 'Big Tech in Finance: Opportunities and Risks' (2019) <https://www.bis.org/publ/arpdf/ar2019e3.pdf> accessed 01 June 2020.

d boyd and K Crawford, 'Six Provocations for Big Data' (2011) <https://ssrn.com/abstract=1926431> accessed 01 June 2020.

P Bracke et al, 'Machine Learning Explainability in Finance: An Application to Default Risk Analysis' (2019) Bank of England Staff Working Paper No. 816 <https://bit.ly/2TyIk0d> accessed 01 June 2020.

M A Bruckner, 'The Promise and Perils of Algorithmic Lenders' Use of Big Data' (2018) 93(1) Chicago-Kent Law Review 3.

G Buchak, G Matsos and A Seru, 'Fintech, Regulatory Arbitrage and the Rise of Shadow Banks' (2018) <http://www.nber.org/papers/w23288> accessed 01 June 2020.

R Calo, 'The Boundaries of Privacy Harm' (2011) Indiana Law Journal 86.

R Calo, 'Digital Market Manipulation' (2014) 82 George Washington Law Review 995.

J Y Campbell et al, 'Consumer Financial Protection' (2011) 25(1) Journal of Economic Perspectives 91.

CGFS and Financial Stability Board, 'FinTech Credit: Market Structure, Business Models and Financial Stability Implications' (2017) <https://bit.ly/2W6yGF5> accessed 01 June 2020.

J Cheney-Lippold, *We Are Data: Algorithms and the Making of Our Digital Selves* (New York University Press 2017).

S Claessens et al, 'Fintech Credit Markets Around the World: Size, Drivers and Policy Issues' (2018) <https://www.bis.org/publ/qtrpdf/r_qt1809e.htm> accessed 01 June 2020.

J E Cohen, 'What Is Privacy For' (2013) 126 Harvard Law Review 1904.

J Cornaggia, B Wolfe and W Yoo, 'Crowding Out Banks: Credit Substitution by Peer-To-Peer Lending (2018) <http://dx.doi.org/10.2139/ssrn.3000593> accessed 01 June 2020.

J Danielsson, R Macrae and A Uthemann, 'Artificial Intelligence and Systemic Risk' (2019) <http://dx.doi.org/10.2139/ssrn.3410948> accessed 01 June 2020.

S Y Deku, A Kara and P Molyneux, 'Access to Consumer Credit in the UK' (2016) 22(10) European Journal of Finance 941.

Deloitte, 'Platform Banking as a New Business Model' (2019) <https://www2.deloitte.com/us/en/pages/financial-services/articles/platform-banking-as-a-new-business-model.html> accessed 01 June 2020.

C Dwork et al, 'Calibrating Noise to Sensitivity in Private Data Analysis', in S Halevi and T Rabin (eds) *Theory of Cryptography: Third Theory of Cryptography Conference* (Springer 2006).

Experian, '5.8m Are Credit Invisible, and 2.5m Are Excluded from Finance by Inaccurate Data. How Data and Analytics Can Include All' (2019) <https://bit.ly/38AS9QQ> accessed 01 June 2020.

FCA, 'Price Discrimination in Financial Services. How Should We Deal with Wuestions of Fairness?' (2018) <https://bit.ly/2W783jl> accessed 01 June 2020.

FCA, 'PS18/19: Assessing Creditworthiness in Consumer Credit – Feedback on CP 17/27 and Final Rules and Guidance' (2018) <https://www.fca.org.uk/publication/policy/ps18-19.pdf> accessed 01 June 2020.

FCA, 'PS19/14: Loan-based ("Peer-to-peer") and Investment-based Crowdfunding Platforms: Feedback to CP18/20 and Final Rules' (2019) <https://bit.ly/2SmeSei> accessed 01 June 2020.

Federal Trade Commission, 'Equifax to Pay $575 Million as Part of Settlement with FTC, CFPB, and States Related to 2017 Data Breach' (2019) <https://bit.ly/3aMZxKe> accessed 01 June 2020.

L Floridi, 'The Informational Nature of Personal Identity' (2011) 21(4) Minds and Machines 549.

S Freedman and G Jin, 'Learning by Doing with Asymmetric Information: Evidence from Prosper.com' (2011) <http://www.nber.org/papers/w16855> accessed 01 June 2020.

J Frost et al, 'BigTech and the Changing Structure of Financial Intermediation' (2019) BIS Working Papers no. 779 <https://www.bis.org/publ/work779.pdf> accessed 01 June 2020.

A Fuster et al, 'Predictably Unequal? The Effects of Machine Learning on Credit Markets' (2020) <http://dx.doi.org/10.2139/ssrn.3072038> accessed 01 June 2020.

H Hau et al, 'How FinTech Enters China's Credit Market' (2019) 109 AEA Papers and Proceedings 60 <https://www.aeaweb.org/articles?id=10.1257/pandp.20191012> accessed 01 June 2020.

J Hirshleifer, 'The Private and Social Value of Information and the Reward to Inventive Activity' (1971) 61(4) The American Economic Review 561.

HM Treasury, 'Review of the Money Advice Service' (2015) <https://www.gov.uk/government/publications/review-of-the-money-advice-service> accessed 01 June 2020.

S Hunt, 'From Maps to Apps: The Power of Machine Learning and Artificial Intelligence for Regulators' (2017) <https://fca.org.uk/publication/documents/from-maps-to-apps.pdf> accessed 01 June 2020.

M Hurley and J Adebayo, 'Credit Scoring in the Era of Big Data' (2016) 18 Yale Journal of Law and Technology 148.

J Jagtiani, L Lambie Hanson and T Lambie-Hanson, 'Fintech Lending and Mortgage Credit Access' (2019) <https://doi.org/10.21799/frbp.wp.2019.47> accessed 01 June 2020.

J Jagtiani and C Lemieux, 'Do Fintech Lenders Penetrate Areas That Are Underserved by Traditional Banks' (2018) <https://ssrn.com/abstract=3178459> accessed 01 June 2020.

J Jagtiani and C Lemieux, 'The Roles of Alternative Data and Machine Learning in Fintech Lending: Evidence from the Lending Club Platform' (2018) Federal Reserve Bank of Philadelphia Working Paper No. 18-15 <https://ssrn.com/abstract=3178461> accessed 01 June 2020.

M Kearns and A Roth, *The Ethical Algorithm* (OUP 2020).

D Kingsford-Smith and O Dixon, 'The Consumer Interest and the Financial Markets' in N Moloney, E Ferran and J Payne (eds), *The Oxford Handbook of Financial Regulation* (OUP 2015).

J Kleinberg et al, 'Human Decisions and Machine Predictions' (2018) 133(1) The Quarterly Journal of Economics 237.

J Kroll et al, 'Accountable Algorithms' (2017) 165 University of Pennsylvania Law Review 633.

Y LeCun, Y Bengio and G Hinton, 'Deep Learning' (2015) 251 Nature 436.

V Mak, 'Financial Services and Consumer Protection' in C Twigg-Flesner (ed), *Research Handbook on EU Consumer and Contract Law* (Edward Elgar 2016).

V Mayer-Schönberger and K Cukier, *Big Data: A Revolution That Will Transform How We Live, Work and Think* (John Murray 2013).

Monzo, 'Monzo Limited Annual Report and Group Financial Statements' (2019) <https://monzo.com/static/docs/annual-report-2019.pdf> accessed 01 June 2020.

N Negroponte, *Being Digital* (Alfred A. Knopf 1995).

C O'Neil, *Weapons of Math Destruction: How Big Data Increases Inequality and Threatens Democracy* (Random House 2016).

H Nissenbaum, 'Privacy as Contextual Integrity' (2004) 79 Washington Law Review 119.

C Odinet, 'Consumer Bitcredit and Fintech Lending' (2018) 69(781) Alabama Law Review 100.

C Odinet, 'Securitizing Digital Debts' (2020) 52 Arizona State Law Journal 505.

T O'Neill, 'The Birth of Predictor – Machine Learning at Zopa' (2016) <https://blog.zopa.com/2016/10/21/the-birth-of-predictor/> accessed 01 June 2020.

Oxera, 'The Economics of Peer-to-peer Lending' (2016) <https://www.oxera.com/wp-content/uploads/2018/03/The-economics-of-P2P-lending_30Sep_.pdf-1.aspx.pdf> accessed 01 June 2020.

F A Pasquale, *The Black Box Society: The Secret Algorithms That Control Money and Information* (Harvard University Press 2015).

M Petersen and R Rajan, 'Does Distance Still Matter? The Information Revolution in Small Business Lending' (2002) LVII(6) The Journal of Finance 2533.

T Philippon, 'The FinTech Opportunity' (2016) <https://www.nber.org/papers/w22476> accessed 01 June 2020.

E Posner and R M Hynes, 'The Law and Economics of Consumer Finance' (2001) John M. Olin Program in Law and Economics Working Paper No. 117 <https://ssrn.com/abstract=261109> accessed 01 June 2020.

J Proudman, 'Supervisor-centred Automation – the Role of Human-centred Automation in Judgement-centred Prudential Supervision' (2020) <https://bit.ly/2W8xn6S> accessed 01 June 2020.

Runnymede Trust, 'Financial Exclusion and Ethnicity – An Agenda for Research and Policy Action' (2008) <https://www.runnymedetrust.org/uploads/publications/pdfs/FinancialInclusion-2008.pdf> accessed 01 June 2020.

M J Sandel, *What Money Can't Buy: The Moral Limits of Markets* (Penguin 2012).

C Sandvig et al, 'Auditing Algorithms: Research Methods for Detecting Discrimination on Internet Platforms' (2014) <https://bit.ly/1tGotry> accessed 01 June 2020.

J Stiglitz and A Weiss, 'Credit Rationing in Markets with Imperfect Information' (1981) 71(3) The American Economic Review 393.

J Stiglitz and A Weiss, 'Asymmetric Information in Credit Markets and Its Implications for Macro-Economics' (1992) 44(4) Oxford Economic Papers 694.

P Swire, 'Financial Privacy and the Theory of High-Tech Government Surveillance' (1999) 77 Washington University Law Quarterly 461.

U.S. Bureau for Consumer Financial Protection, 'Request for Information Regarding Use of Alternative Data and Modeling Techniques in the Credit Process' (2017) 82 FR 11183 <https://bit.ly/2IMH7NK> accessed 01 June 2020.

S Wachter and B Mittelstadt, 'A Right to Reasonable Inferences: Re-Thinking Data Protection Law in the Age of Big Data and AI' (2019) 2 Columbia Business Law Review 494.

G Wagner and H Eidenmüller, 'Down by Algorithms? Siphoning Rents, Exploiting Biases and Shaping Preferences – The Dark Side of Personalized Transactions' (2019) 86 University of Chicago Law Review 581.

Y Yadav and C Brummer, 'Fintech and the Innovation Trilemma' (2019) 107(2) Georgetown Law Journal 235.

D Zetsche et al, 'From FinTech to Techfin: The Regulatory Challenges of Data-Driven Finance' (2017) University of Hong Kong Faculty of Law Research Paper No. 2017/007 <https://papers.ssrn.com/sol3/papers.cfm?abstract_id=2959925> accessed 01 June 2020.

B Zhang et al, 'The 5th UK Alternative Finance Industry Report' (2018) <https://bit.ly/3dl9ekV> accessed 01 June 2020.

S Zuboff, *The Age of Surveillance Capitalism* (Profile Books 2019).

Part III

Fintech and payment services

9 EU payment services regulation and international developments

Alan Brener

1 Introduction

Cross-border card payments in Europe are mainly made through two international card payment schemes: Visa and MasterCard ... new players have emerged in the payments market, spurred by ... the new regulatory environment driven by the PSD2. In the near future, innovation ... might also spur alternatives to the existing card schemes.[1]

Payment services have largely avoided European Union (EU) regulation until relatively recently. However, regulation can 'when drafted and applied correctly ... be an effective tool for creating incentives to increase innovation, economic development and competition'.[2] The Payment Services Directive II (PSD II) has the potential to disrupt the world of payment services and banking across the EU. This Directive is a clear example of a conceptual approach to employing regulation to shape a market. Some have seen it as the EU firing the 'starting gun for banks vs. fin-tech fight over payments'.[3] It is both 'another step towards a digital single market in the EU' and a move to introduce more competition into the EU's payments market and to break the banks' control over customer transaction information.[4] It has been described as a seminal in both encouraging competition and innovation, both within EU member states and across borders.[5] As considered later, it has also become the benchmark against which to measure parallel legislation in other jurisdictions across the globe.

Consolidating a fragmented market into a single-market framework is central to the PSD II.[6] It also aims to break the controlling hold of payment service incumbents by allowing challenger firms to use 'the services of the technical infrastructures' of incumbent payment systems providers on matching terms without discrimination.[7]

In parallel with PSD II there is a move in a number of jurisdiction towards 'open banking' which requires banks to provide their customer data in a secure, standardised form so

1 European Central Bank, 'Card Payments in Europe – Current Landscape and Future Prospects: A Eurosystem Perspective' (17 April 2019).
2 Inna Romānova and others, 'The Payment Services Directive II and Competitiveness: The Perspective of European Fintech Companies' (2018) 21 European Research Studies Journal 3–22, 20.
3 Reuter, 'EU Fires Starting Gun for Banks vs. Fintech Fight over Payments' (27 November 2017).
4 Valdis Dombrovskis, Vice-President responsible for Financial Stability, Financial Services and Capital Markets Union, European Commission press release 'Payment Services: Consumers to Benefit from Cheaper, Safer and More Innovative Electronic Payments' Brussels, 12 January 2018.
5 Alan Brener, 'Payment Service Directive II and Its Implications' in T Lynn (ed), *Disrupting Finance,* (Cham, Switzerland: Springer 2018).
6 Mary Donnelly, 'Payments in the Digital Market: Evaluating the Contribution of Payments Services Directive II' (2016) 32 Computer Law and Security Review 827–839, 829.
7 PSD I, Recital 16, Directive on payment services in the internal market (PSD I), (2007/64/EC).

that it can be passed to authorised third parties and also used to make online payments direct to suppliers of good and services. This information is usually abstracted using a standardised computing 'application programming interface' (API).

One industry innovator expects that in ten years' time all 'banking will be open' and while credit and debit cards will not have entirely disappeared open payments systems will predominate.[8] In their view the 'capture' of detailed personal information on each customer will result in the 'demise of off-the-shelf banking products' and 'will have enabled full commercial roll-out of personalised financial products'.[9]

This chapter considers the key elements of the PSD II, PSD II developments in the UK and other potential new business opportunities, PSD II as a global regulatory model, a number of key risks and the current consumer perspective in the UK on these changes.

2 PSD II: key elements

2.1 *The concepts behind 'open banking' and PSD II*

There are three main conceptual influences on 'open banking' and, possibly, a fourth underpinning PSD II. First, Henry Chesbrough, writing in 2011 set out the risks of current business models with global competition making current business products and services 'commodities' with firms only able to compete on price.[10] In his view 'open services innovation can deliver both better products and better services for a business's customers and better economics for that business'.[11] Chesbrough, as professor and the faculty director of the Garwood Center for Corporate Innovation at the Haas School of Business at the University of California, Berkeley, is credited with devising the 'open innovation' concept and has been highly influential in setting out the vision of an 'open' innovative economy. Second, there is a growing appreciation that customer data has a value and, for example, it is anti-competitive for established banks to restrict access to this information. As a result, in the UK, the Competition and Markets Authority (CMA) issued a report saying that they want to 'significantly accelerate the pace of change by harnessing technology. In particular, we are requiring banks to allow their customers to share their own bank data securely with third parties using an open banking standard. This change … will help customers to find and access better value services and enable them to take more control of their finances. This will also enable new entrants and smaller providers to compete on a more level playing field and increase the opportunities for new business models to develop'.[12] Finally, as alluded to by both Chesbrough and the CMA, changes in technology and how customers interact with it provide both an impetus and an opportunity for change. Specifically, it allows new market entrants to segment existing customer services and to develop new services and products for customers changing what is known in the marketing world as the 'value proposition'.

---

8 Steve Kirsch, CEO Token, Open Banking Expo.

9 Ibid., (Kirsch).

10 Henry Chesbrough, 'Open Services Innovation: Rethinking Your Business to Grow and Compete in a New Era' (San Francisco, California: Jossey-Bass 2011) 1.1.

11 Ibid., (Chesbrough), 1.1.

12 Competition and Markets Authority, 'Making Banks Work Harder for Customers' (August 2016), 1–2.

All of this needs to be seen in the context of current legal, economic and sociological debates on who 'owns' customer data, what does 'ownership' mean, developing and changing notions of 'privacy', the fracturing of jurisdictional control of data and information flows, the growing global dominance of huge IT services firms and the use of regulation to shape economies and business structures and model. These are all substantive subjects which go beyond the scope of this chapter but, nevertheless, underpin its detail.

These changes may also raise, and exacerbate cultural issues by, for example, increasing the 'digital divide' between those 'fluent' in technology and those who are not and between those with access to internet services and those who live in more isolated areas.[13] Others are concerned about the threat of that data users exploiting consumers.[14]

Finally, there is a broad theme summarised as a 'clash of cultures between traditional bankers (who understand what regulators expected of them but struggle to understand the ways in which fintech can be used and abused) and the fintech pioneers (who often come from non-regulated worlds, who are impatient to get on with things, and don't recognise conduct risks)'.[15] Again, this wider issue is evident in anecdotal examples of comments in the industry of fintech innovators 'bumping into' data protection and financial services regulation.

Regulation can be used for a variety of reasons including controlling, prohibiting, protecting and in other ways limiting possible actions. However, PSD II and other legislation in a range of jurisdictions, to a greater or lesser extent, it is much more 'dirigist' – adopting a form of 'high tech colbertism'.[16] The regulations permit, encourage and guide innovation and competition. The legislators appreciate the risks and provide protective guiderails overseen by a set of regulators. Each jurisdiction has approached the issues differently and the rest of this chapter considers aspects of these approaches.

2.2 *Background, objectives and outline*

The first EU Payment Services Directive (PSD I) came into force in 2009.[17] An EU commissioned review of the Directive was highly critical of its effectiveness.[18] A number of EU states had managed to thwart the Directive's central objectives of increasing innovation and competition in payment services. The review found that the consumers were concerned by the risk of unauthorised payments. While Article 61 of the Directive limited customer liability to €150 except in circumstances involving customer fraud or gross negligence the

---

13 In 2018 smartphone penetration in the UK, USA and Germany is around 80% but in other western countries the figures are very much less, Newzoo website, 'Top countries by smartphone users'.

14 Mick McAteer, 'Fintech, Big Data, and the Open Banking "Revolution"', speech given on 1 February 2017, Financial Inclusion Centre, http://inclusioncentre.co.uk/wordpress29/speeches-and-presentations.

15 Ibid., (McAteer).

16 Elie Cohen, 'Industrial Policies in France: The Old and the New' (2007) 7 Journal of Industry, Competition and Trade 213–227, 226.

17 Supra note 7 (PSD I).

18 Study on the impact of Directive 2007/64/EC on payment services in the internal market and on the application of Regulation (EC) NO 924/2009 on cross-border payments in the Community, Final Report.

interpretation of the latter varied widely across jurisdictions.[19] Confidence was also undermined by different consumer complaints handling arrangements across EU states and difficulties in obtaining refunds.[20]

A subsequent EU Commission consultation was heavily influenced by this report and the pace of change in banking and payments technology. Following this consultation the EU issued PSD II.[21] This repealed and replaced all the measures in PSD I. However, many articles in the original Directive were re-enacted in PSD II.

PSD II was published at the end of 2015 and required implementation in local law by January 2018.

The aims of the new Directive were to:

- assist in the integration of the EU's payments market,
- promote competition by encouraging new participants in the market including fintech and the development of mobile and internet payment services across the EU,
- encourage lower prices for payments,
- increase customer confidence in making more efficient electronic payments by introducing better customer protection against fraud and other abuses and error. This would require enhanced security arrangements.[22]

The main themes in the Directive were to increase security measures and other customer protections, level the competitive playing field by reducing the various exemptions from payment services regulation and to permit two new innovative arrangements: 'account information service providers' (AISPs) and 'payment initiation service providers' (PISPs). These are considered in more detail later.

While it is possible to see the Directive as aimed at the banks, it is more likely that the targets were the powerful and profitable US-based credit card companies.[23] The ECB has said that 'European banks and institutions currently have little control over the cross-border payments market, or even the national market if relying on an international card scheme'.[24] The Central Bank has expressed a desire for 'an alternative payment route subject to European governance' and the need to promote 'the creation of a European card scheme, which would offer its services at the pan-European level in competition with international card schemes'.[25] Hence the EU's wish 'to launch innovative, safe and easy-to-use digital payments services and to provide consumers and retailers with effective, convenient and secure payments methods in the Union'.[26]

Besides requiring payment services institutions to be authorised and supervised by 'home' state regulators the European Banking Authority has the task of publishing a

---

19 Ibid., (Impact Study), 242.
20 Ibid., (Impact Study), 243–245.
21 Directive on payment services in the internal market (PSD II, (2015/2366/EC)).
22 European Commission – Fact Sheet, Payment Services Directive: frequently asked questions.
23 'Visa and Mastercard to Cut Foreign Card fees in EU: Latest Concession in Payment Companies' Long-running Antitrust Battle with Brussels', Financial Times, 29 April 2019, 'Mastercard Was Fined 570.6 million Euros ($648 million) by the European Union for Imposing Rules That Regulators Said May Have Artificially Raised the Costs of Card Payments in the Region', Bloomberg, 'MasterCard fined $648 million for High EU Card Dees' (22 January 2019).
24 Supra note 1, (Card payments in Europe), Section 2.1.
25 Supra note 1, (Card payments in Europe), Section 2.1.
26 PSD II, Recital 4.

central public register of authorised payment services firms.[27] The Directive contains various other customer protection measures such as those relating to the transparency of charges and prohibitions on discrimination, based on nationality or place of residence, against those resident legally in the EU.[28] The consumer protection elements are discussed in more detail later.

2.3 *Open banking and new types of customer service*

As mentioned earlier, the Directive created two new types of regulated businesses. First, the Directive permits the creation and operation of 'account information services' (AIS). These organisations collect, aggregate and analyse information from customer payments transactions.

The second type of business, described in the Directive as a 'payment initiation service' (PIS), act as a 'software bridge between the website of the merchant and the online banking platform' of the customer initiating a payment across to the merchant's account.[29] The Directive defines this as 'a service to initiate a payment order at the request of the payment service user with respect to a payment account held at another payment service provider'.[30] It is a secure messaging system. The PIS provider never has access to the transactions funds. Providers of such services are termed 'payment initiation service providers' (PISPs) and 'account information service providers' (AISPs). They are also known collectively as third-party providers (TPPs).[31] The Directive also refers to the bank, or similar, holding the customer's account as the 'account servicing payment service provider' (AS PSP).

It is fundamental to these arrangements that the customer gives explicit consent. There is no requirement for a contract between the customer and either the PISP or AISP. Nor is a contracted necessary between the PISP and the merchant supplying goods or services to the customer.[32] Customer agreements with PSP can be either ad hoc, good for a single transaction or set-up under a continuing contract which can be terminated without charge with, at most, a month's notice.[33] The Directive imposes data protection requirements on both the PISPs and AISPs. Additionally, in order to prevent anti-competitive behaviour AS PSPs are required to treat payment orders and data requests transmitted via a PISP or AISP 'without any discrimination other than for objective reasons'.[34]

Finally, in this section, it is worth mentioning the new 'fund availability confirmation service' highlighted by the Directive. It allows a third party with the customer's express permission to obtain confirmation from the customer's AS PSP (ie, their bank) that sufficient funds are available to enable a payment to be made. It only requires a 'yes/no' response.[35]

27 PSD II, Art. 15.
28 PSD II, Art. 98 and Title III.
29 PSD II, Recital 26–29.
30 PSD II, Art. 4(15).
31 PSD II, Art. 4.
32 PSD II, Recital 30.
33 PSD II, Art. 55.
34 PSD II, Recital 33.
35 PSD II, Art. 65.

2.4 *The requisite safeguards for liberalising the payments markets*

2.4.1 *Introduction*

As mentioned earlier, PSD II establishes trust as a necessary condition for innovation. Consequentially, following a path-dependent route, it requires a regulator to authorise new commercial institutions operating in a market with roles clearly defined by legislation. User trust is further enhanced by the provision of information, ease of redress if things go wrong and robust fund and data security arrangements. Markets may as a result flourish and paradoxically; empirical research has found that trust lowers demand for further government intervention.[36] Aspects of these protections are considered in more detail below.

2.4.2 *Consumer protection*

Increased competition in the payments market will only be achieved if customers trust the providers and the services they provide. PSD II develops consumer protection further than PSD I with the focus on protecting individual 'real' personal customers. However, EU member states are permitted to extend the Directive's safeguards to 'micro-enterprises'.[37]

Customers are expected to communicate, as soon as possible, any incorrect or unauthorised payments.[38] The Directive requires that any alleged unauthorised transaction is immediately reimbursed unless there is a 'high suspicion' that an 'unauthorised transaction results from fraudulent behaviour' by the customer.[39] The suspicion must be based on 'objective grounds'. These must be passed to the national regulator and the PSP should 'conduct, within a reasonable time, an investigation before refunding the payer'.[40] Customers have eight weeks to make a claim for a refund.[41]

Unless the customer has acted fraudulently or was grossly negligent they should only be liable for a maximum of €50 for any loss of their 'payment instrument' (eg, a payment access card) prior to their notifying the PSP.[42] What constitutes 'gross negligence' will be a matter for national law. Any contractual attempt by a PSP to change or shift the burden of proof against the customer will be nugatory.[43]

The customer's PSP or PISP should assume responsibility for any failure in the payments chain.[44] However, if the customer has used the wrong payee's identifier the PSP will not be liable but 'should be obliged to cooperate in making reasonable efforts to recover the funds' including providing information to the customer to help trace the missing funds.[45]

---

36 Paolo Pinotti, 'Trust, Regulation and Market Failures' (2012) 94 The Review of Economics and Statistics 650–658, 650.
37 PSD II, Art. 4(36).
38 PSD II, Arts. 73–74.
39 PSD II, (Arts. 73–74).
40 PSD II, (Arts. 73–74).
41 PSD II, Art. 77.
42 PSD II, Art. 74.
43 PSD II, Recital 72.
44 PSD II, Art. 90.
45 PSD II, Recital 88.

In terms of liability, in the event of an unauthorised, non-executed, defective or late-executed payment initiated via a PISP, the AS PSP is required to refund the customer immediately. There is an obligation on the PISP to compensate the AS PSP where the former is liable, with the burden of proof lying with the PISP 'to prove that, within its sphere of competence, the payment was authenticated, accurately recorded and not affected by a technical breakdown or other deficiency', linked to the payment service of which it is in charge.[46]

The Directive stipulates that the full amount transferred should arrive intact without any charges being levied beyond those agreed at the outset.[47]

All payment made in Euros or other member state currencies should be executed within, at most one day. All other payments should also be completed within the same time period unless otherwise agreed.[48]

2.4.3 *Complaints handling*

The Directive requires that member states have an 'easily accessible, independent, impartial, transparent and effective alternative disputes resolution arrangement for issues between customers and PSPs'.[49] PSPs must have dispute resolution procedures and must respond to complaints within fifteen business days of a complaint being received.[50]

2.4.4 *Security*

The Directive contains extensive requirements on security. These are reinforced by EBA Regulatory Technical Standard (RTS) on home/host state cooperation and the reporting of fraud by PSPs to local competent authorities.[51] There is also guidance on security measures and strong customer authentication (SCA) and incident reporting. This chapter does not consider SCA in any detail other than to note that this requirement exists as part of the overarching strategy to protect customers and build their trust in using these innovative services. The foundation of SCA is to authenticate the identity of the customer and their right to make the transaction – before an electronic payment can be made.[52] Nevertheless, open banking systems, including APIs, present what has been described as an 'attack surface … any service accessible via the Internet is going to be attacked by people wanting to exploit it for nefarious purposes'.[53] However, SCA is to be used proportionately and, for example, low value transactions such as that used for contactless payments at terminals should not require SCA.[54]

---

46 PSD II, Art. 72.
47 PSD II, Art. 81.
48 PSD II, Art 83.
49 PSD II, Art 102.
50 PSD II, Art 101.
51 The EBA has stated that it will be 'analysing regulatory sandboxes [safe regulatory areas for testing innovative products, services and operations] and innovation hubs with a view to developing a set of best practices to enhance consistency and facilitate supervisory coordination', EBA, 'Fintech Roadmap' (March 2018), 4.
52 EU Commission delegated legislation supplementing Directive 2015/2366 of the European Parliament and of the Council with regard to regulatory technical standards for strong customer authentication and common and secure open standards of communication.
53 Steve Mansfield-Devin, 'Open Banking: Opportunity and Danger' (2016) Computer Fraud and Security, 8–13, 10.
54 Ibid., (Mansfield-Devin), 17.

3 PSD II market developments in the UK

The innovative proposals for AISPs and PISPs set out by the PSD II 'may be sufficient to improve user experience and cost to a significant extent '.[55] How extensive this may be, seen at this early stage, is considered in the next sections.

3.1 *Account information service providers*

There are a number of firms offering account information services in the UK. For example, PocketSmith proves a variety of services to consumers who use its app. These include: live feed bank transactions, financial activity labelling to categorise spending, financial budgeting and forecasting, cashflow analysis, net-worth information and a number of graphical information formats.[56] PocketSmith is a New Zealand company operating in Australasia, Canada and the UK. The company uses Yodlee, a US based firm, to collect and supply live bank information. Yodlee is one of a number of companies supplying this service. Others include Moven, Intuit Mint, MX, Finicity etc.

PocketSmith makes its money in three ways: although it provides a very basic, free, service the most useful service, with the bank information feeds, costs the consumer just under $10 per month. The firm also says that based on the consumer's information 'the service may also present information relating to third-party products or services' to the consumer. It may be assumed that the company gets some form of payment for this from these third-party suppliers. Finally, the firm may 'provide aggregate statistics about the use of PocketSmith to our community'.[57] It is assumed that the latter are other businesses PocketSmith has contracted with to provide this data for a fee.

PocketSmith has a number of competitors including Mint, Fentury, a brand of Salt Edge Inc, a Canadian firm and Mobills, a Brazilian firm. UK based firms include Money Dashboard which, like other businesses, 'provides insight and market research services to help companies better understand trends in consumer behaviour. We identify shifts in consumer preferences using anonymised spending information from Money Dashboard users. Money Dashboard may offer suggestions for products and services like credit cards, home loan offers or insurance providers that can save you money. If you select a product based on our suggestion, Money Dashboard may receive a fee from the product provider'.[58] Another example, is Plum. This is the trading name of Plum Fintech Limited which is an 'appointed representative' of Resolution Compliance Limited. It works by analysing the financial data of its individual customers and calculating how much they can save. With the customer's agreement, a direct debit on their bank account transfers this money into a savings vehicle. The latter invests in one of three funds selected by the customer (technology stocks, ethical investments and emerging market securities). These investments are a balance between bonds and equity holdings depending on the customer's level of acceptable risk.[59] There is a fee for these investments which goes to Plum.[60]

---

55 Iris H-Y Chiu, 'A New Era in Fintech Payment Innovations? A Perspective from the Institutions and Regulation of Payment Systems' (2017) 9 Law, Innovation and Technology 190–234, 212.
56 'About Pocketsmith' at https://www.pocketsmith.com.
57 https://www.pocketsmith.com/legal/privacy-policy/.
58 https://www.moneydashboard.com.
59 https://withplum.com under 'Investments'.
60 https://intercom.help/withplum/en/articles/2568684-how-much-does-plum-cost.

Another example is Digital Moneybox ('Moneybox'), which is authorised by the FCA both as an AISP and as a provider of investment products. Besides arranging and managing tax incentivised investments it enables its customers to round up their spending and to transfer the excess into the firm's investment products. It has also agreed with Santander Bank to link the latter's payment cards to the Moneybox app so that a customer making a payment can transfer the roundup excess direct to a Moneybox investment product.[61] Many other banks provide this rounding-up facility but only into product they provide or support.

3.2 *Payment initiation service providers*

The development of payment initiation service providers (PISPs) is still at a very early stage. There are a number of business models. For example, Trustly, a Swedish payments business, has recently taken over PayWithMyBank, a Californian firm.[62] This gives Trustly both access across the EU as a 'passported' operation and also in the US. PISPs, unlike, say the traditional PayPal arrangements, do not require customers to set up an account. The customer can select the goods and services they require on-line; click on payment options and using the PISP app make the payment, with sufficient customer authentication, direct from their bank to the merchant. There are many other firms, such as Stripe, Worldpay and SagePay, which offer payment services for businesses. Although many are based in California, they operate in a number of jurisdictions and are developing their PSD II/ PISP operations. PSD II may result in more competitive pricing with firms such as iZettle and Square charging the merchant 2.5% of the transaction value. Others are a bit cheaper at 1.4% plus a flat fee of 20p for Stripe and 1.9% plus 20p for PayPal.

Klarna, a Swedish firm, has adopted another strategy. As a Swedish bank with passporting rights across the EU, it is able to offer credit to customers which select it as the preferred payments option. Rather than project the business as simply an on-line payment services firm able to offer credit Klarna seeks to use its brand based around the products of its merchant partners to engage the emotions of its customers. It sums this up as:

> 'our tonality adapts, mirroring where the customer is in our model. For example, in the attract phase we grab their attention with our smooth products, while further down into the engage phase, we guide them more, explaining why our product is smooth. This process ensures that we create a natural flow from a consumer first hearing about Klarna, all the way to them joining the Klarna ecosystem'.[63]

It is important to note that in the UK, under s75 of the Consumer Credit Act 1974, that when, within certain limits, a customer uses a credit card to purchase goods or services, the credit card company is jointly and severally liable for any breach of contract or misrepresentation by the supplier of the goods or services. This is a very valuable piece of consumer protection which does not apply to consumers using PISPs. It allows the consumer to seek redress from the credit card company for, say, a failure to deliver the goods ordered from the supplier.

---

61 https://www.moneyboxapp.com.
62 https://www.paywithmybank.com.
63 https://www.klarna.com/international/, 'visual identity guidelines'.

Evidently, PSD II provides a clear business opportunity, but the field is crowded with a number of, largely, US technology companies. It may be that firms that can distinguish themselves with innovative models that are more difficult to replicate, such as emotional engagement, may succeed.

4 Other potential new business opportunities

There are many examples of potential new business areas available under PSD II and 'open banking'. These largely revolve around threatening the traditional credit card model. The main out-comes could include:

- card networks dis-intermediated by PISPs including the loss of customer transaction data as payments are carried out without the use of credit cards;
- PISPs operations reduce the profitability of card firms. For example, currently an interchange fee of, say, 0.2% will go to the card issuing bank, the card network fee may be 0.24% and the merchant acquiring bank gets 0.24%. In total, this represents a charge of some 0.68% for the merchant. However, a PISP might do the whole transaction for a fee of 0.2% charged to the merchant. The customer bank will not be able to discriminate between a PISP mediated transaction and another payment operating through a traditional route[64];
- this may provide opportunity for PISPS to create on-line market places for suppliers of goods and services to offer products not available elsewhere or at a discount. PISPs could offer customers incentives such as access to credit, no-hassle guarantees, insurance, bulk buyer clubs, privileges access to on-line events (eg, live streams) etc.;
- it could provide opportunities for existing major internet firms such as Amazon and Google to move directly into the payments market and to take some of the margin currently given to credit card companies. This could include providing small businesses, for example, with supplier and payment services including finance options;
- for AISPs, the individual and aggregated data, collected with the customers' permission, has a value. This information can be sold on. AISPs could also, for example, develop their own customer data analytical services with real-time data feeds. ASIP would be able to know a lot about both individual customers and cohorts of spenders. Expenditure-pattern algorithms might suggest other goods or services. For example, payment for an insurance product gives immediate knowledge of the likely product renewal date. This can be combined with other customer 'signals' to prompt the latter to buy from an insurance supplier at just the right point;
- information on other bank accounts and assets is likely to be especially valuable to banks where the individual or business is currently a customer since it will allow them to refine their targeting to attract these deposits, investments etc.;
- it is also possible, for example, that government agencies might be interested in this data;
- potential mortgage borrowers would not be required to spend two to three hours going through mortgage affordability assessments since all the data would be easily

---

64 See Robert Maximilian Grüschow, Jan Kemper and Malte Brettel, 'How Do Different Payment Methods Deliver Cost and Credit Efficiency in Electronic Commerce?' (2016) 18 Electronic Commerce Research and Applications 27–36. This looks at the costs to merchants of different payments methods.

available and would, likely, be more accurate than customers' recollections of their individual areas of expenditure;

- it is too early to know how useful the 'funds availability confirmation service', mentioned earlier, will be in practice. It does not address issues relating to assessing customer credit worthiness. Nevertheless, it may help those selling goods and services to know that the customer actually has sufficient funds in their account just before a payment is due to be taken from the customer's account;

- customer payments data can also be used to reinforce an individual's engagement with a brand. Most obviously this could include showing customers complementary products and services (eg, 'customers like you who bought x also liked y'). It could also involve asking customers to become part of the business strategy team to help with decision making. For example, customers could be asked for their help in deciding which of, say, four potential new suppliers should next be signed-up to the payments scheme. Customer's votes could be displayed in real-time and the outcomes actually implemented and customers thanked for their help.

While AISPs may be able to assist customers who operate a number of bank accounts it is worth noting that the number of multiple accounts varies widely across Europe.[65] On average only 19% of customers have more than two bank accounts.[66] Often one account is used for current expenditure and income while the other operates as a savings account. It would be particularly useful for incumbent banks to provide this service to their customers and at the same time see the details of various other accounts held.

One group of consultants consider 'Europe has not seen any significant shifts in this part of the supply side just yet, and a successful model has still to emerge that is able to draw meaningful volumes from the system'.[67] Nevertheless, some 9% of bank retail payments revenue may be under threat by 2020.[68]

In view of the fast-changing nature of the market and technology the EU will probably keep PSD II under close review. Much will depend on the level of trust demonstrated by customers and this, in turn, will depend on the level of fraud, both actual and perceived, by customers.[69]

5 PSD II as a global regulatory model

The EU's PSD II is the 'gold standard' for the development of 'open banking' and this Directive is considered in more detail later. A number of other jurisdictions have considered PSD II and have taken their own paths which focus on aspects relevant to their own circumstances.[70] A number of these are considered next.

---

65 Financial Times, 'One in Four UK Consumers Has More Than One Current Account', the percentage of customers with more than one active bank account varies widely across Europe: 25% 'in the UK, 62% in Germany, 40% in Italy etc.' (17 July 2015).

66 EY, 'The customer takes control: Global Consumer Banking Survey 2012', 10–11.

67 Oliver Wyman, 'EU Retail and SME Payments: The State of the Industry' (2016), 54.

68 Olly Jackson, 'PSD2 Gives Banks Chance to Evolve' (2018) International Financial Law Review 1–4, 4.

69 European Payments Council, '2017 Payment Threats and Fraud Trends' (2018), 40–41.

70 Brian Yap, 'New EU Payment Services Rules Spur New Regulation in Japan' (2017) International Financial Law Review 1–4.

5.1 *Mexico*

The payments infrastructure is poorly developed in Mexico with more than half the population not having a bank account.[71] This falls to less than six percent in rural areas.[72] According to the Bank of International Settlements, in 2012, only thirteen card transactions were carried out per inhabitant, eight of which were made with debit cards, and five with credit cards; fewer than in, for example, Brazil, Turkey or Russia.[73] The government of former President Peña Nieto wanted to significantly increase financial inclusion and with the Council on National Inclusion, a Federal government body, determined, among other strategies to move to an 'open banking' system to encourage greater access to financial services. As a consequence, in 2018, the Federal government enacted legislation to facilitate 'open banking' under the supervision of the National Banking and Securities Commission (CNBV, its Spanish initials).[74]

For example, in concert with this approach, BBVA, a large Spanish bank, has recently agreed an 'open banking' arrangement with Uber in Mexico allowing Uber drivers to access an on-line bank account which 'will "live" on a third party's platform'.[75] The hope that this will enable the on-line based business to grow with more customers using electronic payments systems. This may help to move much of the economy away from informal employment and cash-based arrangements.

Mexico is currently piloting 'open banking' and will issue a further tranche of legislation in this area in March 2020. It is possible that its technical standards may be based on those adopted in the UK. The government of the current President, Andres Manuel Lopez Obrador recently announced plans for a central bank operated mobile phone payments system known as CoDi.[76] The new system will allow consumers to make payments direct to buy goods and services. However, it requires them to have an account at an existing payments provider. This includes, currently, the established banks, while others will need to apply for payment licences to operate this service.[77]

5.2 *Australia*

Australia is also concerned with the need to increase competition in financial services and in ensuring that consumers 'got a "fairer deal".[78] However, the government has focused on consumer data rather than payments.

As a result, of three Australian government reports (the Murray Inquiry in 2014, the Harper Review in 2015, and the Coleman Report in 2016) in 2018 the House of Representatives Standing Committee on Economics recommended that personal and business customers be

71 World Bank, 'Mexico: More Than Half of the Households Don't Have a Bank Account' (12 December 2012).
72 Ibid., (World Bank – Mexico).
73 Consejo Nacional De Inclusión Financiera, *Financial Inclusion Report 2014*, 119.
74 Department of Finance website, 'Ley Para Regular Las Instituciones de Tecnología Financieral' (March 2018).
75 https://www.bbva.com/en/.
76 Reuters, 'Mexico Pushes Mobile Payments to Help Unbanked Consumers Ditch Cash' (19 February 2019).
77 Ibid., (Reuters).
78 Australian Parliament, 'The Standing Committee on Economics will inquire into and report on a review of Australia's Four Major Banks'.

given the right to access and transfer their bank data to designated third parties.[79] This new Consumer Data Right (CDR) regime will be supervised by the Australian Competition and Consumer Commission (ACCC) since the primary aim is to increase competition in the payment services market. The Australian plans follow the UK's data transfer arrangements.[80] The CDR came into effect for the four largest Australian banks in 2019 for all data relating to credit and debit cards and deposit and transaction accounts. The CDR will be extended to other banks and products through 2020 and 2021.[81]

5.3 *Canada*

The Canadian Department of Finance has issued a consultation paper on 'open banking' asking some very broad questions on whether and to what extent 'open banking' might provide 'meaningful benefits; how should risks be managed and what should be the role of the Federal government?'[82] The Canadian focus is mainly on the benefits and risks to consumers and small businesses with little emphasis on developing fintech and financial services firms.[83]

The Canadian's have emphasised the use of consumer data with little mention of payment services. However, the Canadian consultation does acknowledge what is happening in a number of other jurisdictions including the EU and UK. Consequently, a small section of the consultation is devoted to considering payment services: 'Payments Canada is currently working towards the modernization of the infrastructure for retail and large value payments systems. Should the Government proceed with "open banking", appropriate staging and alignment with payments modernization would be undertaken'.[84] Although Canada's national payment systems provider considers that 'open banking' may one day increase competition it is clear that thought in this area is at a very early stage.[85]

5.4 *Japan*

Japan lacks a generally accepted payment services network equivalent, for example, to China's Alipay and WeChat Pay with the consequence that most transactions are undertaken using cash.[86] Japan's Banking Act (Act No. 59 of 1981) was amended in 2018 to encourage the development of 'open banking'. The new legislation is similar to PSD II but its application for banks is voluntary. Moreover, most current services provide read-only access to account information.[87] The Japanese government expects that most of the banks will open up to APIs by 2020.

---

79 Australian Treasury, 'Review into Open Banking in Australia Issues Paper' (August 2017), 1.
80 Ibid., (Issues Paper), 2 and 3.
81 https://treasury.gov.au/sites/default/files/2019-03/Review-into-Open-Banking-_For-web-1.pdf.
82 Canadian Department of Finance, 'Consultation Document: Review into the Merits of Open Banking' (January 2019), ii.
83 Ibid., (Canadian consultation), 1.
84 Ibid., (Canadian consultation), 5–6.
85 Payments Canada, 'Open Banking for the Common Good?' (20 June 2019).
86 Sean Creehan and Paul Tierno, 'The Slow Introduction of Open Banking and APIs in Japan' (2 May 2019), Federal Reserve Bank of San Francisco, https://www.frbsf.org/banking/asia-program/pacific-exchanges-podcast/open-banking-apis-japan/.
87 Ibid., (Creehan and Tierno) and Fingleton and Open Data Institute, 'Open Banking Preparing for Lift-off' (July 2019), 20.

6 Risks

6.1 *Operational risks*

Both AISPs and PISPs, and the providers of similar forms of customer payments and data sharing services across a number of jurisdictions, must ensure that customer information is protected and not disclosed without the customer's express consent and that payments will be made for the right amount to the right person, on time in accordance with the customer's express command.

Operationally, meeting these requirements may be difficult. There may be system design and implementation failures. Additionally, there are many individuals and organisations that may frequently seek to disrupt the process and abstract data and divert funds. Defeating these attacks requires, sound processes and structures, highly trained and trustworthy staff and fast and transparent actions and communications both to prevent and limit any damage.

6.2 *De-risking and non-discrimination requirements*

There are further issues relating to anti-money laundering, sanctions enforcement and reputational risk revolving around banks 'de-risking' their connection with various payment intermediaries. 'In recent years, the international remittance services industry has been subject to the so-called 'de-risking' phenomenon. Banks believe that anti-money laundering and counter financing of terrorism regulations and enforcement practices have made serving money transfer operators too risky from a legal and reputational perspective'.[88] Much of this concern has its origins in increased US aggressive enforcement actions which besides bank capital threating fines has resulted in the forced expulsion of senior bank executives.[89] These risks need to be balanced with the non-discrimination requirements embedded in PSD II.[90] The FCA has attempted to address this aspect by requiring firms to assess granting 'access on a proportionate, objective and non-discriminatory basis ... [and] has applied its criteria consistently ... The FCA acknowledge[s] that credit institutions will each have their own established criteria reflecting, for example, business need and risk appetite'.[91] The FCA further states that 'credit institutions are not under any compulsion to provide the products or services in question'.[92]

6.3 *Internal systems of control*

Although service providers may not require large capital and liquidly reserves they do need to have all the other attributes of a sound business such as good governance, ethics and

---

88 Marco Nicoli, 'De-risking and Remittances: The Myth of the "Underlying Transaction" Debunked', World Bank (13 June 2013).
89 'The New York State Department of Financial Services is announcing BNP Paribas has agreed to, among other things, terminate or separate from the bank 13 employees, including the Group Chief Operating Officer and other senior executives', US Department of Justice website 'BNP Paribas Agrees to Plead Guilty and to Pay $8.9 Billion for Illegally Processing Financial Transactions for Countries Subject to U.S. Economic Sanctions' (30 June 2014).
90 PSD II, Article 35.
91 FCA, 'Implementation of the Revised Payment Services Directive' (PS17/19), 62.
92 Ibid., (PS17/19), 62.

culture, risk management and people policies and practice.[93] In carrying out its supervisory role the FCA will be heavily dependent on market information and the very detailed reporting requirements from individual regulated entities.[94]

6.4 *Changing business models and data protection*

Many of the existing payment institutions are determined not to be 'out-flanked' by significant new entrants into the payments market. The evidence is that they are buying up potential competitors or coopting them.[95] The European Banking Authority has noted that some traditional payments firms are developing new business models around customer data-analytics.[96] This information is being used for customer profiling, marketing etc. and this 'may pose privacy concerns that need to be understood and addressed in order to prevent detriment to consumer protection. Data access and customer consent are becoming prominent, placing customer trust as one of the cornerstones of the upcoming data-driven environment'.[97] Established banks have carried out these activities for many years devising, for example, 'customer propensity to buy models' using their in-house data. PSD II and 'open banking' provides an opportunity for them to use a much wider swathe of information to plug into their models.

6.5 *Regulatory focus*

The likelihood of PSD II and 'open banking' being successful and meeting their objectives depends heavily on close regulatory attention. It is not clear, for example, from its public statements, that these areas are high priorities for the FCA. There is almost no mention of them in the regulator's most recent Business Plan and the perception is that the FCA have other, more pressing concerns.[98] This is also evident from recent speeches by FCA staff.[99]

7 The current consumer's perspective

It is central to the success of the PSD II that the offering provided by businesses are attractive to consumers. Initial reaction in the UK is one of indifference.[100] This may be due to simple lack of awareness or it may be that the potential benefits accrue to others rather than the consumer. Only 14% of those aged between 18 and 24 years had heard of the term and even when clearly explained to all age groups only 18% understood of ways in which they might usefully use the facilities and only 14% believed that it would benefit consumers generally.[101] The main issue was a lack of trust in data security with only 12% saying that they would be prepared to share their financial data in return for access to new and innovative products and services.[102]

---

93 Ibid., (PS17/19), 73 and following.
94 Ibid., (PS17/19), 74 and following.
95 EBA, 'Impact of Fintech on Payment Institutions' (July 2019), 32.
96 Ibid., (EBA), 32.
97 Ibid., (EBA), 32.
98 FCA Business Plan 2019/20, 22.
99 Nick Cook, FCA Director of Innovation, 'From Innovation Hub to Innovation Culture' (speech on 5 June 2019) <https://www.fca.org.uk/news/speeches/innovation-hub-innovation-culture> accessed 26 December 2019.
100 Yougov, 'Three Quarters of Britons Haven't Heard of Open Banking' (1 August 2018).
101 Ibid., (Yougov survey).
102 Ibid., (Yougov survey).

8 Conclusion

PSD II and 'open banking' are being developed for a range of purposes across the globe. These stretch from social engineering in Mexico to potentially undermining the role of the global credit card companies. It represents the use of regulation to restructure markets and, in some cases, society. In a continuing pursuit of these objectives, and as technology changes, there may be further regulatory iterations of PSD II.

Bibliography

Australian Treasury, 'Review into open banking in Australia Issues Paper' (August 2017) <https://treasury.gov.au/sites/default/files/2019-03/Review-into-Open-Banking-IP.pdf> accessed 22 October 2019.

Bloomberg, 'MasterCard Fined $648 million for High EU Card Fees' (22 January 2019) <https://www.bloomberg.com/news/articles/2019-01-22/mastercard-fined-648-million-for-ramping-up-card-fees-in-europe> accessed 14 October 2019.

Alan Brener, 'Payment Service Directive II and Its Implications' in T Lynn (ed), *Disrupting Finance*, (Cham, Switzerland: Springer 2018).

Canadian Department of Finance, 'Consultation Document: Review into the Merits of Open Banking' (January 2019) <https://www.fin.gc.ca/activty/consult/2019/ob-bo/pdf/obbo-report-rapport-eng.pdf> accessed 23 October 2019.

Henry Chesbrough, *Open Services Innovation: Rethinking Your Business to Grow and Compete in a New Era* (San Francisco, California: Jossey-Bass 2011).

Iris H-Y Chiu, 'A New Era in Fintech Payment Innovations? A Perspective from the Institutions and Regulation of Payment Systems' (2017) 9(2) Law, Innovation and Technology 190–234.

Elie Cohen, 'Industrial Policies in France: The Old and the New' (2007) 7 Journal of Industry, Competition and Trade 213–227.

Competition and Markets Authority, 'Making Banks Work harder for Customers' (August 2016) <file:///N:/Downloads/overview-of-the-banking-retail-market.pdf> accessed 26 December 2019.

Nick Cook, FCA Director of Innovation, 'From Innovation Hub to Innovation Culture' (speech on 5 June 2019) <https://www.fca.org.uk/news/speeches/innovation-hub-innovation-culture> accessed 26 December 2019.

Sean Creehan and Paul Tierno, 'The Slow Introduction of Open Banking and APIs in Japan' (2 May 2019), Federal Reserve Bank of San Francisco website <https://www.frbsf.org/banking/asia-program/pacific-exchanges-podcast/open-banking-apis-japan/> accessed 21 October 2019.

Dombrovskis, Valdis, Vice-President responsible for Financial Stability, Financial Services and Capital Markets Union, European Commission press release 'Payment Services: Consumers to Benefit from Cheaper, Safer and More Innovative Electronic Payments', Brussels (12 January 2018) <http://europa.eu/rapid/press-release_IP-18-141_en.htm> accessed 30 October 2019.

Mary Donnelly, 'Payments in the Digital Market: Evaluating the Contribution of Payments Services Directive II' (2016) 32 Computer Law and Security Review 827–839.

European Banking Authority, 'Fintech Roadmap' (March 2018) <https://www.eba.europa.eu/documents/10180/1919160/EBA±FinTech±Roadmap.pdf> accessed 23 October 2019.

European Banking Authority, 'Impact of Fintech on Payment Institutions' (July 2019) <https://eba.europa.eu/eba-assesses-impact-of-fintech-on-payment-institutions-and-e-money-institutions-business-models> accessed 27 December 2019.

European Central Bank, 'Card Payments in Europe – Current Landscape and Future Prospects: A Eurosystem Perspective' (17 April 2019) <https://www.ecb.europa.eu/pub/pubbydate/2019/html/ecb.cardpaymentsineu_currentlandscapeandfutureprospects201904~30d4de2fc4.en.html#toc1> accessed 14 October 2019.

European Commission, 'Fact Sheet – Payment Services Directive II: Frequently asked questions' (2018) <http://europa.eu/rapid/press-release_MEMO-15-5793_en.htm> accessed 28 October 2019.

European Commission, 'Study on the impact of Directive 2007/64/EC on payment services in the internal market and on the application of Regulation (EC) NO 924/2009 on cross-border payments in the Community', Final Report (2013) <https://paymentinstitutions.eu/wp-content/uploads/2017/08/130724_study-impact-psd_en.pdf> accessed 14 October 2019.

European Payments Council, '2017 Payment Threats and Fraud Trends' (2018) <https://www.europeanpaymentscouncil.eu/document-library/guidance-documents/2018-payment-threats-and-fraud-trends-report> accessed 29 October 2019.

EY, 'The Customer Takes Control: Global Consumer Banking Survey' (2012) <http://www.ey.com/Publication/vwLUAssets/ey-global-consumer-banking-survey-2012/$FILE/ey-global-consumer-banking-survey-2012.pdf> accessed 28 October 2019.

Financial Conduct Authority, 'Implementation of the Revised Payment Services Directive', (PS17/19) (2017) <https://www.fca.org.uk/publications/policy-statements/ps17-19-implementation-revised-payment-services-directive> accessed 27 December 2019.

Financial Conduct Authority, Business Plan 2019/20 (2019) <https://www.fca.org.uk/publication/business-plans/business-plan-2019-20.pdf> accessed 26 December 2019.

Financial Times, 'One in Four UK Consumers Has More Than One Current Account' (17 July 2015) <https://www.ft.com/content/c814328c-2bc0-11e5-8613-e7aedbb7bdb7> accessed 19 October 2019.

Financial Times, 'Visa and Mastercard to Cut Foreign Card Fees in EU: Latest Concession in Payment Companies' Long-running Antitrust Battle with Brussels' (29 April 2019) <https://www.ft.com/content/a2b9544a-6a73-11e9-a9a5-351eeaef6d84> accessed 14 October 2019.

Fingleton and Open Data Institute, 'Open Banking Preparing for Lift-off' (July 2019) <https://www.openbanking.org.uk/wp-content/uploads/open-banking-report-150719.pdf> accessed 23 October 2019.

Robert Maximilian Grüschow, Jan Kemper and Malte Brettel, 'How Do Different Payment Methods Deliver Cost and Credit Efficiency in Electronic Commerce? (2016) 18 Electronic Commerce Research and Applications 27–36.

Olly Jackson, 'PSD2 Gives Banks Chance to Evolve' (January 2018) International Financial Law Review 1–4.

Steve Mansfield-Devin, 'Open Banking: Opportunity and Danger' (October 2016) Computer Fraud and Security 8–13.

Mick McAteer, 'Fintech, Big Data, and the Open Banking "Revolution"' (speech given on 1 February 2017), Financial Inclusion Centre web-site <http://inclusioncentre.co.uk/wordpress29/speeches-and-presentations> accessed 26 December 2019.

Mexico, Consejo Nacional De Inclusión Financiera, Financial Inclusion Report 2014 <https://www.cnbv.gob.mx/en/Inclusion/Documents/Reportes%20de%20IF/Reporte%20de%20Inclusión%20Financiera%206.pdf> accessed 21 October 2019.

Marco Nicoli, 'De-risking and Remittances: The Myth of the "Underlying Transaction" Debunked', World Bank website (13 June 2013) <https://blogs.worldbank.org/psd/de-risking-and-remittances-myth-underlying-transaction-debunked> accessed 27 December 2019.

Paolo Pinotti, 'Trust, Regulation and Market Failures' (August 2012) 94(3) The Review of Economics and Statistics 650–658.

Inna Romānova and others, 'The Payment Services Directive II and Competitiveness: the Perspective of European Fintech Companies' (2018) XXI(2) European Research Studies Journal 3–22.

UK Government, 'Boost for Small Businesses Seeking Finance Thanks to Government Data Sharing Scheme' (April 2016) <https://www.gov.uk/government/news/boost-for-small-businesses-seeking-finance-thanks-to-government-data-sharing-scheme> accessed 29 October 2019.

Oliver Wyman, 'EU Retail and SME Payments: The State of the Industry' (2016) <http://www.oliverwyman.com/content/dam/oliver-wyman/v2/publications/2016/Nov/European-Retail-and-SME-Payments-web.pdf> accessed 28 October 2019.

Brian Yap, 'New EU Payment Services Rules Spur New Regulation in Japan' (2017) International Financial Law Review 1–4.

Yougov 'Three Quarters of Britons Haven't Heard of Open Banking' (1 August 2018) <https://yougov.co.uk/topics/finance/articles-reports/2018/08/01/three-quarters-britons-havent-heard-open-banking> accessed 19 October 2019.

10 Current and future liability concepts in European financial market regulation

Marte Eidsand Kjørven

1 Introduction[1]

The relationship between European financial market regulation and national civil law rules on contracts and torts has been debated extensively over the past decade.[2] EU law has traditionally favoured public enforcement of financial market regulation.[3] Hence, for a long time, it did not address questions related to private law liability. While the obligations of financial service providers are often regulated in detail, the private law implications of non-compliance are dealt with by the Member States of the European Union, who are required to comply with the principles of equivalence and effectiveness.[4] While the European legal framework for financial services does not provide a coherent regulatory policy for liability, a number of specific rules nevertheless apply.

Discussions concerning liability in European financial market regulation form part of a more general discussion about the role of liability rules in European law. In particular, the development of new technologies raises the question of whether the European legal framework facilitates the development of a digital single market in which consumers are sufficiently protected against the inherent risks of new technologies while

---

1 My preliminary ideas on the topic of this chapter were presented at the international conference 'Innovation and other Contemporary Pivotal Issues in Financial Markets Law and Company Law – Selected National, International, European and Comparative Views' at Sapienza University of Rome, 13 December 2019. I am grateful to Professor Gudula Deipenbrock and Professor Paola Chirulli for the invitation.

2 Danny Busch, 'Why MiFID Matters to Private Law – the Example of MiFID's Impact on an Asset Manager's Civil Liability' (2012) 7 Capital Markets Law Journal 386; Olha O Cherednychenko, 'Public and Private Enforcement of European Private Law in the Financial Services Sector' (2015) 4 European Review of Private Law 621; Christos Hadjiemmanuil, 'The Banking Union and Its Implications for Private Law: A Comment' (2015) 16 European Business Organization Law Review 383; Danny Busch, 'The Private Law Effect on MiFID: The Genil Case and Beyond' (2017) 13 European Review of Contract Law 70; Gudula Deipenbrock, 'Private Enforcement in the Realm of European Capital Markets Law Revisited and the Case of Credit Rating Agencies from the Perspective of European and German Law' (2018) 29 European Business Law Review 549; Federico Della Negra, *MiFID II and Private Law: Enforcing EU Conduct of Business Rules* (Bloomsbury Publishing 2019); Marnix Wallinga, 'Why MiFID & MiFID II Do (Not) Matter to Private Law: Liability to Compensate for Investment Losses for Breach of Conduct of Business Rules' (2019) 3 European Review of Private Law 515; Olha O Cherednychenko, 'Rediscovering the Public/private Divide in EU Private Law' [2019] European Law Journal 1 <https://doi.org/10.1111/eulj.12351> accessed 18 June 2020.

3 Della Negra (n 2) 25.

4 See Court of Justice of the European Union, Case C-604/11 *Genil 48 SL Comercial Hostelera de Grandes Vinos SL v Bankinter SA Banco Bilbao Vizcaya Argentaria SA* [2013] OJ C 225/25.

technological innovation is still encouraged. The European Commission (Commission) recently published a report on the safety and liability implications of artificial intelligence (AI), the Internet of Things (IoT) and robotics (Liability AI Report), concluding that the current legal framework was insufficient.[5] This is also highly relevant to liability questions related to financial services. AI is already widely deployed in financial services – in the fields of credit scoring, fraud prevention and portfolio management, for example.[6] As emphasised by the Commission, these technological developments challenge traditional European and national liability rules and in particular the concept of fault in the case of loss caused by AI.[7]

In this chapter, we consider the different approaches to liability in current European financial market regulation, in order to assess whether there is a need for new liability concepts in light of regulatory objectives. The chapter is organised as follows: Section 2 explores the role of liability rules in European financial market regulation in light of regulatory objectives. It is argued that, given the objectives of financial stability and consumer and investor protection, questions of liability should be addressed by European law. Section 3 discusses current approaches to liability in European financial market regulation. In Section 4, we focus on important challenges posed by the current liability concepts in European financial market regulation and some possible solutions. The chapter argues that the current fragmentation in the realm of liability provisions is inappropriate. It calls upon European legislators to develop new liability concepts, particularly in order to address safety issues linked to the use of new technologies in financial services.

2 The role of liability rules in European financial market regulation in light of regulatory objectives

Prior to the 2008 financial crisis, financial market regulation was concerned mainly with market-based governance.[8] The crisis made it evident that this approach was untenable. In the last decade, financial market regulation appears to have taken a more risk-based approach, focusing primarily on systemic risk and financial stability.[9] It is not yet entirely clear how the contours of financial stability as an objective of financial market regulation should be defined, but its central purpose seems to be the mitigation and allocation of risk

---

5 Commission, 'Report on the Safety and Liability Implications of Artificial Intelligence, the Internet of Things and Robotics (Liability AI Report)' COM(2020) 64 final.
6 Crispin Coombs and Raghav Chopra, 'Artificial Intelligence and Data Analytics: Emerging Opportunities and Challenges in Financial Services' (2019) CAPCO The Capco Institute Journal of Financial Transformation 54, 54.
7 Commission, COM(2020) 64 final (n 5) 13.
8 Mads Andenas and Iris H-Y Chiu, *The Foundations and Future of Financial Regulation: Governance for Responsibility* (Routledge 2014) 18; Niamh Moloney, *EU Securities and Financial Markets Regulation* (3rd edn, Oxford University Press 2014) 3.
9 Andenas and Chiu (n 8) 18; Moloney (n 8) 4–6. According to Recital 3 of Regulation (EU) 2019/2176 of the European Parliament and of the Council of 18 December 2019 amending Regulation (EU) No 1092/2010 on European Union macro-prudential oversight of the financial system and establishing a European Systemic Risk Board [2019] OJ L 334/146 (Systemic Risk Regulation) the 'ESRB should contribute to preventing or mitigating systemic risks to financial stability in the Union and thereby to achieving the objectives of the internal market'.

in financial markets.[10] In recent years, consumer and investor protection have also become independent goals of financial market regulation, above and beyond their role in achieving efficiency in financial markets.[11] The precise purpose of consumer and investor protection is not entirely clear, but it involves ensuring that financial institutions treat their customers fairly and with transparency, such that consumers and investors are given clear and relevant information and are provided with financial products that match their individual needs.[12]

To enhance financial stability and consumer and investor protection, financial market regulation must address the risk of insufficient cybersecurity and of cybercrime.[13] Hence, deterrence and mitigation of risk related to cybercrime in financial markets have also become increasingly important.[14] In fact, recognising the potential threat to financial stability, the European Parliament has called upon the Commission 'to make cybersecurity the number one priority in the FinTech action plan'.[15] Moreover because the consequences of cybercrime can be personally and economically devastating, the Commission has emphasised that individual protection against such crime is also a fundamental rights issue.[16]

The objectives of financial stability on the one hand and investor and consumer protection on the other are closely related, since a failure to protect individual investors or consumers may also have systemic effects.[17] This was evident in the 2008 financial crisis, caused amongst other things by the widespread mis-selling of financial products. The International Organization of Securities Commissions (IOSCO) explains how systemic risk can take the form of a 'gradual erosion of market trust caused by inadequate investor protection

10 For more information on the objective of financial stability and how it relates to systemic risk, see Andenas and Chiu (n 8) 27–42. On the objective of financial stability under EU law, see more specifically Gianno Lo Schiavo, *The Role of Financial Stability in EU Law and Policy* (Wolters Kluwer 2017). According to Article 1(1)c of the Systemic Risk Regulation, systemic risk is defined as 'a risk of disruption in the financial system with the potential to have serious negative consequences for the real economy'.
11 Della Negra (n 2) 7. According to the Commission, the objectives for the European financial services policy is to 'contribute to an environment that protects consumers, promotes market integrity and supports investment, growth and jobs'; see <https://ec.europa.eu/info/business-economy-euro/banking-and-finance/financial-reforms-and-their-progress/financial-services-policy_en> accessed 16 March 2020.
12 ESMA on investor protection, see <https://www.esma.europa.eu/regulation/mifid-ii-and-investor-protection> accessed June 2020. UK Financial Conduct Authority, *A New Regulator for the New Millennium* (FCA January 2000) identifies prudential risk, bad faith risk and complexity/unsuitability risk as forms of risk where the FSA has a role to play in identifying and reducing risk as part of the consumer protection objective. For more information on the relationship between investor protection and consumer protection, see Niamh Moloney, 'The Investor Model Underlying the EU's Investor Protection Regime: Consumers or Investors?' (2012) 13 European Business Organization Law Review 169.
12 Andenas and Chiu (n 8) 135–136.
13 Commission, 'FinTech Action Plan: For a More Competitive and Innovative European Financial Sector', COM(2018) 109 final, 2–3.
14 For more information on cybersecurity as a key issue in progressing digitalisation, see Gudula Deipenbrock, 'Fintech – Unbearably Lithe or Reasonably Agile?' (2020) 31 European Business Law Review 3.
15 Commission, COM(2018) 109 final (n 13) 16.
16 Commission, 'A Digital Single Market Strategy for Europe', COM(2015) 192 final, 12.
17 Andenas and Chiu (n 8) 135–136; Hilary J Allen, 'Financial Stability Regulation as Indirect Investor/Consumer Protection Regulation: Implications for Regulatory Mandates and Structure' (2016) 90 Tulane Law Review 1113.

standards, lax enforcement, insufficient disclosure requirements, inadequate resolution regimes or other factors'.[18]

Liability rules aim to mitigate and allocate individual economic risk. As emphasised by the Commission in the Liability AI Report, liability rules 'play a double role in society: on the one hand, they ensure that victims of a damage caused by others get compensation and, on the other hand, they provide economic incentives for the liable party to avoid causing such damage'.[19] Hence, in combination with rules on market behaviour, liability rules might contribute to the goal of consumer and investor protection in both a preventive and a compensatory way. For example, mis-selling of investment products is addressed ex-ante by the product governance requirements under Article 16(3) of Directive 2014/65/EU on markets in financial instruments (MiFID II)[20] which aims to ensure that financial instruments are designed to meet the needs of an identified category of clients. Rules on liability after the mis-selling of unsuitable investment products might provide an additional incentive to comply with the product governance rules, while also ensuring that investors are individually compensated in situations of mis-selling.

If a considerable amount of damage is avoided as a result of the preventive function of liability rules, such rules contribute to financial stability by mitigating the risk of damage. Liability rules might also contribute to financial stability in a more indirect way by helping to enhance trust in financial markets. The observed shift from market governance to risk governance and consumer and investor protection has highlighted the role of liability issues in financial market regulation.

However, the compensatory function of liability rules may also endanger financial stability, in particular if claims for damages are directed on a large scale against systemically important financial institutions. Hence, we see that ex-ante investor protection through liability rules may conflict with the objective of financial stability. The European Security and Markets Authority (ESMA) has addressed this conflict of objectives in the context of securities markets with the liability rules for depositaries under Directive 2011/61/EU on alternative investment fund managers (AIFMD)[21].[22] The need to strike this balance might lead to somewhat contradictory results, with the introduction of liability rules aimed at enhancing investor protection in fact leading to decreased investor protection in some Member States. This is because EU law interferes with national concepts of liability, which may go further in protecting consumers or investors than the European liability rule.

---

18 Technical Committee of the International Organization of Securities Commissions (OICV-IOSCO), 'Mitigating Systemic Risk: A Role for Securities Regulators Discussion Paper' OR01/11 (February 2011).

19 Commission, COM(2020) 64 final (n 5) 12.

20 Directive 2014/65/EU of the European Parliament and of the Council of 15 May 2014 on markets in financial instruments and amending Directive 2002/92/EC and Directive 2011/61/EU [2014] OJ L173/349 (MiFID II).

21 Directive 2011/61/EU of the European Parliament and of the Council of 8 June 2011 on Alternative Investment Fund Managers and amending Directives 2003/41/EC and 2009/65/ EC and Regulations (EC) No 1060/2009 and (EU) No 1095/2010 [2011] OJ L174/1 (AIFMD).

22 ESMA, 'Final report ESMA's technical advice to the European Commission on possible implementing measures of the Alternative Investment Fund Managers Directive', ESMA /2011/379 (16 November 2011): 'ESMA has strived to strike the right balance between the Directive's objective to set strict rules ensuring a high level of investor protection while at the same time not putting the entire responsibility on the depositaries, as this would be potentially counterproductive by creating the incentive for regulatory arbitrage and in some cases leading to increased systemic risk'.

3 Different approaches to liability in current European financial market regulation

3.1 *General remarks*

European financial market regulation lacks a coherent approach when dealing with issues of liability. The chapter now looks into some of the different approaches to issues of liability in current European financial market regulation. Section 3.2 considers the approach under MiFID II and Directive 2009/65/EC relating to undertakings for collective investments in transferable securities (UCITS),[23] where Member States are obliged to provide instruments of private enforcement, without stipulating a specific liability concept. The European financial market regulation also contains some fragmented rules on liability regarding non-performance of different types of specific obligations. In Section 3.3, we will look briefly into liability rules under Directive (EU) 2015/2366 on payment services in the internal market (PSD2),[24] AIFMD, Directive 2014/92/EU related to payment accounts (PAD)[25] and Regulation (EU) No 462/2013 on credit rating agencies (CRA Regulation).[26] Though the liability concepts under these directives and regulations differ, they all concern liability for non-performance of obligations. Then, under Section 3.4, we will explore the approach to strict liability for loss following unauthorised payment transactions under PSD2.

3.2 *General obligation to establish private enforcement tools*

The general principles of equivalence and effectiveness, as codified in Article 19(1) of the Treaty on European Union (TEU),[27] imply a duty for Member States to provide remedies sufficient to ensure effective legal protection in the fields covered by EU law. Whether this implies a duty for Member States to have mechanisms for private enforcement of financial market regulation has been debated.[28] However, MiFID II introduced an important provision to foster private enforcement of EU financial market regulation. It

---

23 Directive 2009/65/EC of the European Parliament and of the Council of 13 July 2009 on the coordination of laws, regulations and administrative provisions relating to undertakings for collective investment in transferable securities [2009] OJ L302/32 (UCITS).

24 Directive (EU) 2015/2366 of the European Parliament and of the Council of 25 November 2015 on payment services in the internal market, amending Directives 2002/65/EC, 2009/110/EC and 2013/36/EU and Regulation (EU) No 1093/2010, and repealing Directive 2007/64/EC [2015] OJ L337/35 (PSD2).

25 Directive 2014/92/EU of the European Parliament and of the Council of 23 July 2014 on the comparability of fees related to payment accounts, payment account switching and access to payment accounts with basic features [2014] OJ L257/214 (PAD).

26 Regulation (EU) No 462/2013 of the European Parliament and of the Council of 21 May 2013 amending Regulation (EC) No 1060/2009 on credit rating agencies [2013] OJ L146/1 (CRA Regulation).

27 Consolidated Version of the Treaty on European Union [2012] OJ C362/13.

28 See Mads Andenas and Federico Della Negra, 'Between Contract Law and Financial Regulation: Towards the Europeanisation of General Contract Law' (2017) 28 European Business Law Review 499, 511ff. In Case C-604/11 (n 4), the CJEU held that it was for the internal legal order of each Member State to determine, under the observance of the principles of effectiveness and equivalence, the contractual consequences of non-compliance with the obligations to perform an appropriateness and suitability test under Art 19 of Directive 2004/39/EC of the European Parliament and of the Council of 21 April 2004 on markets in financial instruments amending Council Directives 85/611/EEC and 93/6/EEC and Directive 2000/12/EC of the European Parliament and of the Council and repealing Council Directive 93/22/EEC [2004] OJ L145/1 (MiFID).

follows from Article 69 of MiFID II that Member States must implement mechanisms to 'ensure that compensation may be paid or other remedial action be taken in accordance with national law for any financial loss or damage suffered as a result of an infringement of this Directive'.[29] Originally, the Commission proposed to introduce specific liability rules under MiFID II.[30] Due to differing opinions amongst the Member States and particularly strong objections to such liability rules, the proposed liability rules were eventually removed from the revised directive.[31]

A similar approach is taken in Article 24(1) of UCITS, which provides that a depositary shall, 'in accordance with the national law of the UCITS home Member State, be liable to the management company and the unit-holders for any loss suffered by them as a result of its unjustifiable failure to perform its obligations or its improper performance of them'.

These provisions under MiFID II and UCITS oblige Member States to provide instruments of private enforcement, while refusing to stipulate a specific liability concept. This approach necessarily leads to different solutions in different Member States. Hence, the level of investor and consumer protection as regards private enforcement will differ. Different solutions will also challenge the level playing field. However, the approach makes it possible to ensure seamless integration with national rules on contract and tort.

3.3 *Liability for non-performance of obligations*

European financial market regulation contains some fragmented rules on liability regarding non-performance of different types of specific obligations, including rules under PSD2, AIFMD, PAD and under the CRA Regulation. Article 89 of PSD2 states that where a payment order is initiated directly by the payer, the payer's payment service provider shall be liable to the payer for 'correct execution of the payment transaction'. According to recital 88 of PSD2, a payment transaction is correctly executed when it is executed in accordance with the payment order given by the payment service user. Liability under Article 89 of PSD2 is best understood as contractual liability for non-performance of contractual obligations. However, because PSD2 also defines what constitutes the correct execution of these services to some degree (see, eg, Articles 64 and 88 of PSD2), the liability rule indirectly provides grounds for liability for non-compliance with regulatory duties on how payment transactions must be executed.

When liable under Article 89 of PSD2, the payment service provider must refund to the payer the amount of the non-executed or defective payment transaction and, where applicable, restore the debited payment account to the state in which it would have been had the defective payment transaction not taken place. The liability of the payment service provider for the correct execution of payment transactions is strict, regardless of whether the payment service provider is at fault. However, it follows from Article 93 of PSD2 that no liability arises in cases of abnormal and unforeseeable circumstances beyond the control of the party pleading for the application of those circumstances, the consequences of which

---

29 For more information on Art 69 of MiFID II, see Federico Della Negra, 'The Effects of the ESMA's Powers on Domestic Contract Law' in Mads Andenas and Gudula Deipenbrock (eds), *Regulating and Supervising European Financial Markets: More Risks than Achievements* (Springer 2016) 155.

30 Commission, 'Consultation on the review of the Markets in Financial Instruments Directive (MiFID)' (Public consultation) (8 December 2010) 63.

31 Della Negra (n 29) 155.

would have been unavoidable despite all efforts to the contrary, or where a payment service provider is bound by other legal obligations covered by EU or national law.

This implies strict liability with a force majeure exception for the correct execution of payment services. Recital 85 of PSD2 refers here to the fact that it is the payment service provider that provides the payment system, makes arrangements to recall misplaced or wrongly allocated funds and decides, in most cases, on the intermediaries involved in the execution of a payment transaction.

A similar liability concept follows from Article 21(12) of AIFMD, which imposes strict liability with a force majeure exception for the loss of financial instruments held in custody by a depositary on behalf of investors in an alternative investment fund. For breach of the obligation to keep the financial instruments safe, the depositary is liable regardless of fault. However, in all other situations, liability arises under Article 21(12) of AIFMD for losses suffered 'as a result of the depositary's negligent or intentional failure to properly fulfil its obligations pursuant to this Directive'. Hence, except for the obligation to keep financial instruments safe, liability for loss following the breach of other obligations is based on fault. The difference in the choice of liability concept may be explained by the character of the different obligations. The obligation to keep financial instruments safe is, after all, the core contractual obligation a depositary has towards the alternative investment fund and its investors.

AIFMD also regulates liability for professionals who act as external valuers. According to Article 19(10) of AIFMD, an external valuer will be liable for losses as a result of 'negligence or intentional failure to perform its tasks'. The directive gives no guidance as to how the concept of fault should be understood. While AIFMD regulates liability for depositaries and external valuers, questions of liability for other actors remain unregulated. Hence, the fund management company's obligation to ensure the proper execution of the fund management service is not covered by the directive.

In order to enhance competition between payment service providers and protect consumers, PAD harmonises the process of switching payment accounts. According to Article 10 of PAD, payment service providers are obliged to offer consumers a clear, quick and safe procedure to switch payment accounts. Article 13 of PAD imposes strict liability with a force majeure exception for losses incurred from non-compliance with obligations under Article 10 in relation to the process of switching payment accounts. Here then, the liability concept is similar to the liability rules under PSD2 and AIFMD described above.

Article 35a of the CRA Regulation provides that an investor or issuer may claim damages from a credit rating agency where the latter has committed – intentionally or with gross negligence – any of the infringements listed in Annex III as having an impact on a credit rating. Instead of trying to define what terms such as 'damage', 'gross negligence' and 'intention' mean, Article 35a of the CRA Regulation states that these terms should be 'interpreted and applied in accordance with the applicable national law as determined by the relevant rules of private international law'. The result is a semi-harmonised liability concept, which depends partly on European law and partly on national concepts of liability, leading to potentially unpredictable results. The liability regime under the CRA Regulation has been extensively analysed by Deipenbrock, who concluded that it constituted an 'example of an ill-conceived private enforcement tool'.[32] The argument is that this liability regime is complex and raises more questions

---

32 Deipenbrock (n 2) 575.

than it solves, in particular with regard to the interplay with national rules on liability and private international law.[33]

3.4 *Strict liability for loss following unauthorised payment transactions*

As explained in section 3.3, PSD2 includes rules on liability for the correct execution of payment transactions. However, PSD2 also sets out a detailed liability regime for unauthorised payment transactions, with the main rules following from Articles 73 and 74.[34] The rules impose strict liability for payment service providers for loss caused by an unauthorised payment transaction. In particular, this places the risk associated with unsecured technical solutions for the execution of payment transactions on the payment service provider. For example, if payment card credentials are misused by a fraudster to initiate an unauthorised payment transaction, the default rule is that liability for the resulting loss lies with the payment service provider. Article 74(1) of PSD2 clarifies the consequences of contributory negligence by stating that the 'payer shall bear all of the losses relating to any unauthorised payment transactions if they were incurred by the payer acting fraudulently or failing to fulfil one or more of the obligations set out in Art. 69 with intent or gross negligence'.[35]

The PSD2 liability regime for unauthorised payment transactions places the risk related to insufficient cybersecurity in digital payment services on the payment service provider, regardless of fault or compliance with duties. A number of technical standards exist for payment services, including those set out in Regulation (EU) 2018/389 with regard to regulatory technical standards for strong customer authentication and common and secure open standards of communication.[36] However, even when strong customer authentication is used in compliance with this technical standard, the payment service provider remains liable for loss resulting from third-party fraud or technical problems. This may have contributed to the technical innovations that we have witnessed in the area of fraud detection, which go well beyond legal technical requirements. For example, we have seen a revolution in the development of systems based on AI to prevent fraudulent payment transactions from going through.[37] Using such systems is not legally required under European law but the liability regime under PSD2 has certainly encouraged the development of such systems.

---

33 Deipenbrock (n 2) 575.
34 For a thorough discussion of the liability regime for unauthorised payment transactions under PSD2, see Marte Eidsand Kjørven, 'Who Pays When Things Go Wrong Online: Financial Fraud and Consumer Protection in Scandinavia and Europe' (2020) 31 European Business Law Review 77.
35 PSD2 leaves the concept of intent and gross negligence undefined, leaving it up to national traditions and decision makers to determine its interpretation on a rather ad hoc basis, see Kjørven (n 34) 97.
36 Commission Delegated Regulation (EU) 2018/389 of 27 November 2017 supplementing Directive (EU) 2015/2366 of the European Parliament and of the Council with regard to regulatory technical standards for strong customer authentication and common and secure open standards of communication [2017] OJ L 69/23.
37 Louis Colombus, 'How AI Is Protecting against Payments Fraud' *Forbes* (5 September 2019) <www.forbes.com/sites/louiscolumbus/2019/09/05/how-ai-is-protecting-against-payments-fraud/#5b-1887ba4d29> accessed 18 June 2020.

4 Development of future liability concepts in European financial market regulation

Following the discussion in Section 3, we can see that the liability rules in the field of European financial market regulation are both fragmented and inconsistent. They include a general obligation to put in place private enforcement mechanisms for some financial services, but not for others. Certain liability rules apply to non-compliance, but only for some financial services and some contractual or regulatory duties. These specific liability rules rely on fault in some situations and on strict liability in others. The legal framework includes a detailed liability regime for unauthorised payment transactions, with protection against online financial fraud in payment transactions, but no liability rules for unauthorised transactions with regard to other financial services. Based on these observations, it seems clear that the current liability regimes in European financial market regulation are ill-equipped to achieve the regulatory objectives described in Section 2.[38] More research and evidence on how liability rules can be developed to better achieve the regulatory objectives are needed. In this section, we present some preliminary thoughts on what such new concepts might look like.

Liability rules based on fault, like those under Article 19(10) of AIFMD and Article 35a of the CRA Regulation, seem to be somewhat reactionary in light of the growing complexity of digitalised financial markets and increasing use of AI and algorithms. In its Liability AI Report, the Commission points out that the characteristics of emerging technologies like IoT and AI:

> could make it hard to trace the damage back to a human behaviour, which could give grounds for a fault-based claim in accordance with national rules. This means that liability claims based on national tort laws may be difficult or overly costly to prove and consequently victims may not be adequately compensated.[39]

These more general observations on liability where emerging technologies are concerned are particularly relevant for financial services.[40] Rather than a concept based on fault, a better idea might be to further develop liability rules based on strict liability for the non-performance of obligations, as has been done under Articles 89 and 93 of PSD2, Article 21(12) of AIFMD and Article 13 of PAD. Strict liability with a force majeure exception is also a common liability concept in European consumer contract law. It can be found, for example, in Article 14(3)(c) of the Directive (EU) 2015/2302 on package travel (Package

---

38 It is beyond the scope of this chapter to go into the general legal-political discussions on the EU's power to legislate questions of private enforcement and whether or not they should do so. For further discussion of these issues, see Cherednychenko (n 2); Hans W Micklitz, 'The Transformation of Enforcement in European Private Law: Preliminary Considerations' (2015) 23 European Review of Private Law 491.

39 Commission, COM(2020) 64 final (n 5) 13.

40 For more general discussions on liability issues related to AI in particular, see Iria Giuffrida, 'Liability for AI Decision-Making: Some Legal and Ethical Considerations' (2019) 88 Fordham Law Review 439; Brian Tang, 'Forging a Responsibility and Liability Framework in the AI Era for RegTech' in Janos Barberid and others (eds), *The REGTECH Book: The Financial Technology Handbook for Investors, Entrepreneurs and Visionaries in Regulation* (Wiley 2019).

Travel Directive)[41] and Article 5(3) of Regulation (EC) No 261/2004 on passenger rights (Passenger Rights Regulation).[42] Because the concept of strict liability for the non-performance of obligations has been used in European consumer contract law for a while, the Court of Justice of the European Union (CJEU) has already decided several cases in which non-performance was excused because it followed from an impediment beyond control.[43] Harmonisation is easier to achieve when using a liability concept developed within EU law rather than concepts, like that in the CRA Regulation, which refer to national law.

However, a liability concept based on the non-performance of obligations might not adequately address the risks related to rapid technological and financial innovation, even when the concept relies on strict liability for non-performance. A focus on compliance creates a regime of 'tick-box' rules that may not provide sufficient protection. Regulators are likely to find themselves always one step behind. This was evident in the run-up to the 2008 financial crisis where regulators did not adequately assess the risks inherent in the financial innovation of new products.

In particular, consumers are poorly protected under European law against the risk of cybercrime due to insufficient cybersecurity in the digital use of financial services.[44] The PSD2 liability regime for unauthorised payment transactions provides important consumer protection against loss following cybercrime related to payment services. However, online financial fraud is a growing problem in relation to other financial services as well. Such fraud often includes the misuse of systems for digital authentication and digital signatures. With the information needed to authenticate or sign in another person's name, a fraudster can empty the victim's accounts, obtain credit cards and loans, and make unauthorised investment transactions in the name of the victim.[45] When such fraud does not include an unauthorised payment transaction, the allocation of losses between the financial services provider and the consumer are based on relevant national law. This has had devastating consequences for consumers in Norway, Denmark and Sweden, who are systematically held responsible in credit agreements based on identity theft.[46] If these systems are not providing sufficient security – and it seems they are not if one risks such severe economic losses – one might wonder whether a form of product liability would not be a better solution.

The European Parliament has stressed the need to assess to what extent the existing liability framework – and in particular the Directive 85/374/EEC concerning

---

41 Directive (EU) 2015/2302 of the European Parliament and of the Council of 25 November 2015 on package travel and linked travel arrangements, amending Regulation (EC) No 2006/2004 and Directive 2011/83/EU of the European Parliament and of the Council and repealing Council Directive 90/314/EEC [2015] OJ L326/1 (Package Travel Directive).

42 Regulation (EC) No 261/2004 of the European Parliament and of the Council of 11 February 2004 establishing common rules on compensation and assistance to passengers in the event of denied boarding and of cancellation or long delay of flights, and repealing Regulation (EEC) No 295/91 Regulation (EC) No 261/2004 on passengers rights [2004] OJ L46/1 (Passenger Rights Regulation).

43 See, for example, Court of Justice of the European Union, Cases C-159/18 *André Moens v Ryanair Ltd* [2018] OJ C166/23 and C-315/15 *Marcela Pešková and Jiří Peška v Travel Service a.s.* [2015] OJ C414/12.

44 See Kjørven (n 34) for a thorough analysis of the allocation of losses following online financial fraud under European and Scandinavian law.

45 Kjørven (n 34) 81.

46 Kjørven (n 34) 104.

liability for defective products (Product Liability Directive)[47] – needs to be updated in order to guarantee effective consumer protection and legal clarity for business.[48] According to Article 1 of the Product Liability Directive, the producer is liable for damage caused by a defect in his product. A product is defective under Article 6 of the Product Liability Directive when it does not provide the safety a person is entitled to expect. According to Article 9 of the Product Liability Directive, 'damage' refers to loss caused by death, personal injuries or damage to property. The European Parliament has urged the Commission to examine whether definitions and concepts such as 'products', 'producer' and 'damage' need to be updated due to the specific characteristics of AI applications (namely, complexity, autonomy and opacity). A broader concept of product liability – which might include liability for software – would better protect consumers against risks associated with the digital use of financial services and, in particular, different forms of online financial fraud.

Another idea might be to extend the scope of the liability regime for unauthorised payment transactions under PSD2 to include unauthorised transactions in other financial services. Both the concepts of product liability under the Product Liability Directive and the concept of liability for unauthorised payment transactions under PSD2 share the objectives of promoting loss allocation, reducing transaction costs and enhancing investment in product safety.[49] The second recital of the Product Liability Directive points out that 'liability without fault on the part of the producer is the sole means of adequately solving the problem, peculiar to our age of increasing technicality, of a fair apportionment of the risk inherent in modern technological production'. Correspondingly, the PSD2 liability regime for unauthorised payment transactions allocates the loss resulting from security vulnerabilities in the payment system to payment service providers. In addition, the system encourages payment service providers to enhance safety so as to avoid loss caused by third-party fraud. Because these concepts focus on the mitigation and allocation of risk – rather than assigning moral responsibility – they are better suited to the objectives of financial market regulation than a liability concept based on fault.

In Norway, the legislator is about to extend the scope of the PSD2 liability regime to unauthorised transactions in all types of financial services.[50] In particular, the proposed liability rule will protect against the consequences of online financial fraud, including, for example, unauthorised investment transactions or situations where credit agreements are concluded based on identity theft. As explained, in the Scandinavian countries, consumers are currently held responsible for credit contracts concluded by others in their name

47 Council Directive 85/374/EEC of 25 July 1985 on the approximation of the laws, regulations and administrative provisions of the Member States concerning liability for defective products [1985] OJ L210/29.

48 European Parliament, 'Draft Opinion of the Committee on the Internal Market and Consumer Protection for the Committee on Legal Affairs on Civil Liability Regime for Artificial Intelligence' (28/04/2020) 2020/2014(INL) 3. See also Commission, 'Evaluation of Council Directive 85/374/EEC of 25 July 1985 on the Approximation of the Laws, Regulations and Administrative Provisions of the Member States Concerning Liability for Defective Products' SWD(2018) 157 final, 37.

49 Kathleen M Nilles, 'Defining the Limits of Liability: A Legal and Political Analysis of the European Community Products Liability Directive' (1985) 25 Virginia Journal of International Law 729, 758.

50 Norwegian Ministry of Justice and Public Security, Prop. 92 LS (2019–2020) [2020]. I was employed at the Norwegian Ministry of Justice and Public Security from 2016 to 2017 and worked on the proposal during this time. The proposal is further discussed in Kjørven (n 34) 106–109.

based on a misuse of identification technologies, with devastating consequences for the victims.[51] If the risk of such fraud lay with the financial institution, this would incite financial institutions to enhance security, without the need for regulators to decide precisely how institutions should go about this. The proposal combines this liability rule with another liability rule based on strict liability with a force majeure exception for non-compliance with regulatory duties.

The financial industry in Norway has opposed the proposal. Finance Norway (the central organisation for the financial industry in Norway, representing 240 companies) has demanded that both liability rules be rejected.[52] In their submission, they argue that the proposal will put financial institutions at great risk because there are no limits to their potential responsibility.[53] Under PSD2, the payment service providers' liability is limited to the debit or credit amount available on the account. If the same liability regime is applied to credit-agreement fraud, for example, the potential responsibility for financial institutions would be unlimited. This is an interesting argument because the unlimited risk referred to here already exists. The proposal only shifts the risk from individual consumers – ill-equipped to deal with unlimited risk – to financial institutions.

The Norwegian proposal is interesting in the sense that it suggests liability concepts that are unique in a European context, which disregard traditional distinctions between products and services, between contractual and non-contractual liability, and between 'pure economic loss' and other economic loss. It is often unclear whether we are dealing with a financial product or a service. And it makes little sense that damage to your mobile phone should merit better protection from liability rules than the 'pure economic loss' of losing all your life savings. These distinctions seem unsuited to a complex financial market. The Norwegian proposal raises the question of the appropriate liability concept in financial market regulation. Perhaps it is time for European regulators to start asking some of these questions too?

Bibliography

H J Allen, 'Financial Stability Regulation as Indirect Investor/Consumer Protection Regulation: Implications for Regulatory Mandates and Structure' (2016) 90 Tulane Law Review 1113.

M Andenas and F Della Negra, 'Between Contract Law and Financial Regulation: Towards the Europeanisation of General Contract Law' (2017) 28 European Business Law Review 499.

M Andenas and IHY Chiu, *The Foundations and Future of Financial Regulation: Governance for Responsibility* (Routledge 2014).

D Busch, 'Why MiFID Matters to Private Law – the Example of MiFID's Impact on an Asset Manager's Civil Liability' (2012) 7 Capital Markets Law Journal 386.

D Busch, 'The Private Law Effect on MiFID: The Genil Case and Beyond' (2017) 13 European Review of Contract Law 70.

O O Cherednychenko, 'Public and Private Enforcement of European Private Law in the Financial Services Sector' (2015) 4 European Review of Private Law 621.

---

51 Kjørven (n 34) 104.
52 Finans Norway, *Høringsuttalelse ny finansavtalelov* (15 December 2017) 62 <www.regjeringen.no/ no/dokumenter/horing—revisjon-av-finansavtaleloven/id2569865/?uid=af7f501c-5781-4635-b9b4-1f72c4a14fa4> accessed 18 June 2020.
53 Finans Norway (n 52) 2.

O O Cherednychenko, 'Rediscovering the Public/private Divide in EU Private Law' (2019) European Law Journal 1.

L Colombus, 'How AI Is Protecting against Payments Fraud' *Forbes* (5 September 2019).

Commission, 'Consultation on the Review of the Markets in Financial Instruments Directive (MiFID)' (Public consultation) (8 December 2010).

Commission, 'A Digital Single Market Strategy for Europe', COM(2015) 192 final.

Commission, 'Evaluation of Council Directive 85/374/EEC of 25 July 1985 on the Approximation of the Laws, Regulations and Administrative Provisions of the Member States Concerning Liability for Defective Products', SWD(2018) 157 final.

Commission, 'FinTech Action Plan: For a More Competitive and Innovative European Financial Sector', COM(2018) 109 final.

Commission, 'Report on the Safety and Liability Implications of Artificial Intelligence, the Internet of Things and Robotics (Liability AI Report)', COM(2020) 64 final.

C Coombs and R Chopra, 'Artificial Intelligence and Data Analytics: Emerging Opportunities and Challenges in Financial Services' (2019) CAPCO The Capco Institute Journal of Financial Transformation 54.

G Deipenbrock, 'Private Enforcement in the Realm of European Capital Markets Law Revisited and the Case of Credit Rating Agencies from the Perspective of European and German Law' (2018) 29 European Business Law Review 549.

G Deipenbrock, 'Fintech – Unbearably Lithe or Reasonably Agile?' (2020) 31 European Business Law Review 3.

F Della Negra, 'The Effects of the ESMA's Powers on Domestic Contract Law' in M Andenas and G Deipenbrock (eds), *Regulating and Supervising European Financial Markets: More Risks than Achievements* (Springer 2016).

F Della Negra, *MiFID II and Private Law: Enforcing EU Conduct of Business Rules* (Bloomsbury Publishing 2019).

ESMA, 'Final Report ESMA's Technical Advice to the European Commission on Possible Implementing Measures of the Alternative Investment Fund Managers Directive', ESMA/2011/379 (16 November 2011).

European Parliament, 'Draft Opinion of the Committee on the Internal Market and Consumer Protection for the Committee on Legal Affairs on Civil Liability Regime for Artificial Intelligence' (28/04/2020) 2020/2014(INL).

Finans Norway (the industry organisation for the financial industry in Norway), *Høringsuttalelse ny finansavtalelov* (15 December 2017).

I Giuffrida, 'Liability for AI Decision-Making: Some Legal and Ethical Considerations' (2019) 88 Fordham Law Review 439.

C Hadjiemmanuil, 'The Banking Union and Its Implications for Private Law: A Comment' (2015) 16 European Business Organization Law Review 383.

M E Kjørven, 'Who Pays When Things Go Wrong Online: Financial Fraud and Consumer Protection in Scandinavia and Europe' (2020) 31 European Business Law Review 77.

G Lo Schiavo, *The Role of Financial Stability in EU Law and Policy* (Wolters Kluwer 2017).

H W Micklitz, 'The Transformation of Enforcement in European Private Law: Preliminary Considerations' (2015) 23 European Review of Private Law 491.

N Moloney, 'The Investor Model Underlying the EU's Investor Protection Regime: Consumers or Investors?' (2012) 13 European Business Organization Law Review 169.

N Moloney, *EU Securities and Financial Markets Regulation* (3rd edn, Oxford University Press 2014).

K M Nilles, 'Defining the Limits of Liability: A Legal and Political Analysis of the European Community Products Liability Directive' (1985) 25 Virginia Journal of International Law 729.

B Tang, 'Forging a Responsibility and Liability Framework in the AI Era for RegTech' in J Barberid and others (ed), *The REGTECH Book: The Financial Technology Handbook for Investors, Entrepreneurs and Visionaries in Regulation* (Wiley 2019).

Technical Committee of the International Organization of Securities Commissions (OICV-IOSCO), 'Mitigating Systemic Risk: A Role for Securities Regulators Discussion Paper' OR01/11 (February 2011).

UK Financial Conduct Authority, *A New Regulator for the New Millennium* (FCA January 2000).

M Wallinga, 'Why MiFID & MiFID II Do (Not) Matter to Private Law: Liability to Compensate for Investment Losses for Breach of Conduct of Business Rules' (2019) 3 European Review of Private Law 515.

Part IV

Fintech, investment and insurance services

11 Robo advice – Legal and regulatory challenges*

*Wolf-Georg Ringe and
Christopher Ruof*

1 Introduction

Machines and automated processes are replacing human beings in many areas. 'Robo advice' is the catchphrase for a new phenomenon in the world of investment advice: automatic, web-based tools that help individuals with their investments into certain types of financial assets. Robo advisors will not fully replace human interaction with their clients – far from it – but they have gained a considerable market share over the past several years and are predicted to grow at least at the same pace. The advantages for investors are obvious: they promise higher speed and significantly lower costs in comparison with regular investment services provided by humans. Moreover, their availability is around the clock, and automated advice holds the promise of an unbiased and neutral approach that is free from human error or prejudice.

While the availability of robo advice is clearly a welcome addition to the choices available for many investors, its merits warrant close scrutiny. The main target group of robo advice is retail investors acting in their personal capacity. Such consumers have limited capacity to assess the soundness of the advice, and are prone to make hasty, unverified investment decisions. Moreover, financial advice based on rough and broad classifications, as used by robo advisors, may fail to take into account the individual preferences, situations and specific needs of the investor. On a more general scale, where automated services recommend certain asset classes to investors on a similar pattern, this bears the risk of large-scale parallel behaviour, the development of bubbles and ultimately the emergence of systemic risks.

Regulation, which should address these concerns, is of little help. The key elements of the EU body of financial regulation concerning investment advice are still written with the leitmotif of human interaction in mind. Many categories used by the Markets in Financial Instruments Directive (MiFID)[1] are difficult to match to the activities of this new breed of

---

* Parts of this chapter are part of a wider research project and led to a working paper 'A Regulatory Sandbox for Robo Advice' (EBI Working Paper Series no. 26/2018, available at https://ssrn.com/abstract=3188828). For a related publication, see Wolf-Georg Ringe and Christopher Ruof, 'Regulating Fintech in the EU: the Case for a Guided Sandbox', (2020) 11 European Journal of Risk Regulation 604.

1 See Directive 2004/39/EC of the European Parliament and of the Council of 21 April 2004 on markets in financial instruments amending Council Directives 85/611/EEC and 93/6/EEC and Directive 2000/12/EC of the European Parliament and of the Council and repealing Council Directive 93/22/EEC, [2004] OJ L145/1 ('Mifid I'); Directive 2014/65/EU of the European Parliament and of the Council of 15 May 2014 on markets in financial instruments and amending Directive 2002/92/EC and Directive 2011/61/EU, [2014] OJ L173/349 ('Mifid II').

investment advisors. Worse still, parts of the European framework have been implemented differently across EU Member States. Even where harmonisation has been achieved, rules are partly interpreted differently by national authorities. The result is a patchwork of different rules and requirements that applies to robo advisors, depending on which Member State they are operating in, creating great uncertainty not only among robo advisors and investors, but also on the side of the regulators.

This chapter is organised as follows. Section 2 introduces the phenomenon of robo advice and discusses its significance. Section 3 then turns to explore the risks and promises of this new business practice, and Section 4 will argue that the current regulatory situation is inappropriate for dealing with robo advice. Section 5 concludes.

2 What is robo advice?

There is no standard definition of 'robo advice'. For the purpose of this chapter, we use the term to refer to applications that combine digital interfaces and algorithms in order to provide services ranging from automated financial recommendations to portfolio management to their users.[2] The rise of robo advisors began roughly ten years ago, when two American online wealth managers called Betterment and Wealthfront began offering automated digital advice to public investors.[3] It then took about two years for robo advice to reach the European market with the first one launching in the UK in 2012.[4] Since then, the market has seen a number of launches with a significant increase since 2014.[5] In terms of global market share, the United States is still leading by far: as of 2018, the United States comprised about $440.9 billion, which amounts to almost 79% of assets under management (AuM) from robo advisors globally.[6] It is however unlikely that this dominance sustains in the nearer future. Especially the Chinese market (being the second biggest) is catching up fast, showing impressive growth rates of 500% just in the last two years (2017–2019).[7] Compared to the United States, the European market is still underdeveloped with an

---

2 This definition mostly resembles the definition regularly used in publications by the Financial Stability Board (FSB) and the Bank for international settlements. While robo tools and algorithms are (and have been for a while) also used internally by financial advisors of all sorts, we concentrate on 'client-facing' tools, being the newer and from a regulatory perspective more important phenomenon. We also limit our definition of robo advice to those advising in investment products (excluding inter alia advice in mortgages, insurance, credits).

3 See John Stein, 'The History of Betterment: Changing an Industry (*Betterment*, 20 July 2016) <https://www.betterment.com/resources/the-history-of-betterment/> and <https://www.wealthfront.com/origin>. Call-off date for all hyperlinks, unless stated otherwise, is 03 July 2020.

4 See Businesswire, 'Robo Advice in the UK and Europe – Revolution or Evolution? Including: Robo Advice, Automated Financial Planning, Financial Advice, Brokerage, Fund Platforms – Research and Markets' (Businesswire, 10 November 2016) <http://www.businesswire.com/news/home/20161110006318/en/Robo-Advice-UK-Europe—Revolution-Evolution>.

5 Jill Fisch, Marion Labouré and John Turner, 'The Economics of Complex Decision Making: The Emergence of the Robo Adviser' in Julie Agnew and Olivia S Mitchell (eds), *The Disruptive Impact of Fintech on Retirement Systems* (OUP 2019) 13, 29 f. In the United States, the growth has been particularly impressive, seeing an eight-fold increase in AuM from 2013 to Q1 2017 (see Orçun Kaya, 'Robo-advice – A True Innovation in Asset Management' Deutsche Bank Research (10 August 2017).

6 Statista, *Fintech 2019 – Digital Market Outlook – Market Report* (2019) 35.

7 Data available on subscription at Statista, 'Robo advisors', see <https://www.statista.com/outlook/337/117/robo-advisors/china#market-revenue>.

approximated AuM of about $15.5 billion as of end 2018.[8] The dissemination within the European market varies strongly: while having a relatively significant presence in especially the UK and German market, in some (other) Member States robo advice is not (yet) an economic concern at all.[9]

Globally, robo advice is predicted to keep growing at fast pace and will increasingly become a significant force in financial markets.[10] This trend also has not gone unnoticed by major regulators: The US Securities and Exchange Commission (SEC) reacted by including robo advice in its examination priorities,[11] whereas the UK Financial Conduct Authority (FCA), noticing the potential of robo advice, established an 'Advice Unit' providing regulatory feedback to robo advisors.[12]

Substantially, the advice provided by the robo advisor is mostly based on two key elements: the input information provided by the user and the algorithm. The former is commonly collected via an online questionnaire that asks the user to provide personal information (eg, age, profession, monthly net income) and some investment related data (eg, investment experience, risk aversion, investment goals). Subsequently, based on the user's answers, the algorithm constructs a portfolio proposal with various investment products, in which the user can invest. The composition of the output differs among providers; however, it typically and predominantly consists of passive exchange-traded funds (ETFs) based on the stock, currency or commodity markets[13] along with some mutual funds. The weighting of such components of a portfolio depends on the user's answers, especially on those relating to risk appetite. As to the process, the investor has to create an account and transfer funds to it. The subsequent processing depends on the characteristics of the respective robo advisor. Some provide continuous monitoring and evaluation of the investment strategies followed by corresponding transaction proposals to the investor, whereas others offer automatic reallocating or rebalancing of the portfolio according to the stated preferences of the investor and the information they provided. In the majority of cases, investors retain the option to (manually) adjust their portfolio or recalibrate their preferences.

The costs for robo advice services typically range from an annual fee between 0.25% and 1% of the investor's account value.[14] Other providers charge provision-based fees. In addition to the advisory fee, customers regularly also pay a fee for the acquired investment product, which generally is the fee charged for the purchase of an ETF or a mutual fund.

8 See Orçun Kaya, 'German Robo-advisors – Rapid Growth, Robust Performance, High Cost' Deutsche Bank Research (12 February 2019).

9 For an overview of robo advisors' dissemination in Europe, see TechFluence, 'Map of Robo Advisors in Germany/ Europe' (*TechFluence*, 13 December 2017) <http://www.techfluence.eu/investtech.html>.

10 See eg, Statista (n 6).

11 See SEC, Investment Guidance Update (February 2017) <https://www.sec.gov/investment/im-guidance-2017-02.pdf>.

12 See FCA, 'Advice Unit' (*FCA*, Last updated 10 December 2019) <https://www.fca.org.uk/firms/advice-unit>.

13 Kaya (n 5) states that the final set of ETFs for robo-advisory purposes comes down to only app. 3–6% of all available ETFs.

14 Average fee in Europe: app. 0.8%, whereas in the United States only 0.4%: see Kaya (n 5) 1.

3 Promises and risks

The established goals of financial regulation in most jurisdictions around the world include investor protection and financial stability, with an increasing focus on the latter, especially since the 2008 financial crisis.[15] Good regulation, however, should not only focus on addressing potential risks, but also identify desirable developments in the financial market and promote them. In the following, we discuss the benefits of robo advice that regulation should support.

3.1 *Key advantages*

As mentioned above, the key promise of robo advice is to deliver convenient, unbiased financial advice at significantly lower costs than those charged by human financial advisors. The promise of low costs appears the most evident one. Whereas robo advisors charge average fees between 0.4% (mainly in the United States) and 0.8% (mainly in Europe), the fee for human financial advice usually amounts to 1–2%.[16] The reason is simple: robo advisors make use of economies of scale. The 'advice' is provided by one algorithm, meaning decreasing marginal costs with an increasing number of customers. In addition to that, there are other financial aspects that make robo advisors more attractive for customers: firstly, robo advisors tend to recommend investment in low-cost passive funds (mostly ETFs), which are substantially cheaper and at the same time often perform better than their active counterparts.[17] Human financial advisers on the other hand often recommend actively managed funds, which regularly generate higher commissions.[18]

Secondly, unlike human financial advisors,[19] robo advisors usually require no or relatively little minimum investment volume.[20] Consequently, this makes their advice accessible to a wider range of investors. This would be true for both, individuals who have not yet participated in the financial market at all and for those who have invested without relying on any (professional) advice. Especially in Europe, a big share of households still keeps their savings in a bank deposit, rather than investing it in the capital market.[21] In times of dramatically low interest rates, robo advice might be a convenient way to invest that capital. Regarding those who participate in the financial market

---

15 See for example John Armour and others, *Principles of Financial Regulation* (OUP 2016) 64ff.

16 Note that fees vary by geographical region. An overview of fees charged by a selection of German robo advisors can for instance be found at Brokervergleich, 'Robo-Advisor – Vergleich und Erfahrungen 2020' (*Brokervergleich*, regularly updated) <https://www.brokervergleich.de/robo-advisor/#fuer-wen-eignet-sich-ein-robo-advisor-nicht>.

17 See for example graph no 13 at Kaya (n 5) 10.

18 Fisch and others (n 5) 19 f. For an analysis of the total cost advantage of robo advisors, see Philippe Rohner and Matthias W Uhl, 'Robo-Advisors vs. Traditional Investment Advisors – an Unequal Game' (2017) 21 The Journal of Wealth Management 44.

19 In contrast, human financial advisors (in the United States) often require a minimum asset volume of more than USD 500,000 (see Larry Ludwig, 'Best Robo Advisor for 2020' (2020) <https://investorjunkie.com/35919/robo-advisors/>).

20 See for instance Kaya (n 5) 9 or Morgan Lewis, 'The Evolution of Advice: Digital Investment Advisers as Fiduciaries' (October 2016) <https://www.morganlewis.com/~/media/files/publication/report/im-the-evolution-of-advice-digital-investment-advisers-as-fiduciaries-october-2016.ashx>.

21 See OECD, 'Household financial assets' (*OECD*, 2020) <https://data.oecd.org/hha/household-financial-assets.htm>.

without any advice, robo advice has the potential to improve their investment performance. Numerous empirical studies have shown that individual investors with low financial literacy are particularly prone to behavioural biases, resulting in suboptimal investment choices.[22] Robo advisors hold the promise to provide more rational and sounder investing in such a case. This is corroborated by a recent empirical study showing that a robo advising tool mitigates well-known biases and improves the overall performance of the investor's portfolio.[23]

What makes robo advice so convenient for users is the simplicity and accessibility of the advice. In contrast to opening hours of banks, robo advice is available around the clock, each day of the year, and from any location in the world, provided there is a well-functioning internet connection. Further, the user might receive the advice after about 15 minutes, without having to go through the traditional client onboarding process, often involving extensive paperwork.

Automatisation is further likely to make financial advice more neutral and transparent, reducing internal agency conflicts that often arise between human financial advisors and their clients.[24] Since robo advisors typically do not sell the products they advise in, they are not as prone to the selection bias otherwise prevalent in financial advice.[25]

3.2 *Performance*

To our knowledge, no comprehensive study on the performance of robo advisors compared to their human equivalents has been conducted to date. Nevertheless, it appears likely that the quality of automated advice does benefit consumers.[26] Analytics firm BackEnd has started to collect some data on the performance of robo advisors in their 'Robo Report'. The 2017 report showed a decent performance of the respective providers: one-year returns[27] ranged from 12.39% to 16.47%[28]. In their Q2 2018 report, Backend

---

22 Well-documented biases of individual investors include for example the deposition effect, trend chasing and rank effect. See eg, Francesco D'Acunto, Nagpurnanand Prabhala and Alberto G Rossi, 'The Promises and Pitfalls of Robo-advising' (2019) 32 The Review of Financial Studies 2006ff. See also example Rohner and Uhl (n 18) 44, 50f. with further references. Further, see Jan Henrik Wosnitza, 'Robo-Advising Private Investors on German Mid-Cap Bonds' (2018) 7 Corporate Finance 220 in regard of a prevailing 'home bias' that could be averted by using a robo advisor.
23 Francesco D'Acunto and others (n 22). It has to be noted that this study was based on an automated portfolio optimiser that only invested in individual securities and stocks, so not exactly the classic type of a robo advisor.
24 Fisch and others (n 5) 25 f. In terms of transparency however, new problems may arise with the increasing use of AI and ML (see below at 3.7).
25 It should be noted that this is for 'stand-alone' robo advisors, not belonging for instance to an investment bank.
26 This applies to consumers not (yet) participating in the financial market at all as well as those receiving advice from human advisors (for the arguments see above at 3.1.).
27 Excluding those where the returns could for various reasons not be assessed.
28 BackEnd Benchmarking, *The Robo Report* (Q4 2017) 8. The Q2 2018 report shows slightly decreasing returns. This is explained by general market conditions – inter alia increasing fluctuation in the equity markets as well as decreasing returns in fixed-income, especially sovereign bond markets, amidst a rising dollar and trade concerns.

have begun comparing the robo advisors' returns against a normalised benchmark.[29] This comparison reveals that the majority of robo advisors in a two-year period stays slightly below that benchmark. The subsequent reports mostly confirm that picture.[30] Notably, a look at the fourth quarter of 2018 reveals that robo advisors were able to handle the market downturn rather well.[31] Even though having produced losses during that period, most robo advisors performed better than the benchmark and a fortiori better than the S&P 500.[32] Another study in regard of the German robo advisor market has been conducted by online platform 'brokervergleich.de'.[33] Inter alia, it compared the performance of German robo advisors with two benchmark portfolios that represent common risk-averse portfolios as recommended by a human advisor, showing that the robo advisor were not able to outperform those portfolios.

This picture is surely far from being representative for the entire robo advice market and, since investors take a long-term outlook on their investments, gives an incomplete picture, but it may be useful to give us an idea of their capabilities. Finally, research in diverse fields demonstrates that even simple algorithms may outperform humans in their respective task. There is ample reason to believe that the same is true for automated financial advice.[34]

3.3 *Macroeconomic implications*

Besides those (more obvious) potential benefits for investors some commentators also highlight the broader implications that result from the emergence of robo advice.

First, robo advisors could enhance access to financial markets for consumers and therefore promote financial inclusion.[35] This seems desirable for several reasons: as opposed to the United States, most European jurisdictions still primarily rely on state-run pension schemes. Looking at the demographic development in Europe, it seems inevitable that the current system has to be supplemented by private retirement provision through capital market participation. Robo advice bears the potential to play a key role in this development as it opens a low-cost possibility to invest. Secondly, mid-income households

---

29 Normalised Benchmarking is a method to compare portfolios with differing equity and fixed income allocations. It allows portfolios to be measured against each other by their return above or below the benchmark. For a more detailed description of the methodology, see BackEnd Benchmarking, *The Robo Report* (Q2 2018) 18–19.

30 BackEnd Benchmarking, *The Robo Report* (Q4 2019) 21f.

31 The fourth quarter of 2018 ended an overall volatile year on the stock markets with exceptionally big losses, seeing for instance the S&P 500 plunge 13.97% in the quarter. See Fred Imbert, 'US stocks post worst year in a decade as the S&P 500 falls more than 6% in 2018' (*CNN*, 31 December 2018) <https://www.cnbc.com/2018/12/31/stock-market-wall-street-stocks-eye-us-china-trade-talks.html>.

32 BackEnd Benchmarking, *The Robo Report* (Q4 2018) 8ff.

33 See Brokervergleich, 'Robo-Advisor im Echtgeld-Test 2020' (*Brokervergleich*, regularly updated) <https://www.brokervergleich.de/robo-advisor/echtgeld-test/>. Brokervergleich.de states that they would 'generally' use a balanced risk profile. The composition of the respective portfolios is disclosed in the test.

34 See Tom Baker and Benjamin Dellaert, 'Regulating Robo Advice Across the Financial Services Industry' (2018) 103 Iowa Law Review 713, 716 with further references at footnote 10.

35 See above at Section 3.1.

are and feel increasingly economically left behind, as real wages remain mostly static and bank deposits do not yield any substantial interest, while firms and high-net-worth individuals prosper.[36] By offering a way to participate in economic growth, robo advisors could potentially mitigate this rising inequality. Not least, enhancing participation in the capital market would enhance liquidity and provide capital for productive economic activity,[37] having beneficial effects for the overall economy. In sum, encouraging those households to access the financial market is a confluence of political as well as private interests of the financial sector.[38]

From an EU perspective, this promise seems to be particularly appealing. In 2015 the European Commission adopted an action plan on building a Capital Markets Union (CMU).[39] The CMU project was initially launched since EU capital markets were and still are relatively underdeveloped and fragmented, in particular when compared to the United States. While the EU economy is almost as big as the US one, the EU's equity market comprises only less than half its size. Promising to facilitate access to the capital markets for many not yet participating consumers, robo advice and other fintechs could play an important role in completing CMU.[40] Not less, its reduced geographical proximity and promotion of access to cross-border investments may also make an important contribution to the CMU agenda.[41] Further strengthening and integrating the EU capital market may have become 'more important than ever',[42] since the UK as the Member State with the largest capital market has decided to leave the EU.[43]

Robo advisors might have another positive impact on the financial market by enhancing competition, which it traditionally lacks.[44] However, as it seems the market trend is going more in the direction of collaboration and consolidation, than seeing an increase in

36 For more on this and many other reasons for the increasing economic pressure on the middle-class, see OECD, *Under Pressure: The Squeezed Middle Class* (OECD Publishing 2019).
37 For example, in Germany investing in real estate is very common, which is often not considered to be a productive form of investment.
38 Also Iris H-Y Chiu, 'Fintech and Disruptive Business Models in Financial Products, Intermediation and Markets – Policy Implications for Financial Regulators' (2016) 21 Journal of Technology Law & Policy 55, 71.
39 European Commission, '*Action Plan on Building a Capital Market Union*' COM (2015) 468 final.
40 Maria Demertzis, Silvia Merler and Guntram B Wolff, 'Capital Markets Union and the Fintech Opportunity' (2018) 4 Journal of Financial Regulation 157.
41 See also European Commission, '*Fintech: a more competitive and innovative European financial sector*' (Consultation Document 2017) 7.
42 Huw Jones, 'Europe's slow-moving capital markets plan gets Brexit reboot' (8 June 2017) <https://www.reuters.com/article/us-eu-markets-regulations/europes-slow-moving-capital-markets-plan-gets-brexit-reboot-idUSKBN18Z18W?il=0>.
43 On the implications of Brexit for European financial integration see Wolf-Georg Ringe, 'The Irrelevance of Brexit for the European Financial Market' (2018) 19 European Business Organization Law Review 1; Wolf-Georg Ringe, 'The Politics of Capital Markets Union: From Brexit to Eurozone' in Franklin Allen and others (eds), *Capital Markets Union and Beyond* (MIT Press 2019) 341.
44 Positive effects of more competition in the financial advisory market could be better prices, more efficiency and innovation. FSB, 'FinTech and market structure in financial services: Market developments and potential financial stability implications' (14 February 2019) however also draws attention to potential risks of increased competition, namely increased risk taking due to pressure on margins and their ability to accumulate capital through retained earnings.

competition.[45] Nonetheless, an important survey demonstrates that the majority of wealth managers do feel pressure on their margins and fear losing part of their business due to robo advisors.[46]

3.4 *Investor risks*

In the following, we will analyse the risks associated with robo advice, as it is usually them triggering the need for regulatory action.

The most prevalent risk for investors seems to be the potential unsuitability of the advice, meaning that the output does not appropriately respond to the *actual* situation and risk preferences of the robo advice user. One problem that may lead to such unsuitability is the design of the advice process. Since the robo advisor's output directly depends on what information it seeks and what information the investor provides, it may not assess the investor's situation exhaustively, taking into account all individual conditions.[47] A 'one-size-fits-all' questionnaire may be too narrow in some cases, as opportunities for investors to include additional or connected information to supplement their responses are limited. According to an FCA report, some robo advisors do not properly evaluate their clients' knowledge and experience, investment objectives or capacity for loss.[48] Further, online questionnaires are often not able to provide follow-up questions to address any inconsistencies.[49] In a similar vein, a recent study demonstrates that when answering the questionnaire, customers are particularly susceptible to certain biases (in particular overconfidence, familiarity bias and rules of thumb), resulting in a wrongful self-assessment.[50] Besides, a recent study has shown

---

45 EBA, *Report on the impact of fintech on institutions' business models* (03 July 2018) 24ff. identifies forming partnerships as the predominant type of relationship between incumbent institutions and fintechs. See also Joint Committee of the European Supervisory Authorities (ESAs), *Joint Committee Report on the results of the monitoring exercise on 'automation in financial advice'* (JC 2018-29, 5 September 2018) 10 observing an increase in partnerships between robo advisors and incumbents.

46 See Pricewaterhouse Coopers (PwC), 'Beyond Automated Advice: How FinTech Is Shaping Asset & Wealth Management' Global Fintech survey 2016 (July 2016).

47 The problem is addressed by Marika Salo and Helena Haapio, 'Robo-Advisors and Investors: Enhancing Human-Robot Interaction Through Information Design' in Erich Schweighofer and others (eds), *Trends and Communities of Legal Informatics. Proceedings of the 20th International Legal Informatics Symposium IRIS 2017* (2017) 443 ff.

48 FCA, 'Automated Investment Services – Our Expectations' (21 May 2018) <https://www.fca.org.uk/ publications/multi-firm-reviews/automated-investment-services-our-expectations>. Notably, the FCA only looked at 10 robo advisors operating in the UK.

49 See also Dan Ryan and others, 'PwC discusses SEC's Increased Scrutiny of Robo-Advisors' CLS Blue Sky Blog (8 November 2017) <http://clsbluesky.law.columbia.edu/2017/11/08/pwc-discusses-secs-increased-scrutiny-of-robo-advisers/>.

50 See Florian Wedlich, 'Wie wirken sich Verhaltensanomalien von Anlegern auf Robo-Advisory aus?'(2018) 7 Corporate Finance 225. Wedlich also offers ideas on the design of the questionnaire in order to mitigate those biases. There is however plenty of research on how these biases could be addressed, eg, by 'choice architecture'. See eg, Dominik Jung, Edgar Erdfelder and Florian Glaser, 'Nudged to Win: Designing Robo-Advisory to Overcome Decision Inertia' (29 November 2018) ECIS 2018 Proceedings proposing specific tools to address investors decision inertia.

that the impact of the given answers on the investment recommendation varies wide-ly.[51] There are cases where only a single answer determines the outcome (more spe-cifically, the recommended portfolio was directly correlated to the customer's chosen risk level).[52] On top of that, research in behavioural economics has shown that people often behave in non-rational ways when self-assessing, particularly casting doubts on the robo advisor's approach to measuring risk tolerance and risk perception-related questions.[53] Not least, in some situations the individual situation of the customers simply does not fit into one of the pre-defined categories of the robo advisor.[54] An FCA review further demonstrates that robo advisors frequently fail to appropriately disclose information.[55] In particular, in the FCA sample, fees and service-related disclosure were often unclear or even misleading. Such failures do not allow a customer to make an informed decision.

Not least, unsuitability of the advice can also be caused by the malfunctioning of the tool or its underlying algorithm.[56] This can be due to flaws in the design of the algorithm, but also be caused by third-party manipulation.[57] Due to the digital business model of the robo advisor, this would much likely affect a large number of customers and cause much greater damage than a flawed human financial advice. Given the still small size of many robo advisors, even in the case it is held liable, most customers will probably not get compensated.

Moreover, Jill Fisch and others have identified an advantage of human financial advisors over robo advisors in what they call the 'warm body effect', claiming that the availability of a person to talk to, especially in times of market stress, has some intrinsic value.[58] Inter alia, automated advisors might do less well than human financial advisers in preventing the cli-ent from trend chasing and overreacting to certain movements in the market. If consumers are able to adjust their portfolio and preferences without the consultation of a human pro-fessional, they might be more prone to various 'hypes' in the market. Also, not all aspects of traditional investment advice are yet covered by robo advice. To date, robo advisors largely focus on the matching and rebalancing function, while this represents only a part of the service human advisors (optimally) provide. Humans may help clients with how much they

---

51 Michael Tertilt and Peter Scholz, 'To Advise, or Not to Advise – How Robo-Advisors Evaluate the Risk Preferences of Private Investors' (2018) 21(2) Journal of Wealth Management 70.

52 Tertilt and Scholz (n 51) 78.

53 See Stephen L Deschenes and P Brett Hammod, 'Matching FinTech Advice to Participant Needs' in Julie Agnew and Olivia S Mitchell (eds), *The Disruptive Impact of Fintech on Retirement Systems* (OUP 2019). However, the authors also present studies showing that risk self-assessments and val-idated questionnaires better determine risk tolerance than a financial advisors' assessment (see on p 178).

54 Joint Committee of the ESAs, '*Joint Committee Discussion Paper on Automation in Financial Advice*' (JC 2015 080, 4 December 2015) 25. It should be noted, that human financial advisors also often work with pre-defined categories and risk profiles. See Rohner and Uhl (n 18) 44, 48.

55 See FCA (n 48).

56 ESAs (n 54) 26 f. and the corresponding 2016 Report (Joint Committee of the ESAs, '*Report on Automation in Financial Advice*' (16 December 2016)). See also FSB, '*Financial Stability Implications from Fintech: Supervisory and Regulatory Issues that Merit Authorities' Attention*' (27 June 2017) 45. The most recent 2018 report on automation in financial advice (n 45) found that the risks and benefits that had been originally identified in the 2015 paper and the 2016 report seem to be still valid.

57 For example, ESAs report (n 56) 13.

58 Fisch and others (n 5) 21.

should save, create plans, set up structures and counsel those clients who fall short of their plans etc.[59] Those coaching and relationship aspects are harder to automate and therefore basically not (yet) provided by robo advisors.[60]

This might explain the recent development towards hybrid models[61]: some of the major US financial management companies offer robo-advisory services with the (additional) possibility to contact a certified financial planner 24/7.[62] While fees for such services are often comparable to those of traditional robo advisors, the account minimums of hybrid models are usually significantly higher,[63] potentially even up to that of a (fully) human financial advisor.

3.5 *Systemic risk*

In addition to these risks, there are also potential *systemic risks* linked to the phenomenon of robo advice. Relevant for policymakers are particularly financial stability and cyber risks. As automation in financial advice is currently not widely distributed, the aforementioned risks might not materialise in the near future.[64] However, due to the rapid growth of robo advice, they should be scrutinised as early as possible.

In this context, a predominant concern is the so-called 'herding risk'.[65] Most robo advisors to a certain degree operate similarly when processing and evaluating their customers' data due to similarities in the composition of the portfolios and the workings of their algorithms.[66] Assuming that risk models used by the algorithms are highly correlated, robo advice has the potential to trigger greater herding behaviour than human financial advice. Herding behaviour can increase the amplitude of swings in asset prices and lead to an increased incidence of unidirectional portfolio shifts.[67] Also, correlated algorithms may similarly react to external shocks, leading to solvency problems that can affect the entire financial system. Robo advisors may withdraw from the market during periods of

---

59 See also Baker and Dellaert (n 34) 729.
60 It is however noteworthy that automated advice constantly evolves in that regard: US provider Wealthfront, for example, is currently developing tools to offer goal-based advice tied to asset allocation decisions, ultimately providing a product akin to 'self-driving money'. See Samuel Steinberger, 'Here's How One Robo Provides Goals-Based Planning' (29 June 2018) <https://www.wealthmanagement. com/technology/here-s-how-one-robo-provides-goals-based-planning>.
61 Hybrid models are basically robo advisors, added with the possibility of consulting a (human) financial adviser.
62 See for example Fisch and others (n 5) 26 f.
63 For example, Vanguard charges a fee of 0.3% for their service and require an account minimum of 50,000 USD (see <https://investor.vanguard.com/financial-advisor/personal-advisor-services>).
64 FSB (n 56) 2; ESAs Report (n 56) and confirmed by the 2018 report (n 45).
65 See for example: FSB (n 56) 46; Baker and Dellaert (n 34) 742 f.; ESAs Report (n 56) 11; FSB, '*Artificial Intelligence and Machine Learning in Financial Services*' (1 November 2017) 25. Also, Jens Weidmann, President of the German Bundesbank, warned against the herding risk in a speech at the G20 conference, however saw it as not yet prevalent (see Jens Weidmann, 'Digital Finance – Reaping the benefits without neglecting the risks' (Welcoming remarks at the G20 conference, Wiesbaden, 25 January 2017) available at <https://www.bundesbank.de/Redaktion/EN/Reden/2017/2017_01_25_weidmann.html>).
66 Kaya (n 5) states that robo advisors usually use mean-variance optimisation (see on p. 6). In this context, EBA (n 45) identifies another risk that stems from the reliance on similar underlying technology, more specifically on the technology provider: A development as such could contribute to the creation of systemically important unregulated technology suppliers (see on p. 21).
67 FSB (n 56) 20, 45f.; ESAs (n 54) 27.

market stress when liquidity demands are high and thereby increase asset price volatility.[68] Moreover, predictable patterns in the workings of algorithms could be used by cybercriminals to manipulate market prices.[69]

The effects of correlated algorithmic behaviour might have already been observed during several so-called 'flash crashes',[70] the most prominent of which took place in 2010.[71] The 2010 flash crash lasted for approximately half an hour during which time the American stock indices collapsed and dropped by about 9%.[72] Even though the stock market recovered quickly, the event caused substantial uncertainty among investors and regulators. While the primary cause of this event was a (now banned) trading method called 'spoofing', the intensity of the drop is said to be algorithms reacting to the actions of the trader. Ultimately, this flash crash could be a pretaste of how unexpected market drops can lead to high-speed selling spirals caused by algorithms.

As current robo advisors were trained during times of predominantly low volatility, it remains rather unclear how they will react to a major shock in the markets. That is, whether they will lack flexibility to effectively handle the shock, or rather react in a more prudent, long-sighted way.

It could be argued that the outcome of the UK referendum on Brexit in June 2016 was a first test for the performance of robo advisors, as it led to one of the most significant shocks in the financial markets in recent years.[73] From an investor's perspective, however, most robo portfolios mastered the challenge well. The way it was overcome, however, may give some ground for critique: major robo advice firms decided to halt trading for several hours on that day to prevent investor overreaction.[74] Naturally, this intervention provoked fundamental critique as being patronising, arguing that investors should be the ones to decide when to trade. More importantly though, that reaction revealed an inherent weakness of robo advisors: the inability of the programme itself to solve a comparable situation without the need for human interaction. It would have been interesting to see how the algorithms had reacted to that event, had they not been halted.

In another investigation, it was analysed how robo advisors dealt with the stock market crash that occurred on 5 February 2018, where the Dow Jones lost almost 1,600 points in one day – the biggest slump in its history.[75] While data on German robo advisors suggests that the shock did not cause any prompt reactions (like fire sales),[76] the crash revealed another problem: clients of robo advisors apparently did not remain calm, causing the websites of Betterment and Wealthfront to crash due to massive log-in numbers.[77] Besides

---

68 FSB (n 56) 20.
69 FSB (n 56) 25.
70 The term 'flash crash' refers to a sudden fall in stock prices caused by manual or algorithmic errors.
71 Notably, there are also other factors that contribute to a flash-crash. The concrete mechanisms of their occurrence are not yet fully understood.
72 For more information on these events, see SEC, 'Findings Regarding the Market Events of May 6, 2010' (30 September 2010).
73 Kaya (n 5) 11.
74 Kaya (n 5).
75 See for example Matt Eagen, 'Dow Plunges 1,175 – Worst Point Decline in History' (5 February 2018) <https://money.cnn.com/2018/02/05/investing/stock-market-today-dow-jones/index.html>.
76 See Brokervergleich.de (n 33).
77 See for example Frank Chaparro, 'Betterment and Wealthfront Websites Crash during Market Bloodbath' *Business Insider* (5 February 2018) <https://www.businessinsider.de/betterment-and-wealthfront-crash-during-market-bloodbath-2018-2>.

apparent technological shortcomings, this again underlines the still prevailing lack of trust towards automated advice.

Risks may also occur not only due to actual events, but also in consequence of wrongly propagated information (so called fake news).[78] Given the trend of algorithms to increasingly incorporate also non-financial data in their decision-making, they may overreact to certain false information.[79]

3.6 *Cyber risks*

Another issue that merits regulatory attention, not only in regard of robo advice, but rather concerning the fintech phenomenon as a whole, is the problem of cyber risk. The cyber risk susceptibility of financial market actors is high due to the level of interconnectedness. Given that fintech start-ups are frequently not in possession of a proper cyber-security system comparable to those of big financial institutions, cyber risk is an issue that merits further attention.[80] On the other hand, in case of more diversity and less concentration in the market that may come along with the rise of fintech, a singular cyber-attack may be less systemically relevant where it can be contained to the attacked entity or context.

3.7 *Artificial intelligence*

One factor that plays a great role in the future development of robo advice, bearing great potential for its quality, but also posing serious risks, is the increasing use of state-of-the-art Artificial Intelligence (AI) and machine learning solutions. These technologies can be fed with stacks of data consisting of parameters about individual investors, such as their credit history, employment history, assets, purchasing history as well as data that stems from social media, for example, Facebook or Twitter.[81] Also, the algorithm may use data about macroeconomic parameters, such as market movements and collective behaviour during volatility.

With datasets about the individual, robo advisors using AI could design a portfolio more tailored to the individual preferences, that is, give a more customised advice.[82] Some commentators see the inclusion of AI and machine learning as the yet missing piece in the puzzle that will allow robo advisors to widely replace human financial advisors.[83] Obviously, it could present an opportunity to overcome the problems associated

78 This concern is also raised by the FSB. See FSB (n 56) 11.
79 For example, in April 2013, markets significantly reacted to a false tweet, which was sent from the hacked Associated Press twitter account, reporting of two explosions at the White House. Robo advisors could exacerbate such patterns.
80 FSB (n 56).
81 See also Sviatoslav Rosov, 'Machine Learning, Artificial Intelligence and Robo-Advisers: The Future of Finance?' (4 August 2017) CFA Institute Talk <http://www.cityam.com/269679/machine-learning-artificial-intelligence-and-robo-advisers>.
82 See also FSB (n 65) 27.
83 Michael Rozanski, 'How AI will cause robo advice to completely outperform human advice' (*fintechcircle*, 10 July 2017) <http://fintechcircle.com/insights/ai-will-cause-robo-advice-completely-outperform-human-advice/>; Patrick Hunger, 'Was Robo-Advisors von der Automobilindustrie lernen können' (16 September 2017) <https://www.nzz.ch/wirtschaft/vermoegensverwaltung/was-robo-advisors-von-der-automobilindustrie-lernen-koennen-ld.1316075>.

with the use of a questionnaire that we described earlier. The robo advisor could use various datasets to verify clients' answers to the questionnaire and thereby address certain biases prevalent in the answering process.[84] Even more audaciously, future robo advisors might refrain from using a questionnaire altogether and instead solely rely on data on the user that they retrieved from other sources. The interaction with the client would thus be limited to exploring risk tolerances and investment goals. Such an approach would potentially make the advice more precise, but certainly more convenient and faster. Also, AI could enable robo advisors to offer a more comprehensive product to the customer and automate parts of the financial advice service that are to date reserved for human financial advisors.[85] Feeding the algorithm with macroeconomic data could enable it to even anticipate market movements and the occurrence of shocks and to better estimate certain risks. On the other hand, since an algorithm is always 'trained' on historical data, it might fail to anticipate utterly novel categories of risks.[86] Relying on the algorithm irrespectively may pose an idiosyncratic risk: algorithms using machine learning develop their own dynamics, which can lead to the problem that commentators commonly refer to as 'black boxes' in decision making.[87] This describes a decision made by algorithm which humans find difficult or impossible to trace and understand.[88] Such black box decisions pose difficult questions in relation to liability, auditability and – of course – regulation. Also, as a consequence of unpredictable and unexpected decisions, in the absence of data (and a better explanation) market movements may be ascribed to AI and interpretation of market shocks may therefore be hampered.[89]

On balance, robo advice combines several important benefits, for investors as well as for the financial market as a whole. However, many risks are still unresolved, notably the risk for investors to receive unsuitable advice and the market risks of increasing volatility and potential flash crashes. For both, risks and benefits, we may see some interesting developments with AI and machine learning in the near future. Again, more data and time are necessary to comprehensively assess the phenomenon of robo advice exhaustively.

4 Regulatory status quo

One of the foremost objectives of financial regulation is to ensure the functioning of the financial system. To that end, regulators and legislatures have identified a number of common objectives along which a regulatory framework is developed. Among these are to ensure consumer and investor protection, to enhance financial stability and to promote (good) competition.[90] In this part, we analyse the regulatory framework for robo advisors in the EU and show that at least in the context of robo advice it fails to strike the right

---

84 See also Wedlich (n 50) 227f.
85 As described earlier (see item 3.4. of this chapter), these parts largely consist of relationship management and coaching.
86 See also FSB (n 65) 34.
87 See for example Rosov (n 81). Also EBA (n 45) sees that risk specifically in respect to robo advice (see on p. 21).
88 FSB (n 65) 26.
89 FSB (n 65) 30.
90 See for example OECD (2009) 'Policy Framework for Effective and Efficient Financial Regulation' 17; Armour and others (n 15).

balance between these objectives. With the aim of (primarily) furthering consumer/investor protection, the current regime entails high market barriers, making it difficult for new players to gain foot in the market. Unfit rules further create regulatory uncertainty leading all-together to a highly innovation-unfriendly regulatory environment. At the same time, actual risks remain unaddressed.

At the EU level, regulatory standards that are relevant for robo advice are primarily those provided in the Market in Financial Instruments Directive (MiFID II)[91] framework. Even though robo advice is not explicitly mentioned in this Directive, MiFID II generally applies to automated advice as well as to all other entities which qualify as investment firms under MiFID II.

Firms that provide *investment advice* or *portfolio management* (whether automated or not) generally fall within the scope of MiFID II including all its corresponding obligations. One exception may be available under Article 3 of MiFID II, with the effect that the robo advisor is only subject to the national regulatory regime.[92] However, whereas under MiFID I[93] the regulation of firms meeting requirements of Article 3 was entirely within the responsibility of the national initiatives, MiFID II sets out new requirements, referred to as 'analogue' requirements,[94] entailing an obligation catalogue comparable to that of MiFID II. In the context of Article 3 of MiFID II, the distinction between *investment advice* and *portfolio management* plays a role, since the exemption is only available for firms providing investment advice.

The application of MiFID involves some substantial legal obligations for regulated firms.[95] First, firms must be authorised by the national competent authority.[96] For this, they need to satisfy various requirements, for instance having a sufficient initial capital endowment. Further, several conduct of business standards have to be met when providing the service. Those standards for example consist of obligations to provide information to the client about the firm and the service and to collect relevant information from the client in order to be able to give a suitable recommendation ('*suitability test*').[97] The latter is considered to be one of the most important requirements for investor protection. Also, all necessary steps to prevent a conflict of interest have to be taken by the firm.[98] Since MiFID II became applicable, robo advisors and other institutions see themselves confronted with additional regulatory burdens: the new law prescribes large amounts of

---

91 See above n 1. MiFID II was finalised at the beginning of 2014 and entered into force on 2 July 2014. At that time, also the use of robo advice grew increasingly thereby drawing the attention of lawmakers and regulators. ESMA explicitly referred to robo advice for the first time in its Guidelines on MiFID II (ESMA, '*Guidelines on Certain Aspects of the MiFID II Suitability Requirement*' (Consultation Paper [July 2017]).

92 For example, the firm is limited in the range of financial products it is allowed to recommend to the client.

93 See n 1.

94 MiFID II article 3(2) requires national regulation to be 'at least analogous' to the provisions in respect of authorisation and supervision, conduct of business and organisational requirements.

95 The exact obligations under MiFID II can vary according to the specific service the robo advisors provides and the products he is recommending, respectively investing in. For a detailed account of the different obligations under MiFID II, see eg, (in German) Bianca Lins, 'Robo Advice: Aufsichtsrechtliche Pflichten der digitalen Anlageberatung und Vermögensverwaltung' (2020) 20 Zeitschrift für Bank- und Kapitalmarktrecht (BKR) 181.

96 MiFID II Article 5.

97 MiFID II Article 25(2), and Articles 54 and 55 of Commission Delegated Regulation 2017/565; see also ESAs Report (n 56) 11.

98 MiFID II Article 23.

information to be obtained about the client,[99] to be presented to the client[100] and to be documented.[101] Broadly speaking, with MiFID II the regulatory framework was rendered significantly more complex and demanding, which is not least demonstrated by the 5-fold increase in length compared to its predecessor.[102]

One of the most pressing issues in the regulation of robo advice seems to be regulatory uncertainty.[103] Firstly, firms have huge difficulties complying with the panoply of obligations.[104] Not only has the sheer magnitude of the rule book an overwhelming effect on small start-ups, making it worse, some rules appear not to be technology-neutral and hence hard to reconcile with the (digital) service of robo advisors.[105]

Moreover, pre-defined categories and fine distinctions make it hard for new forms of financial advice to assess their regulatory situation, as new innovative approaches may be hard to fit into existing categories.[106] After all, the more innovative the service, the harder it is to reconcile it with existing categories, and ultimately the greater becomes the uncertainty.

A 2017 EBA Discussion Paper[107] seems to corroborate these arguments, showing that out of a sample of robo advisors 35% are under no regulatory regime, whereas 41% are regulated under EU law and 24% under a national regime.[108] First, considering that the common robo advisor is supposed to be regulated by MiFID II,[109] the relatively high number of unregulated robo advisors seems striking.[110] Secondly, the data implies that firms are subject to different regulatory treatment, even though they offer the same service. This indicates that there are most likely divergences in the

---

99 For example, information about the risk tolerance and the ability to bear losses (Article 25(2)).

100 For instance, firms are now obliged to inform the client whether or not the advice is independent (Article 24(4) lit. a). They must further explain why their advice is qualified as independent or non-independent by clarifying the differences (further specified in Article 52(3) of the Implementing Directive).

101 Under Article 25(6) a suitability report has to be conducted and made available for the client (generally) prior to the transaction.

102 Karel Lannoo, 'MiFID II and the New Market Conduct Rules for Financial Intermediaries: Will Complexity Bring Transparency?' (26 May 2017) ECMI Policy Brief No 24, 5f.

103 See ESAs Report (n 56) 18–19; Mark Battersby, 'Regulatory Uncertainty Frustrates Pace of Robo-advice Growth (*International Advisor*, 15 October 2015) <http://www.international-adviser.com/news/1025395/regulatory-uncertainty-frustrates-pace-robo-advice-growth>; Gregor Dorfleitner, Lars Hornuf, *Fintech in Germany* (Springer 2017) referring to new technologies in the financial sector in general, see eg, European Financial Services Round Table, 'EFR Paper on Regulatory Sandboxes' (September 2016).

104 See eg, FCA (n 48) in particular concerning disclosure obligations and the suitability requirement. Even though ESMA issued guidelines on the suitability requirement (n 91), also regarding robo advice, its applicability still remains a major issue.

105 European Commission, '*Detailed Summary of Individual Responses to the Public Consultation on Fintech: A More Competitive and Innovative European Financial Sector*' 39.

106 See also FCA (n 48). For a detailed analysis of this problem and the regulatory situation of robo advisors in general, see Wolf-Georg Ringe and Christopher Ruof, 'A Regulatory Sandbox for Robo Advice' (2018) EBI Working Paper no 26/2018, 28ff.

107 EBA, 'Discussion Paper on EBA's approach to financial technology (FinTech)' (4 August 2017).

108 A similar trend was observed by EIOPA for the insurance sector. See EIOPA, 'Sixth Consumer Trends Report' (2017).

109 Meaning here regulated under MiFID directly or by the national regime, using the exemption under Article 3 of MiFID.

110 EBA, 'The EBA's Fintech Roadmap' (15 March 2018) builds on the findings of the Discussion Paper. The Roadmap casts doubt on the representativeness of this number against the background of the limited sample (see p 10). Nonetheless, EBA plans to further analyse the matter (see p 20).

treatment of robo advisors across the EU. Similar concerns were raised by respondents to the European Commission's fintech consultation.[111] Given the fact that the regulatory framework is widely harmonised by EU law, this indicates that there is also substantial uncertainty among regulators regarding the application of current regulation to new technologies. This not only runs contrary to the regulatory objectives of investor protection and of preserving financial stability, it also adversely affects innovation. Ultimately, uncertainty on the side of regulators necessarily intensifies the uncertainty among regulated firms.

The effects of high regulatory uncertainty are manifold: first of all, it constitutes a substantial market barrier for potential market entrants. The threat of being sanctioned when introducing a new technology to the market or (in the worst case) being forced to cease business may lead fintechs to be cautious with innovation and may prevent them from entering the market in the first place.[112] Evidence from other areas suggests that time-to-market can be increased by about a third in this way, at a cost of about 7 or 8% of product lifetime revenue.[113]

Regulatory uncertainty also creates a barrier for (potential) investors[114] as they try to factor in risk which, under those circumstances, they are not well placed to assess.[115] In other words, investing in a fintech that has not yet been licensed bears great risks. There is evidence from another sector, the pharma industry, that regulatory uncertainty can have a significant impact on the firm's ability to attract capital from investors.[116] And this does not include cases of firms failing to raise any funding at all. Thus, under regulatory uncertainty it becomes hard for firms to raise fresh capital, which ultimately slows down innovation.

The inconsistent application of regulation (or deviations in domestic regulation) mentioned above can additionally lead to regulatory arbitrage. Robo advisors may shop for the jurisdiction whose regulatory system or enforcement appear more favourable to them, potentially causing the well-known 'race to the bottom' as a result of regulatory competition.[117] This might simultaneously bare risks for investors, because the service might not be properly evaluated by the respective authority.

Aside from regulatory uncertainty, another main obstacle of the current framework appears to be licensing requirements.[118] As stated above, to receive a regular licence, among other things an initial capital endowment is required, as specified in the Capital Requirements Regulation (CRR) and the Capital Requirements Directive IV (CRD IV).[119]

---

111 European Commission (n 105) 42.
112 Notably, the firm seeking to enter the market may (informally) consult the competent authority beforehand. This process however might be slow and is often not able to fully eliminate the uncertainty.
113 Ariel D Stern, 'Innovation under regulatory uncertainty: Evidence from medical technology' (2017) 145 Journal of Public Economics 181, 189.
114 Hereby referring to investors for firms (ie, robo advisors).
115 See FCA, 'Regulatory Sandbox' (November 2015) 5.
116 See Deloitte, 'A Challenging Future for Biopharmaceutical Innovation' (2014) <https://www2.deloitte.com/content/dam/Deloitte/us/Documents/life-sciences-health-care/us-lshc-biopharma-ceutical-innovation-in-the-face-of-uncertainity.pdf>.
117 Wolf-Georg Ringe, 'Regulatory Competition in Global Financial Markets – The Case for a Special Resolution Regime' (2016) 1 Annals of Corporate Governance 175.
118 As shown above, out of the EBA sample, 65% of all robo advisors have an authorisation.
119 Regulation (EU) No 575/2013 of the European Parliament and of the Council of 26 June 2013 on prudential requirements for credit institutions and investment firms [2013] OJ EU L 176/1 (CRR) and Directive 2013/36/EU of the European Parliament and of the Council of 26 June 2013 on access to the activity of credit institutions and the prudential supervision of credit institutions and investment firms [2013] OJ EU L 176/338. See MiFID II Article 15, which refers to CRR.

Especially for small fintechs constantly struggling to find investors and to raise capital, this poses a considerable barrier to enter the market. Insiders estimate that the total costs for operating a fintech until the receipt of a licence amounts to roughly €20 million, which is a significant sum to come up with for any start-up.[120]

As a consequence of this, many robo advisors sought the option that was provided by MiFID I Article 3.[121] However, as this has now been tightened further under MiFID II (see above) the exemption under Article 3 has become more of an 'empty shell' than a considerable opportunity for robo advisors in the long term. This should explain why barely any robo advisor is regulated under Article 3 anymore. It might also be a partial explanation for the recent trend of engaging in partnerships with incumbent players: when obtaining a licence becomes too costly, the fintech firm could effectively be forced into this dependant partnership to be able to enter the market at all. This might in effect undermine the regulator's competition objective. In the end, it also stifles innovation, because as soon as the robo advisor is under the control of an incumbent, the incentive to 'disrupt' is much smaller.

With regard to investor protection, the regulation generally applicable to financial advice primarily relies on the suitability requirement, the prevention of conflicts of interest and the education of the customer by obliging the firms to provide a stack of information.

While the suitability requirement certainly has the potential to ensure a certain quality of the advice, it is yet far from clear how this is supposed to apply to robo advisors.[122]

Regarding disclosure obligations, the automated and digital nature of robo advisors could be an advantage, potentially simplifying the provision of required information. However, the effectiveness of comprehensive disclosure requirements for robo advisors can also be questioned. There are studies showing that especially in an online setting, people tend to 'skip and skim' information[123], which is for example being attributed to the respondents losing concentration or patience.[124] The more information is provided the greater the risk of being skipped. Meanwhile, there is also evidence that the design of information has a huge influence on the probability of it being read at all.[125] Hence, the focus of regulation should not only lie on whether and what kind of information is provided, but also on the (genuinely) necessary amount of information and especially how it is provided.

In sum, the present EU regulatory framework includes rules applicable to robo advice, however causes a number of concerns. While a highly prescriptive, rule-based approach is

---

120 See Philippe Gelis, 'Why Fintech Banks Will Rule the World' in Susanne Chishti and Janos Barberis (eds), *The Fintech Book: The Financial Technology Handbook for Investors, Entrepreneurs and Visionaries* (Wiley 2016) 237. Unfortunately, there are no exact numbers specifically in regard of robo advisors. As 'fintech' encompasses a huge variety of different services, the variation in upfront costs is presumably high. This number can therefore at best work as an indicator.

121 See for example Jürgen App, 'Regulation von Fintech' (*Private Banker*, 22 April 2016) <http://private-banker.online/news/die-app-kolumne.html> showing that half of robo-advisors (from his sample) are regulated under the German Trade Regulation Code (*GewO*), which is mainly the German domestic regime for those robo advisors that benefit from the exemption of article 3 MiFID.

122 According to the Directive, the advice must always take into account the individual situation of the customer. Concerns especially arise against the backdrop of the abovementioned limits of the questionnaire and available portfolio compositions.

123 Salo and Haapio (n 47) 442. Further, see EBA (n 110) (proposing for example, a 'time-lag' between provision of information and continuing, videos or quizzes on p. 50); ESAs (n 54) 22, 28.

124 See Kaya (n 5) 3. Moreover, a recent study documented that visitors of a website had a dwell time on average before leaving the website, 80% had a dwell time of less than 100 seconds (see Nicola Barbieri, Fabrizio Silvestri and Mounia Lalmas, 'Improving Post-Click User's Engagement on Native Ads via Survival Analysis' in *Proceedings of the World Wide Web Conference* (2016) 761ff).

125 Salo and Haapio (n 47) 448ff. with further references.

intended to further regulatory certainty, we can observe that the opposite is true. Adding the immense regulatory burden, the current framework creates high market barriers for robo advisors. At the same time, actual risks remain often unaddressed.

5 Conclusion

This chapter has explored the phenomenon of 'robo advice' – the automated provision of financial advice, typically based on algorithms, without human intervention. Robo advice holds the promise of cheap, convenient and fast investment services for consumers and investors, free from human error or bias. However, retail investors have limited capacity to assess the soundness of the advice, and are prone to make hasty, unverified investment decisions. Moreover, financial advice based on rough and broad classifications may fail to take into account the individual preferences and needs of the investor. On a more general scale, robo advice and recommendations based on algorithms can become a source of new systemic risk. At this stage, the existing EU regulatory framework is of little help. Neither does it adequately address these concerns, nor does it support the development of robo advisors.

Bibliography

J Armour, D Awrey, P Davies, L Enriques, J N Gordon, C Mayer and J Payne, *Principles of Financial Regulation* (Oxford University Press 2016).

T Baker and B Dellaert, 'Regulating Robo Advice Across the Financial Services Industry' (2018) 103 Iowa Law Review 713–750.

N Barbieri, F Silvestri and M Lalmas, 'Improving Post-Click User's Engagement on Native Ads via Survival Analysis' in Proceedings of the 25th International Conference on World Wide Web (Geneva, Switzerland 2016) 761–770.

I H Y Chiu, 'Fintech and Disruptive Business Models in Financial Products, Intermediation and Markets – Policy Implications for Financial Regulators' (2016) 21 Journal of Technology Law & Policy 55–112.

F D'Acunto, N Prabhala and Alberto G Rossi, 'The Promises and Pitfalls of Robo-advising' (2019) 32 Review of Financial Studies 1983–2020.

M Demertzis, S Merler and GB Wolff, 'Capital Markets Union and the Fintech Opportunity' (2018) 4 Journal of Financial Regulation 157–165.

S P Deschenes and P B Hammod, 'Matching FinTech Advice to Participant Needs' in Julie Agnew and Olivia S Mitchell (eds), *The Disruptive Impact of Fintech on Retirement Systems* (OUP 2019) 172–189.

G Dorfleitner, L Hornuf, M Schmitt and M Weber, *The Fintech Market in Germany* (Springer 2017).

European Banking Authority, 'Discussion Paper on EBA's approach to financial technology (FinTech)' (EBA/DP/2017/02, 4 August 2017).

European Banking Authority, 'The EBA's Fintech Roadmap' (15 March 2018) <https://eba.europa.eu/sites/default/documents/files/documents/10180/1919160/79d2cbc6-ce28-482a-9291-34cfba8e0c02/EBA%20FinTech%20Roadmap.pdf?retry=1>.

European Banking Authority, Report on the Impact of Fintech on Institutions' business models (3 July 2018) <https://eba.europa.eu/sites/default/documents/files/documents/10180/2270909/1f27bb57-387e-4978-82f6ece725b51941/Report%20on%20the%20impact%20of%20Fintech%20on%20incumbent%20credit%20institutions%27%20business%20models.pdf?retry=1>.

European Commission, 'Action Plan on Building a Capital Market Union' (COM (2015) 0468, 30 September 2015) <https://eur-lex.europa.eu/legal-content/EN/TXT/?uri=CELEX%3A52015 DC0468>.

European Commission, 'Fintech: A More Competitive and Innovative European Financial Sector' (Consultation Document, 16 March 2017) <https://ec.europa.eu/info/sites/info/files/2017-fintech-consultation-document_en_0.pdf>.

European Commission, 'Detailed Summary of Individual Responses to the "Public Consultation on Fintech: A More Competitive and Innovative European Financial Sector"' (12 September 2017) (ANNEX).

European Financial Services Round Table, 'EFR Paper on Regulatory Sandboxes' (September 2016) <www.efr.be/documents/news/99.2.%20EFR%20paper%20on%20Regulatory%20Sandboxes %2029.09.2016.pdf>.

European Insurance and Occupational Pensions Authority, 'Sixth Consumer Trends Report' (2017) <https://op.europa.eu/de/publication-detail/-/publication/1a9cb27b-437d-11e8-a9f4-01aa75ed71a1>.

European Securities and Markets Authority, 'Guidelines on Certain Aspects of the MiFID II Suitability Requirement' (ESMA35-43-748, July 2017).

Financial Conduct Authority, 'Regulatory Sandbox' (November 2015) <https://www.fca.org.uk /publication /research/regulatory-sandbox.pdf>.

Financial Stability Board (FSB), 'Artificial Intelligence and Machine Learning in Financial Services' (1 November 2017) <https://www.fsb.org/wp-content/uploads/P011117.pdf>.

Financial Stability Board (FSB), Financial Stability Implications from Fintech: Supervisory and Regulatory Issues that Merit Authorities' Attention (27 June 2017) <https://www.fsb.org/wp-content/uploads/R270617.pdf>.

Financial Stability Board (FSB), 'FinTech and Market Structure in Financial Services: Market Developments and Potential Financial Stability Implications' (14 February 2019) <https://www.fsb.org/wp-content/uploads/P140219.pdf>.

J E Fisch, M Labouré and J Turner, 'The Economics of Complex Decision Making: The Emergence of the Robo Adviser' in Julie Agnew and Olivia S Mitchell (eds), *The Disruptive Impact of Fintech on Retirement Systems* (OUP 2019) 13–37.

P Gelis, 'Why Fintech Banks Will Rule the World' in S Chishti and J Barberis (eds), *The Fintech Book: The Financial Technology Handbook for Investors, Entrepreneurs and Visionaries* (Wiley 2016).

Joint Committee European Supervisory Authorities, Joint Committee Discussion Paper on automation in financial advice (JC 2015 080, 4 December 2015).

Joint Committee European Supervisory Authorities, 'Report on Automation in Financial Advice' (16 December 2016) <https://esas-joint-committee.europa.eu/Publications/ Reports/EBA%20BS%202016%20422%20(JC%20SC%20CPFI%20Final%20Report%20on%20auto-mated%20advice%20tools).pdf>.

Joint Committee European Supervisory Authorities, Joint Committee Report on the results of the monitoring exercise on 'automation in financial advice' (JC 2018-29, 5 September 2018).

D Jung, E Erdfelder and F Glaser, 'Nudged to Win: Designing Robo-Advisory to Overcome Decision Inertia' (29 November 2018) ECIS 2018 Proceedings, <https://core.ac.uk/download/pdf/301378642.pdf>.

O Kaya, 'Robo-advice – a True Innovation in Asset Management' Deutsche Bank Research (10 August 2017) <https://www.dbresearch.com/PROD/RPS_EN-PROD/PROD0000000000449125/Robo-advice_%E2%80%93_a_true_innovation_in_asset_managemen.pdf?undefined-&realload=Zxq2vBDA13B9`7nSBtgThJNr7r7cDd7Q53ksin4VS5w6znJkqrWn77X0dghf6PxCIusLin4vMaDDVzxBOdmmfw==>.

O Kaya, 'German Robo-advisors – Rapid Growth, Robust Performance, High Cost' Deutsche Bank Research (12 February 2019) <https://www.dbresearch.com/ PROD/RPS_EN-PROD/PROD0000000000487351/German_robo-advisors%3A_ Rapid_growth%2C_ robust_perform.PDF?undefined&realload=6ZKrbK~w8u5n1CWQ8f/ ZKJ1VV8iAgRqsSm6vGlSvd2cPiROrCaufJYeAb~7F/iUVYzSejqQqHwAcDNkZhxmHaA==>.

K Lannoo, 'MiFID II and the New Market Conduct Rules for Financial Intermediaries: Will Complexity Bring Transparency?' (26 May 2017) ECMI Policy Brief No 24.

B Lins, 'Robo Advice: Aufsichtsrechtliche Pflichten der digitalen Anlageberatung und Vermögensverwaltung' (2020) 20 Zeitschrift für Bank- und Kapitalmarktrecht (BKR) 181.

OECD, *Under Pressure: The Squeezed Middle Class* (OECD Publishing 2019).

W G Ringe, 'Regulatory Competition in Global Financial Markets – The Case for a Special Resolution Regime' (2016) 1 Annals of Corporate Governance 175–247.

W G Ringe, 'The Irrelevance of Brexit for the European Financial Market' (2018) 19 European Business Organization Law Review 1–34.

W G Ringe, 'The Politics of Capital Markets Union: From Brexit to Eurozone' in F Allen, E Faia, M Haliassos and K Langenbucher (eds), *Capital Markets Union and Beyond* (MIT Press 2019) 341-352.

W G Ringe and C Ruof, 'A Regulatory Sandbox for Robo Advice' (2018) EBI Working Paper no 26/2018 <https://ssrn.com/abstract=3188828>.

P Rohner and M W Uhl, 'Robo-Advisors vs. Traditional Investment Advisors – an Unequal Game' (2017) 21 The Journal of Wealth Management 44–50.

D Ryan, J Courbe, A Gilbert, M Alix and R Rodriguez, 'PwC discusses SEC's Increased Scrutiny of Robo-Advisors' (8 November 2017) CLS Blue Sky Blog.

M Salo and H Haapio, 'Robo-Advisors and Investors: Enhancing Human-Robot Interaction Through Information Design' in E Schweighofer, F Kummer, W Hötzendorfer and C Sorge (eds), *Trends and Communities of Legal Informatics. Proceedings of the 20th International Legal Informatics Symposium IRIS 2017* (Österreichische Computer Gesellschaft 2017).

SEC, 'Findings Regarding the Market Events of May 6, 2010' (30 September 2010).

A D Stern, 'Innovation Under Regulatory Uncertainty: Evidence from Medical Technology' (2017) 145 Journal of Public Economics 181–200.

M Tertilt and P Scholz, 'To Advise, or Not to Advise – How Robo-Advisors Evaluate the Risk Preferences of Private Investors' (2018) 21(2) Journal of Wealth Management 70–84.

F Wedlich, 'Wie wirken sich Verhaltensanomalien von Anlegern auf Robo-Advisory aus?' (2018) 7 Corporate Finance 225–230.

J H Wosnitza, 'Robo-Advising Private Investors on German Mid-Cap Bonds' (2018) 7 Corporate Finance 220–225.

12 Insurance and the legal challenges of automated decisions

An EU perspective

Paola Manes

1 From Big Data to automated decisions

1.1 *Data management and new technologies*

Over the past two decades, data has, to a large extent, increased in several business sectors, such as insurance and financial services (just to name a few).[1]

Although data has been analysed for millennia, the rise of so-called 'Big Data'[2] has led to the emergence of a specific discipline that studies how to analyse large datasets and turn them into meaningful information that we can make use of, for example, to make predictions: 'Data Science'.[3]

Data Science can be considered as an amalgamation of classical disciplines such as statistics, Artificial Intelligence (AI), mathematics and computer science; it combines existing

---

1 From the rich literature on this topic, see eg, Phil Simon, *Too Big to Ignore. The Business Case for Big Data* (Wiley 2013) 7; Viktor Mayer-Schönberger and Kenneth Cukier, *Big Data: A Revolution that Will Transform How We Live, Work, and Think* (Houghton Mifflin Harcourt 2013) 6–7; International Association of Insurance Supervisors (IAIS), *FinTech Developments in the Insurance Industry* (2017) 32 <https://www.iaisweb.org/file/65625/report-on-fintech-developments-in-the-insurance-industry> (Call-off date for all hyperlinks, unless stated otherwise: 30 June 2020); Giovanni Comandé, 'Regulating Algorithms' Regulation? First Ethico-Legal Principles, Problems, and Opportunities of Algorithms' in Tania Cerquitelli and others (eds), *Transparent Data Mining for Big and Small Data* (Springer 2017) 169; Antonella Cappiello, *Technology and the Insurance Industry: Re-configuring the Competitive Landscape* (Springer 2018) 9–10; Davide Mula, 'Big Data vs Data Privacy' in Giusella Finocchiaro and Valeria Falce (eds), *Fintech: diritti, concorrenza, regole. Le operazioni di finanziamento tecnologico* (Zanichelli Editore 2019) 355–356; Marco Delmastro and Antonio Nicita, *Big Data. Come stanno cambiando il nostro mondo* (Il Mulino 2019) 14; Viktoria Chatzara, 'FinTech, InsurTech, and the Regulators' in Pierpaolo Marano and Kyriaki Noussia (eds), *InsurTech: A Legal and Regulatory View* (Springer 2020) 3; The Economist, 'An understanding of AI's limitations is starting to sink in' (2020) Technology Quarterly <https://www.economist.com/technology-quarterly/2020/06/11/an-understanding-of-ais-limitations-is-starting-to-sink-in>.
2 The term 'Big Data' was introduced under the massive increase of global data. Initially the idea behind 'Big Data' was that the volume of information had grown so large that the quantity being examined no longer fit into the memory that computers use for processing, so engineers needed new tools for analysing it all; that is the origin of new processing technologies that let one manage far larger quantities of data than ever before. See eg, Mayer-Schönberger and Cukier (n 1) 6–7.
3 See eg, Mike Loukides, *What is Data Science?* (O'Reilly Media 2011) 2, who explains that '*data scientists are involved with gathering data, massaging it into a tractable form, making it tell its story, and presenting that story to others*'. See also Nils J Nilsson, *The Quest for Artificial Intelligence. A History of Ideas and Achievements* (Cambridge University Press 2010) 398; Mayer-Schönberger and Cukier (n 1) 6–7.

approaches with the aim of turning abundantly available data into value for individuals, organisations and society.[4]

Today, just like, in order to obtain a small amount of precious material, a large volume of soil and raw material needs to be extracted from a mine, large volumes of data can be processed to construct a simple model with valuable use (eg having high predictive accuracy).[5]

The concept of 'Data Mining' intertwines with that of 'Machine Learning' (ML). Although over time, the difference between the two has become less relevant and boundaries are beginning to blur, rather simplistically, Data Mining aims at finding knowledge from data, while ML aims at 'teaching' a machine how to do it.[6]

In particular, the core aim of Machine Learning is making inference from example data or experience, using the theory of statistics in building mathematical models;[7] ML methods today are thus playing an increasingly important role in data analysis, as they can deal with massive amounts of data.[8]

ML studies algorithms[9] that can learn from data to obtain knowledge from experience and to generate decisions and predictions; in its most basic form, an algorithm can be described as a set of instructions or rules given to a computer to follow and implement.[10]

The ability of algorithms to identify, select and determine information of relevance beyond the scope of human decision-making creates a new kind of decision optimisation; the level of accuracy of decisions, however, depends both on the design of the algorithm itself and on the data it is based on.[11]

1.2 *Automated decisions: the insurance perspective*

Advances in technology and the capabilities of AI and ML have made it easier for organisations to create profiles and make automated decisions with the potential to increase efficiencies and save resources.[12]

---

4 See eg, Nilsson (n 3) 398; Jerry Kaplan, *Artificial Intelligence. What Everyone Needs to Know* (OUP 2016) 12; Arvind Narayanan and Dillon Reisman, 'The Princeton Web Transparency and Accountability Project' in Tania Cerquitelli and others (eds), *Transparent Data Mining for Big and Small Data* (Springer 2017) 46.

5 Ethem Alpaydın, *Introduction to Machine Learning* (3rd edn, MIT Press 2014) 3.

6 See eg, Toon Calders and Bart Custers, 'What Is Data Mining and How Does It Work?' in Bart Custers and others (eds), *Discrimination and Privacy in the Information Society. Data Mining and Profiling in Large Databases* (Springer 2013) 29.

7 See eg, Narayanan and Reisman (n 4) 46.

8 See eg, Calders and Custers (n 6) 27; Kaplan (n 4) 12; Narayanan and Reisman (n 4) 46.

9 From the rich literature on this topic, see eg, Alpaydın (n 5) 1; Bruno Lepri and others, 'The Tyranny of Data? The Bright and Dark Sides of Data-Driven Decision-Making for Social Good' in Tania Cerquitelli and others (eds), *Transparent Data Mining for Big and Small Data* (Springer 2017) 6–7.

10 See eg, Pedro Domingos, *The Master Algorithm: How the Quest for the Ultimate Learning Machine Will Remake Our World* (Penguin 2015) 6.

11 See eg, Nilsson (n 3) 495; Alpaydın (n 5) 3.

12 See eg, Nilsson (n 3) 495; Simon (n 1) 46; Delmastro and Nicita (n 1) 8.

Although insurance companies have traditionally been slower in embracing technological change than other industries, new technologies have the potential to make the insurance experience on-demand,[13] faster and more affordable for customers.[14]

Combining the tools of AI and ML with the large amount of data at their disposal,[15] insurers might thus be able to provide more tailored and flexible services and premiums that reflect customers' characteristics (eg, health, habits), and cover new risk scenarios by taking a more proactive role in customers' risk management.[16]

An interesting example of the evolution of insurance services thanks to new technologies is telematics car insurance.[17]

Actuarial ratings determine traditional car insurance; insurance companies use actuarial science to quantify the risks based on the driver demographic variables (eg, age, income) and on vehicle characteristics.[18]

Emerging technologies in telematics provide new opportunities for data mining and the creation of new products and services based on better perception of customer behaviour.[19] In particular, new car telematics devices allow insurers to target driving risk classes more effectively and model premiums by combining factors of usage and driving behaviour (eg, speed, driving time).[20]

---

13 On-demand insurance allows policy-holders to quickly insure their life, health, homes, objects and vehicles for a short period of time using a mobile application. This type of insurance is becoming more and more popular among users, as it allows to insure their belongings temporarily, while saving significantly. See eg, Vasyl Soloshchuk and Yuri Kartashov, 'InsurTech Trends – Why Regionalization Matters' in Sabine L B VanderLinden and others (eds), *The InsurTech Book: The Insurance Technology Handbook for Investors, Entrepreneurs and FinTech Visionaries* (Wiley 2018) 108–110.

14 See eg, Capgemini and Efma, *World Insurance Report 2020* (2020) 13 <https://worldinsurancereport. com/resources/world-insurance-report-2020/>. See also Valentino Ricciardi, 'InsurTech Definition as Its Own Manifesto' in Sabine L B VanderLinden and others (eds), *The InsurTech Book: The Insurance Technology Handbook for Investors, Entrepreneurs and FinTech Visionaries* (Wiley 2018) 7.

15 Traditionally, insurers collect a large amount of their customers' specific data in order to provide their services. For example, insurers gather data during the quote process, where very specific questions are asked and then enriched with specific data services. See eg, Visesh Gosrani, 'Data Changes Everything' in Sabine L B VanderLinden and others (eds), *The InsurTech Book: The Insurance Technology Handbook for Investors, Entrepreneurs and FinTech Visionaries* (Wiley 2018) 171.

16 IAIS (n 1) 32; Organisation for Economic Co-operation and Development (OECD), *Technology and Innovation in the Insurance Sector* (2017) 26–27; Capgemini and Efma (n 14) 13. See also Ricciardi (n 14) 7; Rosaria Romano, 'Intelligenza Artificiale, decisioni e responsabilità in ambito finanziario; snodi problematici' in Giusella Finocchiaro and Valeria Falce (eds), *Fintech: diritti, concorrenza, regole. Le operazioni di finanziamento tecnologico* (Zanichelli Editore 2019) 318–319; Piotr Tereszkiewicz, 'Digitalisation of Insurance Contract Law: Preliminary Thoughts with Special Regard to Insurer's Duty to Advise' in Pierpaolo Marano and Kyriaki Noussia (eds), *InsurTech: A Legal and Regulatory View* (Springer 2020) 130–131.

17 Modern vehicles are equipped, or can be retrofitted, with a set of sensors that can infer information about a vehicle's state and its surrounding environment. The data collected from these sensors are known as telematics data. See eg, Manda Winlaw and others, 'Using Telematics Data to Find Risky Driver Behaviour' (2019) 131 Accident Analysis and Prevention 131.

18 See eg, Simon (n 1) 1–2; Philippe Baecke and Lorenzo Bocca, 'The Value of Vehicle Telematics Data in Insurance Risk Selection Processes' (2017) 98 Decision Support Systems 72–73; Yiyang Bian and others, 'Good Drivers Pay Less: A Study of Usage-based Vehicle Insurance' (2018) 107 Transportation Research Part A 21.

19 See eg, OECD (n 16) 26–27. See also Simon (n 1) 3; Baecke and Bocca (n 18) 72–73; Bian and others (n 18) 21; Cappiello (n 1) 12–13; Romano (n 16) 319–20; Tereszkiewicz (n 16) 131.

20 See eg, Simon (n 1) 3; Baecke and Bocca (n 18) 72–73; Bian and others (n 18) 21.

Furthermore, several auto insurers incorporate behaviour-based credit scores from credit bureaus into their analysis, based on empirical evidence that people who pay their bills on time are also safer drivers.[21]

In general, credit scoring is a system creditors use to label credit applicants as either 'good credit' that is likely to repay financial obligation or 'bad credit' who has a high possibility of defaulting on financial obligation.[22] Although credit-scoring methods are widely used for loan applications in financial and banking institutions, they can be useful for other types of organisations, such as insurance companies, for predicting late payments.[23]

Modern credit scoring models, benefiting from new Data Mining techniques, provide an estimate of a counterparty's credit risk;[24] in the field of insurance, such models assess the probability of an individual filing an insurance claim while under coverage.[25] The score is determined by the individual's credit rating and will affect the premiums they pay for the coverage, based on the assumption that an individual with a low score has a greater propensity for filing an insurance claim.[26]

Hence, recourse to new technologies can be a precious tool for insurers, allowing to reveal patterns and correlations, generate new solutions and predict certain events or behaviours in a more accurate and timely manner.[27]

2 New technologies, new problems

2.1 *The legal challenges of automated decisions*

As policymakers are now introducing guidelines for the use of automated decision-making techniques,[28] it is becoming increasingly important to be able to verify whether intelligent systems comply with existing legal framework.

---

21 See eg, OECD (n 16) 26–27. See also Bruce Kellison and Patrick Brockett, 'Check the Score: Credit Scoring and Insurance Losses: Is There a Connection?' (2003) Special Issue 2003 Texas Business Review 1.

22 See eg, Kellison and Brockett (n 21) 1; Shweta Arya and others, 'Anatomy of the Credit Score' (2013) 95 Journal of Economic Behavior & Organization 176; Wang Bao and others, 'Integration of Unsupervised and Supervised Machine Learning Algorithms for Credit Risk Assessment' (2019) 128 Expert Systems With Applications 301–302.

23 See eg, Kellison and Brockett (n 21) 1; Arya and others (n 22) 176; Bao and others (n 22) 301–302.

24 Francesca Mattassoglio, 'La valutazione del merito creditizio e l'innovazione tecnologica" in Maria-Teresa Paracampo (ed), *Fintech. Introduzione ai profili giuridici di un mercato unico tecnologico dei servizi finanziari. Volume II* (2nd edn, Giappichelli 2019) 197. See also Alpaydın (n 5) 5; Bao and others (n 22) 301–302.

25 Kellison and Brockett (n 21) 4–5; Bao and others (n 22) 301–302.

26 Kellison and Brockett (n 21) 4–5; Arya and others (n 22) 176.

27 IAIS (n 1) 32. See also Simon (n 1) 3–4; Tereszkiewicz (n 16) 132.

28 See eg, the Council of Europe, *Guidelines on the Protection of Individuals with Regard to the Processing of Personal Data in a World of Big Data* (T-PD(2017)01, 2017) par 7.3 <https://rm.coe.int/t-pd-2017-1-bigdataguidelines-en/16806f06d0>, which affirm that '*where decisions based on Big Data might affect individual rights significantly or produce legal effects*' the data subject has the right to ask for '*the reasoning underlying the processing*'. See also the European Parliament Committee on Legal Affairs, *European Civil Law Rules on Robotics* (2015/2103 (INL), 2016) 10; the European Commission for the Efficiency of Justice, *European Ethical Charter on the Use of Artificial Intelligence in Judicial Systems and Their Environment* (CEPEJ(2018)14) Principle 4; G20, *AI Principles* (Annex to G20 Ministerial Statement on Trade and Digital Economy, 2019) 11 <https://trade.ec.europa.eu/doclib/docs/2019/june/tradoc_157920.pdf>.

In particular, transparency and explainability are amongst the most demanding issues related to the use of automated decision-making systems.[29]

A 'right to an explanation' for data subjects might be observed within the General Data Protection Regulation (GDPR),[30] in the combination of several dispositions.[31]

First, the GDPR states that data subjects have the right to access information collected about them, and require data processors to ensure data subjects are notified about the data collected.[32]

Second, Article 22 of the GDPR affirms that the data subject shall have the right not to be subject to an assessment based solely on automated processing,[33] and the associated Recital 71 gives them the right to obtain an explanation of the decision reached after such assessment and to challenge it.[34]

The Working Party on the protection of individuals with regard to the processing of personal data (Article 29 Working Party)[35] further specified that in case of automated

29 See eg, Jenna Burrell, 'How the Machine "Thinks": Understanding Opacity in Machine Learning Algorithms' (2016) 3(1) Big Data & Society 2; Gianclaudio Malgieri and Giovanni Comandé, 'Why a Right to Legibility of Automated Decision-Making Exists in the General Data Protection Regulation' (2017) 7(4) International Data Privacy Law 243; Zachary C Lipton, 'The Mythos of Model Interpretability' (2018) 16(3) Queue – Machine Learning 2; Mike Ananny and Kate Crawford, 'Seeing without Knowing: Limitations of the Transparency Ideal and Its Application to Algorithmic Accoun tability' (2018) 20(3) New Media & Society 5; Wojciech Samek and Klaus-Robert Müller, 'Towards Explainable Artificial Intelligence' in Wojciech Samek and others (eds), *Explainable AI: Interpreting, Explaining and Visualizing Deep Learning* (Springer 2019) 7; Giusella Finocchiaro, 'Intelligenza Artificiale e protezione dei dati personali' in Enrico Gabrielli and Ugo Ruffolo (eds), *Intelligenza Artificiale e diritto* (Giurisprudenza Italiana, 2019) 1674.
30 Regulation (EU) 2016/679 of the European Parliament and of the Council of 27 April 2016 on the protection of natural persons with regard to the processing of personal data and on the free movement of such data, and repealing Directive 95/46/EC (General Data Protection Regulation) [2016] OJ L 119/1, Recital 71 and Art. 13–15 and 22.
31 From the rich literature on this topic, see eg, Bryce Goodman and Seth Flaxman, 'European Union Regulations on Algorithmic Decision-making and a "Right to Explanation"' (2017) 38(3) AI Magazine 50–57; Maja Brkan, 'Do Algorithms Rule the World? Algorithmic Decision-Making in the Framework of the GDPR and Beyond' (2019) 27(2) International Journal of Law and Information Technology 93; Mula (n 1) 365; Malgieri and Comandé (n 29) 243; Annarita Ricci, 'I diritti dell'interessato' in Giusella Finocchiaro (ed), *Il nuovo Regolamento europeo sulla privacy e sulla protezione dei dati person-ali* (Zanichelli Editore 2017) 181. It should be noted that not all scholars agree on the existence of a right to an explanation of algorithmic decisions in EU data protection law. In particular, it has been observed that Article 22 of the GDPR provides to prevent only processing of a particular kind and to require human intervention for that, but it does not require any kind of explanation of how processing was carried out or result achieved. See eg, Sandra Wachter and others, 'Why a Right to Explanation of Automated Decision-Making Does Not Exist in the General Data Protection Regulation' (2017) 7(2) International Data Privacy Law 79; Lilian Edwards and Michael Veale, 'Slave to the Algorithm? Why a "Right to an Explanation" is Probably Not the Remedy You Are Looking for' (2017) 16(1) Duke Law & Technology Review 45–49; Giusella Finocchiaro, 'Riflessioni su intelligenza artificiale e protezione dei dati personali', in Ugo Ruffolo (ed), *Intelligenza Artificiale – Il diritto, i diritti, l'etica* (Giuffrè Francis-Lefebvre 2020) 242–246.
32 GDPR, Art. 13–15.
33 GDPR, Art. 22.
34 GDPR, Recital 71.
35 The Article 29 Working Party was an advisory body made up of a representative from the data protec-tion authority of each EU Member State, the European Data Protection Supervisor and the European Commission. On 25 May 2018, the European Data Protection Board (EDPB) replaced it in compliance with the GDPR.

decisions as described in Article 22(1) of the GDPR, the controller must *'provide meaningful information about the logic involved'* and *'explain the significance and envisaged consequences of the processing'*.[36]

These provisions potentially present a number of practical challenges for the design and deployment of ML algorithms.

In particular, Article 22 and Recital 71 of the GDPR, interpreted narrowly, might prohibit a wide range of algorithms currently in use, for example, in credit and insurance risk assessment.[37]

Hence, Insurance Europe[38] issued a Position Paper recommending Article 29 Working Party to re-shape its Guidelines in order to account for the peculiarities of the insurance business.[39] In particular, Insurance Europe suggested that Article 29 Working Party acknowledged in its Guidelines that recourse to profiling and automated decision-making processes should not be challenged in cases of insurance contracts, where such processes are necessary for the assessment of the client's risk.[40]

The Article 29 Working Party did not follow Insurance Europe's recommendations: however, at the national levels, there are a few interesting cases of legislation implementing the GDPR with focus on the peculiarities of the insurance sector.[41]

For example, the German Federal Data Protection Act (BDSG) considers the decisions for the provision of insurance services pursuant to an insurance contract a specific case of permitted automated decision-making; however, it specifies that the exception shall apply only if the request of the data subject receives a positive outcome.[42]

Similar dispositions can be found in the Liechtenstein Data Protection Act.[43]

2.2 *Algorithms: new gold or 'black-boxes'?*

Although ML algorithms have successfully made their way into several practical applications in the insurance field, some of their features raise several concerns.

First, the quality of data, the way the data is input into the system, and the way the system is 'trained' to analyse the data can have disparate effects on the validity, accuracy, and usefulness of the information generated by the algorithm at the basis of an automated decision-making process.[44]

---

36 Article 29 Working Party, *Guidelines on Automated Individual Decision-making and Profiling for the Purposes of Regulation 2016/679* (2018) 16.
37 See eg, Goodman and Flaxman (n 31) 50–57; Brkan (n 31) 91.
38 Insurance Europe is the European insurance and reinsurance federation. Its member bodies are the national insurance associations, and it represents different types of insurance and reinsurance undertakings (eg, pan-European companies, monoliners, mutuals and SMEs).
39 Insurance Europe, *Insurance Europe Comments on the Article 29 Working Party's Draft Guidelines on Automated Individual Decision-making & Profiling* (Position Paper, 2019) 2–3.
40 Insurance Europe (n 39) 2–3.
41 Bundesdatenschutzgesetz (BDSG) (2017) BGBl. I S. 2097, Section 37, official English translation <https://www.gesetze-im-internet.de/englisch_bdsg/englisch_bdsg.html#p0310>.
42 BDSG, Section 37 (n 41). If the outcome is negative the automated decision is permitted only if: (1) the decision is based on the application of binding rules of remuneration for therapeutic treatment; and (2) the controller takes suitable measures to safeguard the data subject's legitimate interests.
43 Datenschutzgesetz (DSG) (2018) LGBl-Nr 2018.272, Art. 37 <https://www.gesetze.li/konso/2018272000?search_text=datenschutz&search_loc=titel&lrnr=&lgblid_von=&observe_date=11.04.2019>.
44 See eg, Finocchiaro (n 29) 1674.

Second, even when the data is accurate, individuals training the algorithm could infuse their own biases into the system.[45] Algorithms can thus lead to discriminatory results, for instance if they are trained on historical examples that reflect past prejudice or implicit bias, or on data that offers a statistically distorted picture of groups comprising the overall population.[46]

As the accuracy of an algorithm is dependent on both the programming and the data, in case of doubts about the results of an automated decision, how can one inspect and analyse the underlying programming? As Pearl noted, ML has its own dynamics and gives the right results most of the time: *'but when it doesn't, you don't have a clue about what went wrong and what should be fixed'*.[47]

Today ML models reach impressive prediction accuracy; however, often their structure makes them highly non-transparent, so that it is not clear what information in the input data makes them actually arrive at their decisions. Hence, these models are typically regarded as 'black-boxes'.[48]

Many observers argue that current frameworks are not well adapted for situations in which a potentially incorrect, unjustified or unfair outcome emerges from a computer, as often algorithms are unintelligible by individuals, and sometimes by their data controller as well.[49]

Credit scoring represents a typical example of the difficulties often encountered in trying to interpret many modern automated decision-making systems.[50]

From a business perspective, studies have been conducted to show that, statistically speaking, the poorer an individual's credit history, the higher the expected losses that the individual will generate for the insurance company (thus justifying a higher premium for people with poorer credit histories and a lower premium for people with better credit histories).[51] However, approached carelessly, credit scoring algorithms (even if not voluntarily programmed to do

---

45 See eg, OECD (n 16) 34. See also Cathy O'Neil, *Weapons of Math Destruction: How Big Data Increases Inequality and Threatens Democracy* (Crown/Archetype 2016) 25; Solon Barocas and Andrew D Selbst, 'Big Data's Disparate Impact' (2016) 104 California Law Review 687; Comandé (n 1) 172; Dino Pedreschi and Ioanna Miliou, *Artificial Intelligence (AI): New Developments and Innovations Applied to E-commerce. Challenges to the Functioning of the Internal Market* (Policy Department for Economic, Scientific and Quality of Life Policies Directorate-General for Internal Policies, European Parliament, 2020) 12 <https://www.europarl.europa.eu/RegData/etudes/IDAN/2020/648791/IPOL_IDA(2020)648791_EN.pdf>.

46 See eg, OECD (n 16) 34. See also O'Neil (n 45) 162; Barocas and Selbst (n 45) 687; Comandé (n 1) 172; James Grimmelmann and Daniel Westreich, 'Incomprehensible Discrimination' (2017) 7 California Law Review Online 176; Pedreschi and Miliou (n 45) 12.

47 Judea Pearl, 'The Limitations of Opaque Learning Machines' in John Brockman (ed), *Possible Minds. 25 Ways of Looking at AI* (Penguin Press 2019) 15.

48 Frank Pasquale, *The Black Box Society: The Secret Algorithms That Control Money and Information* (Harvard University Press 2015) 19.

49 See eg, Joshua A Kroll and others, 'Accountable Algorithms' (2016) 165(3) University Of Pennsylvania Law Review 633; Sandra Wachter and Brent Mittelstadt, 'A Right to Reasonable Inferences: Re-Thinking Data Protection Law in the Age of Big Data and AI' (2019) 2019(2) Columbia Business Law Review 494.

50 Brenda Reddix-Smalls, 'Credit Scoring and Trade Secrecy: An Algorithmic Quagmire or How the Lack of Transparency in Complex Financial Models Scuttled the Finance Market' (2011) 12(87) U.C. Davis Business School Law Journal 117–118. See also O'Neil (n 45) 162; Bao and others (n 22) 303.

51 See eg, Kellison and Brockett (n 21) 4–5; Arya and others (n 22) 176.

so) might reproduce existing patterns of discrimination, inherit the prejudice of prior decision makers or simply reflect the widespread biases that persist in society.[52]

In compliance with Recital 71 and Article 22 GDPR, the Italian Data Protection Authority (*Garante per la protezione dei dati personali*) recently approved a Code of Conduct for the management of consumer credit information systems, providing that, in case of denial of credit based on automatic assessment, consumers have the right to request the reasons behind the algorithmic decision-making process.[53]

Domains such as credit scoring have rooted in the public mind the awareness that challenging a decision involves a right to an explanation of how such a decision was reached.[54]

However, compliance with the GDPR and the data subjects' right to an explanation pose serious practical issues for the design and deployment of ML algorithms.

Explaining the functionality of complex automated decision-making systems and their rationale in specific cases is still a technically challenging problem, as often the decisional rule emerges automatically from the specific data under analysis, in ways that no human can explain.[55]

The most straightforward way to get to interpretable ML is to use only a subset of algorithms that create simple, intrinsically interpretable models.[56] However, when the task is more daunting, simple models need to be substituted by more complex ones, which are more difficult for a user to interpret.[57]

The trade-off between model accuracy and interpretability often implies that one cannot use a model whose behaviour is very complex, yet expect humans to fully comprehend it.

To solve this trade-off, some scholars assert that tools that permit oversight and review shall always be preferred to less intelligible ones, irrespective of predictive accuracy.[58]

Other scholars support the idea of trying to create simple approximations of 'black-box' algorithms able to accurately model the decision given the current inputs and that are comprehensible to humans.[59]

According to others, the key to 'unlock' what is inside the 'black-boxes' is a combination of skills from a variety of areas; in order to seek explanation, therefore, one should look at

52 See eg, Reddix-Smalls (n 50) 117–118; O'Neil (n 45) 162; Barocas and Selbst (n 45) 673; Edwards and Veale (n 31) 38; Samek and Müller (n 29) 7; Lepri and others (n 9) 8.
53 Garante per la protezione dei dati personali, *Provvedimento del 12 settembre 2019 – Codice di condotta per i sistemi informativi gestiti da soggetti privati in tema di crediti al consumo, affidabilità e puntualità nei pagamenti* (2019) <https://www.garanteprivacy.it/web/guest/home/docweb/-/docweb-display/docweb/9141941>. Within this context, the Italian *Consiglio di Stato* (the body that ensures the legality of public administration in Italy) affirmed that, although algorithms pose several advantages linked to process automation, in order to comply with general principles protecting individuals such as transparency and reasonableness, every algorithmic decision shall be explainable. See Consiglio di Stato section VI, *ruling n. 22708* (2019).
54 See eg, Reddix-Smalls (n 50) 117–118; Edwards and Veale (n 31) 38; Bao and others (n 22) 301–302.
55 See eg, Kroll and others (n 49) 633; Burrell (n 29) 2; Pedreschi and Miliou (n 45) 13.
56 Nilsson (n 3) 500.
57 See eg, Lipton (n 29) 2; Samek and Müller (n 29) 12.
58 See eg, Jialnlong Zhou and Fang Chen, '2D Transparency Space – Bring Domain Users and Machine Learning Experts Together', in Jianlong Zhou and Fang Chen (eds), *Human and Machine Learning: Visible, Explainable, Trustworthy and Transparent* (Springer 2018) 12.
59 See eg, Jan Chorowski and Jacek M Zurada, 'Top-Down Induction of Reduced Ordered Decision Diagrams for Neural Networks' in Timo Honkela and others (eds), *Artificial Neural Networks and Machine Learning – ICANN 2011: 21st International Conference on Artificial Neural Networks, Espoo, Finland, June 14–17, 2011, Proceedings* (Springer 2011) 309.

the external inputs and outputs of an algorithmic decision process, rather than at its inner workings.[60]

Within this framework, a new field of research called 'Machine Behaviour' has recently emerged.

According to this approach, to study the behaviour of 'black-box' algorithms in real-world settings, one should integrate knowledge from across a variety of scientific disciplines.[61] The solution to ML interpretability could thus be found by bringing together a new interdisciplinary community of empirical researchers, journalists, and ethical scholars, not only computer scientists.[62]

3 New problems, new solutions

Although explaining the functionality of complex automated decision-making systems is still a challenging problem, several techniques may already help in the post-hoc interpretation of 'black-box' models.[63] Unfortunately, however, most state-of-the-art explanation methods are still complicated and costly to obtain, and require some domain knowledge or expertise.[64]

As such, current regulations and guidelines that require an explanation of the internal logic of automated decision-making systems to be conveyable to data subjects could thus prohibit the use of many standard approaches, also because they often fail to clarify how such explanation should be shaped in practical terms.[65]

The European Commission's Expert Group on Regulatory Obstacles to Financial Innovation (ROFIEG)[66] addressed these issues in its recent report containing recommendations on regulation, innovation and finance.[67]

---

60 See eg, Ananny and Crawford (n 29) 9.

61 Iyad Rahwan and others, 'Machine Behaviour' (2019) 568 Nature 477–486.

62 Rahwan and others (n 61) 477–486. See also, eg, Narayanan and Reisman (n 4) 47; Zhou and Chen (n 58) 12; Pedreschi and Miliou (n 45) 14–15.

63 From the rich literature on this topic, see eg, Marco Tulio Ribeiro and others, '"Why Should I Trust You?": Explaining the Predictions of Any Classifier' in KDD '16 Proceedings of the 22nd ACM SIGKDD International Conference on Knowledge Discovery and Data Mining (ACM 2016) 1135; Lipton (n 29) 2; Zhou and Chen (n 58) 6; Samek and Müller (n 29) 12.

64 See eg, Sandra Wachter and others, 'Counterfactual Explanations without Opening the Black Box: Automated Decisions and the GDPR' (2018) 31(2) Harvard Journal of Law & Technology 842; Mayer-Schönberger and Cukier (n 1) 178; Zhou and Chen (n 58) 6.

65 See eg, Wachter and others (n 64) 861; Kroll and others (n 49) 885. See also Raffaella Messinetti, 'La tutela della persona umana versus l'intelligenza artificiale. Potere decisionale dell'apparato tecnologico e diritto alla spiegazione della decisione automatizzata' (2019) 3 Contratto e impresa 881; Ugo Ruffolo, 'Le responsabilità da *artificial intelligence*, algoritmo e *smart product*: per i fondamenti di un diritto dell'intelligenza artificiale *self-learning*' in Ugo Ruffolo (ed), *Intelligenza Artificiale – Il diritto, i diritti, l'etica* (Giuffrè Francis-Lefebvre 2020) 93–98.

66 The ROFIEG is an expert group set up by the European Commission in June 2018, with the aim to assist the Commission by providing high-level expertise on EU financial services legislation in relation to financial technology.

67 ROFIEG, *30 Recommendations on Regulation, Innovation and Finance* (Final Report to the European Commission, 2019) 38–41.

In its report, the ROFIEG asked the Commission to develop measures clarifying the circumstances under which requirements aiming at explainability of AI and associated technologies, in their concrete applications, are appropriate.[68]

The ROFIEG also suggested a clear elaboration of the concept of explainability and a calibration of the relevant obligations towards stakeholders, based on the type of stakeholder and the different contexts in which AI, Big Data and ML may be used.[69]

With particular reference to credit-scoring, the ROFIEG invited European Supervisory Authorities to develop guidelines on the use of new technologies in this context, ensuring their applicability to any type of financial institution, with a view to promoting high standards concerning outcomes and transparency towards consumers with respect to the general decision-making process.[70]

A possible approach to address these challenges could be represented by the advent of a constructive cooperation among regulators, supervisory authorities and industry players.[71]

In line with this view is the position of the European Commission's White Paper on AI, which affirms that the regulatory framework for AI should be shaped based on a comprehensive dialogue with all concerned parties (Member States civil society, industry and academics), in order to strike a balance among the competing interests at stake.[72]

In Italy a similar position was taken by the Italian Insurance Supervisory Authority (*Istituto per la Vigilanza sulle Assicurazioni – IVASS*), which acknowledged that the best way for regulators to regulate without posing excessive limitations to insurers is through enhanced cooperation among national and international institutions and open and constructive dialogue with the insurance industry.[73]

A useful tool to foster dialogue among regulators, supervisory authorities and industry players in the fields of insurance and financial services may be represented by innovation facilitators.[74]

Innovation facilitators typically take the form of 'innovation hubs' and 'regulatory sandboxes'. Innovation hubs provide a dedicated point of contact for firms to raise enquiries with competent authorities and to seek non-binding guidance on regulatory and supervisory expectations.[75] Regulatory sandboxes, on the other hand, are schemes to enable firms to test, pursuant to a specific testing plan agreed and monitored by a dedicated function of the competent authority, innovative financial products, financial services or business models.[76] Innovation facilitators may thus represent an opportunity for supervisory authorities

68 ROFIEG (n 67) 38–41.
69 ROFIEG (n 67) 38–41.
70 ROFIEG (n 67) 38–41.
71 See eg, IAIS (n 1) 36–37; Chatzara (n 1) 5. See also Laura Carmichael and others, 'Data Mining and Automated Discrimination: A Mixed Legal/Technical Perspective' (2016) 31(6) IEEE Intelligent Systems 53; Andreas Kaplan and Michael Haenlein, 'Rulers of the World, Unite! The Challenges and Opportunities of Artificial Intelligence' (2020) 63(1) Business Horizons 37.
72 European Commission, *White Paper on Artificial Intelligence – A European Approach to Excellence and Trust* (COM(2020) 65 final, 2020) 17.
73 IVASS, Relazione sull'attività svolta dall'Istituto nell'anno 2018. Considerazioni del Presidente Fabio Panetta (2019) 11 <https://www.ivass.it/pubblicazioni-e-statistiche/pubblicazioni/relazione-annuale/2019/Considerazioni_Presidente_IVASS_2018.pdf>.
74 Joint Committee of the European Supervisory Authorities (Joint Committee of the ESAs), *FinTech: Regulatory Sandboxes and Innovation Hubs* (JC 2018 74, 2018) 3.
75 Joint Committee of the ESAs (n 74) 3; OECD (n 16) 29.
76 Joint Committee of the ESAs (n 74) 3; OECD (n 16) 29.

and insurance companies to work in parallel; on the one hand, companies may propose and test solutions, while on the other hand supervisors may indicate existing applicable rules or propose new rules, in line with the needs expressed by business operators.[77]

4 Conclusion

Automated decision-making systems are becoming precious tools for insurers and for companies in general.

However, these systems tend to be opaque, and users are often neither aware of their capabilities nor of their limitations, leading to a lack of trust and concerns towards innovative technologies.[78]

As persons immediately affected by decisions of an automated system may feel the need of a better explanation than '*the computer said so*', regulation shall become a driving force for more transparency in this field.[79]

However, although European and national regulators and policymakers are more and more concerned about algorithmic explainability,[80] it is often not clear how regulatory requirements should be translated in technical terms.

As the majority of the policy challenges regarding AI and ML relate to technologies which are still difficult to understand by non-expert, effective regulation necessarily entails a deep understanding of the technical features at the basis of algorithms and their explanation methods.[81] With particular reference to insurance, this would require ad hoc regulation able to balance customer protection and the specific characteristics of the insurance business.

Tools such as innovation facilitators, expert groups and new multidisciplinary research fields represent precious occasions for different players to interact and foster the interchange of knowledge in order to balance the competing interests at stake.

Hence, dialogue and cooperation among regulators, domain experts and industry players, is probably the best solution in order to define rules and guidelines able to face the challenges posed by AI and ML systems.

Bibliography

E Alpaydın, *Introduction to Machine Learning* (3rd edn, MIT Press 2014).

M Ananny and K Crawford, 'Seeing Without Knowing: Limitations of the Transparency Ideal and Its Application to Algorithmic Accountability' (2018) 20(3) New Media & Society 1.

Article 29 Working Party, *Guidelines on Automated Individual Decision-making and Profiling for the Purposes of Regulation 2016/679* (2018).

S Arya, 'Anatomy of the Credit Score' (2013) 95 Journal of Economic Behavior & Organization 175.

---

77 OECD (n 16) 29.
78 See eg, Samek and Müller (n 29) 6; Comandé (n 1) 169; Lepri and others (n 9) 16; Delmastro and Nicita (n 1) 14–17.
79 See eg, Grimmelmann and Westreich (n 46) 176.
80 See eg, Goodman and Flaxman, (n 31) 50–57.
81 See eg, Mayer-Schönberger and Cukier (n 1) 179–182 who underline the need of regulators and supervisory authorities to rely on the help of expert '*algorithmists*' to manage the techniques related to new technologies and draft solid guidelines in this field. See also Andrew Tutt, 'An FDA for Algorithms' (2017) 69(1) Administrative Law Review 85.

P Baecke and L Bocca, 'The Value of Vehicle Telematics Data in Insurance Risk Selection Processes' (2017) 98 Decision Support Systems 69.

W Bao, 'Integration of Unsupervised and Supervised Machine Learning Algorithms for Credit Risk Assessment' (2019) 128 Expert Systems with Applications 301.

S Barocas and A D Selbst, 'Big Data's Disparate Impact' (2016) 104 California Law Review 671.

Y Bian, 'Good Drivers Pay Less: A Study of Usage-Based Vehicle Insurance' (2018) 107 Transportation Research Part A 20.

M Brkan, 'Do Algorithms Rule the World? Algorithmic Decision-Making in the Framework of the GDPR and Beyond' (2019) 27(2) International Journal of Law and Information Technology 91.

J Burrell, 'How the Machine "Thinks": Understanding Opacity in Machine Learning Algorithms' (2016) 3(1) Big Data & Society 1.

T Calders and B Custers, 'What Is Data Mining and How Does It Work?' in B Custers and others (eds), *Discrimination and Privacy in the Information Society. Data Mining and Profiling in Large Databases* (Springer 2013).

Capgemini and Efma, *World Insurance Report 2020* (2020).

A Cappiello, *Technology and the Insurance Industry: Re-Configuring the Competitive Landscape* (Springer 2018).

V Chatzara, 'FinTech, InsurTech, and the Regulators' in P Marano and K Noussia (eds), *InsurTech: A Legal and Regulatory View* (Springer 2020).

J Chorowski and J M Zurada, 'Top-Down Induction of Reduced Ordered Decision Diagrams for Neural Networks' in T Honkela and others (eds), *Artificial Neural Networks and Machine Learning - ICANN 2011: 21st International Conference on Artificial Neural Networks, Espoo, Finland, June 14-17, 2011, Proceedings* (Springer 2011).

G Comandé, 'Regulating Algorithms' Regulation? First Ethico-Legal Principles, Problems, and Opportunities of Algorithms' in T Cerquitelli and others (eds), *Transparent Data Mining for Big and Small Data* (Springer 2017).

Council of Europe, *Guidelines on the Protection of Individuals with Regard to the Processing of Personal Data in a World of Big Data* (T-PD(2017)01, 2017).

M Delmastro and A Nicita, *Big Data. Come Stanno Cambiando Il Nostro Mondo* (Il Mulino 2019).

P Domingos, *The Master Algorithm: How the Quest for the Ultimate Learning Machine Will Remake Our World* (Penguin 2015).

L Edwards and M Veale, 'Slave to the Algorithm? Why a 'Right to an Explanation' Is Probably Not the Remedy You Are Looking for' (2017) 16(1) Duke Law & Technology Review 18.

European Commission, *White Paper on Artificial Intelligence – A European Approach to Excellence and Trust* (COM (2020) 65 final, 2020).

European Commission for the Efficiency of Justice, *European Ethical Charter on the Use of Artificial Intelligence in Judicial Systems and Their Environment* (CEPEJ (2018)14, 2018).

European Parliament Committee on Legal Affairs, *European Civil Law Rules on Robotics* (2015/2103 (INL), 2016).

Expert Group on Regulatory Obstacles to Financial Innovation (ROFIEG), *30 Recommendations on Regulation, Innovation and Finance* (Final Report to the European Commission, 2019).

G Finocchiaro, 'Intelligenza Artificiale e protezione dei dati personali' in G Gabrielli and U Ruffolo (eds), *Intelligenza Artificiale e diritto* (Giurisprudenza Italiana 2019).

G Finocchiaro, 'Riflessioni su intelligenza artificiale e protezione dei dati personali' in U Ruffolo (ed), *Intelligenza Artificiale - Il diritto, i diritti, l'etica* (Giuffrè Francis-Lefebvre 2020).

G20, *AI Principles* (Annex to G20 Ministerial Statement on Trade and Digital Economy 2019).

B Goodman and S Flaxman, 'European Union Regulations on Algorithmic Decision-Making and a "Right to Explanation"' (2017) 38(3) AI Magazine 50.

V Gosrani, 'Data Changes Everything' in S L B VanderLinden and others (eds), *The InsurTech Book: The Insurance Technology Handbook for Investors, Entrepreneurs and FinTech Visionaries* (Wiley 2018).

J Grimmelmann and D Westreich, 'Incomprehensible Discrimination' (2017) 7 California Law Review Online 164.

Insurance Europe, *Insurance Europe Comments on the Article 29 Working Party's Draft Guidelines on Automated Individual Decision-making & Profiling* (Position Paper 2019).

International Association of Insurance Supervisors (IAIS), *FinTech Developments in the Insurance Industry* (2017) <https://www.iaisweb.org/file/65625/report-on-fintech-developments-in-the-insurance-industry>.

Istituto per la Vigilanza sulle Assicurazioni (IVASS), *Relazione sull'attività svolta dall'Istituto nell'anno 2018* (2019) <https://www.ivass.it/pubblicazioni-e-statistiche/pubblicazioni/relazione-annuale/2019/RELAZIONE_IVASS_2018.pdf>.

Joint Committee of the European Supervisory Authorities, *FinTech: Regulatory Sandboxes and Innovation Hubs* (JC 2018 2018).

J Kaplan, *Artificial Intelligence. What Everyone Needs to Know* (OUP 2016).

A Kaplan and M Haenlein, 'Rulers of the World, Unite! The Challenges and Opportunities of Artificial Intelligence' (2020) 63(1) Business Horizons 37.

B Kellison and P Brockett, 'Check the Score: Credit Scoring and Insurance Losses: Is There a Connection?' (2003) Special Issue 2003 Texas Business Review 1.

J A Kroll, J Huey, S Barocas, EW Felten, JR Reidenberg, DG Robinson and H Yu, 'Accountable Algorithms' (2016) 165(3) University of Pennsylvania Law Review 633.

B Lepri and others, 'The Tyranny of Data? The Bright and Dark Sides of Data-Driven Decision-Making for Social Good' in T Cerquitelli and others (eds), *Transparent Data Mining for Big and Small Data* (Springer 2017).

Z C Lipton, 'The Mythos of Model Interpretability' (2018) 16(3) Queue - Machine Learning 1.

M Loukides, *What Is Data Science?* (O'Reilly Media 2011).

G Malgieri and G Comandé, 'Why a Right to Legibility of Automated Decision-Making Exists in the General Data Protection Regulation' (2017) 7(4) International Data Privacy Law 243.

F Mattassoglio, 'La valutazione del merito creditizio e l'innovazione tecnologica' in M T Paracampo (ed), *Fintech. Introduzione ai profili giuridici di un mercato unico tecnologico dei servizi finanziari. Volume II* (2nd edn, Giappichelli 2019).

V Mayer-Schönberger and K Cukier, *Big Data: A Revolution That Will Transform How We Live, Work, and Think* (Houghton Mifflin Harcourt 2013).

R Messinetti, 'La tutela della persona umana versus l'intelligenza artificiale. Potere decisionale dell'apparato tecnologico e diritto alla spiegazione della decisione automatizzata' (2019) 3 Contratto e impresa 861.

D Mula, 'Big Data vs Data Privacy' in G Finocchiaro and V Falce (eds), *Fintech: Diritti, Concorrenza, Regole. Le Operazioni Di Finanziamento Tecnologico* (Zanichelli Editore 2019).

A Narayanan and D Reisman, 'The Princeton Web Transparency and Accountability Project' in T Cerquitelli and others (eds), *Transparent Data Mining for Big and Small Data* (Springer 2017).

N J Nilsson, *The Quest for Artificial Intelligence. A History of Ideas and Achievements* (Cambridge University Press 2009).

C O'Neil, *Weapons of Math Destruction: How Big Data Increases Inequality and Threatens Democracy* (Crown/Archetype 2016).

F Pasquale, 'Beyond Innovation and Competition: The Need for Qualified Transparency in Internet Intermediaries' (2010) 104(1) Northwestern University Law Review 105.

F Pasquale, *The Black Box Society: The Secret Algorithms That Control Money and Information* (Harvard University Press 2015).

J Pearl, 'The Limitations of Opaque Learning Machines' in J Brockman (ed), *Possible Minds. 25 Ways of Looking at AI* (Penguin Press 2019).

D Pedreschi and I Miliou, *Artificial Intelligence (AI): New Developments and Innovations Applied to E-Commerce. Challenges to the Functioning of the Internal Market* (Policy Department for Economic, Scientific and Quality of Life Policies Directorate-General for Internal Policies, European Parliament 2020).

I Rahwan, 'Machine Behaviour' (2019) 568 Nature 477.

B Reddix-Smalls, 'Credit Scoring and Trade Secrecy: An Algorithmic Quagmire or How the Lack of Transparency in Complex Financial Models Scuttled the Finance Market' (2011) 12(87) U.C. Davis Business School Law Journal 117.

M T Ribeiro, S Singh and C Guestrin, '"Why Should I Trust You?": Explaining the Predictions of Any Classifier' in Association for Computing Machinery (ed), *KDD '16 Proceedings of the 22nd ACM SIGKDD International Conference on Knowledge Discovery and Data Mining* (ACM 2016).

A Ricci, 'I Diritti dell'interessato' in G Finocchiaro (ed), *Il Nuovo Regolamento Europeo Sulla Privacy E Sulla Protezione Dei Dati Personali* (Zanichelli Editore 2017).

V Ricciardi, 'InsurTech Definition as Its Own Manifesto' in S L B VanderLinden and others (eds), *The InsurTech Book: The Insurance Technology Handbook for Investors, Entrepreneurs and FinTech Visionaries* (Wiley 2018).

R Romano, 'Intelligenza Artificiale, decisioni e responsabilità in ambito finanziario; snodi problematici' in G Finocchiaro and V Falce (eds), *Fintech: diritti, concorrenza, regole. Le operazioni di finanziamento tecnologico* (Zanichelli Editore 2019).

U Ruffolo, 'Le responsabilità da *artificial intelligence*, algoritmo e *smart product*: per i fondamenti di un diritto dell'intelligenza artificiale *self-learning*' in U Ruffolo (ed), Intelligenza Artificiale - Il diritto, i diritti, l'etica (Giuffrè Francis-Lefebvre 2020).

W Samek and K-R Müller, 'Towards Explainable Artificial Intelligence' in W Samek, G Montavon, A Vedaldi, L K Hansen and K-R Müller (eds), *Explainable AI: Interpreting, Explaining and Visualizing Deep Learning* (Springer 2019).

P Simon, *Too Big to Ignore. The Business Case for Big Data* (Wiley 2013).

V Soloshchuk and Y Kartashov, 'InsurTech Trends – Why Regionalization Matters' in S L B VanderLinden (ed), *The InsurTech Book: The Insurance Technology Handbook for Investors, Entrepreneurs and FinTech Visionaries* (Wiley 2018).

P Tereszkiewicz, 'Digitalisation of Insurance Contract Law: Preliminary Thoughts with Special Regard to Insurer's Duty to Advise' in P Marano and K Noussia (eds), *InsurTech: A Legal and Regulatory View* (Springer 2020).

The Economist, 'An Understanding of AI's Limitations Is Starting to Sink in' (2020) Technology Quarterly.

A Tutt, 'An FDA for Algorithms' (2017) 69(1) Administrative Law Review 83.

S Wachter and B Mittelstadt, 'A Right to Reasonable Inferences: Re-Thinking Data Protection Law in the Age of Big Data and AI' (2019) 2019(2) Columbia Business Law Review 1.

S Wachter, B Mittelstadt and L Floridi, 'Why a Right to Explanation of Automated Decision-Making Does Not Exist in the General Data Protection Regulation' (2017) 7(2) International Data Privacy Law 76.

S Wachter, B Mittelstadt and C Russels, 'Counterfactual Explanations without Opening the Black Box: Automated Decisions and the GDPR' (2018) 31(2) Harvard Journal of Law & Technology 841.

M Winlaw and others, 'Using Telematics Data to Find Risky Driver Behaviour' (2019) 131 Accident; Analysis and Prevention 131.

Working Party on the protection of individuals with regard to the processing of personal data, *Guidelines on Automated Individual Decision-making and Profiling for the Purposes of Regulation 2016/679*, 17/EN WP251rev.01 (2018).

J Zhou and F Chen, '2D Transparency Space – Bring Domain Users and Machine Learning Experts Together' in J Zhou and F Chen (eds), *Human and Machine Learning: Visible, Explainable, Trustworthy and Transparent* (Springer 2018).

13 Exchange-traded funds (ETFs) and FinTech

Market efficiency and systemic risk

Jay Cullen

1 Introduction

Exchange-traded funds (ETFs) are by common consensus amongst the most innovative financial products to have been introduced to financial markets over the past few decades. Indeed, they have disrupted investment patterns to the point that passive fund management rivals active fund management in scale. ETFs' share of passive fund assets has reached 40% and continues to grow, whilst passive management vehicles by at least one estimate controls over 50% of the US stock market.[1] ETF assets in the United States will reach around $5 trillion by the end of 2020, with this number predicted to hit $50 trillion by 2030.[2] Significant growth is also expected in European ETF markets.[3]

The advent of the ETF sector has coincided with the nascent adoption in financial markets of a variety of FinTech applications. These technologies exhibit considerable heterogeneity, yet a number interact at multiple levels with passive investment products. Robo-advisory services and algorithmic trading technologies, for example, have introduced channels which heighten trading speed and opportunities, by removing human intermediation from the investment process and allowing rapid turnover of securities. These markets have also grown extraordinarily in recent years, with at least $1.5 trillion employed in algorithmic trading strategies alone.[4] Implicitly, such technologies enjoy synergies with the ETF market, which is characterised by passively managed, low-cost financial products requiring minimal human operational intervention. This also means that technological developments may create feedback effects between FinTech applications and the ETF market. Indeed, ETF functionality depends upon algorithmic traders and arbitrage between ETFs and related futures, options and underlying securities.

Taken together, these technologies represent a paradigmatic shift in the operation of financial markets. Growth has been so rapid in the respective sectors that the risk calculus attendant to their potential impacts is changing. As Omarova has noted, these technologies

1 J Cox, 'Passive Investing Automatically Tracking Indexes Now Controls Nearly Half the US Stock Market' (14 March 2019) https://www.cnbc.com/2019/03/19/passive-investing-now-controls-nearly-half-the-us-stock-market.html.
2 C Reinicke, 'The ETF Market Will Hit $50 trillion by 2030, Bank of America Says' (13 December 2019) https://markets.businessinsider.com/news/stocks/etf-market-grow-50-trillion-assets-2030-bank-america-passive-2019-12-1028763048.
3 K Lamont, '4 Key Trends in the European ETF Market' (22 January 2020) https://www.morningstar.co.uk/uk/news/198984/4-key-trends-in-the-european-etf-market.aspx.
4 R Wigglesworth, 'Volatility: How 'Algos' Changed the Rhythm of the Market' Financial Times (9 January 2019) https://www.ft.com/content/fdc1c064-1142-11e9-a581-4ff78404524e.

share features with many other financial innovations of the last 30 years, whereby products are designed to synthesise economic interests and scale up transaction volume(s).[5] Conceptually, Omarova's framework of pooling,[6] layering,[7] acceleration[8] and compression[9] may be applied to a variety of financial products and techniques, including ETFs and FinTech applications. ETFs in general, for example, pool and layer tradable assets through agglomerating securities within an index or exchange, which allows for the acceleration of investments tracking relevant benchmarks. Algorithmic trading and robo-advice share some of these accelerant properties, by providing ways in which to scale up financial asset trading.[10]

These technologies also mark a qualitative shift in the function and interpretation of information in financial markets. Whilst trading becomes quicker, nimbler and more voluminous under passive investment strategies augmented by automation, the role of information also changes in subtle ways. Specifically, under these conditions, financial market prices will become increasingly self-referential; that is to say, investors in markets will no longer make investment decisions based upon information gathered by themselves or others which is, as shall be explained, a hallmark of the efficient markets hypothesis (EMH), but through acting on the trading of a smaller and smaller group of active traders. In such circumstances, misinformed trades by active traders in the markets may not be countered by other informed investors; rather, they would trigger more misinformed automated trades. This, in turn, may undermine the price formation mechanism, especially if the composition of views amongst informed traders is skewed by trading biases favouring a particular direction, thereby compounding informational gaps in the market.

In generating supplemental trading activity, robo-advice and algorithmic trading also raise financial stability concerns regarding possible herding behaviour.[11] The Global Financial Crisis (GFC) demonstrated the rapidity with which panic-selling became contagious across global markets as liquidity in many short-term debt and structured finance markets evaporated amid widespread herding.[12] Other recent market crashes have also been attributed to information problems, most notably the stock market collapse of 2002.[13] Importantly, the disruptive impact of certain automated trading further reduces the incentive for information gathering, as these algorithmically driven vehicles free-ride on research by active traders and use their resources and speed to front-run their trades. One effect of these developments is a reduction in the informativeness of financial market pricing, which, if persistent enough, may cause systemic instability.

---

5 S T Omarova, 'New Tech v New Deal: Fintech as a Systemic Phenomenon' (2019) 36 Yale J on Reg 735.
6 'The technique of combining multiple financial assets with certain shared characteristics'. Omarova (n 5) 762.
7 'The technique of synthesizing financial assets in a manner that creates a chain of hierarchically linked claims, so that the performance of each new asset "layer" is determined by reference to the combined performance of pooled financial assets underlying it' Omarova (n 5) 763.
8 '[This] occurs whenever the speed of transacting is increased (the velocity of trading), thus allowing more trades to be executed (the volume of trading)' Omarova (n 5) 764–765.
9 'The technique of aggregating and compacting risk exposures and obligations associated with multiple trades in a manner that de facto transforms them into a single economic transaction' Omarova (n 5) 765–766.
10 Omarova (n 5) 787.
11 Omarova (n 5) 788–789.
12 See G Gorton and A Metrick, 'Securitized Banking and the Run on Repo' (2012) 104 J Fin Econ 425.
13 R Shiller, *Irrational Exuberance* (3rd edn, Princeton University Press 2016).

Importantly, although these informational gaps have been discussed before, they have not been linked explicitly to the FinTech revolution. As FinTech's footprint expands in a similar manner to ETFs interesting questions arise concerning interactions with passive investment structures. Regulators have highlighted the potential financial stability benefits beyond a reduction in intermediation costs from the widespread adoption of FinTech. These benefits include decentralisation and diversification, heightened transparency and improved access to, and convenience of, financial services for retail and business market participants.[14] On the surface, these purported benefits are not particularly related to financial stability. Indeed, financial market products which share these features have in the past been extolled as financial stability enhancing, an assumption which often turned out to be erroneous.[15] Rather, the increased automation and programmatic systems in trading arising from expanded use of FinTech applications have the potential to exacerbate herding behaviour and investment correlations in financial markets, in particular when compounded by the prevalence of passive investment structures engaged in rudimentary momentum trades.

The framework I rely upon in this chapter builds on the classic analysis of securities market efficiency mechanisms by Gilson and Kraakman, which is arguably the most influential law and economics exposition of this topic in the field.[16] I depart from their analysis, however, by suggesting that the aggregative information function of ETFs, and the increasing prevalence of their use by investors, combined with the increasing financial flows facilitated by certain financial technologies, pose a unique challenge to regulators in maintaining financial stability. Whilst central banks have become more accustomed to preventing such episodes from spilling over into systemic crises, the threat posed by passive investment strategies remains potent and is growing. Given these risks, the anticipated widespread adoption of robo-advice and automated trading, and the explosion in investment in the ETF asset class over the last decade by retail investors, pension funds and other institutions, increased regulatory scrutiny of their contribution to market instability is justified.

2 The ETF landscape

2.1 *Passive asset management: theory*

Whilst the development of passive asset management strategies took decades to occur, their widespread adoption is unsurprising. Modern portfolio theory has been recognised as the most appropriate and cost-effective investment strategy for most investors for over half a century. First articulated by Markowitz in 1952, modern portfolio theory asserts that it is possible to construct an efficient portfolio offering the maximum possible expected return for a pre-determined level of risk.[17] As noted by Bhattacharya and O'Hara, a basic insight from this theory 'is that an asset's price can be decomposed into two factors: (1) an idiosyncratic factor specific to the asset and (2) a systematic factor common to all assets in the

14 Financial Stability Board, 'Financial Stability Implications from FinTech: Supervisory and Regulatory Issues that Merit Authorities' Attention' (June 2017) https://www.fsb.org/wp-content/uploads/R270617.pdf.

15 N Gennaioli, A Shleifer and R W Vishny, 'Neglected Risks, Financial Innovation and Financial Fragility' (2012) 104 J Fin Econ 452.

16 R J Gilson and R H Kraakman, 'The Mechanisms of Market Efficiency' (1984) 70 Virginia L Rev 549.

17 H Markowitz, 'Portfolio Selection' (1952) 7 J Fin 77.

market'.[18] The implication is that an 'efficient' portfolio is the market portfolio, because by investing in all assets, idiosyncratic factors are neutralised. Such passive investment, in contrast to active management therefore moves the emphasis in investing away from the notion that 'better' managers are able to generate 'alpha' from investing (ie, a consistent excess return over the performance of the wider segment or index). These features led Paul Samuelson, one of the leading post-War economists to opine acidly that: 'respect for evidence compels me to incline toward the hypothesis that most portfolio decision makers should go out of business – take up plumbing, teach Greek, or help produce the annual GNP by serving as corporate executives'.[19]

2.2 ETFs: the basics

ETFs are investment funds which hold assets of varying descriptions including bonds, commodities, and even other investment assets, such as Real-Estate Investment Funds (REITs) although the most common by far are listed stocks. They are designed to provide access to markets to those who may not otherwise be able to purchase securities directly, and to those who wish to gain exposure to bespoke market portfolios across geographical regions, sectors or asset types (importantly, these motivations may not be mutually exclusive).[20]

A crucial difference between ETFs and many other index tracking products is the fact that ETFs, like stocks, are fully tradable, and can be bought and sold at any time during trading hours. This stands in contrast to mutual funds and unit trusts, which may only be sold at the end of a trading day. For these reasons, ETFs are attractive both to long-term investors and to traders who wish to take short-term positions in assets and want the flexibility to trade out of those assets quickly. Investors may sell ETF shares short, create options referencing the ETF and limit losses via stop-loss orders. ETFs are also tax-efficient, and in general levy very low operating fees on investors. Most ETFs are passive funds, although there has been growth in actively managed ETFs over the past decade or so. Equities-focused ETFs comprise the lion's share of the ETF universe, with over three-quarters of the total, but more niche sectors have also experienced rapid growth, particularly bond-focused ETFs, the market for which now stands at over $1 trillion.[21] Such volumes provide additional liquidity to those markets; indeed, the liquidity function of ETFs is often heralded as one of their key financial stability advantages. In tandem, however, in thinly traded markets, ETFs may amplify illiquidity during periods of market stress.[22]

---

18 A Bhattacharya and M O'Hara, *ETFs and Systemic Risks* (CFA Institute Research Foundation January 2020) 1 https://www.cfainstitute.org/-/media/documents/article/rf-brief/etfs-and-systemic-risks.ashx.

19 P A Samuelson, 'Challenge to Judgment' (1974) 1 J Portfolio Man 17, 17.

20 R Srichander, 'Market Structures and Systemic Risks of Exchange-Traded Funds' (2011) BIS Working Papers No 343 https://www.bis.org/publ/work343.pdf.

21 See Blackrock, 'Visualising the ETF Universe' (September 2019) https://www.blackrock.com/lu/individual/etfs-and-indexing/visualizing-the-expanse-etf-universe?switchLocale=y&siteEntry-Passthrough=true.

22 P Chatwell, 'The Liquidity "Doom Loop" in Bond Funds Is a Threat to the System' Financial Times (25 March 2020) https://www.ft.com/content/b7c15426-6e1b-11ea-89df-41bea055720b.

2.2.1 *ETF investment*

The investing process in an ETF may be complex, with multiple layers of intermediaries between the securities which comprise the relevant ETF and the end investor. The ETF market is divided into two segments. In the primary market, ETFs are constructed – in what are often termed 'creation units' – by large institutional finance houses in collaboration with a fund management company. In the secondary market, ETFs are traded on an exchange. The institutional players are registered as 'authorised participants' and act as market makers in the ETFs, ensuring liquidity for the ETF shares and that the ETF intraday market price approximates the net asset value of the underlying assets. Once the ETF is constructed, buying and selling is facilitated on a stock exchange and the price of the ETF is adjusted based upon the movement of the underlying securities prices. Typically, if the ETF price departs significantly from its net asset value, then arbitraging authorised participants will step in to close the gap. Authorised participants profit from arbitraging price differences between the ETF and underlying markets, and the design of the product ensures that the risks faced by these arbitrageurs are considerably less than in relation to comparable index products. On the strength of this innovation, ETFs have been able to tap new illiquid markets that had previously been largely inaccessible to many investors.

There are broadly two categories of ETF: physical and synthetic. Physical or traditional ETFs – the more common category – are 'plain vanilla' products, which attempt to replicate an index by physically holding the securities which comprise the relevant benchmark weighted appropriately. In contrast, synthetic ETFs have a legal structure more akin to structured finance products than vanilla index tracker funds. Synthetic ETFs are designed to indirectly replicate a relevant index by means of a swap transaction (total return swap),[23] a form of OTC derivative. The ETF concerned enters into an agreement with a financial house – often a bank or securities dealer – which is obliged to construct and deliver an indexed product (the synthetic ETF) in exchange for a fee. The swap counterparty is then obliged to pay over the index return plus dividends to the ETF.

The funds of a synthetic ETF are invested in other securities which serve as collateral for the swap counterparty, which often do not correspond with the basket of securities of the replicated index. Moreover, such agreements introduce counterparty risk to the ETF; if the swap counterparty defaults, then the transaction may result in losses for the parties involved. Typically, such products are provided by the asset management divisions of banks and broker-dealers, which have access to large volumes of securities. Growth in synthetic ETFs was particularly acute in the EU around a decade ago, where synthetic ETFs comprised 45% of all ETF assets under management.[24] This growth was driven by regulatory and tax advantages which are not available in the United States. However, by 2016 the proportion of assets under management in EU synthetic ETFs dropped to around 20% in particular following pressure from the Bank for International Settlements and the Financial Stability Board to reduce possible complexities in their structure(s).[25]

---

23 A Total Return Swap is a contract between two parties who agree to exchange (or swap) the returns from a financial asset with a fee payment based upon a set rate.
24 Financial Stability Board, 'Potential Financial Stability Issues Arising from Recent Trends in Exchange-Traded Funds' (June 2011) https://www.fsb.org/wp-content/uploads/r_110412b.pdf.
25 FSB (n 24).

2.3 FinTech: automated advice and algorithmic trading

FinTech is defined by the FSB as 'technology-enabled innovation in financial services that could result in new business models, applications, processes or products with an associated material effect on the provision of financial services'.[26] The World Economic Forum organises FinTech activities into five categories of financial services: (i) payments, clearing and settlement; (ii) deposits, lending and capital raising; (iii) insurance; (iv) investment management and (v) market support.[27]

For the present analysis, this chapter focuses exclusively on investment management services. In this context the FSB claims indicatively that 'the costs of executing trades in financial markets may be prohibitively high for individual investors, and more efficient to execute through collective investment vehicles'.[28] According to the FSB, therefore, the primary purpose of FinTech is to reduce financial frictions which increase transaction costs for households and businesses, which arise through information asymmetries, incomplete markets, negative externalities, misaligned incentives, network effects and/or behavioural distortions.[29]

2.3.1 Robo-advice

Techniques which assist in this process include automated advising (often termed 'robo-advice') and algorithmic trading. Robo-advisors combine digital interfaces and algorithms, often incorporating machine learning, offering a range of automated services including financial product recommendations and portfolio management. In the context of investment advice, the inputs to these robo-advisors are usually derived from questionnaires concerning the investor's particulars and risk appetite(s). Based upon this information the robo-advisor constructs a portfolio using an algorithm derived from portfolio models. Changes made to the portfolio are also actioned based upon such models. Importantly, investment by robo-advisors is often made in ETFs.

Robo-advisors typically employ algorithms to action investments. Algorithmic trading reflects, broadly, the use of pre-programmed and delimited computerised instructions which execute trades with no human intervention.[30] Trading therefore occurs automatically, based upon computer programs which contain certain pre-defined risk management practices and executory instructions. The algorithms employed attempt to make sense of market data to produce a usable output which may be used as the basis for trading, built upon a preset strategy. These algorithms use established valuation methodologies from finance theory which far exceed the computational capacity of human traders.[31]

---

26 FSB (n 14) 7.
27 World Economic Forum, 'The Future of Financial Services: How Disruptive Innovations Are Reshaping the Way Financial Services Are Structured, Provisioned and Consumed' Final Report (June 2015) http://www3.weforum.org/docs/WEF_The_future__of_financial_services.pdf
28 FSB (n 14) 8.
29 FSB (n 14) 7–8.
30 Y Yadav, 'How Algorithmic Trading Undermines Efficiency in Capital Markets' (2015) 68 Vanderbilt L Rev 1607, 1619.
31 Yadav (n 30) 1622.

2.3.2 *Automated trading*

At the macro-level, the encroachment of automation promises more efficient financial markets, almost entirely free of intermediation and transaction costs. By removing human interaction in the trading process, investors are now presented with algorithms which increase the speed of trading exponentially, whilst the threat of behavioural influences on investment decisions is correspondingly reduced. On this basis, algorithmic trading has become established as a major vehicle for securities trading. Indeed, the recent development of market infrastructure including hyper-fast computers which can process data at tremendous speed and fiber cabling which may transmit instructions in milliseconds, has facilitated the expansion of algorithmic 'high-frequency trading' (HFT) to the point that HFT now dominates trading across several securities markets, including equities.[32]

Although human decision-making is removed at the point of trading, significant input from designers and modellers is required to establish an algorithmic trading program. Automated trading requires establishing a pre-set trading strategy via a programmed execution model. They also require some 'decision-making' capacity which will determine what instruction they will issue (eg, buy/sell) given a particular set of circumstances and data interpretation. This requires algorithms to possess some level of artificial intelligence, which can not only act according to pre-set stylised instructions but can also learn as market movements develop. Programmers (under advice from traders) also set the parameters within which their algorithms operate. These parameters determine what form of data the algorithm may collect, how the algorithm interprets that data, in which form the data must be aggregated, what model is used to determine the viability of a trade and so on. Such instructions also set limits on when an algorithm must stop trading (often referred to as 'stop-loss orders').

3 ETFs, automated trading and financial market efficiency

This section will begin by outlining the mechanisms through which information is incorporated into financial market prices. It will then proceed to analyse the potential effects upon these mechanisms brought about by the widespread utilisation of passive investment vehicles such as ETFs, and by the introduction of certain FinTech tools, in particular automated trading. Given the spectacular growth of ETFs and the burgeoning FinTech sector, the systemic risks associated with these markets have been comparatively under-studied. Many regulatory analyses have pointed to the role of ETFs and algorithmic trading in accentuating steep and rapid but infrequent and temporary drops in exchange prices – so-called 'flash-crashes' – but systemic risk is frequently regarded as tangential to these episodes. Because of this, few enquiries have concentrated on the potential for ETFs to exacerbate, or cause, broader and enduring systemic risk events.[33] Similarly most recent studies on the risks from FinTech are confined to examining risks at the micro-level; for

---

32 I Aldridge and S Krawciw, *Real-Time Risk: What Investors Should Know About Fintech, High-Frequency Trading and Flash Crashes* (Wiley 2017).

33 Exceptions include a recent paper from the European Systemic Risk Board. See M Pagano, A Sánchez Serrano and J Zechner, 'Can ETFs Contribute to Systemic Risk?' European Systemic Risk Board Reports of the Advisory Scientific Committee No. 9 (June 2019) https://www.esrb.europa.eu/pub/pdf/asc/esrb.asc190617_9_canetfscontributesystemicrisk~983ea11870.en.pdf.

example, the risk of losses incurred by individual consumers from faulty automated advice, privacy concerns or cybersecurity risks.[34]

The neglect of systemic risks from these technologies, on the face of it, is not surprising. By increasing the speed of transactions, removing intermediation costs and increasing competition, financial innovations such as ETFs and algorithmic trading are assumed in almost all circumstances to augment market efficiency. Because the most popular ETFs are designed to mimic a wide market portfolio – often an entire securities or bond exchange – there is normally no question of relative price efficiency that is, the question of whether collectively, investments exhibit efficiency in relation to one another. Hence, studies on ETFs frequently find that inclusion of a security in an ETF improves its informational efficiency.[35]

Despite these findings however, the effects of higher investment volumes made through passive vehicles may impact the informational efficiency of securities prices in the aggregate, through two distinct, but linked, phenomena. First, as capital allocators, ETFs will amplify existing market movements. ETFs are at root pure momentum traders and will buy or sell securities depending upon prevailing market conditions, exacerbating any mispricing which occurs.[36] Because ETF trading requires commensurately lower capital commitments to execute, and the underlying securities of an ETF are less liquid, taking large directional bets on an index is facilitated by ETF vehicles.

Second, as ETFs and certain forms of automated trading continue to proliferate, informed trading – as a mechanism for correcting mispricing through arbitrage and other techniques – will become less likely to deliver returns because the mass of capital flows that such arbitrage strategies must correct are potentially much larger. Such processes are already recognised in algorithmically traded markets; informed traders have fewer incentives to participate in algorithmic markets and to correct informational deficits. As passive investment techniques continue to dominate active trading, price discovery processes will be undermined, making asset value swings more likely.

3.1 *Information costs and market efficiency*

Classic expositions of market operation centre on information problems as a source of inefficiency.[37] Information asymmetries and a lack of information dispersal may result in imperfect market functioning and these inefficiencies have been central to recent stock market collapses and financial crises.[38]

Readers will be familiar with Fama's efficiency form trichotomy: 'strong'; 'semi-strong' and 'weak'.[39] Each of these forms assumes that markets are fundamentally efficient, but each to different degrees, based upon the speed through which information is incorporated into

---

34 Indicatively, see M Demertzis, S Merler and G B Wolff, 'Capital Markets Union and the Fintech Opportunity' (2018) 4 J Fin Reg 157.

35 L Glosten, S Nallareddy and Y Zou, 'ETF Activity and Informational Efficiency of Underlying Securities' (forthcoming 2020) Man Sci https://pubsonline.informs.org/doi/10.1287/mnsc.2019.3427.

36 D Israeli, C Lee and S A Sridharan, 'Is There a Dark Side to Exchange Traded Funds? An Information Perspective' (2017) 22 Rev Acc Stud 1048.

37 G Akerlof, 'The Market for Lemons: Quality Uncertainty and the Market Mechanism' (1970) 84 Q J Econ 488.

38 B Holmstrom, 'Understanding the Role of Debt in the Financial System' BIS Working Paper No. 479 (January 2015) https://www.bis.org/publ/work479.pdf.

39 E F Fama, 'Efficient Capital Markets: A Review of Theory and Empirical Work' (1970) 25 J Fin 383.

prices. The strong-form EMH hold that securities prices reflect all available information, both public and private, and therefore no trader may earn excess returns even where they trade on private information. The semi-strong version holds that securities prices reflect all publicly known information and adjust instantaneously to the production of new information. Profit from trading on private information is therefore possible, but the window for profit is tightly constrained. The weak version of the EMH holds that prices reflect only historically relevant information to the securities concerned. Therefore, traders may make profit on private information-gathering, but cannot outperform the market for consistently long periods.[40] The importance of the EMH to the study of financial markets is 'its prediction that, even though all information is not immediately and costlessly available to all participants, the market will act *as if* it were'.[41]

3.1.1 *Gilson and Kraakman: explaining the mechanisms of market efficiency*

Gilson and Kraakman offer the canonical law and economics account of the processes through which information is impounded into price. They provide a cogent explanation for the significance of the distribution of information amongst categories of traders, and why this distribution is an important factor in the determination of market functioning. The level of market efficiency with respect to particular information depends on which of several market mechanisms operates to impound that information in market price. Their taxonomy of trading comprises:

  i Universally informed trading: trading which takes place on the basis of both historical and new information which is disseminated to the entire marketplace;
 ii Professionally informed trading: trading which is undertaken by those who have invested resources to engage in information mining and interpretation, as well as the possible impact of this information on the securities' market price;
iii Derivatively informed trading: trading which takes one of two forms: (a) 'trade decoding', where traders observe and mimic the trades of other traders they perceive to have superior information; and (b) 'price decoding', where traders respond to anonymous trading data and volumes; and
 iv Uninformed trading: trading which occurs where traders are subject to uncertainty and fall back upon secondary judgments and observations of price patterns to gauge value.[42]

The price formation process relies heavily upon the timely and complete disclosure of information to participants, many of whom expend considerable resources in gathering and analysing that information. Traders undertake these efforts because they make returns over and above the costs involved; if they did not, they would do so, or would continue to lose money until they reached insolvency. Implicit in Gilson and Kraakman's work is that trader behaviour conforms to the rational expectations hypothesis, which assumes that investors' financial decisions are based upon full assimilation of all available information and do not make systematic mistakes (so-called 'unbounded rationality').

---

40 Fama (n 39).
41 Gilson and Kraakman (n 16) 552 [emphasis in original].
42 Gilson and Kraakman (n 16).

3.1.2 *The distribution of information and its effects on market efficiency*

Crucially, the relative distribution of the relevant information amongst the taxonomy of traders determines to what extent the market approaches full efficiency and explains how more sophisticated groups of traders profit from information gathering. For example, in markets where all traders are universally or professionally informed, prices should reflect available information quickly and accurately and should not be subject to any bias. In contrast, in markets containing large proportions of derivatively informed or uninformed traders, information is not fully assimilated or distributed and therefore prices may not necessarily reflect fundamental value. Whilst uninformed trading may contribute to market efficiency in certain circumstances, the value of uninformed prices rests upon the assumption that although each trader's own forecasts and beliefs are skewed, such random biases are expected to wash out at the aggregate level, leaving a single, best estimate price. In contrast, where the aggregate forecasts of uninformed traders remain biased in a particular direction, their presence will impede the process through which new information becomes impounded in prices.[43]

Based upon Gilson and Kraakman's taxonomy of traders, passive investment like that exemplified in the ETF market may damage the process of price discovery because passive ETF trades are not based on any information gathering whatsoever. Instead, ETFs implicitly employ 'derivatively informed' trading strategies; they simply track and attempt to mimic the market portfolio at a given time. Although such vehicles may add liquidity to financial markets, it is plausible that non-fundamental trades at the ETF level could transmit to the securities underlying ETFs and lead to mispricing. Moreover, the agglomeration of large volumes of trading capital amongst derivatively informed or uninformed traders has the potential to produce group behaviour which is irrational. Whilst passive asset management has always posed theoretical risks of this type, the widespread adoption of ETFs has accentuated this threat.

As Gilson and Kraakman acknowledge, their four capital market mechanisms operate on a qualitative spectrum and 'function with decreasing relative efficiency'.[44] In other words, the greater the proportion of derivatively or uninformed trading occurring in a market, the greater the chance of mispricing. Price discovery depends upon numerous and diverse active traders; elsewhere, Gilson and Kraakman claim that '[a]n implicit qualification of the [efficient markets hypothesis] is that one cannot expect informationally efficient prices without active trading ... It is active trading that aggregates information in price'.[45] Where markets do not provide returns to informed traders because their trades are overwhelmed by momentum, they have less incentive to engage in information mining. ETF investors also have no incentives to overcome the 'lemons' problem inherent in any market, because they are buying the entire index, and thus shielding themselves from idiosyncratic risk.[46] The pertinent question then becomes what proportion of trading in a market is being performed by those with financial information relevant to the underlying securities, and to what extent securities trading is being executed on a non-fundamental basis.

---

43 D Awrey, 'The Mechanisms of Derivatives Market Efficiency' (2016) 91 NYU L Rev 1104.
44 Gilson and Kraakman (n 16) 592.
45 R J Gilson and R H Kraakman 'Market Efficiency after the Financial Crisis: It's Still A Matter of Information Costs' (2014) 100 Virginia L Rev 313, 325.
46 Akerlof (n 37).

3.2 *Irrational investors and market inefficiency*

Whilst both the rational expectations hypothesis and Gilson and Kraakman's 'derivatively' and 'uninformed' trader exemplars allow for irrational biases amongst individual traders, each claims these biases will cancel one another out, or be arbitraged away, until a price based upon fundamentals is formed. Gilson and Kraakman recognise that investors may make such errors when uninformed but claim that they will learn from such mistakes as they observe market behaviour. In this view trading activity will be conditioned not simply on subjective assessments of value but on price. This learning will be added to the mix in determining how prices are set, as individual estimates of value move towards consensus predictions. Accordingly, in the absence of information asymmetries and where traders conform to the rational expectations hypothesis, trading is expected to lead to market efficiency.

3.2.1 *Herding, feedback loops and momentum trading*

In spite of these claims, however, there is convincing evidence that markets are often dominated by herding and momentum tendencies and little-to-no aggregate learning occurs. In less than perfectly informed markets others' behaviour may presumably be based upon better information regarding the future of prices.[47] Market actors subsequently rely upon the actions of others as they believe those others to have superior information which they themselves do not; in effect, this contagion is 'concerned with short-term behaviour where agents do not have time to interpret news and may spontaneously follow other market participants'.[48] Where relevant information is defined objectively, such contagion may not occur. However, in conditions where derivatively informed and uninformed trading dominate, a significant proportion of the relevant information traders use to inform trading becomes speculation on the beliefs of other traders. Such speculation is routinely fed by the subjective under- or over-estimation of particular probabilities generated by investor behaviour, a process often referred to as a 'feedback loop'.[49] Positive feedback loops in trading occur when an initial increase in prices due to precipitating factors yields ever increasing price inflation and a self-repeating cycle develops. The mechanism is strengthened precisely the more players act upon it simultaneously: the more they synchronise, the greater the amplitude of the feedback effect(s).[50]

Traders employing these strategies are often referred to in the literature as 'noise' traders, who 'are not fully rational and [whose] demand for risky assets is affected by their beliefs or

---

47 This is known as an 'informational cascade', which occurs 'when it is optimal for an individual, having observed the actions of those ahead of him, to follow the behavior of the preceding individual without regard to his own information'. See S Bikhchandani, D Hirshleifer and I Welch, 'A Theory of Fads, Fashion, Custom and Cultural Change as Informational Cascades' (1992) 100 J Pol Econ 992, 994.

48 See R Topol, 'Bubbles and Volatility of Stock Prices: Effect of Mimetic Contagion' (1991) 101 Econ J 786, 787 note 1.

49 M Wyarta and J P Bouchaud, 'Self-referential Behaviour, Overreaction and Conventions in Financial Markets' (2007) 63 J Econ Behav'r & Organ'tion 1.

50 J P Zigrand, H S Shin and D Beunza, 'Feedback Effects and Changes in the Diversity of Trading Strategies' UK Government Foresight Review: The Future of Computer Trading in Financial Markets (2011) https://assets.publishing.service.gov.uk/government/uploads/system/uploads/attachment_data/file/289030/11-1221-dr2-feedback-effects-and-changes-in-diversity-of-trading-strategies.pdf.

sentiments that are not fully justified by fundamental news'.[51] They are therefore prone to systematic biases which are not fully justified by the relevant information. Where the trades of noise traders are uncorrelated, they cancel each other out and the arbitrage mechanism is unaffected. However, where investor sentiment propels enough noise traders to engage in the same trading strategies, they may move markets. In Gilson and Kraakman's words, '[a]lthough individual traders will attach biased weights because each knows only a fraction of the relevant information, the cumulative weights will be unbiased unless trading volume is itself skewed toward the views of one set of uninformed traders'.[52]

In these circumstances, any market movements will be uncorrelated to changes in fundamentals to some degree because those traders that are driving the movements are not fully rational. Indeed, as noted by the European Systemic Risk Board, the high liquidity and low transaction fees of ETFs enable investors to take 'large, short-term directional positions in entire asset classes, which, if driven by market sentiment, may have adverse consequences for market stability'.[53] Where ETFs and other passive management vehicles do not comprise large proportions of the market, such derivatively trading effects may not be significant enough to cause efficiency problems.[54] Crucially, however, if the volume of passive traders reaches levels which prevent those with more information from arbitraging the market to profit from closing the efficiency loophole, herding and momentum effects will come to dominate.

3.2.2 *Herding and automated trading*

Such factors are recognised potential transmission mechanisms for unidirectional price movements in markets where human interaction is limited. Many studies concentrate on the potential for automation to contribute to procyclicality and contagion risks where automated trading leads to greater herding behaviour than that exhibited by managed portfolios.[55] This risk may be particularly significant where models used to execute trades are highly correlated due to the incorporation of similar algorithms. Trading algorithms have actions hard-wired into their coding that lead directly to positive feedback effects. Where automated trading comprises larger and larger portions of a market, such non-fundamental herding behaviour may place considerable pressure on asset prices, in particular in stressed market conditions. By virtue of the fact that computer algorithms can process large amounts of information rapidly and interrogate common data-sets, they are more likely to engage in co-ordinated trading strategies.[56] When financial institutions which employ similar algorithms in trading are hit by a common shock, they may be forced to liquidate their securities holdings simultaneously into illiquid markets. As a result, even small initial fundamental shocks may be amplified by algorithmic trading and lead to firesales of assets. Indeed, such dynamics may even occur where the behaviour of algorithms is individually prudent, as mechanistic electronic programs quickly generate destabilising trading trends at the macro level.

51 A Shleifer and L H Summers, 'The Noise Trader Approach to Finance' (1990) 4 J Econ Persp 19.
52 Gilson and Kraakman (n 16) 581.
53 Pagano et al (n 33) 20.
54 K Gavriilidis, G N Gregoriou and V Kallinterakis, 'Exchange-Traded Funds: Do They Promote or Depress Noise Trading?' in F Economou, K Gavriilidis and V Kallinterakis (eds), *Handbook of Investors' Behavior During Financial Crises* (Academic Press 2017) 335–361.
55 C Avery and P Zemski, 'Multidimensional Uncertainty and Herd Behavior in Financial Markets' (1998) Am'can Econ Rev 724.
56 Zigrand et al (n 50).

3.3 *ETFs, automation and the effects of 'mistakes' on market pricing*

Any widespread mistake or error in forecasting can generate bias amongst investors with respect to accurate probability estimation. At the same time, where information is not widely available, or uncertainty prevails, uninformed trading will dominate valuation. ETFs, by their nature, focus on the systematic factor over the idiosyncratic factor. In any aggregation of securities, the idiosyncratic factors are cancelled out by one another, with the residual systematic factor as the main determinant of price. However, as noted by Bhattacharya and O'Hara, 'when index products become the chief driver of markets, the systematic factor becomes the key mover of not just index prices but also all underlying asset prices'.[57]

As asset prices lose some of their informational power, the likelihood of traders engaging in herding strategies increases. Indeed, the power of herding is demonstrated by research which confirms that investors will herd even when they know that their peers are not fully informed.[58] In relation to ETFs, Bhattacharya and O'Hara have shown that herding equilibria may arise where the signal from an ETF overwhelms any signal from the underlying assets or the signal from underlying assets overwhelms the ETF signal.[59] Similarly, ETFs increase volatility of the securities in their baskets, which is not accompanied by increased price discovery at the stock level.[60] Further research shows that ETFs contribute to equity return co-movement[61] and increased co-movement of underlying stocks.[62]

Because the composition of equity markets is rapidly becoming dominated by ETFs, and those ETFs in general are entirely passive, capital flow volumes have begun to supplant fundamental analysis as the primary driver of security market prices. Indeed, because market trends are amplified by passive trading, asset overvaluation becomes much more likely. Where ETFs are programmed simply to mimic the movements of a stock index, they will buy shares that even a rational investment manager perceives to be overvalued. These dynamics are even more damaging when market prices begin to fall: as investors liquidate their holdings, outflows from ETFs may impact other markets as ETF sponsors begin to sell. In periods of market stress, ETF participants may be confronted with a significant number of investors selling ETF shares, thereby depressing their price. These sales may amplify negative price movements and lead to price spirals and spillovers into other markets; indeed, funds in the ETF sector experienced greater volatility (in both price and fund flows) during recent bouts of market turbulence than those experienced in other passive investment fund sectors.[63]

This is particularly concerning in the light of the complex network of trading platforms and entities at work in the modern financial marketplace, which mean that relatively small initial shocks may be amplified into much deeper and damaging events. For example, the market may not realise that dislocation is being caused only by an automated trading program which is inducing other automated traders to mimic its

---

57 Bhattacharya and O'Hara (n 18) 2.

58 Topol (n 48).

59 A Bhattacharya and M O'Hara, 'Can ETFs Increase Market Fragility? Effect of Information Linkages in ETF Markets' (2018) https://ssrn.com/abstract=2740699.

60 I Ben-David, F Franzoni and R Moussawi, 'Do ETFs Increase Volatility?' (2018) 73 J Fin 2471.

61 Z Da and S Shive, 'Exchange Traded Funds and Asset Return Correlations' (2018) 24 Eur Fin Man 136.

62 Israeli et al (n 36).

63 V Susko and G Turner, 'The Implications of Passive Investing for Securities Markets' (March 2018) BIS Quarterly Review 113 https://www.bis.org/publ/qtrpdf/r_qt1803j.pdf.

trades. Shocks in human-dominated trading systems are usually much less difficult to arrest because market participants are able to observe the actions of others and can react accordingly. Where information is asymmetric and it is impossible to know why selling is occurring, trading which is being directed rapidly on an automated basis might be impossible to stop. The speed of the trading in question means that even if the initial distress was unwarranted, the precipitating sales may lead to indirect self-fulfilling feedback effects which cannot be unwound.[64] Because trades are routinely executed automatically and under identical trading algorithms, further distress is likely during periods of correlated selling.[65]

3.4 *Limits to arbitrage in passive, automated markets*

In normal circumstances, arbitrage by informed traders would be expected to correct such market mispricing. However, in markets increasingly squeezed by momentum investors, there may be too few active arbitrageurs to stabilise falling markets by purchasing under-valued assets. Indeed, even where a money manager recognises that a security is overvalued, they will not realise a gain on the asset unless a majority of their peers also hold the same view and begin to sell the relevant shares. If arbitrage activity fails to correct a precipitous price fall caused by short selling, the majority of market actors may feel compelled to imitate short sellers' trades, adding further downward pressure on prices.

More importantly in the context of ETFs and FinTech, informed traders may lose interest in acquiring stock-specific information, leading to less informationally rich prices. Arbitraging a large, momentum-based passively driven market may require huge capital outlays and the assumption of large credit risks. Even where an overvaluation persists, an investment manager who sells his position in a market may, in the short-term, appear to be underperforming his rivals. Similarly, in this situation an arbitrageur who spots a gap between fundamental value and price may even be bankrupted before the resulting market correction takes place.[66] Over the longer-term, as ETFs purchase greater volumes of securities, the outstanding shares become increasingly concentrated in the hands of ETF sponsors, rather than individual traders, further discouraging information searches by traders without the resources to expend on correcting mis-valuations, even where those mis-valuations can be spotted. As shown by Israeli et al, the supply of relevant individual securities dries up as ETFs capture higher volumes of shares outstanding, thus preventing traders from transacting at the firm-specific level. Moreover, ETFs themselves attract uninformed traders, who would otherwise trade the underlying securities and reduces firm-level liquidity.[67]

Perversely, automated trading techniques also reduce incentives for information acquisition. The rapidity of automated trading imposes costs on informed investors: high-speed programmatic trading reduces the gains available to informed traders, reducing their incentives to gather and trade upon information, causing some to withdraw from investing and leaving a less-informed rump market. In free-riding on the

64 Zigrand (n 50).
65 I H-Y Chiu, 'Fintech and Disruptive Business Models in Financial Products, Intermediation and Markets – Policy Implications for Financial Regulations' (2016) 21 J Tech L & Pol'y 55.
66 S L Schwarcz, 'Rethinking the Disclosure Paradigm in a World of Complexity' (2004) U Illinois L Rev 1.
67 Israeli et al (n 36).

search costs of others, automated traders capture part of the gain(s) derived from information acquisition by active traders. This strips away advantages derived from information acquisition, diminishing the incentives for information-acquisition. The effect is that informed traders will reduce their trading activity, with some even withdrawing from the market. Naturally, this imposes substantial limitations on the Gilson and Kraakman schema.

A key question for regulators and market observers is what happens when ETFs reach a critical level of market control. In the context of this analysis, conventional accounts recognise that information acquisition is a fundamental component of efficient markets. ETFs in particular, may blunt the incentives for such informed trading. Even where the gains from informed trading are not eroded, because ETFs generally employ rudimentary momentum strategies and automation has led to greater speed in trade execution, levels of uninformed and derivatively informed trading will inevitably become elevated. In these circumstances, market arbitrage becomes more costly. Consequently, herding and asset price swings will likely occur more frequently.

4 Conclusion: regulatory philosophy

In isolation, ETFs and automated trading are unlikely to be sources of systemic crises. Instead, they amplify extant forces in markets, and may undermine their efficiency. However, if the ETF sector continues to grow apace, these considerations will become much more acute, in particular as the near-total automation of finance appears inevitable. Automation is of course not necessarily unwelcome, as FinTech opens up a wide range of possibilities for reducing the rent-seeking behaviour of financial insiders and improving access to finance. Equally, replacing human decision-making in investment management is not prima facie problematic; people are infinitely more prone to behavioural biases and incentive conflicts than computer programs.

Financial regulators have shown concerted support for the evolution of financial technologies in all guises, as demonstrated by the introduction of fast-tracked regulatory sandboxes for new market applications.[68] Paradoxically, many of these innovations rely upon the fact that financial market stability remains continually buttressed by the state, in particular through the extensions of lines of liquidity by the financial authorities accessible to financial innovators in periods of market stress. Historically, such liquidity facilities have directly backstopped ETFs[69] and model-driven investment funds[70] and prevented the eventuation of systemic crises.

The price of lower transaction costs and greater retail participation in financial markets may therefore be that central bank liquidity facilities are extended ever further to supporting private market innovations. Central banks have shown themselves willing to

68 Deloitte, 'A Journey Through the FCA Regulatory Sandbox: The Benefits, Challenges, and Next Steps' (2018) https://www2.deloitte.com/content/dam/Deloitte/uk/Documents/financial-services/deloitte-uk-fca-regulatory-sandbox-project-innovate-finance-journey.pdf.

69 J Rennison, 'How the Fed helped bond ETFs meet their biggest challenge' *Financial Times* (26 March 2020) https://www.ft.com/content/3f65cb22-28c9-493b-8313-434ab5fcd730.

70 J Smialek and D B Solomon, 'A Hedge Fund Bailout Highlights How Regulators Ignored Big Risks' *N.Y. Times* (23 July 2020) https://www.nytimes.com/2020/07/23/business/economy/hedge-fund-bailout-dodd-frank.html.

support certain markets or firms, whenever events threaten financial stability.[71] These episodes provide salutary lessons for the regulation of ever-more complex financial products, technologies and strategies. As noted in this chapter, developments in product markets and investment management may produce unforeseen interconnectedness and complementarities between institutions and markets which are later revealed to be unmanageable.

It is therefore incumbent upon regulators to monitor the development of the ETF sector, its continued interface with FinTech's automated trading tools, and wider liquidity management functions. Financial regulation must recognise that the expansion of large, rapid automatic trading and the removal of human discretion from large swathes of the investment management sector make it impossible to provide effective risk management oversight.[72] At the most fundamental level, regulators ought to wean market participants off the promise of constant liquidity provision, which is routinely called upon in times of market stress. Wider co-movement of asset prices, which is made more likely by both ETFs and algorithmic trading, increases the likelihood of capital losses amongst investors simultaneously, giving rise to additional contagion risk. At the least, this requires higher capital funding of capital positions and heightened disclosure by large investors of their trading positions. If large and correlated positions are unwound at large costs to leveraged investors, default may ensue. Whilst such vulnerabilities are not unique to ETFs or automated trading systems, the dynamics discussed in this chapter make systemic crises emanating from securities markets more likely. Requiring investors to cover a greater proportion of their potential losses *ex ante* will at least shield the financial authorities from the full costs of providing contingent and functionally unbounded liquidity insurance to yet more corners of the financial markets.

Bibliography

G Akerlof, 'The Market for Lemons: Quality Uncertainty and the Market Mechanism' (1970) 84 Q J Econ 488.

I Aldridge and S Krawciw, *Real-Time Risk: What Investors Should Know About Fintech, High-Frequency Trading and Flash Crashes* (Wiley 2017).

C Avery and P Zemski, 'Multidimensional Uncertainty and Herd Behavior in Financial Markets' (1998) 88 Am'can Econ Rev 724.

D Awrey, 'The Mechanisms of Derivatives Market Efficiency' (2016) 91 NYU L Rev 1104.

I Ben-David, F Franzoni and R Moussawi, 'Do ETFs Increase Volatility?' (2018) 73 J Fin 2471.

A Bhattacharya and M O'Hara, 'Can ETFs Increase Market Fragility? Effect of Information Linkages in ETF Markets' (2018) <https://ssrn.com/abstract=2740699> accessed 15 August 2020.

A Bhattacharya and M O'Hara, *ETFs and Systemic Risks* (CFA Institute Research Foundation January 2020) <https://www.cfainstitute.org/-/media/documents/article/rf-brief/etfs-and-systemic-risks.ashx> accessed 19 August 2020.

S Bikhchandani, D Hirshleifer and I Welch, 'A Theory of Fads, Fashion, Custom and Cultural Change as Informational Cascades' (1992) 100 J Pol Econ 992.

---

71 For example, even prior to the widespread central bank support for economies and markets in the wake of the Covid-19 pandemic, the US central bank was forced to prop up short-term debt (repo) markets. See A Samson, J Rennison, L Noonan and R Wigglesworth, 'Fed plans second intervention to ease funding squeeze' Financial Times (17 September 2019) https://www.ft.com/content/2c11a972-d941-11e9-8f9b-77216ebe1f17.

72 A A Kirilenko and A W Lo, 'Moore's Law versus Murphy's Law: Algorithmic Trading and Its Discontents' (2012) 27 J Econ Persp 51.

Blackrock, 'Visualising the ETF Universe' (September 2019) <https://www.blackrock.com/lu/individual/etfs-and-indexing/visualizing-the-expanse-etf-universe?switchLocale=y&siteEntryPassthrough=true> accessed 14th July 2020.

P Chatwell, 'The Liquidity "Doom Loop" in Bond Funds Is a Threat to the System' (Financial Times, 25 March 2020) <https://www.ft.com/content/b7c15426-6e1b-11ea-89df-41bea055720b> accessed 12th June 2020.

I H-Y Chiu, 'Fintech and Disruptive Business Models in Financial Products, Intermediation and Markets – Policy Implications for Financial Regulations' (2016) 21 J Tech L & Pol'y 55.

J Cox, 'Passive Investing Automatically Tracking Indexes Now Controls Nearly Half the US Stock Market' (14 March 2019) <https://www.cnbc.com/2019/03/19/passive-investing-now-controls-nearly-half-the-us-stock-market.html> accessed 15 January 2020.

Z Da and S Shive, 'Exchange Traded Funds and Asset Return Correlations' (2018) 24 Eur Fin Man 136.

Deloitte, 'A Journey Through the FCA Regulatory Sandbox: The Benefits, Challenges, and Next Steps' (2018) <https://www2.deloitte.com/content/dam/Deloitte/uk/Documents/financial-services/deloitte-uk-fca-regulatory-sandbox-project-innovate-finance-journey.pdf> accessed 15 January 2020.

M Demertzis, S Merler and G B Wolff, 'Capital Markets Union and the Fintech Opportunity' (2018) 4 J Fin Reg 157.

E F Fama, 'Efficient Capital Markets: A Review of Theory and Empirical Work' (1970) 25 J Fin 383.

Financial Stability Board, 'Potential Financial Stability Issues Arising from Recent Trends in Exchange-Traded Funds' (June 2011) <https://www.fsb.org/wp-content/uploads/r_110412b.pdf> accessed 17 August 2020.

Financial Stability Board, 'Financial Stability Implications from FinTech: Supervisory and Regulatory Issues that Merit Authorities' Attention' (June 2017) <https://www.fsb.org/wp-content/uploads/R270617.pdf> accessed 21 August 2020.

K Gavriilidis, G N Gregoriou and V Kallinterakis, 'Exchange-Traded Funds: Do They Promote or Depress Noise Trading?' in F Economou, K Gavriilidis and V Kallinterakis (eds), *Handbook of Investors' Behavior During Financial Crises* (Academic Press 2017) 335–361.

N Gennaioli, A Shleifer and R W Vishny, 'Neglected Risks, Financial Innovation and Financial Fragility' (2012) 104 J Fin Econ 452.

R J Gilson and R H Kraakman, 'The Mechanisms of Market Efficiency' (1984) 70 Virginia L Rev 549.

R J Gilson and R H Kraakman, 'Market Efficiency after the Financial Crisis: It's Still a Matter of Information Costs' (2014) 100 Virginia L Rev 313.

L Glosten, S Nallareddy and Y Zou 'ETF Activity and Informational Efficiency of Underlying Securities' (forthcoming 2021) Man Sci <https://pubsonline.informs.org/doi/10.1287/mnsc.2019.3427>..

G Gorton and A Metrick, 'Securitized Banking and the Run on Repo' (2012) 104 J Fin Econ 425.

B Holmstrom, 'Understanding the Role of Debt in the Financial System' BIS Working Paper No. 479 (January 2015) <https://www.bis.org/publ/work479.pdf> accessed 16 August 2020.

D Israeli, C Lee and S A Sridharan, 'Is There a Dark Side to Exchange Traded Funds? An Information Perspective' (2017) 22 Rev Acc Stud 1048.

A A Kirilenko and A W Lo, 'Moore's Law versus Murphy's Law: Algorithmic Trading and Its Discontents' (2012) 27 J Econ Persp 51.

K Lamont, '4 Key Trends in the European ETF Market' (22 January 2020) <https://www.morningstar.co.uk/uk/news/198984/4-key-trends-in-the-european-etf-market.aspx> accessed 25 January 2020.

H Markowitz, 'Portfolio Selection' (1952) 7 J Fin 77.

S T Omarova, 'New Tech v New Deal: Fintech as a Systemic Phenomenon' (2019) 36 Yale J on Reg 735.

M Pagano, A Sánchez Serrano and J Zechner, 'Can ETFs Contribute to Systemic Risk?' European Systemic Risk Board Reports of the Advisory Scientific Committee No. 9 (June 2019) <https://www.esrb.europa.eu/pub/pdf/asc/esrb.asc190617_9_canetfscontributesystemicrisk~983ea11870.en.pdf> accessed 12 August 2020.

C Reinicke, 'The ETF Market Will Hit $50 trillion by 2030, Bank of America Says' (13 December 2019) <https://markets.businessinsider.com/news/stocks/etf-market-grow-50-trillion-assets-2030-bank-america-passive-2019-12-1028763048> accessed 16 August 2020.

J Rennison, 'How the Fed Helped Bond ETFs Meet Their Biggest Challenge' *Financial Times* (26 March 2020) <https://www.ft.com/content/3f65cb22-28c9-493b-8313-434-ab5fcd730> accessed 15 April 2020.

A Samson, J Rennison, L Noonan and R Wigglesworth, 'Fed Plans Second Intervention to Ease Funding Squeeze' *Financial Times* (17 September 2019) <https://www.ft.com/content/2c11a972-d941-11e9-8f9b-77216ebe1f17> accessed 21 August 2020.

P A Samuelson, 'Challenge to Judgment' (1974) 1 J Portfolio Man 17.

S L Schwarcz, 'Rethinking the Disclosure Paradigm in a World of Complexity' (2004) U Illinois L Rev 1.

R Shiller, *Irrational Exuberance* (3rd edn, Princeton University Press 2016).

A Shleifer and L H Summers, 'The Noise Trader Approach to Finance' (1990) 4 J Econ Persp 19.

J Smialek and D B Solomon, 'A Hedge Fund Bailout Highlights How Regulators Ignored Big Risks' *The New York Times* (23 July 2020) <https://www.nytimes.com/2020/07/23/business/economy/hedge-fund-bailout-dodd-frank.html> accessed 15 August 2020.

R Srichander, 'Market Structures and Systemic Risks of Exchange-Traded Funds' (2011) BIS Working Papers No 343 <https://www.bis.org/publ/work343.pdf> accessed 15 March 2020.

V Susko and G Turner, 'The Implications of Passive Investing for Securities Markets' (March 2018) BIS Quarterly Review 113 <https://www.bis.org/publ/qtrpdf/r_qt1803j.pdf> accessed 12 August 2020.

R Topol, 'Bubbles and Volatility of Stock Prices: Effect of Mimetic Contagion' (1991) 101 Econ J 786.

R Wigglesworth, 'Volatility: How 'Algos' Changed the Rhythm of the Market' *Financial Times* (9 January 2019) <https://www.ft.com/content/fdc1c064-1142-11e9-a581-4ff78404524e> accessed 21 August 2020.

World Economic Forum, 'The Future of Financial Services: How Disruptive Innovations Are Reshaping the Way Financial Services Are Structured, Provisioned and Consumed' Final Report (June 2015) <http://www3.weforum.org/docs/WEF_The_future__of_financial_services.pdf> accessed 25 August 2020.

M Wyarta and J P Bouchaud, 'Self-Referential Behaviour, Overreaction and Conventions in Financial Markets' (2007) 63 J Econ Behav'r & Organ'tion 1.

Y Yadav, 'How Algorithmic Trading Undermines Efficiency in Capital Markets' (2015) 68 Vanderbilt L Rev 1607.

J P Zigrand, H S Shin and D Beunza, 'Feedback Effects and Changes in the Diversity of Trading Strategies' (2011) UK Government Foresight Review: The Future of Computer Trading in Financial Markets <https://assets.publishing.service.gov.uk/government/uploads/system/uploads/attachment_data/file/289030/11-1221-dr2-feedback-effects-and-changes-in-diversity-of-trading-strategies.pdf> accessed 18 August 2020.

Part V

Fintech, financial inclusion and sustainable finance

14 FinTech, financial inclusion and the UN Sustainable Development Goals[*]

Ross P Buckley, Dirk A Zetzsche, Douglas W Arner, and Robin Veidt

1 Introduction

Sustainable development is one of the most important shared objectives globally, and today increasingly centres on the United Nations Sustainable Development Goals (UN SDGs). The UN SDGs provide a framework of detailed objectives and criteria in pursuing sustainable development.

Central banks and financial regulators around the world are likewise considering how to enhance sustainable development in the context of their wider mandates for financial and economic development, while also balancing their other primary objectives, including monetary and financial stability, financial integrity and consumer protection. COVID-19 – as an existential sustainability crisis – has reinforced the need to focus on sustainability challenges and to use the crisis to improve existing systems and infrastructure.

Today, there are three major approaches emerging to sustainability and the UN SDGs.

The first approach views climate change and the other UN SDGs from the standpoint of the traditional financial services' policy focus on risk and related disclosure and particularly centres around environmental, social and corporate governance (ESG). Going forward, using the UN SDGs as the core framework for defining, monitoring and evaluating, ESG investment has great potential to redirect existing resources towards achieving the SDGs.

The second approach views the UN SDGs (particularly climate change, biodiversity, inequality and poverty reduction) as relating to new sources of potential risk; for example, climate change is now identified by the global insurance industry as perhaps the greatest risk facing the industry going forward. This leads to policy changes and significant research into risk modelling, management and mitigation, all resulting in substantial redirection of resources to support the SDGs.

We focus on the third approach, which is in its early stages and involves thinking about how to restructure or even redesign the financial system, thereby transforming

[*] This chapter draws upon and reflects a series of work from the authors: Douglas W Arner, Ross P Buckley, Dirk A Zetzsche and Robin Veidt, 'Sustainability, FinTech and Financial Inclusion' (2020) 21 European Business Organization Law Review 7–35; Dirk A Zetzsche, Ross P Buckley and Douglas W Arner, 'FinTech for Financial Inclusion: Driving Sustainable Growth' in Julia Walker, Alma Pekmezovic and Gordon Walker, *Sustainable Development Goals: Harnessing Business to Achieve the SDGs through Finance, Technology and Law Reform* (Wiley 2019) 179–204; and Douglas W Arner, Ross P Buckley and Dirk A Zetzsche, *FinTech for Financial Inclusion: A Framework for Digital Financial Transformation*, Special Report, Alliance for Financial Inclusion/Group of 24 (September 2018). Financial support was provided by the Hong Kong Research Grants Council Senior Fellowship programme.

finance to support the UN SDGs. To answer this question, we turn to two other leading foci for central banks and financial regulators: financial inclusion and financial technology.

As the increasing focus on sustainability and the UN SDGs has emerged, so has a related focus on financial inclusion, bringing finance to all parts of societies to maximise benefits.

Over the past decade, regulators have had to face yet another challenge: the digital transformation of finance around the world by FinTech.[1] The most recent waves of FinTech development pose new regulatory challenges because of the unprecedented speed of technological development including Big Data, Artificial Intelligence, enhanced connectivity and storage technologies such as distributed ledger technologies, blockchain and cloud services.[2] FinTech brings with it not only major opportunities to transform finance positively but also major new risks which potentially impact regulatory objectives. COVID-19 has accelerated all of these pre-existing trends and also magnified resulting risks.

Sustainable Finance and *FinTech* are now major policy focuses of most regulators, as demonstrated by (1) a range of initiatives promoted by the European Commission[3] and some EU Member States,[4] and (2) an abundant stream of research on both sustainability[5] and FinTech.[6] Yet few have linked the two fields.

---

1   See on the evolution of the FinTech sector Douglas W Arner, Janos N Barberis and Ross P Buckley, 'The Evolution of Fintech' (2016) 47 GeoJ Int'l L 1271; Douglas W Arner, Janos Barberis and Ross P Buckley, 'FinTech, RegTech and the Reconceptualization of Financial Regulation' (2017) 37 NwJ Int'l L Bus 371, 377–378.

2   See Dirk A Zetzsche, Ross P Buckley, Douglas W Arner, Janos N. Barberis, 'From FinTech to TechFin' (2018) 14 NYUJ Int'l L Bus 393; Arner, Barberis and Buckley (n 1) 373.

3   See Commission, 'FinTech Action Plan' COM(2018) 109 final, 8 March 2018; Commission, 'Action Plan: Financing Sustainable Growth' COM(2018) 97 final, 8 March 2018.

4   Prominent EU examples include the Luxembourgish Green Finance initiative and the sustainability agendas of France, the Netherlands and Germany, which seek to steer capital flows into sustainable financial products.

5   See eg, Panagiotis Delimatsis, 'Sustainable Standard-Setting, Climate Change and the TBT Agreement' in *Research Handbook on Climate Change and Trade Law* (Edward Elgar 2016) 148 (arguing that a 'discomfort with the functioning, working methods and certain rigidities of the global standardizing bodies such as the ISO led to a mushrooming of a new generation of private standard-setters at the transnational level'). The European Commission is working on an own taxonomy, see Commission, 'Action Plan: Financing Sustainable Growth' (n 3) work programme in Annex II and III; see also Max M Schanzenbach and Robert H Sitkoff, 'Reconciling Fiduciary Duty and Social Conscience' (2020) 72 Stan L Rev 381 (arguing that ESG investing is only possible for trusts if the trustee reasonably concludes and solely acts because of the fact that the ESG investment will be directly beneficial for the beneficiary by improving risk-adjusted return); Beate Sjåfjell and Christopher M Bruner (eds), *The Cambridge Handbook of Corporate Law, Corporate Governance and Sustainability* (CUP 2019) (discussing the mismatch between global markets and territorially rooted national sustainability regulation).

6   Rather than referring to the large volume of legal work in this field (including our own), we refer to some key economic research, including Bruno Biais and others, 'The Blockchain Folk Theorem' (2019) 32 Rev Financ Stud 1662 (analysing economics of Blockchain technology); Lars Hornuf and Armin Schwienbacher, 'Market Mechanisms and Funding Dynamics in Equity Crowdfunding' (2018) 50 JCorpF 556; Greg Buchak and others, 'Fintech, Regulatory Arbitrage, and the Rise of Shadow Banks' (2018) 130 JFinEcon 453 (measuring the impact of technologies); Maya Bacache and others, 'Taxation and the Digital Economy' (2015) <https://www.strategie.gouv.fr/sites/strategie.gouv.fr/files/atoms/files/ficalite_du_numerique_10_mars_corrige_final.pdf> accessed 01 December 2020 (as example for related topics such as taxation of the digital economy).

We aim at linking the two topics, using a third as a catalyst: *Financial Inclusion*. Similar to sustainable finance and FinTech, financial inclusion is at the centre of current global policy attention, driven for example, by the G20,[7] the World Bank[8] and major development organisations.[9]

Why focus on financial inclusion? As of 2017, 1.7 billion adults, some 31% of the world's population, lacked access to a financial or mobile money account.[10] Significantly, though, between 2010 and 2017, 1.2 billion people gained a financial or mobile money account for the first time, with most located in developing countries.[11] Much of this progress came from the impact of technology in finance. For example, mobile money has played a major role in increasing financial inclusion in Kenya and East Africa.[12] China has rapidly developed into perhaps the world's most digitised financial system.[13] India has dramatically increased financial access by building the infrastructure for a new digital economy, leading to hundreds of millions people gaining accounts.[14]

From the legal perspective, most research has focused on the three fields as separate, unrelated silos of knowledge. Financial inclusion has become an economic research topic[15] – with a focus in microfinance[16] – but with few exceptions,[17] much less a legal one. Where

---

7 See GPFI, 'G20 High-Level Principles for Digital Financial Inclusion' (2016) <www.gpfi.org/publications/g20-high-level-principles-digital-financial-inclusion> accessed 01 December 2020.

8 See The World Bank's financial inclusion policy work at www.worldbank.org/en/topic/financialinclusion.

9 Including the IMF, the OECD and others, NGOs, such as AFI, The Toronto Centre and Microfinance Centre, as well as the state-sponsored development banks (EIB, ADB, IDB, FDIC, etc.).

10 Asli Demirguc-Kunt and others, *The Global Findex Database 2017* (2018) <https://elibrary.worldbank.org/doi/pdf/10.1596/978-1-4648-1259-0> accessed 01 December 2020.

11 See World Bank, 'The Global Findex Database 2017' <https://globalfindex.worldbank.org/> accessed 01 December 2020.

12 GSMA, 'Mobile Money as a Driver of Financial Inclusion in Sub-Saharan Africa' (7 June 2017) <https://www.gsma.com/mobilefordevelopment/programme/mobile-money/mobile-money-driver-financial-inclusion-sub-saharan-africa/> accessed 01 December 2020; Ashenafi Beyene Fanta and others, 'The Role of Mobile Money in Financial Inclusion in the SADC Region' (2016) RP 03/2016 <https://www.finmark.org.za/wp-content/uploads/2016/12/mobile-money-and-financial-inclusion-in-sadc.pdf> accessed 01 December 2020.

13 Jennifer Chien and Douglas Randall, 'Key Lessons for Policymakers from China's Financial Inclusion Experience' (*WBB*, 15 February 2018) <https://blogs.worldbank.org/psd/key-lessons-policymakers-china-s-financial-inclusion-experience> accessed 01 December 2020; see also Weihuan Zhou, Douglas W Arner and Ross P Buckley, 'Regulation of Digital Financial Services in China' (2015) 8 Tsinghua China LR 25.

14 For a detailed discussion, see Douglas W Arner, Dirk A Zetzsche, Ross P Buckley and Janos N Barberis, 'The Identity Challenge in Finance' (2019) 20 EBOR 55, 64 et seq.

15 See eg, Rajiv Lal and Ishan Sachdev, 'Mobile Money Services-Design and Development for Financial Inclusion' (2015) HBS WP 15-083 <https://www.hbs.edu/faculty/Publication Files/15-083_e7db671b-12b2-47e7-9692-31808ee92bf1.pdf> accessed 01 December 2020.

16 See eg, with regard to technology Arvind Ashta (ed), *Advanced Technologies for Microfinance: Solutions and Challenges* (IGI Global 2010).

17 See eg, Michael S Barr, 'Microfinance and Financial Development' (2004) 26 Mich J Int Law 271 <https://repository.law.umich.edu/articles/61> accessed 01 December 2020; Michael S Barr, 'Banking the Poor' (2004) 21 Yale J Reg <https://digitalcommons.law.yale.edu/cgi/viewcontent.cgi?article=1160&context=yjreg> accessed 01 December 2020; Michael S Barr, *No Slack* (Brookings Press 2012); Emily Lee, 'Financial Inclusion: A Challenge to the New Paradigm of Financial Technology, Regulatory Technology and Anti-Money Laundering Law' (2017) JBL 473, as well as the contributions in Michael S Barr, Anjali Kumar and Robert E Litan (eds), *Building Inclusive Financial Systems* (Brookings Press 2007).

legal scholars focus on financial inclusion, they have studied (1) bank access for underprivileged people in developed societies,[18] (2) the regulatory set-up of mobile money service providers,[19] (3) regulatory preconditions for microfinance institutions[20] and (4) the role of central banks in financial inclusion.[21] We also note a scarcity of legal work relating to sustainable finance: while a plethora of studies discuss sustainable finance or the steering effects of the UN SDGs in general,[22] few academics have studied the link between *law* and sustainable finance with the exception of the impact of climate change on financial institutions.[23] A lot of attention (including our own[24]) has been devoted to the legal environment governing certain financial technologies such as initial coin offerings,[25] artificial intelligence,[26]

18 See in particular Barr, *No Slack* (n 17) and the contributions in Barr, Kumar and Litan (n 17), as well as Rebecca M Blank and Michael S Barr (eds), *Insufficient Funds* (RSF 2009).

19 See eg, Ross P Buckley, Jonathan Greenacre and Louise Malady, 'The Regulation of Mobile Money in Malawi' (2015) 14 Global Stud L Rev 435; Louis de Koker, Supriya Singh and Jonathan Capal, 'Closure of Bank Accounts of Remittance Service Providers' (2017) UQLJ 119; Lal and Sachdev (n 15); Jane K Winn, 'Mobile Payments and Financial Inclusion: Kenya, Brazil, and India as Case Studies' in John A Rothchild (ed), *Research Handbook on Electronic Commerce Law* (Edward Elgar 2016); Zhou, Arner and Buckley (n 13).

20 See Basel Committee on Banking Supervision (BCBS), 'Microfinance Activities and the Core Principles for Effective Banking Supervision' (2010) <https://www.bis.org/publ/bcbs175.pdf> accessed 01 December 2020; Veronica Trujillo, Fernando Rodriguez-Lopez and Victoria Muriel-Patino, 'Microfinance Regulation and Market Development in Latin America' (2014) 4 BE J Econ AP 1615; Verónica Trujillo-Tejada, Victoria Muriel-Patino and Fernando Rodríguez-López, 'How Is Microfinance Being Regulated in Latin America?' (2015) 26 E Dev Mfin 343; Jay K Rosengard, 'Oversight Is a Many-Splendored Thing' in Beatriz Armendáriz and Marc Labie (eds), *The Handbook of Microfinance* (World Scientific 2011).

21 See Adrienne Harris and Michael S Barr, 'Central Bank of the Future' (2019) <https://ssrn.com/abstract=3422860> accessed 01 December 2020.

22 See Frank Biermann, 'A New Paradigm for Global Sustainability Governance' (2019) 28:1 GAIA 52–53; Norichika Kanie and Frank Biermann (eds), *Governing through Goals – Sustainable Development Goals as Governance Innovation* (MIT Press 2017) (with contributions on the governance function and implementation of the UN SDGs).

23 See the ground-breaking report by Kern Alexander, 'Stability and Sustainability in Banking Reform' (2014) <https://www.cisl.cam.ac.uk/resources/publication-pdfs/stability-and-sustainability-basel-iii-final-repor.pdf> accessed 01 December 2020 (assessing the link between systemic environmental risks and financial stability, and offering insights into how some members of the Basel Committee are already acting on these links).

24 See Dirk A Zetzsche, Ross P Buckley, Douglas W Arner and Linus Föhr, 'The ICO Goldrush – a Challenge for Regulators' (2019) 60 Harv Int Law J 267; Douglas W Arner, Ross P Buckley and Dirk A Zetzsche, 'The Rise of Global Technology Risk' in Douglas W Arner, Emilios Avgouleas, Ross P Buckely and Steven Schwarcz (eds), *Systemic Risk in the Financial Sector: Ten Years after the Great Crash* (CIGI 2019); Ross P Buckley, Douglas W Arner, Dirk A Zetzsche and Rolf Weber, 'The Road to RegTech: The (Astonishing) Example of the European Union' (2019) 21 J Bank Regul 26; Arner and others (n 14); Zetzsche and others (n 2); Dirk A Zetzsche, Ross P Buckley and Douglas W Arner, 'The Distributed Liability of Distributed Ledgers: Legal Risks of Blockchain' (2018) Univ Ill LRev 1361.

25 See eg, Iris HY Chiu, 'Decoupling Tokens From Trading' (2018) 3 IBLJ 265.

26 Cf. Mark Fenwick, Erik PM Vermeulen and Marcelo Corrales, 'Business and Regulatory Responses to Artificial Intelligence: Dynamic Regulation, Innovation Ecosystems and the Strategic Management of Disruptive Technology' in Marcelo Corrales, Mark Fenwick and Nikolaus Forgó (eds), *Perspectives in Law, Business and Innovation* (Springer 2018).

crowdfunding,[27] blockchain[28] and new payment methods.[29] However, besides furthering competition and innovation, and balancing the former with traditional objectives of financial regulation,[30] little attention has so far been focused on how to ensure financial inclusion as a wider objective of the promotion of FinTech.

While our cross-disciplinary analysis is a radical step away from traditional disciplinary boundaries of legal scholarship,[31] we follow the practical approach undertaken by development bodies. *Their* interdisciplinary tendency is demonstrated by widely recognised reports issued, for example, by the G20 and the United Nations.[32]

In line with this approach, we show why FinTech is important for sustainable development and how regulators and governments can design a comprehensive strategy to support digital financial transformation, using both FinTech and financial inclusion as *tools* to build a sustainable future.

27 Cf. Lars Hornuf and Armin Schwienbacher, 'Should Securities Regulation Promote Equity Crowdfunding?' (2017) 49 Small Bus Econ 579.
28 See Philipp Paech, 'The Governance of Blockchain Financial Networks' (2017) 80 MLR 1073; Mark Fenwick and Erik PM Vermeulen, 'Technology and Corporate Governance - Blockchain, Crypto, and Artificial Intelligence' (2019) 48 Tex J Bus L 1; Emilios Avgouleas and Aggelos Kiayias, 'The Promise of Blockchain Technology for Global Securities and Derivatives Markets' (2019) 20 EBOR 81; Michèle Finck, *Blockchain Regulation and Governance in Europe* (CUP 2018).
29 Cf. Iris HY Chiu, 'A New Era in Fintech Payment Innovations?' (2017) 9 LIT 190.
30 See Hilary J Allen, 'Regulatory Sandboxes' (2019) 87 Geo Wash L Rev 579; Emilios Avgouleas, 'The Role of Financial Innovation in EU Market Integration and the Capital Markets Union' in Emilios Avgouleas, Danny Busch and Guido Ferrarini (eds), *Capital Markets Union in Europe* (OUP 2018); Chris Brummer, 'Disruptive Technology and Securities Regulation' (2015) 84 Fordh Law Rev 977; Chris Brummer and Yesha Yadav, 'Fintech and the Innovation Trilemma' (2019) 107 Geo LJ. 235; Iris HY Chiu, 'Fintech and Disruptive Business Models in Financial Products, Intermediation and Markets' (2016) 21 JTLP 55; Lars Hornuf and Christian Haddad, 'The Emergence of the Global Fintech Market: Economic and Technological Determinants' (2019) 53 Small Bus Econ 81; Saule T Omarova, 'New Tech v. New Deal: Fintech As A Systemic Phenomenon' (2019) 36 Yale J Reg 735; William Magnuson, 'Regulating Fintech' (2018) 71 Vand LRev 1167; Wolf-Georg Ringe and Christopher Ruof, 'A Regulatory Sandbox for Robo Advice' (2018) <https://ssrn.com/abstract=3188828> accessed 01 December 2020.
31 To our knowledge, two exceptions apply, see Dirk A Zetzsche, Ross P Buckley and Douglas W Arner, 'FinTech for Financial Inclusion: Driving Sustainable Growth' in Julia Walker, Alma Pekmezovic and Gordon Walker (eds), *Sustainable Development Goals: Harnessing Business to Achieve the SDGs through Finance, Technology, and Law Reform* (Wiley 2019), as well as the article by *Chiu and Greene* proposing ICO-style fund-raising in order to achieve greater marketisation of sustainable and social finance products, see Iris H Y Chiu and Edward F Greene, 'The Marriage of Technology, Markets and Sustainable (and) Social Finance' (2019) 20 EBOR 139.
32 See eg, GPFI, 'Digital Financial Inclusion: Emerging Policy Approaches' (2018) <http://www.gpfi.org/sites/gpfi/files/documents/Digital Financial Inclusion-CompleteReport-Final-A4.pdf> accessed 01 December 2020, a follow up to GPFI, (n 7), as well as GPFI, 'G20 Policy Guide Digitisation and Informality' (2018) <http://www.gpfi.org/sites/gpfi/files/documents/G20_Policy_Guide_Digitisation_and_Informality.pdf> accessed 01 December 2020, endorsed in August 2018. See also UNCDF, 'Improving Distribution of Digital Financial Services in Rural Areas' (2019) <https://www.uncdf.org/article/4542/improving-distribution-of-digital-financial-services-in-rural-areas> accessed 01 December 2020; World Bank, 'Financial Inclusion Beyond Payments' (2019) <http://documents.worldbank.org/curated/en/467421555393243557/pdf/Financial-Inclusion-Beyond-Payments-Policy-Considerations-for-Digital-Savings-Technical-Note.pdf> accessed 01 December 2020.

2 Financial inclusion and sustainability

This section examines FinTech, its relationship with financial inclusion and how FinTech for financial inclusion relates to sustainability.

2.1 *Financial inclusion: two sides of the same coin*

Financial inclusion involves delivering financial services at an affordable cost to all parts of society.[33] It enables people to manage their financial obligations efficiently, reduces poverty and supports wider economic growth.[34]

It has been argued that financial inclusion is a mere 'mechanism through which finance capitalism extracts value from the socially excluded'.[35] It is true that a lack of financial literacy coupled with the use of loans for personal consumption instead of value creation can lead to over-indebtedness of newly included individuals.[36] Paradoxically, promoting financial inclusion by giving access to a bank account and credit can indeed lead to financial exclusion in the long run.[37]

Financial inclusion, and especially access to credit, therefore introduces individuals to a new array of financial risks.[38] The success of any financial inclusion strategy therefore depends on factors such as a basic general level of financial literacy and the transparency of financial services, allowing customers to easily calculate risk and return of any financial product.[39] We argue that the fundamental advantages of financial inclusion – especially when part of a wider public policy approach as detailed in Section 4 – may limit over-indebtedness and certainly outweigh the potential financial risks, for four reasons. First, being financially included reduces individuals' vulnerability. For instance, by facilitating saving inclusion allows people to weather shocks and invest in their education and health. Second, inclusion can greatly increase the efficiency of daily life: bills can be paid electronically without taking time off work. Third, financial inclusion does not end with saving and credit provision alone. It can lead to the socialisation and diversification of peoples' financial risks through advanced financial instruments. For instance, breadwinner insurance can prevent people

---

33 FATF, 'Anti-Money Laundering and Terrorist Financing Measures and Financial Inclusion' (2013) 12 <http://www.fatf-gafi.org/media/fatf/documents/reports/AML_CFT_Measures_and_Financial_Inclusion_2013.pdf> accessed 01 December 2020.

34 CFI, 'Financial Inclusion 2020' <https://www.centerforfinancialinclusion.org/about/what-we-do/financial-inclusion-2020> accessed 01 December 2020

35 Guido Comparato, *The Financialisation of the Citizen: Social and Financial Inclusion through European Private Law* (Hart studies in commercial and financial law, Hart Publishing 2018) 60. Also see the contributions in Isabelle Guérin, Solène Morvant-Roux and Magdalena Villarreal (eds) *Microfinance, Debt and Over-Indebtedness* (Routledge, 2014) and their conclusion in Ch. 14 (stating that 'debt and credit have always been a historical motor of both oppression and emancipation').

36 Comparato (n 35) 51, also see p. 43 (stating that 'consumption credit [...] will generally not be reinvested in productive activities by the consumer, so that the possibility to repay the debt cannot depend on the viability of a business plan but on [...] income, any loan guarantees and – most paradoxically – the availability of further credit').

37 Ibid 142.

38 See eg, Aaron Mehrotra and James Yetman, 'Financial inclusion – Issues for Central Banks' (2015) <https://www.bis.org/publ/qtrpdf/r_qt1503h.pdf> accessed 01 December 2020 ('if financial inclusion is associated with excessive credit growth, or the rapid expansion of unregulated parts of the financial sector, financial risks may rise').

39 Also see Comparato (n 35) 51.

falling back into poverty. Fourth, financial inclusion supports economic growth through increasing financial resources to support real economic activity, particularly for individuals and small and medium enterprises (SMEs).

Financially excluded individuals are not exposed to the risks of the financial market, but they lack tools to prepare for and manage the burden of life's challenges, including sickness, crime, poverty, etc. For instance, farmers without access to electronic payment systems worry about theft, and may consume more immediately rather than take the risk. Health insurance can secure one's long-term working capacity. Savings can fund children's educations and provide for old age. Financial exclusion takes from people the opportunity to think, plan and *act* long-term. Where risks that could be avoided, hedged or socialised through the financial system materialise we force the excluded to think and act *short*-term, often unsustainably. Financial inclusion and sustainability are two sides of the same coin, aimed at the UN SDG's core objective: promoting prosperity while balancing risks. The experiences of COVID-19 have dramatically highlighted the importance of account and electronic payment access in the context of government support as well as in the context of e-commerce and an ever-increasing range of cashless and non-face-to-face transactions.

While financial inclusion is not a UN SDG *per se*, it underlies success in all the SDGs and therefore should be seen as a key underlying objective in seeking balanced sustainable development (see Table 14.1).

2.2 *Financial inclusion: a developing country topic?*

Formal financial exclusion is less widely spread in developed countries, but this does not mean that the population in developed countries know how to use their bank access well: as of 2014, only 33% of all adults globally (and only 38% of account-owning adults) are *financially literate* (among them 57% in major advanced economies, and 30% in major emerging economies).[40] Financial literacy means the ability to manage one's finances independently, without a financial advisor.[41] Assuming that approximately 1/3 of the world's population are children and subtracting the 1.7 billion formally excluded from the financial illiterate *approximately 1.7 billion adults* globally remain that cannot put their financial services access to good use. Beyond financial literacy, COVID-19 highlighted the importance of government delivery of financial support and other programmes remotely, with some of the greatest weaknesses in the US response the result of the substantial number of people without financial access. Financial inclusion thus has a key role in all economies.

FinTech, if rightly designed and applied can provide the 'rails' for delivery of payments across the population while at the same time having the potential to improve financial literacy (eg, through robo-advisors). However, according to Eurostat, as recently as 2016, 37% of EU individuals over age 65 had never used the internet.[42] The UK Financial Conduct

40 See Leora Klapper, Annamaria Lusardi and Peter Van Oudheusden, 'Financial Literacy Around the World' (2015) 16 <https://gflec.org/wp-content/uploads/2015/11/Finlit_paper_16_F2_singles.pdf> accessed 01 December 2020.

41 See ibid.

42 UK FCA, 'Access to Financial Services in the UK' (2016) 13 <https://www.fca.org.uk/publication/occasional-papers/occasional-paper-17.pdf> accessed 01 December 2020.

Table 14.1 Financial inclusion and the UN SDGs

No.	Goals	Impact (direct = D; indirect = I)	How financial inclusion can further goal
1	No poverty	I	Access to finance supports poverty reduction
2	Zero hunger	I	Enhance financial stability; stabilise cash-flows through saving and lending
3	Good health and well-being	I	Provide health insurance and financial stability
4	Quality education	I	Enable financial planning and saving for school fees
5	Gender equality	D	Strengthening female entrepreneurship and financial control
6-7	Clean water and sanitation; affordable and clean energy	I	Financing development and maintenance of infrastructure
8	Decent work and economic growth	D	Availability of finance supports entrepreneurship, SMEs and innovation
9	Industry, Innovation and Infrastructure	D	Provide financing for development and maintenance of infrastructure
10	Reduced inequalities	D	Enable funding of education and savings which provide the best opportunity for greater participation
11	Sustainable cities and communities	I	Finance is key to achieving all the targets; increases the domestic and international resources available to focus on infrastructure development
12	Responsible consumption and production	I	Key to achievement is financing of research and development as well as infrastructure and education; increases resources – domestic and international – available
13	Climate action	D	Identifying and managing both new forms of existing risk as well as new risks and creating systems which expand financial resources available
14	Life below water	I	Providing alternatives to unsustainable production
15	Life on land	I	Ibid
16	Peace, justice and strong institutions	I	Economic development strengthens peace and civil institutions
17	Partnerships	D	Allows for engagement of private actors, multiplying assistance of public or state-supported actors

Authority (as example of an advanced economy) estimates that one in five consumers lack the digital skills to use digital financial services.[43] At a time where bank branches are being closed,[44] and more bank branches are about to close in poor quarters than in rich,[45]

---

43 Ibid.
44 See report by consultancy firm McKinsey cited in Tim Wallace, 'Thousands More UK Bank Branches Could Face Closure' (14 September 2015) <https://www.telegraph.co.uk/finance/newsbysector/banksandfinance/11863736/Thousands-more-UK-bank-branches-could-face-closure.html> accessed 01 December 2020.
45 See Miles Brignall, 'Banks Accused of Abandoning England's Poorest Communities' (22 July 2019) <https://www.theguardian.com/business/2019/jul/22/banks-accused-abandoning-england-poorest-communities> accessed 01 December 2020.

technological exclusion translates into financial exclusion.[46] This highlights the importance of the foundation of digital inclusion through communications technology for financial inclusion and sustainable development more broadly.

Despite many national and EU initiatives,[47] an analysis of how legislation, with help of technology, could respond to financial illiteracy is sorely needed.[48] Multiple regulators seek to draw lessons from (and implement) the UN's digital literacy framework[49] – with Kenya's Three-Step-System of (1) familiarising consumers, (2) assisting their usage and (3) creating and programming software as a good example.[50] But despite all these efforts, due to its enormous dimensions both digital and financial illiteracy is here to stay. Financial law has to accept widespread illiteracy as a given regulatory precondition and needs to reflect this reality when determining the necessary level of consumer protection and information requirements in FinTech regulation.[51] In light of this, ensuring FinTech for financial inclusion is a crucial intermediate goal on the road towards a long-term, sustainable, yet prosperous world.

3 FinTech, financial inclusion and sustainability

This section analyses the role of FinTech in the relationship between financial inclusion and sustainability in terms of underpinning the achievement of the UN SDGs.

3.1 *FinTech and financial inclusion*

The 2008 financial crisis prompted sweeping regulatory responses coordinated by the G20 aimed at building a resilient global financial system. This led to the establishment of the Financial Inclusion Experts Group ('FIEG'),[52] Global Partnership for Financial Inclusion

---

46 See Hoai-Luu Q Nguyen, 'Do Bank Branches Still Matter?' (2014) <https://www.fdic.gov/regulations/laws/rules/5000-3830.html> accessed 01 December 2020 (stating that closings have prolonged negative impact on credit supply to local small businesses, even after the entry of new banks), as well as Hoai Luu Q Nguyen, 'Are Credit Markets Still Local? Evidence from Bank Branch Closings' (2019) 11 AEJ Applied 1 (stating that bank branch closings in the USA during the 2000s lead to a persistent, but local decline in small business lending for six years).

47 See the overview on the European Commission's online platform for adult learning, Commission, 'Financial Literacy | EPALE' <https://epale.ec.europa.eu/en/themes/financial-literacy> accessed 01 December 2020.

48 See the recent proposal by Safeguarding Ireland, taken from the website of the Commission, 'Scoping of a Regulatory Framework for Adult Safeguarding Welcomed' <https://epale.ec.europa.eu/en/content/scoping-regulatory-framework-adult-safeguarding-welcomed-call-establishment-national> accessed 01 December 2020.

49 UNESCO, 'A Global Framework of Reference on Digital Literacy Skills for Indicator 4.4.2' (2018) <http://uis.unesco.org/sites/default/files/documents/ip51-global-framework-reference-digital-literacy-skills-2018-en.pdf> accessed 01 December 2020.

50 See the Kenyan Ministry of ICT, 'Update on the Digital Literacy Programme' <http://icta.go.ke/update-on-the-digital-literacy-programme-being-implemented-by-the-ict-authority/> accessed 01 December 2020.

51 See Comparato (n 35) 18.

52 G20 FIEG, 'Innovative Financial Inclusion' (2010) <https://www.findevgateway.org/sites/default/files/publications/files/mfg-en-paper-innovative-financial-inclusion-may-2010.pdf> accessed 01 December 2020; GPFI, 'Innovative Financial Inclusion: Principles and Report on Innovative Financial Inclusion' (2010) <http://www.gpfi.org/sites/gpfi/files/documents/Principles and Report on Innovative Financial Inclusion_0.pdf> accessed 01 December 2020.

('GPFI') and the endorsement of the first Financial Inclusion Action Plan ('FIAP') by G20 leaders in 2010, which has been revised in 2017.[53]

GPFI recognised digital financial solutions as critical to facilitate global financial inclusion in 2016[54] and introduced the G20 High Level Principles for Digital Financial Inclusion ('HLPs').[55] Alongside the Recommendations for Responsible Finance[56] and the ID4D,[57] the HLPs encourage and guide governments to embrace digital approaches to financial inclusion. In 2017, the FIAP was updated to reflect the pivotal role of digitisation.[58]

The Alliance for Financial Inclusion ('AFI') was established in 2008 by the central banks of developing countries. In 2012, its members signed the historic Maya Declaration on Financial Inclusion, by which developing countries committed to financial inclusion targets and national policy changes and other agreements have followed.[59] In 2018, AFI endorsed its FinTech for Financial Inclusion ('FinTech4FI') strategy.

The UN established the Task Force on Digital Financing in November 2018 to develop strategies that promote financial technology to advance the SDGs. It is committed to 'put people at the centre', that is, it supports the view expressed herein that FinTech is an important, possibly the most important, single accelerator for attainment of the SDGs.[60]

3.2 *FinTech and sustainability*

Digital finance and FinTech play three core roles in relation to achieving the SDGs.

The first is enhancing the allocation of existing financial resources by redirecting financial resources globally and in individual countries to provide SDG-related finance. Examples include ESG and Green investment strategies, and the rapid growth in the EU, China and Japan in ESG-related financing.

53 For the latest version see GPFI, '2017 Financial Inclusion Action Plan' (2017) <https://www.gpfi.org/publications/g20-financial-inclusion-action-plan-fiap-2017> accessed 01 December 2020; Ross P Buckley, 'The G20's Performance in Global Financial Regulation' (2014) 37 UNSW Law Journal 63 <www.cifr.edu.au> accessed 01 December 2020.
54 GPFI, 'Launch of the G20 Basic Set of Financial Inclusion Indicators' (22 April 2013) <http://www.gpfi.org/featured/launch-g20-basic-set-financial-inclusion-indicators> accessed 01 December 2020.
55 GPFI (n 7).
56 See ASBA, 'Best Practices and Recommendations on Financial Consumer Protection, ATN/ME-11612-RG'(2012)<https://responsiblefinanceforum.org/wp-content/uploads/2014/04/ASBA_Consumer-Protection.pdf> accessed 01 December 2020.
57 See World Bank, 'Identification for Development' <https://id4d.worldbank.org/> accessed 01 December 2020.
58 Beatrice Timmermann and Philipp Gmehling, 'Financial Inclusion and the G20 Agenda' (2017) <https://www.bis.org/ifc/events/ifc_isi_2017/06_timmermann_paper.pdf> accessed 01 December 2020.
59 AFI, 'Maya Declaration' <https://www.afi-global.org/maya-declaration> accessed 01 December 2020; AFI, 'Maya Declaration Continues to Evolve' (6 November 2017) <https://www.afi-global.org/news/2017/11/maya-declaration-continues-evolve-financial-inclusion-commitments-66-countries> accessed 01 December 2020.
60 UNSG, 'Task Force on Digital Financing of Sustainable Development Goals' <https://www.un.org/sg/en/content/sg/personnel-appointments/2018-11-29/task-force-digital-financing-sustainable-development> accessed 01 December 2020.

The second involves the expansion of resources in the financial system generally, which can in turn support the SDGs. This takes place through financial inclusion and financial sector development, which together can increase the amount of financial resources available.

The third involves the use of digital finance and FinTech to directly achieve the SDGs themselves. This occurs through the use of new technologies and regulatory technology (RegTech) to design better financial and regulatory systems to achieve policy objectives.

Table 14.2[61] presents how FinTech contributes directly or indirectly to the UN SDGs.

If financial markets are sufficiently mature, providing financial services supporting financial inclusion contributes to *all* 17 UN SDGs. This makes evident that financial inclusion through FinTech is perhaps *the most important* intermediate step economies can take on their journey to achieving the UN SDGs.

4 Four pillars of digital financial transformation

An ever-increasing range of international development organisations are focusing on the role of FinTech and digital financial transformation in supporting broader developmental objectives today, including the United Nations Secretary General's (UNSG) Task Force on Digital Financing of the SDGs,[62] AFI,[63] the World Bank and Consultative Group to Assist the Poor (CGAP),[64] and many regional development banks.[65]

This section addresses two questions: which types of FinTech are most likely to advance balanced sustainable growth and financial inclusion and what lessons have we learned.[66]

The immediate answer to the first is mobile money – the provision of e-money on mobile phones – of which the paradigmatic example is M-Pesa. The longer-term answer is more complex. The real opportunity FinTech affords is developing an entire infrastructure for a digital financial ecosystem underpinning the SDGs and financial development, inclusion, stability and integrity.

Lessons can be taken from India's FinTech strategy, India Stack. It is a set of APIs which form a digital infrastructure used by the government, businesses and other entities to provide paperless and cashless services.[67] India Stack involves four main levels.[68] First is a national biometric identification system. Second is the establishment of bank accounts to

---

61 The Table draws on the authors' own research and experience. That digital financial services support the UN SDGs is very broadly accepted: see UNCDF, 'DFS and the SDGs' <https://www.uncdf.org/mm4p/dfs-and-the-sdgs> accessed 01 December 2020.

62 See UNSG's DFTF, 'UNSG's Task Force on Digital Financing of the SDGs' <https://digitalfinancingtaskforce.org/> accessed 01 December 2020.

63 See the AFI special report by lead authors Douglas W Arner, Ross P Buckley and Dirk A Zetzsche, 'Fintech for Financial Inclusion' (2018) <https://ssrn.com/abstract=3245287> accessed 01 December 2020.

64 World Bank, 'FinTech and Financial Inclusion' <http://pubdocs.worldbank.org/en/877721478111918039/breakout-DigiFinance-McConaghy-Fintech.pdf> accessed 01 December 2020.

65 We know of FinTech initiatives by the Asian Development Bank, the Islamic Development Bank, the European Investment Bank and the Financial Development Corporation.

66 GPFI, 'Digital Financial Inclusion: Emerging Policy Approaches' (n 32).

67 'About – IndiaStack' <https://www.indiastack.org/about/> accessed 01 December 2020.

68 Abhijit Bose, 'India's Fintech Revolution Is Primed to Put Banks out of Business | TechCrunch' (14 June 2016) <https://techcrunch.com/2016/06/14/indias-fintech-revolution-is-primed-to-put-banks-out-of-business/> accessed 01 December 2020.

Table 14.2 How FT4FI could further the UN SDGs

No.	Goals	Impact (direct = D; indirect = I)	How FT4FI can further goal
1	No poverty	I	Allow for online financing, including credit and crowdfunding; create new income opportunities through online markets and payments; reduce impact of disasters with local impact
2	Zero hunger	I	Enhance financial stability; stabilise cash-flows through saving and lending
3	Good health and well-being	I	Provide health insurance and financial stability
4	Quality education	I	Provide financial planning and savings for school fees
5	Gender equality	D	Strengthening female entrepreneurship and financial controls
6	Clean water and sanitation	I	Provide financing for development and maintenance of infrastructure; further education for local sustainability expertise
7	Affordable and clean energy	I	Ibid
8	Decent work and economic growth	D	Allow for online financing, including credit and crowdfunding; create new (online) income opportunities; ensure funding and use symmetry (long-term for long-term projects, short-term for short-term projects)
9	Industry, Innovation and Infrastructure	D	Provide financing for development and maintenance of infrastructure
10	Reduced inequalities	D	See on gender at UN SDG 5. Re regional, economic and educational equality, education and savings provide the best opportunity for greater participation for most societies; both are furthered by FT4FI
11	Sustainable cities and communities	I	FT4FI assists the development of and investment in sustainable technology and transformation
12	Responsible production and consumption	I	Ibid
13	Climate action	I	Ibid
14	Life below water	I	Ibid
15	Life on land	I	Ibid
16	Peace, justice and strong institutions	I	Robust economic development strengthens peace and civil institutions
17	Partnerships	D	FT4FI allows for engagement of private actors, multiplying assistance by public or state supported actors

deliver national services. Third is a common payment API. Fourth is a series of electronic KYC initiatives allowing individual identification.

Based on India's experience and other successful examples, we argued in our major study for AFI that economies must focus on four pillars of digital financial infrastructure to support digital financial transformation, built on the foundation of digital access through communications, in particular mobile phones, smart phones and internet access.[69]

4.1 *Pillar I: digital ID and eKYC – establishing the foundation*

Customer identification has been particularly challenging in developing countries where substantial numbers of people lack formal identification documents.[70]

India's Aadhaar system is the first level of India Stack and involves issuing a 12-digit randomised number to all residents for access to government and other services.[71] Difficulties in implementation should not detract from the potential of a national biometrically-based identification system to create the solid foundation of any digital financial ecosystem.

The experiences of the UN and Jordan with developing a digital identity solution for refugees illustrates good system design and synergistic development.[72] IrisGuard converts an iris image into a unique code which is then used to identify the individual.[73] Since 2016, IrisGuard's EyePay platform has been used by the UN to deliver financial aid and enable beneficiaries to receive food vouchers, withdraw cash and transfer funds without a bank account.

Base digital ID needs to extend as broadly as possible to maximise efficiencies. Particularly when linked electronically with other golden source data (such as tax information), it provides the basis of a simple eKYC system. The core objective is to make account openings for most people and entities simple and cheap, thereby allowing resources to be focused on higher risk customers and protection of market integrity.

In the European Union, the 2014 eIDAS Regulation was adopted to provide mutually recognised digital identity for cross-border interactions between European citizens, companies and government institutions.[74] It aims at making it 'possible to open a bank account on-line while meeting the strong requirements for customer identity'.[75] This includes accepting electronic identification for meeting customer due diligence (CDD) requirements.

Such systems – while technically feasible – may not be politically feasible everywhere.[76] Systems of optional digital identity, supported by sovereign identification systems, may hold the greatest transformative potential.[77]

---

69 Arner and others (n 63).
70 See for an extensive analysis of ID techniques and regulation Arner and others (n 14).
71 Government of India, 'Unique Identification Authority of India' <https://uidai.gov.in/about-uidai/unique-identification-authority-of-india/about.html> accessed 01 December 2020.
72 See Irisguard, 'IFC and Irisguard to Support Financial Inclusion and Syrian Refugees in Jordan' (13 February 2018) <https://www.irisguard.com/node/39> accessed 01 December 2020.
73 Ibid.
74 See for more information Arner and others (n 14) s. 4.3.
75 Commission, 'Consumer Financial Services Action Plan' (2017) 13–14 COM(2017) 139 final 23 March 2017.
76 See Arner and others (n 14) 58.
77 Ibid s. 4.4.2.

4.2 *Pillar II: open, interoperable electronic payment systems – building connectivity*

A mobile money ecosystem is one way FinTech can help developing countries to leapfrog bricks-and-mortar bank branches with a seamless digital financial system that provides the fundamental infrastructure for money to flow through their economies.

4.2.1 *Mobile money*

Mobile money enables mobile phones to be used to pay bills, remit funds and save, using e-money[78], mostly issued by telecommunication companies ('telcos'). The service currently exists in over 89 developing countries and is growing rapidly.[79]

M-Pesa is a major success in providing financial services to a sizable proportion of the Kenyan population.[80] However, mobile money success has not been consistent across countries. This is due to the differing needs of consumers in different countries, the inability of service providers to adapt to different markets,[81] a tendency of central banks to over-regulate these services,[82] a lack of trained payments professionals in many markets[83] and cultural and anthropological reasons.

Mobile money services, often do not initially pose systemic stability concerns and at least initially do not in many cases require, traditional levels of banking regulation.[84] However, such services have the potential to grow rapidly, particularly when introduced by a dominant telco, meaning that risks and the consequent need for regulation can develop very quickly.

4.2.2 *Regulatory infrastructure for an open electronic payments system*

In China, Alipay and WeChat Pay show the power of facilitating new entrants and the digitisation of the traditional payments system among banks.

---

78 For a definition of e-money, see eg, AFI MFSWG, 'Mobile Financial Services: Basic Terminology' (2013) <https://www.afi-global.org/sites/default/files/publications/mfswg_gl_1_basic_terminology_finalnewnew_pdf.pdf> accessed 01 December 2020.
79 Claire Scharwatt and others, 'State of the Industry 2014, GSMA Report' (2015) <https://www.gsma.com/mobilefordevelopment/wp-content/uploads/2015/03/SOTIR_2014.pdf> accessed 01 December 2020.
80 By 2016, over 75% of adults in Kenya had access to formal financial services, a 26.7% increase from a decade earlier, Njuguna Ndung'u, 'M-Pesa – a Success Story of Digital Financial Inclusion' (2017) <https://www.geg.ox.ac.uk/publication/practitioners-insight-m-pesa-success-story-digital-financial-inclusion> accessed 01 December 2020.
81 Ross P Buckley and Sarah Webster, 'FinTech in Developing Countries' (2016) 44 J Fin Transformation 151.
82 The Central Bank of Kenya however applied a 'light-touch' approach.
83 Ross P Buckley and Ignacio Mas, 'The Coming of Age of Digital Payments as a Field of Expertise' (2016) J L Tech Pol'y 71.
84 Arner and others (n 63) 12. Also see the in-depth analysis by GSMA, 'The Impact of Mobile Money on Monetary and Financial Stability in Sub-Saharan Africa' (2019) 20 et seq. <https://www.gsma.com/mobilefordevelopment/wp-content/uploads/2019/03/The-impact-of-mobile-money-on-monetary-and-financial-stability.pdf> accessed 01 December 2020.

Alibaba established Alipay in 2004 as a payment method for its ecommerce business. Yu'e Bao was established with Alipay in 2013, providing the opportunity to make small investments, and is now one of the world's largest money market funds.[85]

WeChat was established as a messaging platform by Tencent in 2011. Cash transfers and in-store cashless payments became possible in 2014,[86] and by 2017, 92% of survey respondents were using mobile payment systems like this for retail payments.[87]

The People's Bank of China ('PBoC') has since 2017 subjected mobile wallet services to increasing regulation.[88] Mobile payment institutions are now required to channel payments through a centralised clearing house[89] and their reserve funds ratios are gradually being increased to 100%.[90] Payment institutions must now also obtain permits to offer barcode payments.[91]

These Chinese experiences highlight how payments providers should be subject to appropriate proportional regulation to address risks and provide a level playing field.

4.3 *Pillar III: electronic government provision of services – expanding usage*

While various governments have experimented with electronic provision of services and mandatory account approaches, their effect is often limited unless built upon Pillar I and II infrastructure.

The electronic provision of government salaries and services may support financial inclusion, empowerment and savings, while also dramatically reducing leakage and improving tax collection, facilitating and supporting all aspects of achieving the UN SDGs. The Pillar I-II-III infrastructure can also support national pension systems, which enhance the financial safety net and provide additional financial resources to support growth.

4.3.1 *Electronic payment: government salaries and transfers*

Digital financial transformation policies focused on government payments first enable governments to shift from in-kind assistance (food, water supply) to inexpensive cash transfers.[92]

---

85 Eric Mu, 'Yu'ebao: A Brief History of the Chinese Internet Financing Upstart' (*Forbes*, 18 May 2014) <https://www.forbes.com/sites/ericxlmu/2014/05/18/yuebao-a-brief-history-of-the-chinese-internet-financing-upstart/#25c898583c0e> accessed 01 December 2020.
86 Steven Millward, '7 Years of WeChat' (*Tech in Asia*, 21 January 2018) <https://www.techinasia.com/history-of-wechat> accessed 01 December 2020.
87 Technode, 'WeChat User & Business Ecosystem Report 2017' (24 April 2017) <https://technode.com/2017/04/24/wechat-user-business-ecosystem-report-2017/> accessed 01 December 2020.
88 See Zhou, Arner and Buckley (n 13) 28 et seq. ('discussing China's last mover advantage').
89 Jinshan Hong, 'How China's Central Bank Is Clamping Down On The Mobile Payment Industry' (*Forbes*, 18 August 2017) <https://www.forbes.com/sites/jinshanhong/2017/08/18/how-chinas-central-bank-is-clamping-down-on-the-mobile-payment-industry/#5fa0a13b50be> accessed 01 December 2020.
90 Yue Wang, 'China Tightens Regulation Over Mobile Payment Apps' (*Forbes*, 3 January 2018) <https://www.forbes.com/sites/ywang/2018/01/03/china-tightens-regulation-over-mobile-payment-apps-whats-next-for-tencent-and-ant-financial/#47e526ae7f1d> accessed 01 December 2020.
91 'China Looks for Right Balance between Financial Innovation, Risk' (*China Daily*, 30 December 2017) <http://www.chinadaily.com.cn/a/201712/30/WS5a46fd55a31008cf16da4599.html> accessed 01 December 2020.
92 Guy Stuart, 'Government to Person Transfers' (2016) <https://www.centerforfinancialinclusion.org/government-to-person-transfers> accessed 01 December 2020.

Second, accounts established for support payments can be used for non-government payments. Third, the need to use the technology to receive government payments can break down cultural attachment to cash.

As of 2016 at least 19 Government-to-Person ('G2P') payment programmes operated in developing countries.[93] However, most of these projects are at best half-digital: according to CGAP, '31 percent of accounts in low-income countries [...] [are] used for only one or two withdrawals per month'.[94] Potential reasons including use limitations of accounts and insufficient recipient and agent training.[95]

The Centre for Financial Inclusion highlights the need for payment processes to 'align with customer life patterns'.[96] For instance, in a Pakistani G2P women's programme, only 53% of transactions were initiated by women; the rest were by male representatives.[97] Consequently, the Pakistan government adopted biometric technology, thereby hopefully empowering women to decide how to use the money.[98]

G2P payments can further financial inclusion and the UN SDGs, *if properly designed*. In particular, the three following features must be addressed:

1 Government-designed account procedures should facilitate later unrestricted payments.
2 The digital-to-real gap must be bridged well. If merchants cannot do business without accepting e-money, they will provide devices to accept e-money efficiently, with or without incentives.
3 Functionality must be simple. The learning required to receive government support must enable one to make and receive other transfers.

4.3.2 *Electronic payment and provision: other core services*

The combination of the foundation of digital access combined with Pillars I–III supports many service payments, particularly for utilities and telecommunications, that improve the lives of individuals. They offer endless potential for e-government and the infrastructure also supports ecommerce, with significant benefits for SMEs.

Governments can support digital transformation by setting limits for cash transactions in the real economy, and requiring merchants to accept digital payments at low or no cost to customers.

More transformational, integrated strategies integrating Pillars I–III have the potential to transform government revenue, delivery of services and trust and confidence.

93 Ibid 29 (citing policy reports from PFIP, CGAP, Gates Foundation and others).
94 Silvia Baur-Yazbeck, 'Accessible, Robust, Integrated' (*CGAP*, 12 December 2016) <https://www.cgap.org/blog/accessible-robust-integrated-identifying-good-payment-programs> accessed 01 December 2020.
95 Ibid.
96 Stuart (n 92) 2.
97 Ibid 19.
98 See BISP, 'Biometric Verification' (2019) <https://bisp.gov.pk/SiteImage/Misc/files/PR-10-10-2019-1.pdf> accessed 01 December 2020.

4.4 *Pillar IV: design of financial market infrastructure and systems*

Additional forms of digital financial infrastructure, combined with the foundations of Pillars I–III can support access to finance, financial stability and market integrity. Digitised systems for securities trading, clearing and settlement can also provide greater access to investment products and support financial sector development.

4.4.1 *Transforming credit provision: from collateral and microfinance to cash-flow*

Since credit risk analysis was historically deemed uncommercial for many individuals and SMEs, banks traditionally rely on collateral, which is difficult in developing countries where property rights may be weak or non-existent.

Digitalisation has changed this. Providers with accurate customer data are well placed to price credit through datafication, that is, the process of analysing and using data.[99] Superior data may derive from social media services, search engines, e-commerce platforms and telcos.[100]

The potential benefits are huge and may lead to a 're-personalisation' of the financial relationship between credit providers and their clients by adjusting credit rates based on individuals' real risk profiles.[101] However, the emergence of such platforms also brings new challenges, some of which threaten attainment of the UN SDGs. For example, there is little to prevent scoring tools from inadvertently using innocuous data points as proxies for sensitive attributes such as race.[102] Also, when dealing with Big-Data scoring systems that may integrate thousands of variables, it may prove practically impossible for consumers to verify the accuracy of their scores and reports.[103] This means that approaches to the interaction between data regulation and financial regulation must be considered very carefully.

4.4.2 *Adding insurance and investments to savings and credit*

While online payments and lending are the core of most financial inclusion strategies, extensions into the investment sector are necessary. Digitalisation can increase access and overall efficiency, while also reducing transaction costs.[104] Accenture expects banks to potentially save between 20% and 25% across IT operations, including infrastructure, maintenance and development costs, because of process automation and the use

---

99 For an overview of the alternative credit-scoring market see Mikella Hurley and Julius Adebayo, 'Credit Scoring in the Era of Big Data' (2017) 18(1) Yale Journal of Law and Technology 148, 157 et seq. For possible dangers of the use of AI in Finance, see Ross P Buckley, Douglas W Arner, Dirk A Zetzsche, and Brian W Tang, 'Artificial Intelligence in Finance: Putting the Human in the Loop', Sydney Law Rev (2021), *in press* <https://ssrn.com/abstract=3531711> accessed 01 December 2020.
100 Zetzsche and others (n 2) 406 et seq.
101 Ibid 420.
102 Hurley and Adebayo (n 99) 199.
103 Ibid 189.
104 See eg, for the cost benefits of Robo-Advisors Facundo Abraham, Sergio L Schmukler and José Tessada, 'Robo-Advisors: Investing through Machines' (World Bank, 2019) 2 et seq. <http://documents.worldbank.org/curated/en/275041551196836758/Robo-Advisors-Investing-through-Machines> accessed 01 December 2020.

of Artificial Intelligence.[105] Digitalisation, done well, may also reduce biases in investments,[106] strengthen capital markets through enhanced savings rates and bring new resources into the financial system while, done poorly, particularly by relying on biased or otherwise unsuitable data, this process may have a range of negative impacts. The main risk digitalisation brings arises in the uncertainty and complexity which are inherent in investments. Lessening the trust divide – as investors must trust intermediaries to control risk – lies at the heart of developing liquid financial markets.

5 Developing a comprehensive strategy

5.1 *Strategic approach*

The starting point is that the power of the foundation and these pillars is greatest when all are pursued and become mutually reinforcing.

5.2 *The challenge of technology*

Any FinTech-based approach must accept that technology is not perfect. Three consequences follow.

First, technology may operate beyond its developers' intentions. Self-learning algorithms may enhance biases existing in the data.[107] This may either be due to data selection issues ('dashboard myopia') or data reflecting biases persisting in society at large (eg, that males are more likely to work in tech).[108] Perfect technologies to control this tendency do not yet exist. Hence, providers must constantly test the outcomes of algorithmic data interpretation. A number of ethical questions with a particular financial services dimension should be addressed by future legislation so as to make AI-driven financial services stable and sound, and their risks balanced.[109] In order to ensure constant testing, we suggest that responsibility frameworks for senior management should be expanded to specifically incorporate responsibility for AI in regulated activities, thus mandating a 'human-in-the-loop'.[110]

Second, technology may do exactly what the developers intend, and the problem is the developers. Financial history is replete with fraud. Every new technology will be abused by some. A recent example is the use of initial coin offerings for defrauding investors/participants.[111]

Third, ever-accelerating technology facilitates ever more new entrants, making regulators' roles ever more challenging. This will likely require regulators to use RegTech for automation

---

105 See Accenture, 'Redefine Banking with Artificial Intelligence' (2018) 9 <https://www.accenture.com/_acnmedia/pdf-68/accenture-redefine-banking.pdf> accessed 01 December 2020.
106 For risks and present biases of robo-advisors see Abraham and others (n 104) 3.
107 See eg, Hope Reese, 'How Data and Machine Learning Are "Part of Uber's DNA"' (*Techrepublic*) <https://www.techrepublic.com/article/how-data-and-machine-learning-are-part-of-ubers-dna/> accessed 01 December 2020.
108 See Zetzsche and others (n 99) 18 et seq. Also see Tom C W Lin, 'Artificial Intelligence, Finance, and the Law' (2019) 88 Fordh L Rev 531 (summarising risks and limitations of AI in light of financial regulation).
109 See Buckley and others (n 99) 22.
110 Ibid 44.
111 Zetzsche and others, 'The ICO Gold Rush' (n 24).

and data-driven analysis of internal control systems and internal and external reporting to improve their own regulatory capabilities and enhance regulatory outcomes.

5.3 *Building innovation ecosystems*

Policymakers and regulators need to develop methods to understand new technologies and the related risks and opportunities. They also increasingly have to consider how they can better use technology in redesigning their systems for the regulation of FinTech.

One recent development to potentially assist digital financial transformation is regulatory sandboxes.[112] The sandbox creates an environment for businesses to test products without having to meet the full panoply of regulation. In return, regulators require appropriate safeguards.

We note, however, that most regulators practice, under the sandbox label, something we find more akin to an innovation hub, that is, a structured way of communication with innovative firms that results in guidance to the firm and mutual learning, without automatically granting regulatory privilege; further, while innovation hubs require substantial resources, they often function without changes to legislation and can have a more important impact in many financial systems than sandboxes, which in turn function best when combined with an innovation hub.[113] Other ways to respond to innovation include more structured approaches to waivers, no-action letters, piloting and testing and small business exemptions.

6 Towards inclusive and balanced sustainable growth

Digital financial transformation is *one* important answer to how regulators and government can support achievement of the UN SDGs by potentially generating additional financial resources, by more efficiently using financial resources and in some cases by directly supporting achievement.

What sorts of approaches work? A comprehensive digital financial transformation strategy based on four pillars, including digital ID, open interoperable payment systems, FinTech for G2P programmes, and long-term development of sophisticated financial market infrastructure, is key. These pillars in turn rest on the broader foundation of digital access, in particular through mobile phones, smart phones and the internet.

From the standpoint of transforming all aspects of society and development, the most powerful technology which has emerged is the mobile phone, particularly when combined with internet access. Major barriers remain though, particularly regarding the last mile and in much of Africa where feature phones still prevail and internet access is mixed. Because of their foundational effect, this is a core area for focus in seeking rapid transformation going forward, especially in combination with digital identification.

These foundational technologies offer the potential for other interventions, of which interoperable mobile payment systems have been among the most important from the standpoint of achieving the SDGs.

---

112 Dirk Zetzsche, Ross P Buckley, Douglas W Arner and Janos N Barberis, 'Regulating a Revolution' (2017) 23 Fordh J Corp Fin L 31 <https://ir.lawnet.fordham.edu/jcfl/vol23/iss1/2>.

113 For a detailed analysis of regulatory sandboxes around the globe, see Ross P Buckley, Douglas W Arner, Robin Veidt and Dirk Zetzsche, 'Building Financial Ecosystems' (2020) 61 WashU J L&Pol'y 55.

Combining these allows governments, businesses and others to provide better services to people, with important successes in the context of displaced persons through the UNHCR's use of digital delivery of aid. Other examples of mitigation and development include forms of digital crop insurance, and pooled digital insurance for catastrophes. COVID-19 has clearly demonstrated the value and importance of digital finance and the value of building the necessary foundations and infrastructure, in both developed and developing countries.

Looking forward, the power of digital finance is greatest in those countries which are furthest behind but are able to leapfrog to higher levels of development. This strategy of digital financial infrastructure development rests fundamentally on availability of communications' infrastructure. While digital infrastructure will not solve all challenges – for instance, we may face a new digital divide between the technologically able and others – it does provide the core elements of an enabling framework to support the achievement of the UN SDGs and to better withstand not only COVID-19 but also future sustainability crises.

Bibliography

F Abraham, S L Schmukler and J Tessada, 'Robo-Advisors: Investing through Machines' (2019) World Bank <http://documents.worldbank.org/curated/en/275041551196836758/Robo-Advisors-Investing-through-Machines> accessed 01 December 2020.

Accenture, 'Redefine Banking with Artificial Intelligence' (2018) <https://www.accenture.com/_acnmedia/pdf-68/accenture-redefine-banking.pdf> accessed 01 December 2020.

K Alexander, 'Stability and Sustainability in Banking Reform: Are Environmental Risks Missing in Basel III?' (16 October 2014) University of Cambridge Institute for Sustainability Leadership (CISL) <https://www.cisl.cam.ac.uk/resources/sustainable-finance-publications/banking-regulation> accessed 01 December 2020.

H J Allen, 'Regulatory Sandboxes' (2019) 87(3) Geo Wash Law Rev 579–645.

Alliance for Financial Inclusion (AFI) Mobile Financial Services Working Group, 'Mobile Financial Services: Basic Terminology' (1 August 2014) <http://www.afi-global.org/library/publications/mobile-financial-services-basic-terminology-2013> accessed 01 December 2020.

Alliance for Financial Inclusion (AFI), 'Maya Declaration' (2017) <https://www.afi-global.org/maya-declaration> accessed 01 December 2020.

Alliance for Financial Inclusion (AFI), 'Maya Declaration Continues to Evolve with Financial Inclusion Commitments from 66 Countries' (6 November 2017) <https://www.afi-global.org/news/2017/11/maya-declaration-continues-evolve-financial-inclusion-commitments-66-countries/> accessed 01 December 2020.

D W Arner, J N Barberis and R P Buckley, 'The Evolution of FinTech: A New Post-Crisis Paradigm?' (2016) 47(4) Georget J Int Law 1271–1319.

D W Arner, J N Barberis and R P Buckley, 'FinTech, RegTech and the Reconceptualisation of Financial Regulation' (2017) 37(3) Northwestern J Int Law Bus 371–413.

D W Arner, R P Buckley and D A Zetzsche, 'FinTech for Financial Inclusion: A Framework for Digital Financial Transformation' (2018) Alliance for Financial Inclusion (AFI) Special report <https://www.afi-global.org/publications/2844/FinTech-for-Financial-Inclusion-A-Framework-for-Digital-Financial-Transformation> accessed 01 December 2020.

D W Arner, D A Zetzsche and R P Buckley, 'FinTech, RegTech and Systemic Risk: The Rise of Global Technology Risk' in L Schwarcz, E Avgouleas, D Busch and D W Arner (eds), *Systemic Risk in the Financial Sector: Ten Years after the Global Financial Crisis* (Waterloo: CIGI Press 2019) Ch 4.

D W Arner, D A Zetzsche, R P Buckley and J Barberis, 'The Identity Challenge in Finance: from Analogue Identity to Digitized Identification to Digital KYC Utilities' (2019) 20(1) EBOR 55–80.

B F Ashenafi, M Kingstone, G Roelof, E Matthew and K Nikki, 'The Role of Mobile Money in Financial Inclusion in the SADC Region' FinMark Trust (December 2016) Pol Research Paper No 03/2016 <https://www.researchgate.net/publication/311576448_The_role_of_mobile_money_in_financial_inclusion_in_the_SADC_region> accessed 01 December 2020.

A Ashta, *Advanced Technologies for Microfinance: Solutions and Challenges* (Hershey: IGI Global 2010).

A Avgouleas, 'The Role of Financial Innovation in EU Market Integration and the Capital Markets Union: A Re-Conceptualisation of Policy Objectives' in E Avgouleas, D Busch, G Ferrarini (eds), Capital Markets Union in Europe (Oxford: Oxford University Press 2018) 171–192.

A Avgouleas and A Kiayias, 'The Promise of Blockchain Technology for Global Securities and Derivatives Markets: The New Financial Ecosystem and the "Holy Grail" of Systemic Risk Containment' (2019) 20 EBOR 1–30.

M Bacache et al, Taxation and the digital economy: A survey of theoretical models (2015). 26 February 2015 <https://www.strategie.gouv.fr/sites/strategie.gouv.fr/files/atoms/files/ficalite_du_numerique_10_mars_corrige_final.pdf> accessed 01 December 2020.

M S Barr, 'Microfinance and Financial Development' (2004a) 26 Mich J Int Law 271–296.

M S Barr, 'Banking the Poor' (2004b) 21 Yale J Reg121–237.

M S Barr, *No Slack: the Financial Lives of Low-Income Americans* (Washington, DC: Brookings Press 2012).

M S Barr, A Kumar and R Litan (eds), *Building Inclusive Financial Systems – a Framework for Financial Access* (Washington DC: Brookings Press 2007).

Basel Committee for Banking Supervision (BCBS), Microfinance activities and the core principles for effective banking supervision (2010). BIS August 2010 <https://www.bis.org/publ/bcbs175.htm> accessed 01 December 2020.

B Biais, C Bisière, M Bouvard and C Casamatta, 'The Blockchain Folk Theorem' (2019) 32(5) Rev Fin Studies 1662–1715.

F Biermann, 'A New Paradigm for Global Sustainability Governance: Inside look from the Trenches of the SDGs Negotiation Arena' (2019) 28(1) GAIA 52–53.

R Blank and M S Barr, *Insufficient Funds: Savings, Assets, Credit and Banking Among Low-Income Households* (New York: Russel Sage2009).

A Bose, India's Fintech revolution is primed to put banks out of business (2016). TechCrunch, 14 June 2016 <https://techcrunch.com/2016/06/14/indias-fintech-revolution-is-primed-to-put-banks-out-of-business/> accessed 01 December 2020.

M Brignall, Banks accused of abandoning England's poorest communities (2019). *The Guardian*, 22 July 2019 <https://www.theguardian.com/business/2019/jul/22/banks-accused-abandoning-england-poorest-communities> accessed 01 December 2020.

C Brummer, 'Disruptive Technology and Securities Regulation' (2015) 84 Fordh Law Rev 977–1052.

C Brummer and Y Yadav, 'FinTech and the Innovation Trilemma' (2019) 107 Georget Law J 235–307.

G Buchak, G Matvos, T Piskoski and A Seru, 'Fintech, Regulatory Arbitrage, and the Rise of Shadow Banks' (2018) 130(3) JFE 453–483.

R P Buckley, 'The G20's Performance in Global Financial Regulation' (2014) 37(1) UNSW Law J 63–93.

R P Buckley, J Greenacre and L Malady, 'The Regulation of mobile Money in Malawi' (2015) 14(3) Wash Univ Global Stud Law Rev 435–497.

R P Buckley and I Mas, 'Coming of Age of Digital Payments as a Field of Expertise' (2016) 1 J Law Technol Policy 71–87.

R P Buckley and S Webster, 'FinTech in Developing Countries: Charting New Customer Journeys' (2016) 44 Journal for Financial Transformation 151–159.

R P Buckley, D W Arner, D A Zetzsche and R Weber, 'The Road to RegTech: The (Astonishing) Example of the European Union' (2019) J Bank Regul. doi: 10.1057/s41261-019-00104-1.

R P Buckley, D W Arner, R Veidt and D A Zetzsche, 'Building FinTech Ecosystems: Regulatory Sandboxes, Innovation Hubs and Beyond' (2020) 61 Wash J Law Policy 55–98.

Center for Financial Inclusion (CFI), About financial inclusion 2020 (2019) <http://www.centerforfinancialinclusion.org/fi2020/about-fi-2020> accessed 01 December 2020.

J Chien and D Randall, Key lessons for policymakers from China's financial inclusion experience (2018). World Bank Blogs, 15 February 2018 <http://blogs.worldbank.org/psd/key-lessons-policymakers-china-s-financial-inclusion-experience> accessed 01 December 2020.

China Tech Insights, WeChat user & business ecosystem report 2017 (2017). Technode, 24 April 2017 <https://technode.com/2017/04/24/wechat-user-business-ecosystem-report-2017/> accessed 01 December 2020.

I Chiu, 'Fintech and Disruptive Business Models in Financial Products, Intermediation and Markets – Policy Implications for Financial Regulators' (2016) 21(1) J Technol Law Policy 55–112.

I Chiu, 'A New Era in Fintech Payment Innovations? A Perspective from the Institutions and Regulation of Payment Systems' (2017) 9(2) Law Innovation Technol 190–234.

I Chiu, 'Decoupling Tokens from Trading: Reaching Beyond Investment Regulation for Regulatory Policy in Initial Coin Offerings' (2018) 3 IBLJ 265–287.

I Chiu and E F Greene, 'The Marriage of Technology, Markets and Sustainable (and) Social Finance: Insights from ICO Markets for a New Regulatory Framework' (2019) 20(1) EBOR 139–169.

G Comparato, *The Financialisation of the Citizen: Social and Financial Inclusion Through European Private Law* (Hart Publishing 2018).

L de Koker, S Singh and J Capal, 'Closure of Bank Accounts of Remittance Service Providers – Global Challenges and Community Perspectives in Australia' (2017) 36(1) Univ Queensland Law J 119–154.

P Delimatsis, 'Sustainable Standard-Setting, Climate Change and the TBT Agreement' in P Delimatsis (ed), *Research Handbook on Climate Change and Trade Law* (Cheltenham: Edward Elgar 2016) 148–180.

A Demirguc-Kunt, L Klapper, D Singer, S Ansar and J Hess, *The Global Findex Database 2017: Measuring Financial Inclusion and the Fintech Revolution* (Washington DC: World Bank 2018) <https://openknowledge.worldbank.org/handle/10986/29510> accessed 01 December 2020.

S Desai and N Jasuja, India Stack: the bedrock of a digital India (2016). Medium, 28 October 2016 <https://medium.com/wharton-fintech/the-bedrock-of-a-digital-india-3e96240b3718> accessed 01 December 2020.

European Commission, Consumer financial services action plan: better products, more choice (2017). 23 March 2017 <https://ec.europa.eu/info/publications/consumer-financial-services-action-plan_en> accessed 01 December 2020.

European Commission, FinTech action plan: for a more competitive and innovative European financial sector (2018). 8 March 2018 <https://ec.europa.eu/info/publications/180308-action-plan-fintech_en> accessed 01 December 2020.

European Commission, Action plan: financing sustainable growth (2018). 8 March 2018 <https://eur-lex.europa.eu/legal-content/EN/TXT/?uri=CELEX%3A52018DC0097> accessed 01 December 2020.

Financial Action Task Force (FATF), FATF guidance: anti-money laundering and terrorist financing measures and financial inclusion (2013). February 2013 <http://www.fatf-gafi.org/media/fatf/documents/reports/AML_CFT_Measures_and_Financial_Inclusion_2013.pdf> accessed 01 December 2020.

M Finck, *Blockchain Regulation and Governance in Europe* (Cambridge: Cambridge University Press 2018).

G20 Financial Inclusion Experts Group, Innovative financial inclusion (2010). ATISG report, 25 May 2010 <https://www.findevgateway.org/library/innovative-financial-inclusion> accessed 01 December 2020.

G20 Global Partnership for Financial Inclusion (GPFI), Principles and report on innovative financial inclusion (2010). 25 May 2010 <http://www.gpfi.org/publications/principles-and-report-innovative-financial-inclusion> accessed 01 December 2020.

G20 Global Partnership for Financial Inclusion (GPFI), Launch of the G20 basic set of financial inclusion indicators (2013). 22 April 2013 <http://www.gpfi.org/featured/launch-g20-basic-set-financial-inclusion-indicators> accessed 01 December 2020.

G20 Global Partnership for Financial Inclusion (GPFI), G20 high-level principles on financial inclusion (2016) <https://www.gpfi.org/sites/gpfi/files/documents/G20%20High%20Level%20Principles%20for%20Digital%20Financial%20Inclusion%20-%20Full%20version-.pdf> accessed 01 December 2020.

G20 Global Partnership for Financial Inclusion (GPFI), Financial inclusion action plan (FIAP) 2017 (2017) <https://www.gpfi.org/publications/g20-financial-inclusion-action-plan-fiap-2017> accessed 01 December 2020.

G20 Global Partnership for Financial Inclusion (GPFI), Digital financial inclusion: emerging policy approaches (2018) <http://www.gpfi.org/sites/gpfi/files/documents/Digital%20Financial%20Inclusion-CompleteReport-Final-A4.pdf> accessed 01 December 2020.

G20 Global Partnership for Financial Inclusion (GPFI), Financial inclusion policy guide on digitisation and informality (2018) <http://www.gpfi.org/sites/gpfi/files/documents/G20_Policy_Guide_Digitisation_and_Informality.pdf> accessed 01 December 2020.

Government of Pakistan and Benazir Income Support Programme (BISP), BISP develops a robust and transparent biometric verification based payment solution to facilitate beneficiaries (2019). 10 October 2019 <https://bisp.gov.pk/SiteImage/Misc/files/PR-10-10-2019-1.pdf> accessed 01 December 2020.

GSMA, Mobile money as a driver of financial inclusion in Sub-Saharan Africa (2017). 7 June 2017 <https://www.gsma.com/mobilefordevelopment/programme/mobile-money/mobile-money-driver-financial-inclusion-sub-saharan-africa/> accessed 01 December 2020.

GSMA, The impact of mobile money on monetary and financial stability in Sub-Saharan Africa (2019). March 2019 <https://www.gsma.com/mobilefordevelopment/wp-content/uploads/2019/03/The-impact-of-mobile-money-on-monetary-and-financial-stability.pdf> accessed 01 December 2020.

C Haddad and L Hornuf, 'The Emergence of the Global Fintech Market: Economic and Technological Determinants' (2019) 53(1) Small Bus Econ 81–105.

A Harris and M S Barr, Central bank of the future (2019). Univ of Michigan Public Law Research Paper No 1, July 2019 <https://ssrn.com/abstract=3422860> accessed 01 December 2020.

J Hong, How China's central bank is clamping down on the mobile payment industry (2017). *Forbes*, 18 August 2017 <https://www.forbes.com/sites/jinshanhong/2017/08/18/how-chinas-central-bank-is-clamping-down-on-the-mobile-payment-industry/#5fa0a13b50be> accessed 01 December 2020.

L Hornuf and A Schwienbacher, 'Market Mechanisms and Funding Dynamics in Equity Crowdfunding' (2017) 50 J Corp Financ 556.574.

L Hornuf and A Schwienbacher, 'Should Securities Regulation Promote Equity Crowdfunding?' (2017) 49(3) Small Bus Econ 579–593.

M Hurley and J Adebayo, 'Credit Scoring in the Era of Big Data' (2017) 18(1) Yale J Law Technol 148–216.

India Infoline News Service, Axis Bank introduces a paperless eKYC based a/c opening (2014). 26 February 2014 <https://www.indiainfoline.com/article/news/axis-5875391291_1.html> accessed 01 December 2020.

N Kanie and F Biermann (eds), *Governing Through Goals – Sustainable Development Goals as Governance Innovation* (Cambridge: MIT Press 2017).

L Klapper, A Lusardi and P van Oudheusden, Financial literacy around the world: Insights from the Standard & Poor's Ratings Services Global Financial Literacy Survey (2015). GFLEC working paper <https://gflec.org/wp-content/uploads/2015/11/Finlit_paper_16_F2_singles.pdf> accessed 01 December 2020.

R Lal and I Sachdev, Mobile money services – design and development for financial inclusion (2015). Harvard Business School Working Paper No 15-083 <http://www.hbs.edu/faculty/Publication%20Files/15-083_e7db671b-12b2-47e7-9692-31808ee92bf1.pdf> accessed 01 December 2020.

E Lee, 'Financial Inclusion: A Challenge to the New Paradigm of Financial Technology, Regulatory Technology and Anti-Money Laundering Law' (2017) 6 J Bus Law 473–498.

T Lin, 'Artificial Intelligence, Finance, and the Law' (2019) 88 Fordh L Rev 531.

W J Magnuson, 'Regulating Fintech' (2018) 71 Vanderbilt Law Rev1168–1226.

A Mehrotra and J Yetman, Financial inclusion – issues for central banks (2015). BIS Quarterly Review March 2015 <https://www.bis.org/publ/qtrpdf/r_qt1503h.pdf> accessed 01 December 2020.

S Millward, 7 years of WeChat (2018). Tech in Asia, 21 January 2018 <https://www.techinasia.com/history-of-wechat> accessed 01 December 2020.

E Mu, Yu'ebao: A brief history of the Chinese internet financing upstart (2014). *Forbes*, 18 May 2014 <https://www.forbes.com/sites/ericxlmu/2014/05/18/yuebao-a-brief-history-of-the-chinese-internet-financing-upstart/#25c898583c0e> accessed 01 December 2020.

N Ndung'u, M-Pesa – a success story of digital financial inclusion (2017). Blavatnik School of Government Practitioner's Insight <https://www.geg.ox.ac.uk/publication/practitioners-insight-m-pesa-success-story-digital-financial-inclusion> accessed 01 December 2020.

H Q Nguyen, Do bank branches still matter? The effect of closings on local economic outcomes (2014). MIT Working Papers <http://economics.mit.edu/files/10143> accessed 01 December 2020.

H Q Nguyen, 'Are Credit Markets Still Local? Evidence from Bank Branch Closings' (2019) 11(1) AEJ: Applied Economics 1–32.

S T Omarova, 'New Tech v. New Deal: Fintech as a Systemic Phenomenon' (2019) 36 Yale J Regul 735–793.

P Paech, 'The Governance of Blockchain Financial Networks' (2017) 80(6) Mod Law Rev 1073–1110.

H Reese, How data and machine learning are 'part of Uber's DNA' (2016). TechRepublic, 21 October 2016 <https://www.techrepublic.com/article/how-data-and-machine-learning-are-part-of-ubers-dna> accessed 01 December 2020.

Responsible Finance Forum, Best practices and recommendations on financial consumer protection (2011). Association of Supervisors of Banks of the Americas (ASBA) ATN/ME-11612-RG <https://responsiblefinanceforum.org/publications/best-practices-recommendations-financial-consumer-protection/> accessed 01 December 2020.

W Ringe and C Ruof, A regulatory sandbox for robo advice (2018). EBI Working Paper No 26/2018 <https://ssrn.com/abstract=3188828> accessed 01 December 2020.

J K Rosengard, 'Oversight Is a Many-Splendored Thing: Choice and Proportionality in Regulating and Supervising Microfinance Institutions' in B Armendariz and M Labie (eds), *The Handbook of Microfinance* (Singapore: World Scientific 2011) 159–171.

M M Schanzenbach and R H Sitkoff, Reconciling fiduciary duty and social conscience: The law and economics of ESG investing by a trustee (2019). Nw Law & Econ Research Paper No 18-22 <https://ssrn.com/abstract=3244665>. 72(2) Stanf Law Rev 381–454.

C Scharwatt, A Katakam, J Frydrych, A Murphy and N Naghavi, State of the industry 2014 – mobile financial services for the unbanked (2015). GSMA report <https://www.gsma.com/mobilefordevelopment/wp-content/uploads/2015/03/SOTIR_2014.pdf> accessed 01 December 2020.

B Sjafjell and C M Bruner (eds), *Cambridge Handbook of Corporate Law, Corporate Governance and Sustainability* (Cambridge: Cambridge University Press 2019).

G Stuart, Government to person transfers – on-ramp to financial inclusion? (2016) Center for Financial Inclusion <https://www.centerforfinancialinclusion.org/Government-to-Person-Transfers/> accessed 01 December 2020.

B Timmermann and P Gmehling, Financial inclusion and the G20 agenda (2017). Paper presented at the International Statistical Institute Regional Statistics Conference, Bali, 22–24 March 2017 <https://www.bis.org/ifc/events/ifc_isi_2017/06_timmermann_paper.pdf> accessed 01 December 2020.

V Trujillo, M V Muriel-Patino and F R López, 'How Is Microfinance Being Regulated in Latin America?' (2015) 26(4) Enterprise Dev Microfinance 343–357.

V Trujillo, F Rodríguez and V Muriel, 'Microfinance Regulation and Market Development in Latin America' (2014) 14(4) BEJEAP 1615–1644.

UK Financial Conduct Authority (UKFCA), Access to financial services in the UK (2016). Occasional Paper 17 <https://www.fca.org.uk/publication/occasional-papers/occasional-paper-17.pdf> accessed 01 December 2020.

UNESCO, A global framework of reference on digital literacy skills for indicator 4.4.2 (UN digital literacy framework) (2018). Information Paper No 51, UIS/2018/ICT/IP/51 <http://uis.unesco.org/sites/default/files/documents/ip51-global-framework-reference-digital-literacy-skills-2018-en.pdf> accessed 01 December 2020.

United Nations Capital Development Fund (UNCDF), Improving distribution of digital financial services in rural areas (2019). 13 May 2019 <https://www.uncdf.org/article/4542/improving-distribution-of-digital-financial-services-in-rural-areas> accessed 01 December 2020.

United Nations Secretary General (UNSG), Task force on digital financing of sustainable development goals (2018). 29 Nov 2018 <https://www.un.org/sg/en/content/sg/personnel-appointments/2018-11-29/task-force-digital-financing-sustainable-development/> accessed 01 December 2020.

E Vermeulen and M Fenwick, 'Technology and Corporate Governance: Blockchain, Crypto, and Artificial Intelligence' (2019) 48(1) Tex J Bus Law 1–15.

E Vermeulen, M Fenwick and M Corrales, 'Business and Regulatory Responses to Artificial Intelligence: Dynamic Regulation, Innovation Ecosystems and the Strategic Management of Disruptive Technology' in M Corrales, M Fenwick and N Forgó (eds), *Robotics, AI and the Future of Law* (Singapore: Springer Nature 2018) 81–103.

T Wallace, Thousands more UK bank branches could face closure (2015). Telegraph, 14 September 2015 <http://www.telegraph.co.uk/finance/newsbysector/banksandfinance/11863736/Thousands-more-UK-bank-branches-could-face-closure.html> accessed 01 December 2020.

Y Wang, China tightens regulations over mobile payment apps – What's next for Tencent and Ant Financial? (2018) *Forbes*, 3 January 2018 <https://www.forbes.com/sites/ywang/2018/01/03/china-tightens-regulation-over-mobile-payment-apps-whats-next-for-tencent-and-ant-financial/#47e526ae7f1d> accessed 01 December 2020.

J Winn, 'Mobile Payments and Financial Inclusion: Kenya, Brazil, and India as Case Studies' in J A Rothchild (ed), *Research Handbook on Electronic Commerce Law* (Cheltenham: Edward Elgar 2016) 62–90.

World Bank, The Global Findex database 2017 (2017) <https://globalfindex.worldbank.org/> accessed 01 December 2020.

World Bank, Financial inclusion beyond payments – policy considerations for digital savings (2019) <http://documents.worldbank.org/curated/en/467421555393243557/pdf/Financial-Inclusion-Beyond-Payments-Policy-Considerations-for-Digital-Savings-Technical-Note.pdf> accessed 01 December 2020.

Xinhua, China looks for right balance between financial innovation, risk (2017). China Daily, 30 December 2017 <http://www.chinadaily.com.cn/a/201712/30/WS5a46fd55a31008cf16da4599.html> accessed 01 December 2020.

D A Zetzsche, D W Arner, R P Buckley and B W Tang, Artificial Intelligence in Finance: Putting the Human in the Loop (2021) Sydney Law Rev, in press <https://ssrn.com/abstract=3531711> accessed 01 December 2020.

D A Zetzsche, R P Buckley and D W Arner, 'The Distributed Liability of Distributed Ledgers: the Liability Risks of Blockchain' (2018) 2018 Univ Ill Law Rev 1361–1407.

D A Zetzsche, R P Buckley and D W Arner, 'FinTech for Financial Inclusion: Designing Infrastructure for Financial Transformation' in J Walker, A Pekmezovic and G Walker (eds), *Sustainable Development Goals – Harnessing Business to Achieve the SDGs Through Finance, Technology and Law Reform* (Hoboken: Wiley & Sons 2019) 179–214.

D A Zetzsche, R P Buckley, D W Arner and J Barberis, 'Regulating a Revolution: from Regulatory Sandboxes to Smart Regulation' (2017) 23(1) Fordh J Corp Fin Law 31–103.

D A Zetzsche, R P Buckley, D W Arner and J Barberis, 'From FinTech to TechFin: The Regulatory Challenges of Data-Driven Finance' (2018) 14(2) NY Univ J Law Bus 393–446.

D A Zetzsche, R P Buckley, D W Arner and L Föhr, 'The ICO Goldrush – a Challenge for Regulators' (2019) 60(2) Harv Int Law J 267–315.

W Zhou, D W Arner and R P Buckley, 'Regulation of Digital Financial Services in China: Last Mover Advantage?' (2015) 8(1) Tsinghua China Law Rev 25–62.

15 Digital transformation and financial inclusion

Kern Alexander and Xenia Karametaxas

1 Introduction

Financial technology – commonly referred to as 'fintech' – links together the delivery of financial services with digital technology. While the financial services industry has always relied on technological advances to spur innovation in the provision of services and the allocation of capital, recent data-based fintech developments, such as blockchain, mobile payment systems, peer-to-peer lending platforms, crowdfunding and other internet-based financial services, are radically transforming the financial services industry by challenging the traditional business models of incumbent financial institutions and the institutional and operational infrastructure of the financial system. Indeed, fintech has given rise to new forms of currencies and new ways of allocating capital, managing risks and carrying out financial transactions. This digital transformation of the financial sector provides consumers with better targeted services and lower prices, facilitates access to credit for small and medium-sized enterprises (SMEs), enhances productivity of traditional financial institutions and, more fundamentally, offers new possibilities of including more individuals and enterprises into the financial system.[1]

From this perspective, fintech offers great promise in its potential to democratise financial services by expanding access to previously unbanked or underserved groups and individuals. The process of integrating economic agents into the financial system by providing them with useful and affordable financial products and services delivered in a responsible and sustainable way is known as financial inclusion.[2] Even though access to financial services has drastically improved in the last decade across both developed and developing countries, most recent data suggests that about one third of the world's adult population (around 1.7 billion individuals) still do not have a transaction account at a formal financial institution or through a mobile money provider, and is therefore excluded from the formal financial system.[3] In many emerging or developing economies, the share of unbanked adults has reached nearly 90%.[4] Yet, two-thirds of these unbanked individuals (approximatively 1.1 billion) have a mobile phone, which technically enables them to gain access to financial

---

1 See Mark Carney, 'The Promise of FinTech – Something New Under the Sun?' (G 20 conference on 'Digitising Finance, Financial Inclusion and Financial Literacy', Wiesbaden, 25 January 2017) <www.bankofengland.co.uk/speech/2017/the-promise-of-fintech-something-new-under-the-sun> accessed 26 May 2020.
2 World Bank Group, 'Financial Inclusion' <www.worldbank.org/en/topic/financialinclusion> accessed 26 May 2020.
3 Asli Demirgüç-Kunt and others, *Global Findex Database 2017: Measuring Financial Inclusion and the Fintech Revolution* (World Bank Group 2018) 35.
4 Aaron Mehrotra and James Yetman, 'Financial Inclusion – Issues for Central Banks' (BIS Quarterly Review 2015) 83.

products and services.[5] Although financial inclusion closely relates to expanding the reach into financial services, the two concepts are not synonymous. Some individuals may have access to financial services without utilising such services, whether due to prohibitively high prices, regulatory barriers or a combination of market, institutional and cultural phenomena.[6] Access to financial services varies widely between developing and developed economies, knowing that in the latter almost all economic agents are included in the formal financial system; but in most developing countries only a small percentage has such access. Most of these unbanked or underserved individuals are in specific societal groups[7]: for instance, women are more likely to be financially excluded, so are people with poorer education and those living in rural areas, due to the lack of infrastructure and poor economic conditions.

The purpose of the present contribution is to explore the potential of the digital transformation through the lens of social sustainability, an aspect of sustainable finance that often remains in the shadow of the political and academic debate on environmental sustainability. This chapter analyses some of the main regulatory concerns and market barriers that arise from the digital transformation of the financial services industry. Focus is on how some developing and emerging market countries are confronting the challenges to achieving financial inclusion and, ultimately, at putting forward policy recommendations to make sure that new technologies create equal opportunities for all, while minimising the unintended risks and consequences.

Assuming that innovation in financial products and technology should go hand in hand with adequate regulation that benefits society, we discuss how policymakers and financial regulators should respond to the fast-changing development in financial technologies. Part 2 begins by analysing how financial inclusion has become an important public policy objective and by exploring the potential of financial inclusion to contribute to financial and social sustainability. Part 3 then analyses to what extent fintech is a driver for financial inclusion and highlights some of the main advantages and risks of the digital transformation. We will analyse the different regulatory approaches of China and India to digital financial transformation, which, as we argue, illustrate some of the advantages and disadvantages for countries in addressing these challenges. Finally, Part 4 discusses how policymakers and international standard setters have been coordinating on a cross-border level to develop principles and standards for regulating the provision of data-based financial services so that it can more effectively enable sustainable and socially inclusive economic development. Part 5 then concludes.

2 Financial inclusion as a public policy concern

Financial inclusion is a public policy concern that directly relates to the objectives and activities of central banks and international financial standard-setting bodies.[8] Advocates of financial inclusion, including the World Bank and some financial institutions, unequivocally stress that the process of integrating more individuals and businesses into the financial system contributes to income equality, alleviates poverty, influences saving rates and

5 Ibid.
6 World Bank Group, 'Global Financial Development Report 2014: Financial Inclusion' (World Bank 2013) 2.
7 Eugenia Macchiavello, *Microfinance and Financial Inclusion: The Challenge of Regulating Alternative Forms of Finance* (Routledge 2018) 9.
8 Mehrotra and Yetman (n 4) 4.

investment decisions and improves overall economic welfare. From an economic perspective, financial inclusion is considered one of the major enablers of economic development.[9] The access to useful and safe financial products may allow previously unbanked individuals to invest in assets, including their own education and training, potentially reducing income inequality.[10] Conversely, financial exclusion increases the risk of poverty and, thus, is a key barrier to development.[11] Moreover, by making saving and investment decisions more efficient and facilitating the functioning of the economy, financial inclusion also reinforces monetary and financial stability.[12]

The indirect macroeconomic argument behind financial inclusion is that expanding access to finance benefits society as a whole because it leads to economic growth and, thus, to a more stable monetary and financial system.[13] According to Mehrota and Yetman, enhanced inclusion should lead to a more efficient allocation of capital, and support central bank efforts to maintain price stability.[14] Further, increased access to credit and investment services boosts firm performance and enhances economic well-being. In that sense, the members of the Alliance for Financial Inclusion (AFI)[15] stated in the Maya Declaration on Financial Inclusion (Maya Declaration) that financial inclusion has a critical role in improving 'national and global financial stability and integrity' and in contributing to 'strong and inclusive growth in developing and emerging market countries'.[16] In addition, financial inclusion and sustainability were brought to the fore of international financial policymakers efforts in the wake of the 2007/08 financial crisis when the G20 Heads of State at the Pittsburgh Summit stated that a core aim of international financial reforms was to 'generate strong, sustainable and balanced global growth'.[17] Prior to the 2007/08 financial crisis, most financial market regulators and standard-setting bodies refrained from taking into account regulatory objectives that did not appear to be directly related to the stability of the financial system and investor protection, as there was little appreciation for the role of regulation in mitigating social risks and contributing to financial equity and more

---

9 Asli Demirgüç-Kunt and Leonora Klapper, 'Measuring Financial Inclusion: The Global Findex Database' (2012) World Bank Policy Research Paper 6025; Minjin Kim and others, 'Mobile Financial Services, Financial Inclusion, and Development: A Systematic Review of Academic Literature' (2018) 84(5) Electronic Journal of Information Systems in Developing Countries 1 <https://onlinelibrary.wiley.com/doi/10.1002/isd2.12044> accessed 26 May 2020; Oksana Kabakova and Evgeny Plaksenkov 'Analysis of Factors Affecting Financial Inclusion: Ecosystem View' (2018) 89 Journal of Business Research 198.

10 Mehrotra and Yetman (n 4) 83.

11 Kim and others (n 9) 2.

12 Irving Fisher, 'Measures of Financial Inclusion – A Central Bank Perspective' (Committee on Central Bank Statistics, Bank for International Settlements 2016) 4.

13 Philip Mader, 'Contesting Financial Inclusion' (2018) 49 (2) Development and Change 461, 469.

14 Mehrotra and Yetman (n 4) 83.

15 The AFI is a network of financial inclusion policy members. Its members are central banks and other financial regulatory institutions from more than 80 emerging and developing economies. The mission of the AFI is to empower policymakers to increase access and usage of quality financial services for the underserved, through formulation, implementation and global advocacy of sustainable and inclusive policies.

16 Alliance for Financial Inclusion, '2018 Maya Declaration Progress Report' (2018) 3 <https://www.afi-global.org/sites/default/files/publications/2018-09/AFI_Maya_report_2018_AW_digital.pdf> accessed 26 May 2020.

17 G20 Research Group, 'G20 Leaders Statement: The Pittsburgh Summit' (2009) Preamble no 13 <www.g20.utoronto.ca/2009/2009communique0925.html> accessed 26 May 2020.

inclusive growth through wider access to financial services.[18] Post-crisis regulatory reforms, however, are premised on the inter-linkages between financial institutions and the broader financial system and economy and the use of macro prudential tools to control and limit the systemic risks.[19]

Several think tanks, standard-setting bodies and policymakers have begun to actively address the challenges related to financial inclusion.[20] In 2006, the UN declared that 'access to a well-functioning financial system can economically and socially empower individuals, in particular poor people, allowing them to better integrate into the economy of their countries, actively contribute to their development and protect themselves against economic shocks'.[21] The Global Partnership for Financial Inclusion (GPFI), through its three key partners AFI, the Consultative Group to Assist the Poor (CGAP) and the International Finance Corporation (IFC), have led international efforts to promote financial inclusion. Launched in 2010 at the G20 Summit in Seoul, the GPFI endorsed a Financial Inclusion Action Plan and spurred initial policy actions by publishing the G20 Principles for Innovative Financial Inclusion as a platform for knowledge sharing, policy advocacy and coordination.[22] In 2011, the AFI promulgated the Maya Declaration, an initiative to reach the world's unbanked individuals (2.5 billion at that time) and to encourage national financial inclusion commitments by central banks in partnership with private sector actors. Also, the Better than Cash Alliance, a UN-based partnership of governments (mainly from developing economies), foundations, companies and international organisations, was created in 2012 with the aim to accelerate the transition from cash to digital payments in order to reduce poverty and promote inclusive growth.[23]

Financial inclusion has also made its entry into the United Nation's 2030 sustainable development agenda (2030 SDG Agenda).[24] While not a sustainable development goal (SDG) in itself, financial inclusion is considered an enabler of other SDGs, where it is featured as a target in 8 of the 17 goals. Accordingly, financial inclusion is supposed to help eradicate poverty and hunger, to achieve food security and to promote sustainable agriculture (SDG 1 & 2). Further, financial inclusion also supports health and well-being (SDG 3), promotes gender equality by economically empowering women (SDG 5), boosts economic growth and development (SDG 8), supports industry, innovation and infrastructure (SDG 9) and reduces inequality (SDG 10). In addition, SDG 17's strengthening the means

---

18 Macchiavello (n 7) 14.
19 Kern Alexander, *Principles of Banking Regulation* (CUP 2019) 396; Gudula Deipenbrock, 'Is the Law Ready to Face the Progressing Digital Revolution? – General Policy Issues and Selected Aspects in the Realm of Financial Markets from the International, European Union and German Perspective' (2019) 118 Zeitschrift für vergleichende Rechtswissenschaft 285, 303; Emily Jones and Peter Knaack, 'Global Financial Regulations: Shortcomings and Reform Options' (2019) 10 Global Policy 193.
20 Kabakova and Plaskenkov (n 9) 198; M Mostak Ahamed and Sushanta Mallick, 'Is Financial Inclusion Good for Bank Stability? International Evidence' (2019) 157 Journal of Economic Behavior & Organization 403.
21 United Nations, 'Building Inclusive Financial Sectors for Development' (Joint Report by the United Nations Department of Economic and Social Affairs and the United Nations Capital Development Fund 2006) 4.
22 About the work and the mission of the GPFI, see: James Pearse, 'About GPFI' (25 November 2013) <http://gpfi.org/about-gpfi> accessed 26 May 2020.
23 About the work, members and mission of the Better than Cash Alliance, see: Better than Cash Alliance, 'About the Better than Cash Alliance' <www.betterthancash.org/> accessed 11 May 2020.
24 United Nations, 'Transforming Our World: The 2030 Agenda for Sustainable Development' (2015) <https://sustainabledevelopment.un.org/post2015/transformingourworld> accessed 26 May 2020.

of implementation implies a role for greater financial inclusion through greater savings mobilisation for investment and consumption that can stimulate growth.[25]

The emphasis on financial inclusion in the 2030 SDG agenda is premised on the important role that the financial system plays in the shift towards a circular and more sustainable economy. In this vein, financial inclusion has also caught the attention of international financial institutions and central banks. In 2016, the primary global standard setter for the prudential regulation of banks, the Basel Committee on Banking Supervision, published its 'Guidance on the application of the core principles for effective banking supervision to the regulation and supervision of institutions relevant to financial inclusion'.[26] In the same year, the G20 supported its initial 2010 Principles for Innovative Financial Inclusion by endorsing the G20 High-Level Principles for Digital Financial Inclusion, where the focus is placed on providing a basis for national action plans to leverage the potential offered by digital technologies.[27] The World Bank Group implemented in 2017 the Financial Inclusion Global Initiative (FIGI) to support and accelerate the implementation of country-led reform actions to meet national financial inclusion targets.[28]

These international initiatives are premised on the key assumption that the expansion of financial markets and the availability of financial services is vital for a country – particularly developing and emerging market countries – in promoting economic development and poverty reduction. It comes as no surprise therefore that the fintech and information technology (IT) sectors, backed by institutions such as the World Bank, the World Economic Forum (WEF) and the Bill and Melinda Gates Foundation, are enthusiastic about financial inclusion. The growing role of Big Tech firms – such as Google, Amazon and Facebook – along with the existing influence of incumbent financial institutions in providing financial services are leading a transformation of the traditional banking and financial system to a data-driven banking and finance business model that is resulting in a 'Big Bang' in data-driven financial services.[29] This has highlighted one of the greatest challenges for the global financial services industry that involves how to reconcile the objectives and the tools of data regulation and financial regulation. The proponents of this 'Big Bang' in data-driven financial services and its broad scope of application argue that it will enhance financial inclusion

---

25 The relationship between expanding access to financial services and achieving the SDGs has been discussed extensively in a 2016 working paper published by the Consultative Group to Assist the Poor (CGAP): CGAP, 'Achieving Sustainable Development Goals: The Role of Financial Inclusion' (2016) 2 <www.cgap.org/sites/default/files/researches/documents/Working-Paper-Achieving-Sustainable-Development-Goals-Apr-2016_0.pdf> accessed 26 May 2020.

26 Basel Committee on Banking Supervision, 'Guidance on the Application of the Core Principles for Effective Banking Supervision to the Regulation and Supervision of Institutions Relevant to Financial Inclusion' (Bank for International Settlements September 2016) <www.bis.org/bcbs/publ/d383.htm> accessed 26 May 2020.

27 G20, 'G20 High-Level Principles for Digital Financial Inclusion' (2016) www.gpfi.org/sites/gpfi/files/documents/G20%20High%20Level%20Principles%20for%20Digital%20Financial%20Inclusion%20-%20Full%20version-.pdf> accessed 26 May 2020.

28 World Bank Group, 'Financial Inclusion Global Initiative (FIGI)' (18 July 2019) <www.worldbank.org/en/topic/finan-cialinclusion/brief/figi> accessed 26 May 2020.

29 The US Federal Trade Commission (FTC) has addressed some of the important questions about how to regulate finance, data and technology in ways that do not inhibit the development of the digital economy. The FTC adopted in 2019 broad new requirements for financial institutions to protect the privacy and security of customers' data. See: FTC, 'FTC Seeks Comment on Proposed Amendments to Safeguards and Privacy Rules' (2019) <www.ftc.gov/news-events/press-releases/2019/03/ftc-seeks-comment-proposed-amendments-safegu-ards-privacy-rules> accessed 26 May 2020.

by widening access to financial services resulting in improved living standards and poverty alleviation because of reduced transaction costs in the provision of capital and credit to a larger number of individuals and firms.[30]

Nonetheless, policymakers and regulators should refrain from an overly optimistic view about financial inclusion through digitalisation as a strategy for poverty alleviation and development. The hypothesis that financial inclusion leads to improved standards of living is not without controversy and risks.[31] Skeptics point out that financial inclusion is a mere re-branding for microfinance, which appeared in the 1970s and, following initial praise,[32] developed into a 'global finance-development hybrid specialized in making high interest loans'.[33] Microfinance institutions have come under scrutiny for a variety of reasons, notably their high-interest rates and their fixation on credit, which leads to over-indebtedness.[34] Although microfinance and financial inclusion are related concepts,[35] the analogy is not entirely accurate. With community-based programmes, cooperative institutions, technology firms, mobile network operators and credit card companies on board, financial inclusion involves a new set of players and practices that have little in common with microfinance.[36] In addition, with the impetus of sustainable development, financial inclusion blends financial logics with the idea of social justice and equality.[37] The fervour of financial inclusion steers the focus away from the fundamental question about the responsibility of financial markets in creating inequality. Indeed, incorporating underprivileged and often poorly educated people into the financial system through advances in technology may exacerbate existing inequalities and lead to an increase in indebtedness.

In view of the quest for social justice, regulators and policymakers should make sure that data-driven financial services and related fintech innovations do not lead to a development hybrid that puts even greater power in the hands of financial market actors. A sustainable financial system calls for a transformative system change and not for incremental measures that merely mitigate the symptoms of poverty by extending services to the poor as a goal itself. Therefore, new policies and regulations should focus on the needs and the protection of those excluded from the financial system by adopting policies that maximise the opportunities and minimise the risks for society.

---

30 Tavneet Suri and William Jack, 'The Long-run Poverty and Gender Impacts of Mobile Money' (2016) 354 Science 1288, 1288ff.

31 For a critical view on financial inclusion, see Mader (n 13), 461ff; Milford Bateman, Maren Duvendack and Nicholas Loubere, 'Is Fin-tech the New Panacea for Poverty Alleviation and Local Development? Contesting Suri and Jack's M-Pesa Findings Published in Science' (2019) 161 Review of African Political Economy 480.

32 The UN and the World Bank regarded microfinance as a 'miraculous tool to spur development' (Macchiavello (n 7) 82). See also United Nations, 'Monterrey Consensus on Financing for Development' (2003) 8 point 18, <www.un.org/en/development/desa/population/migration/generalassembly/docs/globalcompact/A_CONF.198_11.pdf> accessed 26 May 2020; Ousa Sananikone, 'Microfinance and the Millennium Development Goals' (CGAP donor brief no 9 2002) <http://documents.worldbank.org/curated/en/960981468140964497-/Microfinance-and-the-millennium-development-goals> accessed 26 May 2020.

33 Mader (n 13) 463.

34 Mader (n 13) 463.

35 On the interrelationship between financial inclusion and microfinance, see Macchiavello (n 7), 18f and 82ff.

36 Mader (n 13) 464.

37 Ibid.

3 Advantages and risks of the technological transformation

If financial inclusion means delivering financial services and products to unbanked and underserved groups in a sustainable way, it is critical to monitor the providers of innovative financial products and services. Through technologically enabled mobile and online plat-forms, innovative fintech providers make financial operations both less expensive and more convenient to their customers. An important feature fintech innovations have in common is their potential to increase proximity with customers, given their ability to bypass financial intermediaries by connecting services directly with consumers. The boundaries between financial providers and consumers become increasingly blurred, which challenges tradi-tional legal categories and, therefore, the validity of current legal regulatory approaches.[38]

For example, crowdfunding companies have disrupted the business of raising capital and challenged the traditional monopoly large banks have had in deciding which companies and individuals receive loans and investment. Another example are software and mobile phone applications that match borrowers with lenders without a traditional intermediary. These so-called peer-to-peer lending platforms have been highly successful in China where they expanded exponentially in just a decade, from a single platform in 2007 to almost 2000 in 2017.[39] The benefits are an easier access to capital for SMEs and consumers. With capital from multiple sources being pooled, default risk is spread out and decentralised. Consequently, large banks find themselves under competitive pressure, which supposedly improves overall economic efficiency.

The shortcut of the intermediary chain facilitates substantially the access to financial products and services by drastically reducing information asymmetry and transaction costs. In that perspective, one of the promises of the digital transformation is not only the crea-tion of highly efficient economically and socially integrated ecosystems, but also its poten-tial to provide access to financial products and services to economic agents who lack access to a formal transaction account and hence were excluded from the financial system.

Considering the above, the link between expanding access to financial products and services and development seems unquestioned.[40] However, while fintech innovations create a wide variety of possibilities to include more people and businesses into the financial system, it does not necessarily lead to a more sustainable financial system. Indeed, the prospects of fintech to increase financial inclusion are extensive, it also creates multiple micro- and macro financial risks, as well as social risks, to which low-income populations are exposed to a larger extent.

First, fintech innovations raise concerns about consumer protection and over-indebtedness. While the digital transformation of the financial sector spurs financial inclusion of low-income households and businesses by boosting their incomes and savings, it also leads to a higher debt of individuals and SMEs. One example of this phenomenon is the mobile payment provider M-Pesa in Kenya. Founded in 2007 and internationally celebrated for its transformative power to lift 'thousands of households out of poverty',[41] M-Pesa substan-tially facilitated digital cash transfers by providing mobile banking access through standard text messages. Monetary value can be stored on a mobile phone and then be sent to other users, without the need of a smart phone. In a country where many people had cell phones but no debit cards and, especially in rural areas, where poor infrastructure made going

---

38 Macchiavello (n 7), 213. See also Deipenbrock (n 19) 303.
39 James Guild, 'Fintech and the Future of Finance' (2017) 10 Asian Journal of Public Affairs 52, 59.
40 CGAP (n 25) 9.
41 Suri and Jack (n 30) 1288ff.

to the bank burdensome, M-Pesa appeared as a leading example of a fintech company responding to an unmet market need. M-Pesa is often cited as a successful example of financial inclusion in a developing country, having lifted nearly 10% of Kenya's poorest households out of poverty.[42] Yet, M-Pesa and other microcredit and fintech institutions have also made it easier for individuals and small businesses to increase debts, an aspect which often is ignored in the debate. According to Bateman and Duvendack (2019), Kenya is facing 'high and growing levels of over-indebtedness' as a result of the operations of M-Pesa and similar fintech institutions.[43]

Another risk for customers is the misuse of their digital data. Most individuals underestimate the privacy risks that cheap financial products entail. Indeed, fintech providers use algorithms to make decisions about their customers, which may reinforce existing disparities and financial exclusion.[44] Whereas traditional financial institutions are bound by a detailed regulatory framework to protect the use of their customer's data, fintech companies often do not fit into existing legal categories which allows them to avoid compliance with burdensome regulation. In considering the linkages between regulating both finance and data, the European Union's (EU) implementation of the General Protection of Data Regulation (EU GPDR) has resulted in a fundamental change in how firms are required to manage personal data and applies to all EU markets and citizens and also extraterritorially to all non-EU persons and firms dealing with EU markets and firms.[45] The EU places great emphasis on a privacy-oriented approach to data protection and privacy that provides uniquely stronger safeguards for customer data protection and portability than almost any other large economic jurisdiction.

In contrast, China has taken a different approach to data regulation and privacy that has allowed the emergence of a small group of Big Tech and financial technology companies who dominate market share while being subject to much less stringent regulations in respect to data protection and privacy in the financial sector.[46] China's regulation of data-driven finance emerged from a largely laissez-faire approach prior to 2014 in which a small number of major tech firms, with state acquiescence, became dominant market players with little supervisory oversight. This changed in 2015 and 2016 when the People's Bank of China, responding to the growth of new fintech corporates, such as Ant Financial and Tencent, took steps to limit their market growth by imposing risk-based regulations for solvency, liquidity and related governance controls.[47] Despite these regulations, financial

---

42 UNSGSA, 'UNSGSA 2017 Annual Report' (2017) 8 <www.gpfi.org/publications/unsgsa-2017-annual-report> accessed 26 May 2020.

43 Bateman, Duvendack and Loubere (n 31) 486.

44 UNSGSA (n 42) 9.

45 See Regulation (EU) 2016/679 of the European Parliament and of the Council of 27 April 2016 on the protection of natural persons with regards to the processing of personal data and on the free movement of such data, and repealing Directive 95/46/EC (General Data Protection Regulation) (2016) OJ L119/1, 1–88.

46 See generally Dirk Zetsche and others, 'The Future of Data Driven Finance: Financial Regulation, Data Regulation, and RegTech' (*The CLS Blue Sky Blog*, 15 April 2019) <https://clsbluesky.law.columbia.edu/2019/04/15/the-future-of-data-driven-finance-financial-regulation-data-regulation-and-regtech/> accessed 26 May 2020. See also Andrew Liu, 'An Analysis of the PBOC's New Mobile Payment Regulation', (2019) 39 1 Cato Journal 87, 88.

47 Weihuan Zhou, Douglas W Arner and Ross P Buckley, 'China's Regulation of Digital Financial Services: Some Recent developments' (2016) 90 issue 5 Australian Law Journal 297. See also Dirk A Zetzsche and others, 'Regulating a Revolution: From Regulatory Sandboxes to Smart Regulation' (2017) 23 Fordham Journal of Corporate & Financial Law 31, 44.

intermediaries in China (as financial institutions did in the United States) were allowed to collect large amounts of data from and about their customers.[48] Data-driven financial firms acquired dominant market share based on network effects and economies of scale and scope, resulting in an oligopolistic market structure in consumer payment platform services.[49] In the case of mobile payment companies, such as Alipay and WeChat, Liu (2019) states that '[b]y gaining access to the billions of proprietary consumer data points collected by mobile payment providers, the CCP [Chinese Communist Party] and PBOC gain incredible insight into the behavior of the hundreds of millions of Chinese citizens that use mobile payment platforms'.[50] Liu (2019) further observes that

> [t]he government has a myriad of uses for this data. First, officials can now more easily track down and find incriminating evidence for political opponents by tracking their monetary transfers through mobile payment platforms. In addition, with the full-fledged implementation of the social credit system on the horizon, the government will be able to monitor its citizens on a more granular level and have more data on which to base its social credit scores.[51]

Moreover, the Australian Strategic Policy Institute published a report, entitled 'Engineering Global Consent – The Chinese Communist Party's data driven power expansion' in which it is argued that the Chinese tech companies, such as Global Tone Communications Technology Co. Ltd (GTCOM), conduct

---

48 Liu (n 46) 88–89; also, the United States has no explicit right to data protection either in the US (federal) constitution nor in federal statutes, except for the Bank Secrecy Act of 1970 and the Financial Privacy Act of 1978 that applies only to regulated financial institutions, and not to data-tech companies, such as Facebook, Google or Amazon. See Bank Secrecy Act of 1970 31 USC §§5311–5330; Financial Privacy Act of 1978 12 USC §§3401–3422; see also the recent ruling by the ECJ in Data Protection Commissioner v Facebook Ireland and Maximillian Schrems in which the EU–US Data Protection Shield was ruled inadequate. C-311/18 *Data Protection Commissioner v Facebook Ireland Limited, Maximillian Schrems* (2020) 559.

49 Leading international organisations have observed that the Chinese fintech/e-commerce market has an oligopolistic market structure. See Financial Stability Board (FSB), 'FinTech and market structure in financial services: Market developments and potential financial stability implications' (FSB 2019) 30; Longmei Zhang, Sally Chen, 'China's Digital Economy: Opportunities and Risks' (2019) IMF Working Paper 19/16 11; Lin Chen, 'Who Can Break the Oligopoly of E-commerce in China?' (China Europe International Business School (CEIBS) 15. April 2020) <https://www.ceibs.edu/new-papers-columns/who-can-break-oligopoly-e-commerce-china> accessed 24 July 2020 and Zhang observing that AliPay and WeChat have 94% of the mobile payment market. Maggie Zhang, 'China Sets Up Clearing House for AliPay and TenPay' South China Morning Post (7 August 2017) <https://www.scmp.com/business/companies/article/2105825/china-sets-clearing-house-online-payment-services-alipay-and> accessed 24 July 2020; Qiang Xiaoji, 'Baidu, Tencent, Alibaba Forming Oligopoly on Chinese Internet' *China Daily* (18 February 2011) <http://www.chinadaily.com.cn/bizchina/2011-02/18/content_12042514.htm#:~:text=An%20Internet%20oligopoly%20is%20forming,a%20research%20report%20on%20Internet> accessed 24 July 2020; Gabriel Wildau, 'China Targets Mobile Payments Oligopoly with Clearing Mandate' *Financial Times* (9 August 2017).

50 Liu (n 46), 88, citing Alyssa Abkowitz, 'The Cashless Society Has Arrived – Only It's in China'. *Wall Street Journal* (4 January 2018) <https://www.wsj.com/articles/chinas-mobile-payment-boom-changes-how-people-shop-borrow-even-panhandle-1515000570> accessed 24 July 2020.

51 Liu (n 46) 88, citing Alexandra Ma 'China Has Started Ranking Citizens with a Creepy "Social Credit" System: Here's What You Can Do Wrong, and the Embarrassing, Demeaning Ways They Can Punish You' *Business Insider* (29 October 2018) <www.businessinsider.com/china-social-credit-system-punishments-and-rewards-explained-2018-4> accessed 24 July 2020.

[b]ulk data collection in conjunction with the ability to leverage AI processing – which is GTCOM's business model – creates the capability to quickly turn large amounts of data into usable information. The PRC's smart cities equipment, for instance, both provides an advertised service and generates information that contributes to the party's social stability risk assessments. The same information that allows for traffic management or public safety can also be directed to products that allow the party to optimise its capacity for control.[52]

China's growing intrusiveness in how it regulates personal data should be compared with India's centralised approach to finance and data – known as 'India Stack'[53] – adopted in 2016 that revolves around a centralised strategy for managing its digital financial transformation. Until recently, India trailed other large jurisdictions, such as the EU, China and the United States, in its sophistication for the regulation of finance and data-driven finance. With the development and implementation of India Stack, however, India has put into practice a comprehensive approach to providing the infrastructure necessary to support the development of digital financial transformation and data-driven finance. The India Stack strategy combines a system of digital identification that supports a digital payment system that facilitates interoperability across traditional and new payment technologies and providers. An important part of India Stack is the Aadhaar system that is operated by the Unique Identification Authority of India (UIDAI). The Aadhaar system provides a unique 12-digit randomised identification number to all residents on a voluntary basis. Since 2016, almost all of India's 1.3 billion people have been registered with numbers.[54] These numbers make it more administratively efficient for the government to provide access to government services, including social insurance and welfare payments, and banking, insurance and other services. The Aadhaar system has proven beneficial for the government and for individuals and small firms who were previously excluded from the formal financial system. Prior to Aadhaar, it is estimated that 45% of Indian government payments reached the wrong payee. Moreover, fraudulent payments related to government transfer payments have been reduced by US$5 billion a year.

India Stack also provides a know-your-customer ('KYC') e-system, known as 'eKYC', to support the integrity of account opening and ongoing account transactions.[55] The eKYC system can also be used to verify and confirm a number of other government financial functions such as tax and salary payments, crediting and debiting vendor accounts and ensuring welfare payments to society's most vulnerable. The creation of this data infrastructure, including personal accounts with identification numbers for all individuals and firms who make tax payments or receive payments from the government, has caused a massive digitalisation and datafication of the Indian financial system that has enhanced financial inclusion, and generated a substantial digital financial transformation of society.

---

52 Samantha Hofmann, 'Engineering Global Consent – The Chinese Communist Party's Data Driven Power Expansion' (Australian Strategic Policy Institute) 18.

53 See India Stack, 'What is India Stack?' <https://www.indiastack.org/about/> accessed 26 May 2020.

54 Kathryn Henne, 'Surveillance in the name of governance: Aadhar as a Fix for Leaking Systems in India' in Blayne Haggart, Kathryn Henne and Natasha Tusikov (eds), *Information, Technology and Control in a Changing World – Understanding Power Structures in the 21st Century* (Palgrave Macmillan 2019) 224.

55 See the eKYC process at: India Stack, 'About eKYS API' <https://www.indiastack.org/ekyc/> accessed 26 June 2020.

The Aadhaar system has made access to financial accounts much easier, thereby improving financial inclusion. It is used by almost every business (online or offline) to link bank accounts and tax identification numbers and to authenticate bank accounts for the eKYC process resulted in legal actions alleging breach of data privacy.[56] It has facilitated the digitisation of payments and services for the government and the financial sector, reducing losses due to corruption and enabling the vast majority of the population to have a government financial account that can be used for opening bank and investment accounts.

Nevertheless, there have been implementation problems, particularly regarding data protection and privacy. Critics have described Aadhaar as mass surveillance technology and legal petitions challenged its constitutionality before the Indian Supreme Court.[57] The Indian Supreme Court ruled that the government's use of the data was lawful, but it also held that the use of the data by private firms was not undertaken in conformity with privacy safeguards.[58] One result of this decision was that the government's use of the data was required to be proportional to the public policy objectives of financial inclusion and reducing financial crime and tax evasion. The judgment identified privacy of personal data to be a fundamental constitutional right and that any infringement of that right in order to achieve valid public policy objectives had to be proportional.[59]

In response to the Indian Supreme Court decision, the President of India approved in March 2019 an ordinance that allows voluntary use of Aadhaar as proof of identification for obtaining mobile SIM cards and opening bank accounts. Also, the Aadhaar Act and other related legislation were amended in 2019, and the Aadhaar (Pricing of Aadhaar Authentication Services) Regulations, 2019) resulting in private entities being able to use data collected through Aadhaar scheme for eKYC after making a payment per transaction to the Aadhaar authority Unique Identification Authority of India.[60]

The Aadhaar system's problems in addressing data protection and fraud demonstrate the inherent weaknesses of such technologies, particularly in developing countries where data is much more limited and in certain cases easier to misrepresent and misuse. This is why fintech innovations, despite innovations, should be scrutinised closely for their compliance with data protection, anti-money laundering and cyber-security regulations.[61] Compliance with anti-financial crime regulations is also important from a financial inclusion perspective since economic agents who are not using formal deposit-taking banks are even more vulnerable to frauds and misuse of data. Recently, scandals erupted over frauds and abusive practices by fintech companies, involving the use of mobile phones to make payments. In 2015, a Chinese peer-to-peer lending company has revealed itself to be part of a fraudulent scheme that misappropriated over $5.5 billion.[62]

---

56 Kathryn Henne (n 54) 226–227.
57 Ibid 224. The case in question is: Justice K S Puttaswamy (Retd) and Anr vs Union of India and Ors, Writ Petition (Civil) no 494 of 2012 (2017 SCC OnLine SC 996).
58 Ibid 226–228.
59 Ibid.
60 For a detailed discussion of the amended legislation and the ordinance, see: Press Trust of India, 'President's Nod to Ordinance for Voluntary Use of Aadhaar as ID Proof for Bank a/c, SIM' *Times of India* (New Delhi 3 March 2019).
61 Machiavello (n 7) 214.
62 Emily Feng, 'Chinese Government Faces Peer-to-Peer Lending Scandals Dilemma' *Financial Times* (12 November 2018).

From a systemic point of view, decentralised and rapidly evolving technologies may pose a risk to the stability of the financial system.[63] Certainly, the arrival of new depositors generates more diversity on the lending market which, at first glance, may contribute to financial stability. Yet, the expansion of financial access also leads to rapid and excessive credit growth with inadequate lending standards and, potentially, to instability in lending markets.[64] The fact that fintech companies are usually small, dispersed and difficult to monitor raises other systemic risks than the ones that led to the financial crisis of 2007/08. In fact, an under-appreciated systemic risk in the fintech sector has been that its fast paced growth creates the risk that the fintech industry skips the intermediary stage of being 'too large to ignore' by evolving directly from 'to small to care' to 'too big to fail'.[65]

4 Turning digital transformation into inclusive growth

The above-mentioned risks and unintended consequences of fintech innovations raise important policy questions about appropriate regulation and supervision. From a public policy perspective, the challenge is to ensure that fintech develops in a way that maximises the opportunities and minimises the risks for society.[66] This is all the more relevant, as fintech companies and individuals or small businesses are not operating in a level playing field.

What is the role of global financial governance in mitigating these risks? How can regulatory frameworks facilitate the process of expanding access to finance for low-income countries (or in general underserved groups)? Financial regulators, central banks and standard-setting bodies in global finance hold the reins to control many of the levers that can drive financial inclusion, without simultaneously endanger financial stability. These actors play also a relevant role in the process of financial inclusion, given their access to data, information, currencies and payment infrastructures.

Directing fintech innovation towards inclusive growth and increased social equity involves a coordination on an international level that brings together all relevant stakeholders such as fintech companies, standard-setting bodies and national financial regulators. As a first step, the United Nations suggest the development of good practices for regulating and monitoring fintech innovation.[67]

Financial markets are increasingly interconnected, yet financial systems remain primarily administered on a national level. In order to unleash the full potential for fintech to contribute to sustainable and inclusive growth, financial regulators and central banks need to take into account the international dimension of fintech and coordinate their actions on a global level. Magnuson identified three principles for an 'internationally minded regulatory approach' to fintech regulation.[68] First, with consumers, investors and providers dispersed around the globe, fintech activity is implicitly detached from national borders. Since multiple regulators are having an interest in regulating the activities of fintech providers, fintech

63 William Magnuson, 'Regulating Fintech' (2018) 71 Vanderbilt Law Review 1167, 1199ff.
64 Mehrotra and Yetman (n 4) 84 and 92; Magnuson (n 63) 1200.
65 Douglas W Arner, Janos Nathan Barberis and Ross P Buckley, 'The Evolution of Fintech: A Post-Crisis Paradigm?' (2015) University of Hong Kong Faculty of Law Research Paper no 2015/047, UNSW Law Research Paper no 2016-62, 35 <https://papers.ssrn.com/sol3/papers.cfm?abstract_id=2676553> accessed 26 May 2020.
66 Carney (n 1).
67 See UNSGSA (n 42).
68 Magnuson (n 63) 1222.

regulation needs to have a substantial extraterritorial dimension.[69] Second, the regulatory approach of one country necessarily affects other countries, for there are important distributional effects of choosing one regulatory regime over another.[70] This means that jurisdictions are in competition with each other, which may lead to a 'race to the bottom', given that a specifically burdensome regulatory approach may cause fintech activity to shift from one country to another. Third, and despite this regulatory competition between jurisdictions, financial regulators are advised to establish ties with their peer institutions in other jurisdictions, in order to share useful information with respect to their experience with fintech regulation. By building networks for formal and informal exchanges of information, financial regulators could benefit from the lessons other financial authorities learned.[71]

When it comes to the bottom line in considering possible policy pathways to boost financial inclusion through technological innovation, proportionality is key. How can we shape regulation in a way not to unduly restrict inclusion? What is the optimal level of regulation for the market? On the one hand, regulatory safeguards are necessary with a view to mitigate the risks that arise with fintech innovation. On the other hand, given that, regulation raises prices for products and services, regulatory intervention should not infringe the fundamental rights, such as the freedom to conduct business, which includes the interest to dispose of one's property and to keep sensitive information confidential.[72] At the same time, as Zilioli points out, the freedom to conduct a business should not unduly threaten regulatory objectives, such as consumer protection and the stability of the financial system.[73]

The Basel Committee on Banking Supervision acknowledged the principle of proportionality as one of the core principles for effective banking supervision.[74] Accordingly, the risks from fintech players for the financial systems call for a well-calibrated regulatory and supervision approach.[75]

Most policymakers and market participants would agree that regulatory intervention should be proportional, but proportionality is an elastic concept with a different meaning in different jurisdictions. International standards for fintech need to be readily adjusted for use in a variety of jurisdictions. Since developed and developing economies have a very different starting point, with the latter being characterised by higher inequality and weaker institutional structures, it becomes apparent that there is no one-size-fits-all

---

69 Magnuson (n 63) 1222.

70 Ibid 1223.

71 Ibid.

72 Chiara Zilioli, 'Proportionality as the Organizing Principle of European Banking Regulation' in Theodor Baums and others (eds), *Zentralbanken, Währungsunion und stabiles Finanzsystem – Festschrift für Helmut Siekmann* (Duncker und Humblot 2019) 257.

73 Ibid, quoting Article 1(1) of Council Regulation (EU) No 1024/2013 of 15 October 2013 conferring specific tasks in the European Central Bank concerning policies relating to the prudential supervision of credit institutions (2013) OJ L287/63.

74 Basel Committee on Banking Supervision, 'Core Principles for Effective Banking Supervision' (Bank for International Settlements September 2012) principle 8 – Supervisory approach: 'An effective system of banking supervision requires the supervisor to develop and maintain a forward-looking assessment of the risk profile of individual banks and banking groups, proportionate to their systemic importance; identify, assess and address risks emanating from banks and the banking system as a whole; have a framework in place for early intervention; and have plans in place, in partnership with other relevant authorities, to take action to resolve banks in an orderly manner if they become non-viable'.

75 Mehrotra and Yetman (n 4) 88.

solution for regulatory intervention. In this regard, it is important to ensure that developing countries are able to express their voice in global standard setting. In theory, according to the principle of equivalence of global governance, those who 'are affected by a global public good or bad should have some say in its provision or regulation'.[76] Yet, given the unequal distribution of power in global financial markets, there is 'a rigid divide between standard-setters and standard-takers'.[77] Greater autonomy on the national or regional level would be of limited help, because in practice, the unequal distribution of power in global financial markets, would give the jurisdictions of the financial hubs the leeway to dictate the standards of the market.[78] Emerging and developing economies, for which financial inclusion is a particular concern, would follow the rules and standards of the market. Therefore, the principle of proportionality is the glue that ties together the regulation with the inclusiveness objective.

A proportionate regulatory response is also a matter of the right timing, since regulatory requirements should not unnecessarily suppress financial innovation at an early stage. Yet, if new service providers become economically important, to the extent that they could pose potential financial stability risk, regulators should intervene.[79] An example to illustrate the importance of the right timing of regulatory intervention is the reaction of the Kenyan Central Bank following the emergence of M-Pesa. In 2009, that is two say two years after the emergence of M-Pesa, the Central Bank of Kenya acknowledged that digital payment systems should not be subject to the same requirements as banking services, which paved the way for a lighter intervention without burdensome capital and compliance requirements. According to Guild, this proceeding 'clarified regulatory confusion allowed the service to confidently pursue an expansion strategy'.[80] In addition to the regulatory gap at this early stage, M-Pesa benefited from low start-up requirements, since the technology used the existing telecom network, meaning that there was no need to invest in or build out infrastructure. According to a study led by Suri/Jack,[81] M-PESA raised long-term consumption levels per capita and lifted nearly one in? Ten of Kenya's poorest households out of poverty, with an even higher impact for female-headed households.[82] In general, the emergence of mobile money in Kenya increased financial resilience and saving and allowed a more efficient allocation of labour. Ten years after the emergence of M-Pesa, mobile cash service has reached approximately 90% of the Kenyan population.[83]

In order to give developing countries a voice in global financial standard-setting, it is of paramount importance to ensure that they are sufficiently represented in international standard-setting bodies. The Financial Stability Board (FSB), took a step in that direction

76 David Held and Kevin Young, 'The World Crisis: Global Financial Governance: Principles of Reform' (IDEAS reports – special reports, Nicholas Kitchen (ed) LSE IDEAS 2009) 17 <http://eprints.lse.ac.uk/43602/1/The%20world%20crisis_%20global%20financial%20governance(lsero).pdf> accessed 1 June 2020.
77 Jones and Knaack (n 19) 200.
78 Ibid.
79 Mehrotra and Yetman (n 4) 88.
80 Guild (n 39) 10.
81 Suri and Jack (n 30) 1288.
82 UNSGSA (n 42) 8.
83 Guild (n 39) 10.

in 2014, by allocating more seats to officials from emerging market member jurisdictions.[84] Some authors even suggest more radical measures, such as a merger of the FSB with the International Monetary and Financial Committee[85] or the creation of an international treaty under the umbrella of the International Monetary Fund (IMF) for the integration of micro and macro prudential supervisory institutions.[86]

Another reform proposal for global financial regulation worth exploring in the future is the creation of a new standard setting body for the prudential supervision of digital financial services. Instead of integrating the supervision of fintech providers into an existing organisation, Jones and Knaack suggest that such a new organisation should be placed under the auspices of the FSB and operate with a dual mandate to balance financial stability with the objective of inclusive growth.[87]

5 Conclusion

The chapter analysed some of the main issues related to how policymakers and standard setters are addressing the challenges of the digitalisation of finance (fintech) and financial inclusion. While fintech offers a myriad of different opportunities to include the unbanked around the world, it is also a Pandora's Box unleashing a number of risks that can undermine the stability and integrity of the financial system, in particular for developing economies. Developing country and emerging market regulators are confronted with the need to find a balance between allowing advances in technology to develop more options for consumers and businesses for data-based financial services and the regulation of such services to achieve regulatory objectives, such as financial stability, consumer protection and privacy rights. The principle of proportionality is key for policymakers in finding the right balance between the extent and scope of regulation to achieve these objectives while recognising that the adoption of such measures can lead to increased costs in the provision of finance and thus to further financial exclusion.[88]

India has adopted the most centralised and comprehensive strategy to enhance financial inclusion. Indeed, the India Stack strategy provides an alternative model for a developing and emerging market country that seeks to adopt a centralised strategy for addressing the financial risks associated with financial exclusion but nevertheless confronts institutional and legal challenges regarding data protection and privacy. In contrast, China has taken a different approach to data regulation and privacy that allowed a small group of Big Tech and financial technology companies to dominate the market in providing consumer financial and payment services while being subject to much less stringent regulations

---

84 Financial Stability Board (FSB), 'Report to the G20 Brisbane Summit on the FSB's Review of the Structure of Its Representation' (FSB, 15–16 November 2014) 2 <www.fsb.org/wp-content/uploads/Report-to-the-G20-Brisbane-Summit-on-the-FSB%E2%80%99s-Review-of-the-Structure-of-its-Representation.pdf> accessed 26 May 2020.
85 Mervyn King, 'Mervyn King Speech at the University of Exeter' (Exeter, 19 January 2010) 8 <www.bankofengland.co.uk/speech/2010/mervyn-king-speech-at-the-university-of-exeter> accessed 26 May 2020: '[...] the legitimacy and leadership of the G20 would be enhanced if it were seen as representing views of other countries too. That could be achieved if the G20 were to metamorphose into a Governing Council for the IMF, and at the same time acquire a procedure for voting on decisions'.
86 Emilios Avgouleas, *Governance of Global Financial Markets: The Law, the Economics, the Politics* (CUP 2012) 440ff.
87 Jones and Knaack (n 19) 203.
88 Macchiavello (n 7) 229.

in respect to data protection and privacy. International initiatives to adopt principles and standards for regulating the provision of data-driven financial services will need to be developed further to support countries in finding the right balance in utilising data-driven finance to enhance financial inclusion while ensuring that other regulatory objectives are met.

Bibliography

A Abkowitz, 'The Cashless Society Has Arrived — Only It's in China' *Wall Street Journal* (4 January 2018).

M M Ahamed and S Mallick, 'Is Financial Inclusion Good for Bank Stability? International Evidence' (2019) 157(issue C) Journal of Economic Behavior & Organization 403.

K Alexander, *Principles of Banking Regulation* (CUP 2019).

Alliance for Financial Inclusion, 'Maya Declaration – The AFI Network Commitment to Financial Inclusion' (2011).

Alliance for Financial Inclusion, '2018 Maya Declaration Progress Report' (2018).

D W Arner, J N Barberis and R P Buckley, 'The Evolution of Fintech: A Post-Crisis Paradigm?' (2015) University of Hong Kong Faculty of Law Research Paper no 2015/047, UNSW Law Research Paper no 2016-62.

E Avgouleas, *Governance of Global Financial Markets: The Law, the Economics, the Politics* (CUP 2012).

Basel Committee on Banking Supervision, 'Core Principles for Effective Banking Supervision' (Bank for International Settlements September 2012).

Basel Committee on Banking Supervision, 'Guidance on the Application of the Core Principles for Effective Banking Supervision to the Regulation and Supervision of Institutions Relevant to Financial Inclusion' (Bank for International Settlements September 2016).

M Bateman, M Duvendack and N Loubere, 'Is Fin-Tech the New Panacea for Poverty Alleviation and Local Development? Contesting Suri and Jack's M-Pesa Findings Published in Science' (2019) 161 Review of African Political Economy 480.

Better than Cash Alliance, 'About the Better than Cash Alliance'.

M Carney, 'The Promise of FinTech – Something New Under the Sun?' (G 20 conference on 'Digitising finance, financial inclusion and financial literacy' 25 January 2017).

L Chen, 'Who Can Break the Oligopoly of E-commerce in China?' (China Europe International Business School (CEIBS) 15 April 2020).

Consultative Group to Assist the Poor (CGAP), 'Achieving Sustainable Development Goals: The Role of Financial Inclusion' (2016).

G Deipenbrock, 'Is the Law Ready to Face the Progressing Digital Revolution? – General Policy Issues and Selected Aspects in the Realm of Financial Markets from the International, European Union and German Perspective' (2019) 118 Zeitschrift für vergleichende Rechtswissenschaft 285.

A Demirgüç-Kunt and L Klapper, 'Measuring Financial Inclusion: The Global Findex Database' (2012) World Bank Policy Research Paper 6025.

A Demirgüç-Kunt and L Klapper, Global Findex Database 2017: Measuring Financial Inclusion and the Fintech Revolution (World Bank Group 2018).

E Feng, 'Chinese Government Faces Peer-to-peer Lending Scandals Dilemma' *Financial Times* (18 November 2018).

Federal Trade Commission (FTC), 'FTC Seeks Comment on Proposed Amendments to Safeguards and Privacy Rules' (2019).

Financial Stability Board (FSB), 'Report to the G20 Brisbane Summit on the FSB's review of the structure of its representation' (15–16 November 2014).

Financial Stability Board (FSB), 'FinTech and Market Structure in Financial Services: Market Developments and Potential Financial Stability Implications' (FSB 2019).

I Fisher, 'Measures of Financial Inclusion – A Central Bank Perspective' (Committee on Central Bank Statistics, Bank for International Settlements 2016).

G20 Research Group, 'G20 Leaders Statement: The Pittsburgh Summit' (2009).

G20, 'G20 High Level Principles for Digital Financial Inclusion' (23–24 July 2016).

J Guild, 'Fintech and the Future of Finance' (2017) 10(1) Asian Journal of Public Affairs 52.

D Held and K Young, 'The World Crisis: Global Financial Governance: Principles of Reform' (IDEAS reports – special reports, Nicholas Kitchen (ed) LSE IDEAS 2009).

K Henne, 'Surveillance in the Name of Governance: Aadhar as a Fix for Leaking Systems in India' in B Haggart, K Henne and N Tusikov (eds), *Information, Technology and Control in a Changing World – Understanding Power Structures in the 21st Century* (Palgrave Macmillan 2019) 223–245.

S Hofmann, 'Engineering Global Consent – The Chinese Communist Party's Data Driven Power Expansion' (Australian Strategic Policy Institute).

India Stack, 'About eKYS API'.

India Stack, 'What is India Stack?'

E Jones and P Knaack, 'Global Financial Regulations: Shortcomings and Reform Options' (2019) 10 Global Policy 193.

O Kabakova and E Plaksenkov, 'Analysis of Factors Affecting Financial Inclusion: Ecosystem View' (2018) 89 Journal of Business Research 198.

M Kim, H Zoo, H Lee and J Kang, 'Mobile Financial Services, Financial Inclusion, and Development: A Systematic Review of Academic Literature' (2018) 84 (5) Electronic Journal of Information Systems in Developing Countries.

M King, 'Mervyn King Speech at the University of Exeter' (19 January 2010).

A Liu, 'An Analysis of the PBOC's New Mobile Payment Regulation' (2019) 39(1) Cato Journal 87.

A Ma 'China Has Started Ranking Citizens with a Creepy "Social Credit" System: Here's What You Can Do Wrong, and the Embarrassing, Demeaning Ways They Can Punish You' Business Insider' (29 October 2018).

E Macchiavello, *Microfinance and Financial Inclusion: The Challenge of Regulating Alternative Forms of Finance* (Routledge 2018).

P Mader, 'Contesting Financial Inclusion' (2018) 49(2) Development and Change 461.

W Magnuson, 'Regulating Fintech' (2018) 71 Vanderbilt Law Review 1167.

A Mehrotra and J Yetman, 'Financial Inclusion – Issues for Central Banks' (BIS Quarterly Review March 2015).

J Pearse, 'About GPFI' (25 November 2013).

T Philippon, 'On Fintech and Financial Inclusion' (2019) National Bureau of Economic Research, Working Paper 26330.

Press Trust of India, 'President's Nod to Ordinance for Voluntary Use of Aadhaar as ID Proof for Bank a/c, SIM' Times of India (3 March 2019).

O Sananikone, 'Microfinance and the Millennium Development Goals' (CGAP donor brief no. 9, World Bank 2002).

T Suri and W Jack, 'The Long-Run Poverty and Gender Impacts of Mobile Money' (2016) 354 Science 1288.

United Nations, 'Monterrey Consensus on Financing for Development' (2003).

United Nations, 'Building Inclusive Financial Sectors for Development' (Joint Report by the United Nations Department of Economic and Social Affairs and the United Nations Capital Development Fund 2006).

United Nations, 'Transforming Our World: The 2030 Agenda for Sustainable Development' (2015).

United Nations Secretary-General's Special Advocate for Inclusive Finance for Development, 'Annual Report to the Secretary General' (2017).

G Wildau, 'China Targets Mobile Payments Oligopoly with Clearing Mandate' *Financial Times* (9 August 2017).

World Bank Group, 'Global Financial Development Report 2014: Financial Inclusion' (World Bank 2013).

World Bank Group, 'Financial Inclusion Global Initiative (FIGI)' (18 July 2019).

Q Xiaoji, 'Baidu, Tencent, Alibaba Forming Oligopoly on Chinese Internet' China Daily (18 February 2011).

L Zhang and S Chen, 'China's Digital Economy: Opportunities and Risks' (2019) IMF Working Paper 19/16 11.

D A Zetsche and others, 'The Future of Data Driven Finance: Financial Regulation, Data Regulation, and RegTech' (*The CLS Blue Sky Blog* 15 April 2019).

D A Zetsche, D P Arner, R P Buckley and R H Weber, 'The Future of Data-Driven Finance and Regetech: Lessons from EU Big Bang II' (March 2019).

D A Zetsche and others, 'Regulating a Revolution: From Regulatory Sandboxes to Smart Regulation' (2017) 23 Fordham Journal of Corporate & Financial Law 31.

M Zhang, 'China Sets Up Clearing House for AliPay and TenPay' South China Morning Post (7 August 2017).

W Zhou, D W Arner and R P Buckley, 'China's Regulation of Digital Financial Services: Some Recent Developments' (2016) 90 Australian Law Journal 297.

C Zilioli, 'Proportionality as the Organizing Principle of European Banking Regulation' in T Baums and others (eds) *Zentralbanken, Währungsunion und stabiles Finanzsystem – Festschrift für Helmut Siekmann* (Duncker und Humblot 2019).

16 Disintermediation in fund-raising

Marketplace investing platforms and EU financial regulation

Eugenia Macchiavello

1 Introduction: 'platform economy' and disintermediation in fund-raising

In recent years, the so-called platform economy[1] has emerged, characterised by 'a digital service that facilitates interactions between two or more distinct but interdependent sets of users (whether firms or individuals) who interact through the service via the Internet' ('multi-sided platforms').[2]

This phenomenon has also impacted the financial sector on the back of growing distrust towards traditional finance and a consequent demand for 'democratised'/'direct' finance.[3] In the capital markets area, this has entailed the emergence of 'disintermediation', that is, the elimination of traditional financial intermediaries and the creation of 'P2P-marketplaces' in both: (1) the fund-raising/primary market, with, for instance, investment-based crowd-funding (IBC) and lending-based crowdfunding (LBC),[4] Initial Coin Offerings (ICOs) and Security Token Offerings (STOs) (cutting out underwriters and distributors); (2) the secondary market, with P2P exchanges of crowd-loans/crowd-investments previously subscribed on the same platform or transfers of tokens directly through the blockchain or decentralised/automated exchanges (eliminating market operators). ICOs/STOs, which rely on blockchain and smart contracts, are considered as evolutions of IBC, entailing more liquidity and more disintermediation/decentralisation (smart contracts instead of intermediary-platforms), but as regards the latter aspect, the differences may be a matter of degree.[5]

---

1 Orly Lobel, 'The Law of the Platform' (2016) 101(1) Minn L Rev 87.
2 OECD, *An Introduction to Online Platforms and Their Role in the Digital Transformation* (OECD 2019) 20–21, <https://doi.org/10.1787/53e5f593-en>. Call-off date for all hyperlinks, unless stated otherwise: 03/02/2020.
3 OECD, 'Initial Coin Offerings (ICOs) for SME Financing' (2019) 20, 30 <www.oecd.org/finance/ICOs-for-SME-Financing.pdf>.
4 See Eugenia Macchiavello, 'Peer-to-peer Lending and the "Democratization" of Credit Markets: Another Financial Innovation Puzzling Regulators' (2015) 21(3) CJEL 521; Macchiavello, 'Financial-Return Crowdfunding and Regulatory Approaches in the Shadow Banking, Fintech and Collaborative Finance Era' (2017) 14(4) ECFR 662.
5 In fact, also in an ICO/STO context, new intermediaries and Initial Exchange Offerings (with exchanges selecting and sponsoring offerings) have emerged and, on the other hand, in crowdfund-ing, we start to see security-tokens offerings and automated/decentralised offerings (eg, STOKR) and markets (eg, RealMarket). See also FSB, 'Decentralised Financial Technologies. Report on Financial Stability, Regulatory and Governance Implications' (6 June 2019) 1ff <www.fsb.org/wp-content/uploads/P060619.pdf>; OECD (n 3) 26ff.

Disintermediated finance challenges current financial regulation, conceived with traditional intermediaries and centralised systems in mind. Supervisors now have to assess whether such disintermediated activities correspond to mere information/technical services[6] or rather to new professional services that require special regulation or, instead, are equivalents of regulated services ('re-intermediation')[7] and, in this last case, whether existing rules are fit to regulate them.

The present chapter will focus on and analyse IBC and its original features within the landscape of business fund-raising, assessing whether it represents a new form of intermediation and/or deserves specific regulation, with particular regard to EU financial regulation.[8]

2 Investment-based crowdfunding: main features

2.1 *Main classifications and market description*

Crowdfunding typically entails an open call from entrepreneurs, organisations or consumers to a multitude of internet users (the 'crowd') to raise funds (in the form of donations, rewards, loans or investments) for specific projects, generally through specialised online platforms. The financial contribution to each project from a single crowd-funder is usually individually small.[9] IBC is a form of financial-return crowdfunding (FRC, together with LBC/marketplace lending), where contributors participate, with the aim of financial profit, in the form of either equity (eg, shares or equivalent forms of participation to the ownership of a firm; equity-based crowdfunding-EBC[10]), debt-securities (eg, bonds, minibonds) or other forms of investment (eg, profit-sharing investment contracts recognising

---

6 Exempted under Art. 2(a) e-commerce Directive (No. 2000/31 [2000] OJ L178/1); Art. 2(2)(d) Services in the Internal Market Directive (2006/123/CE [2006] OJ L 376/36), Art. 56 TFEU. The answer by the ECJ to the question in the text has been differentiated case-by-case (and depending on the sector: transportation, hospitality): Eugenia Macchiavello, 'The European Crowdfunding Service Providers Regulation and the Future of Marketplace Lending and Investing in Europe: The "Crowdfunding Nature" Dilemma' (April 10, 2020) forthcoming in EBLR, 34 (fn 105), 10 (fn 36) <https://papers.ssrn.com/sol3/papers.cfm?abstract_id=3594353>.

7 Iris Chiu, 'Fintech and Disruptive Business Models in Financial Products, Intermediation and Markets' (2016) 21 J Tech L & Pol'y 55, 85–86.

8 More extensively: Eugenia Macchiavello, 'What to Expect When You Are Expecting' a European Crowdfunding Regulation: The Current "Bermuda Triangle" and Future Scenarios for Marketplace Lending and Investing in Europe' (2019) EBI Working Paper 55 <https://ssrn.com/abstract=3493688>; Macchiavello, 'Financial-Return' (n 4); Guido Ferrarini and Eugenia Macchiavello, 'Investment-based Crowdfunding: Is MiFID II Enough?' in Danny Busch and Guido Ferrarini (eds), *Regulation of EU Financial Markets: MiFID II* (OUP 2017) 668.

9 For an unofficial EU description of crowdfunding: Commission, 'Impact Assessment Accompanying the Document Proposal for a Regulation [...] on European Crowdfunding Service Providers (ECSP) for Business-Staff Working Document' (8 March 2018) SWD(2018) 56 final, 7; Commission, 'Unleashing the Potential of Crowdfunding in the European Union' (Communication) COM(2014) 172 final 2, 3. For renowned definitions inspiring the Commission, see Armin Schwienbacher and Benjamin Larralde, 'Crowdfunding of Small Entrepreneurial Ventures' in Douglas Cumming (ed), *The Oxford Handbook of Entrepreneurial Finance* (OUP 2012) 369, 370–371.

10 Some platforms (eg, Crowdcube) also allow offerings of dual-class shares: Douglas Cumming and Sophia Johan, *Crowdfunding. Fundamental Cases, Facts, and Insights* (Academic Press 2019) 151, 264ff.

a right to a share of future sales – royalty – not of the company's ownership).[11] In some cases, crowd-investors invest only indirectly in firms, buying a security issued by a collective investment fund or SPV (generally one per project) which invests in companies (eg, Seedrs-UK). Other models allow crowd-investors to invest along with business angels (eg, MyMicroInvest–Belgium).[12] The investees are generally unlisted, seed or start-up companies.[13]

Some platforms have recently started offering security tokens (digital representation of securities on a blockchain, a form of STO; eg, Austrian Conda[14]) or accept virtual currencies from crowd-investors (eg, Italian Opstart).

IBC has been growing in terms of volumes but remains small compared to LBC.[15] Looking at the global volumes of IBC, the United States and the United Kingdom (UK) are the main markets for volumes, with Europe ranking only third.[16] Within Europe, the IBC market is dominated, besides the UK, by Benelux, France and Nordic countries,[17] but the list of top countries changes depending on the subtype.[18] The prevailing IBC-subtype is EBC (especially the fast-growing segment of real estate), while debt-securities and, in particular, profit-sharing models present negligible figures (except in the UK).[19]

The term crowdfunding derives from 'crowdsourcing'[20] and similarly indicates that a certain relevant activity is provided – also thanks to new technologies and in particular, Web 2.0 – by individuals (consumers) instead of, as typically happens in the traditional sector, professional and specialised providers. In the investment area, crowdfunding has allowed individuals to directly invest in firms, with a consequent elimination of several layers of the typical infrastructure for capital fund-raising and Initial Public Offerings (IPOs), which involves underwriters (performing due diligence on companies, pricing the financial instrument, organising the distribution process, etc.), distributors (investment firms distributing financial instruments based on an agreement with underwriters), including brokers (acting upon clients' orders) or investment advisors (suggesting certain specific

---

11 Some taxonomies separate real estate crowdfunding (investment in shares and debt-securities of real estate ventures) within the IBC area: see Tania Ziegler et al, 'The Global Alternative Finance Market Benchmarking Report' (2020) 31 <https://www.jbs.cam.ac.uk/fileadmin/user_upload/research/centres/alternative-finance/downloads/2020-04-22-ccaf-global-alternative-finance-market-benchmarking-report.pdf>: see also Commission, 'Impact' (n 9) 11.
12 About IBC models and characteristics: Eleanor Kirby and Shane Worner, 'Crowd-funding: An Infant Industry Growing Fast' (2014) IOSCO Research Department Staff Working Paper 3/2014 <www.iosco.org/research/pdf/swp/Crowd-funding-An-Infant-Industry-Growing-Fast.pdf>; ESMA, 'Opinion on Investment-based Crowdfunding' ESMA/2014/1378, 7; Macchiavello, 'Financial-return' (n 4) 668; Ferrarini and Macchiavello (n 8) 660; Cumming and Johan (n 10) 150.
13 ESMA (n 12) 8; Kirby and Worner (n 12) 8–9.
14 See <https://medium.com/crwdnetwork/first-security-token-issued-in-austria-97e3c0ea000a>.
15 LBC represents the 90% of global alternative finance (USD 78.9 billion), while IBC the 6.5% (USD 8.2 billion): Ziegler et al (n 11) 39–40.
16 Respectively (USD millions): 2,500; 883.82; 833.32: Ziegler et al (n 11) 41.
17 Respectively (USD millions): 352; 226; 169: Ziegler et al (n 11) 77.
18 See Ziegler et al (n 11) 82–83.
19 The figures for Europe (UK excluded) are (in USD million): 600.1 (68%) real-estate crowdfunding; 278.1 (31%) EBC; 167.8 (3%) debt-securities; 42.8 (1%) mini-bonds (relevant almost only in the Netherland and France); 3.5 (0%) revenue sharing. For the UK (in USD million): 484.7 (56%) EBC; 264.9 (30%) real estate crowdfunding; 102.2 (12%) revenue sharing; 529.8 (6%) debt-securities; 0.1 (0%) mini-bonds: Ziegler et al (n 11) 42–43, 78.
20 Schwienbacher and Larralde (n 9) 373.

financial instruments to clients based on the latter's investment objectives, experience, risk and financial profile), credit rating agencies, analysts, etc. More recently, the term 'marketplace investing' has emerged to also signal the presence of institutional investors as crowd-investors, although the 'institutionalisation' trend is still limited as regards IBC (contrary to LBC).[21]

Nevertheless, platforms perform key services: they generally screen applicants (performing certain due diligence activities such as background, credit and cross-checks to exclude frauds or even, sometimes, select the 'best'), support them in preparing business plans and making projects visible on the website (or sometimes even providing additional promotion/marketing support). Furthermore, they channel information about entrepreneurs to crowd-investors, provide standard contracts and create and maintain communication channels among users as well as handle post-contractual parties' relationships.[22]

Start-up and seed companies' shares (unlisted) appear highly illiquid (exits are limited to liquidation, a future IPO or acquisition by venture capital – VC – funds) and systems are needed to allow crowd-investors to identify other users interested in buying previously subscribed crowd-investments (bulletin boards) or even to match interests and conclude the sale directly on the platform (closer to secondary markets). Nonetheless, only a few platforms (eg, Seedrs) have made available such systems and with limitations (eg, only periodic and short 'trading cycles').[23] The above-mentioned security-tokens experiences within the crowdfunding sector have been regarded as a potential solution to such liquidity issues.[24]

2.2 *Opportunities offered and risks raised by IBC*

Crowdfunding is considered an important alternative form of finance for consumers and small and medium-sized enterprises (SMEs), expanding access to finance and partially filling SMEs' financing gap, especially in the post-financial crisis and post-COVID-19 scenario.[25] In particular, EBC seems to bridge start-up (especially fast-growing ones) and established small companies from family and friends' financing to private equity (PE) and

21 Institutional investors' participation in 2018 for IBC is the following (respectively, globally/EU): 16%/12% for real-estate crowdfunding and 23%/7% for EBC but 31%/53% for debt-securities and 70%(/NA) for revenue-sharing: Ziegler et al (n 11) 52, 87.
22 See Yannis Pierrakis and Liam Collins, 'Crowdfunding: A New Innovative Model of Providing Funding to Projects and Businesses' (2013) <https://papers.ssrn.com/sol3/papers.cfm?abstract_id=2395226>; Douglas Cumming, Sofia A. Johan and Yelin Zhang, 'The Role of Due Diligence in Crowdfunding Platforms' (2019) 108 Journal of Banking and Finance 1.
23 See <www.seedrs.com/pages/secondary-market-terms>. In 2014, only 9.5% of European EBC platforms had a form of secondary market for their products (*versus* 29% for LBC): Giuliana Borello et al, 'The Funding Gap and The Role of Financial Return Crowdfunding: Some Evidence from European Platforms' (2015) 20(1) JIBC 1, 13, 16. See also Armin Schwienbacher, 'Equity Crowdfunding: Anything to Celebrate?' (2019) 21(1) Venture Capital 65, 71.
24 Schwienbacher (n 23) 70.
25 About SMEs dependence on banks' funding and obstacles to other financing sources, see Peter Schammo, 'Market Building and the Capital Markets Union: Addressing Information Barriers in the SME Funding Market' (2017) 2 ECFR 271.

VC or even to public markets,[26] entailing lower costs for the same[27] but also access to a potentially large public (with significant network effects, as other platform-based systems).[28] Furthermore, crowdfunding appears an opportunity also for entrepreneurs to test and give visibility to their products as well as to leverage investments from other sources.[29] Although evidence is not always conclusive, crowdfunding might also be able to lead to a more democratic distribution of funds – compared to IPOs – across territories, gender and minorities.[30] From an investor's perspective, FRC is appealing in terms of diversification (as an alternative and therefore more resilient market) and types of returns (also non-financial, rewarding through the sense of involvement and the idea of supporting firms which share the same principles/vision). Finally, the financial system might benefit from increased competition among different operators, investment diversification and innovation.[31]

Nonetheless, several risks are attached to IBC. The most significant are observed from the investor's perspective and are linked to its 'direct' character: crowd-investors, because of their inexperience in start-up and seed companies (fields where typically only business angels, VC and PE are at ease) and in the absence of professional intermediaries performing due diligence, pricing and information functions, might suffer from the effects of market failures (asymmetric information and moral hazard). They may not realise the risks involved in relying on incomplete or misleading information and lose their money because of fraud or investee or platform defaults. Conflicts of interest between the platform and investors, although potentially minimised by reputation concerns and incentives to reinforce the network effects of the platform, might arise especially in case of remuneration schemes based on the volume/number of transactions. Although investors investing small sums in each project mitigate risks through diversification, this creates disincentives to gather information, monitor and seek legal enforcement (coordination problem). Platforms have tried to mitigate some of these risks through different market-based solutions: from imposing diversification (across projects, sectors, geographies, etc.), to platform's co-investing or crowd-investing along with business angels or other sophisticated investors, to supporting the 'wisdom of the crowd' through feedback and rating systems and other forms of signalling (investment by social network's backers, high retention rates, etc.).[32]

As regards investees' risks, firms might face governance problems related to the sudden increase in the number of owners. Moreover, investees might be discriminated (eg, based

26 Pierrakis and Collins (n 22) 5–6; Commission, 'Proposal for a Regulation of the European Parliament and of the Council on European Crowdfunding Service Providers (ECSP) for Business' (8 March 2018) COM(2018)113, 1.
27 Business angels financing absorbs 40–45% of capital raised in various fees, IPOs 7% (more if SMEs), crowdfunding only 4–5%: Cumming and Johan (n 10) 5.
28 Commission, 'Impact' (n 9) 13ff.
29 Schwienbacher and Larralde (n 9) 373ff.
30 Andrew Schwartz, 'Crowdfunding Issuers in the United States' (2020) 61 Journal of Law & Policy 155. But see Douglas Cumming, Michele Meoli and Silvio Vismara, 'Does Equity Crowdfunding Democratize Entrepreneurial Finance?' (2019) Small Bus Econ <https://doi.org/10.1007/s11187-019-00188-z> (rejecting the hypothesis that EBC increases female entrepreneurs' opportunities).
31 About benefits and risks of crowdfunding see also Ajay Agrawal, Christian Catalini and Avi Goldfarb, 'Some Simple Economics of Crowdfunding' (2013) NBER Working Paper 19133/2013, 10ff <https://www.nber.org/papers/w19133>; Commission, 'Unleashing' (n 9) 5; ESMA (n 12) 10ff; John Armour and Luca Enriques, 'The Promise and Perils of Crowdfunding: Between Corporate Finance and Consumer Contracts' (2018) 81(1) Modern Law Review 51.
32 See also Agrawal et al (n 31) 22ff; Cumming and Johan (n 10) Chs 2 and 10; references in Macchiavello 'Financial-return' (n 4) 677–678.

on gender or ethnicity) during an opaque selection process and be required to publish unprotected corporate information. Finally, the financial system might have to deal with the increased risk of fraud, cyber-crimes or money laundering and financing terrorism (if platforms are not subject to existing anti-money laundering rules: see item 3.2). At present, systemic risk remains low, although this might change as the area grows and increases its interconnections with the mainstream sector.

3 Main legal issues and regulatory trends in Europe

3.1 *EU financial regulation: application of existing rules*

In the EU, IBC may be captured by the European Prospectus Regulation (PR),[33] MiFID II[34] or collective investments regimes (eg, UCITS and AIFMD).[35] This chapter will look at this legal framework[36] before discussing the need for bespoke regulation, recently also introduced at EU level (see item 4).

As regards the PR, burdensome disclosure obligations apply to issuers/offerors in public offerings of transferable securities unless certain exemptions or exclusions apply (eg, private offers – to less than 150 people or reserved to qualified investors). Although some Member States have extended Prospectus obligations to the offering of investment products other than transferable securities (see Italy, Austria and Germany; since 2018, Belgium), the main issue is therefore whether IBC products have to be considered transferable securities, which Article 4(1)44 MiFID II defines as:

> those classes of securities which are negotiable on the capital market, with the exception of instruments of payment, such as: (a) shares in companies and other securities equivalent to shares in companies, partnerships or other entities, and depositary receipts in respect of shares; (b) bonds or other forms of securitised debt, including depositary receipts in respect of such securities; (c) any other securities giving the right to acquire or sell any such transferable securities [...].

The transferability of securities and their ability to be exchanged in 'all contexts where buying and selling interest in securities are met' appear key identifying characteristics,[37] but some interpreters include the standardisation of the conditions attached to the product (allowing for the formation of a market). Although the same article (Art. 4(2) MiFID II) empowers the Commission to adopt delegated acts to specify technical elements of these

---

33 Regulation 2017/1129/EU [2017] OJ L168/12.

34 Directive 2014/65/EU [2014] OJ L173/349.

35 Directives 2009/65/EC OJ [2009] L303/32 and 2011/61 OJ [2011] L174/1. Subcategories are Directives: EuVECA No. 345/2013/EU, EuSEF No. 346/2013/EU, ELTIF No. 2015/760.

36 About IBC and EU financial regulation: Eugenia Macchiavello, 'Financial-return' (n 4) 680ff; Id (n 6); Ferrarini and Macchiavello (n 8); Matthias Klaes et al, *Identifying Market and Regulatory Obstacles to Crossborder Development of Crowdfunding in the EU* (European Commission 2017); Dirk Zetzsche and Christine Preiner, 'Cross-Border Crowdfunding – Towards a Single Crowdfunding Market for Europe' (2018) 19(2) EBOR 217; Sebastian Hooghiemstra and Kristof de Buysere, 'The Perfect Regulation of Crowdfunding: What Should the European Regulator Do?' in Dennis Brüntje and Oliver Gajda (eds), *Crowdfunding in Europe* (Springer 2016) 135.

37 Commission, 'Questions on Single Market Legislation'– Definitions, 'transferable securities', Art. 4(1) (18) of Dir. 2004/39/EC, ID 150 (Internal reference 2) and ID 285 (Internal reference 115).

definitions 'to adjust them to market developments, technological developments […] and to ensure the uniform application' of the Directive, the identification of transferable securities and specification of their characteristics[38] have traditionally been carried out by national authorities, and significant national variations in this regard have proliferated as in corporate laws in general.[39]

Furthermore, the most important exemption from the PR in an IBC context is a total consideration in 12 months not exceeding €1 million (with reference to the same product issued by the same issuer) though Member States may set higher thresholds up to €8 million, leading again to differences among countries in the availability of exemption.[40]

Where crowdfunding products are considered transferable securities (see above) or more generally financial instruments (including, in addition, eg, financial derivatives and units in collective investment undertakings[41]), we should also ascertain whether platforms offer one or more investment services reserved to investment firms under MiFID II.[42] In fact, in this case, they would need to seek an authorisation from the national competent authority (NCA) and comply with extensive capital, organisational (including conflict of interest rules, corporate governance rules, remuneration rules, product governance, records), disclosure and other conduct requirements (general duty to act honestly, fairly and in the best interest of clients plus specific conduct duties differentiated based on the type of investment service).

Regulatory application is complicated by the variety of IBC business models and by the lack of detailed definitions of most investment services in EU legislation and consequent national interpretative differences. Nonetheless, considering the services generally offered by crowdfunding platforms (see item 2.1), the activity most likely to be carried out by crowdfunding platforms, also according to the European Securities and Markets Authority (ESMA), is reception and transmission of orders (Art. 4(1)5 MIFID II) between investors

---

38 For instance, under a restrictive approach, certain similarities with the securities exemplified in MiFID II (eg, voting rights attached, transferability rules, etc.) and/or negotiability on regulated trading venues.

39 Significant differences exist in the classification as financial instruments of, for example, silent partnerships, participations in private limited companies and subordinated profit-participating loans as well as in private limited companies forms and legal possibility to offer their participations to the public or creditors' protection measures, etc. For further discussion and references, see Macchiavello, 'Financial-return' (n 4) 698; Macchiavello, 'FinTech Regulation from a Cross-sectoral Perspective', in Veerle Colaert, Danny Busch and Thomas Incalza (eds), *European Financial Regulation: Levelling the Cross-Sectoral Playing Field* (Hart 2019) 69.

40 Articles 1(2)h and 3(2)e PR. In Belgium, the general exemption used to be €100,000 in total consideration but crowdfunding exemptions have been introduced since 2014 and the prospectus law of 11 July 2018 raised the general exemption to €5 million but an information note (concise, comprehensible, clear) is required for offers of securities between €500,000 and €5 million provided that the investor subscribes up to €5,000, while below €500,000 an information document can be omitted. Germany previously had €2.5 million as maximum threshold, while France and Italy had €5 million. However, all three countries raised their thresholds to €8 million in 2018 (but requiring a national information note and, sometimes, investment limits for offers above €1 million): Macchiavello (n 8) 30–31; <https://www.esma.europa.eu/sites/default/files/library/esma31-62-1193_prospectus_thresholds.pdf>.

41 Annex 1, Section C, MiFID II.

42 Annex 1, Section A.

and issuers, which is accompanied by limited initial capital,[43] general conduct duties and appropriateness/execution-only rules, with the availability of Art. 3(1) exemption where no clients' money or assets are held. However, jurisdictions tend to exclude such qualification when the platform only brings together an issuer with potential sources of funding and the deal is concluded 'elsewhere'. Where the platform concludes the deal on the investors' behalf, it would also perform the execution of orders service (which presents own funds requirements and does not benefit from the Art. 3 exemption).[44]

Some countries might also consider platforms performing the service of placing without firm commitment – not defined in EU legislation – for performing due diligence, giving visibility to a project on their website and sending e-mails marketing the same based on a remunerated agreement with the issuer. This qualification would negatively affect platforms' activity in terms of capital requirements and Prospectus liability. Nonetheless, the elements required to identify such a service significantly differ among Member States.[45]

Similarly, a few countries have left the door open to the classification as investment advice (personal recommendation regarding a specific financial instrument) when platforms rate/rank projects and market them to users as 'the best for you',[46] potentially covered by Art. 3 exemption but otherwise subject to strict conduct rules (eg, suitability test).

Finally, in case of indirect investments, when crowdfunding involves the pooling of contributions from many crowd-investors not taking part in day-to-day decisions, based on a defined investment policy with a view to generate a return for the pool (unless it is a holding with a certain industrial objective or a securitisation SPV or exempted for assets-under-management below €100,000 – with leverage – or €500,000 – without leverage), the activity may be recognised as a collective investment undertaking regulated under the AIFMD (or sub-categories, see above), with certain national differences.[47] In this case, the platform needs to obtain an authorisation (with an initial capital of €300,000/€125,000), have an authorised depositary and comply with other organisation and conduct requirements

---

43 The initial capital requirements used to be €125,000 or, without holding clients' assets, €50,000 (CRDIV 30–31(1)). With the Investment Firms Regulation (IFR 2019/2033) and Directive (IFD 2019/2034) (OJ [2019] L314/1-114), it will be, respectively, €150,000 and €75,000 (Art. 9 IFD). No own funds requirement existed, while under IFD/IFR it will correspond to the highest between the required minimum capital, the 25% of their fixed overheads and (except for class-3 firms) the Risk-to-Client risk, calculated based on the value of client orders handled (K-COH) and client money held (K-CMH) (Art. 9, 11–14 IFR).

44 FCA, 'The Perimeter Guidance Manual – Chapter 13 – Guidance on the scope of MiFID and CRD IV', 13.3 (Q13–Q15).

45 In France – where placing/underwriting is characterised by the existence of a service rendered to an issuer and the act of finding subscribers/purchasers – a platform can avoid the placing/underwriting classification when allowing access to project descriptions only to registered users passing a test, not actively searching for subscribers for specific projects and being regulated as EBC providers or investment consultant: see Macchiavello 'Financial-return' (n 4) 701–702; in Belgium, the main elements of the placing service have been identified in the existence of an agreement between the issuer and the intermediary acting on behalf of the issuer and a consideration paid by the issuer to the intermediary but the FSMA has recently clarified that also an assistance during the entire process, including financial flows management, is required, while Art. 4(3) of *loi du 18 décembre 2016* (*loi crowdfunding*) and Art. 56 Prospectus Law allow platforms to commercialise financial instruments (ie, to present the same with the view of incentivising the subscription of financial instruments): CrowdfundingHub, 'Crowdfunding Crossing Borders' (2016) 32 <https://drive.google.com/file/d/0B7uykMX1rDrWU3BRZTBMNzF-wLVE/view>; Klaes et al (n 36) 37, 217–218.

46 See about France, Macchiavello 'Financial-return' (n 4) 702.

47 ESMA (n 12) 21ff.

(including conflicts of interest, investors' best interest, remuneration practices, risk management, valuation of assets, liquidity, disclosure to investors), including marketing to professional clients-only, unless national laws state differently.

Business models structured as allowing the automatic matching of subscription and issuing orders (marketplace model) or the creation of 'secondary' marketplaces to re-sell financial instruments, can trigger the regulation of trading venues unless they function as mere bulletin boards, therefore only advertising buying and selling interests, without matching multiple orders in a way to result in a contract.[48]

Therefore, depending on national interpretations and their flexibility as well as different business models, it might not be straightforward to reconnect crowdfunding activities to MiFID II investment services, conceived with traditional infrastructures and providers in mind. In fact, IBC could entail certain aspects and functions of investment services (eg, transfer of economic resources for financing productive activities; information asymmetry reduction) in a simplified way, combining at times different aspects (eg, mixing fragments of placing, reception/transmission and markets). IBC also significantly relies on technology, different communication methods (simple documents, video, pitches, forums and feed-backs) and rules (eg, 'all-or-nothing'; 'signalling'). In doing so, it reduces costs and the distance between investees (smaller private companies instead of big public companies) and investors (reducing the number of intermediaries and entailing a sense of involvement and a lower level of separation between ownership and control[49]), while shrinking SMEs' financing gap.[50]

If we completely fit IBC into existing regulatory regimes, we may deny its innovative character and positive effects (SMEs' funding). Furthermore, both PR and MiFID II, conceived with the traditional sector in mind, might, on the one hand, not improve investor protection (conveying complex and numerous information under the assumption of an intermediary assistance, without specific warnings) and, on the other, represent a disproportionate burden for platforms and small issuers.

Finally, crowdfunding STOs raise the additional issues (addressing which would require a separate chapter) about the legal qualification of the blockchain and token-exchanges under EU financial law, the applicability of the latter to such new structures (partially decentralised), the identification of the governing law considering the global ramification of DLT-networks, the variety of both securities transferability rules and regulatory responses in Member States.[51]

---

48 See recital 8 MiFIR (600/2014, OJ [2014] L173/84). Lithuania prohibits crowdfunding platforms to manage systems allowing the trade of crowdfunding financial instruments (while unregulated markets of loans or other investment products are permitted) unless organised as MTFs and managed by authorised investment firms or MTF operators (Art. 5(2)–(3) Law on Crowdfunding of 3 November 2016); Italy allows platforms to set up bulletin boards pertaining to financial instruments (equity and bonds) only in a separate section of the platform's website and in the form of 'windows' for buy/sell interests without any facilitation by the platform (new Art. 25b Consob Crowdfunding Regulation No. 18592/2013 as modified by Consob Resolution of 6 February 2020): see Macchiavello 'Financial-return' (n 4) 702; Macchiavello (n 6) 15–16.

49 About the related scarce success of dual-class shares in crowdfunding: Cumming and Johan (n 10) Ch 12.

50 On the differences between crowdfunding and traditional intermediaries see also Arash Gholamzadeh, 'Equity Crowdfunding: Beyond Financial Innovation', in Brüntje and Gadja (n 36) 201ff; Pierrakis and Collins (n 22) 3–4.

51 See chapters by Schilling and Lee in this Book.

3.2 *Special national crowdfunding regulations*

Some countries have decided to introduce special regimes for IBC,[52] distinguishing it from MiFID investment services (eg, Spain) or assimilating it either to the reception and transmission of orders (eg, Italy, Germany) or investment advice (France) or both (Belgium), without the holding of clients' assets, and therefore recurring to Art. 3(1)-(2) MiFID II exemption. Certain Member States apply the same special regime for both IBC and LBC (Spain, Portugal, Belgium).

The procedure and requirements to obtain the authorisation under these special regimes are simple: the governance requirements are that managers and major shareholders must be fit and proper and certain minimum initial capital or professional insurance requirements must be met. The regimes are generally quite light and focused on disclosure. The disclosure document focuses on concise and clear information about risks, costs, selection criteria and performance, with warnings about specific risks and lack of authority's approval. Other business conduct rules apply, such as fair conduct and efficient orders management, while due diligence in recipients' selection is required only in France and Spain. Only the UK and Lithuania envisage a prudential 'own funds' requirement. On the other hand, the activities that platforms may carry out are limited,[53] such as prohibition to offer other investment products,[54] services and holding clients' money/securities. Most countries – except in France, Italy and Lithuania – have also introduced limits to the sums that retail or nonsophisticated investors (except when receiving regulated advice: Spain and UK) may invest per project and per year. An investor test or appropriateness assessment is required in Italy, UK (when retail, in absence of regulated advice), the Netherlands, Lithuania and Belgium. A suitability assessment is instead mandatory in France (where platforms are investment advisors) and Belgium (only when platforms offer investment advice).

Additional investor protection measures for retail investors have been implemented in some countries, such as withdrawal rights (eg, Italy, UK, Austria, Germany and Netherlands) or redress mechanisms/ADRs (Portugal, France, Netherlands and the UK), while only Italy has introduced tag-along rights in case of change of control and the mandatory pre-investment by professional investors. Some countries expressly apply anti-money laundering (AML/CT) regulations to platforms (UK, Austria, Portugal and Germany).

---

52 Austria, Belgium, Netherlands, Spain, France, UK, Italy, Germany, Portugal, Finland, Lithuania.

53 For example, maximum offering size ranging from €1 million (eg, Portugal) to €2/2.5 million (Spain, Netherlands, Germany) or €5 million (France, having raised both the general and, since AMF *Ordonnance 2019*-1067, crowdfunding ones to €8 million): Macchiavello (n 6); Macchiavello, 'Financial-return' (n 4).

54 For instance, in France, first, only ordinary shares, fixed-interest bonds and '*bons de caisse*' were covered, then also mini-bonds (even transferable through blockchain), preference shares, convertible bonds, participation instruments and shares in cooperative limited companies (Art. L547-1 and D547-1 *CMF* as lastly modified by *Décret* No. 2019-1097); in Italy, originally, only shares of innovative start-ups but progressively also shares of all SMEs (s.p.a. or s.r.l.) and, since law 145/2018, also bonds of the same companies; in Austria, various investment products (shares, bonds, participations in private liability companies and cooperatives, participation rights, silent partnerships) below a certain size threshold, but only subordinated loans to SMEs (Art. 1, § 2 *AltFG*; § 3(1)10a *Kapitalmarktgesetz*), not to violate the banking monopoly; in Germany, for the same reasons, only subordinated loans and profit-participation loans but, starting July 2019, also profit participation rights, below certain thresholds (Sections 1(2) and 2(a) *VermAnIG*).

Most regimes also allow traditional financial institutions to conduct crowdfunding operations (except Spain) but generally subject the same, in addition to their regime, to the specific crowdfunding requirements.[55]

4 The introduction of the European crowdfunding service providers regulation

The Commission has been looking at crowdfunding as an important alternative source of funding for SMEs and, after recognising significant obstacles to cross-border activity, especially in terms of regulatory fragmentation,[56] presented in March 2018 a proposal for a regulation on European Crowdfunding Service Providers (ECSPs),[57] within its Capital Markets Union program and FinTech Action Plan.

Nonetheless, the legislative process progressed slowly, also because of the differing views about FRC among the Commission, European Parliament[58] and Council[59] that emerged during trilateral negotiations. The final version, which revises the original Proposal in several important aspects, was eventually agreed on 19th December 2019. At the time of writing, the Council has adopted the agreed version on 20th July 2020, but adoption by the European Parliament is outstanding before being published in the Official Journal.[60] This paragraph discusses the main aspects of the Regulation based on the version adopted by the Council on 20th July 2020.[61]

The ECSPs Regulation will introduce a mandatory European regime for crowdfunding platforms, requiring any legal person willing to offer crowdfunding services covered by such Regulation to apply (once the transitional period expires) for new authorisation from the NCA of the Member State of establishment.[62] This applies also, after a (second optional) transitional period, in the case of platforms operating only nationally. The authorisation, ensuring a European passport, is conditional on certain

---

55 See in Italy and Belgium (Art. 5§2 *loi crowdfunding*) as regards conduct rules and in Lithuania as regards prudential and fit & proper requirements (Art. 7(6) and 8(7) Crowdfunding Law); France, instead applies to regulated providers their own regime only (L547-1, IV): Macchiavello (n 6) 18 (ft 62).

56 Commission (n 26) 3–7; Klaes et al (n 36). About updated data on cross-border activity: Ziegler et al (n 11) 88.

57 Commission (n 26).

58 European Parliament, 'Legislative Resolution of 27 March 2019 on the Proposal for a Regulation [...] on [...] ECSP for Business' <http://www.europarl.europa.eu/RegData/seance_pleniere/textes_adoptes/provisoire/2019/03-27/0301/P8_TA-PROV(2019)0301_EN.pdf>.

59 Council of the EU, 'Proposal for a Regulation [...] on ECSP for Business. Mandate for Negotiations with the European Parliament-Compromise Proposal' (24 June 2019) <https://data.consilium.europa.eu/doc/document/ST-10557-2019-INIT/en/pdf>.

60 <https://www.consilium.europa.eu/en/press/press-releases/2020/07/20/capital-markets-union-council-adopts-new-rules-for-crowdfunding-platforms/>.

61 Position of the Council at first reading with a view to the adoption of a Regulation [...] on European crowdfunding service providers for business, and amending Regulation (EU) 2017/1129 and Directive (EU) 2019/1937, available at <https://data.consilium.europa.eu/doc/document/ST-6800-2020-INIT/en/pdf>. For a more detailed analysis and references: Macchiavello (n 8); Macchiavello (n 6).

62 The Commission had originally not only proposed an optional regime (label-like, in competition with national and MiFID-regimes) but also ESMA as supervisory authority, while the Parliament/Council (and agreed version) subsequently favoured a national competence, assigning ESMA only a role to ensure consistent procedures/practices in the authorisation process, coordinating cooperation, with data collection and binding dispute resolution powers.

ordinary requirements, such as business plan, adequate internal organisation, 'fit and proper' managers, business continuity arrangements, professional insurance cover, and, under the revised text, the description and evidence of certain prudential safeguards and of adequate systems for complying with other conduct and organisational requirements (including managing operational risk, data processing, complaint handling, outsourcing; verifying the completeness, correctness and clarity of the information and the respect of investment limits).[63]

The status as ECSPs would apply to both business-LBC and IBC platforms but, as regards the latter, only when pertaining to transferable securities and – a new category of – 'admitted instruments' (ie, shares of limited liability companies not considered financial instruments under national law), and for offers not exceeding €5 million in total consideration within 12 months.[64] The regime, in exemption from MiFID II, only covers crowdfunding activities, defined as 'the matching of business funding interest of investors and project owners through the use of a crowdfunding platform'. These are only identified, as regards IBC, with the services corresponding to the MiFID II placing without firm commitment and reception and transmission of orders combined (with filtering systems based on objective criteria not accounting as investment advice and the pricing -of debt-instruments-being allowed but conditional on additional requirements). Considering the difficulties and national differences in reconnecting crowdfunding services with investment ones, *ad hoc* definitions or clarifications would have appeared preferable to simply accommodating under MiFID II.

Systems allowing the exchange among clients of products previously subscribed through the platform ('bulletin boards') are also permitted but cannot present characteristics that resemble trading venues. In particular, platforms can only publish on their website indications of the clients' buy/sell interests, specifying that they are not regulated trading venues, that the exchanges are under the exclusive responsibility of investors and, where a price is suggested, that this is not binding. The requirement to conclude the transaction offline, obviously reduces bulletin boards' effectiveness and market liquidity.

ECSPs will be allowed to offer additional services (complying with the relevant laws), but if they perform other regulated services such as payment, custodian or banking services and other investment services, they would need separate authorisation. This chapter argues that Regulation (or its secondary acts) still needs to clarify the boundaries between the ECSPs regime and other regimes, in particular whether national crowdfunding regimes can survive.[65]

ECSPs are subject to a regime mimicking the MiFID one but simplified. Under the original proposal, it was primarily based on general conduct rules, such as to act honestly, fairly and professionally in accordance with the best interests of their clients, in addition to

---

63 Art. 12ff.

64 Initially, the Commission had proposed €1 million, while the Parliament and the Council raised the threshold to €8 million, the latter introducing the possibility for Member States to set lower limits according to their transposition of the PR (and, in case, also to prohibit offers above €5 million from raising any capital from their residents), with a significant risk of fragmentation, hindering cross-border activities. The approved version now allows Member States to maintain lower thresholds in line with their Prospectus rules only for a transitional period of 24 months (new Art. 1(2) and 49).

65 For example, in case of natural persons operating IBC platforms; reception/transmission of orders only or investment advice exempted under Art. 3 MiFID II; investment funds; offers between €5 million and €8 million, etc.

disclosure obligations. Nonetheless, the adopted version, following the Council's suggestions, has significantly extended ECSPs' duties also in terms of organisational, risk management and prudential requirements.

As regards disclosure obligations, ECSPs have to provide clients (and potential clients),
before they enter into the contract, with information (including marketing information)
about themselves, the costs, the financial risks and charges related to crowdfunding services
or investments, the crowdfunding project selection criteria and the nature and risks associated with crowdfunding services (including capital loss, illiquidity and insolvency risk).
They also need to inform their clients about the lack of a deposit guarantee or securities
compensation coverage, the four-day reflection period for un-sophisticated investors (see
below) and, when the platform performs credit scoring/pricing, the calculation method
used. All information must be fair, clear and not misleading, and, depending on the type,
published on a clearly identified section of their website or prominent place of medium, in
a non-discriminatory manner.

With reference to single offers, ECSPs have to provide clients with a Key Investor
Information Sheet (KIIS), based on the KID-PRIIPs (Regulation No 1286/2014 on pack-
aged retail and insurance-based investment products) model (six pages maximum, without
footnotes) and prepared by the project owner. The original Commission proposal required
ECSPs to only verify the completeness and clarity of the KIIS but the current version also
refers to the 'correctness' of the document (an expression requiring further clarifications).[66]
This position shows anyway policy-makers' intention to ensure that platforms act not only
as intermediaries but also as gatekeepers for investor protection. Besides certain fundamental information about the specific project owner, instrument and conditions of the offer,
in particular as regards risks, main terms, price and fees, the KIIS will contain several
warnings, such as about the lack of control/approval by supervisory authorities, of deposit/
investment guarantee schemes or of a proper appropriateness test, about the specific risks
as well as about the opportunity not to invest more than 10% of their own net worth (see
below).

The final version of the Regulation, following the Council's suggestions, introduces the
new category of 'non-sophisticated' investors[67] and provides for them special protections.
In particular, ECSPs, before allowing non-sophisticated investors to access the offers,
must perform an 'entry-knowledge test'. This test aims at verifying whether and which
crowdfunding services are appropriate for them considering their past investments in transferable securities, admitted instruments and loans and their understanding of risks and
professional experience about crowdfunding investments.[68] Non-sophisticated investors
must also use platforms' systems to simulate their ability to bear loss, calculated as 10% of

---

66 Art. 23(11).
67 Non-sophisticated investors are those not included in the categories of professional investors and
   sophisticated investors. In particular, while the former category is defined in MiFID II, the latter consists in investors declaring to be aware of the relative consequences and with certain evidences of high
   net worth or investment experience (eg, legal entities in terms of own funds/turnover/balance sheet;
   natural persons in terms of gross income and financial portfolio): Annex II.
68 New Art. 21(1)-(4). The entry-knowledge test (to be repeated every two years) resembles a form of
   appropriateness test (assessment of knowledge, skills and experience; in case of a negative result, issuance of a warning with client's acknowledgement) but less product-specific and performed at an earlier
   stage. The final version incoherently requires ECSPs to collect information also about clients' financial
   situation (needed however for the loss simulation test) and investment objectives (like a 'digital' suitability test: see Parliament's version), also with potential GDPR implications.

their net worth.[69] Additional measures for non-sophisticated investors added are an explicit warning in case of investment above €1,000 or 5% of the client's net worth, which must be agreed to by the investor, and a four-day withdrawal right.[70]

ECSPs are also subject to organisational requirements[71]: adequate measures to ensure an effective and prudent management, including the segregation of duties, business continuity and conflict of interest prevention and management; management of operational risk coming from outsourcing; complaints handling. Special requirements apply in case of pricing services, for example, that platforms present policies and procedures ensuring reasonable prices, using factors and criteria indicated by EBA and ESMA. ECSPs cannot have any financial participation in the offers, not even when aligning platforms' and clients' interests. They can accept their managers, employees and controlling shareholders only as investors (not as project owners) and conditional on disclosure and equal terms. The final version of the Regulation also requires ECSPs to undertake a minimum level of due diligence in respect of project owners, as regards criminal records (for infringements of commercial, insolvency, financial services, AML/CT, fraud laws and professional obligations) and whether there is establishment in non-cooperative jurisdictions (in AML/CT terms). Finally, the current version has also embraced the Council's suggestion to introduce prudential safeguards for operational risk, mainly consisting in CET1 requirements, in alternative to or combination with a professional insurance.[72] This chapter considers that the Regulation could have also provided explicit cyber security and certain direct AML/CT obligations. The regime will be detailed and completed by a number of ESMA/EBA's technical standards.[73]

Regulated providers (banks, investment firms, payment services and e-money providers) are allowed to access the ECSPs regime through a simplified procedure. Furthermore, they are exempt from the above-mentioned prudential safeguard for crowdfunding services when already subject to capital adequacy requirements for operational risk.[74] Although the Regulation is not explicit is this regard, they might need to comply only with conduct of business and investor protection requirements specific to ECSPs Regulation.

5 Conclusions

The functions performed by IBC platforms resemble in some respects but are partially different from regulated investment firms. Arguably, IBC deserves a different treatment based on certain differences from the traditional sector, such as in relation to small unlisted issuers, the absence of traditional protections (eg, guarantee schemes and authority's checks, and consequent low level of investor reliance), new techniques for evaluation and mitigation of issuer risk (eg, co-investing, feed-backs, small ticket-size and diversification, etc.), special risks and the need for lowering funding costs for SMEs (especially in this post-crisis-financial and COVID-19 era). Nonetheless, designing such a regime for diversified models of 'intermediation without intermediaries' while protecting investors appears difficult.

---

69 Art. 21(5)-(6). This might recall a suitability test but does not pertain to investment objectives and a negative result does not impede the investment, only requiring an acknowledgement from the client.

70 New Art. 21(7) and 22.

71 New Art. 4–8.

72 The higher between €25,000 and ¼ of overheads of the previous year.

73 For example, about pricing/scoring criteria and factors; governance and procedures for risk management and complaint handling.

74 Art. 11(3).

The original ECSPs Proposal had tried to characterise IBC – not without certain contradictions – as mid-way between a minimalist intermediary[75] and more 'involved' intermediation.[76] It had intended to balance investor protection with ECSPs and project owners' costs, designing, on the one hand, a light regime with relevant limitations in terms of maximum offering size, permissible products and activities; on the other hand, new, technologically based and simplified (but, hopefully, effective) investor protection measures (eg, entry-knowledge test, loss simulation system) and synthetic and comprehensible documents with warnings. In doing so, it had created an 'alternative' segment of the financial sector where investors would be considered more self-responsible and trusted with taking informed decisions despite investing in risky companies.

The approved version seems to share the same vision only partially. On the one hand, it correctly clarifies and extends the Regulation coverage, improves and focuses the protections around non-sophisticated investors and introduces a minimum due diligence obligation on platforms as regards project owners, as suggested in my previous contributions. On the other hand, it substantially increases and details ECSPs requirements and responsibilities (but more significantly for marketplace lending), making the authorisation process and regime more rigid and complex and, consequently, the compliance with the same expensive. This seems to significantly 're-intermediate' IBC, making it less 'alternative', but might appear justified by an investor protection rationale. Nonetheless, it might end up excessively reassuring investors, while limiting both the financial inclusion effect of and the need for such Regulation since platforms, obtaining a MiFID II licence, would be able to offer more services, with fewer restrictions but similar requirements (with the relevant exception of product governance requirements).

Anyway, considering the rise of ICOs/STOs even in the crowdfunding sector and the additional issues raised, an EU position also on the regulatory treatment of such phenomena, also in connection with the ECSP Regulation, cannot be postponed any further.

Bibliography

A K Agrawal, C Catalini and A Goldfarb, 'Some Simple Economics of Crowdfunding' (2013) NBER Working Paper 19133/2013.

J Armour and L Enriques, 'The Promise and Perils of Crowdfunding: Between Corporate Finance and Consumer Contracts' (2018) 81(1) Mod L Rev 51.

G Borello et al, 'The Funding Gap and The Role of Financial Return Crowdfunding: Some Evidence from European Platforms' (2015) 20(1) JIBC 1.

I H Chiu, 'Fintech and Disruptive Business Models in Financial Products, Intermediation and Markets-Policy Implications for Financial Regulators' (2016) 21(1) J Tech L & Pol'y 55.

CrowdfundingHub, 'Crowdfunding Crossing Borders' (2016), <https://drive.google.com/file/d/0B7uykMX1rDrWU3BRZTBMNzFwLVE/view>.

D Cumming and S Johan, *Crowdfunding. Fundamental Cases, Facts, and Insights* (Academic Press 2019).

D Cumming, M Meoli and S Vismara, 'Does Equity Crowdfunding Democratize Entrepreneurial Finance?' (2019) Small Bus Econ, <https://doi.org/10.1007/s11187-019-00188-z>.

D Cumming, S Johan and Y Zhang, 'The role of due diligence in crowdfunding platforms' (2019) 108 J Bank Finance 1.

---

75 See for instance the classification as reception and transmission of orders, strict conflicts of interest policy and lack of platform's responsibility for the KIIS or explicit due diligence checks.

76 See the classification also as placing, the possibility to use discretion on orders and only the duty to make available to investors (not necessarily to perform) the loss-simulation test.

European Commission, 'Unleashing the Potential of Crowdfunding in the European Union' (Communication), COM (2014) 172 final.

European Securities and Markets Authority (ESMA), 'Opinion on Investment-based Crowdfunding' ESMA/2014/1378 (2014).

G Ferrarini and E Macchiavello, 'Investment-Based Crowdfunding: Is MiFID II Enough?' in D Busch and G Ferrarini (eds), *Regulation of EU Financial Markets: MiFID II* (OUP 2017).

Financial Stability Board (FSB), 'Decentralised Financial Technologies. Report on Financial Stability, Regulatory and Governance Implications' (2019) <www.fsb.org/wp-content/uploads/P060619.pdf>.

S Hooghiemstra and K de Buysere, 'The Perfect Regulation of Crowdfunding: What Should the European Regulator Do?' in Dennis Brüntje and Oliver Gajda (eds), *Crowdfunding in Europe* (Springer 2016).

E Kirby and S Worner, 'Crowd-funding: An Infant Industry Growing Fast' (2014) IOSCO Research Department Staff Working Paper 3/2014.

M Klaes et al, *Identifying Market and Regulatory Obstacles to Crossborder Development of Crowdfunding in the EU* (European Commission 2017).

O Lobel, 'The Law of the Platform' (2016) 101(1) Minn L Rev 87.

E Macchiavello, 'Peer-To-Peer Lending and the "Democratization" of Credit Markets: Another Financial Innovation Puzzling Regulators' (2015) 21(3) CJEL 521.

E Macchiavello, 'Financial-Return Crowdfunding and Regulatory Approaches in the Shadow Banking, Fintech and Collaborative Finance Era' (2017) 14(4) ECFR 662.

E Macchiavello, 'What to Expect When You Are Expecting' a European Crowdfunding Regulation: The Current "Bermuda Triangle" and Future Scenarios for Marketplace Lending and Investing in Europe' (2019) EBI Working Paper 55/2019.

E Macchiavello, 'FinTech Regulation from a Cross-Sectoral Perspective' in V Colaert, D Busch and T Incalza (eds), *European Financial Regulation: Levelling the Cross-Sectoral Playing Field* (Hart 2019).

E Macchiavello, 'The European Crowdfunding Service Providers Regulation and the Future of Marketplace Lending and Investing in Europe: The "Crowdfunding Nature" Dilemma' (2021) forthcoming in EBLR <https://papers.ssrn.com/sol3/papers.cfm?abstract_id=3668590>.

Organization for Economic Co-operation and Development (OECD), 'Initial Coin Offerings (ICOs) for SME Financing' (2019) <http://www.oecd.org/finance/ICOs-for-SME-Financing.pdf>.

Organization for Economic Co-operation and Development (OECD), *An Introduction to Online Platforms and Their Role in the Digital Transformation* (OECD 2019).

Y Pierrakis and L Collins, 'Crowdfunding: A New Innovative Model of Providing Funding to Projects and Businesses' (2013) <https://papers.ssrn.com/sol3/papers.cfm?abstract_id=2395226>.

P Schammo, 'Market Building and the Capital Markets Union: Addressing Information Barriers in the SME Funding Market' (2017) 2 ECFR 271.

A Schwartz, 'Crowdfunding Issuers in the United States' (2020) 61 J Law Policy 155.

A Schwienbacher, 'Equity Crowdfunding: Anything to Celebrate?' (2019) 21(1) Venture Capital 65.

A Schwienbacher and B Larralde, 'Crowdfunding of Small Entrepreneurial Ventures' in D Cumming (ed), *The Oxford Handbook of Entrepreneurial Finance* (OUP 2012).

D A Zetzsche and C Preiner, 'Cross-Border Crowdfunding – Towards a Single Crowdfunding Market for Europe' (2018) 19(2) EBOR 217.

T Ziegler et al, 'The Global Alternative Finance Market Benchmarking Report' (2020) <https://www.jbs.cam.ac.uk/fileadmin/user_upload/research/centres/alternative-finance/downloads/2020-04-22-ccaf-global-alternative-finance-market-benchmarking-report.pdf>.

Part VI

Cryptocurrencies and cryptoassets

17 Cryptoassets in private law

Jason Grant Allen

1 Introduction

So-called 'cryptoassets' are becoming a mainstream lawyerly concern. The rise of cryptoassets is perhaps not the most important aspect of current developments in financial technology ('Fintech') – they remain, after all, a relatively small asset class in the scheme of the global financial system.[1] But it is no longer possible to dismiss them as insignificant, as it may have been some years ago, for (at least) three reasons. First, a broader cross-section of market participants now has some kind of exposure to the cryptoasset market, including an increasing number of financial intermediaries. Secondly, cryptoassets are thus interacting with conventional legal institutions (like the trust and the corporation), and parties to cryptoasset transactions have already begun to seek vindication of their legal rights in the courts.[2] Finally, if the more enthusiastic cryptoasset proponents are taken seriously, the cryptoassets currently circulating are but a harbinger of things to come – the technology they utilise, in the near to middle term, may fundamentally change the financial system and will compound with other developments in Fintech such as the application of artificial intelligence ('AI').

A literature has grown up around the topic, including on the legal and regulatory issues cryptoassets potentially raise. Much of this literature, however, focuses on regulatory rather than private law issues. Core questions, such as whether and how cryptoassets can be owned, and whether the 'owner' of cryptoassets can avail herself of proprietary remedies, were somewhat overlooked in the first instance, but have been attracting more attention more recently.[3] In a recent analysis, Sir Geoffrey Vos drew two distinctions in the context of 'smart contracts' and cryptoassets in English law – the first between 'law' and 'regulation' and the second between 'rights' and 'remedies':

> One must understand the underlying legal position before one starts to regulate the use of smart contracts and cryptoassets. What will ultimately be of most significance to those using smart contracts will be the remedies that they can obtain when things go wrong. But, like regulation, one cannot reliably ascertain the appropriate remedies, before one has properly analysed the legal rights with which one is dealing.[4]

---

1 See BIS, 'Basel Committee invites comments on the design of a prudential treatment for crypto-assets' (BIS Press Release 12 December 2019) https://www.bis.org/press/p191212.htm. (Call-off date for all URLs: 25 March 2020).
2 See eg, *AA v Persons Unknown* (2019) EWHC 3556 (Comm) (Bryan J).
3 See eg, David Fox and Sarah Greene (eds), *Cryptocurrencies in Public and Private Law* (Oxford University Press 2019).
4 Sir Geoffrey Vos, 'End-to-End Smart Legal Contracts: Moving from Aspiration to Reality' (2020) 26(1) Journal of Law, Information and Science EAP 1, EAP 6.

In this chapter, I will focus on the legal rather than the regulatory position of cryptoassets, although I will discuss both rights and remedies.

The structure of this chapter is as follows: Section 2 deals with the appropriate definition of 'cryptoassets'. The terminology has changed over the years, as a result of both market practices and regulatory interventions. The definition I adopt is that advocated in the *CCAF Global Regulatory Landscape Study* of 2018.[5] This definition distinguishes between 'cryptoassets, properly so called' and 'digital assets' more generally, which may or may not utilise some kind of distributed ledger technology (DLT). This is an alternative approach to the familiar trichotomy of 'payment', 'security' and 'utility' tokens.

Sections 3 to 6 then discuss specific issues in private law. I have structured each section around a verb that may or may not apply straightforwardly to cryptoassets: 'owning', 'holding', 'transferring', and 'encumbering'. The specific private law issues raised by cryptoassets will differ from legal system to legal system, as will the responses possible within each legal system. Generally, the theme is of the interaction between conventional, established legal categories and new socio-technical phenomena. Of all the issues raised by cryptoassets in private law, the property law issues are foundational. Section 7 deals briefly with the question of 'smart contracts', that is, the software processes that automate many of these legal operators and thus may need to be taken into account in cryptoasset-related cases.

Some words of delimitation are appropriate. First, this chapter is comparative, from the perspective of a common lawyer. That, in itself, presents an initial challenge – it is difficult to compare legal systems, both because the range of issues to explore is thereby increased and because the methodology of comparison is contested.[6] But the transnational nature of the subject matter requires such scope.[7] There are precedents for rigorous comparative property law,[8] and even a garden-variety Commonwealth lawyer could be said to be a native comparatist in a limited sense.[9] At the risk of being a tourist,[10] it is also useful to contrast

---

5 Apollin Blandin, Ann Sofie Cloots, Hatim Hussain, Michel Rauchs, Rasheed Saleuddin, J G Allen, Bryan Zhang and Katherine Cloud, 'Global Cryptoasset Regulatory Landscape Study' (Cambridge Centre for Alternative Finance and Nomura Research Institute April 2019) <https://www.jbs.cam. ac.uk/fileadmin/user_upload/research/centres/alternative-finance/downloads/2019-04-ccaf-global-cryptoasset-regulatory-landscape-study.pdf>.

6 See Martin van Hoeke, 'Methodology of Comparative Legal Research' (2015) *Law and Method*, DOI: 10.5553/REM/.000010, 1.

7 See J G Allen and R M Lastra, 'Border Problems: Mapping the Third Border' (2020) 83(3) Modern Law Review 505.

8 See in particular Christian von Bar, *Gemeineuropäisches Sachenrecht Band I* (CH Beck 2015); see also Sjef van Erp, 'From "Classical" to Modern European Property Law' in Faculty of Law of the National and Kapodostrian University of Athens (ed), *Essays in Honour of Konstantinos D Kerameus* (Sakkoulos/Bruylant 2009).

9 'In a historical sense it may well be true to say that common lawyers are comparative lawyers despite themselves and even though they may not know it, because their whole training is based on the comparative development of principles derived from English law'. R H Graveson, 'The Task of Comparative Law in Common Law Systems' (1959) 34(4) Indiana Law Journal 573, 578.

10 '[C]omparatists often act like tourists who visit a foreign city and notice that things are different, be it to some extent similar too, compared to their home-town. After their visit they will be able to describe what they have seen to their family and friends at home, but they will lack a more general framework used, for instance, by specialists in architecture or art historians to describe the same sights in a (very) different way'. Martin van Hoeke, 'Methodology of Comparative Legal Research' (2015) *Law and Method*, DOI: 10.5553/REM/.000010, 7.

the common law approach with the conceptual schemes found in the Civilian property law tradition. This chapter cannot be taken as an exhaustive treatment of the subject matter in any given jurisdiction, but rather as a roadmap for terrain that might have to be explored soon.

Secondly, I will focus on national private law issues in a comparative perspective, and will for the most part bracket out private international law aspects from the present treatment. Private international law adds a further layer of complexity, comprising rules of national law that refer, in some cases, to the application of the substantive private law of another jurisdiction.

Thirdly, while this chapter presents some of the solutions that have been proposed to the problems identified, it will not attempt any systematic comparison of those solutions, their relative merits or their suitability for use in other legal systems. That said, it is immediately apparent that some issues will be more easily solved in some legal systems than in others, and that some solutions are more readily transplantable. At one end of the spectrum are the persuasive reasons given by one common law court in a judgment. At the other end are significant changes to fundamental legal concepts in codified jurisdictions. Some solutions, for example, would simply entail too high a 'systemic cost' to be considered seriously in the immediate term – they would require a sustained law reform process. By this, I mean the degree of intervention required in the prevailing law, and the degree of risk of disruption, to accommodate cryptoassets. At a fairly high level of abstraction, then, I will permit myself some observations on the kind of solution possible in different legal systems, but will not develop this analysis – that is work, ultimately, for scholars of the relevant national law.

Finally, this chapter will not deal with the regulatory and public law aspects of cryptoassets, including, for example, capital markets, consumer protection, anti-money laundering. Nor will it deal with questions arising from the use of cryptoassets as money – for example, with questions of monetary law arising from certain applications of cryptoassets as media of payment or stores of value.[11] Nor will it deal with procedural law issues.[12]

In other words, the aim of this chapter is to get the basic categorisation of cryptoassets right, such that they can be integrated without undo friction (eg, without changing the law more than is strictly necessary) into the complex mechanics of private law transactions; further, it aims to introduce the range of private law issues on which work must be done both by lawyers working within a national law, comparatists working across national law and those involved in the development of transnational and international legal norms.

11 See generally Simon Gleeson, *The Legal Concept of Money* (Oxford University Press 2019); see also David Fox and Sarah Green (eds), *Cryptocurrencies in Public and Private Law* (Oxford University Press 2019).
12 See eg, Marc Schmitz and Patrick Gielen (eds), *Avoris dématérialisés et exécution forcée. Digital Assets and Enforcement* (Bruylant 2019).

2 Definitions

The definition of 'cryptoassets' is not straightforward, and several definitions are now current in the literature.[13] As with any definition, perhaps the most important things are to remain consistent with the definition one adopts, and to avoid speaking at cross-purposes on the basis of divergent definitions. If these two rules are followed, getting the definition 'absolutely' right is often not strictly necessary. However, the definition of cryptoassets is very important, and skipping this preliminary issue compounds the difficulty of issues that inevitably arise later.

Taxonomies of the new digital 'tokens'[14] that have emerged often express some version of the trichotomy of 'payment', 'security', and 'utility' tokens. This approach looks attractive, at first blush, because it refers to the function of the token and brings certain tokens effectively under existing regulation. However, these regulatory-driven taxonomies fail to identify what is truly novel – and therefore legally challenging – about 'cryptoassets' from a private law perspective. The focus of this chapter is therefore on the nature and substance of 'cryptoassets', that is, on the rights and obligations they confer on their holder, and on their main economic purpose. The fact that a given asset may take different forms does not change the nature of the asset: a company share that takes the form of a 'security token' is still a company share.

The first substantive question, then, is whether we should distinguish between 'cryptoassets' and 'digital assets' as a more general category that also includes conventional entities. The approach one adopts to answering this question depends on assumptions about the desirability (and feasibility) of technology neutrality and the level of conceptual generality to which we aspire. Counter-intuitively, these taxonomies obscure the central question and rather lead to less technology neutrality – suggesting a difference between conventional digital company shares and 'security tokens', for example. Again, counter-intuitively, a degree of technology-*specificity* in the first instance might actually help to identify the salient differences in the subject matter and yield a more rational approach overall.[15]

In my view, it is necessary to distinguish between (i) data-based objects 'endogenous' to an open, permissionless DLT system, which play an indispensable role in the economic incentive design of the underlying shared ledger and (ii) data-based objects that represent something 'exogenous' to that system, be it a right against a counter-party or rights in

13 I take it as a given that we should not discuss 'cryptocurrencies' in the first instance, as that is question-begging; we are concerned with 'cryptoassets' which may or may not be used in a currency-like way. This is the direction of travel in the official terminology, too: see Apollin Blandin, Ann Sofie Cloots, Hatim Hussain, Michel Rauchs, Rasheed Saleuddin, J G Allen, Bryan Zhang and Katherine Cloud, 'Global Cryptoasset Regulatory Landscape Study' (Cambridge Centre for Alternative Finance and Nomura Research Institute April 2019) 35 for an instructive visual chart.

14 I use 'tokens' with reservation because the term has very different connotations in computer science and payments law, respectively. In the former, a 'token' is a programming object that represents the ability to *perform an action* in a software system. To this extent, 'token' is entirely appropriate. However, the word at least connotes a tangible object (such as a banknote) and the term can be misleading, for example, in the phrase 'token-based payment system'. See also David Fox, 'Cryptocurrencies in the Common Law of Property' in David Fox and Sarah Green (eds), *Cryptocurrencies in Public and Private Law* (Oxford University Press 2019) para 6.18.

15 See in particular Chris Reed, 'Taking Sides on Technology Neutrality' (2007) 4(3) SCRIPT-ed 264.

something like a commodity.[16] Data-based objects in category (ii) should not be referred to as 'cryptoassets' at all. Nothing is gained by so calling them. DLT enables new kinds of expressiveness and functionality, and may raise new questions of ownership, custody and transfer; there may be different mechanics for the transfer, loss, theft or forgery of the company share, but it is not categorically different to a company share in a non-DLT digital information repository. It does not need a new legal category but can, in my view, fit within existing categories like *res incorporales* and *choses in action*.[17]

That is not the case for 'cryptoassets' properly so called. They are not easily subsumed within existing categories in any legal system, as I explain in Section 3, below.

In other words, the crucial difference is whether the 'token' represents *exogenous value*, not whether it utilises DLT. What the narrow approach makes clear is that the definitive characteristic of 'cryptoassets' is their stand-alone nature; a cryptoasset, unlike a conventional financial asset that is recorded using DLT, does not represent anything external to the technical system in which it operates. It 'represents' only itself, the fact of its own existence. Further, such cryptoassets play an essential role in the technical functioning of the system. This is for the simple reason that if they did not play an essential role in the function of the system, no one would treat them as being worth anything at all. This is the essential starting point from which analyses of cryptoassets and other digital assets should proceed. In the balance of this chapter, I will focus on cryptoassets narrowly defined, although my analysis will necessarily touch on digital assets more broadly.

3 Owning cryptoassets

Perhaps the cardinal question is whether cryptoassets can be property, or, in a more Civilian idiom, whether they can be *objects of property rights*. In general terms, the answer to this is a fairly obvious 'yes', but there are a number of qualifications necessary depending on the context. Logically, there are a number of approaches available to us. Previously I argued:

> When confronted with an entity that defies straightforward placement in our catalogue of all that exists and is the case, we have three options: (i) we can deny the intuitive fact that it exists (ie, it is a legally cognisable entity) at all; (ii) we can shoehorn it into an existing category; or (iii) we can reform our catalogue.[18]

---

16 See Apollin Blandin, Ann Sofie Cloots, Hatim Hussain, Michel Rauchs, Rasheed Saleuddin, J G Allen, Bryan Zhang and Katherine Cloud, 'Global Cryptoasset Regulatory Landscape Study' (Cambridge Centre for Alternative Finance and Nomura Research Institute April 2019) 16. The distinction between endogenous and exogenous data objects was a point of discussion among experts at a joint UNCITRAL/UNIDROIT workshop on 10–11 March 2020; while different views were presented, this criterion was identified as perhaps the most important single characteristic for developing a taxonomy of digital assets.

17 *Res incorporales* (literally 'incorporeal things') is the traditional concept for reified rights in the Civilian tradition. *Choses in action* (literally and alternatively 'things in action') are intangible objects that can only be 'had' by taking legal action; this is the traditional concept for reified rights in the common law tradition. See generally J G Allen, 'Property in Digital Coins' (2019) 8(1) European Property Law Journal 64.

18 J G Allen, 'Property in Digital Coins' (2019) 8(1) European Property Law Journal 64, 76. See also Sjef van Erp, 'Ownership of Digital Assets and the Numerus Clausus of Legal Objects' (2017) 6 Property Rights Conference Journal 235.

There, I argued that it is perhaps time to revise our catalogue of 'objects of property rights' in order to accommodate digital objects – including but not limited to cryptoassets – and that recent developments provide a good context for some much-needed housekeeping.

Here, the importance of the 'narrow view' becomes clear: different questions arise in the context of the ownership of cryptoassets. All legal systems have some way of reifying certain intangible, incorporeal, non-spatial objects (usually rights) and treating them as objects of property rights up to and including ownership. In the Civilian legal tradition, the concept of *res incorporales* has traditionally recognised that (certain) rights can be the object of property rights.[19] In the common law tradition, several types of intangible real and personal property are recognised, including 'incorporeal hereditaments' and '*choses in action*'. Civilian legal systems in the Germanic tradition take a restrictive approach to the category of *res incorporales*.[20] However, even in these systems things like company shares are treated as objects of some property rights, if not the right of ownership, as I explain below.

This being the case, it seems to me that while significant doctrinal work might be needed to bring pre-modern and early modern conceptual frameworks into the digital era,[21] there is no fundamental impediment to incorporating DLT-based data objects into the catalogue of 'objects of property rights'. In the first instance, this will be a matter of recognising that they are *res incorporales* or *choses in action* (as appropriate) in the relevant system of property law. The same devices that have been used for the past several decades to incorporate older digital assets will be available for DLT-based digital assets. This may require some finessing, but does not present any 'system-breaking' challenges. Recent efforts at the international level towards a sensible regulation of 'electronic transferable records' may also serve as a guideline and encourage harmonisation across legal systems.[22] This is not to say that the existing regimes are entirely satisfactory, either conceptually or practically, or that they are future-proof. Problems exist concerning intermediation, for example, and the exact nature of the property rights in question – especially in a cross-border context. But the point is that a legal regime, such as it is, is in principle available for DLT-based digital assets that evidence rights in some underlying asset, whether that asset be (i) rights against a counter-party or (ii) rights in another asset (be it a physical object, a right against a counter-party, or indeed a cryptoasset).

The same cannot be said of cryptoassets narrowly defined, which do not evidence anything except their own existence, in the technical system. Cryptoassets either exist as an object of value in their own right, or they do not exist in the eyes of the law at all.

The concrete challenges this presents will differ from legal system to legal system. We can (very roughly) group the world's systems into three camps. At one end we have the common law systems, where the question is really about the breadth of the category of *choses in action*. The conventional wisdom is that personal property cleaves neatly into *choses in action* and *choses in possession*, and that 'the law knows no *tertium quid* between the

---

19 See generally G L Gretton, 'Ownership and Its Objects' (2007) 71 Rabels Zeitschrift 802.

20 See Christian von Bar, *Gemeineuropäisches Sachenrecht Band I* (CH Beck 2015) 140–141.

21 Particularly in in those systems that insist on a paper global certificate. See Part II of Eva Micheler, *Property in Securities: A Comparative Study* (Cambridge University Press 2007), and Ch 12 in particular. For example, the German Civil Code §793 requires a paper certificate for 'negotiable instruments' [*Schuldverschreibungen auf Inhaber*, literally 'debt writings to bearer'].

22 See UNCITRAL Model Law on Electronic Transferable Records (2017) <https://uncitral.un.org/en/texts/ecommerce/modellaw/electronic_transferable_records>.

two'.[23] The choice is between making the category *choses in action* broad enough to cover bitcoins (for example) and recognising a third category. Whichever of these approaches is taken, however, common law systems law should not struggle to recognise property rights in cryptoassets.[24]

On the other end of the spectrum, as alerted to above, cryptoassets directly challenge the position in legal systems like Germany, Greece, Portugal, the Netherlands, Hungary, Japan and Poland, which all adopt a conception of 'thing' that excludes intangible objects and expressly restrict the right of ownership to 'things'.[25] To take German law as an example, cryptoassets might be recognised as 'objects' [*Gegenstände*] of lesser property rights, they are not 'things' [*Sachen*] and cannot be the object of the right of ownership [*Eigentum*].[26] It seems fairly clear that proprietary remedies like *vindicatio* cannot extend to cryptoassets in such systems, as the well-known Mt Gox insolvency proceedings in Japan illustrate.[27] *Prima facie* to make cryptoassets 'things' capable of being objects of the right of ownership as such under the German civil code (for example) would require amendment of § 90 in the General Part.[28] This would cut against the grain of the system built around it, and entail consequences that are difficult to foresee.[29]

In the middle of my rough classification would fall the Civilian and mixed legal systems that are more accommodating of *res incorporales*, but adopt a confusing terminological and conceptual apparatus. For example, French law makes various types of incorporeal objects moveable property '*par la determination de la loi*'.[30] There may be a need for some more fundamental re-evaluation of the existing categories in such systems,[31] but at least the fundamental obstacle faced by systems in the Germanic tradition is not present.

This notwithstanding, I think it is less of a question of *whether* cryptoassets will be recognised by legal systems as objects of property rights, and rather a question of how to solve the practical and conceptual difficulties that arise from the *way they are recognised*. In this regard, we can contrast two approaches by early moving jurisdictions. In England and Wales, the UK Jurisdiction Taskforce of the LawTech Delivery Panel *Legal statement on cryptoassets and smart contracts*,[32] which has been followed by the High Court of England

---

23 *Colonial Bank v Whinney* (1885) 30 Ch D 261 (Court of Appeal), 285 (Fry LJ). See UK Jurisdiction Taskforce, *Legal statement on cryptoassets and smart contracts* (UK LawTech Delivery Panel November 2019) 66–84.

24 See *AA v Persons Unknown* (2019) EWHC 3556 (Comm), [59] (Bryan J).

25 See Christian von Bar, *Gemeineuropäisches Sachenrecht Band I* (CH Beck 2015) 86, 140–145.

26 German law, for example, deals with incorporeal objects under the indefinite category of 'objects' [*Gegenstände*] as opposed to 'things' [*Sachen*]. I harbour misgivings about the internal coherence of this approach, but that is something for another day. See also generally Daniel Carr, 'Cryptocurrencies as Property in Civilian and Mixed Legal Systems' in David Fox and Sarah Greene (eds), *Cryptocurrencies in Public and Private Law* (Oxford University Press 2019) Ch 7 on 'cryptocurrencies' as *res* in Civilian and mixed systems.

27 An English paraphrase of the judgment of the Tokyo District Court is available at <https://www.law.ox.ac.uk/sites/files/oxlaw/mtgox_judgment_final.pdf>.

28 § 90 BGB reads: 'Concept of the thing. Only corporeal objects are things as defined by law'.

29 A literature is growing in German law concerning the work-around. See eg, Sebastian Omlor and Alexandra Spiegel, 'Blockchain-basierte Zahlungsmittel im Geld- und Währungsrecht' in Florian Möslein and Sebastian Omlor, *FinTech Handbuch: Digitalisierung, Recht, Finanzen* (CH Beck 2019).

30 French *Code Civil* Art. 529.

31 See eg, Myriam Rousille, 'Le bitcoin: object juridique non identifié' (2014) 158 Banque et Droit 27.

32 UK Jurisdiction Taskforce, *Legal statement on cryptoassets and smart contracts* (UK LawTech Delivery Panel November 2019).

and Wales, has taken the approach of incorporating cryptoassets into the general law of property.[33] Liechtenstein, by way of contrast, has enacted a special legislative regime that accommodates cryptoassets under the concept of *Wertrechte* (literally 'value rights' derived from the German word for securities, *Wertpapiere*, literally 'value papers').[34] Because the Liechtenstein property law restricts the concept of 'things' to corporeal objects, recognition of cryptoassets would require a 'deep intervention' in the general law with wide-ranging consequences; the decision was thus taken to create a parallel 'autonomous' regime to govern property rights in tokens based on 'trustworthy technology' (eg, blockchain).[35] The merit of this approach in the short to medium term is obvious. Whether problems will arise in the longer term remains to be seen; I would feel some unease about 'autonomous' regimes proliferating in parallel. A broadly similar approach is currently under consideration in Germany, where § 2 (3) of a proposed Statute on Electronic Securities [*Gesetz über elektronische Wertpapiere*] deems certain electronic securities to 'count as things within the meaning of § 90 of the German civil code'.[36] Such an approach implicitly undermines the choice to define 'things' axiomatically and presents the risk that similar objects may be treated differently under the law of property and various laws of pseudo-property, respectively.

4 Holding cryptoassets

It is common to speak of 'holding' a cryptoasset, which would seem to imply having some kind of right in the cryptoasset. This should not be taken to lead automatically to concepts like 'holder in due course', for reasons I will explain below, but rather to an analogy with 'holding' a right. It expresses the idea – whether descriptive or aspirational – that the 'holder' of a cryptoasset has rights in it, which reveals the core assumption: that changes to the state of a distributed ledger effect changes in the state of legal reality, such that the legal position of parties is changed.

Sometimes it is difficult to talk about performing legal operations with cryptoassets at all, because the verbs we use beg the very question. For example, as we have seen, referring to someone as the 'owner' of bitcoins is not straightforward in many important legal

---

33 For example, see *AA v Persons Unknown* (2019) EWHC 3556 (Comm) (Bryan J) [57]: '[T]he legal statement is not in fact a statement of the law. Nevertheless, in my judgment, it is relevant to consider the analysis in that Legal Statement as to the proprietary status of crypto currencies because it is a detailed and careful consideration and, as I shall come on to, I consider that that analysis as to the proprietary status of crypto currencies is compelling and for the reasons identified therein should be adopted by this court'.

34 On the different terminology used for 'securities', see Giuliano G. Castellano, 'Towards a General Framework for a Common Definition of 'Securities': Financial Markets Regulation in Multilingual Contexts' (2012) XVII Uniform Law Review 449.

35 See Ministerium für Präsidiales und Finanzen, *Vernehmlassungsbericht der Regierung betreffend die Schaffung eines Gesetzes über auf Vertrauenswürdigen Technologien (VT) beruhende Transaktionssysteme (Blockchain-Gesetz; VT-Gesetz; VTG) und die Abänderung weitere Gesetze* (16 November 2018) <https://www.llv.li/files/srk/vnb-blockchain-gesetz.pdf>; see also Gesetz vom 3. Oktober 2019 über Token und VT-Dienstleister <https://www.gesetze.li/konso/pdf/2019.301> and in English <https://www.regierung.li/media/medienarchiv/950_6_08_01_2020.pdf?t=2>.

36 See *Referentenentwurf des Bundesministeriums der Justiz und für Verbraucherschutz und des Bundesministeriums der Finanzen Entwurf eines Gesetzes zur Einführung von elektronischen Wertpapieren,* https://www.bmjv.de/SharedDocs/Gesetzgebungsverfahren/Dokumente/RefE_Einfuehrung_elektr_Wertpapiere.pdf?__blob=publicationFile&v=1.

systems, and should be avoided. Likewise, the concept of 'possession' differs considerably between legal systems, but is generally defined in terms that presuppose a tangible object; it is not clear that the law of possession can carry over to incorporeal objects at all.[37] The classic example from English law is the ruling in *OBG v Allan*[38] that intangibles cannot be the subject matter of the tort of conversion, because that tort requires possession.[39] While it might be possible to stretch the concept of possession to embrace data objects, less is gained than is potentially lost. In my view, the major cost of 'stretching' is the lost opportunity of developing concepts tailored to the digital nature of cryptoassets. In this context, then, it is best to say what one actually means. What we mean in the context of cryptoassets is surely something like 'control', that is, that if I have the private key, I control the ledger entry which represents the notional cryptoasset. 'Control' was adopted in the UNCITRAL Model Law on Electronic Transferable Records for this reason.[40] In my view, it provides a better starting point for thinking about how one 'holds' cryptoassets.

The details of how cryptoassets are 'held' will, like ownership, be jurisdiction-specific. They will also depend on the technological features and business models employed in the market. The major distinction to notice here is between 'custodial' and 'non-custodial' control. 'Custody' is used loosely to describe a variety of different arrangements. Cryptoassets, as I have defined them, all use public-key cryptography. In such systems, value is stored at an 'address' (akin to an account number) derived from one's public key, and a private key (akin to a password) is used to authorise ('sign') a change to the state of the ledger moving value from one address to another. Software programs, so-called 'wallets', handle the management of these key pairs. There are different types of wallet. 'Hot storage' refers to a wallet connected to the Internet; 'cold storage' refers to arrangements where the private keys are stored in a non-connected, physical storage medium. Another important difference is whether the wallet is 'custodial' or 'non-custodial'. The former involves the storage of private keys by a third-party service provider.[41] In some cases the custodian can authorise changes to the state of the ledger unilaterally; in so-called 'multisig' systems, the 'holder' of the cryptoasset will need to provide a signature too. The main point to make in this regard is that the 'custodian' holds the *private keys, not the cryptoassets* (whatever the latter are said to be); in other words, the custodian holds the password that allows modifications of the ledger, not the value represented in ledger-entries. This makes 'custody' somewhat inapt, as custody connotes a relationship where one person keeps a thing for another.

Custody arrangements add a further level of complexity to analyses of the ownership situation set out in Section 3, above. Where a wallet provider, for example, controls the

---

37 See J G Allen, 'Negotiability in Digital Environments' (2019) 7 Butterworths Journal of International Banking and Finance Law 459; Christian von Bar, *Gemeineuropäisches Sachenrecht Band I* (CH Beck 2015) 80; *Gray v G-T-P Group Ltd* [2010] EWHC 1772 (Ch) (Vos J). See *contra* Geoffrey Yeowart, Robin Parsons, Edward Murray and Hamish Patrick, *Yeowart and Parsons on the Law of Financial Collateral* (Edward Elgar 2016) Ch 8.

38 [2007] UKHL 21.

39 See *contra* Sarah Green, 'To Have and to Hold? Conversion and Intangible Property' (2008) 71(1) Modern Law Review 114.

40 See Elena Christina Zaccaria, 'An Enquiry into the Meaning of Possession and Control over Financial Assets and the Effects on Third Parties' (2018) 18(1) Journal of Corporate Law Studies 217, 221; see also *Gray v G-T-P Group Ltd* (2010) EWHC 1772 (Ch) (Vos J).

41 See Michel Rauchs, Apolline Blandin, Kristina Klein, G C Pieters, Martino Recanati and Bryan Zhang, *2nd Global Cryptoasset Benchmarking Study* (Cambridge Centre for Alternative Finance 12 December 2018) 49 <https://ssrn.com/abstract=3306125>.

private keys of 'my' cryptoassets, the correct legal analysis might be that the wallet provider is the owner and that I have some other right – whether 'real' or 'obligational' – against them. It will also complicate the analysis of 'transfer', which I deal with immediately below. In custodial arrangements, transfers of cryptoassets occur 'off-chain', which means that the wallet provider remains in control of the private keys that control the relevant cryptoasset values, and when I buy and sell cryptoassets I am merely trading rights against the wallet provider (presumably obligational, rather than real) without any changes to the ledger. Such situations rely wholly, if implicitly, on the assumption that the ambient law, presumably the law of some state, takes care of the necessary legal mechanics. This means that there is a whole segment of the cryptoasset ecosystem which has less to do with blockchain and more to do with the conventional law than is commonly recognised. In my view, the legal framework for this segment is at this stage radically under-determined.

5 Transferring cryptoassets

Accepting that one holds (and possibly even owns), one's cryptoassets, the next question is how one 'transfers' them to another user within the system. Here, again, the terminology is not completely satisfactory. When I 'transfer' a bitcoin to you, for example, there is no endurant thing that passes from me to you. The 'coin' is purely notional, as David Fox explains: the 'coin' representing input to the transaction at public key A is destroyed and replaced by another 'coin' representing transaction output at public key B; in this system, value flows by the 'consumption and creation of distinct informational entities at each public key'.[42] What we are really talking about in the 'transfer' of cryptoassets is the *legal and economic meaning* that the community of users ascribe to changes of the state of the Bitcoin blockchain.

However, we routinely talk of 'transferring' bank account deposits ('book-money') to each other, and the law can tolerate the implicit metaphor in this type of usage. It should be remembered that no cryptoasset is actually a 'digital bearer instrument' (let alone 'digital cash') to the extent that nothing subsists through the transfer of *value* from one public key 'address' to another. Our analysis, then, should look at the transactional details of the 'transfer' in light of the technology it uses and the legal relationships at play.[43] There are many issues that could be discussed under this heading – for example, the intricacies of 'transfer' of cryptoassets held in a 'cold' versus 'hot' wallet or in a custodial versus a non-custodial wallet. These will surely raise difficult questions in the context of national law and, to the extent that it may be difficult to locate a distributed ledger, private international law as well.[44]

Instead of trying to gloss all these issues, however, I will focus on the core question: whether, and, if so, why changes to the state of a distributed ledger should effect changes to the state of legal reality – to the *legal* position of parties – at all.

42 David Fox, 'Cryptocurrencies in the Common Law of Property' in David Fox and Sarah Greene (eds), *Cryptocurrencies in Public and Private Law* (Oxford University Press 2019) 6.18.
43 See eg, Tatiana Cutts, 'Modern Money Had and Received' (2018) 38(1) Oxford Journal of Legal Studies 1.
44 See eg, Matthias Lehmann 'Who Owns Bitcoin? Private Law Facing the Blockchain' (2019) 21 Minnesota Journal of Law, Science & Technology 93; Michael Ng, 'Choice of Law for Property Issues Regarding Bitcoin under English Law' (2019) 15(2) Journal of Private International Law 315.

In ledger, registry and account systems, the entry of data in a repository plays a constitutive role in the creation of financial assets (which as we have seen are really reified rights against a counterparty or in another asset). With cryptoassets, the establishment of the distributed ledger also creates the notional 'coins' which, although they do not represent rights to anything, are treated by the market as 'tokens' of value. In ledger, registry and account systems, alteration of the data stored in the repository is constitutive of changes in the legal title to the assets it presents. In English law, for example, changes by a company secretary to the Register of Members of an English limited liability company creates and transfers 'company shares'.

Conventional ledgers, registers and accounts have required a central counterparty to instantiate the repository and ensure that only amendments compliant with the system are made to it, such that a degree of legal effect can be given to the register. Certain forms of DLT circumvent the need for a central 'clerk' to keep the ledger – but they have not changed the essential nature of a ledger. Absent the clerk, however – who is a target for regulation and legal accountability – it is an open question what legal effect any given change to the state of the ledger ought to be given. There are several options available: a change to the ledger might be (i) legally irrelevant, (ii) evidential, with a greater or lesser degree of probity or (iii) dispositive, such that the ledger is taken to be indefeasible proof of the legal state of affairs.

One encounters arguments based on the technical 'immutability' of blockchain technology that claim the third kind of legal effect. But the fact that a record is tamperproof with a high degree of probabilistic certainty is, frankly, nothing to the point. There are plenty of scenarios – involving dodgy custodians, common or garden fraud, or buggy 'smart contracts' – that will, in my view, lead parties to seek assistance from the law to reverse cryptoasset dealings on blockchains because they claim that the state of the ledger does not reflect the proper state of affairs in legal reality. In my view, distributed ledgers (like all ledgers) will almost always be relevant, but they will never be dispositive – they will always be of evidential value only.

There is one other important issue in the context of transferring cryptoassets. One sometimes reads that cryptoassets should be considered as something like 'digital bearer instruments'.[45] In my view, this approach is mistaken. The law of negotiable instruments is an ingenious way to transfer intangible financial assets (ie, rights) by enclosing them in a paper instrument, such that the financial assets move from the transferor to the transferee of the paper instrument 'free and clear' even when the transferor's title was somehow defective. But the law of negotiable instruments presupposes an *instrument*; without the tangible paper instrument, there is no need for the mechanics of negotiable instruments law to achieve the situation that the transferee gets better title than the transferor had.[46] Looking at the substance of a cryptoasset transaction, we are more concerned with the law of *registers*. A register, too, can provide *prima facie* or even indefeasible evidence of title such that the same outcome is achieved, and it is to the law of registers that I think we should turn if analogies are needed.

45 See eg, R3, Shearman & Sterling LLP and BAFT, 'Code is not Law: The Legal Background for Trade Finance Using Blockchain' (6 July 2018).
46 See in this regard the numerous writings of J S Rogers, including J S Rogers, 'Negotiability, Property, and Identity' (1990) 12 Cardozo Law Review 472 and J S Rogers, *The End of Negotiable Instruments: Bringing Payment Systems Law Out of the Past* (Oxford University Press 2012).

6 Encumbering cryptoassets

Finally, the question arises whether and how – short of transferring my title in cryptoassets *holus bolus* – I might grant a third-party rights over them. For example, I might wish to grant a lender a security interest in the current balance of my bitcoin wallet in order to obtain a USD loan, or I might want to declare a trust over cryptoassets in favour of my nephew. The scenarios that will arise will be diverse, not least because different legal systems recognise a different catalogue of 'partial', 'lesser', or 'accessory' rights that can encumber title. There might appear a common core of property rights that can encumber another's right of ownership – familiar faces such as pledges, usufructs, charges, etc., crop up in many different legal systems. But there are great differences in how these rights are conceptualised and catalogued in legal systems around the world, and this will impact on the way that cryptoassets are treated in private law. We have seen that not all legal systems straightforwardly recognise ownership of cryptoassets; there is a high degree of idiosyncrasy in which of the 'lesser' rights can be held in intangibles, too.[47]

Again, I am unable to offer any systematic analysis of these issues. I will make a few brief points. The first is that interesting cases are likely to arise in situations where a party wishes to treat cryptoassets in 'cold storage' separately from the storage medium. What would we make of a trust settlement that purported to give a computer to A and the cryptoassets in 'cold storage' on its hard drive to B, for example? Such questions require us to engage more closely with the legal treatment of data and force us to articulate a more satisfactory theory of what it is about cryptoassets that makes them more than 'just' data.[48] Questions of this nature are likely to arise in the context of insolvency proceedings, where priority is an important and hard-fought issue. With reference to Section 5 above, encumbrances on cryptoassets are likely to arise in cases where transferees seek title free and clear despite an admitted defect in the transferor's title. Such cases are difficult, because they deal with the competing interests of two innocent parties.

Encumbrances are particularly difficult in the case of cryptoassets (narrowly defined) because the systems on which the encumbrance is said to operate will often have been designed with the exclusion of 'conventional law' in mind. There is no readily obvious way for a judge to make an order to amend the state of a blockchain to reflect the fact that a party's cryptoassets are encumbered with third party rights, or indeed for anyone to enforce such an order on recalcitrant counterparties. As cryptoassets become increasingly mainstream, and parties turn to the courts for assistance, this might begin to seem more like a bug than a feature.

7 Smart contracts

There is a close connection between cryptoassets and what have become known as 'smart contracts'. Here, too, lurk difficult definitional questions. What we are actually talking about in this context is software that manipulates the records assumed to evidence property rights in digital assets within a DLT system, on the occurrence of conditions but without

47 For examples, see Christian von Bar, *Gemeineuropäisches Sachenrecht Band I* (CH Beck 2015) 316–319.
48 See UK Jurisdiction Taskforce, *Legal statement on cryptoassets and smart contracts* (UK LawTech Delivery Panel November 2019) 59 and following.

necessary human intervention. The alternative nomenclature of 'transactional scripts' has recently been suggested, quite sensibly in my view.[49]

These transactional scripts are assumed to interact with the ambient legal order(s) in which they operate, but the exact mode of their interaction is contested. In some seminal contributions by Nick Szabo, 'smart contracts' interact minimally with legal order – they provide a parallel, technical regime that achieves the same outputs as law, but better.[50] The position advanced more recently by legal scholars is quite different. It is that, to the extent that transactional scripts (or any other technological artefact) automate performance, they implicitly encode the terms of the legal relationship in the context of which performance takes place, and therefore comprise part of a legal 'contract stack'.[51]

Transactional scripts will add complexity and urgency to the legal analysis of all the questions set out above. The most important thing to remember is that the state of a ledger is, from the legal perspective, only ever evidential. There may be practical issues in dealing with automated transactions, and in some cases the technical features of open, permissionless DLT systems might effectively preclude recourse to state courts. But these issues will be practical, rather than conceptual.

8 Conclusion

This chapter has moved through a number of issues at a trot, and at the high level of abstraction necessary to ensure relevance in different legal systems. The most important point is that, for the purposes of analysing private law issues, a narrow definition of cryptoassets should be adopted. This is somewhat orthogonal to the trichotomies of 'security', 'utility' and 'exchange' tokens that tend to circulate in the context of regulation.

Adopting this narrow definition is essential to clear-eyed analysis of the private law issues that arise in the context of financial assets that just happen to utilise DLT, which are susceptible of much more conventional legal analysis, and in the context of cryptoassets such as bitcoins, which raise novel issues.

These issues will differ considerably from system to system. Some of them, in some systems, may be achieved through private law means (eg, appropriate drafting) and others by courts and other authorities taking a pro-active interpretative approach; others, in other systems, may require dedicated legislative intervention and the model of this intervention will likely track the path-dependencies and legacy structures within the relevant system.

It is not necessarily straightforward to apply all the usual legal verbs to cryptoassets; lawyers in both transactional and litigious work and legal scholars should consider carefully what any given operator *actually involves* in the context of open, permissionless DLT systems and adjust the terminology and conceptual apparatus as appropriate. One should prefer 'control' to 'possession' and similar words, for example. In particular, it is important to use analogies carefully and to choose the appropriate category from which

---

49 Shaanan Cohney and D A Hofmann, 'Transactional Scripts in Contract Stacks' (2020) Faculty Scholarship at Penn Law 2138. Ethereum co-founder Vitalik Buterin has expressed a preference for a term like 'persistent scripts' <https://twitter.com/vitalikbuterin/status/1051160932699770882?lang=en>.

50 See eg, Nick Szabo, 'Formalising and Securing Relationships on Public Networks' (originally published 1997) <https://nakamotoinstitute.org/formalizing-securing-relationships/>.

51 See also J G Allen, 'Wrapped and Stacked: "Smart Contracts" and the Interaction of Natural and Formal Language' (2018) 14(4) European Review of Contract Law 307.

to draw analogies. The law of registers, for example, may be more apt than the law of negotiable instruments to achieve indefeasible transfers of title despite a defect in the transferor's title.

Bibliography

J G Allen, 'Wrapped and Stacked: "Smart Contracts" and the Interaction of Natural and Formal Language' (2018) 14(4) European Review of Contract Law 307.

J G Allen, 'Negotiability in Digital Environments' (2019) 7 Butterworths Journal of International Banking and Finance Law 459.

J G Allen, 'Property in Digital Coins' (2019) 8(1) European Property Law Journal 64.

J G Allen and R M Lastra, 'Border Problems: Mapping the Third Border' (2020) 83(3) Modern Law Review 505.

C von Bar, *Gemeineuropäisches Sachenrecht Band I* (CH Beck 2015).

BIS, *Basel Committee Invites Comments on the Design of a Prudential Treatment for Crypto-Assets* (BIS Press Release 12 December 2019).

A Blandin, A S Cloots, H Hussain, M Rauchs, R Saleuddin, J G Allen, B Zhang and K Cloud, *Global Cryptoasset Regulatory Landscape Study* (Cambridge Centre for Alternative Finance and Nomura Research Institute 2019).

G Castellano, 'Towards a General Framework for a Common Definition of "Securities": Financial Markets Regulation in Multilingual Contexts' (2012) XVII Uniform Law Review 449.

S Cohney and D A Hofmann, 'Transactional Scripts in Contract Stacks' (2020) Faculty Scholarship at Penn Law 2138.

T Cutts, 'Modern Money Had and Received' (2018) 38(1) Oxford Journal of Legal Studies 1.

S van Erp, 'From "Classical" to Modern European Property Law' in Law Faculty of the National and Kapodostrian University of Athens (ed), *Essays in Honour of Konstantinos D Kerameus* (Sakkoulos/Bruylant 2009).

S van Erp, 'Ownership of Digital Assets and the Numerus Clausus of Legal Objects' (2017) 6 Property Rights Conference Journal 235.

D Fox and S Green (eds), *Cryptocurrencies in Public and Private Law* (Oxford University Press 2019).

S Gleeson, *The Legal Concept of Money* (Oxford University Press 2019).

R H Graveson, 'The Task of Comparative Law in Common Law Systems' (1959) 34(4) Indiana Law Journal 573.

S Green, 'To Have and to Hold? Conversion and Intangible Property' (2008) 71(1) Modern Law Review 114.

G L Gretton, 'Ownership and Its Objects' (2007) 71 Rabels Zeitschrift 802.

M van Hoeke, 'Methodology of Comparative Legal Research' (2015) Law and Method, DOI: 10.5553/REM/.000010.

M Lehmann, 'Who Owns Bitcoin? Private Law Facing the Blockchain' (2019) 21 Minnesota Journal of Law, Science & Technology 93.

E Micheler, *Property in Securities: A Comparative Study* (Cambridge University Press 2007).

Ministerium für Präsidiales und Finanzen Liechtenstein, *Vernehmlassungsbericht der Regierung betreffend die Schaffung eines Gesetzes über auf Vertrauenswürdigen Technologien (VT) beruhende Transaktionssysteme (Blockchain-Gesetz; VT-Gesetz; VTG) und die Abänderung weitere Gesetze* (16 November 2018).

F Möslein and S Omlor, *FinTech Handbuch: Digitalisierung, Recht, Finanzen* (CH Beck 2019).

M Ng, 'Choice of Law for Property Issues Regarding Bitcoin under English Law' (2019) 15(2) Journal of Private International Law 315.

R3, Shearman & Sterling LLP and BAFT, 'Code is not Law: The Legal Background for Trade Finance Using Blockchain' (6 July 2018).

M Rauchs, A Blandin, K Klein, G C Pieters, M Recanati and B Zhang, *2nd Global Cryptoasset Benchmarking Study* (Cambridge Centre for Alternative Finance 12 December 2018).

C Reed, 'Taking Sides on Technology Neutrality' (2007) 4(3) SCRIPT-ed 264.

J S Rogers, 'Negotiability, Property, and Identity' (1990) 12 Cardozo Law Review 472.

J S Rogers, *The End of Negotiable Instruments: Bringing Payment Systems Law Out of the Past* (Oxford University Press 2012).

M Rousille, 'Le Bitcoin: Object Juridique non Identifié' (2014) 158 Banque et Droit 27.

M Schmitz and P Gielen (eds), *Avoris dématérialisés et exécution forcée. Digital Assets and Enforcement* (Bruylant 2019).

N Szabo, 'Formalising and Securing Relationships on Public Networks' (1997) <https://nakamotoinstitute.org/formalizing-securing-relationships/>.

UK Jurisdiciton Taskforce, *Legal Statement on Cryptoassets and Smart Contracts* (UK LawTech Delivery Panel November 2019).

Sir G Vos, 'End-to-End Smart Legal Contracts: Moving from Aspiration to Reality' (2020) 26(1) Journal of Law, Information and Science EAP 1.

G Yeowart, R Parsons, E Murray and H Patrick, *Yeowart and Parsons on the Law of Financial Collateral* (Edward Elgar 2016).

E C Zaccaria, 'An Enquiry into the Meaning of Possession and Control over Financial Assets and the Effects on Third Parties' (2018) 18(1) Journal of Corporate Law Studies 217.

18 Cryptocurrencies

Development and perspectives

Michael Anderson Schillig

1 Introduction

What happens when Alice pays Bob in cash in discharge of a payment obligation? By handing over cash, Alice obtains an immediate and irreversible discharge of a pre-existing liability. For Alice it is impossible to retrieve her money without Bob's cooperation or a court order. Conversely, Bob does not have to enquire whether Alice was the rightful owner of the coins and notes received[1]; at the same time the discharging effect of payment will be final.[2] As a consequence, trust between the parties is irrelevant; all that matters is that both parties have trust in the underlying cash: in the sense that both are confident that it can be used for the immediate discharge of Alice's obligation to Bob and of Bob's own obligations to his creditors.[3] Since time immemorial, payment between parties who are not present in the same geographical location at the same time, could only be effectuated by relying on trusted third parties. Compared to payment in cash, this has a number of weaknesses: in addition to the risk that the third party acts maliciously, there is an inherent risk of uncertainty: Alice may still be able to revoke her payment order under certain circumstances.[4] Non-reversible payments for non-reversible services are not really possible under a system that relies on third-party intermediaries.[5] Attempts to electronically replicate (some of) the attributes of cash by relying on cryptographic primitives go back to 1983, culminating in David Chaum's DigiCash. However, all earlier attempts relied on a central authority acting as a clearinghouse for transaction verification and processing.[6] The original contribution of Satoshi Nakamoto[7] was the combination of existing technologies (distributed databases, public-key cryptography, cryptographic hash functions and Merkle trees) to create a peer-validated decentralised system for secure value transfers without central control: the blockchain as a 'new technological milestone'.[8] Over the last decade,

---

1 S Gleeson, *The Legal Concept of Money* (OUP 2018) 7.29–7.35.
2 Ibid., para 7.84.
3 Ibid., para 1.48.
4 For example, *Rekstin v Severo* (1933) 1 KB 47 (CA); *Momm v Barclays Bank International Ltd* (1977) QB 790.
5 S Nakamoto, 'Bitcoin – A Peer-to-Peer Electronic Cash System' (2008) https://bitcoin.org/bitcoin.pdf, 1.
6 A Narayanan, J Bonneau, E Fleten, A Miller and S Goldfeder, *Bitcoin and Cryptocurrency Technologies* (Princeton University Press 2016) XIII–XVIII; P De Filippi and A Wright, *Blockchain and the Law: The Rule of Code* (Harvard University Press 2018) 18–19.
7 Nakamoto (2008).
8 P Tasca and C Tessone, 'Taxonomy of Blockchain Technologies. Principles of Identification and Classification' (2017) https://papers.ssrn.com/sol3/papers.cfm?abstract_id=2977811, 2.

Bitcoin and some altcoins came to represent substantial amounts of value and crypto-currencies have emerged as a new asset class.[9] As an area of constant innovation, the cryptocurrency ecosystem is expanding very quickly, the surrounding policy debates keep shifting and legal development is trying to keep pace. Section 2 charts the emergence of cryptocurrencies with a focus on their underlying technological properties and provides an overview of important current legal issues. Section 3 discusses the most recent iterations within the cryptocurrencies space and tries to anticipate the legal challenges that may arise in the future. Section 4 concludes.

2 The emergence of cryptocurrencies

Bitcoin was launched in January 2009 after decades of experimenting with unsuccessful digital cash systems. Today coinmarketcap.com lists more than 800 cryptocurrencies and tokens with a market capitalisation exceeding $1,000,000 each.[10] These various 'altcoins' seek to offer superior cryptocurrency properties and/or additional function-alities. With improvements to transaction throughput[11] and decreased volatility[12] the acceptance of cryptocurrencies, not just as speculative assets, but also as stores of value and media of exchange is likely to become ever more widespread.[13] It is therefore inev-itable that, in addition to regulatory concerns, fundamental legal issues of general pri-vate and commercial law arise.

2.1 *Bitcoin and early altcoins*

Bitcoin seeks to replicate the advantages of a cash payment for online value transfers, 'allowing any two willing parties to transact directly with each other without the need for a trusted third party'.[14] The Bitcoin protocol tracks value[15] as a chain of transaction outputs.[16] At the protocol level, there are no coins or tokens, no senders or recipients and no balances or accounts. All these concepts are constructed by applications that provide the user interface and operate on top of the Bitcoin protocol.[17] Each transac-tion references as input a previous transaction and creates outputs of certain amounts with specific conditions for spending these unspent transaction outputs (UTXO). Spending conditions, in their simplest form, consist of a 'bitcoin address' derived from the 'recipient's' public key, so that the output value can be unlocked (spend) by

---

9 C Proctor, 'Cryptocurrencies in International and Public Law Conceptions of Money' in D Fox and S Green (eds) *Cryptocurrencies in Public and Private Law* (OUP 2019) 33, 40.

10 https://coinmarketcap.com/all/views/all/.

11 As 'Layer 2' technologies, the Lightning Network (https://cointelegraph.com/lightning-network-101/what-is-lightning-network-and-how-it-works) or Plasma (https://www.theblockcrypto.com/post/10793/understanding-plasma-part-1-the-basics) operating on top of the Bitcoin and Ethereum blockchains, allow transactions to be processed in seconds.

12 Section 3.1 below.

13 'Over 700% Surge in Worldwide Venues accepting Bitcoin in the Last 5 years' (February 2019) available at https://bitcoin.co.uk/over-700-percent-surge-worldwide-venues-accepting-bitcoin-last-5-years/.

14 Nakamoto (2008) 1.

15 In the sense of Gleeson (2018) para 1.48.

16 Nakamoto (2008) 2.

17 A Antonopoulus, Mastering Bitcoin (2nd edn, O'Reilly 2017) 145–148.

providing the matching digital signature derived from the corresponding private key as proof of 'ownership' of the output value.

Without more, the 'recipient' of an UTXO would still be able to spend the same value twice by creating two conflicting transaction messages that both reference the same UTXO as input, but contain divergent spending conditions in form of different 'bitcoin addresses'.[18] In order to address the double-spending problem, the Bitcoin protocol chains together blocks of data items, creating a chain of data blocks or blockchain, which has to be published widely so as to prove that the respective data existed at a certain moment in time (when the block was added to the chain).[19] This requires decentralisation: the relevant data must be publicly announced and, following announcement, must be independently stored in multiple places; otherwise a data controller would be able to change already published data without others being able to easily verify whether such tampering has occurred. Consequently, transactions are bundled together in blocks and the blocks are chained together through cryptographic hashes. A hash is taken of the block header, which includes a hash of the previous block (header) and a summary of all transactions contained in the current block in form of their Merkle root.[20] Transmitting the block across the peer-to-peer network provides proof that a particular transaction, spending an UTXO, was included in the block. The hash of each subsequent block includes the hash of the previous block, linking them together.[21] When a new transaction is submitted, the nodes in the network scan the entire chain of previous blocks to ascertain whether the referenced input UTXO has already been spent in a previous transaction, in which case the transaction will be rejected as 'invalid'.[22] This requires that all participating nodes agree on a single version of the transaction history. In a distributed peer-to-peer network without a coordinating central authority, this is achieved through computer software that provides the decision-making process in form of a consensus protocol. Trust is shifted from a central authority to the consensus protocol instead. Bitcoin relies on a 'proof-of-work' consensus: (some) participating nodes (miners) expend computing power to solve a 'cryptographic puzzle', in the form that the hash of a new block (header) must fall below a certain target range of value (must start with a certain number of 0s). This can only be achieved by trial and error: the transaction data of the new block and the hash of the previous block are repeatedly hashed together with a changing random variable (*nonce*) until the hash meets the prescribed target requirement. The miner who solves the puzzle first proposes the new block to be added to the chain and, if accepted by the peers, will earn the mining reward and transaction fees (of the transactions included in the block). Miners will work on, and seek to add to, the longest chain of blocks so that consensus is achieved around the transaction history that has absorbed the greatest amount of computing power.[23]

The Bitcoin protocol relies on cryptographic techniques at two critical junctures: (i) the integrity of the value chain through the construction of transaction messages; and (ii) in addressing the double spending problem through establishing decentralised consensus on a tamper-resistant transaction history. The cryptographic techniques utilised by Bitcoin are

---

18 Nakamoto (2008) 2.
19 Ibid.
20 Antonopoulus (2017) 201–202; Narayanan et al, 12–15.
21 Nakamoto (2008) 2.
22 Ibid., 3.
23 Ibid.

public-key cryptography[24] and proof of data authenticity (digital fingerprints)[25] through cryptographic hash functions,[26] primarily the Secure Hash Algorithm 256 (SHA-256).

Early altcoins generally sought to improve on some of Bitcoin's actual or perceived weaknesses.[27] For example, Litecoin, launched in 2011,[28] uses a different consensus algorithm based on a 'memory-hard' puzzle that requires fast access to large amounts of memory.[29] The underlying rationale was to preserve CPU-mining and thus a more democratic peer-to-peer system. In the end, Litecoin's mining puzzle turned out to be unable to resist adoption of ASICs (Application-Specific Integrated Circuits) mining, although the move to GPUs and ASICs occurred somewhat later than in Bitcoin.[30] Peercoin was launched in 2012 with a view to providing a more sustainable consensus mechanism.[31] In 2019, Bitcoin's proof-of-work consensus algorithm had an annualized estimated electricity consumption similar to Austria (71.42TWh) and a carbon footprint comparable to Denmark (33.93 Mt CO_2).[32] Peercoin is the first cryptocurrency that uses a proof-of-stake consensus algorithm. Proof-of-stake is based on the idea of allocating 'voting' power directly in proportion to the amount of cryptocurrency held by participants, who have a proportionate incentive to act loyally, thereby, reducing the 'wasteful' use of energy and equipment.[33] Peercoin relies on a hybrid proof-of-work/proof-of-stake mechanism. Stake is determined by 'coin age' as the product of the UTXO amount and the number of blocks the UTXO has remained unspent. The proof-of-work element of the minting process requires solving a SHA-256 based computation similar to Bitcoin. However, the difficulty of the mining puzzle is reduced in accordance with the 'coin age' a minter is willing to put at stake. The more 'coin age' is consumed, the easier the proof-of-work puzzle, so that new blocks can be found with standard computer hardware and low energy consumption.[34] A number of altcoins since have adopted a variety of different design alternatives, notably Delegated Proof of Stake (DPOS) which is also envisaged for Ethereum's proof-of-stake system called Beacon Chain, which has recently been activated with a view to being merged with the current Ethereum mainnet in due course.[35]

2.2 *Smart contracts on the ethereum virtual machine*

In Bitcoin, the capacity for coding complex spending conditions into UTXOs is limited.[36] By contrast, Ethereum, launched in 2015, combines a general-purpose data storage public blockchain with a Turing-complete programming language (*Solidity*) to create the Ethereum Virtual Machine (EVM). The EVM has memory to store both data and machine readable instructions, it can run this code and track and store the resulting state

24 Antonopoulus (2017) 55–56.
25 Ibid., 55.
26 Narayanan et al (2016) 2–9.
27 Ibid., 243.
28 https://litecoin.org/.
29 Narayanan et al (2016) 193–194.
30 https://litecoin.info/index.php/Litecoin.
31 https://docs.peercoin.net/#/consensus-algorithm.
32 https://digiconomist.net/bitcoin-energy-consumption.
33 Narayanan et al (2016) 207.
34 https://docs.peercoin.net/#/proof-of-stake.
35 Tasca and Tessone (2017) 12–13; https://www.binance.vision/blockchain/ethereum-casper-explained.
36 Antonopoulus (2017) 149–169; Narayanan et al (2016) 60–64.

changes on the Ethereum blockchain. The EVM operates as if it were a global single-instance computer, running on every participating node. State is, thus, distributed globally and state changes are governed by the rules of consensus.[37] Whereas Bitcoin is transaction-based – tracking the value chain of UTXOs – Ethereum is account-based, distinguishing between 'externally owned accounts' (EOA) and (smart) 'contract accounts'. EOAs are controlled by private keys, allowing the 'owner' to send and receive ether and to create and activate smart contract code. By contrast, contract accounts are controlled solely by the logic of the machine-readable instructions recorded on the Ethereum blockchain. Like an EOA, a contract account can send and receive ether; however, only an EOA can initiate transactions. By sending a transaction to a contract address, the contract can be triggered to run on the EVM. This may take the form of sending ether to an EOA or contract address or the calling and triggering of other contracts.[38] Ethereum stores the account balances of every EOA and contract account; every block contains a summary of the current state of every EOA (balance of ether, and transaction count by *nonce*) and of every contract account (balance of ether, storage, and smart contract code) in form of a Merkle Patricia tree as a serialized hashed data structure, more complex than Bitcoin's Merkle tree.[39]

State changes and contract execution can only be triggered by transaction messages sent from EOAs. The transaction 'payload' may consist of value, data, both or neither. A transaction with value only constitutes a simple payment; a transaction with only data is the invocation of a smart contract, calling the function named in the data payload.[40] The digital signature, derived from the private key that controls the EOA, proves authorisation of the transaction by the 'owner' of the account.[41] Transactions are propagated across the network, and if valid eventually included in a newly mined block, effectuating state changes either by modifying the ether balance of an EOA (payment) or by invoking a smart contract and changing its internal state (invocation and execution).[42]

In Ethereum, smart contracts are simply computer programs, written in a high-level programming language and compiled into machine-readable bytecode, that run on the EVM.[43] A smart contract can be deployed by creating a contract account under which the smart contract can receive ether and be called on for execution. This requires the sending of a contract creation transaction from an EOA to a special contract creation address (*zero* address). Smart contracts lie dormant until their execution is triggered by the data payload of an invocation transaction sent from an EOA (or their functionality is called upon by another smart contract).[44] The ease with which smart contracts can be deployed on Ethereum has greatly facilitated a tendency of 'tokenisation'.[45] A common classification dis-

---

37 A Antonopoulos and G Wood, *Mastering Ethereum* (O'Reilly 2019) 6–8. Ethereum's current proof-of-work algorithm *Ethash* is a memory-hard consensus protocol dependent on maintaining and frequently accessing a large data structure; ibid., 321–322.
38 Ibid., 26–27.
39 Ibid., 7, 297, 303.
40 Ibid., 108–111.
41 Ibid., 115.
42 Ibid., 123–124.
43 Ibid., 127.
44 Ibid., 128–129.
45 Ibid., 221.

tinguishes between payment tokens, utility tokens and security tokens.[46] Ether and Bitcoin are payment tokens that operate at the protocol level, but there is now a wide range of application tokens, including currency tokens, that are built on Ethereum's smart contract capability. At the protocol level Ethereum knows nothing about 'owning' and sending these tokens. Whereas, a change in ether balances is recorded as a state change of EOAs and contract accounts on the Ethereum platform, the creation, transfer and recording of token balances takes place at the smart contract level.[47] Under the ERC20 token standard, a smart contract's internal table maps token balances by 'owner' and records a transfer as a deduction from one balance and addition to another balance.[48] Consequently, token transfers occur within the specific token contract state. The destination of a token transfer is the token contract address, not the recipient's EOA. A token transfer only changes the state of the token contract account, not the state of the sender's or recipient's EOAs.[49]

Ethereum has opened up of a wide space for experimentation with applications that go far beyond general purpose cryptocurrencies, ranging from the tracking and transfer of extrinsic assets of all shapes and sizes to decentralised autonomous organisations (DAOs) and smart property.

2.3 Current legal issues – an overview[50]

Cryptocurrencies as an asset class give rise to a range of issues of general commercial law. These have to be addressed with the traditional toolbox of legal categories, in particular 'property', 'money' and 'contract'. The treatment in private international law of value held and transferred across a globally distributed network is particularly problematic.

2.3.1 Property

Whether and to what extent an item of value should[51] be treated as 'property' is relevant in a wide range of contexts, including the law of succession, matrimonial and family law, and insolvency law.[52] In any legal system, whether an item is property or not may entirely depend on the legal context.[53] However, in order to be considered as a candidate for property at all, an item must have certain characteristics, neatly expressed for English law by Lord Wilberforce in National Provincial Bank v Ainsworth.[54] Accordingly, '[b]efore a right or an interest can be admitted into the category of property … it must be definable, identifiable by third parties, capable in its nature of assumption by third parties, and have some

---

46 Finma, Guidelines for enquiries regarding the regulatory framework for initial coin offerings (ICOs) (16 February 2018) (available https://www.finma.ch/en/news/2018/02/20180216-mm-ico-wegleitung/) para 3.1.
47 Antonopoulos and Wood (2019) 227.
48 Ibid., 229–231.
49 Ibid., 242.
50 For a more detailed discussion of some of these issues see chapters by Lee and Allen in this volume.
51 These are normative questions; the law is by no means settled on these issues; J Sarra and L Gullifer, 'Crypto-claimants and Bitcoin Bankruptcy: Challenges for Recognition and Realization' (2019) 28 International Insolvency Review 233, 242.
52 The LawTech Delivery Panel, Legal Statement on Cryptoassets and Smart Contracts (November 2019) para 36–37.
53 Ibid., 39.
54 [1965] AC 1175 (HL), 1247-8.

degree of permanence or stability'. UTXOs are definable and identifiable through their unique transaction IDs. As soon as a transaction is included in a newly mined block, the UTXOs it contains become increasingly more stable and irreversible the longer the blockchain becomes. Whereas a specific UTXO is not strictly speaking transferable – it is merely used up as an input in a transaction that creates new UTXOs – the value it represents is transferable to third parties in a way not dissimilar to an electronic funds transfer within the banking system.[55] Although an UTXO meets Lord Wilberforce's characteristics,[56] English law has traditionally recognised only two types of personal property: things in possession and things in action.[57] As an intangible, and absent a special statutory provision, an UTXO cannot be a thing in possession.[58] However, it also does not represent a claim against anyone and is therefore not enforceable by legal action against an issuer. Consequently, an UTXO can be categorised as property only if English law either recognises a third category of 'other intangible property' or things in action serve as a kind of default category.[59] There is authority for treating non-traditional assets such as export quotas,[60] milk quotas[61] and carbon trading allowances[62] as intangible property. Given the pragmatism of English common law, it can reasonably be assumed that courts would find UTXOs to be property.[63] Legal systems of the civilian tradition face similar issues.[64]

2.3.2 *Transfer*

From a technical perspective, the transfer of value in Bitcoin is clear: the sender of a transaction message references a previously unspent transaction output, provides his private-key-derived digital signature as spending condition, and addresses a newly created UTXO to the recipient, who can subsequently spend this new UTXO by referencing it in a new transaction signed with the recipient's digital signature. The transactions are recorded on the blockchain, with ever increasing computational irreversibility. Subjecting such a 'transfer' of value to the law on choses in action – transfer by way of assignment – or on choses in possession – transfer by way of delivery – or a different regime altogether[65] would not solve all potentially ensuing legal problems. For example, what if the sender was incapacitated at the time she hit the send button in her wallet? What if the wallet was stolen and the thief sends the UTXO? What if a debtor sends UTXO post-commencement

---

55 LawTech Delivery Panel (2019) para 45.
56 Sarra and Gullifer (2019) 242–244.
57 *Colonial Bank v Whinney* (1885) 30 Ch D 261 (CA), 285 per Fry LJ.
58 *OBG Ltd v Allan* [2007] UKHL 21.
59 *Colonial Bank v Whinney* (1986) 11 App Cas 426 (HL), 440 per Lord Blackburn.
60 *Attorney General of Hong Kong v Nai-Keung* [1987] 1 WLR 1339.
61 *Dairy Swift v Dairywise Farms Ltd* [2000] 1 WLR 1177.
62 *Armstrong DLW GmbH v Winnington* [2012] EWHC 10.
63 LawTech Delivery Panel (2019) para 85.
64 D Carr, 'Cryptocurrencies as Property in Civilian and Mixed legal Systems' in D Fox and S Green (eds) *Cryptocurrencies in Public and Private Law* (OUP 2019) 177. See Tokyo District Court, Reference number 25541521, Case claiming the bitcoin transfer etc., Tokyo District Court, Heisei 26 (Year of 2014), (Wa)33320, Judgement of Civil Division 28 of 5th August 2015 (Year of Heisei 27), Date of conclusion of oral argument; 10th June 2015, translation available at https://www.law.ox.ac.uk/sites/files/oxlaw/mtgox_judgment_final.pdf.); Ninth Arbitrazh Court of Appeals (No. 9AP-16416/18 in Case No. A40-124668/17, 15 May 2018).
65 Sarra and Gullifer (2019) 245.

of an insolvency process?[66] With assets other than cryptocurrency units, depending on the applicable law, the transfer may be void or voidable. Applied to cryptocurrencies, this would potentially mean that following a void transfer the ledger would be wrong. From a practical perspective, this would be unsatisfactory. Bitcoin is a global decentralised network; neither sender nor recipient nor the court can undo a confirmed transaction as such. What is possible, however, is a 're-transfer' by way of a new transaction that creates a new UTXO spendable by the previous sender. Therefore, in order to preserve the integrity of the ledger, it seems preferable to treat the ledger as a correct representation of the allocation of value and address problematic scenarios on the basis of either a restitutionary claim for retransfer or compensation.

2.3.3 *Money*

If UTXOs are classified as property pursuant to the applicable law the question arises as to whether UTXOs are also 'money' as a type of property with unique characteristics in law.[67] In addition to regulatory questions – deposit-taking of cryptocurrency and associated payment services as regulated activities[68] – a number of issues of general private and commercial law may arise. For example, in English law an action in debt for failure to pay a sum of money is treated radically differently from an action in damages for failure to deliver goods or provide services.[69] If Alice is obliged to pay Bob 5BTC, Bob's action in debt if UTXOs are money will be for that exact amount; if Bob's action is in damages he may sue for a Sterling amount factoring in the price increase (or decrease) of BTC against the £ since the agreed delivery date. Moreover, the remedies of the Sale of Goods Act 1979 will only be available where the buyer contracts 'for a money consideration, called the price'. If Alice buys goods from Bob in exchange for BTC, this will be a sale of goods only if BTC is classified as 'money' for the purposes of the Sale of Goods Act 1979, otherwise the transaction would be barter. Perhaps the most significant legal characteristic of money as a category of property is money's currency or negotiability.[70] Where cash has been passed by delivery to a person who has obtained possession of it honestly and in good faith, the rule of *nemo dat quod non habet* does not apply and a fresh and indefeasible title arises in the person of the transferee.[71]

Statutes will normally define legal tender, for English law: English banknotes[72] and English coins,[73] but this would not seem to prevent courts from recognising other items as 'money' in appropriate circumstances, for example foreign currency under the Sale of Goods Act 1979[74]; and generally bank credits as the most common form of payment.[75] The various social theories on the origins of money are of little help in individual cases. Of the three generally accepted indicia of money-ness – common unit of account, store of value

---

66 For example, Insolvency Act 1986, Sec.127(1).
67 Gleeson (2018) para 7.01.
68 Ibid., para 10.29–10.30.
69 Ibid.
70 E McKendrick (ed), *Goode on Commercial Law* (5th edn, Penguin 2016) 489.
71 *Miller v Race* (1758) 1 Burr 452.
72 Currency and Bank Notes Act 1954, Sec.1.
73 Coinage Act 1971, Sec.2.
74 Gleeson (2018) para 7.04.
75 Ibid., para 7.08.

and generally accepted medium of exchange – the latter is usually regarded as the defining feature of money.[76] But it immediately raises the question: 'generally accepted' by whom? For the State theory of money general acceptance must be prescribed top-down by the sovereign; the Societary theory adopts a bottom-up approach and relies on the empirical fact of an item being commonly and continuously accepted as payment in exchange for goods and services within society.[77] There is no rule of law that would mandate the application of the State theory of money in all circumstances[78]; and ascertaining empirically whether an item has found common acceptance as a medium of exchange within society may be difficult. On that basis it seems preferable to adopt a case-by-case approach[79] and in accordance with commercial law in general have recourse to the intention of the parties, subject to public policy concerns.[80] If Alice sells goods to Bob in exchange for BTC, there seems to be no good reason to deny Bob the remedies available under the Sale of Goods Act 1979. If Bob fails to pay the sales price in BTC, Alices' action would be in debt for the price in BTC. By contrast, where Alice seeks to buy BTC for speculative purposes and Bob fails to deliver, Alice may sue for damages. Moreover, in line with what has been said earlier, maintaining the integrity of the ledger requires the disapplication of the *nemo dat* rule: the ledger is correct even though the sender lacked the capacity or authority to send the relevant transaction message, which does not preclude the availability of restitutionary remedies in appropriate cases.

2.3.4 *Contract*

The recourse to 'smart contracts' as a key innovation within the cryptocurrency world has resulted in some confusion between lawyers and programmers. It is generally accepted, and has often been repeated, that smart contracts 'are neither smart nor legal contracts'; and that the use of the term in the context of Ethereum and similar platforms is perhaps somewhat unfortunate.[81] Within Ethereum, 'smart contracts' are nothing more than simple computer programs; they have no legal significance and operate within a limited execution context, based on their own state, the transactions that invoked them and information available on the blockchain.[82] For Nick Szabo, the cryptographer who coined the phrase in 1997, the 'basic idea behind smart contracts is that many kinds of contractual clauses … can be embedded in the hardware and software we deal with, in such a way as to make breach of contract expensive (if desired, sometimes prohibitively so) for the breacher'.[83] In this sense, like the mechanism of a vending machine, smart contracts are merely devices for the automated performance of contractual obligations. In order for them to have the legal

---

76 S Fiedler, K-J Gern and U Stolzenburg, 'The Impact of Digitalisation on the Monetary System' in European Parliament, The Future of Money – Compilation of Papers, Study requested by the ECON committee (December 2019) 6, 11; F Hayek, *Denationalisation of Money – The Argument Refined* (3rd edn, Institute of Economic Affairs 1990) 67.

77 Financial Markets Law Committee (2019) 12–14.

78 Gleeson (2018) para 7.06.

79 See Case C-264/14 *Skatteverket v Hedqvist* ECLI:EU:C:2015:718 para 53: Bitcoin as equivalent to 'currency, banknotes and coins' for the purposes of Art 135(1)(e) of the VAT Directive (2006/112/EC).

80 Gleeson (2018) para 7.12–7.25.

81 Antonopoulos and Wood (2019) 127.

82 Ibid., 127–128.

83 N Szabo, 'Formalizing and Securing Relationships on Public Networks' (1997) 9 First Monday, https://firstmonday.org/ojs/index.php/fm/article/view/548/469.

significance envisaged by Szabo there has to be an agreement between the parties in accordance with traditional contract law principles. In order to be automatable, an obligation has to be of a state-contingent nature, it must follow a deterministic 'if X then Y' logic.[84] All X must be data accessible by the smart contract: the state of the smart contract account (in-contract token balances of the parties); the state of the parties' EOAs, possibly also the state of other contract accounts and EOAs; off-chain data may be pushed onto the Ethereum blockchain through oracles. Y can only be in the form of sending ether from the smart contract account to another smart contract account or EOA; calling another smart contract; or modifying the in-contract token balances of the parties. Despite these limitations, developers have been able to simulate the entire lifecycle of complex derivative contracts on Ethereum.[85] In any case, a smart contract obtains legal significance as automated performance device only within the context of a traditional contractual agreement between the parties, following traditional contract law doctrine.[86]

2.3.5 *Private international law*

An important overarching question concerns the rule of private international law that determines the applicable law. Since the parties can freely determine the law that governs their contract on the basis of choice of law, contract law issues are unlikely to cause major issues. Property law is generally governed by the conflicts rule of *lex situs*. Identifying the *situs* of an intangible asset is at best difficult if not nonsensical and the law has to rely on pragmatic fictions.[87] As a starting point and in parallel with the conflicts rule for choses in action it makes sense to have recourse to enforceability, that is, the proprietary effects of holding and transferring cryptocurrency units should be governed by the law of the country where the relevant network participant resides or carries on business at the relevant time.[88] This is of course not a perfect solution for each and every case, it is however an approximation hat can be refined over time, perhaps through statutory intervention following international cooperation.[89]

3 The next generation

Large value fluctuations over short periods of time have hampered the acceptance of cryptocurrencies as media of exchange and rendered them more akin to speculative assets.[90] Stablecoins have emerged as a potential remedy and can be thought of as tokens that rely on a range of different stabilisation mechanisms in order to minimise price fluctuations against

---

84 ISDA and King & Wood Mallesons, *Whitepaper Smart Derivatives Contracts: From Concept to Construction* (October 2018) 12.
85 'A deeper look into a financial derivative on the Ethereum blockchain' (2016) https://medium.com/@vishakh/a-deeper-look-into-a-financial-derivative-on-the-ethereum-blockchain-47497bd64744.
86 LawTech Delivery Panel (2019) para 136.
87 Gleeson (2018) para 9.70–9.83.
88 A Dickinson, 'Cryptocurrencies and the Conflict of Laws' in D Fox and S Green (eds) *Cryptocurrencies in Public and Private Law* (OUP 2019) 93, 132.
89 LawTech Delivery Panel (2019) para 99.
90 Fiedler et al (2019) 10; A Kriwoluzky and C H Kim, 'Public or Private? The Future of Money' in European Parliament, The Future of Money – Compilation of Papers, Study requested by the ECON committee (December 2019) 6267.

certain reference currencies or commodities.[91] Most stablecoins are issued as ERC-20 compliant Ethereum tokens.[92] The oldest and by market capitalisation largest stablecoin, USD Tether, has been in existence since 2014.[93] However, since the launch of Facebook's *Libra* (now *Diem*) project in June 2019,[94] interest in this area has been growing, and the creation of a widely accepted privately issued global stablecoin has become a real possibility. Given the potential impact on monetary policy, various central banks have started to explore the options for issuing their own Central Bank Digital Currencies (CBDC) as a possible counter measure.

3.1 *(Global) stablecoins*

Bullmann et al offer a neat classification of stablecoins based on the relevant stabilisation mechanism.[95] 'Tokenisation of funds' as the most common and least innovative stabilisation mechanism involves a token being issued on receipt of funds in fiat currency, representing a claim on the issuer backed by the funds received which, depending on the underlying terms of service, may be redeemable at par.[96] This setup relies on a trusted entity, the issuer, at the centre and is plugged into the traditional banking system.[97] Representing a claim on the issuer in fiat currency, the token may amount to electronic money in the sense of the Electronic Money Directive (2009/110/EU).[98] Tether as the currently dominant stablecoin operates a tokenised system for both USD and EUR[99]; whereas EURT is an Ethereum token, USDT uses the Omni Layer protocol[100] operating on top of the Bitcoin blockchain.

Similar to tokenised funds, off-chain collateralised stablecoins are backed by assets that are held off-chain by custodians in the form of deposits or intermediated securities. Whereas tokenized funds can be redeemed at par in the referenced fiat currency, the off-chain collateral may constitute a basket of currencies and/or other financial assets that may fluctuate in value over time against the price of the reference currency. In order to ensure that every token is backed by collateral valued (at least) at par in the reference currency, the stablecoin must allow for margin calls on every user if the value of collateral falls below a certain threshold of (normally over-)collateralisation.[101] Depending on the specific design features, the coin may qualify as a collective investment scheme or deposit.[102] Facebook's *Libra* proposal constitutes an off-chain collateralised (global) stablecoin. As a cryptocurrency, *Libra* would be backed by a reserve of 'real assets' in form of a basket of fiat

91 D Bullmann, J Klemm and A Pinna, 'In Search of Stability in Crypto-Assets: Are Stablecoins the Solution?' (2019) ECB Occasional Paper Series No 230 (August 2019) 9; Financial Stability Board (FSB), Addressing The Regulatory, Supervisory and Oversight Challenges Raised by 'Global Stablecoin' Arrangements – Consultative Document (14 April 2020) 7.
92 https://cryptoslate.com/cryptos/stablecoin/.
93 https://cryptoslate.com/coins/tether/.
94 https://libra.org/en-US/white-paper/.
95 Bullmann et al (2019) 10.
96 Ibid., 12.
97 Ibid.
98 Ibid., 39.
99 https://tether.to/wp-content/uploads/2016/06/TetherWhitePaper.pdf.
100 https://www.omnilayer.org/.
101 Bullmann et al (2019) 16–18.
102 FSB (2020) 15.

currencies and sovereign debt securities held by geographically diverse custodians.[103] The *Libra* reserve would be managed by the *Libra* Association,[104] which would also act as issuer of the Libra token, by 'minting' and redeeming ('burning') *Libra* according to supply and demand.[105] Local authenticated resellers would exchange local currency into *Libra* and *vice versa*. Libra transactions would be verified in blocks on a permissioned blockchain with the founding members of the *Libra* Association acting as validating nodes based on proof-of-authority, eventually transitioning to a permission-less network with proof-of-stake.[106] Given Facebook's global reach and massive user base, the proposal had regulators' alarm bells ringing. Immediately upon its launch, *Libra* could be systemically important.[107] With US regulators cracking down on the project,[108] a number of high-profile supporters subsequently withdrew. In April 2020, the Libra Association (now Diem Association) has issued a revised Whitepaper v2.0.[109] The project has been watered down somewhat and now envisages the offering of single-currency stablecoins (in addition to a multi-currency coin) and forgoes the future transitioning to a permission-less network; whilst offering an enhanced compliance framework.[110] In anticipation of its launch in 2021, and to demonstrate organizational independence from Facebook, as of December 2020 the project has been renamed and rebranded as *Diem*.[111]

Stablecoins based on tokenised funds and off-chain collateralisation are simple representations of traditional assets in form of electronic money or shares in investment funds.[112] Their operation and functionality depend on accountable issuers and reliable custodians in the traditional sense. This is different for on-chain collateralised stablecoins and algorithmic stablecoins. The former are collateralised by cryptocurrency units on-chain. As a consequence, issuance, redemption and margining can be handled entirely by a network of interacting smart contracts, constituting a DAO.[113] The latter rely on smart contract technology to automatically adjust the supply of tokens so as to maintain parity with the price of the reference currency, amounting to an 'algorithmic central bank' with its own 'algorithmic monetary policy'.[114] Algorithmic stablecoins constitute a major step in the development of the cryptocurrency theme, but currently remain largely at the experimental stage. On-chain collateralised stablecoins are at an early stage of development and currently of limited significance in terms of market capitalisation.[115]

---

103 https://libra.org/en-US/about-currency-reserve/#the_reserve.
104 https://libra.org/en-US/association/#founding_members.
105 https://libra.org/en-US/white-paper/#the-libra-association.
106 https://developers.libra.org/docs/assets/papers/the-libra-blockchain/2019-09-26.pdf.
107 G Claeys and M Demertzis, 'The Next Generation of Digital Currencies: In Search of Stability' in European Parliament, The Future of Money – Compilation of Papers, Study requested by the ECON committee (December 2019) 83, 91–92.
108 United States House of Representatives Committee on Financial Services, Letter to Mark Zuckerberg et al of July 2, 2019, https://financialservices.house.gov/uploadedfiles/07.02.2019_-_fb_ltr.pdf.
109 https://libra.org/en-US/white-paper/#cover-letter.
110 See also the FSB's recommendations for effective regulation of global stablecoins; FSB (2020) 24–33, and Section 3) below.
111 https://www.diem.com/en-us/.
112 G7 Working Group on Stablecoins, Investigating the Impact of Stablecoins (October 2019) Annex A.
113 Bullmann et al (2019) 20–26.
114 Ibid., 26–29, 43.
115 G7 Working Group on Stablecoins (2019) Annex A.

3.2 *Central bank digital currencies*

The prospect of a widely used privately issued global stablecoin has engendered an important policy debate on the desirability of CBDC.[116] The introduction of a CBDC as a third category of base money, complementing cash and reserves, would allow households and businesses to hold claims in digital form against the central bank directly, providing an additional and widely available instrument for retail payments.[117] A CBDC may be either account-based or token-based. An account-based CBDC could be easily introduced and would largely resemble the current system of deposits at commercial banks, except that accounts would be held directly with the central bank.[118] By contrast, a token-based CBDC as a fiat cryptocurrency could replicate some of the features of a cash payment. The tokens representing claims on the central bank could be transferred cash-like peer-to-peer with some degree of anonymity depending on the wallet software. This could be achieved on the basis of a permissioned DLT network maintained by the central bank.[119] However, whether CBDC may be implemented as a fiat cryptocurrency remains to be seen. Systems based on centralised settlement technology may prove to be more efficient.[120]

3.3 *Legal challenges*

The operation of tokenised and off-chain collateralised stablecoin systems depends on an entire ecosystem of entities with specialised functions,[121] some of which may fall within various regulatory perimeters.[122] The issuer may need to obtain licences as payment services provider and/or electronic money provider; a banking licence may be necessary where the issuer or custodians accept deposits. If the stablecoin set-up is interpreted as a collective investment fund it may require a licence as such. Custodians may require licences for the custody and safekeeping of reserve assets. Depending on the regulatory classification of the respective coin – money, security, commodity and/or derivative –, market-makers and exchanges may need a licence as investment firms; and management of the pool of reserve assets may require an asset manager licence.[123] These regulatory regimes ensure a minimum of user protection and address to some extent operational, market, credit and liquidity risks. Outside these various regulatory perimeters, the protection of users depends entirely on the generally applicable law and contractual documentation.

In the absence of a robust statutory underpinning, the relationships between the various participants need to be firmly specified by contractual arrangements. For example, the

---

116 Fiedler et al (2019) 10; T Mancini-Griffoli, M Soledad Martinez Peria, I Agur, A Ari, J Kiff and A Popescu, 'Casting Light on Central Bank Digital Currency' (2018) IMF Staff Discussion Note SDN/18/08 (November 2018) 6.

117 Fiedler et al (2019) 17; Mancini-Griffoli et al (2018) 7.

118 Fiedler et al (2019) 18; Mancini-Griffoli et al (2018) 8.

119 Fiedler et al (2019) 18; Mancini-Griffoli et al (2018) 9.

120 E Gerba and M Rubio, 'Virtual Money: How much do Cryptocurrencies Alter the Fundamental Functions of Money' in European Parliament, The Future of Money – Compilation of Papers, Study requested by the ECON committee (December 2019) 3155.

121 For example, Libra 2.0 (https://libra.org/en-US/white-paper/#cover-letter).

122 In addition, there are issues of anti-money laundering/countering the financing of terrorism, data protection, tax compliance and many more, for a comprehensive overview G7 Working Group on Stablecoins (2019); FSB (2020) 14–20, Annex 2 and 3.

123 Zetzsche et al (2019) 17–23; Gleeson (2018) para 10.01–10.71; FSB (2020) 14–20.

legal entitlement of a user vis-à-vis the issuer may be a personal claim for an amount in the reference currency, or it may be, or secured by, a proprietary interest in a segregated pool of assets.[124] Segregation of reserve assets or holding them through a bankruptcy remote special purpose vehicle will have to be clearly set out in the agreement between the issuer and any custodians, if not mandated by applicable regulation.[125] Users will be interested in whether any profits will be distributed to the issuer and validating nodes only, or whether the users themselves will participate.[126] The system's governance arrangements have to set out the allocation of decision-making power between the issuer and other holders of key functions.[127] At the user interface, there is the general issue of the applicability of consumer and investor protection laws.[128] Without a clear specification of the nature and allocation of legal entitlements across the participating entities, the failure of any key function may not only bring down the whole system, but any attempt at disentangling the various positions may be difficult and chaotic.

On-chain collateralised stablecoins and algorithmic stablecoins may engender legal challenges of an entirely novel kind. Where issue, redemption and margining are entirely controlled by a DAO the question as to the legal nature of this set-up immediately arises with significant consequences for users, initiators and validating nodes. For lack of registration a DAO is unlikely to be a corporate type entity. Depending on the allocation of rights and obligations, a DAO may constitute a commercial partnership, at least in certain jurisdictions, with initiators and/or validating nodes and/or users as partners. This raises the issue of liability, not just for initiators, but potentially also for validating nodes and even users.[129] Overall, the delineation of the legal responsibilities of all constituencies involved requires careful consideration.

The allocation and use of stablecoins that run on globally distributed ledger systems will rarely be confined to a single jurisdiction. Effective cross-border regulation and supervision will require enhanced international cooperation. The otherwise ensuing fragmentation of the regulatory landscape may incentivise arbitrage attempts and result in inefficiencies in cross-border settings.[130] Regulatory concerns are amplified for stablecoins with a potentially global reach.[131] Facebook's 2.5 billion active users provide a massive incentive for online and offline retailers to accept *Libra* (now *Diem*) as a means of payment. The network effects that would normally hamper the adoption of alternative currencies actually work in *Libra's* (*Diem's*) favour.[132] A global stablecoin, issued by Facebook or other Tech giants, may or may not be systemically important from day one; it certainly has the potential of getting there sooner rather than later. Trust in a stablecoin depends on users' confidence that each coin is continuously backed by an adequate amount of reserve assets, which can only be achieved through robust measures addressing market, credit and liquidity risks.[133] At the same time, stablecoin providers face a constant conflict of interest between maintaining redeemability

---

124 G7 Working Group on Stablecoins (2019) 6.
125 Bullmann et al (2019) 12.
126 Zetzsche et al (2019) 7.
127 Ibid., 7–9; G7 Working Group on Stablecoins (2019) 6.
128 G7 Working Group on Stablecoins (2019) 10.
129 Zetzsche et al (2017) 36–37.
130 Zetzsche et al (2019) 26; FSB (2020) 20.
131 G7 Working Group on Stablecoins, Investigating the Impact of Stablecoins (October 2019) 11.
132 Zetsche et al (2019) 15–16.
133 G7 Working Group on Stablecoins (2019) 12–13; FSB (2020) 11–14.

at par and profit maximisation through deviations from full collateralisation.[134] The users' realisation of this conflict of interest – perhaps triggered by weak mechanisms to redeem value, ambiguous legal obligations of the issuer, inadequate legal remedies, and poor governance arrangements – may result in a loss of confidence in the stablecoin, which may also be caused by reputational damage resulting from the issuer's other lines of business (data breaches, political scandals). The resulting run of users to redeem their coins at par may be akin to conventional bank runs, however without deposit insurance and lender of last resort backing.[135] In fact there might be numerous feedback loops between a stablecoin and the traditional banking system. A run on a stablecoin may necessitate the liquidation of the reserve portfolio at fire sale prices with potentially systemic effects on the banking system. On the other hand, the stablecoin itself may be exposed to the credit and liquidity risks of the banks that maintain deposit accounts as part of the reserve. Liquidity issues at the bank may affect redeemability at par of the stablecoin with an ensuing loss of confidence. Also, where confidence in one or more banks has been eroded, the ready availability of a global stablecoin may exacerbate the fragility of the banking system: bank deposits may decline, and bank funding may shift into more expensive and volatile wholesale funding.[136] Thus, the interactions and potential spillovers between a global stablecoin system and the traditional financial system are manifold. Systemic risk may lurk in many corners. In order for a global stablecoin to be a safe alternative, a robust legal and regulatory framework will have to be developed over time.[137]

A widely accepted global stablecoin would weaken the effect of monetary policy on domestic interest rates and credit conditions.[138] It is therefore not surprising that numerous central banks have explored the option of a CBDC. The implications for the financial system are hard to predict.[139] Units of CBDC compete directly with bank deposits. Presumably, they would be legal tender without counterparty credit risk or run risk, rendering CBDC superior to bank deposits. As a consequence, commercial banks would have to find alternative sources of funding, and in order to remain attractive to customers would have to offer additional benefits and services, perhaps higher interest rates on deposits. Whereas deposits would become less reliable as a source of funding for commercial banks, CBDC could provide an alternative payment system that is immune to systemic crises.[140] In any case, a CBDC would be disruptive to the financial system and require a comprehensive rethink in both economic and legal terms.[141]

4 Conclusion

With the rise of cryptocurrencies and their ongoing refinement, currency competition[142] may soon become a reality. What precise shape it will take and impact it may have on the financial system remains to be seen. It has been predicted that it may result in an

134 Claeys and Demertzis (2019) 93.
135 G7 Working Group on Stablecoins (2019) 13–14.
136 Ibid.; FSB (2020) 11–14.
137 FSB (2020) 24–33.
138 G7 Working Group on Stablecoins (2019) 15–16.
139 Zetsche et al (2019) 16.
140 Fiedler et al (2019) 19–20.
141 Zetsche et al (2019) 16.
142 Hayek (1990).

'unbundling' of the separate functions of money – for example, fiat currency as a unit of account, interest bearing bank deposits as a store of value, and a global stablecoin as a transnational medium of exchange; combined with a 're-bundling' with specific platform services.[143] In any case, cryptocurrencies have the potential of reshaping numerous networks of economic interaction, both domestically and internationally.[144] To do so safely and soundly, law and regulation will have a major part to play.

Bibliography

A Antonopoulus, *Mastering Bitcoin* (2nd edn, O'Reilly 2017).

A Antonopoulos and G Wood, *Mastering Ethereum* (O'Reilly 2019).

D Awrey and K van Zwieten, 'The Shadow Payment System' (2018) 43 Journal of Corporation Law 101.

M Brunnermeier, H James and J-P Landau, 'The Digitalization of Money' (2019) https://scholar.princeton.edu/sites/default/files/markus/files/02c_digitalmoney.pdf (accessed 02 December 2020).

D Bullmann, J Klemm and A Pinna, 'In Search of Stability in Crypto-assets: Are Stablecoins the Solution?' (2019) ECB Occasional Paper Series No 230 (August 2019).

D Carr, 'Cryptocurrencies as Property in Civilian and Mixed Legal Systems' in D Fox and S Green (eds), *Cryptocurrencies in Public and Private Law* (OUP 2019) 177.

G Claeys and M Demertzis, 'The Next Generation of Digital Currencies: In Search of Stability' in European Parliament, The Future of Money – Compilation of Papers, Study requested by the ECON committee (December 2019) 83.

P De Filippi and A Wright, *Blockchain and the Law: The Rule of Code* (Harvard University Press 2018).

A Dickinson, 'Cryptocurrencies and the Conflict of Laws' in D Fox and S Green (eds), *Cryptocurrencies in Public and Private Law* (OUP 2019) 93.

S Fiedler, K-J Gern and U Stolzenburg, 'The Impact of Digitalisation on the Monetary System' in European Parliament, The Future of Money – Compilation of Papers, Study requested by the ECON committee (December 2019) 6.

Financial Markets Law Committee, Issues of Legal Uncertainty Arising in the Context of Virtual Currencies (July 2016), http://fmlc.org/wp-content/uploads/2018/03/virtual_currencies_paper_-_edited_january_2017.pdf (accessed 02 December 2020).

Financial Stability Board (FSB), Addressing the regulatory, supervisory and oversight challenges raised by 'global stablecoin' arrangements – Consultative Document (14 April 2020), https://www.fsb.org/wp-content/uploads/P140420-1.pdf (accessed 02 December 2020).

Finma, Guidelines for enquiries regarding the regulatory framework for initial coin offerings (ICOs) (16 February 2018) https://www.finma.ch/en/news/2018/02/20180216-mm-ico-wegleitung/ (accessed 02 December 2020).

G7 Working Group on Stablecoins, Investigating the impact of stablecoins (October 2019).

S Gleeson, *The Legal Concept of Money* (OUP 2018).

E Gerba and M Rubio, 'Virtual Money: How much do Cryptocurrencies Alter the Fundamental Functions of Money' in European Parliament, The Future of Money – Compilation of Papers, Study requested by the ECON committee (December 2019) 31.

F Hayek, *Choice in Currency: A Way to Stop Inflation* (Institute of Economic Affairs 1976).

---

143 M Brunnermeier, H James and J-P Landau, 'The Digitalization of Money' (2019) https://scholar.princeton.edu/sites/default/files/markus/files/02c_digitalmoney.pdf.

144 Ibid., 18.

F Hayek, *Denationalisation of Money – The Argument Refined* (3rd edn, Institute of Economic Affairs 1990).

ISDA and King & Wood Mallesons, Whitepaper Smart Derivatives Contracts: From Concept to Construction (October 2018).

A Kriwoluzky and C H Kim, 'Public or Private? The Future of Money' in European Parliament, The Future of Money – Compilation of Papers, Study requested by the ECON committee (December 2019) 62.

The LawTech Delivery Panel, Legal statement on cryptoassets and smart contracts (November 2019).

T Mancini-Griffoli, M Soledad Martinez Peria, I Agur, A Ari, J Kiff and A Popescu, 'Casting Light on Central Bank Digital Currency' (2018) IMF Staff Discussion Note SDN/18/08 (November 2018).

E McKendrick (ed), *Goode on Commercial Law* (5th edn, Penguin 2016).

S Nakamoto, 'Bitcoin – A Peer-to-Peer Electronic Cash System' (2008) https://bitcoin.org/bitcoin.pdf (accessed 02 December 2020).

A Narayanan, J Bonneau, E Fleten, A Miller and S Goldfeder, *Bitcoin and Cryptocurrency Technologies* (Princeton University Press 2016).

C Proctor, 'Cryptocurrencies in International and Public Law Conceptions of Money' in D Fox and S Green (eds), *Cryptocurrencies in Public and Private Law* (OUP 2019) 33.

J Sarra and L Gullifer, 'Crypto-Claimants and Bitcoin Bankruptcy: Challenges for Recognition and Realization' (2019) 28 International Insolvency Review 233.

N Szabo, 'Formalizing and Securing Relationships on Public Networks' (1997) 9 First Monday https://firstmonday.org/ojs/index.php/fm/article/view/548/469 (accessed 02 December 2020).

P Tasca and C Tessone, 'Taxonomy of Blockchain Technologies. Principles of Identification and Classification' (2017) https://papers.ssrn.com/sol3/papers.cfm?abstract_id=2977811 (accessed 02 December 2020).

D Zetzsche, R Buckley and D Arner, 'The Distributed Liability of Distributed Ledgers: Legal Risks of Blockchain' (2017) USNW Law Research Series 52, http://ssrn.com/abstract=3018214 (accessed 02 December 2020).

D Zetzsche, R Buckley and D Arner, 'Regulating Libra: The Transformative Potential of Facebook's Cryptocurrency and Possible Regulatory Responses' (2019) UNSW Law Research Series 47, http://ssrn.com/abstract=3414401 (accessed 02 December 2020).

19 Distributed ledger technology and sovereign financing

Astrid Iversen

1 Introduction

This chapter examines recent developments in financial technology – more specifically, distributed ledger technology (DLT) – in the area of sovereign financing.

In simple terms, DLT is a growing list of data records, often referred to as blocks, interlinked by unbreakable cryptography, which is a kind of a mathematical puzzle.[1] Blockchain was the first widely known DLT and underpins the cryptocurrency called Bitcoin. The term 'Blockchain' is often used interchangeably with the more general term DLT because of its descriptive name (data blocks in a chain).

Two core characteristics are key in describing DLT: (i) decentralisation and (ii) consensus.[2] First, in a distributed ledger, all transactions take place directly between the participants in the system (peer-to-peer). The transaction information is stored in records – typically referred to as blocks or ledgers – that are held by all participants in a system. The recorded data are then shared across all participants and synchronised. The correctness of new transactions needs to be confirmed by all the participants to be recorded in the blocks and, therefore, is described as being based on a consensus. Second, because the transaction occurs directly between the participants in the system and because the records of all transactions are synchronised across an immutable network, there is no need for intermediaries to safeguard the system. Therefore, the ideal version of the system is decentralised.

There are high expectations attached to the technology's ability to improve existing financial market infrastructures and make them more secure and efficient.[3] In recent years, DLT has also started to be applied in the context of sovereign financing in various ways. Here, sovereign financing refers to various ways in which a sovereign, such as a state, may

---

1 Cryptography is the art of practice of writing in code or cipher. The aim is to protect information and communications so that only those to whom the information is intended can read and process it. See 'Cryptography', Oxford English Dictionary (*oed.com*, 20. February 2020); Sarah Green, 'Cryptocurrencies: The Underlying Technology' in David Fox and Sarah Green (eds), *Cryptocurrencies in Public and Private law* (OUP 2019) 2–5.

2 Green (n 1) 1–2.

3 For example, the Bank of England assumes that central bank digital currency will lead to an increase in the steady-state level of GDP of almost 3% because of reductions in real interest rates in distortionary tax rates and in monetary transaction costs. John Barrdear and Michael Kumhof, 'The Macroeconomics of Central Bank Issued Digital Currencies' (2016) Bank of England Staff Working Paper No. 605, 3.

raise capital, in particular but not limited to sovereign borrowing.[4] In 2018, the World Bank (WB) launched the world's first global bond to be created, allocated, transferred and managed via distributed ledger technology throughout its life cycle.[5] Austria followed this trend later in 2018, using DLT (Ethereum) for its 1.15 billion euro bond auction.[6] Finally, at the 2019 Spring Meetings of the International Monetary Fund (IMF) and the WB, the Central Bank governors of Afghanistan and Tunisia claimed that 'Bitcoin bonds', the issuance of sovereign bonds using a distributed ledger, would help the countries access highly needed capital.[7] The two central bank governors did not elaborate on why Bitcoin bonds would provide access to more capital but assumed that such bonds would be an attractive investment for foreign investors. Another example of the use of DLT in a sovereign financing context is Venezuela's issuance of the Petro in 2018. The Venezuelan government refers to the Petro as a 'cryptocurrency' that is backed by Venezuelan oil reserves.[8] Although it was created as an alternative to the traditional currency system, it is a financial instrument that contributes to raise capital for the Venezuelan state, which has been undergoing a severe economic crisis and does not have access to ordinary international capital markets.[9]

This chapter aims at shedding light on the main benefits of DLT in the context of sovereign financing, in particular by discussing how the technology affects key challenges that the legal framework governing sovereign borrowing currently is facing. The discussion will be linked to the above-mentioned examples of how DLT already has been used in the context of sovereign financing. Section 2 introduces the current framework regulating how states raise capital (borrowing money) and debt crisis resolution. Section 3 discusses the issuance of sovereign bonds using DLT. Section 4 discusses the issuances of so-called cryptocurrencies by states and how some of these issuances can function as a means to raise capital for the state. Sections 3 and 4 examine two separate ways for states to raise capital by using DLT. Finally, Section 5 briefly concludes the findings of the chapter.

4 Borrowing constitutes an essential part of sovereigns' – in particular states' – financing needs The combined gross borrowings of OECD governments from the markets, which peaked at USD 10.9 trillion in 2010 in the wake of the global financial crisis, are set to reach USD 11.4 trillion in 2019. The Organisation for Economic Co-operation and Development (OECD), 'Sovereign Borrowing Outlook for OECD Countries 2020' (2019). The global COVID-19 pandemic has drastically increased states' borrowing needs, and the estimates are therefore likely to be too low.

5 World Bank, 'World Bank Mandates Commonwealth Bank of Australia for World's First Blockchain Bond' (*worldbank.org*, 9 August 2018) <https://www.worldbank.org/en/news/press-release/2018/08/09/world-bank-mandates-commonwealth-bank-of-australia-for-worlds-first-blockchain-bond> accessed 6 June 2020. The bond was created on Ethereum. It raised A$110 million ($73.16 million).

6 APA/ Roman Vilgut, 'Bundesanleihen-Auktion: Österreich setzt auf Ethereum-Blockchain' (*kleinezeitung.at*, 25 September 2018) <https://www.kleinezeitung.at/wirtschaft/5502515/115-Milliarden-Euro_BundesanleihenAuktion_Oesterreich-setzt-auf> accessed 6 June 2020.

7 P K Semler, 'Kabul, Tunis in Sovereign Crypto Bond Race' (*asiatimes.com*, 17 April 2019) <https://asiatimes.com/2019/04/kabul-tunis-in-sovereign-crypto-bond-race/> accessed 6 June 2020.

8 Article 5 of the Venezuelan Constitutional Decree on Cryptoactives and the Sovereign Cryptocurrency Petro (OJ N. 6.370 Extraordinary [2018] April 9). The extent to which it should be defined as a cryptocurrency and whether it is actually backed by oil reserves is debated.

9 The Venezuelan President Nicolas Maduro stated that Venezuela received $735 million in the first day of a pre-sale of the country's 'Petro' cryptocurrency. See 'Venezuela says launch of "petro" cryptocurrency raised $735 million' (*reuters.com*, 21. Feb 2018) <www.reuters.com/article/us-crypto-currencies-venezuela/venezuela-says-launch-of-petro-cryptocurrency-raised-735-million-idUSKCN1G506F> accessed 4 June 2020.

2 The legal framework governing sovereign debt: challenges in contracting with states

2.1 *Introduction*

States borrow money in similar ways as private individuals and corporations. They may borrow money from other states and international finance institutions but also from commercial banks and raise capital through the issuance of bonds in capital markets. This credit is regularly granted in the form of contracts, which confer rights and impose obligations to the respective parties. Similar to corporate debt instruments, sovereign debt instruments are normally governed not by international law but by domestic law.[10] Governing law can be either the laws of the sovereign debtor (local law) or the laws of another jurisdiction. If well used, sovereign borrowing can contribute to economic and social development, helping achieve economic stability in a country.[11] Almost all states borrow to promote development, invest in infrastructure, fund warfare or ensure that the government has sufficient cash reserves at all times.

Like any other debtor, states may default on their payment obligations. There are many reasons why countries default and end up in a debt crisis, including poor economic management, external economic shocks, civil wars and natural disasters. Despite several similarities, important differences exist between the legal framework for debt instruments issued by states and those issued by corporations. In contrast to corporate borrowers, there are no comprehensive frameworks under national or international law regulating sovereign borrowing and insolvency procedures. Because of this regulatory situation, sovereign borrowing regularly faces two profound challenges, which are discussed in the following two sections.

2.2 *Bankruptcy procedure for states and collective action problems*

In contrast to corporate debtors, sovereign debtors facing a debt crisis and solvency problems are not protected by any legally binding bankruptcy procedures because there are no legal insolvency frameworks for sovereign states in international or national law. This implies that there are no mandatory standstills or stays on creditors, there is no mandatory ladder of priority, the state cannot be liquidated and its assets will not be realised and disbursed to creditors holding claims against the state.[12]

For states, one available crisis resolution tool is restructuring the debt, which implies making the debt burden manageable through a renegotiation of outstanding debt

---

10 The Permanent Court of International Justice stated that: '[a]ny contract which is not a contract between States in their capacity as subjects of international law is based on the municipal law of some country', see *Case Concerning the Payment in Gold of the Serbian Federal Loans Issued in France* (France v Kingdom of the Serbs, Croats and Slovenes), Judgment No 14 (1929) PCIJ Series A, para. 86.

11 Yuefen Li and Ugo Panizza, 'The Economic Rationale for the Principles on Promoting Responsible Sovereign Lending and Borrowing' in Carlos Espósito, Yuefen Li and Juan Pablo Bohoslavsky (eds), *Sovereign Financing and International Law: The UNCTAD Principles on Responsible Sovereign Lending and Borrowing* (OUP 2013) 15.

12 For an introduction to sovereign insolvency, see Chapter 25 of Philip R Wood, *Principles of International Insolvency* (2nd edn, Thomson/ Sweet & Maxwell 2008).

agreements.[13] Being that they are contractual renegotiations, restructurings depend on the voluntary acceptance of the creditors involved.[14] This means that the economic losses that inherently come with a debt restructuring are distributed among the creditors consenting to participate in the restructuring, while the creditors refusing to take part ('holdout creditors') retain their original claims.

Although an offer to restructure may be beneficial to the entire group of creditors, individual creditors may benefit from demanding a disproportionately greater payment than the amount received by the other creditors in a restructuring. In other words, holdout creditors can seek to take advantage of the financial concessions granted by fellow creditors to the debtor state during the restructuring process. Other creditors observing that holdout creditors can freeride on their losses might feel less inclined to participate in a restructuring. This leads to the risk that no restructuring agreement will be reached; this is often referred to as a 'collective action problem'.[15]

This ad-hoc system and reliance on voluntary renegotiations to implement a sovereign debt restructuring can make it challenging for the state to reach a sustainable debt level and solve a debt crisis. The IMF has stated that under the current legal framework governing sovereign borrowing, 'debt restructurings have often been too little and too late, thus failing to re-establish debt sustainability and market access in a durable way'.[16]

2.3 *Enforcement challenges*

For creditors holding sovereign debt, the main risk is that a debtor will not fulfil its payment obligation under the loan contract. In the context of sovereign borrowing, this risk is closely related to the rules concerning sovereign immunity and the so-called local law advantage, both of which make it difficult to enforce the original terms of a debt contract. These two factors are discussed in the following.

2.3.1 *Sovereign immunity*

If a dispute arises in connection with a debt instrument, for example, if the issuing state defaults on its payment obligation, a creditor may choose to bring an action against the state to uphold his/her rights under the contract. However, these lawsuits are challenging because states are protected by sovereign immunity rules. Sovereign immunity is a key principle in national and public international law.[17] The rules constitute a procedural bar, deciding whether the national courts of one state may assume jurisdiction in a case involving another state and whether it may use enforcement measures against the other state, such

---

13 See, in general, Lee Buchheit, Guillaume Chabert, Chanda DeLong and Jeromin Zettelmeyer, 'How to Restructure Sovereign Debt: Lessons from Four Decades' (2019) Peterson Institute for International Economics (PIIE) Working Paper May 2019.

14 Loan contracts and sovereign bonds may contain majority-voting clauses, enabling the majority of bondholders to bind minority creditors to a restructuring agreement, see the International Monetary Fund (IMF), 'Strengthening the Contractual Framework to Address Collective Action Problems in Sovereign Debt Restructuring' (2014) IMF Staff Report.

15 Buchheit et al (n 13) 19.

16 IMF, 'Sovereign Debt Restructuring: Recent Developments and Implications for the Fund's Legal and Policy Framework' (2013) IMF Paper, 7.

17 On sovereign immunity, see Hazel Fox and Philippa Webb, *The Law of State Immunity* (3rd edn, OUP 2015).

as attaching its assets. Before the 20th century, most countries in the world had absolute immunity from the jurisdiction of other states, prohibiting claims brought by private citizens against foreign sovereigns before domestic courts.[18] The more states became involved in commercial activities, however, the more restrictive these immunity rules became. It has been argued that when a 'sovereign descends to the market place, he must accept the sanctions of the market place'.[19] Today, it is widely acknowledged that the issuance of a debt instrument in the capital market is a commercial activity not protected by sovereign immunity rules when brought before foreign courts. However, objections made on the grounds of rules concerning immunity from enforcement measures still constitute the main obstacle to creditor claims against states. In practice, ordinary creditors do not have the resources to litigate for full payment because the search for attachable property not protected by sovereign immunity rules is expensive and time-consuming, often entailing multiple court cases conducted around the world. This is also one reason why voluntary debt restructurings are generally the main tool through which a sovereign debtor can resolve its solvency problems and creditors can be repaid, at least in part.

2.3.2 *The local law advantage*

The idea that a state depends on the acceptance of its creditors to restructure its debt is only partly true. States are sovereigns under international law who have legislative powers in their own jurisdiction. In exercising such legislative powers, a sovereign debtor can unilaterally amend the terms of a debt instrument governed by its *own* laws as a crisis resolution measure. In other words, the state, which alters through the exercise of its sovereign rights – here its legislative powers – its own law to escape its contractual obligations to the detriment of the creditor and contrary to the original purpose of the contract, would not necessarily breach the contract according to its own law. This is sometimes referred to as 'the local law advantage'.[20] Unilateral amendments made by a state using its legislative powers can have legitimate aims, such as solving a serious debt crisis, protecting its citizens and other core functions of the state. However, the local law advantage may also be misused by the sovereign debtor state. In sum, a state 'comes into the contractual relationship with its exorbitant powers and sometimes bad manners'[21], implying that contracting with sovereign states encompasses a political risk.[22]

To summarise, the lack of legal insolvency procedures in domestic and international law makes sovereign debtors, in some respects, more vulnerable than private debtors and, in other respects, less vulnerable. On the one hand, if a sovereign state is unable to service its debts, it cannot seek the protection of bankruptcy laws to restructure or delay payments, as

---

18 Fox and Webb (n 17) 131ff.
19 See Philip R Wood, *Conflict of Laws and International Finance* (1st edn, Thomson/Sweet & Maxwell 2007) 557 and 560–570; Fox and Webb (n 17) 399 et sec.
20 If a debt instrument is not governed by the laws of the sovereign debtor, the sovereign debtor will not be able to use the local law advantage. See Lee Buchheit and Mitu Gulati, 'Use of the Local Law Advantage in the Restructuring of European Sovereign Bonds' (2018) 3 University of Bolgona Law Review 2, 173.
21 Patrick Wautelet, 'International Public Contracts: Applicable Law and Dispute Resolution' in Mathias Audit and Stephan Schill (eds) *Internationalization of Public Contracts* (Bruylant 2013) 2.
22 See also Robert Y Jennings, *State Contracts in International Law* (1961) 37 British Yearbook of International Law, 156.

private debtors do. The 'ad-hoc regime' that relies on voluntary renegotiations of outstanding debt burdens makes it challenging for the state to solve sovereign debt crises and reach a sustainable debt level. On the other hand, sovereign debt instruments that are subject to local law (the laws of the sovereign debtor) may be unilaterally amended by the state using its legislative powers. Creditors will also find it difficult to seize non-commercial public assets in lieu of payment for a defaulted sovereign debt because of sovereign immunity rules. The following sections will discuss how DLT may influence these challenges faced by a sovereign debtor and its creditors.

3 Issuance of sovereign bonds on the ledger

3.1 *Ordinary issuance of bonds*

Since the late 1980s, the issuance of sovereign bonds has been one of the most important tools when it comes to states borrowing money.[23]

When issuing ordinary sovereign bonds, a state relies on several intermediaries to ensure that the final beneficiary bondholder receives the benefits from its investment (payment of interest and principal). Bonds issued in common law jurisdictions are normally split into a beneficial and legal title. The *legal* title rests with a nominee and is registered with a registrar.[24] The nominee holds the bond for the clearing system. The *beneficial* title to the bond lies with account holders in the clearing system (the custody). The *ultimate beneficial* holders – the investors – hold their bonds through the custodian. Consequently, there is a chain of intermediaries between the issuance of a bond and the ultimately beneficial holder. The custodian is responsible for creating records for the assets and the money held for each of the ultimate beneficial holders (its clients). The custodian will also have an account for the money of the client. Finally, the issuer's payments of principal and interest under the sovereign bond are made through a paying agent, which is typically an international bank.[25] This is a stylised description of a bond issuance in a common law jurisdiction. The number of intermediaries involved when issuing, settling and reselling such bonds on the secondary market will vary across jurisdictions.

3.2 *Bond issuance recorded on distributed ledger*

If a state issues a sovereign debt instrument denominated in fiat money and records it on a distributed ledger, some of the intermediaries mentioned above would be redundant. The distributed ledger would be recoding both the legal and beneficial ownership of the bonds. Consequently, there would be no need for a separate registrar or nominee.

Other intermediaries remain necessary. When the described bonds are issued on a ledger, investors first must pay fiat money via bank transfer to a custodian's client account. The distributed ledger is then credited with the relevant amount before the issued bond is registered in the issuer state's securities account with a custodian. Upon settlement, when the

---

23 Eduardo Borensztein, Olivier Jeanne, Paolo Mauro, Jeromin Zettelmeyer and Marcos Chamon, 'Sovereign Debt Structure for Crisis Prevention' (2004) IMF Occasional Paper 237, 7–8.

24 A nominee is a person or company, not the owner, in whose name a stock, bond or company is registered.

25 For a more detailed discussion of the issuance of international bonds, see Patrick B G van der Wansem, Lars Jessen and Diego Rivetti, 'Issuing International Bonds A Guidance Note' (2019) Discussion Paper No. 13 2019 World Bank Group

investor's fiat money is transferred to the state's account, the transfer of the ownership over the bonds from the issuer to the investor is recorded on the distributed ledger. This allows the investor (ultimate beneficial holder) to hold both a legal and beneficial title.[26]

The issuance of bonds on a distributed ledger as described here encompasses a so-called tokenisation of fiat money. This means that when the fiat money paid by the investors is immobilised in the client account with the custodian, a token of this value is created for the distributed ledger. The custodian provides an account for the client's money and is responsible for ensuring that the fiat money of the investor is exchanged for tokens representing the fiat money and ownership allocated on the ledger for 'on chain' clearing and settlement. Once the fiat money of the investor is tokenised, the DLT obviates the need for separate records of the assets and money held for clients.

3.3 *Bonds denominated in cryptocurrency issued with DLT*

It is also possible to issue a sovereign bond on a ledger denominated in a cryptocurrency. If denominating a bond in a specific cryptocurrency and making it the accepted form of payment of principal and interest, it is then possible to manage the full life cycle of the bond on the ledger using a smart contract (create, issue, resell, settle and execute payments of principal and interest).[27] In this case, an investor transfers the cryptocurrency from its existing designated cryptocurrency wallet (account) to a cryptocurrency wallet offering the sovereign bond. Upon settlement, the cryptocurrency of the investor is transferred to the address of the issuer, and the bonds are transferred from the issuer's securities wallet to the investor's address.[28] The whole transaction is recorded on the distributed ledger. When comparing the structure of a sovereign bond denominated in fiat money and issued on a distributed ledger with a bond denominated in a cryptocurrency and issued on a distributed ledger described, the latter requires even fewer intermediaries.

Tests of the WB and other institutions in context with issuing ordinary corporate bonds indicate that smart contracts are not yet capable of operating safely with a bond that has many investors and complex contract features going beyond very simple terms concerning the payment of principal and minimum of the interest payments.[29]

3.4 *The effect of DLT on the legal framework of sovereign borrowing*

3.4.1 *Borrowing costs and market access for sovereign debtors*

As mentioned in Section 1.1, the Central Bank Governors of Tunisia and Afghanistan have stated that they believe that so-called crypto bonds, the issuance of sovereign bonds using DLT, can attract international investors. No elaborate explanations were provided to explain why 'crypto bonds' would have such a positive effect on the demand of the two states' sovereign bonds. As discussed above, using DLT when issuing bonds can contribute to a reduction in the transaction costs associated with the issuance of bonds because fewer

---

26 For a general overview of the use of DLT in securities issuances, see Richard Cohen, Philip Smith, Vic Arulchandran and Avtar Sehra, 'Automation and Blockchain in Securities Issuances' (2018) Butterworths Journal of International Banking and Financial Law, 144.
27 Cohen et al (n 26) 146.
28 Cohen et al (n 26) 146.
29 Cohen et al (n 26) 147.

financial intermediaries are necessary. Although using DLT may reduce the cost of issuing bonds for the two states, it is not clear that it is sufficient to increase the number of investors interested in acquiring sovereign crypto bonds. One reason for this is that normally, it is the underlying value of the investment asset that makes an investment attractive to investors, not the investment infrastructure in itself. However, if issuing bonds using DLT can increase the chances that the sovereign debtor will fulfil its payment obligations under the debt instrument or that it is easier for the creditor to enforce the contract, this could make investing in 'crypto bonds' more attractive compared with investing in ordinary bonds (lowering a state's borrowing costs and improving its access to capital). Therefore, the next question is whether DLT may contribute to a reduction in these two legal risks associated with sovereign borrowing.[30]

First, issuing a sovereign bond on a distributed ledger and denominating it in a cryptocurrency does not in and of itself strengthen the creditworthiness of a state that has a fragile economy. When using DLT technology for issuing sovereign bonds, the purchase of a debt instrument, the transfer of tokens or cryptocurrencies in exchange for a legal and beneficial title of a debt instrument, is securely and efficiently handled on the distributed ledger. However, the use of DLT does not mean that the execution of a debt contract – in particular the payment of principal and interest – is guaranteed and automatically effected. The use of DLT does not mitigate against the risk that the debtor may not have sufficient funds to pay according to the terms of the bond. Consequently, similar legal disputes to those arising in the context of ordinary debt instruments related to the payment of interest and principal, as well as potential debt restructuring, may arise. In such situations, the creditor holding a debt instrument registered on a DLT can easily obtain a judgement confirming her/his rights to payment according to the contractual terms. Rather, the problem lies in enforcing the judgement because of sovereign immunity rules. The latter problem continues to exist, regardless of the use of DLT.

Second, if the distributed ledger is permission-less, no one (including the state) can unilaterally amend the record of the transaction or contracts stored on the ledger. However, the sovereign issuer may still amend the laws governing the instrument if it is governed by the laws of the sovereign (local law). An issue related to this is the exchange risk. One may think that purchasing sovereign bonds denominated in a cryptocurrency is more stable compared with, for example, local currency. So far, established 'ecosystems' of both cryptocurrencies and crypto tokens within which investors (and sovereign debtors) can execute transactions and make use of the cryptocurrency as a medium of exchange (for payment purposes) are rare.[31] Therefore, the payment of interest and principal from the sovereign debtor to the investor would have to be exchanged from crypto token to fiat money for the investor to have a functioning medium of exchange. This exchange is associated with a risk for the investor, particularly if the chosen currency is that of the sovereign debtor. The reason is that the sovereign debtor may seek to cause inflation to deflate the real value of its debt burden.[32]

30 These risks are described in Section 2.3.
31 An overview of the jurisdictions where various cryptocurrencies are accepted as legal tender can be found in The Law Library of Congress, 'Regulation of Cryptocurrency Around the World' (2018).
32 The government can influence the inflation rate by creating incentives for growth in the money supply, see, in general, Joshua Aizenman and Nancy Marion, 'Using Inflation to Erode the US. Public Debt' (2009) National Bureau of Economics (NBER) Working Paper No. 15562.

3.4.2 *Eased debt crisis resolution for the sovereign debtor*

The next question is whether DLT may contribute to easing collective action problems among creditors and improve sovereign debt crisis resolutions. When sovereign debt instruments are denominated in fiat money and in a cryptocurrency and then issued on a distributed ledger, the DLT makes it easier for the sovereign debtor to have an overview over the investors who are actually holding a bond at any point in time, regardless of resales in the secondary market. Moreover, DLT can enable the debtor state to communicate directly with all of its bondholders, if necessary. This can help ease the practical problems related to the need for coordinating creditor action. As described in Section 3.2, this is particularly challenging when a sovereign debtor faces economic problems and is in need of communicating swiftly with its creditors, as well as potentially renegotiating the payment schedule, maturity date, interest rate or principal of its debts (restructuring).

Issuing a bond using DLT can also help the sovereign debtor identify different groups of creditors (investors) more efficiently, which is important when designing a debt-restructuring proposal. A restructuring inherently entails economic losses for a creditor, and it can be very important for the sovereign debtor to understand how different types of creditors will be affected by a potential restructuring. Whether the creditors who participate in a debt restructuring are institutional investors or small retail investors, hedge funds, pension funds or foreign and domestic banks will influence the domestic economy and the likelihood of solving an economic crisis.[33]

In sum, DLT can contribute by reducing certain transaction costs associated with issuing and trading sovereign bonds. In particular, it will make it easier for first-time issuers who have not yet developed all standard documentation and procedures needed to contract with a number of various financial intermediaries. Moreover, the book-keeping-like records of investors help ease practical collective action challenges because it can serve as a communication tool between the sovereign debtor and the creditors, as well as among the creditors. This is also the reason why international finance institutions, such as the WB, have engaged in developing and testing the issuances of bonds using DLT; they seek to develop the technology, testing how it can also be applied for low- and medium-income countries in a responsible manner.[34] DLT does not reduce the main risks associated with investing in sovereign debt instruments for either the creditor (investor) or the sovereign debtor itself. There are still no insolvency procedures in domestic or international law that protect a sovereign debtor and enable it to implement crisis resolution measures. It is the contractual terms of a debt instrument that are decisive in terms of how a debt restructuring may be implemented. If the contract terms do not provide for any crisis resolution tools, investors holding sovereign bonds are still free to refuse to partake in a debt restructuring and retain their original terms related to the debt instrument.

---

33 Lee Buchheit, 'The Search for Intercreditor Parity' (2002) 8 Law & Bus Rev Am 73.
34 The World Bank (n 5).

4 Sovereign issuance of 'cryptocurrencies'

4.1 *'Cryptocurrencies' and central bank digital currencies*

Although the main use of DLT in the context of sovereign financing is the issuance of sovereign bonds, as described above in Section 3, a state can also raise capital by issuing a cryptocurrency on a distributed ledger. Before discussing this possibility, it is useful to examine the concept of cryptocurrency more generally.

In simple terms, a cryptocurrency can be described as an asset held electronically on a distributed ledger.[35] There is no universal definition of a cryptocurrency, and there is often some overlap between commonly used terms such as 'cryptoasset', 'crypto token', 'digital currency' and 'cryptocurrency'.[36] Nevertheless, some distinctions should be made between the various types of encrypted assets.

Cryptocurrencies that are issued by private entities, of which Bitcoin is the most well known, are created and held electronically on DLT and normally operate independently from any central bank or public authority. In contrast, 'fiat' money, the ordinary government-issued currency, is highly centralised and issued and supervised by the central bank of a state.[37] Fiat money is a medium of exchange,[38] an asset that can be used for payment purposes (a counter performance) and legal tender[39] in the jurisdiction of the central bank. Currently, fiat money is not backed by a commodity such as gold but rather by the faith in the liquidity of a sovereign government.[40]

---

35 Bank of England, 'What Are Cryptoassets (Cryptocurrencies)' (*bankofengland.co.uk*, undated) <https://www.bankofengland.co.uk/knowledgebank/what-are-cryptocurrencies> accessed 5 June 2020.
36 Depending on the design and content of a cryptoasset, it may fall under the scope of an existing regulation and, for example, qualify as a financial instrument under Council Directive 2004/39/EC of 21 April 2004 on markets in financial instruments amending Council Directives 85/611/EEC and 93/6/EEC and Directive 2000/12/EC of the European Parliament and of the Council and repealing Council Directive 93/22/EEC [2004] OJ L 145/1. It can also be discussed whether a certain cryptoasset falls under the scope of Council Directive 2009/110/EC of 16 September 2009 on the taking up, pursuit and prudential supervision of the business of electronic money institutions amending Directives 2005/60/EC and 2006/48/EC and repealing Directive 2000/46/EC [2009] OJ L 267/94, and Council Directive 2015/2366/EU of 25 November 2015 on payment services in the internal market, amending Directives 2002/65/EC, 2009/110/EC and 2013/36/EU and Regulation (EU) No 1093/2010, and repealing Directive 2007/64/EC [2015] OJ L 337/35.
37 Charles Proctor, *Mann on the Legal Aspects of Money* (7th edn, OUP 2012) 71. Money is traditionally defined as a financial instrument that fulfils three main functions: (1) facilitate the indirect trade of goods and services as a generally accepted medium of exchange, (2) serve as a store of value and (3) provide a common unit of account to accurately compare the value of goods and services. Salmon Fiedler, Klaus-Jurgen Germ and Ullrich Stolzenburg, 'The Impact of Digitalisation on the Monetary System', European Parliament, Monetary Dialogue Papers, December 2019, 8. See also Proctor (n 37) 10.
38 A medium of exchange is something that is used to pay for goods or services. For a system to function as a medium of exchange, it must represent a standard of value, and all parties must accept that standard. 'Medium of exchange', see 'medium of exchange' (*dictionary.cambridge.org*, undated).
39 Here, legal tender refers to the money that can be officially used in a country, see 'legal tender' (*dictionary.cambridge.org*, undated). Be aware that the legal definition of 'legal tender' is debated and may vary across jurisdictions. See 'What is legal tender?' (*bankofengland.co.uk*, undated). See also Bank for International Settlements, Committee on Payments and Market Infrastructures, Markets Committee, 'Central Bank Digital Currencies' (2018) 9.
40 The gold standard was abandoned 15 August 1971 when President Nixon abolished the convertibility of dollars into gold. See Proctor (n 37) 69.

Whether a cryptocurrency is a medium for exchange or only an investment asset depends on whether potential contracting parties are willing to accept it for payment purposes and whether a particular jurisdiction accepts it as legal tender. Currently, cryptocurrencies issued by private entities are normally not accepted as legal tender under domestic law.[41] Because 'cryptocurrencies' cannot necessarily be used to pay for ordinary commodities and services as ordinary fiat currencies, the terms cryptoasset or crypto token are more precise and may be preferable.[42]

Although cryptocurrencies typically are issued by private entities, states – particularly central banks – may also issue assets using DLT. This is often referred to as central bank digital currency (CBDC). There are different potential CBDC models described in the literature. Some detail the establishment of CBDC as electronic cash, others as reserves and some as a combination of both. The difference between the two is that cash is accessible to anyone and meant for payment purposes, while reserves are only accessible to banks.[43] Which model a specific state may choose to implement will likely vary according to its needs. Some states fear the competition from private cryptocurrencies because they may disrupt financial stability, they can be more challenging to monitor and regulate and they may weaken the central bank's monetary policy tools. Consequently, such states (or central banks) may seek to establish CBDC to compete with private cryptocurrencies and ensure that a monetary monopoly is maintained.[44] Other states want to establish a CBDC to increase financial inclusion. This is particularly relevant for states where banks and financial institutions currently are not accessible for major parts of the population and its businesses. The argument is that DLT and digital currencies are easier to establish and will contribute to reduce costs compared with ordinary payments and banking systems.[45] Moreover, a shift from cash towards CBDC could increase the ability of central banks to influence inflation, while competition from digital currencies offered by private third parties, such as Bitcoin, constrains it.[46]

41 For an overview of jurisdictions where various types of cryptocurrencies are accepted as legal tender, see The Law Library of Congress, 'Regulation of Cryptocurrency Around the World' (2018).

42 The European Central Bank (ECB) is critical of referring to cryptocurrencies as currencies and prefers the term 'cryptoassets'. The ECB argues that cryptocurrencies do not reliably provide the standard functions of money and are unsafe to rely on as a medium of exchange or store of value. European Central Bank (ECB) Crypto-Assets Task Force, 'Crypto-Assets: Implications for Financial Stability, Monetary Policy, and Payments and Market Infrastructures' (2019) ECB Occasional Papers Series, 3. See also Bank for International Settlements (n 39) 4.

43 Currently, if non-banks intend to hold non-tangible money, they have to rely on deposits at commercial banks. These deposits represent claims against commercial banks instead of claims against the central bank. Fiedler et al. (n 37) 6. In other words, the models vary first in the sectors that have access to CBDC and second in whether there are entities that provide deposit facilities fully backed by CBDC (as distinct from deposit facilities fully backed by reserves). See in general Michael Kumhof and Clare Noone, 'Central Bank Digital Currencies – Design Principles and Balance Sheet Implications' (2018) Bank of England Staff Working Paper No. 725, in particular 5.

44 Introducing CBDC may also improve the countercyclical monetary policy tools of a central bank in times where the interest rate for a long time has been close to zero. Barrdear and Kumhod (n 3) 12.

45 Bank for International Settlements (n 39) 9.

46 Fiedler et al (n 37) 23.

4.2 *Issuance of cryptocurrencies as a means to raise capital*

States can choose different methods to issue a cryptocurrency or CBDC adapted to its purpose and desired function.[47]

As indicated earlier in this section, depending on the method chosen, the issuance of a cryptocurrency by a state can also be a way for it to raise capital.[48] One example is Venezuela's issuance of the Petro, which it labelled a cryptocurrency.[49]

Venezuela issued the Petro through an initial coin offering (ICO).[50] An ICO is a form of fundraising that issues and allocates (among other things) cryptocurrencies by using DLT in exchange for legal tender or other cryptocurrencies. The typical ICO provides a purchaser with cryptocurrency and access to a platform where the cryptocurrencies can be traded through a crypto exchange, creating a secondary market that makes the cryptocurrency fungible.[51]

In the case of Venezuela, the value of the cryptocurrency to the investor was initially not clear because the Petro did not have a status as legal tender, and it was unclear if it could be used for payment purposes.[52] However, the Venezuelan Supreme Court appears to have forced the Venezuelan legislator to regulate it as legal tender.[53] Nevertheless, and regardless of Venezuela's promises that the Petro may be used for paying taxes and public services payments as well as the purchase of goods,[54] it is still unclear whether investors might benefit from it.[55]

What is clear is that at the time of the creation of the Petro, Venezuela did not have access to capital markets, particularly because of its poor economic situation and relevant US

47 Barrdear and Kumhof (n 3) 10. It is not necessary to withdraw existing currency from circulation to implement new CBDC. If CBDC is created, that is, a reserve available only for certain banks against certain assets, such as government bonds, it will not contribute towards financing the central government.
48 In general, the issuance of CBDC can affect fiscal policy and have real economic outcomes, but not all methods of issuing CBDCs will raise capital for the central bank or the central government directly, Barrdear and Kumhof (n 3) 10.
49 For an overview of the Venezuelan issuance of the Petro, see in general Ignacio Herrera Anchustegui and Tina Soliman Hunter, 'Oil as Currency: Venezuela's Petro, a New "Oil Pattern"?' (2018) ssrn.com, 8.
50 Presidential Decree No 3.353 creating the Cryptocurrency Treasury of Venezuela, S.A. (OJ Extraordinary N. 6.731 9 April 2018).
51 In the case of Venezuela, the secondary market where the Petro can be traded has, like the initial (pre) sale, been characterised by unclarity. Although still facing many uncertainties, allegedly, trading started on state-sanctioned exchanges in 2019. Jose Antonio Lanz, 'The Petro Is Real and Venezuelans Are Slowly Starting to Trade It' (*decrypt.com*, 20 April 2019) <https://decrypt.co/6593/venezuela-trading-petro> accessed 22 June 2020.
52 Articles 106 and 107 of the Venezuelan Central Bank Act. See also Anchustegui and Hunter (n 49) 8
53 Supreme Court of Venezuela, Decreto Constituyente de fecha 4 de abril de 2018, sobre Criptoactivos y la Criptomoneda Soberana Petro, publicado en la Gaceta Oficial de la República Bolivariana de Venezuela N° 6.370 Extraordinario de fecha 9 de abril de 2018. See also Bitcoin News Network (BTCNN), 'The Petro Is Legal Tender, But It Still Lacks A Working Wallet' (*btcnn.com* 19 August 2019) <https://www.btcnn.com/the-petro-is-legal-tender/> accessed 7 July 2020.
54 Gobierno Bolivariano de Venezuela, *Petro; Towards the Economic Digital Revolution* (White Paper, undated) 6. See also Anchustegui and Hunter (n 49) 8.
55 AFP, 'Maduro bids to revive Venezuela's "petro" cryptocurrency' (*france24.com*, 15 January 2020) <https://www.france24.com/en/20200114-maduro-bids-to-revive-venezuela-s-petro-cryptocurrency> accessed 22 June 2020.

sanctions.[56] Therefore, the introduction of the Petro can be assessed as both an attempt to access capital and to create a payment system that can circumvent US sanctions.[57]

Both when a state issues a cryptocurrency and when it issues a sovereign bond, it is issuing a financial asset. If the method applied to issue the cryptocurrency provides the issuing state with capital, it still differs from the issuance of a sovereign bond in essential ways. A state raising capital through the issuance of a cryptocurrency is normally not under any obligation to pay an interest rate to the purchaser of the cryptocurrency as with the issuance of ordinary bonds or loans. Neither will the issuer pay principal (repay the nominal value initially paid for the cryptocurrency).

The capital raised through such an issuance of cryptocurrency comes with few restrictions for the state issuer. If faced with economic problems, the issuer would not have to restructure the cryptocurrency like it would with a debt obligation (bond) to improve its economic situation. Considering this factor alone, it may seem as though state-issued cryptocurrencies can be more predictable investments compared with sovereign bonds. However, a risk that remains when investing in state-issued cryptocurrencies is that the issuing state may amend the laws governing it (the local law), thereby affecting the value of the cryptocurrency. Moreover, whether a state-issued cryptocurrency is attractive among investors and how secure the investment is ultimately depends on its overall design and how the investor can make use of the cryptocurrency. Because there currently are no international common standards for state-issued cryptocurrencies, these factors will vary between jurisdictions.

5 Concluding remarks

DLT already has – and will continue to have – a transformative impact on financial markets, including sovereign financing. This chapter has shown that states may raise capital through the issuance of a 'cryptocurrency'. However, states that consider issuing some sort of encrypted currency are generally prompted to do so for other reasons, such as a wish to retain monetary monopoly or improve financial inclusion for its citizens. The area in which DLT is likely to be of greatest importance in the field of sovereign financing is the issuance of bonds. DLT has the potential to streamline the processes for issuing and trading sovereign bonds and increase efficiency of the operations by making a number of intermediaries and agents redundant. Consequently, the use of DLT can make the process of issuing sovereign bonds easier and cheaper. Although DLT offers benefits, it has also limitations. Issuing sovereign bonds using DLT does not provide a guarantee against default on the side of the state. The legal disputes related to defaults on payment of principal and interest may still arise because creditors will continue to face challenges when enforcing payment claims and judgements because of sovereign immunity rules.

56 Alexandra Ulmer and Deisy Buitrago, 'Enter the "Petro": Venezuela to Launch Oil-backed Cryptocurrency' (*reuters.com*, 3 December 2017) <https://www.reuters.com/article/us-venezuela-economy/enter-the-petro-venezuela-to-launch-oil-backed-cryptocurrency-idUSKBN1DX0SQ> accessed 3 July 2020.
57 By 19 March 2018, Trump and the US administration also implemented sanctions concerning the cryptocurrency Petro, see US Presidential Executive Order 13827 of March 19, 2018.

Bibliography

Joshua Aizenman and Marion Nancy, 'Using Inflation to Erode the US Public Debt' (2009) National Bureau of Economics (NBER) Working Paper No. 15562. <https://www.nber.org/system/files/working_papers/w15562/w15562.pdf> accessed 03 December 2020.

Ignacio Herrera Anchustegui and Tina Soliman Hunter, 'Oil as Currency: Venezuela's Petro, a New "Oil Pattern"?' (2018) ssrn.com.

Bank for International Settlements, Committee on Payments and Market Infrastructures, Markets Committee, 'Central Bank Digital Currencies' (2018) Markets Committee Papers No 174. <https://www.bis.org/cpmi/publ/d174.pdf> accessed 03 December 2020.

John Barrdear and Michael Kumhof 'The Macroeconomics of Central Bank Issued Digital Currencies' (2016) Bank of England Staff Working Paper No. 605. <https://www.bankofengland.co.uk/-/media/boe/files/working-paper/2016/the-macroeconomics-of-central-bank-issued-digital-currencies.pdf> accessed 03 December 2020.

Eduardo Borensztein, Olivier Jeanne, Paolo Mauro, Jeromin Zettelmeyer and Marcos Chamon, 'Sovereign Debt Structure for Crisis Prevention' (2004) IMF Occasional Paper 237. <https://www.imf.org/external/pubs/nft/op/237/op237.pdf> accessed 03 December 2020.

Lee Buchheit, 'The Search for Intercreditor Parity' (2002) 8 Law & Business Review of the Americas 73.

Lee Buchheit, Guillaume Chabert, Chanda DeLong and Jeromin Zettelmeyer 'How to Restructure Sovereign Debt: Lessons from Four Decades' (2019) Peterson Institute for International Economics (PIIE) Working Paper. <https://www.piie.com/publications/working-papers/how-restructure-sovereign-debt-lessons-four-decades> accessed 03 December 2020.

Lee Buchheit and Mitu Gulati, 'Use of the Local Law Advantage in the Restructuring of European Sovereign Bonds' (2018) 3 University of Bologna Law Review 2.

Richard Cohen, Philip Smith, Vic Arulchandran and Avtar Sehra, 'Automation and Blockchain in Securities Issuances' (2018) 3 Butterworths Journal of International Banking and Financial Law 144.

European Central Bank (ECB) Crypto-Assets Task Force, 'Crypto-Assets: Implications for Financial Stability, Monetary Policy, and Payments and Market Infrastructures' (2019) ECB Occasional Papers Series. <https://www.ecb.europa.eu/pub/pdf/scpops/ecb.op223˜-3ce14e986c.en.pdf> accessed 03 December 2020.

Salomon Fiedler, Klaus-Jurgen Gern and Ulrich Stolzenburg 'The Impact of Digitalisation on the Monetary System' (2019) Monetary Dialogue Papers of the European Parliament. <https://www.europarl.europa.eu/cmsdata/190130/PE%20642.361%20Kiel%20publication-original.pdf> accessed 03 December 2020.

Sarah Green, 'Cryptocurrencies: The Underlying Technology' in David Fox and Sarah Green (eds), *Cryptocurrencies in Public and Private Law* (OUP 2019).

The International Monetary Fund (IMF), 'Sovereign Debt Restructuring: Recent Developments and Implications for the Fund's Legal and Policy Framework' (2013) IMF Paper. <https://www.imf.org/-/media/Websites/IMF/imported-full-text-pdf/external/np/pp/eng/2013/_042613.ashx> accessed 03 December 2020.

The International Monetary Fund (IMF), 'Strengthening the Contractual Framework to Address Collective Action Problems in Sovereign Debt Restructuring' (2014) IMF Staff Report. <https://www.imf.org/-/media/Websites/IMF/imported-full-text-pdf/external/np/pp/eng/2014/_090214.ashx> accessed 03 December 2020.

Robert Y Jennings, 'State Contracts in International Law' (1961) 37 British Yearbook of International Law 156.

Michael Kumhof and Clare Noone 'Central Bank Digital Currencies – Design Principles and Balance Sheet Implications' (2018) Bank of England Staff Working Paper No. 725. <https://www.bankofengland.co.uk/-/media/boe/files/working-paper/2018/central-bank-digital-currencies-design-principles-and-balance-sheet-implications> accessed 03 December 2020.

Yuefen Li and Ugo Panizza, 'The Economic Rationale for the Principles on Promoting Responsible Sovereign Lending and Borrowing' in Carlos Espósito, Yufen Li and Juan Pablo Bohoslavsky (eds), *Sovereign Financing and International Law: the UNCTAD Principles on Responsible Sovereign Lending and Borrowing* (OUP 2013).

The Organisation for Economic Co-operation and Development (OECD) 'Sovereign Borrowing Outlook for OECD Countries 2020' (2019). <https://read.oecd.org/10.1787/dc0b6a-da-en?format=pdf> accessed 03 December 2020.

Charles Proctor, *Mann on the Legal Aspects of Money* (7th edn, OUP 2012).

Patrick B G van der Wansem, Lars Jessen and Diego Rivet, 'Issuing International Bonds A Guidance Note' (2019) MTI Global Practice Discussion Paper No. 13 World Bank Group. <https://openknowledge.worldbank.org/handle/10986/31569> accessed 03 December 2020.

Patrick Wautelet, 'International Public Contracts: Applicable Law and Dispute Resolution' in Mathias Audit and Stephan Schill (eds), *Internationalization of Public Contracts* (Bruylant 2013).

Philip R Wood, *Conflict of Laws and International Finance* (1st edn, Thomson/Sweet & Maxwell 2007).

Philip R Wood, *Principles of International Insolvency* (2nd edn, Thomson/Sweet & Maxwell 2008).

20 Law and regulation for a crypto-market

Perpetuation or innovation?

Joseph Lee

1 Introduction

Discussion about the way in which cryptoassets can or should be classified in law, otherwise known as legal taxonomy (LT),[1] has made a significant contribution to the development of an infrastructure for crypto-finance and of its regulation.[2] Legal taxonomy clarifies what cryptoassets are in law so that stakeholders and participants in this developing system can understand how to use them to catalyse socio-economic transformation,[3] how to monetise them,[4] how to mitigate risks[5] and how to regulate the way the system is used.[6]

---

1 Emily Sherwin, 'Legal Taxonomy' (2009) 15 Legal Theory 25, 54; Jens Lausen, 'Regulating Initial Coin Offerings? A Taxonomy of Crypto-Assets' (2019) Association for Information Systems Research Paper <http://aisel.aisnet.org.ecis2019_rp/26>; Rafael Delfin, 'A General Taxonomy for Cryptographic Assets' (2019) <https://assets.ctfassets.net/sdlntm3tthp6/6mqu1HTdBKG46Q6iqa26uE/df09eaf16935053c99c8fcdce658c7ae/General_Taxonomy_for_Cryptographic_Assets.pdf> accessed 05 July 2020.

2 UK HM Treasury, 'Cryptoasset Promotions: Consultation' (2020) <https://assets.publishing.service.gov.uk/government/uploads/system/uploads/attachment_data/file/902891/Cryptoasset_promotions_consultation.pdf> accessed 22 July 2020; Lin Lin and Dora Neo, 'Alternative Investments in the Tech Era' 2020 (3) Singapore Journal of Legal Studies 1, 3; Apolline Balndin et al, 'Global Cryptoasset Regulatory Landscape Study' (2019) Cambridge Centre for Alternative Finance Research Paper <https://www.jbs.cam.ac.uk/fileadmin/user_upload/research/centres/alternative-finance/downloads/2019-04-ccaf-global-cryptoasset-regulatory-landscape-study.pdf>; Global Digital Finance, 'Code of Conduct - Taxonomy for Cryptographic Assets' (2019) <https://www.gdf.io/wp-content/uploads/2018/10/0010_GDF_Taxonomy-for-Cryptographic-Assets_Proof-V2-260719.pdf> accessed on 05 July 2020.

3 Robby Houben et al, 'Cryptocurrencies and Blockchain: Legal Context and Implications for Financial Crime, Money Laundering and Tax Evasion' (2018) Policy Department for Economic, Scientific and Quality of the Politics of the European Parliament Research Paper.

4 Edmund Mokhtarian and Alexander Lindgren, 'Rise of the Crypto Hedge Fund: Operational Issues and Best Practices for an Emergent Investment Industry' (2018) 23 Stanford Journal of Law, Business & Finance 112, 158; Robert Hockett, 'Money's Past and Fintech's Future: Wildcat Crypto, the Digital Dollar, and Citizen Central' (2019) 2 Stanford Journal of Blockchain Law & Policy 1, 11.

5 Regulatory Requirements and Economic Impact Working Group of International Telecommunication Union, 'Regulatory Challenges and Risks for Central Bank Digital Currency' (2019) <https://www.itu.int/en/ITU-T/focusgroups/dfc/Documents/DFC-O-006_Report%20on%20Regulatory%20Challenges%20and%20Risks%20for%20Central%20Bank%20Digital%20Currency.pdf> accessed 05 July 2020.

6 UK HM Treasury, 'Cryptoassets Taskforce: Final Report' (2018) <https://assets.publishing.service.gov.uk/government/uploads/system/uploads/attachment_data/file/752070/cryptoassets_taskforce_final_report_final_web.pdf>; FCA, 'Guidance of Cryptoassets' (2019) Consulation Paper 19/3; European

Previous research has shown that lack of either legal certainty or regulatory intervention can lead to the downfall of a sector,[7] whether mature or developing. The fall of unstable coins markets, such as the Bitcoin market, demonstrates that both legal certainty and regulatory intervention are needed for stable market construction.[8] As supervision has been developed sector by sector in most jurisdictions,[9] legal taxonomy also helps determine which regulator has oversight over dealings in any particular asset.[10] The regulator applies existing laws or develops new ones to bring the asset in question under its regulatory purview.[11] In private law, legal taxonomy directs how parties negotiate contracts for transactions and how lawyers draft documents to provide evidence of their negotiations.[12] Their subsequent actions, including execution, reporting, registration and compliance, will depend on terms embedded in the contract, and these are based on the legal taxonomy of the assets and the regulatory framework that applies to them.[13] For insolvency practitioners and creditors, the legal taxonomy of assets will determine how to safeguard their interest (*ex ante* protection), and also how to assert claims in assets during reorganisation and insolvency proceedings (*ex post* protection).[14]

As new concepts of law and regulation have emerged in this area, software developers have begun to work with lawyers to create smart technologies that link the different functions.[15] Automation can increase the efficiency of the crypto-market as well as monetizing

Banking Authority, 'Report with Advice for the European Commission on Crypto-Assets' (2019) <https://eba.europa.eu/sites/default/documents/files/documents/10180/2545547/67493daa-85a8-4429-aa91-e9a5ed880684/EBA%20Report%20on%20crypto%20assets.pdf?retry=1>; Norman Chan, 'Keynote Speech at Treasury Markets Summit 2018 on Crypto-assets and Money' (2018) <https://www.hkma.gov.hk/eng/news-and-media/speeches/2018/09/20180921-1/>; Securities and Futures Commission of Hong Kong, 'Conceptual Framework for the Potential Regulation of Virtual Asset Trading Platform Operates' (2018) <https://www.sfc.hk/web/EN/files/ER/PDF/App%202_%20Conceptual%20framework%20for%20VA%20tra>; People's Bank of China, 'Notice on Precautions Against the Risks of Bitcoins' (2013) <http://www.miit.gov.cn/n1146295/n1652858/n1652930/n3757016/c3762245/content.html> accessed on 10 July 2020.

7 Tara Mandjee, 'Bitcoin, its Legal Classification and its Regulatory Framework' (2016) 15 Journal of Business and Securities Law 158, 211.
8 Joseph Lee and Lheureux Florian, 'A Regulatory Framework for Cryptocurrency' (2020) 31(3) European Business Law Review, 423–446.
9 International Monetary Fund, 'Evaluating Financial Sector Supervision: Banking, Insurance and Securities Markets', in 'Financial Sector Assessment: A Handbook' (2005).
10 Iris H-Y Chiu, 'Pathways to European Policy and Regulation in the Crypto-Economy' (2019) European Journal of Risk Regulation 738, 765.
11 Johannes Ehrentraud et al, 'Policy Responses to Fintech: A Cross-Country Overview' (2020) Financial Stability Institute on Policy Implementation No. 23; Data Guidance, 'Hong Kong: A New Regulatory Approach for Cryptocurrencies' (2019) <https://www.dataguidance.com/opinion/hong-kong-new-regulatory-approach-cryptocurrencies>; David Lee et al, *Handbook of Blockchain, Digital Finance, and Inclusion* (1st edn, Elsevier 2018) Vol 1 & Vol 2.
12 Carol Goforth, 'The Lawyer's Cryptionary: A Resource for Talking to Clients about Crypto-transactions' (2019) 1 Campbell Law Review 47, 122; Rainer Kulms, 'Blockchain: Private Law Matters' (2020) Singapore Journal of Legal Studies 63, 89.
13 Carla Reyes, '(Un)Corporate Crypto-Governance' (2020) 88 Fordham Law Review 1875, 1922.
14 Janis Sarra and Louise Gullifer, 'Crypto-Claimants and Bitcoin Bankruptcy: Challenges for Recognition and Realization' (2019) 2 International Insolvency Review 233, 272.
15 O Bolotaeva et al, 'The Legal Nature of Cryptocurrency' (2019) IOP Conference Series: Earth and Environmental Science <https://iopscience.iop.org/article/10.1088/1755-1315/272/3/032166/pdf> accessed on 05 July 2020.

new products and services[16] that are generated by, for example, Big Data.[17] Legal taxonomy provides the ground rules within which IT engineers and lawyers design new hardware and software systems. If the market is recognised as a legal construct,[18] legal taxonomy will also determine how stakeholders congregate to create a market for assets, whether physically in a place such as Lloyd's in London,[19] digitally such as on the London Stock Exchange[20] or virtually such as on blockchain for crypto-currency.[21] As a consequence, there are legal implications for the way the market is defined in financial law as well as in competition.

Crypto systems are aimed at creating a boundary-free[22] regional and global space where stakeholders can benefit from the Internet's high-speed transmission of data[23]; in other words, a virtual world.[24] Crypto-finance facilitates the creation of this universal Crypto-Republic.[25] Under the 'law matters' theory,[26] an international standard for the legal taxonomy of crypto-assets can reduce confusion and conflict,[27] and increase competition by developing a rule-based level playing field.[28] Taking current legal and regulatory rules and using them by analogy and extension to support the construction of the crypto-market can be efficient, but to do so without considering the targeted functions and operational matters will stifle development.[29] The rules that are currently in place were not originally designed to regulate crypto-functions.

16 Emmanuelle Ganne, *Can Blockchain Revolutionise International Trade?* (2018) <https://www.wto.org/english/res_e/booksp_e/blockchainrev18_e.pdf> accessed 05 July 2020.

17 Albert Opher, Alex Chou, Andrew Onda and Krishna Sounderrajan, 'The Rise of the Data Economy: Driving Value through Internet of Things Data Monetisation: A Perspective for Chief Digital Officers and Chief Technology Officers' (2016) <https://www.ibm.com/downloads/cas/4JROLDQ7> accessed 07 December 2020.

18 Justin Desautels-Stein, 'The Market as a Legal Concept' (2012) 60 Buffalo Law Review 387, 492.

19 Frederick Martin, *The History of Lloyd's and of Marine Insurance in Great Britain* (London MacMillan 2004).

20 Ranald Michie, *The London Stock Exchange: A History* (Oxford University Press 2003).

21 Joseph Lee and Florian Lheureux, 'A Regulatory Framework for Cryptocurrency' (2020) 31 European Business Law Review 423–446.

22 Garrick Hileman and Michel Rauchs, 'Global Cryptocurrency Benchmarking Study' (2019) <https://www.jbs.cam.ac.uk/fileadmin/user_upload/research/centres/alternative-finance/downloads/2017-04-20-global-cryptocurrency-benchmarking-study.pdf> accessed 06 July 2020.

23 Marco Iansiti and Karim Lakhani, 'The Truth about Blockchain' (2017) Harvard Business Review <https://hbr.org/2017/01/the-truth-about-blockchain> accessed 06 July 2020.

24 Robert Hoogendoorm, 'Virtual Worlds: The Next Frontier for Businesses' <https://dappradar.com/blog/virtual-worlds-the-next-frontier-for-businesses>, accessed 06 July 2020.

25 Thad Kousser and Matthew McCubbins, 'Social Choice, Crypto-Initiatives, and Policymaking by Direct Democracy' (2005) 78 Southern California Law Review 949, 984.

26 Michael Gilbert, 'Does Law Matter? Theory and Evidence from Single-Subject Adjudication' (2011) 40 Journal of Legal Studies 333, 365.

27 OECD, 'The Tokenisation of Assets and Potential Implications for Financial Markets' (2020) OECD Blockchain Policy Series <https://www.oecd.org/finance/The-Tokenisation-of-Assets-and-Potential-Implications-for-Financial-Markets.pdf> accessed 06 July 2020; Michael Ng, 'Choice of Law for Property Issues regarding Bitcoin under English Law' (2019) 15 Journal of Private International Law 315, 338.

28 G7 Working Group, 'Investing the Impact of Global Stablecoins' (2019) <https://www.bis.org/cpmi/publ/d187.pdf> accessed 06 July 2020.

29 Apolline Balndin et al, 'Global Cryptoasset Regulatory Landscape Study' (2019) Cambridge Centre for Alternative Finance Research Paper <https://www.jbs.cam.ac.uk/fileadmin/user_upload/research/centres/alternative-finance/downloads/2019-04-ccaf-global-cryptoasset-regulatory-landscape-study.pdf> accessed 06 July 2020.

This paper will assess the functions and operation of some crypto-assets that are either already on the market[30] or that have been proposed,[31] by looking at attempts to regulate them and discussing regulatory attitudes and policy directions. The main crypto-assets to be analysed against both laws and regulations include exchange tokens (payment tokens), security tokens (asset tokens), utility tokens, fund tokens, commodity tokens, title tokens and hybrid tokens.[32] There are also variations within a single token class. For instance, while share tokens and debt tokens are subsets of security tokens, they should not be treated in the same way, using the same rules, in contexts such as issuance or insolvency. The overall aim is to discover whether legal taxonomy and regulatory intervention can help in the construction of the emerging crypto-asset market with the goal of creating a boundary-free virtual Crypto-Republic.

2 Payment tokens

Payment tokens such as Bitcoin and Ether, also termed exchange tokens, are used as a method of payment, and may be either unstable or stable.[33] Unstable tokens are not linked to any particular asset class recognised by the law and are created through the protocols of the 'mining' process.[34] An unstable token is an intangible, virtual object that can be used for payment as were gold or silver in the past.[35] There is no specific value affixed to this intangible object,[36] unlike fiat money or digital money, both of which have a set value. The value of a payment token is determined by supply and demand in the market and as a result, its price is variable with no stable benchmark to measure its intrinsic value.[37] As payment tokens are not issued

---

30 Apolline Blandin et al, 'Global Cryptoasset Regulatory Landscape Study' (2019) University of Cambridge Faculty of Law Research Paper; Brianne Smith, 'The Life-Cycle and Character of Crypto-Assets: A Framework for Regulation and Investor Protection' (2019) 19 Journal of Accounting and Finance 156, 168.

31 Satoshi Nakamoto, 'Bitcoin: A Peer-to-Peer Electronic Cash System' (2009) <https://www.bitcoin.com/bitcoin.pdf> accessed 06 July 2020; Dominic Worner et al, 'The Bitcoin Ecosystem: Disruption Beyond Financial Services?' (2016) European Conference on Information Systems; FCA, 'Guidance on Cryptoassets' (2019) Consultation Paper 19/3.

32 Robby Houben and Alexander Snyers, 'Crypto-Assets: Key Developments, Regulatory Concerns and Responses' (2020) Study requested by the ECON Committee of the European Parliament <https://www.europarl.europa.eu/RegData/etudes/STUD/2020/648779/IPOL_STU(2020)648779_EN.pdf> accessed on 06 July 2020; Securities and Markets Stakeholder Group and European Securities and Markets Authority, 'Own Initiative Report on Initial Coin Offerings and Crypto-Assets' (2018) <https://www.esma.europa.eu/sites/default/files/library/esma22-106-1338_smsg_advice_-_report_on_icos_and_crypto-assets.pdf> accessed on 06 July 2020.

33 G7 Working Group on Stablecoins, 'Investing the Impact of Global Stablecoins' (2019) <https://www.bis.org/cpmi/publ/d187.pdf> accessed 07 July 2020.

34 Joseph Lee and Florian Lheureux, 'A Regulatory Framework for Cryptocurrency' (2020) 31 European Business Law Review 423–446.

35 Chia Ling Koh, 'The Rise of e-Money and Virtual Currencies: Re-discovering the Meaning of Money from a Legal Perspective' (Osborne Clarke 2018), <https://www.osborneclarke.com/wp-content/uploads/2018/07/The-rise-of-e-Money-and-virtual-currencies.pdf> accessed 07 July 2020.

36 PWC, 'Cryptographic Assets and Related Transactions: Accounting Considerations under IFRS' (2019) PWC Research Report <https://www.pwc.com/gx/en/audit-services/ifrs/publications/ifrs-16/cryptographic-assets-related-transactions-accounting-considerations-ifrs-pwc-in-depth.pdf> accessed 21 January 2021.

37 EY, 'The Valuation of Crypto-Assets: Minds Made for Shaping Financial Services' (2018) <https://assets.ey.com/content/dam/ey-sites/ey-com/en_gl/topics/emeia-financial-services/ey-the-valuation-of-crypto-assets.pdf> accessed 07 July 2020.

by a central bank or a central authority, and there is no defined measure to stabilise their intrinsic value, stabilisation depends on what the participants in the consensus system (the nodes) decide.[38] This can include revision of the original protocols used to create the tokens, which leads to the problem of 'forking' with the opportunity for market manipulation at the expense of anybody unable to participate meaningfully in the revision of the original protocols.[39] To counter the instability of unstable payment tokens, some stable coins have emerged, notable among them being LIBRA, which intends to issue tokens linked to underlying assets that can be used for payment within the network.[40] The aim is to stabilise the value of the issued tokens, possibly with a fixed price, so that people who purchase them with fiat currencies, use them as payment, or receive them as payments or gifts, would have some protection against fluctuations in value. However, as in other fiat currencies, payment tokens can also be used for purposes other than payment. They can be purchased as an investment, expecting the value to go up or to earn interest/dividends when in the custody of intermediaries such as exchanges or banks. They can also be used as a method of transmitting value, though not in retail payment transactions by consumers, for large payments between entities, or in investment. This ability is most likely to be used to facilitate exchanges in criminal activity, particularly if the tokens and the trading space are ungoverned.[41]

Current legal taxonomy and regulatory approaches to payment tokens remain sectoral rather than systematic. They are a taxable asset recognised as a 'unit of account' by the UK tax authority.[42] However, it is not clear how the UK tax authority intends to treat in law, for instance, whether payment tokens can be held in trust and are capable of being passed down from the settler to the ultimate beneficiaries, or how tax rates can be applied to payment tokens that have no face value and a fluctuating intrinsic value.[43] A decision is needed on how legal taxonomy applies to crypto-assets and whatever that decision is, the revenue authorities will have a keen interest in levying taxes on them, as a receipt of payment, an investment or a gift, either legal or illegal.[44] The tax authorities can levy taxes on gains that originate from money laundering, market abuse, insider dealing or bribes.

As payment tokens have been used to facilitate exchanges associated with crime, money laundering laws are necessary in order to cut off financing channels for activities such as the drug trade along the Silk Road.[45] In this context, money-laundering law has been

---

38 G7 Working Group on Stablecoins, 'Investing the Impact of Global Stablecoins' (2019) <https://www.bis.org/cpmi/publ/d187.pdf> accessed 07 July 2020.

39 Vitalik Buterin, 'Decentralised Protocol Monetisation and Forks' (2014) <https://blog.ethereum.org/2014/04/30/decentralized-protocol-monetization-and-forks/> accessed 07 July 2020.

40 The Libra Association Members, 'Libra White Paper' (2020) <https://libra.org/en-US/white-paper/> accessed 07 July 2020.

41 Public-Private Analytic Exchange Programme, 'Risk and Vulnerabilities of Virtual Currency: Cryptocurrency as a Payment Method' (2017) <https://www.dni.gov/files/PE/Documents/9—2017-AEP_Risks-and-Vulnerabilities-of-Virtual-Currency.pdf> accessed 07 July 2020.

42 UK HM Revenue & Customs, 'Cryptoassets: Tax for Individuals' (2019) UK HM Revenue & Customs Research Paper <https://www.gov.uk/government/publications/tax-on-cryptoassets/cryptoassets-for-individuals> accessed on 07 July 2020.

43 Ibid.

44 Peter Chapman and Laura Douglas, 'The Virtual Currency Regulation in the United Kingdom' in Michael Sackheim and Nathan Howell (eds), *The Virtual Currency Regulation Review* (The Law Reviews 2018) 310, 329.

45 David Adler, 'Silk Road: The Dark Side of Cryptocurrency' (2018) Fordham Journal of Corporate and Financial Law <https://news.law.fordham.edu/jcfl/2018/02/21/silk-road-the-dark-side-of-cryptocurrency/> accessed on 07 July 2020.

the first set of laws to recognise the legal status of crypto-assets as money.[46] However, payment tokens are still not systematically recognised as money; Bitcoin, for instance, is not considered to be money in the Sale of Goods Act 1979.[47] When Bitcoin and similar tokens are treated as money, there are two implications. Firstly, since the law is targeted at money laundering, Bitcoin and other similar tokens are included within the parameters of anti-money-laundering regulations.[48] Secondly, it implies that the definition of money used by the anti-money-laundering law is not limited to payment tokens and may be extended to other tokens such as hybrid tokens.

The UK Payment Systems Regulator (PSR), which regulates credit card payments and digital third-party payment providers, does not issue guidance on how payment tokens are to be treated and recognised.[49] There is no reason why payment systems should not have the ability to process payment tokens and be subject to the oversight of the PSR. Although the market operations of payment tokens are different from those of fiat currency and e-money,[50] bringing processing payment tokens under the PSR would enhance the ability of operators to manage risk and promote innovation.[51]

The Information Commissioner's Office, the UK's data protection regulator, also has jurisdiction over payment tokens when they contain personal information. The software design of payment tokens contains information about their origination in blocks on the DLT system, which means that personal information could be revealed.[52] Current encryption technology may not be effective in preventing violations of data protection and privacy.[53]

The discussion above shows that although regulators have begun to exert jurisdiction over payment tokens, they do not take a common approach to LT. The way they share or divide their regulatory oversight largely relies on Memoranda of Understanding to avoid potential legal, organisational or operational conflicts in this sectoral regulatory sphere.[54] It is likely that payment tokens will continue to be regulated in this way and that a single

---

46 Peter Chapman and Laura Douglas, 'The Virtual Currency Regulation in the United Kingdom' in Michael Sackheim and Nathan Howell (eds), *The Virtual Currency Regulation Review* (The Law Reviews 2018) 310, 329.

47 Laurie Korpi and Yasmine Dong, 'Unrivalled Insight into Global Digital Payments Regulation' (2015) <https://gamblingcompliance.com/sites/gamblingcompliance.com/files/attachments/page/PaymentsCompliance%20-%20Payments%20Lawyer%20June%202015.pdf> accessed 06 July 2020.

48 Ibid.

49 FCA, 'Guidance on the Scope of the Payment Services Regulations' (2017) <https://www.handbook.fca.org.uk/handbook/PERG/15.pdf> accessed 07 July 2020.

50 Digital Watch Observatory, *Cryptocurrencies* (2020) <https://dig.watch/issues/cryptocurrencies> accessed 07 July 2020.

51 FCA, 'Innovation in UK Consumer Electronic Payments: A Collaborative Study by Ofcom and the Payment Systems Regulator' (2014) <https://www.fca.org.uk/publication/research/ofcom-psr-joint-study.pdf> accessed 07 July 2020.

52 thinkBLOCKtank, 'The Regulation of Token in Europe: National Legal & Regulatory Frameworks in Select European Countries' (2019) <http://thinkblocktank.org/wp-content/uploads/2019/08/thinkBLOCKtank-Token-Regulation-Paper-v1.0-Part-C.pdf> accessed 06 July 2020.

53 PrivSec Report, 'Preventing Data Breaches and Assisting GDPR Compliance Using Encryption' (2017) <https://gdpr.report/news/2017/12/21/preventing-data-breaches-assisting-gdpr-compliance-using-encryption/> accessed 06 July 2020.

54 Dax Hansen and Sarah Howland, 'Digital Currencies: International Actions and Regulations' (2020) <https://www.perkinscoie.com/en/news-insights/digital-currencies-international-actions-and-regulations.html> accessed 06 July 2020.

regulator will not be able to determine the legal status of payment tokens and claim exclusive oversight. The way in which international regulators will co-coordinate will depend on how assets are legally classified (LT).[55]

3 Utility tokens

Utility tokens allow their holders to access products and services either currently or in the future.[56] They are issued by an individual, an entity or an association, and in this, they differ from payment tokens that have their origin in the 'mining' process according to a pre-designed protocol. Payment tokens have no fixed face value, but utility tokens have a value that is linked to particular products (two meals or three smart technology applications, for example) or services (three hours of legal services, a training course or purchase of clean energy). They are similar to vouchers or membership cards. A voucher can be redeemed for goods (a book) and for services (seeing a film or using the gym facility). The terms and conditions of these vouchers usually make their transferability restricted and time limited.[57] When issuers become defunct due to bankruptcy, insolvency or project failure, voucher holders do not have access to asset pools and are unlikely to have any significant monetary claim.[58] However, some vouchers can be transferable,[59] lack a time limit and are even redeemable for multiple goods and services provided by concerns other than the issuers. If such vouchers are tokenised, they are then similar to payment tokens.

Some membership cards allow their holders to access goods and services.[60] For example, members might access unlimited film viewings at home, gym facilities or benefits provided by golf clubs. When these membership cards are tokenised, they become utility tokens that enable the token holders – individuals or entities – to have access to the utilities provided by the issuer or other third-party partners. Some systems allow membership cards to be sold, even on the open market, and some even allow participation in the decision-making process of the associated business, for example, a golf club.[61] Some membership cards only allow membership to pass to the next-of-kin, others give cardholders priority in the purchase of goods or services at favourable rates, and with further cumulative benefits (the more you use the more benefits you get).

Because of this variety, defining the legal taxonomy of utility tokens is problematic. They can be a transferable or non-transferable voucher (contract), a payment method, a negotiable instrument (a forward contract for commodities or services) or a unit of investment. They can be taxable assets, be used for facilitating criminal proceeds or be used by financial services and other sectors to provide advice. They can also contain personal information. A regulatory model that is built on Memoranda of Understanding between the

---

55 Apolline Blandin et al, 'Global Cryptoasset Regulatory Landscape Study' (2019) University of Cambridge Faculty of Law Research Paper 23/2019.
56 FCA, 'Guidance on Cryptoassets' (2019) FCA Consultation Paper 19/3.
57 Ibid.
58 Gareth Malna and Sarah Kenshall, Chapter 25, in Thomas Frick (ed), *The Financial Technology Law Review* (2nd edn, The LawReviews 2019).
59 Michael Junemann and Johannes Wirtz, 'ICO: Legal Classification of Tokens: Part 4 – Utility Tokens' (2019) <https://www.twobirds.com/en/news/articles/2019/global/ico-legal-classification-of-tokens-utility-token> accessed on 07 July 2020.
60 FCA, 'Guidance on Cryptoassets' (2019) FCA Consultation Paper 19/3.
61 Ibid.

various regulatory bodies can assist regulation and avoid conflict. However, if utility tokens become redeemable for multiple goods and services, and there are entities managing these tokens as well as facilitating the redeeming services, such as loyalty points, a regulatory task force is needed to consider consumer protection since there is no specific regulatory entity with responsibility for consumer protection in access to utilities.[62]

4 Asset tokens

Asset tokens, also known as security tokens, represent underlying assets such as shares, bonds (debt), commodities, units of investment and rights to deal in those assets, such as options and futures.[63] They are issued by entities such as companies, but also by an individual or an association of individuals or entities.[64] If security tokens were treated as securities, it would bring them into the current legal and regulatory framework and securities law would apply to the whole security trading cycle: issuing, trading, clearing and settlement. The current securities law covers the operations of the securities market. It recognises primary and secondary markets, and divides market players into infrastructure providers, issuers, intermediaries, institutional and retail investors, domestic and foreign participants.[65] Securities law broadly divides into the prudential aspect of regulation with a focus on systemic issues, and the conduct aspect with a focus on market integrity, investor protection, consumer protection and market competitiveness.[66]

In addition to securities law, company law governs the internal affairs of a corporate organisation.[67] The major issues arising are capital maintenance for investor protection, particularly minority shareholders and outside creditors, governance of the organisation such as the decision-making process and the right to obtain redress, re-organisation and dissolution of the organisation and dispute resolution.[68] Modern company law accommodates various types of companies, from closely held companies to publicly listed companies. Specific regimes have been created within the company law framework to service companies with different objectives and functions.[69] The aim is to ensure, on the one hand, that capital can continue to be aggregated efficiently through the collective effort of promoters, directors, shareholders, employees and creditors, and, on the other hand, that benefits can

---

62 Deloitte, 'Making Blockchain Real for Customer Loyalty Rewards Programmes' (2016) <https://www.finextra.com/finextra-downloads/newsdocs/us-fsi-making-blockchain-real-for-loyalty-rewards-programs.pdf> accessed 07 July 2020.

63 Deloitte, 'Are Token Assets the Securities Tomorrow?' (2019) <https://www2.deloitte119.com/content/dam/Deloitte/lu/Documents/technology/lu-token-assets-securities-tomorrow.pdf> accessed 08 July 2020.

64 Ibid.

65 Baker McKenzie, 'Global Financial Services Regulatory Guide' (2016) <https://www.bakermckenzie.com/-/media/files/insight/publications/2016/07/guide_global_fsrguide_2017.pdf?la=en> accessed 07 July 2020.

66 Ibid.

67 Deborah Demott, 'Perspectives on Choice of Law for Corporate Internal Affairs' (1985) 45 Law and Contemporary Problems 161, 198.

68 Neal Watson and Beliz McKenzie, 'Shareholders' Right in Private and Public Companies in the UK (England and Wales)' (2019) <https://uk.practicallaw.thomsonreuters.com/5-613-3685?transitionType=Default&contextData=(sc.Default)&firstPage=true> accessed 07 July 2020.

69 Harvard Law School Forum, 'Principles of Corporate Governance' (2016) Harvard Law School Forum on Corporate Governance <https://corpgov.law.harvard.edu/2016/09/08/principles-of-corporate-governance/> accessed 07 July 2020.

be shared equitably among them.[70] New methods, processes and markets have been developed to facilitate the aggregation of capital, including private placement,[71] direct listing,[72] initial public offering,[73] private equity[74] and the newly emerged securities token offering (STO).[75] To ensure that benefits are shared equitably, various mechanisms have been introduced such as minority shareholder protection in closely held companies to corporate governance of listed and quoted companies. Beside these mechanisms, the takeover market has been developed as a way to monitor corporate performance rather than as a way to share the benefits of the company, mainly through the sale of the control premium to the bidders.[76]

Including security tokens under the company law framework poses a manageable legal risk for uncertainty but the problem is whether it would defeat the purpose of issuing asset tokens,[77] namely to ensure efficient capital aggregation and equitable sharing of benefits. In many STO projects, security tokens are offered on the open market to anyone who can access the internet; issue and purchase do not need the traditional financial intermediaries.[78] However, under the current company law framework, only certain companies can issue securities to the general public,[79] needing, for example, a clean three-year trading record.[80] Furthermore, the corporate governance rules in company law and the Corporate Governance Code place significant burdens on issuers who are often not able to afford the expense of governance services such as legal, compliance and auditing costs.[81] Although 'Code as law' seems to be able to mitigate some of these costs through automation,[82] many areas would still require human intervention, especially where cognitive judgement is

70 Paul Davies, 'The Board of Directors: Composition, Structure, Duties and Powers' (2020) Company Law Reform in OECD Countries: A Comparative Outlook of Current Trends.

71 Andrew Baum, 'The Future of Real Estate Initiative' (2020) <https://www.sbs.ox.ac.uk/sites/default/files/2020-01/Tokenisation%20Report.pdf> accessed 07 July 2020.

72 Ran Ben-Tzur and James Evans, 'The Rise of Direct Listings: Understanding the Trend, Separating Fact from Fiction' (2019) <https://ncfacanada.org/the-rise-of-direct-listings-understanding-the-trend-separating-fact-from-fiction/> accessed 07 July 2020.

73 Ryan Zullo, 'Can Tokenisation Fix the Secondary IPO Market?' (2020) <https://www.eisneramper.com/tokenization-secondary-ipo-catalyst-0420/> accessed 07 July 2020.

74 Greenwich Associates, 'The Tokenisation of Financial Market Securities – What's Next?' (2019) Greenwhich Associations Research Report <https://www.r3.com/wp-content/uploads/2019/10/R3.Tokenization.Financial.Market.Securities.Oct2019.pdf> accessed 07 July 2020.

75 Deloitte, 'Are Token Assets the Securities of Tomorrow?' (2019) <https://www2.deloitte119.com/content/dam/Deloitte/lu/Documents/technology/lu-token-assets-securities-tomorrow.pdf> accessed 07 July 2020.

76 David Kershaw, *Principles of Takeover Regulation* (1st edn, Oxford University Press 2018) 44.

77 'Initial Coin Offerings: Issues of Legal Uncertainty Report' (2019) <http://fmlc.org/wp-content/uploads/2019/07/ICOs-paper.pdf> accessed 17 Jan 2021. Ross Buckley et al, 'TechRisk' (2020) 1 Singapore Journal of Legal Studies 35.

78 Jovan Ilic, 'Security Token Offerings: What Are They, and Where Are They Going in 2019?' (2019) <https://medium.com/mvp-workshop/security-token-offerings-sto-what-are-they-and-where-are-they-going-in-2019-cc075aea6313> accessed 07 July 2020.

79 S 755 of Companies Act 2006 provides that 'a private company limited by shares or limited by guarantee and having a share capital must not; (a) offer to the public any securities of the company, or (b) allot or agree to allot any securities of the company with a view to their being offered to the public'.

80 LR 6.3.1R, FCA.

81 OECD, 'Risk Management and Corporate Governance' (2014) <http://www.oecd.org/daf/ca/risk-management-corporate-governance.pdf> accessed 07 July 2020.

82 Gabrielle Patrick and Anurag Bana, 'Rule of Law Versus Rule of Code: A Blockchain-Driven Legal World' (2017) IBA Legal Policy & Research Unit Legal Policy.

required to interpret rules that are based on policy objectives or where there are different acts to be balanced against one another.[83] The reason that STO is attractive to legitimate businesses is its ability to reach the entire internet community without infrastructure obstacles or national boundaries.[84] Bringing them under the current company law framework would compromise this benefit. As an example, the US's Howey test when, applied to DAO (an STO project), would prevent development in security token finance, and encourage underground STO markets.[85] While many countries have created a specific legal and regulatory regime for STO and have provided trading platforms for the investment community, none has been successful.

It is time to reconsider the current legal, regulatory and market infrastructures for security tokens. How do they function? Can they change as required by developments in the market? Who has authority to create the law and to control its development? In particular, since the current legal and regulatory framework is the result of regulatory capture, to what extent are participants in today's security tokens market able to influence the law?

5 Title tokens

There are legal and evidential documents that represent or certify an underlying asset or class of assets.[86] When they are tokenised, they become title tokens. What differentiates them from security tokens is that the title is not recognised as a security such as a land title,[87] documentary title (eg, a bill of lading)[88] or the title to an artwork. There are also intra-organisational titles that represent workload (hours of work), entitlements (right to receive skill-training courses) or the right to inherent contractual relationships (leader in a direct-selling group). Some of these titles can easily be brought into the current legal framework without the need to introduce a new regime; an example of this is the land title in real property law. Tokenising land titles and moving conveyance on to a DLT platform can improve the transparency of land ownership and its history,[89] and can reduce inter-

83 Smart Contract Alliance, 'Smart Contracts: Is the Law Ready?' (2018) Smart Contract Alliance Whitepaper <https://lowellmilkeninstitute.law.ucla.edu/wp-content/uploads/2018/08/Smart-Contracts-Whitepaper.pdf> accessed 07 July 2020.
84 Deloitte, 'Are Token Assets the Securities of Tomorrow?' (2019) <https://www2.deloitte119.com/content/dam/Deloitte/lu/Documents/technology/lu-token-assets-securities-tomorrow.pdf> accessed 07 July 2020.
85 Lennart Ante and Ingo Fiedler, 'Cheap Signals in Security Token Offerings' (2019) Blockchain Research Lab Working Paper Series No. 1 <https://www.blockchainresearchlab.org/wp-content/uploads/2019/07/Cheap-Signals-in-Security-Token-Offerings-BRL-Series-No.-1-update3.pdf> accessed 07 July 2020.
86 The Law Commission, 'Electronic Execution of Documents' (2019) Policy Paper No. 386 <https://s3-eu-west-2.amazonaws.com/lawcom-prod-storage-11jsxou24uy7q/uploads/2019/09/Electronic-Execution-Report.pdf> accessed 07 July 2020.
87 Michael Junemann and Johannes Wirtz, 'ICO: Legal Classification of Tokens: Part 2 – Security Token' (2019) <https://www.twobirds.com/en/news/articles/2019/global/ico-legal-classification-of-tokens-2> accessed 09 July 2020.
88 Marek Dubovec, 'The Problems and Possibilities for Using Electronic Bill of Lading as Collateral' (2006) 23 Arizona Journal of International and Comparative Law 437.
89 Nan Liu et al, 'A Critical Review of Distributed Ledger Technology and Its Applications in Real Estate' (2020) <https://www.rics.org/globalassets/rics-website/media/knowledge/research/research-reports/rics0077-001-distributed-ledger-technology-review-report–final.pdf> accessed 08 July 2020.

mediary fees such as estate agency and legal fees. It can also improve the efficiency of tax collection by the revenue authorities in levying stamp duty.

Documentary titles such as bills of lading can be accommodated in the sale of goods and carriage of goods laws.[90] This can improve transparency, reduce fraud and remove the legal uncertainty of goods in transit. It can also increase the ability of traders to obtain finance from banks through letters of credit.[91] The legal certainty provided by tokenised documentary titles in goods can increase the willingness of banks to remit finance more quickly, and the fees charged by banks can be lower since the risk of legal uncertainty is reduced. Tokenising legal or documentary titles would not pose technical problems in either a centralised or a partly decentralised system, but there would be issues of data protection, privacy protection (including financial privacy) and commercial secrecy protection.[92] The biggest legal challenge is how to transfer the legal interest in the underlying assets of title tokens. The transfer of security tokens, which are recognised as assets, involves registration of interest in distributed ledgers through crediting and debiting, while effecting registration relies on using public and private keys. However, for documentary title transactions, the possession of the titles may or may not be evidence of ownership in the underlying property. For instance, in an international contract for the sale of goods, property passes to the seller from the buyer irrespective of the possession of the bill of lading (the documentary title) if it is a free-on-board contract.[93] In a cost-insurance-freight contract,[94] the transfer of title tokens to a bank (providing the letter of credit) would be necessary for the bank to remit finance, but the bank does not own the goods despite holding the title tokens. The critical question is how transfer of interest in goods can be effected within trade finance market practice, while decoupling it from possession of the title. Market structure and practice may need to be rebuilt if trades based on title tokens are to be made on a DLT network.

For title tokens to represent goods in bulk is legally problematic. Goods in bulk are likely to be split up as they are sold, thus passing from single to multiple ownership with the implication that the tokens need to be similarly subdivided or reissued in order that the new owners can demonstrate their ownership of a component of the original bulk.[95] Without such evidence of a property interest, the buyers may not be able to sell on their new acquisition or to make a claim in insolvency proceedings.

Even for specific goods,[96] tokenised titles can represent a challenge to the market. In the art market where goods are individual and often unique, there is no single legal registration system to evidence ownership. Tokenised titles representing artworks would mean that possession of the artwork itself, such as a painting, is not *prime face* evidence of owning

90 Caslav Pejovic, 'Documents of Title in Carriage of Goods by Sea: International Law and Practice' (1st edn, Informa Law from Routledge 2020) 460, 461.
91 Friederike Niepmann and Tim Schmidt-Eisenlohr, 'International Trade, Risk, and the Role of Banks' (2014) Federal Reserve Bank of New York Staff Reports No. 633.
92 ICO, 'Anonymisation: Managing Data Protection Risk – Code of Practice' 2012 <https://ico.org.uk/media/1061/anonymisation-code.pdf> accessed on 08 July 2020.
93 Martin Davis, 'Delivery and the Passing of Risk' (2014) <https://oxford.universitypressscholarship.com//mobile/view/10.1093/acprof:oso/9780195388183.001.0001/acprof-9780195388183-chapter-5> accessed on 22 January 2021.
94 Ibid.
95 The Law Commission and The Scottish Law Commission, 'Sale of Goods Forming Part of a Bulk' (1965) Policy Paper No. 215/145.
96 Vlad Burilov, 'Regulation of Crypto Tokens and Initial Coin Offerings in the EU' (2019) 6 European Journal of Comparative Law and Governance 146, 186.

the property. A good-faith purchaser may not acquire the legal title in the painting without showing possession of the tokenised title, and, unlike land registration, the purchaser may not know where to find the token holder if there is no centralised system.[97] Furthermore, market practices in the sale of artwork would also need to change, because the shaking of hands in the gallery or the fall of the hammer at an auction would not enable the proprietary interest in the artwork to pass to the buyer because only the transfer of the tokenised title would amount to *prima facie* evidence of such a transfer.

Within an organisation or an association, there may be rules designed to allocate workload and control, and this allocation can be assignable and transferable within the organisation or association. Assigned work and its ownership can be further assigned to others, as in industry's practice of outsourcing. In work that is shared between organisations, a tokenised title representing hours of work (a utility) can demonstrate how the total working hours in a project will be distributed and the hours can be traded among the organisations.[98] The control relationship, if control is to be recognised as a valuable thing or asset, can also be tokenised and assigned. For instance, shareholder agreement on how control is to be exercised or membership agreement on who will be the next controller within the group can be tokenised to show how the control title will be passed. This will doubtlessly raise further legal questions on the transferability, assignability and the ability to delegate these controls (rights and/or duties) as well as public policy issues that give rise to issues of morality, utility and freedom.[99]

It is unlikely a single regulator will be given complete oversight of tokenised titles as they are components of totally different markets ranging from the sale of crude oil to modern artwork, and from shareholders' to workers' agreements on control.

6 Commodity tokens

Commodity tokens represent underlying commodities, such as raw materials, agricultural products or clean energy.[100] In some commodity trades the underlying commodities are securitised with the securities mostly being options and futures – contractual instruments that represent a right to purchase or sell the underlying commodities at a pre-determined price and at a specific time in the future. They do not involve directly securitising a particular asset or an identifiable quantity of asset.[101] Trade, in other types of commodity, involves setting up funds such as exchange-traded-funds,[102] hedge funds or private equity funds.[103] When tokenised, the units of investment in these funds can be classified as asset

---

97 Josias Dewey et al, *Blockchain & Cryptocurrency Regulation* (1st edn, Global Legal Insights 2019) <https://www.acc.com/sites/default/files/resources/vl/membersonly/Article/1489775_1.pdf> accessed 08 July 2020.

98 Dachs Bernhard, 'The Impact of New Technologies on the Labour Market and the Social Economy' (2017) University of Munich MPRA Paper 90519.

99 Josias Dewey et al, *Blockchain & Cryptocurrency Regulation* (1st edn, Global Legal Insights 2019).

100 AAX Academy, 'Tokenising Commodities: It's Possible, But Should We?' (2020) <https://academy.aax.com/en/tokenizing-commodities-its-possible-but-should-we/> accessed 08 July 2020.

101 OECD, 'The Tokenisation of Assets and Potential Implications for Financial Markets' (2020) <http://www.oecd.org/finance/The-Tokenisation-of-Assets-and-Potential-Implications-for-Financial-Markets.pdf> accessed 08 July 2020.

102 Adam Marszk and Ewa Lechman, *Exchange-Traded Funds in Europe* (1st edn, Academic Press 2019).

103 Anne Jansen et al, 'Hedge Funds and Financial Market Dynamics' (1998) Occasional Papers of IMF.

tokens which may be traded in the same way as other security tokens.[104] This means that commodity tokens are not tokenised titles in the underlying asset or commodity and do not represent the title in the goods for both the market and in law. Currently, commodity markets are organised as multilateral trading platforms with their own specific market rules.[105] They are only accessible to institutional investors through trading market members; retail investors do not participate directly. Commodity trades are used not only to purchase the underlying commodity goods but also to hedge against the risk of market volatility.[106] In addition, traders, clearing houses and settlement entities may be involved in trading in order to mitigate default risk, enhance legal certainty and provide liquidity. For instance, default in a settlement would be covered by clearing houses.[107] The types of market described above for trading title tokens are mostly bilateral rather than multilateral and even an auction house, which could be seen as an organised market, is not a multilateral trading platform in the way that commodity markets operate. Failure to deliver goods could result in the award of damages or other remedies by a court or by some other dispute settlement mechanisms.

In law, commodity tokens do not represent the specific titles of goods nor a specifically defined bulk of goods, unlike title tokens. Commodity tokens do not confer ownership of goods or goods in bulk to their holders. This affects contractual claims where there has been default in the delivery of the underlying goods, and also claims in priority in insolvency proceedings,[108] as well as other market rules attached to the tokens. The current commodity trades regulators are likely to continue to oversee tokenised commodity trades, but whether the commodity markets regulator should also have jurisdiction over inter-exchangeable tokenised commodities such as computing power or electricity should be examined further.

7 Hybrid tokens and convertible tokens

Using current legal taxonomy to define the nature of a token may mean that some elements in the token are not covered by conventional legal definitions, and they may also limit its true functionality. The issuers of a token can design it in a way that includes a number of functions and create, for example, a hybrid token that acts both as a payment token and as a utility token.[109] One of the functions of the token might be convertibility – its conversion to another type of token. For instance, a share token issued by a company might be converted into a bond token, or a payment token into a utility token that can then be

104 Deloitte, 'Are Token Assets the Securities Tomorrow?' (2019) <https://www2.deloitte.com/content/dam/Deloitte/lu/Documents/technology/lu-token-assets-securities-tomorrow.pdf> accessed 08 July 2020.
105 European Commission, 'Review of the Markets in Financial Instruments Directive' (2011) <https://ec.europa.eu/commission/presscorner/detail/en/MEMO_11_716> accessed 08 July 2020.
106 Deloitte, 'Commodity Price Risk Management: A Manual of Helping Commodity Price Risk for Corporates' (2018) <https://www2.deloitte.com/content/dam/Deloitte/in/Documents/risk/in-risk-overview-of-commodity-noexp.PDF> accessed 08 July 2020.
107 Ibid.
108 INSOL International, 'Cryptocurrency and Its Impact on Insolvency and Restructuring' (2019) INSOL Special Report.
109 Thijs Maas, 'Why Hybrid Tokens are Superior to Utility Tokens: Comparing Utility Tokens, Security Tokens and Hybrid Tokens' (2019) <https://medium.com/hackernoon/hybrid-tokens-are-superior-to-utility-tokens-heres-why-3bec287c465> accessed 09 July 2020.

converted back to a payment token, or a title token could be converted to a payment token, such as Token Equity Convertible (TEC). For example, *SynchroLife Limited*, a subsidiary of Japanese restaurant *SNS Ginkan*, fundraised by offering convertible equities, which allow investors to exchange the equities for their tokens named SynchroGoin in the future.[110] This means that there is a difference between a hybrid token and a convertible token. The former entitles its holders to a specific range of benefits and rights, and also confers liabilities. The latter turns one type of token into another without renegotiating the terms attached to it, without going through an exchange, and without receiving it as a result of a dispute resolution mechanism. Convertibility is embedded in the original design,[111] so when it could be converted, as well as how and what it might be converted into, would need to be pre-agreed by the parties and pre-determined in the design. This is not the same as the concept of automation in a smart contract which enables issuers to buy back tokenised shares when a certain condition has been triggered,[112] resulting in the tokenised shares being returned to the issuing companies, and payment (or payment tokens) remitted to the original share token holders. Convertibility is something quite different.

There are several benefits associated with convertible tokens. For instance, an insurance token[113] might be converted into a utility voucher, such as a medical voucher or a hotel voucher, when a flight is delayed. A title token representing a worker's hours of work in an organisation might be converted into a utility voucher for clean-energy electricity, or a tokenised green bond. Such convertibility can bypass the need to convert tokens into fiat money through a currency exchange, hence saving costs, and also avoid the need to convert them into payment tokens. Yet, if different token operators were to be linked, the degree of convertibility could be enhanced, thereby bypassing the need to trade them in an open market for the purpose of converting them and eliminating the cost of using intermediaries. The legal imperative is to ensure that all the parties understand convertibility as set out in the contract, and that the event triggering convertibility can be accurately defined in law.[114]

No regulator has yet devised a plan to supervise hybrid tokens or considered the possibility of accepting convertible tokens on the markets. The more likely scenario is that regulators will assert jurisdiction when they perceive that a token contains an element that falls under its regulatory parameter. This situation is likely to create regulatory conflict and competition and it may be that in certain areas, regulators lack the capacity to understand the markets or the ability to resolve disputes.

110 S Nishimura, 'A New Way to Fundraise? – Token Equity Convertible' (2018) <https://medium.com/@vcinsights/a-new-way-to-fundraise-token-equity-convertible-tec-7d3c987e520e> accessed 09 July 2020.

111 PwC, 'Cryptographic Assets and Related Transactions: Accounting Considerations under IFRS' (2019) <https://www.pwc.com/gx/en/audit-serices/ifrs/publications/ifrs-16/cryptographic-assets-related-transactions-accounting-considerations-ifrs-pwc-in-depth.pdf> accessed 09 July 2020.

112 Joseph Lee, 'Smart Contracts for Securities Transaction on the DLT Platform (Blockchain): Legal Obstacles and Regulatory Challenges' (2020) <https://papers.ssrn.com/sol3/papers.cfm?abstract_id=3523317> accessed 09 July 2020.

113 Peter Temperley, 'Using Crypto Tokens in Insurance' (2018) <https://medium.com/@peter.temperley/using-crypto-tokens-in-insurance-7125ccb090eb> accessed 09 July 2020.

114 Robby Houben et al, 'Cryptocurrencies and Blockchian: Legal Context and Implications for Financial Crime, Money Laundering and Tax Evasion' (2018) Policy Department for Economic, Scientific and Quality of Life Policies of the European Parliament Research Paper.

8 Innovation

Law and regulation are critical elements in the development of a market. A mature market is a legal construct but also has a heavily embedded regulatory system. The law defines the products and services that the market is constructed on, for instance the stock market, the insurance market, the commodity market or the energy trading market. Often the markets are supported by technical systems and processes; they have physical buildings and legally defined participants such as issuers, traders, institutional investors and consumers. Regulations can bridge legal gaps, enhance enforcement or even foreclose the market in the case of protectionist regulations. In a developing market which is not yet saturated, there are many competing interests and potential markets. Law can help categorise the market, define the scope of private behaviours and provide the basis for evolution either through doctrinal development that gives legal status to market elements, or through legal transplant to replicate an existing market structure.[115] Mature markets have their own exisiting legal and regulatory infrastructures, however, developing markets need to select appropriate legal and regulatory systems that both suit their intended function and confer competitive advantage.[116] For example, stock markets compete with bond markets and tech companies compete with other retail companies. Newcomers need to differentiate themselves from existing markets in order to compete with them, and their participants must engage in regulatory capture[117] in order to break away, grow and eventually compete successfully. To win the hearts and minds of current participants in the market, they must demonstrate the benefits of engagement in their new market and win on efficiency (more economical) and efficacy (better results). They will need to create a space for regulatory arbitrage[118] where activities prohibited in existing markets can be launched in a new space. New and old markets will engage in regulatory competition at sectoral, regional or international levels, and such competition can result in a race to either the top or the bottom.[119]

What we have witnessed in the development of cryptoasset markets is a breaking away from the traditional thinking that a market is a legal construct in which the aim of regulation is to promote the market.[120] Participants of the crypto-market do not want to be constrained by traditional norms of the main legal systems (either common law or civil

---

115 Alan Watson, 'Legal Transplants and European Private Law' (2000) 4.4 Electronic Journal of Comparative Law (2000) <http://www.ejcl.org/ejcl/44/44-2.html>; Rainer Kulms, 'Blockchain: Private Law Matters' (2020) Singapore Journal of Legal Studies 63, 89.

116 Competition & Market Authority, 'Regulation and Competition: A Review of the Evidence' (2020) <https://assets.publishing.service.gov.uk/government/uploads/system/uploads/attachment_data/file/857024/Regulation_and_Competition_report_-_web_version.pdf> accessed on 09 July 2020.

117 Ibid.

118 Ibid.

119 OECD, 'Striking the Right Balance between Competition and Regulation: The Key is Learning from Our Mistakes' (2002) APEC-OECD Co-operative Initiative on Regulatory Reform: Third Workshop <https://www.oecd.org/regreform/2503205.pdf> accessed 09 July 2020.

120 FCA, 'Guidance on Cryptoassets: Feedback and Final Guidance to CP 19/3' (2019) FCA Policy Statement 19/22 <https://www.fca.org.uk/publication/policy/ps19-22.pdf> accessed 09 July 2020.

law) and do not wish the state to continue acting as a regulator.[121] The borderless nature of the internet and the appeal of anonymity allow a new 'legal and regulatory escape'.[122] The hope is that a space, which is not held back by existing legal doctrines and regulatory ethos, can increase access to goods and services. This explains why it is difficult to capture the nature of a crypto-currency such as Bitcoin while there is an apparent parallel between an initial public offering and an initial coin offering.[123] When traditional legal doctrines prove unable to capture the essence of a new type of token it is termed a hybrid token and the existence of hybrid tokens challenges conventional legal thinking on the definition of goods, securities, ownership titles and other intangibles such as intellectual property.

The nature of the DLT as a consensus network challenges conventional legal doctrines on contract law and the public law concept of social contract.[124] The way the current global regulatory system has developed is the result of activity over many years by the more advanced economies, and it operates to their agenda and in their self-interest. This has led to mistrust by those who feel that 'the establishment' is holding back development and preventing innovation. The regulatory ethos of the crypto-market as a decentralised, consensual and constantly evolving system is seen as a more desirable space for new ways of exchange, communication and living (a virtual life). It is not hard to understand why critics, including myself,[125] immediately cast doubt on the legitimacy, legality, morality and governance of this new form of republic with its promises of total democracy, transparency and freedom. In political terms, the new republic is a response to the frustration of current global governance in the hands of major international powers.[126] One of the results of such global governance is the concentration of resources in the hands of a few powerful nations and entities.[127] This also includes a concentration of capital through globalised financial systems that are furthered by major central banks, by financial exchanges, by circles of institutional investors and the regulatory powers they have taken upon themselves.[128] Placing this Crypto-Republic under the current system of global governance would reduce citizens' ability to innovate, grow and eventually compete.

121 Rain Xie, 'Why China Had to Ban Cryptocurrency but the US Did Not: A Comparative Analysis of Regulation on Crypto-Markets between the US and China' (2019) 2 Washington University Global Studies Law Review 457, 492; Emmanuelle Ganne, 'Can Blockchain Revolutionise International Trade?' (2018) <https://www.wto.org/english/res_e/booksp_e/blockchainrev18_e.pdf> accessed 05 July 2020.
122 Sophia Qasir, 'Anonymity in Cyberspace: Judicial and Legislative Regulations' (2013) 81 Fordham Law Review 3651, 3691.
123 Barbara Jones et al, *The Evolution of Token Offerings and Regulation: From ICO to STO* (2019) <https://www.gtlaw.com/-/media/files/insights/published-articles/2019/12/the-evolution-of-token-offerings-and-regulation-from-ico-to-sto-q4-2019.pdf> accessed 21 January 2021.
124 Telecommunication Standardisation Sector of ITU, 'Distributed Ledger Technology Regulatory Framework' (2019) Telecommunication Standardisation Sector of ITU, Technical Report.
125 Joseph Lee and Florian Lheureux, 'A Regulatory Framework for Cryptocurrency' (2020) 31 European Business Law Review 423–446.
126 Bank for International Settlements, 'Designing a Potential Treatment for Crypto-Assets' (2019) Discussion Paper <https://www.bis.org/bcbs/publ/d490.pdf> accessed 21 January 2021.
127 Emmanuelle Ganne, 'Can Blockchain Revolutionise International Trade?' (2018) World Trade Organisation Research Paper <https://www.wto.org/english/res_e/booksp_e/blockchainrev18_e.pdf> accessed 05 July 2020.
128 Ibid.

The emerging tool of code as law[129] is not an attempt to break away from conventional law and regulation, instead it incorporates laws into smart technologies and uses those technologies to police the market in a system of surveillance capitalism. Experimenting with new regulatory systems as an innovative tool is aimed neither at displacing the current regulatory framework nor at substituting for current legal doctrines. This code as law innovation is more likely to affect organisational structures by moving from human intervention to machine learning and execution.[130] A new form of social contract is required. That social contract should be the basis for the creation of a new Crypto-Republic where assets are created, owned and shared differently from the way they are in 'our world'.

9 Conclusion

This article has discussed how current legal taxonomy (classification) can help define crypto-assets by looking at the function, participants and operation of market structures. The way in which tokens are named can be very different from the way that the law defines them now or in the future, and the way they are regulated can help to clarify their legal status. However, a token's definition that is recognised by one regulator is not necessarily shared by other regulatory agencies or by the courts. The legal fluidity of crypto-assets creates legal confusion. As a result, creating a coherent legal and regulatory framework, either through the application of legal analogy or by extending the current regulatory framework, becomes a challenging task.

The current classification of crypto-assets into payment, utility, security, title, commodity and hybrid tokens is based on their function, the perceptions of market participants and regulatory attitudes towards them. Legal doctrines such as contract and property can help define, or provide a basis for clarification of, rights and obligations as well as the methods of and implications for their transfer and assignment. Statutory definitions of money, insurance, security and units of investment can also provide such a basis. Some crypto-assets are hard to define, so new approaches need to be created to support their development.

Using current legal and regulatory frameworks for crypto-finance will not transform the economy or the market because they have evolved as mechanisms to support the *status quo* in the current financial markets. Extending existing systems to include crypto-assets would merely perpetuate the dominance of existing interests by another form of regulatory capture. A new crypto-asset market structure cannot be created without introducing new laws and rules and this requires the establishment of a social contract for governance based on new legal doctrines that transcend 'contract' and 'property'. A new regulatory form and ethos should be devised because code as law, regtech or legaltech indoctrinated by the current legal and regulatory frameworks are unlikely to generate a true transformation of the market.

129 Primavera De Filippi and Samer Hassan, 'Blockchain Technology as a Regulatory Technology: From Code is Law to Law is Code' (2016) <https://firstmonday.org/ojs/index.php/fm/article/view/7113/5657> accessed 09 July 2020.

130 Darrell West and John Allen, 'How Artificial Intelligence is Transforming the World' (2018) <https://www.brookings.edu/research/how-artificial-intelligence-is-transforming-the-world/> accessed 09 July 2020.

Bibliography

AAX Academy, 'Tokenising Commodities: It's Possible, But Should we?' (2020) <https://academy.aax.com/en/tokenizing-commodities-its-possible-but-should-we/> accessed 08 July 2020.

David Adler, 'Silk Road: The Dark Side of Cryptocurrency' (2018) Fordham Journal of Corporate and Financial Law <https://news.law.fordham.edu/jcfl/2018/02/21/silk-road-the-dark-side-of-cryptocurrency/> accessed on 07 July 2020.

Lennart Ante and Ingo Fiedler, 'Cheap Signals in Security Token Offerings' (2019) Blockchain Research Lab Working Paper Series No. 1 <https://www.blockchainresearchlab.org/wp-content/uploads/2019/07/Cheap-Signals-in-Security-Token-Offerings-BRL-Series-No.-1-update3.pdf> accessed 07 July 2020.

Apolline Balndin et al, 'Global Cryptoasset Regulatory Landscape Study' (2019) Cambridge Centre for Alternative Finance Research Paper <https://www.jbs.cam.ac.uk/fileadmin/user_upload/research/centres/alternative-finance/downloads/2019-04-ccaf-global-cryptoasset-regulatory-landscape-study.pdf> accessed 09 July 2020.

Andrew Baum, *The Future of Real Estate Initiative* (Said Business School, University of Oxford 2020) accessed 07 July 2020.

Ran Ben-Tzur and James Evans, 'The Rise of Direct Listings: Understanding the Trend, Separating Fact from Fiction' (2019) <https://ncfacanada.org/the-rise-of-direct-listings-understanding-the-trend-separating-fact-from-fiction/> accessed 07 July 2020.

O Bolotaeva et al, 'The Legal Nature of Cryptocurrency' (2019) IOP Conference Series: Earth and Environmental Science <https://iopscience.iop.org/article/10.1088/1755-1315/272/3/032166/pdf> accessed on 05 July 2020.

Kelly Buckley, 'Crypto Revolution: Bitcoin, Cryptocurrency and the Future of Money' (2019) Southbank Investment Research.

Ross Buckley et al, 'TechRisk' (2020) Mar (1) Singapore Journal of Legal Studies 35.

Vlad Burilov, 'Regulation of Crypto Tokens and Initial Coin Offerings in the EU' (2019) 6 European Journal of Comparative Law and Governance 146.

Vitalik Buterin, 'Decentralised Protocol Monetisation and Forks' (2014) <https://blog.ethereum.org/2014/04/30/decentralized-protocol-monetization-and-forks/> accessed 07 July 2020.

Peter Chapman and Laura Douglas, 'The Virtual Currency Regulation in the United Kingdom' in Michael Sackheim and Nathan Howell (eds), *The Virtual Currency Regulation Review* (The Law Reviews 2018) 310.

Norman Chan, 'Keynote Speech at Treasury Markets Summit 2018 on Crypto-assets and Money' (2018) <https://www.hkma.gov.hk/eng/news-and-media/speeches/2018/09/20180921-1/> accessed 07 December 2020.

Iris H-Y Chiu, 'Pathways to European Policy and Regulation in the Crypto-Economy' (2019) 10(4) European Journal of Risk Regulation 738.

Competition & Market Authority, 'Regulation and Competition: A Review of the Evidence' (2020) <https://assets.publishing.service.gov.uk/government/uploads/system/uploads/attachment_data/file/857024/Regulation_and_Competition_report_-_web_version.pdf> accessed on 09 July 2020.

Data Guidance, 'Hong Kong: A New Regulatory Approach for Cryptocurrencies' (2019) <https://www.dataguidance.com/opinion/hong-kong-new-regulatory-approach-cryptocurrencies> accessed 09 July 2020.

Bernhard Dachs, 'The Impact of New Technologies on the Labour Market and the Social Economy' (2017) University of Munich MPRA Paper 90519.

Paul Davies, 'The Board of Directors: Composition, Structure, Duties and Powers' (2000) OECD Research Report on Company Law Reform in OECD Countries.

Martin Davis, 'Delivery and the Passing of Risk' (2014) <https://oxford.universitypressscholarship.com//mobile/view/10.1093/acprof:oso/9780195388183.001.0001/acprof-9780195388183-chapter-5> accessed on 22 January 2021.

Primavera De Filippi and Samer Hassan, 'Blockchain Technology as a Regulatory Technology: From Code is Law to Law is Code' (2016) <https://firstmonday.org/ojs/index.php/fm/article/view/7113/5657> accessed 09 July 2020.

Rafael Delfin, 'A General Taxonomy for Cryptographic Assets' (2018) <https://assets.ctfassets.net/sdlntm3tthp6/6mqu1HTdBKG46Q6iqa26uE/df09eaf16935053c99c8fcdce658c7ae/General_Taxonomy_for_Cryptographic_Assets.pdf> accessed 05 July 2020.

Deloitte, 'Making Blockchain Real for Customer Loyalty Rewards Programmes' (2016) <https://www.finextra.com/finextra-downloads/newsdocs/us-fsi-making-blockchain-real-for-loyalty-rewards-programs.pdf> accessed 07 July 2020.

Deloitte, 'Commodity Price Risk Management: A Manual of Helping Commodity Price Risk for Corporates' (2018) <https://www2.deloitte.com/content/dam/Deloitte/in/Documents/risk/in-risk-overview-of-commodity-noexp.PDF> accessed 08 July 2020.

Deloitte, 'Are Token Assets the Securities of Tomorrow?' (2019) <https://www2.deloitte.com/content/dam/Deloitte/lu/Documents/technology/lu-token-assets-securities-tomorrow.pdf> accessed 07 July 2020.

Deborah Demott, 'Perspectives on Choice of Law for Corporate Internal Affairs' (1985) 45 Law and Contemporary Problems 161.

Justin Desautels-Stein, 'The Market as a Legal Concept' (2012) 60 Buffalo Law Review 387.

Josias Dewey et al, 'Blockchain & Cryptocurrency Regulation' (1st edn, Global Legal Insights 2019) <https://www.acc.com/sites/default/files/resources/vl/membersonly/Article/1489775_1.pdf> accessed 08 July 2020.

Marek Dubovec, 'The Problems and Possibilities for Using Electronic Bill of Lading as Collateral' (2006) 23 Arizona Journal of International and Comparative Law 438.

Johannes Ehrentraud et al, 'Policy Responses to Fintech: A Cross-Country Overview' (2020) Financial Stability Institute on Policy Implementation No. 23.

European Banking Authority, 'Report with Advice for the European Commission on Crypto-Assets' (2019) <https://eba.europa.eu/sites/default/documents/files/documents/10180/2545547/67493daa-85a8-4429-aa91-e9a5ed880684/EBA%20Report%20on%20crypto%20assets.pdf?retry=1> accessed 09 July 2020.

European Commission, 'Review of the Markets in Financial Instruments Directive' (2011) <https://ec.europa.eu/commission/presscorner/detail/en/MEMO_11_716> accessed 08 July 2020.

EY, 'The Valuation of Crypto-Assets: Minds Made for Shaping Financial Services' (2018) <https://assets.ey.com/content/dam/ey-sites/ey-com/en_gl/topics/emeia-financial-services/ey-the-valuation-of-crypto-assets.pdf> accessed 07 July 2020.

FCA, 'Innovation in UK Consumer Electronic Payments: A Collaborative Study by Ofcom and the Payment Systems Regulator' (2014) <https://www.fca.org.uk/publication/research/ofcom-psr-joint-study.pdf> accessed 07 July 2020.

FCA 'Guidance on the Scope of the Payment Services Regulations' of PERG Handbook (2017) <https://www.handbook.fca.org.uk/handbook/PERG/15.pdf> accessed 07 July 2020.

FCA, 'Guidance on Cryptoassets' (2019) FCA Consultation Paper 19/3.

FCA, 'Guidance on Cryptoassets: Feedback and Final Guidance to CP 19/3' (2019) Policy Statement 19/22 <https://www.fca.org.uk/publication/policy/ps19-22.pdf> accessed 09 July 2020.

Financial Markets Law Committee, 'Initial Coin Offerings: Issues of Legal Uncertainty Report' (2019) <https://www.comsuregroup.com/news/initial-coin-offerings-issues-of-legal-uncertainty-report-initial-coin-offerings-30-july-2019/> accessed 09 July 2020.

G7 Working Group on Stablecoins' before the title of contribution, 'Investigating the Imact of Global Stablecoins' (2019) <https://www.bis.org/cpmi/publ/d187.pdf> accessed 06 July 2020.

Emmanuelle Ganne, 'Evaluating Financial Sector Supervision: Banking, Insurance and Securities Markets' in International Monetary Fund, *Financial Sector Assessment: A Handbook* (2005).

Emmanuelle Ganne, *Can Blockchain Revolutionise International Trade?* (2018) <https://www.wto.org/english/res_e/booksp_e/blockchainrev18_e.pdf> accessed 05 July 2020.

Geneva Internet Platform, 'Cryptocurrencies' (2020) <https://dig.watch/issues/cryptocurrencies> accessed 07 July 2020.

Michael Gilbert, 'Does Law Matter? Theory and Evidence from Single-Subject Adjudication' (2011) 40 Journal of Legal Studies 333.

Global Digital Finance, 'Code of Conduct- Taxonomy for Cryptographic Assets' (2019) <https://www.gdf.io/wp-content/uploads/2018/10/0010_GDF_Taxonomy-for-Cryptographic-Assets_Proof-V2-260719.pdf> accessed 09 July 2020.

Carol Goforth, 'The Lawyer's Cryptionary: A Resource for Talking to Clients About Crypto-transactions' (2019) 1 Campbell Law Review 47.

Greenwich Associates, 'The Tokenisation of Financial Market Securities – What's Next?' (2019) Research Report of Greenwich Associates <https://www.r3.com/wp-content/uploads/2019/10/R3.Tokenization.Financial.Market.Securities.Oct2019.pdf> accessed 07 July 2020.

Dax Hansen and Sarah Howland, 'Digital Currencies: International Actions and Regulations' (2020) <https://www.perkinscoie.com/en/news-insights/digital-currencies-international-actions-and-regulations.html> accessed 06 July 2020.

Harvard Law School Forum on Corporate Governance, 'Principles of Corporate Governance' (2016) <https://corpgov.law.harvard.edu/2016/09/08/principles-of-corporate-governance/> accessed 07 July 2020.

Garrick Hileman and Michel Rauchs, *Global Cryptocurrency Benchmarking Study* (2019) Cambridge Centre for Alternatvie Finance <https://www.jbs.cam.ac.uk/fileadmin/user_upload/research/centres/alternative-finance/downloads/2017-04-20-global-cryptocurrency-benchmarking-study.pdf> accessed 06 July 2020.

Robert Hockett, 'Money's Past and Fintech's Future: Wildcat Crypto, the Digital Dollar, and Citizen Central' (2019) 2 Banking Stanford Journal of Blockchain Law & Policy 1.

Robert Hoogendoorm, 'Virtual Worlds: The Next Frontier for Businesses' <https://dappradar.com/blog/virtual-worlds-the-next-frontier-for-businesses>, accessed 06 July 2020.

Robby Houben et al, 'Cryptocurrencies and Blockchain: Legal Context and Implications for Financial Crime, Money Laundering and Tax Evasion' (2018) Policy Department for Economic, Scientific and Quality of Life Policies of the European Parliament Research Report.

Robby Houben and Alexander Snyers, 'Crypto-Assets: Key Developments, Regulatory Concerns and Responses' (2020) Study requested by the ECON Committee of the European Parliament <https://www.europarl.europa.eu/RegData/etudes/STUD/2020/648779/IPOL_STU(2020)648779_EN.pdf> accessed on 06 July 2020.

Marco Iansiti and Karim Lakhani, 'The Truth About Blockchain' (2017) 91 (1) Harvard Business Review <https://hbr.org/2017/01/the-truth-about-blockchain> accessed 06 July 2020.

ICO, 'Anonymisation: Managing Data Protection Risk – Code of Practice' <https://ico.org.uk/media/1061/anonymisation-code.pdf> accessed on 08 July 2020.

Jovan Ilic, 'Security Token Offerings: What Are They, and Where Are They Going in 2019?' (2019) <https://medium.com/mvp-workshop/security-token-offerings-sto-what-are-they-and-where-are-they-going-in-2019-cc075aea6313> accessed 07 July 2020.

INSOL International, 'Cryptocurrency and Its Impact on Insolvency and Restructuring' (2019) INSOL Special Report.

Anne Jansen et al, *Hedge Funds and Financial Market Dynamics* (Occasional Papers of the IMF 1998).

Barbara Jones et al, *The Evolution of Token Offerings and Regulation: From ICO to STO* (2019) <https://www.gtlaw.com/-/media/files/insights/published-articles/2019/12/the-evolution-of-token-offerings-and-regulation-from-ico-to-sto-q4-2019.pdf> accessed 21 January 2021.

Michael Junemann and Johannes Wirtz, 'ICO: Legal Classification of Tokens: Part 4 – Utility Tokens' (2019) <https://www.twobirds.com/en/news/articles/2019/global/ico-legal-classification-of-tokens-utility-token> accessed on 07 July 2020.

Michael Junemann and Johannes Wirtz, 'ICO: Legal Classification of Tokens: Part 2 – Security Token' (2019) <https://www.twobirds.com/en/news/articles/2019/global/ico-legal-classification-of-tokens-2> accessed 09 July 2020.

David Kershaw, *Principles of Takeover Regulation* (1st edn, Oxford University Press 2018).

Chia Ling Koh, *The Rise of E-Money and Virtual Currencies: Re-Discovering the Meaning of Money from a Legal Perspective* (Osborne Clarke 2018) accessed 07 July 2020.

Laurie Korpi and Yasmine Dong, 'Unrivalled Insight into Global Digital Payments Regulation' (2015) <https://gamblingcompliance.com/sites/gamblingcompliance.com/files/attachments/page/PaymentsCompliance%20-%20Payments%20Lawyer%20June%202015.pdf> accessed 06 July 2020.

Thad Kousser and Matthew McCubbins, 'Social Choice, Crypto-Initiatives, and Policymaking by Direct Democracy' (2005) 78 Southern California Law Review 949.

Rainer Kulms, 'Blockchain: Private Law Matters' (2020) Singapore Journal of Legal Studies 63.

Jens Lausen, 'Regulating Initial Coin Offerings? A Taxonomy of Crypto-Assets' (2019) Association for Information Systems Research Paper <http://aisel.aisnet.org.ecis2019_rp/26> accessed 09 July 2020.

David Lee et al, Handbook of Blockchain, Digital Finance, and Inclusion (1st edn, Elsevier 2018) Vol 1 & Vol 2.

Joseph Lee, 'Smart Contracts for Securities Transaction on the DLT Platform (Blockchain): Legal Obstacles and Regulatory Challenges' (2020) <https://papers.ssrn.com/sol3/papers.cfm?abstract_id=3523317> accessed 09 July 2020.

Joseph Lee and Florian Lheureux, 'A Regulatory Framework for Cryptocurrency' (2020) 31(3) European Law Review 423.

Lin Lin and Dora Neo, 'Alternative Investments in the Tech Era' (2020) 1 Singapore Journal of Legal Studies 1.

Nan Liu et al, 'A Critical Review of Distributed Ledger Technology and Its Applications in Real Estate' (2020) <https://www.rics.org/globalassets/rics-website/media/knowledge/research/research-reports/rics0077-001-distributed-ledger-technology-review-report–final.pdf> accessed 08 July 2020.

Thijs Maas, 'Why Hybrid Tokens are Superior to Utility Tokens: Comparing Utility Tokens, Security Tokens and Hybrid Tokens' (2019) <https://medium.com/hackernoon/hybrid-tokens-are-superior-to-utility-tokens-heres-why-3bec287c465> accessed 09 July 2020.

Gareth Malna and Sarah Kenshall, 'Chapter 25 United Kingdom' in Thomas Frick (ed), *The Financial Technology Law Review* (2nd edn, The LawReviews 2019).

Tara Mandjee, 'Bitcoin, Its Legal Classification and Its Regulatory Framework' (2016) 15 Journal of Business and Securities Law 158.

Adam Marszk and Ewa Lechman, *Exchange-Traded Funds in Europe* (1st edn, Academic Press 2019).

Frederick Martin, The History of Lloyd's and of Marine Insurance in Great Britain (London MacMillan 2004).

Baker McKenzie, 'Global Financial Services Regulatory Guide' (2016) <https://www.bakermckenzie.com/-/media/files/insight/publications/2016/07/guide_global_fsrguide_2017.pdf?la=en> accessed 07 July 2020.

Ranald Michie, The London Stock Exchange: A History (Oxford: OUP 2003).

Edmund Mokhtarian and Alexander Lindgren, 'Rise of the Crypto Hedge Fund: Operational Issues and Best Practices for an Emergent Investment Industry' (2018) 23 Stanford Journal of Law, Business & Finance 112.

Satoshi Nakamoto, 'Bitcoin: A Peer-to-Peer Electronic Cash System' (2009) <https://www.bitcoin.com/bitcoin.pdf> accessed 06 July 2020.

Michael Ng, 'Choice of Law for Property Issues Regarding Bitcoin under English Law' (2019) 15 Journal of Private International Law 315.

Friederike Niepmann and Tim Schmidt-Eisenlohr, 'International Trade, Risk, and the Role of Banks' (2014) Federal Reserve Bank of New York Staff Reports No. 633.

S Nishimura, 'A New Way to Fundraise? – Token Equity Convertible' (2018) <https://medium.com/@vcinsights/a-new-way-to-fundraise-token-equity-convertible-tec-7d3c987e520e> accessed 09 July 2020.

OECD, 'Striking the Right Balance between Competition and Regulation: The Key is Learning from Our Mistakes' (2002) APEC-OECD Co-operative Initiative on Regulatory Reform <https://www.oecd.org/regreform/2503205.pdf> accessed 09 July 2020.

OECD, 'Risk Management and Corporate Governance' (2014) <http://www.oecd.org/daf/ca/risk-management-corporate-governance.pdf> accessed 07 July 2020.

OECD, 'The Tokenisation of Assets and Potential Implications for Financial Markets' (2020) OECD Blockchain Policy Series <https://www.oecd.org/finance/The-Tokenisation-of-Assets-and-Potential-Implications-for-Financial-Markets.pdf> accessed 06 July 2020.

Albert Opher et al, 'The Rise of the Data Economy: Driving Value through Internet of Things Data Monetisation' 2016.

Gabrielle Patrick and Anurag Bana, 'Rule of Law Versus Rule of Code: A Blockchain-Driven Legal World' (2017) IBA Legal Policy & Research Unit Legal Paper.

Caslav Pejovic, 'Documents of Title in Carriage of Goods by Sea: International Law and Practice' (1st edn, Informa Law from Routledge 2020) 461.

People's Bank of China, 'Notice on Precautions against the Risks of Bitcoins'(2013) <http://www.miit.gov.cn/n1146295/n1652858/n1652930/   n3757016/c3762245/content.html> accessed on 10 July 2020.

PrivSec Report, 'Preventing Data Breaches and Assisting GDPR Compliance Using Encryption' (2017)   <https://gdpr.report/news/2017/12/21/preventing-data-breaches-assisting-gdpr-compliance-using-encryption/> accessed 06 July 2020.

Public-Private Analytic Exchange Programme, 'Risk and Vulnerabilities of Virtual Currency: Cryptocurrency as a Payment Method' (2017) < https://www.dni.gov/files/PE/Documents/9---2017-AEP_Risks-and-Vulnerabilities-of-Virtual-Currency.pdf> accessed 07 July 2020.

PwC, 'Cryptographic Assets and Related Transactions: Accounting Considerations under IFRS'   (2019)   <https://www.pwc.com/gx/en/audit-services/ifrs/publications/ifrs-16/cryptographic-assets-related-transactions-accounting-considerations-ifrs-pwc-in-depth.pdf> accessed 09 July 2020.

Sophia Qasir, 'Anonymity in Cyberspace: Judicial and Legislative Regulations' (2013) 81 Fordham Law Review 3651.

Regulatory Requirements and Economic Impact Working Group, International Telecommunication Union, 'Regulatory Challenges and Risks for Central Bank Digital Currency' (2019) <https://www.itu.int/en/ITU-T/focusgroups/dfc/Documents/DFC-O-006_Report%20on%20Regulatory%20Challenges%20and%20Risks%20for%20Central%20Bank%20Digital%20Currency.pdf> accessed 05 July 2020.

Carla Reyes, '(Un)Corporate Crypto-Governance' (2020) 88 Fordham Law Review 1875.

Janis Sarra and Louise Gullifer, 'Crypto-Claimants and Bitcoin Bankruptcy: Challenges for Recognition and Realization' (2019) 28 (2) International Insolvency Review 233.

Securities and Futures Commission of Hong Kong, 'Conceptual Framework for the Potential Regulation of Virtual Asset Trading Platform Operates' (2018) <https://www.sfc.hk/web/EN/files/ER/PDF/App%202_%20Conceptual%20framework%20for%20VA%20tra> accessed on 09 July 2020.

Securities and Markets Stakeholder Group, European Securities and Markets Authority, 'Own Initiative Report on Initial Coin Offerings and Crypto-Assets' (2018) <https://www.esma.europa.eu/sites/default/files/library/esma22-106-1338_smsg_advice_-_report_on_icos_and_crypto-assets.pdf> accessed on 06 July 2020.

Emily Sherwin, 'Legal Taxonomy' (2009) 15 (1) Legal Theory 25.

Smart Contract Alliance, 'Smart Contracts: Is the Law Ready?' (2018) Smart Contract Whitepaper <https://lowellmilkeninstitute.law.ucla.edu/wp-content/uploads/2018/08/Smart-Contracts-Whitepaper.pdf> accessed 07 July 2020.

Brianne Smith, 'The Life-Cycle and Character of Crypto-Assets: A Framework for Regulation and Investor Protection' (2019) 19 (1) Journal of Accounting and Finance 156.

Telecommunication Standardisation Sector of ITU, 'Distributed Ledger Technology Regulatory Framework' (2019) Technical Report.

The Law Commission, 'Electronic Execution of Documents' (2019) Policy Paper No. 386 <https://s3-eu-west-2.amazonaws.com/lawcom-prod-storage-11jsxou24uy7q/uploads/2019/09/Electronic-Execution-Report.pdf> accessed 09 July 2020.

The Law Commission and The Scottish Law Commission, 'Sale of Goods Forming Part of a Bulk' (1965) Research Report No. 215/145.

The Libra Association Members, 'Libra White Paper' (2020) <https://libra.org/en-US/white-paper/> accessed 07 July 2020.

thinkBLOCKtank, 'The Regulation of Token in Europe: National Legal & Regulatory Frameworks in Select European Countries' (2019) <http://thinkblocktank.org/wp-content/uploads/2019/08/thinkBLOCKtank-Token-Regulation-Paper-v1.0-Part-C.pdf> accessed 06 July 2020.

Peter Temperley, 'Using Crypto Tokens in Insurance' (2018) <https://medium.com/@peter.temperley/using-crypto-tokens-in-insurance-7125ccb090eb> accessed 09 July 2020.

UK HM Revenue & Customs, 'Cryptoassets: Tax for Individuals' (2019) UK HM Revenue & Customs Policy Paper <https://www.gov.uk/government/publications/tax-on-cryptoassets/cryptoassets-for-individuals> accessed 09 July 2020.

UK HM Treasury et al, 'Cryptoassets Taskforce: Final Report' (2018) <https://assets.publishing.service.gov.uk/government/uploads/system/uploads/attachment_data/file/752070/cryptoassets_taskforce_ final_report_final_web.pdf> accessed 09 July 2020.

UK HM Treasury, 'Cryptoasset Promotions: Consultation' (2020) <https://assets.publishing.service.gov.uk/government/uploads/system/uploads/attachment_data/file/902891/Cryptoasset_promotions_consultation.pdf> accessed 22 July 2020.

Alan Watson, 'Legal Transplants and European Private Law' (2000) 4 Electronic Journal of Comparative Law <http://www.ejcl.org/44/art44-2.html>.

Neal Watson and Beliz McKenzie, 'Shareholders' Right in Private and Public Companies in the UK (England and Wales)' (2019) <https://uk.practicallaw.thomsonreuters.com/5-613-3685?transitionType=Default&contextData=(sc.Default)&firstPage=true> accessed 07 July 2020.

Darrell West and John Allen, 'How Artificial Intelligence Is Transforming the World' (2018) <https://www.brookings.edu/research/how-artificial-intelligence-is-transforming-the-world/> accessed 09 July 2020.

Dominic Worner et al, 'The Bitcoin Ecosystem: Disruption Beyond Financial Services?' (2016) European Conference on Information Systems.

Rain Xie, 'Why China Had to Ban Cryptocurrency but the U.S. Did Not: A Comparative Analysis of Regulations on Crypto-Markets between the U.S. and China' (2019) 2 Washington University Global Studies Law Review 457.

Ryan Zullo, 'Can Tokenisation Fix the Secondary IPO Market?' (2020) <https://www.eisneramper.com/tokenization-secondary-ipo-catalyst-0420/> accessed 07 July 2020.

Part VII

Markets and trading

21 High-frequency trading – regulatory and supervisory challenges in the pursuit of orderly markets[1]

Trude Myklebust

1 Introduction

The frequently used notion of 'fair and orderly markets'[2] captures two essential goals of securities regulation. This chapter focuses on the aspect of orderly markets and discusses the challenges faced by regulatory and supervisory efforts to maintain orderly trading conditions in markets where high-frequency trading (HFT) is present.[3]

It is by now generally acknowledged that HFT exacerbates the risk of disorderly trading and instability in the markets in which it operates, epitomised by so-called *flash crashes*, disturbances to market functionality and excessive volatility. This risk has elicited a number of regulatory responses, including MiFID II[4] in the European Union (EU).

The EU regulatory framework imposes requirements on both high-frequency traders and the market venues that allow high-frequency traders to take part in trading activities through their electronic trading systems. Systematically, these rules belong within securities regulation, which is one of the three main areas of financial regulation.[5] The regulation of HFT employs several of the strategies commonly used in financial regulation,[6] including entry requirements for HFT firms, as well as conduct requirements, information requirements and governance-related requirements, especially with regards to systems

---

1 The author gave a presentation on the topic of this chapter at a seminar organised by Professor Gudula Deipenbrock and Professor Paola Chirulli at Sapienza Università di Roma, on 13 December 2019. I am grateful to Professor Gudula Deipenbrock and Professor Paola Chirulli for this. I would also like to thank Professor Mads Andenæs, for his guidance and many inspiring discussions on this and other issues. All errors remain mine.

2 See for instance Caroline Bradley, 'Disorderly Conduct: Day Traders and the Ideology of "Fair and Orderly Markets"' (2000) 26(1) Journal of Corporation Law 63; Jonathan Macey and David Swensen, 'Recovering the Promise of the Orderly and Fair Stock Exchange' (2017) 42 The Journal of Corporation Law 777.

3 For a discussion of fairness-related questions with regard to the regulation of HFT in MiFID II, see Trude Myklebust, 'Fairness and Integrity in High-Frequency Markets – A Critical Assessment of the European Regulatory Approach' (2020) 31 European Business Law Review 33.

4 Directive 2014/65/EU of the European Parliament and of the Council of 15 May 2014 on markets in financial instruments and amending Directive 2002/92/EC and Directive 2011/61/EU [2014] OJ L173/349 (MiFID II).

5 This regulatory field also encompasses the areas of banking law, and the regulation of insurance companies and occupational pension schemes, among others.

6 John Armour and others, *Principles of Financial Regulation* (First edition, Oxford University Press 2016) 73.

specifications. Entities taking part in HFT activities will also be subjected to enforcement, both with regards to requirements as to self-monitoring and administrative supervision.[7] Although the adopted regulatory package in MiFID II (along with its accompanying regulations and technical standards and enforcement system) is both comprehensive and detailed, it is unclear whether it will bring about the desired result of ensuring orderly trading environments.

The background for this article is the technological, institutional and regulatory changes that have radically transformed the workings of the financial markets over the past decades. The hallmarks of this new market reality include the continuously increasing fragmentation of trade[8] as well as cross-market and cross-border activity. The current trading landscape features high levels of competitive dynamics between market venues of different regulatory status.[9] This, in combination with a host of new market entrants, many of which have adopted advanced computer-based trading systems, results in a situation of unprecedented and highly adaptive capacity and complexity. Thus, regulators' endeavours to safeguard orderly trading conditions and resilient markets take place in a context which diverges in fundamental ways from the traditional factual and legal paradigms[10] of securities trading. This observation motivates the two main research questions of this chapter. First, how can we describe the disorderly trading conditions that arise in HFT markets and what are the implications in terms of systemic risk? Second, what challenges will regulators encounter in their efforts to safeguard orderly market conditions in markets where HFT is present? The chapter then discusses whether the relevant EU regulation adequately responds to these challenges.

2 Exploring the risks to orderly trading in HFT markets

2.1 *The defining features of HFT markets*

Electronic trading techniques have become ubiquitous in current market environments.[11] Traders in global financial markets rely on advanced electronic trading strategies in their day-to-day business. Pre-programmed algorithms make decisions on where, when and how to trade, meaning that much of today's trading decisions are automated and performed without human intervention.[12]

HFT, which is the main focus of this chapter, is a subgroup of algorithmic trading distinguished by its technical properties, its strategies and the nature of its relationship

---

7 See categorisation of various forms of enforcement in Rüdiger Veil, 'Concept and Aims of Capital Markets Regulation' in Rüdiger Veil (ed), *European Capital Markets Law* (2nd edition, Hart Publishing, an imprint of Bloomsbury Publishing Plc 2017) 29.

8 In the current dispersed market environment, the same financial assets will often be traded simultaneously across a range of market platforms. This is further explained in Section 2.1 below.

9 Guido Ferrarini and Niamh Moloney, 'Reshaping Order Execution in the EU and the Role of Interest Groups: From MiFID I to MiFID II' (2012) 13 European Business Organization Law Review 557.

10 See for instance Yesha Yadav, 'Algorithmic Trading and Market Regulation' in Walter Mattli (ed) *Global Algorithmic Capital Markets* (Oxford University Press 2018) <http://www.oxfordscholarship.com/view/10.1093/oso/9780198829461.001.0001/oso-9780198829461-chapter-9> (Call-off date for all hyperlinks, unless stated otherwise: 31 March 2020).

11 For a more comprehensive account of the features of HFT markets, see Myklebust (n 3) 38 et seq.

12 See for instance Marcus P Lerch, 'Algorithmic Trading and High-Frequency Trading' in Rüdiger Veil (ed), *European Capital Markets Law* (2nd edition, Hart Publishing, an imprint of Bloomsbury Publishing Plc 2017) 481.

with the market venues in which it operates. HFT uses highly advanced and complex trading systems which make it possible to move across the trading systems of different market venues with astonishing speed, measured in time units beyond human perception.[13]

As will be discussed in Section 4.2 below, HFT suffers from a lack of conceptual clarity something that causes challenges in several respects. For legal purposes a definition is included in Art. 4(1)(40) of MiFID II:

'high-frequency algorithmic trading technique' means an algorithmic trading technique characterised by:

a   infrastructure intended to minimise network and other types of latencies, including at least one of the following facilities for algorithmic order entry: co-location, proximity hosting or high-speed direct electronic access;

b   system-determination of order initiation, generation, routing or execution without human intervention for individual trades or orders; and

c   high message intraday rates which constitute orders, quotes or cancellations;

Algorithmic trading is defined in Art. 4(1)(39) of MiFID II:

'algorithmic trading' means trading in financial instruments where a computer algorithm automatically determines individual parameters of orders such as whether to initiate the order, the timing, price or quantity of the order or how to manage the order after its submission, with limited or no human intervention, and does not include any system that is only used for the purpose of routing orders to one or more trading venues or for the processing of orders involving no determination of any trading parameters or for the confirmation of orders or the post-trade processing of executed transactions;

High-frequency traders pursue a range of different strategies that span from techniques resembling market making and different modes of arbitrage, to so-called directional trading.[14] HFT is also associated with prohibited, but hard-to-detect, manipulative practices. However, a common denominator of the various strategies is that they critically depend on the speed with which the high-frequency traders place, update and cancel orders in the market venues' trading systems. As a general rule, high-frequency traders do not participate in trading to hold a portfolio of financial assets. They often do not hold open positions at the end of a trading day.[15] The aim of HFT is to secure a financial return from the trading activity itself. Thus, the purpose of trading differs from that of other investors. As the profit potential per transaction is small, HFT posts very large numbers of orders, but also operates with a very high level of cancellations. The penetration of HFT, like that of other forms of

13 The trading speed is measured in milliseconds, microseconds or even nanoseconds, see Walter Mattli, *Darkness by Design: The Hidden Power in Global Capital Markets* (Princeton University Press 2019) 1.

14 For a description of various techniques employed by HFT, see Myklebust (n 3) 42 et seq.

15 See Lerch (n 12) 484.

electronic and automated trading, varies across markets and geographic areas, ranging from 25 to 70 percent according to estimates in a recent report by IMF.[16]

The properties and risks of HFT are best understood when considered as an integral part of the market environments in which it takes place. The traditional role of stock exchanges as the sole venue for the execution of trades in securities issued by companies admitted to the exchange has over the past decades been superseded[17] by a fragmented and dispersed market environment, where the same financial assets can be traded simultaneously across a range of market venues of different regulatory status.[18] Market venues are no longer mutual or member-owned institutions, but have been transformed into for-profit enterprises that compete with each other for trading, liquidity and revenues. These structural changes are advanced by the accelerated technological developments replacing trading techniques performed by humans in interaction and traditional trading floors by electronic trading systems through which orders are placed and matched. Over the years, HFT has expanded its territory from the securities markets to markets for a wide range of financial assets.

The structural changes just described result in part from a regulatory agenda which has sought to decrease the hegemony of the old business model of incumbent stock exchanges by increasing competition and thereby driving down transaction costs in securities markets. However, these regulatory efforts failed to foresee the full range of consequences market fragmentation would have on market evolution and the new business models that would arise in this fragmented space. HFT is a prime example of the latter. With its superior abilities to exploit arbitrage opportunities created by the price discrepancies that inevitably develop in fragmented markets,[19] and its ability to harness the features of the trading system to its own advantage,[20] high-frequency traders have in many respects outcompeted the traditional day traders and market makers.[21] However, the expansion of HFT was only made possible by the specific arrangements agreed with market venues. The latter are interested in attracting HFT activities to their markets, as this leads to an increase in trading activity, liquidity and revenues. In command of the configuration of their own trading systems and the rules that govern trading (the market microstructure), market venues offer special arrangements to HFT, such as co-location, special order and fee structures, and access to market information structured in ways that meet the needs of high-frequency

16 International Monetary Fund 'Global Financial Stability Report: Vulnerabilities in a Maturing Credit Cycle' (April 2019) 51. See also the discussion on measuring problems in Section 4.2 below.
17 This has among others led to a reallocation of regulatory and supervisory powers to avert conflict of interests arising from changed incentives on the side of exchanges to perform self-regulatory activities. See Guido Ferrarini and Paolo Saguato, 'Regulating Financial Market Infrastructures' in Niamh Moloney, Eilís Ferran and Jennifer Payne (eds), *The Oxford Handbook of Financial Regulation* (Oxford University Press 2015) 576.
18 See, for instance, Dariusz Wójcik, *The Global Stock Market: Issuers, Investors, and Intermediaries in an Uneven World* (Oxford University Press 2011). See also Myklebust (n 3) 38 et seq. for a description of how the changes influenced the development of HFT.
19 Maureen O'Hara, 'High Frequency Market Microstructure' (2015) 116 Journal of Financial Economics 257, 258.
20 Thierry Foucault, 'Algorithmic Trading' in Frédéric Abergel and others (eds), *Market Microstructure: Confronting Many Viewpoints* (Wiley 2012) 14.
21 See Lerch (n 12) 515.

traders.[22] However, being proprietary contracts, it is difficult to know the full range and nature of such arrangements.

When it comes to the effects of HFT, evidence within a comprehensive financial literature on the topic is mixed. HFT has been considered to have a positive effect in terms of higher liquidity, improved price efficiency and lower transaction costs, all factors important for the assessment of *market quality* as this term is traditionally used within financial theory and in particular the sub-field of market microstructure theory.[23] However, these findings are not conclusive[24] and are constantly being nuanced by new research.[25] The negative effects of HFT with regard to fairness, integrity and systemic risk have increasingly become the focus of policymakers, practitioners and scholars from different fields.[26]

2.2 *Flash crashes and other disruptive market events*

While market actors and regulators are striving to get a better understanding of the new realities of the fragmented and technologically advanced financial markets, the occurrence of disruptive market events have caused serious concerns as to the risk of, what the International Organization of Securities Commissions (IOSCO) refers to as, 'abnormal (including extreme) volatility in financial markets'.[27] The colloquial term for such incidents is 'flash crash'.

Instances involving extreme market movements have been registered on several occasions. Among the most well-known is the flash crash which took place on the New York Stock Exchange on 6 May 2010.[28] Cespa and Vives point out that flash crashes have become pervasive, ranging from stocks to commodities and even treasury bonds, noting that for US futures markets in the five-year period from 2010, more than one hundred flash events were documented.[29] According to Mattli, 'mini flash crashes' involving erratic price swings in individual stocks over milliseconds occur daily in today's markets.[30]

---

22 Giovanni Cespa and Thierry Foucault, 'Sale of Price Information by Exchanges: Does It Promote Price Discovery?' (2014) 60 Management Science 148.
23 Market quality is a concept developed in economic theory and particularly within the sub-field of market microstructure theory, often focused on the features of efficiency, liquidity, volatility and price formation. See Myklebust (n 3) 50 et seq. with further references.
24 David Easley, Marcos López de Prado and Maureen O'Hara (eds), *High-Frequency Trading: New Realities for Traders, Markets and Regulators* (Risk Books 2013) 209. See also Lerch (n 12) 496 et seq.
25 See for instance Johannes Breckenfelder, 'Competition among High-Frequency Traders, and Market Quality' (2019) ECB Working Paper Series No 2290; Álvaro Cartea and others, 'Ultra-Fast Activity and Intraday Market Quality' (2019) 99 Journal of Banking & Finance 157. ESMA notes that duplicated orders may lead to an overestimation of available liquidity, see ESMA 'Order Duplication and Liquidity Measurement in EU Equity Market – Economic Report No. 1' (2016).
26 For a comprehensive discussion of various effects of HFT, see Myklebust (n 3) 50 et seq. with further references.
27 IOSCO, 'Mechanisms Used by Trading Venues to Manage Extreme Volatility and Preserve Orderly Trading – Final Report' (FR13/18, 2018) 1.
28 Staffs of the Commodity Futures Trading Commission and the Securities and Exchange Commission, 'Findings Regarding the Market Events of May 6, 2010 – Report of the Staffs of the CFTC and SEC to the Joint Advisory Committee on Emerging Regulatory Issues' (30 September 2010) 1. Other notable events are described in IOSCO (n 27) 3.
29 Giovanni Cespa and Xavier Vives, 'High Frequency Trading and Fragility – Working Paper Series 2020' (European Central Bank 2017) 2.
30 Mattli (n 13) 113.

There is strong evidence that HFT and bouts of excessive volatility and sudden liquidity shortages are interrelated.[31] When comparing market conditions before and after the introduction of a market system that facilitated HFT participation, Jain and others found increases in the exposure to systemic risk, particularly during tail-risk[32] events, which could potentially lead to highly destabilised market situations. Farmer and Skouras point out that 'fads in algos are more dangerous than fads in broader trading principles, because by involving extremely systematic trading patterns they can become widespread and can lead to systemic risk because they are highly correlated across many participants'.[33]

There are various ways in which HFT can trigger market dysfunction and lead to flash crashes. Among the potential causal factors are rogue algorithms, algorithms overreacting to market events and the increased pressure on trading systems to cope with the large numbers of orders generated by automated trading.[34] Haldane explains how automatic sell-off by HFT algorithms magnifies the effects of an event through a 'fire-sale forced machine selling'.[35] Furthermore, an increase in volatility can be set off by algorithmic market makers withdrawing liquidity in times of market turmoil.[36] Cyber-attacks may also be a trigger for disruptive events,[37] where HFT can amplify the effects.[38]

The impact of flash crashes may be severe, as emphasised by Madhavan:

> It is difficult to overstate the potential negative consequences of another flash crash. Such an event could dramatically erode investor confidence and participation in the capital markets for years to come, leading to reduced liquidity and higher transaction costs.[39]

31 See Lerch (n 12) 497: 'There is strong evidence that HFT takes liquidity out of the market and increases volatility when markets are under stress. This may cause flash crashes; in fact, 'mini flash crashes' happen frequently already.'

32 Pankaj K Jain, Pawan Jain and Thomas H McInish, 'Does High-Frequency Trading Increase Systemic Risk?' (2016) 31 Journal of Financial Markets 1. 'Tail-risk' is a colloquial term that describes events that have a small estimated probability of occurring, alluding to the ends on either side of normal distribution curves (bell curves). Such events are sometimes referred to as 'Black Swans', see in particular Nassim Nicholas Taleb, *The Black Swan: The Impact of the Highly Improbable* (Penguin Group 2010). See also Andrew G Haldane and Benjamin Nelson, 'Tails of the Unexpected' Speech (8 June 2012) given at the conference *The Credit Crisis Five Years On: Unpacking the Crisis* held at the University of Edinburgh Business School.

33 J Doyne Farmer and Spyros Skouras, 'An Ecological Perspective on the Future of Computer Trading' (2013) 32513 Quantitative Finance 325.

34 European Commission, 'Review of the Markets in Financial Instruments Directive (MiFID) – Public consultation' (2010) 15.

35 Andrew G Haldane, 'The Race to Zero' in Franklin Allen and others (eds) *The Global Macro Economy and Finance* (Palgrave Macmillan 2012) 260.

36 Mattli (n 13) 112–3.

37 Emanuel Kopp, Lincoln Kaffenberger and Christopher Wilson, 'Cyber Risk, Market Failures, and Financial Stability' (2017) 17 IMF Working Papers <http://elibrary.imf.org/view/IMF001/24475-9781484313787/24475-9781484313787/24475-9781484313787.xml>.

38 Gregory Meyer, 'NYSE Owner Warns of Cyber Risk to High-Frequency Trading' Financial Times (13 March 2015) <https://www.ft.com/content/62d9101c-c9a1-11e4-b2ef-00144feab7de>.

39 Ananth Madhavan, 'Exchange-Traded Funds, Market Structure, and the Flash Crash' (2012) 68 Financial Analysts Journal 20, 32. Other adverse effects noted here are severe disruption of closing prices and hence of the pricing of index derivative products, with follow-on effects for foreign markets and the subsequent day's opening.

These findings are supported by those of Foucault, who observes that the extreme price movements are accompanied by a sharp decline in liquidity, thereby leading to both price and liquidity crashes. He also notes that they happen without apparent changes in fundamentals and that multiple assets are affected.[40]

The correlation between HFT and disruptive trading conditions has also been subject of investigations undertaken by policymakers, regulators and supervisors. As will be explained in Section 3 below, particularly the possible negative effects of HFT on various aspects of market functionality led to introducing a regulatory regime for HFT at EU level. IOSCO in particular has, through a series of reports,[41] explored the nature and impact of organisational and technological changes in market environments, focusing among others on how to mitigate extreme volatility and preserve orderly trading.[42] At EU level, concerns related to increased systemic risk in HFT markets were noted in the MiFID review process[43] and later addressed in the ESMA report investigating the level of HFT activity in European financial markets.[44]

2.3 *Market-wide fragility and systemic repercussions*

The changes in market structure (described in Section 2.1 above) have resulted in a trading environment of unprecedented complexity and interconnectedness. Hence, market turmoil and disruptive events as described in Section 2.2 may not be confined to the market venue or the trading engine on which they arise. Concerns about excessive volatility or other disruptive incidents potentially migrating from one market to another due to the interconnectedness of markets, have been raised among others by Sornette and von der Becke. They contend that a consequence of the increasing inter-dependence between various financial instruments and asset classes, is that one can expect more flash crashes involving additional markets and instruments in the future.[45]

This increased level of interconnectedness of the financial system has, apart from other emerging system properties of concern, made policymakers alert to the impact of market-generated adverse incidents on systemic risk in a broad sense. Systemic risk

---

40 Thierry Foucault, 'Where Are the Risks in High Frequency Trading?' (2016) 20 Banque de France Financial Stability Review 53, 62.

41 IOSCO, 'Transparency and Market Fragmentation' (November 2001); IOSCO, 'Regulatory Issues Arising from Exchange Evolution – Final Report' (November 2006); IOSCO, 'Issues Raised by Dark Liquidity – Consultation Report' (CR05/10, 2010); IOSCO, 'Regulatory Issues Raised by the Impact of Technological Changes on Market Integrity and Efficiency – Final Report' (FR09/11, 2011); IOSCO, 'Technological Challenges to Effective Market Surveillance: Issues and Regulatory Tools – Final Report' (FR04/13, 2013).

42 IOSCO (n 27) 5.

43 The Committee of European Securities Regulators (CESR) 'CESR Technical Advice to the European Commission in the Context of the MiFID Review – Equity Markets' (2010) CESR/10-802 <https://www.esma.europa.eu/sites/default/files/library/2015/11/10_802_technical_advice_mifid_review_equity_markets.pdf>.

44 ESMA, 'High-Frequency Trading Activity in EU Equity Markets – Economic Report No. 1' (2014) <https://www.esma.europa.eu/sites/default/files/library/2015/11/esma20141_-_hft_activity_in_eu_equity_markets.pdf.>

45 Didier Sornette and Susanne Von der Becke, 'Crashes and High Frequency Trading – Foresight Driver Review DR 7' (2011) UK Government's Foresight Project: The Future of Computer Trading in Financial Markets 4.

has been a concern of securities regulators for decades.[46] However, the notion that market-wide stress can originate from structural elements of securities markets[47] is a marked departure from the traditional understanding of financial stability which was mostly associated with the banking sector.[48] This changed with the 2008 financial crisis, after which considerations of financial stability were included as governing objectives in securities and market regulation.[49] The same wider, cross-sectoral understanding of the concept of systemic risk, is demonstrated by the mandate of the European Systemic Risk Board (ESRB). Art. 2(c) of the ESRB Regulation[50] states that all types of financial intermediaries, markets and infrastructure may be systemically important to some degree.[51]

Contagion can lead to knock-on effects across markets. This aspect is raised by IOSCO, among others, who notes that the flip side of the price consistency that HFT arbitrage may bring to markets is that extreme price shocks may also be transmitted more easily both between different asset classes and between different trading venues.[52]

A clear understanding of the degree to which HFT firms may exacerbate the transmission of shocks across markets is still lacking.[53] How such contagion may occur will vary across different parts of the economy,[54] but among the potential propagation channels are financial indexes,[55] fire sales, margin cascades in derivatives markets[56] and default clauses that lead to termination of positions and exposures,[57] potentially triggering new rounds of terminations.[58] Schwarcz refers to the speed accelerated by high-speed algorithmic trading technology with which local shocks can travel through the financial system, and points out that the financial system increasingly exhibits the characteristics of

46 See already IOSCO, 'Objectives and Principles of Securities Regulation' (1998) i.
47 See for instance Andrew G Haldane, 'The Age of Asset Management?' Speech (4 April 2014) given at London Business School.
48 Andrew Crockett, 'Why Is Financial Stability a Goal of Public Policy?' (1997) 82 Economic Review – Federal Reserve Bank of Kansas City 4, 7.
49 Niamh Moloney, *EU Securities and Financial Markets Regulation* (3rd edition, Oxford University Press 2014) 5.
50 Regulation (EU) No 1092/2010 of the European Parliament and of the Council of 24 November 2010 on European Union macro-prudential oversight of the financial system and establishing a European Systemic Risk Board [2010] OJ L331/1.
51 See Trude Myklebust, 'Form and Function of the ESRB: A Critical Analysis' in Mads Andenas and Gudula Deipenbrock (eds) *Regulating and Supervising European Financial Markets – More Risks than Achievements* (Springer 2016) 49.
52 IOSCO, Regulatory Issues Raised by the Impact of Technological Changes on Market Integrity and Efficiency – Final Report' (FR09/11, 2011) 31.
53 IOSCO (n 52) 31.
54 See for example an empirical study that focuses on propagation within bond markets: Alberto Manconi, Massimo Massa and Ayako Yasuda, 'The Role of Institutional Investors in Propagating the Crisis of 2007–2008' (2012) 104 Journal of Financial Economics 491.
55 Kathryn Judge, 'Fragmentation Nodes: A Study in Financial Innovation, Complexity and Systemic Risk' (2012) 64 (3) Stanford Law Review 657, 698.
56 Andrew G Haldane, 'Multi-Polar Regulation' (2015) 11 International Journal of Central Banking 385.
57 See for instance Jain and others (n 32), who develop a measurement of systemic risk in HFT markets, referring to the spillover effect from one stock's selling pressure to another stock or the whole stock market.
58 Breckenfelder (n 25).

so-called tight coupling, exacerbating the risk of wider contagion,[59] because the failure of a single firm or market can rapidly propagate throughout the financial system.[60] This is in line with observations made by Kirilenko and Lo:

> The financial system has become much more of a *system* than ever before, with globally interconnected counterparties and privately-owned and – operated infrastructure that facilitates tremendous integration during normal market conditions, but which spreads dislocation rapidly during periods of financial distress.[61]

Similar concerns have been voiced by the European Systemic Risk Board (ESRB) in their response to the ESMA consultation paper on Guidelines on systems and controls in a highly automated trading environment for trading platforms, investment firms and competent authorities:

> The ESRB would also like to draw the attention of the ESMA to the risk that HFT would amplify the transmission of shocks across markets, potentially contributing to one or more financial shocks becoming systemic.[62]

The ESRB substantiated this warning by highlighting two different concerns: the propagation of illiquid market conditions due to fire sales and the increased interconnectedness of markets, which could result in swifter transmission of adverse shocks (contagion) through financial markets.

The risk of cross-market contagion emanating from HFT activity increases the importance of deterring disruptive market events from occurring in the first place. At the same time, the underlying features of the financial markets that may contribute to such developments – complexity, velocity, connectivity and uncertainty among others – also complicate the process of designing appropriate and practicable regulatory responses, something that will be discussed further in Section 4.4.

---

59 See Steven L Schwarcz, 'Regulating Complexity in Financial markets' (2009) 87 Wash. UL Rev. 211, 215, with further reference to Richard Bookstaber, *A Demon of Our Own Design: Markets, Hedge Funds, and the Perils of Financial Innovation* (John Wiley & Sons 2007) 144.

60 Steven L Schwarcz, 'Regulating Financial Change: A Functional Approach' (2016) 100 Minn. L. Rev. 1441, 1477.

61 Andrei A Kirilenko and Andrew W Lo, 'Moore's Law versus Murphy's Law: Algorithmic Trading and Its Discontents' (2013) 27 Journal of Economic Perspectives 51, 53.

62 ESRB, 'ESRB response to the ESMA consultation paper on "Guidelines on Systems and Controls in a Highly Automated Trading Environment for Trading Platforms, Investment Firms and Competent Authorities"' (21 September 2011). The ESMA Guidelines on Systems and Controls in an Automated trading Environment for trading platforms, Investment Firms and Competent Authorities, ESMA/2012/122 (24 February 2012) were issued to ensure a common, uniform and consistent application of MiFID and MAD. The guidelines were withdrawn 26 September 2018 by ESMA based on the subject matter being fully incorporated into MiFID II, MAR and relevant delegated acts. Information about the decision is available at <https://www.esma.europa.eu/document/guidelines-systems-and-controls-in-automated-trading-environment-trading-platforms>.

3 An overview of the EU regulatory responses

At the global level, different types of regulatory responses to HFT have been discussed or implemented, including financial transaction taxes, requirements on minimum resting times for orders, various safeguarding measures against malfunctioning algorithms and other system glitches, and organisational requirements to strengthen oversight and market integrity.[63]

In the EU, rules specifically addressing algorithmic trading, including HFT,[64] are provided in MiFID II with delegated acts, thus replacing and reinforcing the guidelines set out by ESMA in 2012.[65] The European regulation covers several other aspects of HFT than orderly trading. In particular, an important aim is to strengthen market integrity and fair market conditions in markets with HFT presence.[66] In the remainder of this section, the main focus will be on the rules that are of particular relevance for discussions relating to orderly trading and systemic stability.[67]

According to Recitals 63 and 64 of MiFID II, an important purpose was to strengthen the resilience of markets in the light of technological developments and to ensure robust measures were in place to ensure that algorithmic trading or HFT techniques do not create a disorderly market. Recital 62 of MiFID II states that trading technology gives rise to a number of potential risks such as an increased risk of overloading trading systems due to large volumes of orders, the risks of duplicative or erroneous orders, and other malfunctions that might create a disorderly market. Furthermore, Recital 62 of MiFID II emphasised the risk of algorithmic trading systems overreacting to other market events and exacerbating volatility in cases of pre-existing market problems.

To reduce the risks of disorderly trading conditions caused by algorithmic trading in general and HFT in particular, MiFID II addresses both the trading firms that operate such systems and the market venues that facilitate such trading.[68] The rules can be grouped according to the two broad categories set forth by Armour and others: *ex ante* strategies and *ex post* strategies.[69]

Whereas ex ante strategies comprise rules that apply from the moment the activity is carried out, particularly entry, conduct, information, prudential and governance regulation, ex post strategies comprise rules applying if something goes wrong.[70] This categorisation is useful when analysing the rules pertaining to HFT because, as pointed out by Lerch, there is a distinction between normal market circumstances and markets under stress, in which

---

63 For an overview of international responses, see Kee H Chung and Albert J Lee, 'High-Frequency Trading: Review of the Literature and Regulatory Initiatives around the World' (2016) 45 Asia-Pacific Journal of Financial Studies 7.

64 Algorithmic trading and HFT are defined in MiFID II, Arts. 4(1)(39) and 4(1)(40), see Section 2.1 above.

65 See n 62 above.

66 This aspect is discussed in Myklebust (n 3).

67 It is however important to note that the same provision can serve several purposes, for instance the authorisation and organisational requirements. A broader and more detailed description of the totality of the European regulation of HFT is provided in Myklebust (n 3) 55 et seq. with further references (see in particular fn 148).

68 For an overview, see Danny Busch, 'MiFID II: Regulating High Frequency Trading, Other Forms of Algorithmic Trading and Direct Electronic Market Access' (2016) 10 Law and Financial Markets Review 72.

69 Armour and others (n 6) 73.

70 Armour and others (n 6) 73.

the particular market functionalities and influences associated with HFT differ, depending on the market conditions prevalent at a particular time.[71]

Rules reducing the risk of disorderly trading in the *ex ante* category for HFT firms include requirements for firms that apply HFT and are not already authorised as an investment firm to seek such authorisation under Art. 2(1)(d)(iii) of MiFID II.[72] The firm shall according to Art. 7(1) of MiFID II not be granted authorisation unless and until such time as the competent authority is fully satisfied that the applicant complies with all requirements under the provisions adopted pursuant to MiFID II. HFT firms will be subject to the general organisational requirements for investment firms that follow from Art. 16 of MiFID II. Art. 17 of MiFID II lays down additional requirements[73] for firms involved in algorithmic trading (and therefore also HFT, as it is a subgroup of algorithmic trading). With regards to orderly trading, a particularly important element is the systems requirements set forth in Art. 17(1) of MiFID II, whereby an investment firm that engages in algorithmic trading shall have in place effective systems and risk controls suitable to the business it operates to ensure that its trading systems are resilient and have sufficient capacity, are subject to appropriate trading thresholds and limits and prevent the sending of erroneous orders or the systems otherwise functioning in a way that may create or contribute to a disorderly market. Furthermore, the firm shall have in place effective business continuity arrangements to deal with any failure of its trading systems and shall ensure its systems are fully tested and properly monitored to ensure that they meet the requirements laid down in this paragraph.

With regards to the market venues, Art. 48 of MiFID II places systems requirements on regulated markets that in many respects are similar to those described directly above for HFT firms. According to Art. 18(5) of MiFID II, the requirements for regulated markets shall also apply to multilateral trading facilities (MTF) and organised trading facilities (OTF).[74] The Member States shall require the market venues to have in place effective systems, procedures and arrangements to ensure its trading systems are resilient, have sufficient capacity to deal with peak order and message volumes, are able to ensure orderly trading under conditions of severe market stress, are fully tested to ensure such conditions are met and are subject to effective business continuity arrangements to ensure continuity of its services if there is any failure of its trading systems. Furthermore, the trading venues must according to Art. 48(9) of MiFID II also ensure

71 See Lerch (n 12) 496.
72 The criteria for identifying whether a firm is deemed to be applying an HFT technique are detailed in Art. 19 of Commission Delegated Regulation (EU) 2017/565 of 25 April 2016 supplementing Directive 2014/65/EU of the European Parliament and of the Council as regards organisational requirements and operating conditions for investment firms and defined terms for the purposes of that Directive, [2017] OJ L 87/1.
73 Detailed measures are given in Commission Delegated Regulation (EU) 2017/589 of 19 July 2016 supplementing Directive 2014/65/EU of the European Parliament and of the Council with regard to regulatory technical standards specifying the organisational requirements of investment firms engaged in algorithmic trading, OJ [2017] L87/417 (RTS 6).
74 For regulated markets, MTFs and OTFs, general requirements on authorisation and organisation apply for each category. See for instance Moloney (n 49) Ch V. for a description of these rules. Detailed measures are given in Commission Delegated Regulation (EU) 2017/584 of 14 July 2016 supplementing Directive 2014/65/EU of the European Parliament and of the Council with regard to regulatory technical standards specifying organisational requirements of trading venues OJ [2017] L87/350 (RTS 7).

they have trading rules and fee structures that do not create disorderly trading conditions or market abuse associated with HFT participation in their systems. Art. 48(4) of MiFID II requires market venues to be able to reject orders that exceed predetermined volume and price thresholds or that are clearly erroneous. Moreover, they must in accordance with Art. 48(6) of MiFID II provide testing facilities for algorithms to ensure that algorithmic trading systems cannot create or contribute to disorderly trading conditions on the market.

MiFID II also contains regulatory requirements that will bring more transparency to the operations of algorithmic trading. The venues must in line with Art. 48(10) of MiFID II require algorithmic (this also covers HFT) orders to be flagged and must share information relating to the order book with National Competent Authorities (NCAs) so that NCAs can monitor the trade. HFT firms are required to notify NCAs and the relevant trading venues on which they engage in algorithmic trading and are subject to further disclosure requirements regarding the nature and details of their strategies, according to Art. 17(2) of MiFID II.

Rules that fall in the *ex post* category – in this context, rules that are applicable if states of market turmoil and excessive volatility do arise – also impose requirements on both HFT firms and market venues. For both types of entities, these rules focus on measures that are able to stop systems functionality in case of malfunctioning, with the aim of averting further escalation of the situation. For investment firms, Art. 12 of RTS 6[75] requires the firm to be able to cancel immediately, as an emergency measure, any or all of its unexecuted orders submitted to any or all trading venues with which the investment firm is connected ('kill functionality').

For the market venues, Art. 48(5) of MiFID II requires that *circuit breakers* are set up, allowing the venues to *temporarily halt or constrain trading* in situations with severe volatility and cancel or correct orders in exceptional situations. In case of disorderly trading conditions, it follows from Art. 48(6) of MiFID II that the venues shall be able to manage them and have available systems which limit the ratio of unexecuted orders to transactions. In case of imminent overloading of the trading systems, the venues shall be able to slow down the flow of orders.

Regulatory measures have been put in place to reduce the risk of disruptive events related to the widespread HFT trading strategies which are akin to market making. Unlike traditional market makers, HFT market makers have to a less degree been subject to contractual obligations to continuously provide liquidity to the market. To counter concerns that HFT market makers will withdraw abruptly from the market, thereby causing illiquidity Art. 17(3) of MiFID II now requires high-frequency traders carrying out a market-making strategy to continue to do so throughout the day in order to provide regular and predictable liquidity, except under exceptional circumstances. The market venues are according to Art. 48(2) and (3) of MiFID II responsible for having in place written agreements with market makers and ensuring that a sufficient number of firms participate in market maker agreement with the purpose of providing liquidity to the market on a regular and predictable basis.

The responsibility for monitoring and enforcement of HFT activity is partly left to the trading platforms on which the HFT activity takes place.[76] The market venues shall in

75 See n 73.
76 See Lerch (n 12) 514.

line with Art. 48(3) of MiFID II follow up on the market-maker obligations imposed on algorithmic firms, oversee market participation via Direct Electronic Access according to Art. 48(7) of MiFID II, and facilitate the flagging of algorithmic orders according to Art. 48(10) of MiFID II. As to administrative supervision, day-to-day supervision of HFT firms lies with NCAs. The same applies to the MTFs and OTFs, if they operate their trading platforms based on an authorisation as investment firms in accordance with Artt. 19 and 20 of MiFID II. Regulated markets are supervised by the NCAs in the country where the market is domiciled.

4 Regulatory and supervisory challenges to maintaining orderly and stable markets in trading environments with HFT participation

4.1 *Introduction*

Section 3 above shows that regulators are well aware of – and, moreover, see the need to respond to – risks to orderly markets linked to HFT activities. However, the EU regulation does not actively aim at decreasing the prevalence of HFT in the EU markets, but instead puts in place rules that seek to reduce the risks of harmful effects associated with this business practice. The success of this regulatory strategy depends on the efficacy of the rules in question, which again will depend on the appropriateness of the regulatory design, as well as the operational enforcement through supervision and monitoring of the relevant rules.[77] Building on these initial observations, the chapter now selects to discuss the following three issues relevant for the regulation and supervision of HFT: 1) the lack of conceptual clarity and knowledge, 2) conflicting regulatory objectives, and 3) how changes in market structure and market functionality create challenges in terms of designing and enforcing regulation that will successfully mitigate risks to orderly trading conditions.

---

77 See this distinction among others in Niamh Moloney, 'Supervision in the Wake of the Financial Crisis' in Eddy Wymeersch, Klaus J Hopt and Guido Ferrarini (eds), *Financial Regulation and Supervision: A post-crisis analysis* (Oxford University Press 2012) 71 <http://www.oxfordscholarship.com/view/10.1093/acprof:osobl/9780199660902.001.0001/acprof-9780199660902-chapter-4>. Enforcement can include private self-monitoring, private external monitoring (for instance by auditors) as well as supervision and monitoring by public authorities, see Veil (n 7) 29. Also civil liability regimes are important in terms of the efficiency and effectiveness of the relevant rules. For comprehensive studies from other areas of securities law, see Federico Della Negra, *MiFID II and Private Law: Enforcing EU Conduct of Business Rules* (Hart Publishing 2019) and Gudula Deipenbrock, 'The European Civil Liability Regime for Credit Rating Agencies from the Perspective of Private International Law – Opening Pandora's Box?' (2015) International and Comparative Corporate Law Journal, Special Issue: Civil Liability of Credit Rating Agencies in the European Union 3. From a US perspective, see discussion in Stanislav Dolgopolov, 'Legal Liability for Fraud in the Evolving Architecture of Securities Markets: From Marketplaces to Traders' in Walter Mattli (ed), *Global Algorithmic Capital Markets* (Oxford University Press 2018) Ch 10 <http://www.oxfordscholarship.com/view/10.1093/oso/9780198829461.001.0001/oso-9780198829461-chapter-10>.

4.2 *Lack of conceptual clarity and knowledge regarding the nature, scale and scope of HFT*

Mitigation of information asymmetry is one of the main justifications for regulatory intervention in financial markets.[78] Substantial parts of securities regulation reflect the need to increase the amount of information available to market actors and to level out information asymmetries between them.[79] However, information asymmetries are not just an issue for market actors; the work of regulatory and supervisory authorities is also at risk of being obstructed by a lack of insight and information regarding market practices. That risk automatically increases in periods of rapid innovation and change. Deipenbrock describes this problem as the 'FinTech information mismatch', with a view to FinTech and the problem of establishing the facts of the case in particular.[80]

The information mismatch pointed out by Deipenbrock is relevant also with regards to the nature and scope of HFT business strategies and their effects on market quality. The concern has been highlighted by regulators[81] as well as in academic literature.[82]

One particular obstacle seems to be that the definition of HFT varies across markets, and researchers also apply different definitions in their empirical investigations.[83] As noted by ESMA, this causes significant challenges for regulators when analysing HFT activities and its impacts, and moreover, is a significant challenge for regulators who need to define what constitutes HFT activity.[84]

A connected problem is the lack of HFT-related market data available to researchers, thereby limiting the scope of their research. Monaco here explains that only a few datasets allow the identification of HFT, and that most studies are hence based on proxies to detect HFT activity and highlight the effects of HFT on capital markets.[85]

Not only HFT practices are opaque, but also the relationship between high frequency traders and trading venues. The latter is subject of contractual arrangements and trading protocols, and shaped in addition by the structures of the trading system and the mode of communication between the systems of the venues and that of HFT. Such governing and technical arrangements form an integral part of the market microstructure of trading platforms and are to a large extent proprietary.[86] Writing in a different context (HFT-related market abuse), Dolgopolov explains that secret arrangements between trading venues and favoured traders limit the objectivity of the trading process taking place through the electronic matching engines.[87]

---

78 See for instance Armour and others, (n 6) 55 et seq.
79 Relevant sets of rules concern reporting, prospectuses, insider trading, pre- and post-trade transparency, etc.
80 Gudula Deipenbrock, 'FinTech – Unbearably Lithe or Reasonably Agile? – A Critical Legal Approach from the German Perspective' (2020) 31 European Business Law Review 3, 16.
81 ESMA (n 44) 4.
82 Mattli (n 13) ch 5; Myklebust (n 3) 37.
83 Eleonora Monaco, 'What FinTech Can Learn from High-Frequency Trading: Economic Consequences, Open Issues and Future of Corporate Disclosure' in Theo Lynn and others (eds), *Disrupting Finance* (Springer International Publishing 2019) 54 <http://link.springer.com/10.1007/978-3-030-02330-0_4>; Andrew J Keller, 'Robocops: Regulating High Frequency Trading after the Flash Crash of 2010' (2012) 73 Ohio St. LJ 1457, 1477. See also Lerch (n 12) 496.
84 ESMA (n 44) 4.
85 Monaco (n 83) 54.
86 Armour and others (n 6) 148.
87 Dolgopolov (n 77) 267.

The information mismatch raises regulatory challenges. First of all, the lack of insight into the structures and activities taking place on and across markets venues, as well as into the effects and risks entailed by these, limits policymakers' ability to make assessments when determining the appropriate levels of regulation. This is of particular concern to the extent excessive volatility could spread and cause systemic problems across the financial system. The result is that policymakers are prevented from making informed decisions regarding *risk tolerance*, or, what level of risk is *acceptable*,[88] a type of judgement familiar to decision-makers in other policy areas dealing with risks at the societal level.

Furthermore, the opacity surrounding HFT practices complicates the process of designing rules that will effectively achieve their purpose.[89] The statutory definition in Art. 4(1) (40) of MiFID II[90] hinges mostly on technical criteria and hence, does not distinguish between different HFT strategies, whether harmful or benign in terms of market quality.[91] As pointed out by Keller,[92] HFT regulators must begin to understand HFT as a trading method comprised of a variety of strategies with different goals, in order to institute an effective regulatory regime.

Lastly, difficulties in establishing relevant and reliable facts can also pose challenges in terms of performing reviews and assessing the efficacy of regulatory measures, which should form a natural part of a sound regulatory agenda[93] and for HFT is instituted in Art. 90(1)(c) of MiFID II.

4.3 *Conflicting regulatory objectives*

Within the area of securities regulation, the overarching regulatory objectives are commonly stated in terms of market efficiency, investor protection and financial stability.[94] However, the different legal objectives are not always aligned and will often have to be traded off against each other.[95] This section will in particular focus on the relationship between market efficiency and financial stability.[96]

Goal conflicts will require regulators to weigh the different objectives and considerations against each other, in order to reach the overall best result. However, balancing the different considerations within a 'regulatory objective function'[97] is no exact science, and

---

88 Robert Baldwin, Martin Cave and Martin Lodge, *Understanding Regulation: Theory, Strategy, and Practice* (2nd edition, Oxford University Press 2012) 283.
89 As pointed out by Moloney, it is challenging to figure out how to best capture HFT and algorithmic trading within a robust regulatory definition. Moloney (n 49) 552.
90 See Section 2.1 above.
91 Myklebust (n 3) 61.
92 Keller (n 83) 1457, 1477.
93 OECD, 'Policy Framework for Effective and Efficient Financial Regulation, General Guidance and High-Level Checklist' (2010) Section V <https://www.oecd.org/finance/financial-markets/44362818.pdf>.
94 See for instance Veil (n 7) 24. See also IOSCO, 'Objectives and Principles of Securities Regulation (2017)' 3. It is also suggested to broaden the catalogue of objectives, particularly by adding among others fairness, prevention of financial crime and competition, see Armour and others (n 6) 51.
95 Armour and others (n 6) 52.
96 Matters of relevance for investor protection in HFT markets are discussed in Myklebust (n 3).
97 The regulatory objective function is a term suggested by Armour and others to denote a possible framework for regulators when making priorities for resolving goal conflicts, see Armour and others (n 6) section 3.8.4.

may require challenging exercises of judgement and discretion on the part of regulators. Moreover, the objectives may change over time,[98] and thus also their relative weight.

With regards to HFT, it is clear that regulators have seen benefits as well as risks resulting from the business practice.[99] For instance in Recital 62 of MiFID II, positive effects of HFT are listed as wider participation in markets, increased liquidity, narrower spreads, reduced short term volatility and the means to obtain better execution of orders for clients. Such effects[100] are considered beneficial seen from the traditionally much emphasised perspective of market efficiency. On the other hand, Recital 62 notes that trading technology also gives rise to a number of potential risks such as an increased risk of overloading the systems of trading venues due to large volumes of orders, risks of algorithmic trading generating duplicative or erroneous orders or otherwise malfunctioning in a way that may create a disorderly market. These risks to orderly trading are clearly relevant seen from a financial stability objective.

The regulatory strategy chosen in MiFID II can thus be understood as being a compromise between the objectives of market efficiency and financial stability. It allows continued market presence of HFT, with the main features of the business model intact, while in parallel enacting measures intended to curb disorderly results of such activities. The question however arises if that approach reflects an appropriate balance between the objectives in question. This question has practical relevance because some measures that could be effective in reducing the risk of disorderly trading resulting from HFT (eg, reducing the speed, the connectivity across markets or the extent of HFT participation in a given market), at the same time could reduce effects of HFT that so far have been perceived as being beneficial in terms of improved market efficiency (eg, liquidity, price formation and reduced transaction costs).

Scholars have pointed out that algorithmic trading and HFT is a moving target that calls for a dynamic regulatory approach.[101] Changes to the regulation must be expected as markets continue to evolve, and regulators gain more experience with HFT practices and their effects. In the time that has passed since the MiFID II regulation was drafted and adopted, recent research results seem increasingly to question the efficiency-related benefits of HFT, and how they contribute to overall market quality.[102] At the same time, the financial research agenda increasingly seem to consider the risks and consequences of disorderly trading and propagation effects and has brought new and worrisome knowledge into the light.[103] Policymakers' attention towards and understanding of how systemic risk can originate in and propagate from technological developments in the financial sector is increasing.[104] Hence, policymakers should revisit the assessments of the balance between efficiency and stability in regulatory considerations going forward. The result may be a shift in favour of considerations of systemic stability in future regulation.

---

98 Mads Andenas and Iris H-Y Chiu, *The Foundations and Future of Financial Regulation: Governance for Responsibility* (Routledge 2014) 16.
99 See Lerch (n 12) 496.
100 See Section 2.1 above.
101 Lerch (n 12) 498–499 with further references.
102 See Sections 2.2 and 2.3 above.
103 See Sections 2.2 and 2.3 above.
104 See Moloney (n 49) 4–6; See in general, Douglas W Arner, Jànos Barberis and Ross P Buckley, 'FinTech, RegTech, and the Reconceptualization of Financial Regulation' (2017) 37 Northwestern Journal of International Law & Business 371, 403–404.

4.4 *Regulatory challenges raised by current market structure and market functionality*

As described above in Section 2.1 above, markets with HFT presence are characterised by automation, extreme velocity, very high numbers of messages (orders, cancellations and transactions), high levels of connectivity across markets and large investments in sophisticated technology and specialist personnel. The specialised HFT firms participating in the trade have different business models, revenue structures and company cultures when compared to traditional trading firms. These features challenge regulators' and supervisors' ability to uphold orderly markets in several ways, of which some will be discussed here.

First, the complexity of the market structure also leads to a complex task for regulators in judging risks and crafting responses, a task that is further complicated by the information mismatch pointed out in Section 4.2 above. A particular issue relates to the risk that problems which develop locally and within the confines of one specific computer-based trading system, through unforeseen interactions with other trading systems, may propagate and produce unexpected, unpredictable and undesirable price dynamics in markets.[105] These aggregate effects of changed market functionality challenge the traditional perspective and regulatory models of securities law, which so far mainly have been focused on tackling problems at the level of each institution or market.[106]

Second, the cross-market activities common to HFT raise additional concerns in terms of designing effective regulatory interventions and the timely coordination of their implementation. For instance, negative effects may arise if circuit breakers are not effectuated simultaneously across different markets where the same securities are traded. Moreover, the fact that HFT in the same instruments takes place on several trading platforms may obscure the insight supervisors need to assess the totality of any problems that develop. The cross-border dimension of HFT exacerbates this problem as several regulatory agencies in different jurisdictions may be involved with regards to the same episodes and regulated entities.[107] Such problems are of particular concern in an HFT environment, where the speed, complexity and cross-market connectivity mean that problems can develop and propagate in an instant, outrunning mitigating measures which depend on human consideration, intervention and coordination.[108]

A third concern of particular relevance for supervision and enforcement arises due to the costly, complex and sophisticated systems HFT firms and market venues employ. These

---

105 See Sections 2.2 and 2.3 above.
106 This aspect is comprehensively discussed by Saule T Omarova, who highlights how the existing regulatory model developed to tackle isolated micro-level phenomena becomes challenged by macro-level considerations brought on by fintech. Saule T Omarova, 'Technology v Technocracy: Fintech as a Regulatory Challenge' (2020) 6 Journal of Financial Regulation 75 <https://doi.org/10.1093/jfr/fjaa004>.
107 Tietje and Lehman uses the term 'domestic embeddedness' to explain how financial markets products are linked necessarily to a specific legal order. Christian Tietje and Matthias Lehmann, 'The Role and Prospects of International Law in Financial Regulation and Supervision' (2010) 13 Journal of International Economic Law 663, 678. This viewpoint seems equally relevant for market practices, as they also will be a result of contractual obligations entered into under the rules of a specific jurisdiction. That means that coordination between for instance different supervisory agencies can be complicated and take time, not least if the contact relates to jurisdictions outside the EEA area.
108 Lerch (n 12) 497.

systems compete with each other in what has been referred to as an 'arms race'[109] and thus constantly evolve. Supervisory agencies cannot be expected to have the competences and capacities to match these core assets of HFT firms, in terms of personnel and access to technology. It is doubtful whether regulators have attached sufficient weight to the obvious imbalance between the regulated entities and supervisory agencies in this respect. For example, it seems very difficult for supervisory agencies to assess whether the risk-mitigating systems and controls demanded of HFT firms and market venues are 'effective' and 'suitable', as required by Art. 17(1) and Art. 48(1) of MiFID II. Another example is the obligation in Art. 17(2) of MiFID II on HFT firms to provide competent authorities, upon request, with a description of the nature of its algorithmic trading strategies along with several other details of its systems and risk control. Scientists have pointed out the futility of such disclosure, given the vast range of technical descriptions that would have to be made, in combination with the lack of resources among supervisors to meaningfully process such information.[110]

Finally, the incentive structures embedded in the current business models of HFT firms and market venues as pointed out in Section 2.1 above, may impact the efficacy of some elements in the regulatory approach in MiFID II. As described in Section 3 above, MiFID II puts responsibility on the HFT firms and market venues to have in place trading systems that are resilient and uphold orderly trading conditions. Though subject to supervision, the design of these systems will to a large extent be under the influence of the regulated entities, as the configuration of the systems will relate closely to their market microstructure as such. A technique of enrolling market actors in the efforts to achieve regulatory objectives is not uncommon in financial market regulation,[111] but can raise potential conflicts of interest.[112] The characteristics which amplify threats to orderly trading – speed, complexity and connectivity, among others – are at the same time important factors in the competition for market shares and revenue for market venues and for HFT firms. Within private organisations (such as market venues and HFT firms), spending on measures that could reduce risk *ex ante* may lose out to more revenue-generating activities in terms of internal priorities. The same mechanisms could come into play regarding the *ex post* measures as described in Section 3. There could for instance be diverging opinions as to when a price movement is significant enough to warrant a trading halt in accordance with Art. 48(5) of MiFID II. Taken together, these issues lead to a concern that the regulatory techniques applied under MiFID II, with large reliance on the contributions from the market actors in terms of ensuring orderly trading conditions, are vulnerable to incentive problems.

---

109 Andrew G Haldane, 'Financial Arms Races' Speech (14 April 2012) given at the conference *Paradigm Lost* convened by Institute for New Economic Thinking in Berlin <https://www.ineteconomics.org/uploads/papers/haldane-andy-berlin-paper.pdf>.

110 See Dave Cliff, 'Regulatory Scrutiny of Algorithmic Trading Systems: An Assessment of the Feasibility and Potential Economic Impact. Economic Impact Assessment EIA16' (2011) UK Government's Foresight Project: The Future of Computer Trading in Financial Markets 14, building his assessment on a draft version of Art. 17(2) that, in this regard, is comparable to the adopted version, noting that the thinking behind the provision is 'rather naïve'.

111 J Black, 'Enrolling Actors in Regulatory Processes: Examples from UK Financial Services Regulation' (2003) Public Law 62.

112 For a comprehensive discussion, see Jonathan R Macey, 'The Nature and Futility of "Regulation by Assimilation"' in Greg Urban (ed), *Corporations and Citizenship* (University of Pennsylvania Press 2014) <http://www.degruyter.com/view/books/9780812209716/9780812209716.199/9780812209716.199.xml>. See also Lerch (n 12) 515.

5 Conclusion

This chapter has explored the nature, scale and scope of disorderly trading conditions that may develop in financial markets where HFT is present. It seems well documented that the presence of HFT in a market environment heightens the risk of flash crashes and excessive volatility. HFT can also act as a vehicle for the propagation of market turmoil to other market venues. These risks are closely associated with the core properties of the business model – specifically, the unprecedented speed, high messaging rates, complexity and cross-market connectivity that HFT entails – as these unfold in the fragmented, competitive and highly dynamic market environment which has developed over the past decades.

European regulation currently does little to directly restrict the scale and scope of HFT participation in markets. Instead, it aims to curb and control the ensuing risk by introducing a combination of preventive (*ex ante*) measures and emergency (*ex post*) responses. The regulated entities are obliged to participate actively in both, by instigating systems of risk management and response. This way of assimilating the pre-existing features and institutional setup of a business model into regulation is subject to specific risks, particularly where there is a misalignment between the regulated parties' interests and the public interest motivating the regulation. This is particularly relevant to the case at hand: the entities enrolled (HFT firms and market venues) have clear commercial interests in maintaining the high-speed and complex trading environment that has emerged as a result of their mutual interests. This makes the regulatory system vulnerable, undermining the efficacy of the MiFID II regulatory approach. Such concerns are compounded by other challenges faced by regulators and supervisors. The opacity and complexity of the business model lead to an information deficit that may cause regulators to underestimate the real risks behind the business model and furthermore, hamper the work of supervisors. The market structure and market functionality that define the environment in which HFT operates have changed radically over the last decades. New characteristics – namely, the automation, extreme velocity, highly sophisticated electronic systems and cross-market and cross-border activity – challenge regulators and supervisors in novel ways, putting pressure on resources and making it difficult to ensure sufficient oversight so that risks do not develop.

To sum up, the nature, scope and scale of the risks to orderly trading that HFT inflicts on markets may have severe consequences if they materialise. The regulatory challenges associated with the business model are significant. So far, the habitual primacy of efficiency considerations in the regulatory agenda seems to have resulted in a regulatory compromise that favours the existing business model, in spite of the risks it entails for orderly trading. In future policymaking, regulators may need to reconsider the current compromise by attaching more weight to the orderly-market objective, especially given that the positive effects of HFT are increasingly being called into question by recent research. The regulatory objective of ensuring orderly markets could be better served by imposing meaningful restrictions on HFT activity, rather than trying to mitigate risks as they arise.

Bibliography

M Andenas and I H-Y Chiu, *The Foundations and Future of Financial Regulation: Governance for Responsibility* (Routledge 2014).

J Armour, D Awrey, P L Davies, L Enriques, J N Gordon, C P Mayer and J Payne, *Principles of Financial Regulation* (1st edition, Oxford University Press 2016).

D W Arner, J Barberis and R P Buckley, 'FinTech, RegTech, and the Reconceptualization of Financial Regulation' (2017) Northwestern Journal of International Law & Business 371.

R Baldwin, M Cave and M Lodge, *Understanding Regulation: Theory, Strategy, and Practice* (2nd edition, Oxford University Press 2012).

R Bookstaber, *A Demon of Our Own Design: Markets, Hedge Funds, and the Perils of Financial Innovation* (John Wiley & Sons 2007).

C Bradley, 'Disorderly Conduct: Day Traders and the Ideology of "Fair and Orderly Markets"' (2000) 26(1) Journal of Corporation Law 63.

J Breckenfelder, 'Competition among High-Frequency Traders, and Market Quality' (June 2019) ECB Working Paper Series No 2290.

D Busch, 'MiFID II: Regulating High Frequency Trading, Other Forms of Algorithmic Trading and Direct Electronic Market Access' (2016) 10 Law and Financial Markets Review 72.

Á Cartea, R Payne, J Penalva and M Tapia, 'Ultra-Fast Activity and Intraday Market Quality' (2019) 99 Journal of Banking & Finance 157.

G Cespa and T Foucault, 'Sale of Price Information by Exchanges: Does It Promote Price Discovery?' (2014) 60 Management Science 148.

G Cespa and X Vives, *High Frequency Trading and Fragility – Working Paper Series 2020* (European Central Bank 2017) 2.

K H Chung and A J Lee, 'High-Frequency Trading: Review of the Literature and Regulatory Initiatives around the World' (2016) 45 Asia-Pacific Journal of Financial Studies 7.

D Cliff, 'Regulatory Scrutiny of Algorithmic Trading Systems: An Assessment of the Feasibility and Potential Economic Impact. Economic Impact Assessment EIA16' (20 January 2011) UK Government's Foresight Project: The Future of Computer Trading in Financial Markets <https://assets.publishing.service.gov.uk/government/uploads/system/uploads/attachment_data/file/289049/12-1075-eia16-regulatory-scrutiny-of-algorithmic-trading-systems.pdf>.

The Committee of European Securities Regulators (CESR), 'CESR Technical Advice to the European Commission in the Context of the MiFID Review – Equity Markets' (29 July 2010) CESR/10-802.

A Crockett, 'Why Is Financial Stability a Goal of Public Policy?' (1997) 82 Economic Review-Federal Reserve Bank of Kansas City 4.

G Deipenbrock, 'The European Civil Liability Regime for Credit Rating Agencies from the Perspective of Private International Law – Opening Pandora's Box?' (2015) International and Comparative Corporate Law Journal, Special Issue: Civil Liability of Credit Rating Agencies in the European Union 3.

G Deipenbrock, 'FinTech – Unbearably Lithe or Reasonably Agile? – A Critical Legal Approach from the German Perspective' (2020) 31 European Business Law Review 3.

F Della Negra, *MiFID II and Private Law: Enforcing EU Conduct of Business Rules (Hart Publishing* 2019).

S Dolgopolov, 'Legal Liability for Fraud in the Evolving Architecture of Securities Markets: from Marketplaces to Traders' in W Mattli (ed), *Global Algorithmic Capital Markets* (Oxford University Press 2018) 260.

D Easley, M López de Prado and M O'Hara, *High-Frequency Trading: New Realities for Traders, Markets and Regulators* (Risk Books 2013).

European Securities and Markets Authority, 'High-Frequency Trading Activity in EU Equity Markets – Economic Report No. 1' (2014).

European Securities and Markets Authority, 'Order Duplication and Liquidity Measurement in EU Equity Market – Economic Report No. 1' (2016).

European Systemic Risk Board, 'ESRB Response to the ESMA Consultation Paper on "Guidelines on Systems and Controls in a Highly Automated Trading Environment for Trading Platforms, Investment Firms and Competent Authorities"' (21 September 2011).

European Commission, Directorate General Internal Market and Services, 'Review of the Markets in Financial Instruments Directive (MiFID) – Public Consultation' (8 December 2010).

J D Farmer and S Skouras, 'An Ecological Perspective on the Future of Computer Trading' (2013) 13 Quantitative Finance 325.

G Ferrarini and N Moloney, 'Reshaping Order Execution in the EU and the Role of Interest Groups: From MiFID I to MiFID II' (2012) 13 European Business Organization Law Review 557.

G Ferrarini and P Saguato, 'Regulating Financial Market Infrastructures' in N Moloney, E Ferran and J Payne (eds), *The Oxford Handbook of Financial Regulation* (Oxford University Press 2015) 568.

T Foucault, 'Where Are the Risks in High Frequency Trading?' (2016) 20 Banque de France Financial Stability Review 53.

A G Haldane, 'The Race to Zero' in F Allen, M Aoki, J-P Fitoussi, N Kiyotaki, R Gordon and J E Stiglitz (eds), *The Global Macro Economy and Finance* (Palgrave Macmillan 2012) 245.

A G Haldane, 'Financial Arms Races', Speech (14 April 2012) given at the conference *Paradigm Lost* held by Institute for New Economic Thinking in Berlin.

A G Haldane, 'The Age of Asset Management?' Speech (4 April 2014) given at London Business School.

A G Haldane, 'Multi-Polar Regulation' (2015) 11 International Journal of Central Banking 385.

A G Haldane and B Nelson, 'Tails of the Unexpected' Speech (8 June 2012) given at the conference *The Credit Crisis Five Years On: Unpacking the Crisis* held at the University of Edinburgh Business School.

International Monetary Fund 'Global Financial Stability Report: Vulnerabilities in a Maturing Credit Cycle' (April 2019).

International Organization of Securities Commissions (IOSCO), 'Objectives and Principles of Securities Regulation' (1998).

International Organization of Securities Commissions (IOSCO), 'Transparency and Market Fragmentation' (November 2001).

International Organization of Securities Commissions (IOSCO), 'Regulatory Issues Arising from Exchange Evolution – Final Report' (November 2006).

International Organization of Securities Commissions (IOSCO), 'Issues Raised by Dark Liquidity – Consultation Report' (CR05/10, 2010).

International Organization of Securities Commissions (IOSCO), 'Regulatory Issues Raised by the Impact of Technological Changes on Market Integrity and Efficiency – Final Report' (FR09/11, 2011).

International Organization of Securities Commissions (IOSCO), 'Technological Challenges to Effective Market Surveillance: Issues and Regulatory Tools – Final Report' (FR04/13, 2013).

International Organization of Securities Commissions (IOSCO), 'Objectives and Principles of Securities Regulation' (2017).

International Organization of Securities Commissions (IOSCO), 'Mechanisms Used by Trading Venues to Manage Extreme Volatility and Preserve Orderly Trading – Final Report' (FR13/18, 2018).

P K Jain, P Jain and T H McInish, 'Does High-Frequency Trading Increase Systemic Risk?' (2016) 31 Journal of Financial Markets 1.

K Judge, 'Fragmentation Nodes: A Study in Financial Innovation, Complexity and Systemic Risk' (2012) 64 (3) Stanford Law Review 657.

A J Keller, 'Robocops: Regulating High Frequency Trading after the Flash Crash of 2010' (2012) 73 Ohio State Law Journal 1457.

A A Kirilenko and A W Lo, 'Moore's Law Versus Murphy's Law: Algorithmic Trading and Its Discontents' (2013) 27 Journal of Economic Perspectives 51.

E Kopp, L Kaffenberger and C Wilson, 'Cyber Risk, Market Failures, and Financial Stability' (2017) 17 IMF Working Papers.

M P Lerch, 'Algorithmic Trading and High-Frequency Trading' in R Veil (ed), *European Capital Markets Law* (2nd edition, Hart Publishing, an imprint of Bloomsbury Publishing Plc 2017) 477.

J R Macey, 'The Nature and Futility of "Regulation by Assimilation"' in G Urban (ed), *Corporations and Citizenship* (University of Pennsylvania Press 2014).

J R Macey and D Swensen, 'Recovering the Promise of the Orderly and Fair Stock Exchange' (2017) 42 The Journal of Corporation Law 777.

A Madhavan, 'Exchange-Traded Funds, Market Structure, and the Flash Crash' (2012) 68 Financial Analysts Journal 20.

A Manconi, M Massa and A Yasuda, 'The Role of Institutional Investors in Propagating the Crisis of 2007–2008' (2012) 104 Journal of Financial Economics 491.

W Mattli, *Darkness by Design: The Hidden Power in Global Capital Markets* (Princeton University Press 2019).

G Meyer, 'NYSE Owner Warns of Cyber Risk to High-Frequency Trading' *Financial Times* (13 March 2015).

N Moloney, 'Supervision in the Wake of the Financial Crisis' in E Wymeersch, K J Hopt and G Ferrarini (eds), *Financial Regulation and Supervision: A Post-Crisis Analysis* (Oxford University Press 2012) 71.

N Moloney, *EU Securities and Financial Markets Regulation* (3rd edition, Oxford University Press 2014).

E Monaco, 'What FinTech Can Learn from High-Frequency Trading: Economic Consequences, Open Issues and Future of Corporate Disclosure' in T Lynn, J G Mooney, P Rosati and M Cummins (eds), *Disrupting Finance* (Springer International Publishing 2019) 51.

T Myklebust, 'Form and Function of the ESRB: A Critical Analysis' in M Andenas and G Deipenbrock (eds), *Regulating and Supervising European Financial Markets – More Risks than Achievements* (Springer International Publishing 2016) 43.

T Myklebust, 'Fairness and Integrity in High-Frequency Markets – A Critical Assessment of the European Regulatory Approach' (2020) 31 European Business Law Review 33.

Organisation for Economic Co-operation and Development (OECD), 'Policy Framework for Effective and Efficient Financial Regulation; General Guidance and High-Level Checklist' (2010).

M O'Hara, 'High Frequency Market Microstructure' (2015) 116 Journal of Financial Economics 257.

S T Omarova, 'Technology v Technocracy: Fintech as a Regulatory Challenge' (2020) 6 Journal of Financial Regulation 75.

S L Schwarcz, 'Regulating Complexity in Financial Markets' (2009) 87 Washington University Law Review 211.

S L Schwarcz, 'Regulating Financial Change: A Functional Approach' (2016) 100 Minnesota Law Review 1441.

D Sornette and S Von der Becke, 'Crashes and High Frequency Trading – Foresight Driver Review DR 7' (August 2011) UK Government's Foresight Project: The Future of Computer Trading in Financial Markets <https://assets.publishing.service.gov.uk/government/uploads/system/uploads/attachment_data/file/289016/11-1226-dr7-crashes-and-high-frequency-trading.pdf>.

Staffs of the Commodity Futures Trading Commission and the Securities and Exchange Commission, 'Findings Regarding the Market Events of May 6, 2010 – Report of the Staffs of the CFTC and SEC to the Joint Advisory Committee on Emerging Regulatory Issues' (30 September 2010) <https://www.sec.gov/news/studies/2010/marketevents-report.pdf>.

N N Taleb, *The Black Swan: The Impact of the Highly Improbable* (Penguin Group 2010).

C Tietje and M Lehmann, 'The Role and Prospects of International Law in Financial Regulation and Supervision' (2010) 13 Journal of International Economic Law 663.

R Veil, 'Concept and Aims of Capital Markets Regulation' in R Veil (ed), *European Capital Markets Law* (2nd edition, Hart Publishing, an imprint of Bloomsbury Publishing Plc 2017) 23.

D Wójcik, *The Global Stock Market: Issuers, Investors, and Intermediaries in an Uneven World* (Oxford University Press 2011).

Y Yadav, 'Algorithmic Trading and Market Regulation' in M Mattli (ed), *Global Algorithmic Capital Markets* (Oxford University Press 2018) 232.

22 'Trustless' distributed ledgers and custodial services

Matteo Solinas

1 Introduction

A distributed ledger is a database designed to be distributed among many users, to be immutable, to work without oversight from any central authority and to operate without the need for its users to trust each other. The first one, introduced in 2008 to power bitcoin, was the blockchain. Contrary to earlier attempts to use cryptography to create computerised money, the blockchain offered a solution to the problem of preventing users from spending the same digital coin more than once without relying on a trusted authority to check every transaction.[1] Fundamentally, all users ('nodes') have a copy of the records of every transaction performed with the currency, bundled into blocks connected by a chain of cryptographic links maintained by a special group of trusted users called 'miners'. Transactions are processed and validated with the solution of a cryptographic puzzle to be solved in compliance to certain conditions set out in an algorithm designed to generate a one-way hash function (a 'proof-of-work model').[2] In order to have one hash that matches these conditions, a computer has to generate thousands of hashes, employing considerable computational power and energy.[3] Once obtained, a successful hash (ie, one that includes transaction information, a record of the previous block and a timestamp pointing out that the underlying conditions have been met) is disclosed to the network. The nodes then validate the block by cryptographically signing it with the hash of the prior block, hence creating an immutable chain of sequential blocks.[4] Users are incentivised to participate in this process because each successful hash is rewarded with new bitcoins. However, this incentive is designed to become more difficult as the number of users in the network grows,[5] and because the amount of bitcoins released as rewards for successful hashing is predetermined to

---

1 The solution to the 'double spend problem' has its roots in the 'timestamp server'(see Stuart Haber and W Scott Stornetta, 'How to Time-stamp a Digital Document' (1991) 3 Journal of Cryptology 99, 99) and it relies on a cryptographic hash function that ensures that the recorded transactions are not duplicated or manipulated (see Richard P Salgado, 'Fourth Amendment Search and the Power of the Hash' (2006) 119 Harvard Law Review 38, 39; Dennis Martin, 'Demystifying Hash Searches' (2018) 70 Stanford Law Review 691, 695).
2 See Adam Back, 'Hashcash – A Denial of Service Counter-Measure' (*Hashcash*, 1 August 2002) <http://www.hashcash.org/papers/hashcash.pdf> accessed 20 April 2020; Arvind Narayanan and others, *Bitcoin and Cryptocurrency Technologies* (Princeton University Press 2016) 61–67.
3 The costs of bitcoin mining are enormous (four-fifths of mining costs are electricity). For an estimate of bitcoin energy usage, see 'Bitcoin Energy Consumption Index' (*Digiconomist*) <https://digiconomist.net/bitcoin-energy-consumption> accessed 20 April 2020.
4 Satoshi Nakamoto, 'Bitcoin: A Peer-To-Peer Electronic Cash System' (2008) White Paper <bitcoin.org/bitcoin.pdf> accessed 20 April 2020.
5 See Narayanan and others (n 2) 65.

decrease as time goes on.[6] Rewriting the ledger is almost impossible, as it would require control of more than half of the total mining capacity.[7]

As bitcoin's protocol was open-source, others were able to capitalise on the technology and to launch different cryptocurrencies.[8] More importantly perhaps, distributed ledger technology ('DLT') offered support to wider applications involving cryptoassets[9] than just tracking the transaction history of electronic cash. The cryptography that protects entries in a blockchain from tampering has for example been used to build registers of property deeds in Georgia[10] and Ukraine.[11] Big transport and logistics firms have also adopted the technology to shipments of goods,[12] not to mention the applications in the banking sector[13] and finance, including the management of clearing and settlement of equities.[14]

In essence, the revolution brought on by DLT centred on the notion that trust in a central authority could be replaced with trust in computer code and mathematics. Transactions could occur directly between any two users of the software at almost

6 The supply of bitcoins is finite. According to the 'white paper' (Satoshi Nakamoto, 'Bitcoin: A Peer-To-Peer Electronic Cash System' (2008) White Paper <bitcoin.org/bitcoin.pdf> accessed 20 April 2020) (Nakamoto n 4), the total number of bitcoins in existence will never exceed 21 million.

7 See Narayanan and others (n 2) 59.

8 See CoinMarketCap, a website for tracking market capitalisation of various cryptocurrencies, CoinMarketCap 'Top 100 Cryptocurrencies by Market Capitalization' (*CoinMarketCap*) <https://coinmarketcap.com/> accessed 20 April 2020 and Chloe Cornish 'Growing number of cryptocurrencies spark concerns' (*Financial Times*, 10 January 2018) <www.ft.com/content/a6b90a8c-f4b7-11e7-8715-e94187b3017e> accessed 20 April 2020.

9 These are 'cryptographically secured digital representations of value or contractual rights that use some type of distributed ledger technology (DLT) and can be transferred, stored or traded electronically': Financial Conduct Authority, 'CP19/3: Guidance on Cryptoassets' (January 2019) <https://europeanchamberofdigitalcommerce.com/wp-content/uploads/2019/06/Guidance-on-Cryptoassets-Consultation-Paper.pdf> accessed 20 April 2020.

10 In 2016, the National Agency of Public Registry of Georgia launched a blockchain project on land management with the Bitfury Group: 'The Bitfury Group and Government of Republic of Georgia Expand Historic Blockchain Land-Titling Project' (*Bitfury*) <https://bitfury.com/content/downloads/the_bitfury_group_republic_of_georgia_expand_blockchain_pilot_2_7_16.pdf> accessed 20 April 2020.

11 In 2017, the State Land Cadastre of Ukraine switched to the Exonum platform for private blockchains, supported by Bitfury. See Rachel Wolfson 'Purchasing Property Online: The Revolutionary Way Ukraine Uses Blockchain For Real Estate' (*Huffington Post*, 15 October 2017) <www.huffpost.com/entry/purchasing-property-online-the-revolutionary-way-ukraine_b_59933fe7e4b0af-d94eb3f565> accessed 20 April 2020.

12 Adam Green 'Will Blockchain Accelerate Trade Flows?' (*Financial Times*, 10 November 2017) <www.ft.com/content/a36399fa-a927-11e7-ab66-21cc87a2edde> accessed 20 April 2020.

13 Martin Arnold 'European Banks to Launch Blockchain Trade Finance Platform' (*Financial Times*, 27 June 2017) <www.ft.com/content/6bb4f678-5a8c-11e7-b553-e2df1b0c3220> accessed 20 April 2020.

14 Jamie Smyth 'ASX Chooses Blockchain for Equities Clearing' (*Financial Times*, 7 December 2017) <www.ft.com/content/c9b86e8e-dae4-11e7-a039-c64b1c09b482> accessed 20 April 2020. For a discussion of the use of blockchain technology in the area of securities holdings, see Philipp Paech, 'Securities, Intermediation and the Blockchain: an Inevitable Choice between Liquidity and Legal Certainty?' (2016) 21 Uniform Law Review 612; and Eva Micheler and Luke von der Heyde, 'Holding, Clearing and Settling Securities through Blockchain/distributed Ledger Technology: Creating an Efficient System by Empowering Investors' (2016) 31 JIBFL 652.

zero cost and be irreversible once recorded in a permanent and fully public record.[15] Unfortunately, this libertarians' dream of a world where it was possible to replace more and more state regulations with self-enforcing private contracts between individuals[16] collided (at least in its most popular applications – ie, cryptocurrencies) with reality.[17] Notwithstanding the difficulties in extracting hard data, market practice suggests that today the vast majority of cryptocurrency transactions occur 'off-chain' between investors who have accounts at the same exchange or between exchanges.[18] Serious design flaws prevented cryptocurrencies to achieve mass adoption and to become a viable alternative to online payment systems. Ironically, market's evolution undermined the very idea that DLT could cut out the middleman and allow people to deal directly with each other.

The study of these operational changes (and the inherent legal implications) is the focus of this chapter. In particular, with specific emphasis on cryptocurrencies, Part II explains that maintaining ready access to cryptoassets that, unlike physical assets, can exist in a sense simultaneously in many locations is a particularly difficult task. While in theory it is possible to permit users direct availability, there are several practical and economic reasons that point towards more effective alternatives, usually involving the recourse to specialised custodians. Building on those concerns in the light of the typical (indirect) holding arrangements, Part III examines whether market reality substantially transformed the legal nature of investor's rights in cryptoassets. It finds that this has been the case and that, contrary to the orthodox fintech narrative, exchanges and other unregulated custodians operate for the most part as trusted third parties that play the role of banks in the cryptocurrency world getting around transaction settlement simply by netting 'off the blockchain', 'when it becomes cost effective to do so'.[19] The conclusion of the inquiry developed in this chapter is that under the shining veil of scientific progress, 'off-chain' transacting replicates, possibly with increased financial risks hidden behind an apparent transparent ledger, a familiar pattern of holding, trading and collateralising intermediated securities.

15 Michael Casey and others, *The Impact of Blockchain Technology on Finance: A Catalyst for Change* (Vol 21 of Geneva Reports on the World Economy, Centre for Economic Policy Research 2018).

16 Kevin Werbach, *The Blockchain and the New Architecture of Trust* (The MIT Press 2018) 53–71; Nigel Dodd, 'The Social Life of Bitcoin' (2018) 35 Theory, Culture & Society 35, 41–47.

17 Nouriel Roubini, 'The Big Blockchain Lie' (*Project Syndicate*, 15 October 2018) <www.project-syndicate.org/commentary/blockchain-big-lie-by-nouriel-roubini-2018-10?barrier=accesspaylog> accessed 20 April 2020; and Martin Wolf, 'The libertarian fantasies of cryptocurrencies' (*Financial Times*, 13 February 2019) <www.ft.com/content/eeeacd7c-2e0e-11e9-ba00-0251022932c8> accessed 20 April 2020.

18 Ross Anderson and others, 'Bitcoin Redux' (*WEIS 2018*, 28 May 2018) Cambridge University Computer Laboratory, 15 <https://weis2018.econinfosec.org/wp-content/uploads/sites/5/2018/05/WEIS_2018_paper_38.pdf> accessed 20 April 2020.

19 Izabella Kaminska, 'The Currency of the Future Has a Settlement Problem' (*Financial Times*, 18 May 2017) <www.ftalphaville.ft.com/2017/05/17/2188961/the-currency-of-the-future-has-a-settlement-problem> accessed 20 April 2020.

2 The myth of (direct) propriety rights in cryptoassets

2.1 *Holding patterns*

The conventional narrative suggests that investors in cryptoassets have direct and absolute control of them. Starting from the familiar case of bitcoins, the lay perception is that they are usually bought (and sold) in return for traditional currency on cryptocurrency exchanges and directly transferred across the internet from one user to another using appropriate software without the need of intermediation of specialist crypto-custodians. This is the holding mechanism described in the bitcoin 'white paper' and it has rarely been questioned to be an accurate representation of the market reality. A collection of recently published academic papers on cryptocurrencies confirms this view, as alternative holding patterns are not even mentioned.[20] Even the 2019 *Legal statement on cryptoassets and smart contracts* delivered by the UK Jurisdiction Taskforce, while observing that 'many dealings in cryptoassets involve intermediaries such as brokers or custodians', dismisses the issue as negligible in two lines (over a 60-page paper) by declaring that 'what personal and proprietary rights the principal may have against an intermediary will depend on established rules of contract, tort and agency'.[21]

This part of the chapter argues that this picture is a misleading representation of market practice. Building on the findings of authoritative studies that have established that cryptoassets qualify as property in the law,[22] the inquiry below examines at first how investors maintain full control of cryptoassets and direct access to the distributed ledger. The aim is to provide the economic and legal background to understand the limitations of DLT and to address its problematic implementation (and limited developments) in market practice.

2.2 *Storing and using cryptoassets*

According to property law, purchasers of cryptoassets on the blockchain qualify as legal owners and, if adequate precautions are not taken, bear the risk of loss.

In the case of bitcoins transfer is effected by the use of 'public-private key' cryptography that originally enabled the sending of encrypted (and allowed to decrypt) messages without the need for a shared key, according to a scheme where the 'public key' serves as a reference point and the 'private key' operates as a secret password.[23] In essence, the payer issues an

20 David Fox and Sarah Green (eds), *Cryptocurrencies in Public and Private Law* (Oxford University Press 2019).
21 UK Jurisdiction Taskforce, 'Legal Statement on Cryptoassets and Smart Contracts' (*The Law Tech Delivery Panel*, November 2019), para 34 <https://35z8e83m1ih83drye28oo9d1-wpengine.netdna-ssl.com/wp-content/uploads/2019/11/6.6056_JO_Cryptocurrencies_Statement_FINAL_WEB_111119-1.pdf> accessed 20 April 2020.
22 Kelvin F K Low and Ernie G S Teo, 'Bitcoins and Other Cryptocurrencies as Property?' (2017) 9 Law, Innovation and Technology 235, 249–252; David Fox, 'Cryptocurrencies in the Common Law of Property' in David Fox and Sarah Green (eds), *Cryptocurrencies in Public and Private Law* (Oxford University Press 2019) 139, 142–155; UK Jurisdiction Taskforce, 'Legal Statement on Cryptoassets and Smart Contracts' (*The Law Tech Delivery Panel*, November 2019) para 34 <https://35z8e83m1ih83drye28oo9d1-wpengine.netdna-ssl.com/wp-content/uploads/2019/11/6.6056_JO_Cryptocurrencies_Statement_FINAL_WEB_111119-1.pdf> accessed 20 April 2020.
23 W Diffie and M Hellman, 'New Directions in Cryptography' (1976) 22 IEEE Transactions on Information Theory 644; Donald Davies, 'A Brief History of Cryptography' (1977) 2 Information Security Technical Report 14.

instruction on the network using, like a bank account number, a 'public key' to sign the bitcoin, followed by the 'public key' of the recipient. Once the payer's authority to spend the bitcoin has been validated by the miners and the result of the successful miner has been published on the blockchain, the payee, in the same way performed earlier by the payer, is able to activate the payment instruction by signing the bitcoin with the 'private key'. While the system is entirely anonymous in its operation because it does not allow a user to know the identity of a person who has control of a specific 'public key', it is also transparent, as bitcoin transactions can be tracked in the blockchain.

Once cryptoassets are acquired, they have to be stored in a safe location for future use. In the case of bitcoins, the technical mechanism that explains how the direct holding system operates is relatively simple: 'private keys'[24] are stored in a personal account based on a special software (a virtual self-hosted 'wallet') downloaded by owners directly on their hardware, and addresses between users are exchanged by encoding them as a text string[25] or as a QR code (a two-dimensional barcode). This practice may not be ideal, as storing private keys on a local device is not always secure. Mobile devices, for example, can break down or can be lost or stolen.[26] For security reasons, most bitcoins are therefore stored offline in a 'cold storage' and managed via a separate address using different secret keys from a 'hot storage' connected to the blockchain network.[27] Even in this case certain practical concerns emerge, since two separate addresses with different secret keys are necessary, with all the technical difficulties in connecting the cold storage address to the 'hot wallet'.[28]

An alternative method to store and directly manage bitcoins involves 'online wallets', which store the information in the cloud and provide customers access via a web interface on a computer or an app on a smartphone.[29] Under this mechanism, the support of a third party is necessary, as it is the service provider who delivers the code that runs on the computer browser or app and stores the customers' 'private keys'. Online wallets are convenient, enjoy ease of use, operate across multiple devices[30] and do not require the user to download the blockchain software.[31] However, they do raise a number of security concerns due to the level of trust handed over to service providers who store the 'private keys' and maintain control of the code.[32]

---

24 That is, a signing key that can be used to authenticate a transfer of a UTXO (unspent transaction output) to another blockchain address.

25 This is possible by taking the bits of the key and converting them from a binary number to a base-58 number and then using a set of 58 characters to encode each digit as a character (a 'base-58 notation'). See Narayanan and others (n 2) 77.

26 Nathaniel Popper, 'Identity Thieves Hijack Cellphone Accounts to Go After Virtual Currency' (*The New York Times*, 21 August 2017) <www.nytimes.com/2017/08/21/business/dealbook/phone-hack-bitcoin-virtual-currency.html> accessed 20 April 2020.

27 See the description offered in *United States v. Ulbricht*, 858 F.3d 71(2nd Cir, 2018) 116–117.

28 A number of technical solutions are offered by Narayanan and others (n 2) 79–83. A telling example of this issue is described by Robert Armstrong, 'Cryptocurrency Exchange Boss's Death Locks Away $150m in Digital Assets' (*Financial Times*, 5 February 2019) <www.ft.com/content/538b8ece-296e-11e9-a5ab-ff8ef2b976c7> accessed 20 April 2020.

29 See the relevant details on the mechanics provided online for the popular 'Coinbase wallet' (*Coinbase | Wallet*) <https://wallet.coinbase.com/> accessed 20 April 2020.

30 As the wallet is located in the cloud.

31 Christopher Twemlow, 'Why are Securities Held in Intermediated Form?' in Louise Gullifer and Jennifer Payne (eds), *Intermediation and Beyond* (Hart Publishing 2019) 85, 106.

32 Narayanan and others (n 2) 88.

2.3 *The limits of blockchain technology*

The just described (direct) holding pattern does not fairly reflect the current market practice, at least in relation to the circulation of cryptocurrencies. This has progressively moved to more efficient (indirect) holding patterns. The fundamental impetus to that trend has been that the blockchain's capacity as data management technology is too clunky to operate at scale.[33]

The issue of blockchain's inability to handle bitcoin transactions in an effective way has always been familiar to developers. However, it has never been identified as particularly concerning until the system, as the crypto-bubble was inflating in 2017, became so clogged that to ensure that transactions would go through, users had to pay miners an extra fee per transaction to prioritise payments.[34] In theory, it takes approximately 10 minutes for a transaction to be validated by the network and recorded in the blockchain.[35] That limits the network to processing about seven transactions per second (Visa, by contrast, can handle tens of thousands per second). More worryingly perhaps, this is not even what frequently happens, and settlement periods are often longer. Transactions which fail to get the attention of miners sit in a limbo called Mempool[36] until they possibly drop out.[37] The future is also not promising. Settlement problems will be hard to overcome in the short run: with the increase in the number of transactions, the blockchain will grow as will its requirement in terms of storage bandwidth and computational power.[38]

Quite interestingly, this scenario is similar to the one experienced during the 'paper crunch' in the 1970s in the United States[39] and in the 1980s in the UK[40] where the traditional process of delivering paper-based securities against payment in order to fulfil contractual obligations arising out of trading could not keep pace with the increase in the number of transactions. Severe delays in the settlement interval became frequent and backlogs of unsettled trades threatened the integrity of the securities market. As will be described in Part III below, the solution to the settlement problem adopted by market

---

33 Primavera De Filippi and Aaron Wright, *Blockchain and the Law: The Rule of Code* (Harvard University Press 2018) 56–57.

34 Kaminska, 'The Currency of the Future' (n 19).

35 The median time for a transaction to be accepted into a mined block and added to the public ledger is available: 'Median Confirmation Time' (*Blockchain.com*) <www.blockchain.com/en/charts/median-confirmation-time> accessed 20 April 2020.

36 The Mempool is effectively a 'waiting area' for bitcoin transactions that each full node maintains for itself.

37 The number of unconfirmed transactions building up on the bitcoin network on 15 June 2019 was 20,000: 'BTC / Unconfirmed Tx' (*Blockchain.com*) <www.blockchain.com/btc/unconfirmed-transactions> accessed 20 April 2020.

38 Kieren James-Lubin, 'Blockchain Scalability: A Look at the Stumbling Blocks to Blockchain Scalability and Some High-level Technical Solutions' (*O'Reilly Media*, 22 January 2015) <www.oreilly.com/ideas/blockchain-scalability> accessed 20 April 2020; Yoohwan Kim and Juyeon Jo, 'Binary Blockchain: Solving the Mining Congestion Problem by Dynamically Adjusting the Mining Capacity' in Roger Lee (ed), *Applied Computing & Information Technology* (Springer International Publishing 2018) 29; Raphael Auer 'Beyond the Doomsday Economics of "Proof-of-work" in Cryptocurrencies' (2019) BIS Working Papers No 765 <www.bis.org/publ/work765.pdf> accessed 20 April 2020.

39 Richard Smith, 'A Piece of Paper Revisited' (1971) 25 The Business Lawyer 1769; David Donald, 'The Rise and Effects of the Indirect Holding Systems – How Corporate America Ceded its Shareholders to Intermediaries' (2007) Institute for Law and Finance Working Paper Series No 68.

40 The topic is comprehensively covered in Madeleine Yates and Gerald Montagu, *The Law of Global Custody* (4th edn, Bloomsbury Professional 2013) Ch 8.

practice in the case of investment securities is very similar to the one chosen by investors in cryptocurrencies.

2.4 *Empirical evidence and (other) rationales*

While the 'scalability' issue has been the fundamental driver to market changes in the holding and transfer of cryptocurrencies, the relevance of other concurring explanations should not be ruled out. These will be examined below, after offering appropriate reference to the developments that can be observed in market practice.

Abundant evidence points out that the vast majority of small-scale cryptocurrency payments are not currently processed on the blockchain. Most of the transactions (up to 99% according to one authoritative source[41]) occur 'off-chain' between customers at the same exchange (or wallet-provider of specialist crypto-custodian).[42] The fact that off-chain transactions would have become the norm was first highlighted by bitcoin pioneer Hal Finney in 2010 when he declared:

> Bitcoin itself cannot scale to have every single financial transaction in the world be broadcast to everyone and included in the block chain ... Most Bitcoin transactions will occur between banks, to settle net transfers. Bitcoin transactions by private individuals will be as rare as... well, as Bitcoin based purchases are today.[43]

Data assembled by Chainalysis for *The New York Times* on bitcoin's use in 2016 suggests that the direct bitcoin holding models have never been widely adopted.[44] This observation is confirmed by other authoritative sources and can be supported by a simple empirical test. Using data from CoinMarketCap, an authoritative website that provides cryptocurrency market capitalisation rankings,[45] 24-hour trading volumes were around US$130 billion on 4 March 2020. This figure, even with necessary adjustments to take into account probable fake transactions (often the result of 'wash trading', in

41 According to the recent TABB Group research report: Monica Summerville, 'Crypto Trading: Platforms Target Institutional Market' (*TABB Group*, 5 April 2018) <https://research.tabbgroup.com/report/v16-013-crypto-trading-platforms-target-institutional-market/> accessed 20 April 2020.
42 Tuur Demeester, 'Bitcoin: Digital Gold or Digital Cash? Both' (*Medium*, 15 January 2017) <https://medium.com/@tuurdemeester/bitcoin-digital-gold-or-digital-cash-both-382a346e6c79> accessed 20 April 2020; and Ross Anderson and others (n 18).
43 Hal Finney, 'Bitcoin Bank' (*Bitcoin Forum*, 30 December 2010) <https://bitcointalk.org/index.php?topic=2500.msg34211#msg34211> accessed 30 March 2020.
44 Nathaniel Popper, 'How China Took Center Stage in Bitcoin's Civil War' (*The New York Times*, 29 June 2016) <www.nytimes.com/2016/07/03/business/dealbook/bitcoin-china.html> accessed 20 April 2020. Chainalysis has a proprietary method of tying specific transactions to particular businesses: (*Chainalysis*) <www.chainalysis.com> accessed 20 April 2020.
45 CoinMarketCap, 'Top 100 Cryptocurrencies by Market Capitalization' (*CoinMarketCap*) <https://coinmarketcap.com/> accessed 20 April 2020.

which traders buy and sell to each other to create the illusion of volume[46]), is many times greater than the US$1.3 billion corresponding to the trading volumes on the blockchain at the same date.[47] It is also greater than the one generated by decentralised exchanges that facilitate direct swapping of assets between users using peer-to-peer smart contracts.[48] Using data from DEXWatch, a decentralised exchange explorer that captures on-chain data pertaining to decentralised exchanges in real time,[49] 52,000 Ethers were traded per day across the major decentralised exchanges on 4 March 2020. With Ethereum priced at around US$201, this equates to approximately US$10.5 million in trade per day.

Once accepted that the blockchain is not currently able to deal with a large number of users and that this has likely contributed to the rise in off-chain cryptocurrency transactions, the impact of other concurring explanations should not be underestimated. The most relevant of these relate to the technical concerns in downloading the specialist software to keep a copy of the blockchain, which now exceeds 11 gigabytes in size and continues to grow steadily. Moreover, the costs required in updating the hardware, together with the computing power necessary to participate in the mining process,[50] the risk of losing the private key[51] and the fact of being exposed to hackers' attacks, also contributed to prevent this original model to achieve widespread diffusion, especially among retail investors. A well-known example of the risks involved in maintaining the ability to generate the right digital signature with which to sign transactions is the case of Mr Howells, a British crypto enthusiast, who bought 7,500 bitcoins in 2009, when they were nearly worthless, before throwing away the hard drive on which they were stored. By 2013 they were worth millions of dollars. Mr Howells' attempts to recover his hard drive from a

46 See Matthew Hougan, Hong Kim and Micah Lerner, 'Economic and Non-Economic Trading in Bitcoin: Exploring the Real Spot Market for the World's First Digital Commodity' (24 May 2019) Bitwise Asset Management <www.sec.gov/comments/sr-nysearca-2019-01/srnysearca201901-5574233-185408.pdf> accessed 15 March 2020. Similar conclusions were reached by The Block (the leading research, analysis and news brand in the digital asset space): Larry Cermak, 'Up to 86% of Total Reported Cryptocurrency Trading Volume Is Likely Fake, According to Analysis of Exchange Website Visits' (*The Block*, 28 May 2019) <www.theblockcrypto.com/genesis/24878/up-to-86-of-total-reported-cryptocurrency-trading-volume-is-likely-fake-according-to-analysis-of-exchange-website-visits> accessed 15 March 2020. See also Paul Vigna, 'Most Bitcoin Trading Faked by Unregulated Exchanges, Study Finds' (*The Wall Street Journal*, 22 March 2019) <www.wsj.com/articles/most-bitcoin-trading-faked-by-unregulated-exchanges-study-finds-11553259600> accessed 20 April 2020.
47 With bitcoin priced at US$4,950: 'Confirmed Transactions Per Day' (*Blockchain.com*) <www.blockchain.com/en/charts/n-transactions> accessed 20 April 2020.
48 This is a marketplace for trading Ethereum-based tokens where a certain element of the exchange's functionality operates according to Ethereum's decentralised protocol.
49 (*DEXWatch*) <https://dex.watch/> accessed 20 April 2020.
50 The first bitcoin exchange (Mt Gox) was set up when the computing resources required to mine bitcoin became unreasonable and inadequate to meet the demand for bitcoins. See Nathaniel Popper, *Digital Gold: Bitcoin and the Inside Story of the Misfits and Millionaires Trying to Reinvent Money* (HarperCollins 2015) 51.
51 See Hannah Murphy, 'Lost Your Bitcoin Password? Call in the Crypto-hunters' (*Financial Times*, 18 July 2018) <www.ft.com/content/f1b12970-8959-11e8-b18d-0181731a0340> accessed 30 March 2020.

Welsh landfill were not successful.[52] Finally, the relevant transaction costs,[53] and certain technical disadvantages, including the fact that bitcoin's circulation faces severe capacity constraints compared with other payment systems,[54] should also be factored in as possible concurring explanations.

From a rational investor's perspective, there might also be additional economic motives to explain the recent trends in market practice. In particular, with the growth in the number of cryptocurrencies available (and, in the light of their fundamental use as a store of value), cryptocurrency exchanges have become the marketplaces for listing and trading cryptocurrencies. As a basic approach to portfolio diversification would suggest, to trade efficiently rational users would buy multiple digital currencies and exchange them according to various cryptographic protocols when their needs evolve. This will be possible only by combining the operations of an exchange with basic custodial services, centralised order booking and efficient order matching,[55] together with a decentralised cross-chain settlement based on cross-chain cryptographic protocols that allow users to settle transactions across heterogeneous blockchain networks without a 'trusted' third party and without counterparty risk.

2.5 *The developers' response*

There have recently been a number of (so far not particularly successful) attempts to find alternative technical means to overcome the blockchain inability to net and to allow for trading on credit.

The most promising example has been the use of limitless 'off-chain' transactions managed via smart contracts under the 'Lightning Network'.[56] This is simply a second-layer payment protocol that exists on top of blockchain and allows two people

---

52 See Aatif Sulleyman, 'Man Who "Threw Away" Bitcoin Haul Now Worth over 80M Wants to Dig Up Landfill Site' (*The Independent*, 4 December 2017) <www.independent.co.uk/life-style/gadgets-and-tech/news/bitcoin-value-james-howells-newport-landfill-hard-drive-campbell-simpson-laszlo-hanyecz-a8091371.html> accessed 20 April 2020.

53 See Izabella Kaminska, 'But, But ... I thought Bitcoin was Supposed to be Cheap?' (*Financial Times*, 17 March 2017) <https://ftalphaville.ft.com/2017/03/17/2186161/but-but-i-thought-bitcoin-was-supposed-to-be-cheap/> accessed 20 April 2020; and Izabella Kaminska, 'Bitcoin's Fake News Problem' (*Financial Times*, 21 March 2017) <https://ftalphaville.ft.com/2017/03/21/2186260/bitcoins-fake-news-problem/> accessed 20 April 2020.

54 The speed and cost of bitcoins' transaction is not yet competitive with payments in national currency. See Jan Vermeulen, 'Bitcoin and Ethereum vs Visa and PayPal – Transactions per second' (*Mybroadband*, 22 April 2017) <https://mybroadband.co.za/news/banking/206742-bitcoin-and-ethereum-vs-visa-and-paypal-transactions-per-second.html> accessed 20 April 2020. Contrary to debit or credit card transactions, bitcoin transactions are not completed in seconds, but hours, unless a large transaction fee is introduced to persuade bitcoin miners to complete the transfer rapidly; see the British Retail Consortium's Payment Survey 2016 (*BRC*, 2016) <https://brc.org.uk/media/179489/payment-survey-2016_final.pdf> accessed 20 April 2020.

55 And, possibly, margin trading, proprietary lending, and peer-to-peer lending.

56 See Joseph Poon and Thaddeus Dryja, 'The Bitcoin Lightning Network: Scalable Off-Chain Instant Payments' (Draft Version 0.5.9.2, 14 January 2016) <https://lightning.network/lightning-network-paper.pdf>; Izabella Kaminska, 'Blockchain and the Holy Real-time Settlement Grail' (*Financial Times*, 27 February 2016) <https://ftalphaville.ft.com/2016/02/26/2154510/blockchain-and-the-holy-real-time-settlement-grail/> accessed 20 April 2020; and Kaminska, 'The Currency of the Future' (n 19).

to transfer bitcoins directly, rather than via the main bitcoin blockchain.[57] However, while it frees up capacity on the main network, it moves the circulation of cryptocurrencies away from 'real time gross settlements and push payments and into the world of deferred net settlement and pull payments',[58] in this way reinstating an element of intermediation.[59]

The latest addition to market practice has been the introduction of decentralised exchanges. These are non-custodial, peer-to-peer exchanges, with users enjoying total control of their funds, and the ability to trade directly from their own wallets with on-chain settlement without the supervision of any central authority. Trades are executed by a smart contract (a program executing on a blockchain) visible on the Ethereum blockchain, providing the appearance of transparency. As custody and transfer mechanisms are processed and guaranteed by the smart contract, funds cannot be stolen by the exchange operator. The combination of the technology of a centralised custodial exchange with a decentralised cross-chain settlement might allow cryptocurrency traders to obtain the efficiency of a centralised exchange when they need quick and liquid trading for exchanging big volumes, and also the ability to settle a transaction without the supervision of a third party. However, it has been suggested that trading in cryptocurrencies is not fair when it takes place on decentralised exchanges because of certain design flaws arising from numerous arbitrage bots and inherent market-exploiting behaviours that threaten the underlying blockchain security.[60]

3 Indirectly held cryptoassets

3.1 *Trusted (crypto) intermediaries*

Transactions between counterparties effected through the books of the exchanges (or other cryptocurrency custodian firms) offered the solution to the blockchain technical and practical concerns described in Part II. These transactions are instant and operationally convenient as they reduce administration, and the price at which cryptocurrencies are bought or sold is never affected by blockchain congestion.[61] This explains why most of the trade volume in the cryptocurrency space is today effected through traditional custodial

57 See (*Lightning Network*) <https://lightning.network> accessed 20 April 2020. See also the commentary provided by Michael J Casey and Paul Vigna, *The Truth Machine: The Blockchain and the Future of Everything* (St Martin's Press 2018) 95.

58 Izabella Kaminska, 'By Jove! Crypto Has Discovered Netting' (*Financial Times*, 5 December 2019) <https://ftalphaville.ft.com/2019/12/04/1575457459000/By-Jove–Crypto-has-discovered-netting/> accessed 20 April 2020.

59 See also Frances Coppola, 'The Fat Controller of the Lightning Network' (*Coppola Comment*, 17 January 2018) <www.coppolacomment.com/2018/01/lightning-and-fat-controller.html> accessed 20 April 2020.

60 Philip Daian and others, 'Flash Boys 2.0: Frontrunning, Transaction Reordering, and Consensus Instability in Decentralised Exchanges' (*Cornell University arXiv:1904.05234 [cs.CR]*, 10 April 2019) <https://arxiv.org/abs/1904.05234> accessed 20 April 2020; and Izabella Kaminska, 'Don't Bet on Decentralised Exchanges Becoming the New Crypto Frontier …' (*Financial Times*, 11 September 2019) <https://ftalphaville.ft.com/2019/09/11/1568182095000/Don-t-bet-on-decentralised-exchanges-becoming-the-new-crypto-frontier—/> accessed 20 April 2020.

61 Low and Teo (n 22) 264.

exchanges, which, in an increasingly competitive environment,[62] enjoy a tremendous opportunity to profit both by earning management fees for delivering custodian and providing trade execution services.

However, indirect holding and off-chain transactions carried out by institutions that play the role of banks in the cryptocurrency world are not risk-free for investors. Historically, exchanges have been a particularly attractive target for cyberattacks, as was the case in 2014 with Mt Gox where 744,400 bitcoins were lost from a 'malleability-related theft' caused by a bug that created a brief time period in which the unique ID (or 'TXID') of each transaction on the blockchain could be changed.[63] Similarly, the Canada-based Flexcoin (the 'Bitcoin bank') shut down after all 896 bitcoins in its 'hot wallet' were stolen as the result of technical flaws in the code that enabled transfers between its users.[64] Yet another recent example is Japan's cryptocurrency exchange Bitpoint, which reported an unauthorised withdrawal of $32 million in company and customer funds when it tried to make a payment using the cryptocurrency Ripple and got an error message.[65] The true scale of the hacking problem, however, is hard to estimate.[66]

Notwithstanding the significant risks involved, according to a recent survey compiled by Binance Research, 92% of 72 interviewed institutional investors keep their crypto assets on exchanges and not under their own control.[67] Arguably, the percentage is far higher in the case of retail investors who, as suggested above, may not have the resources or the economic interest to operate directly on the blockchain.

3.2 *Indirect holding patterns*

The fact that many users today do not hold cryptoassets directly, but do so through custodians reflects a commercial demand for intermediation, which is characterised (in its simplest version) by a combination of two-tier networks based on a distributed and decentralised scheme where the nodes are represented by exchanges that are connected to the adjacent nodes within the blockchain (ie, a distributed network) and where additional nodes are also formed among investors and the relevant exchanges (ie, a decentralised network).[68]

62 Tomio Geron, 'Companies Compete to Be Cryptocurrency Custodians' (*The Wall Street Journal*, 17 September 2019) <www.wsj.com/articles/companies-compete-to-be-cryptocurrency-custodians-11568772060> accessed 20 April 2020.
63 Ben McLannahan, 'Bitcoin Exchange Mt Gox Files for Bankruptcy Protection' (*Financial Times*, 1 March 2014) <www.ft.com/content/6636e0e8-a06e-11e3-a72c-00144feab7de> accessed 20 April 2020.
64 'Bitcoin Bank Flexcoin Shuts Down After Theft' (*Reuters*, 5 March 2014) <www.reuters.com/article/us-bitcoin-flexcoin/bitcoin-bank-flexcoin-shuts-down-after-theft-idUSBREA2329B20140304> accessed 20 April 2020.
65 See Robin Harding, 'Bitpoint Exchange Says Hackers Stole $32m in Cryptocurrency' (*Financial Times*, 12 July 2019) <www.ft.com/content/c23930d4-a474-11e9-974c-ad1c6ab5efd1> accessed 20 April 2020.
66 Izabella Kaminska, 'Bitcoin Bitfinex Exchange Hacked: The Unanswered Questions' (*Financial Times*, 4 August 2016) <https://www.ft.com/content/1ea8baf8-5a11-11e6-8d05-4eaa66292c32> accessed 20 April 2020.
67 Binance Research, 'Institutional Market Insights – 2nd edition' (*Binance Research*, 22 November 2019) <https://research.binance.com/analysis/institutional-insights-2nd-edition> accessed 20 April 2020.
68 See Paul Baran, 'On Distributed Communications Networks' (1964) 12 IEEE Transactions of the Professional Technical Groups on Communications Systems 1.

There are technically various ways of holding cryptoassets under the rules of the exchanges, usually in offline machines with only a limited number of them transferred to online machines in order to meet the trading requirement each day.

In one way, cryptocurrencies purchased from the exchange are kept by the same exchange in a hosted 'wallet' where the private keys are also stored. In this case, the exchange executes the transactions in relation to identifiable cryptocurrencies held in segregated accounts on behalf of the customers. This is the case of the Hong Kong dollar-based exchange Bitfinex, where user wallets are segregated and the 2016 hack of nearly 120,000 bitcoins resulted in the theft of users' property.[69]

An alternative way, and perhaps today's dominant business model, allows investors to purchase and sell, and provide collateral to secured lenders,[70] on their holdings by means of book entries made in the account kept with the exchange on an unallocated basis,[71] where indirectly held cryptocurrencies are commingled with those of other investors.[72] This is for example the case of the Malta-based OKEx exchange (the world's largest by reported turnover) where the Terms of Service clearly state 'by accepting the Terms, you expressly agree to the pooling of your VFAs [virtual financial assets] with the VFAs of other Users' which are held and safe-kept by Aux Cayes FinTech Co Ltd, a Seychelles-registered company with its head office in Kuala Lumpur, Malaysia.

3.3 *Regulation*

The regulatory framework for holding or administering cryptoassets on behalf of others is very light and rather patchy in the United Kingdom.

In particular, cryptocurrencies are not regulated by the UK Financial Conduct Authority (FCA) as they do not qualify as currencies or commodities for regulatory purposes under Markets in Financial Instruments Directive II (MiFID II), unless they bear characteristics of transferable securities (eg, cryptocurrency derivatives), becoming in that case directly comparable to regulated products.[73]

However, activities carried out by exchanges and specialised custodians have to be authorised when they deal with 'safeguarding of assets belonging to another' and administering 'those assets, or arranging for one or more other persons to carry on that activity' under arts 40 and 64 of the Financial Services and Markets Act 2000 (FSMA) (Regulated

---

69 Izabella Kaminska, 'Legal Tussle Looms for Bitcoin Holders in Hacked Bitfinex' (*Financial Times*, 5 August 2016) <www.ft.com/content/c3b9f89c-5b18-11e6-9f70-badea1b336d4> accessed 20 April 2020. See also Lucy Chambers, 'The Keepers of the Keys: Remedies and Legal Obligations Following Misappropriations of Cryptocurrency' (2016) 11 JIBFL 673.
70 See David Quest, 'Taking Security over Bitcoins and Other Virtual Currency' (2015) 7 JIBFL 401. This is for example the case of Hong Kong-based Bitfinex exchange, where art 3.6 of the Terms of Service clearly states: 'Digital Tokens can be borrowed for purposes of short sales through the Site's peer-to-peer financing functionality': 'Terms of Service' (*Bitfinex*) <www.bitfinex.com/legal/terms> accessed 20 April 2020.
71 That is, there is no link between particular participants and particular bitcoins.
72 'Terms of Service' (*OKEx Support*, 26 October 2018), art 2 <www.okex.com/support/hc/en-us/articles/360021813691-Terms-of-Service> accessed 20 April 2020.
73 Financial Conduct Authority, 'FCA Statement on the Requirement for Firms Offering Cryptocurrency Derivatives to be Authorised' (FCA Statement, 6 April 2018) <www.fca.org.uk/news/statements/cryptocurrency-derivatives> accessed 20 April 2020.

Activities) Order 2001 (RAO).[74] This is rarely the case as for the regulation to apply, both elements of the activity (ie, safeguarding and administering assets) must be conducted together, and conducted in relation to the same investments. Contrary to the guidance regarding the meaning of 'safeguarding' and 'administration' set out in the Guidance Release produced by the SIB (now FCA) in June 1997,[75] art 43 RAO clarifies that certain activities typically performed by crypto exchanges (eg, currency conversion or receiving documents relating to an investment solely for the purposes of onward transmission to, from or at the direction of the owner of the investment) do not constitute 'administration' for the purpose of art 40 RAO.

Moreover, since the safeguarding and administration of assets is a regulated activity only if it consists or includes 'any investment which is a security or contractually based investment',[76] it is likely that, unless custody contemplates items such as options, futures and contracts for differences,[77] cryptocurrencies are not within the scope of art 40 RAO. Should that be the case, it means that crypto-custodians would not have to comply with FCA rules on safeguarding of trust assets established in the High Level Standards,[78] in the Business Standards (CASS) rules[79] and the statutory mechanism under which client assets can be returned to clients in the event of the intermediary's failure.[80]

In relation to the more specific issue of money laundering, the UK regulatory response has been particularly effective. From 10 January 2020, businesses carrying on cryptoasset activity (both cryptoasset exchange providers and custodian wallet-providers) in the UK have to register with the FCA for money laundering and terrorist financing purposes under the Money Laundering, Terrorist Financing and Transfer of Funds (Information on the Payer) Regulations 2017. The speed of the reaction is probably ascribable to the fact that some of the characteristics of cryptocurrencies[81] make them particularly attractive to convert 'dirty cash' from illegal activities into (subdivided smaller amounts of) several virtual currencies to be moved through the crypto-sphere.

Considering the frequency with which cryptocurrency exchanges collapse or are hacked or misappropriate funds, it seems that under the above sketched UK regulatory framework the level of investor's protection is suboptimal. The fundamental economic problem of asymmetry of information between investors and crypto-custodians that operate using DLT is not addressed. This in turn generates agency costs which are not currently rectified

---

74 SI 2001/544 (RAO).

75 Securities Investment Board, 'Custody of Investments under the Financial Services Act 1986' (Guidance Release 5/97, June 1997). See also Financial Conduct Authority, *The Perimeter Guidance Manual* (PERG Handbook, March 2020), PERGs 2.7.9G and 2.7.10G <www.handbook.fca.org.uk/handbook/PERG.pdf> accessed 20 April 2020.

76 RAO, art 40(2)(a).

77 This will rarely be the case since these are contractual arrangements and 'the custodian would therefore have to enter into the relevant contract itself in order to hold the benefit of the contractual obligations': Yates and Montagu (n 40) 142–143.

78 Financial Conduct Authority, 'Principles for Businesses' (PRIN Handbook, 21 April 2016), PRIN 2.10 <www.handbook.fca.org.uk/handbook/PRIN.pdf> accessed 20 April 2020.

79 Financial Conduct Authority, 'Business Standards' (CASS Handbook, 3 January 2018), CASS 6.1 <www.handbook.fca.org.uk/handbook/CASS/6/1.html> accessed 20 April 2020.

80 That is, Investment Bank Special Administration Regime (SAR) SI 2011/245 made under the Banking Act 2009 (as amended by the Investment Bank (Amendment of Definition) and Special Administration (Amendment) Regulations SI 2017/443).

81 For example, global availability, the speed and irreversibility of transactions and the ability to hide identities.

by conduct of business rules and prudential regulation and which might have negative repercussions on the future growth of investments in cryptoassets.

3.4 *Outstanding legal challenges*

The recent operational changes suggest that in order to function, cryptocurrencies rely on countless points of centralisation, like wallet-providers, exchanges and specialist crypto-custodians. From a legal perspective and in the lack of a guiding regulatory framework, if owners do not hold cryptocurrencies directly, the conventional property law analysis underpinning the inquiry outlined in Part II above may become questionable and not capable of providing a correct representation of the legal nature of investors' entitlement over cryptocurrencies. In the case of indirectly held cryptocurrencies on unallocated basis, investors' rights may be personal and not proprietary in nature. The analysis below seeks to clarify this fundamental issue and the associated legal challenges. It highlights how the rules applicable to the circulation of intermediated cryptocurrencies are incomplete, ambiguous and a source of legal risk and, as a consequence, how investors are unable to quantify or to limit their exposure to potentially damaging outcomes. The ideal solution would be to establish clear rules that offer for consistent and predictable solutions to particular fact situations, while maintaining market confidence. Whether this can be achieved by adapting existing legal doctrines or via *ad hoc* legislative intervention in combination with regulatory reform and whether cross border 'compatibility' of different legal systems (when intermediated cryptocurrencies are settled or pledged cross-border) should also be simultaneously promoted, involve the analysis of complex issues *de lege ferenda* that will not be addressed, if not in passing, in the rest of this chapter.

3.4.1 *Nature of intermediated cryptocurrencies*

Although never expressly provided in the terms of service currently available online, a cryptocurrency exchange that operates a crypto account regulated by English law for the benefit of an account holder holds cryptocurrencies of the same kind on trust.[82] This characterisation, recently endorsed in by Gendall J in *Ruscoe v Cryptopia Limited (in liquidation)*[83] in New Zealand, allows the protection of the account holders' cryptocurrencies from the claims of the exchange's creditors. Cryptocurrencies held on trust are outside the trustee's estate and, on the exchange's insolvency, the beneficiary would have a proprietary right that could not be defeated by the exchange's creditors (the same would apply to 'client money' resulting from the sale of cryptocurrencies[84]).

---

82 Same *ratio* in *Re Lehman Brothers International (Europe) (In Administration)* [2010] EWHC 2914 (Ch) [226].

83 [2020] NZHC 728 [134]–[206]. See Matteo Solinas 'Investors' Rights in (Crypto) Custodial Holdings: *Ruscoe v Cryptopia Ltd (in Liquidation)*' (2021) 84 Modern Law Review 155.

84 By analogy with *Re Lehman Brothers International (Europe) (In Administration)* [2012] UKSC 6.

The alternative interpretation of the custodial relationship in terms of bailment is not convincing[85]: bailment arrangements are in fact restricted to tangible assets,[86] and available only where possession is possible.[87] That said, it has been recently argued that a mere wallet-provider could be in the position of a bailee of cryptocurrencies.[88] If the definition of possession under English law is treated to be an anachronism in a context where digital assets are commonplace, and if the legal objectives of the tort of conversion could be achieved by referring to the criteria of excludability and exhaustibility,[89] then a modern notion of possession should be available – a notion that 'is not dependent upon the existence of, or relationship between, individuals for its existence'.[90] Cryptocurrencies should not be regarded as mere claims because the existence of the private key provides to the owner full control access to cryptocurrencies in the same way as provided by physical possession of a tangible object. In this light, it might be said that even intermediated cryptocurrencies are choses in possession amenable to bailment. The greatest concern with this reading is that it is convincing only to the limited extent that user wallets are segregated, and investors are able to maintain direct control of cryptocurrencies under the custodial arrangement with the exchange. These are exceptional cases in market practice and cases where the relevance of intermediation is negligible.

Another possible approach might be one based on banking law.[91] It is a clear principle of banking law that the deposit of cash with a bank establishes the relationship of debtor and creditor between the bank and the depositor.[92] Depositors' money is not held by the bank by way of bailment[93] or trust[94] and the depositors' rights of repayment are not proprietary[95] (ie, on the bank's insolvency, the depositor qualifies as an unsecured creditor[96]). However, even assuming that cryptocurrencies are money at law, the debtor–creditor principle may not apply to non-bank custodians such as cryptocurrency exchanges. This is simply because it would not satisfy the pre-requisites to the creation of a bank-customer contract based on the common law definitions of either 'bank'[97] or a 'customer'.[98]

---

85 Under a bailment relationship, legal title to the deposited assets is not transferred to the intermediary but remains with the client. As the intermediary, the bailee is not the owner of the assets bailed with them but is entitled only to possession. They are a mere custodian and must refrain from denying the bailor's title (*Biddle v Bond* (1865) 6 B&S 225, (1865) 122 ER 1179).

86 *Re Hallett's Estates, Knatchbull v Hallett* (1880) 13 Ch D 696, 708 (Jessel MR) with respect to bearer bonds.

87 *Coggs v Bernard* (1703) 2 Ld Raym 909.

88 Sarah Green and Ferdisha Snagg, 'Intermediated Securities and Distributed Ledger Technology' in Louise Gullifer and Jennifer Payne (eds), *Intermediation and Beyond* (Hart Publishing 2019) 337, 345–348.

89 Sarah Green and John Randall, *The Tort of Conversion* (Hart Publishing 2009) Ch 5.

90 Green and Snagg (n 88) 346.

91 See Christopher Hare, 'Cryptocurrencies and Banking Law: Are There Lessons to Learn?' in David Fox and Sarah Green (eds), *Cryptocurrencies in Public and Private Law* (Oxford University Press 2019) 229, 231–248.

92 *Carr v Carr* (1811) 1 Mer 541n.

93 *Akbar Khan v Attar Singh* [1936] 2 All ER 545 (PC) 548.

94 *Foley v Hill* (1848) 2 HL Cas 28; *Foskett v Mckeown* [2001] 1 AC 102 (HL) 127–128; *Azam v Iqbal* [2007] EWHC 2025 (Admin) [15]–[17], [27]–[29].

95 *Re Hallett's Estate* (n 86) 746 (Thesiger LJ).

96 *Space Investments Ltd v Canadian Imperial Bank of Commerce Trust Co (Bahamas) Ltd* [1986] 1 WLR 1072 (PC).

97 *United Dominions Trust Ltd v Kirkwood* [1966] 2 QB 431, 447, 457–458, 465.

98 *Commissioners of Taxation v English, Scottish and Australian Bank* [1920] AC 683, 687–688.

The legal characterisation for indirectly held cryptocurrencies based on trust operates under the assumption that a valid trust has been created notwithstanding the fact that the cryptocurrencies held by the exchange are aggregated into one commingled account (ie, they are held on an unallocated basis). This is because the fundamental principle of the need for certainty of subject matter for a valid trust to arise[99] is redundant in the context of a commingled pool of cryptocurrencies. There are no relevant differences between cryptocurrencies to require identifying which specific cryptocurrencies are to be the subject matter of the trust,[100] or, alternatively, the account holder's equitable interest may be treated as a co-ownership interest in relation to the entire pool of cryptocurrencies held by the intermediary.[101]

Finally, as Briggs J clarified in *Re Lehman Brothers International (Europe), Lomas v RAB Market Cycles (Master) Fund Ltd*[102] the fact that intermediated securities may be subject to the 'right of use' according to operational arrangements with the custodian is not inconsistent with the existence of a valid trust.[103] The same ratio could be adopted in relation to crypto exchanges that hold cryptocurrencies for the account holders, provided that the practice is allowed in the terms of service.

99 *Knight v Knight* (1840) 3 Beav 148. See also *Re Goldcorp Exchange* [1994] 2 All ER 806 (PC) 814 (Lord Mustill); *Westdeutsche Landesbank Girozentrale v Islington London Borough Council* [1996] AC 669 (HL) 705 (Lord Browne-Wilkinson).

100 The Court of Appeal in *Hunter v Moss* [1993] 1 WLR 934 (CA). Notwithstanding strong academic criticisms (eg, David Hayton, 'Uncertainty of Subject-matter of Trusts' (1994) 110 LQR 335; Mark Ockelton, 'Share and Share Alike?' (1994) CLJ 448; and William Norris, 'Uncertainty and Informality: *Hunter v Moss*' (1995) 1 Private Client Business 43, 45) and the existence of inconsistent authorities on the possibility of creating property rights under a trust without attaching to any particular asset (eg, *Mac-Jordan Construction Ltd v Brookmount Erostin Ltd (in receivership)* [1992] BCLC 350 (CA); *Russell-Cooke Trust Co v Prentis* [2002] EWHC 2227 (Ch) and *Re BA Peters plc (in administration)* [2008] All ER (D) 392; *Re Global Trader Europe Ltd (in liquidation)* [2009] EWHC 602 (Ch)), this *ratio* has been followed with a variety of accents in *Re Harvard Securities (in liquidation)* [1998] BCC 567, [1997] 2 BCLC 369, 388 (Neuberger J); *Re CA Pacific Finance Ltd (in liquidation)* [2000] BCLC 494 (Yuen J); *Holland v Newbury* (1997) 2 BCLC 396; *Re CA Pacific Finance Ltd* [1999] BCLC 494 (Hong Kong); and, more recently, in *Re Lehman Brothers International (Europe), Lomas v RAB Market Cycles (Master) Fund Ltd* [2009] EWHC 2545 (Ch) [56]. See the critical remarks of Michael Bridge, 'Security Financial Collateral Transfers and Prime Broker Insolvency' (2010) 4 LFMR 189, 192.

101 Following the *ratio* in *Re Lehman Brothers* (n 83) [225]–[248] (Briggs J) (upheld in the Court of Appeal judgment *Re Lehman Brothers International (Europe) (in administration)* [2011] EWCA Civ 1544, [69]–[71] (Lloyd LJ)) and *White v Shortall* [2006] NSWSC 1379, [201]–[213] (Campbell J) in symmetrical contrast with *Re Wait* [1927] 1 Ch 606. This interpretation also has some academic support. See Roy Goode, 'Are Intangible Assets Fungible?' in Arianna Pretto and Peter Birks (eds), *Themes in Comparative Law* (Oxford University Press, 2002) 102. The same position is shared by Ben McFarlane and Robert Stevens, 'Interest in Securities: Practical Problems and Conceptual Solutions' in Louise Gullifer and Jennifer Payne (eds), *Intermediated Securities: Legal Problems and Practical Issues* (Hart Publishing 2010) 40; Giles Richardson, 'Lehman Brothers: Traditional Trusts Principles and 21st Century International Bank Failures' (2011) 17 Trusts & Trustees 226; and Michael Bridge, 'Certainty, Identification and Intention in Personal Property Law' in Paul Davies and James Penner (eds), *Equity, Trusts and Commerce* (Hart Publishing 2017) 87, 101–102.

102 [2009] EWHC 2545 (Ch) [64].

103 Joanna Benjamin and Louise Gullifer, 'Stewardship and Collateral: The Advantages and Disadvantages of the No Look Through System' in Louise Gullifer and Jennifer Payne (eds), *Intermediation and Beyond* (Hart Publishing 2019) 215, 227.

3.4.2 *Shortfalls*

Even if the account holders' assets are ring-fenced from the claims of the exchange's creditors, a shortfall may arise in the cryptocurrency exchange's account. This will occur when the cryptocurrencies of the same kind credited on the books of the exchange fall short of the aggregate of the investor's entitlements. The imbalance does not result necessarily from the exchange's fraud or mistake. Under English law, the problem about the allocation of a shortfall among the different investors is relevant only when the exchange is insolvent. A solvent exchange, if it does not decide voluntarily to make up the shortfall for reason of relationship and reputation, is under a legal duty to make good the shortfall, to replace the missing cryptocurrencies or pay damages. It is responsible to account for the cryptocurrencies held on trust and it can be required to restore any deficiency in the trust assets to the trust.[104] Even outside the cases of strict liability when the shortfall is the result of a positive act of the exchange, its duty cannot be contracted out because it concerns the same subject matter of the trust, a duty on which the investor has relied upon. If it is contracted out, the trust is inevitably destroyed.[105]

When the crypto exchange is insolvent, various methods of allocating the shortfall among account holders are available. This is a source of legal uncertainty. Apart from the case of segregated accounts where a shortfall loss affecting a particular account holder is borne entirely by that same account holder, it is not predictable whether competing claims to assets in a pooled fund of cryptocurrencies should be resolved according to traditional tracing rules, to the 'first in first out rule' applied in *Clayton's case*,[106] to a 'rolling charge approach'[107] or to a rateable distribution in proportion to the size of each account holder's holding with the exchange.[108] This last approach allows all investors in cryptocurrencies to share the risk of the exchange's insolvency undertaken at the time of the investment. Considering the arbitrary way in which administrative errors or frauds may affect individual accounts, the *pro rata* rule better captures the commercial expectations, reflecting the common venture of holding securities in a pooled account and the common risk taken by the account holders as to the exchange's integrity and solvency. This is the case of the OKEx exchange mentioned above where the Terms of Service clearly state that 'individual user entitlements may not be identifiable by separate physical documents of title or other electronic record and, in the case of an irreconcilable shortfall, you may not receive your full entitlement and may share in the shortfall pro rata'.[109] Although the *pro rata* solution seems to be the most practical and least arbitrary, it would be open

104 *Re Dawson* [1966] 2 NSWR 211; *Target Holdings Ltd v Redferns (a firm)* [1996] AC 421, 434. See also P J Millett, 'Equity's Place in the Law of Commerce' (1998) 114 LQR 214, 225.
105 See Ben McFarlane, *The Structure of Property Law* (Hart Publishing 2008) 551; *Armitage v Nurse* [1998] Ch 214, 253 (Lord Millett).
106 That is, the first assets into a fund are deemed to have been the first out; 'the first drawings out are attributed to the first payments in': *Devaynes v Noble; Clayton's Case* (1816) 1 Mer 529, 572, (1816) 35 ER 767, 781 (Sir Wm Grant MR). This approach might be particularly helpful in the case of omnibus accounts where the number of securities held fluctuates. See Gabriel Moss, 'Intermediated Securities: Issues arising from Insolvency' in Louise Gullifer and Jennifer Payne (eds), *Intermediated Securities: Legal Problems and Practical Issues* (Hart Publishing 2010) 62.
107 See the discussion on this approach (or 'North American solution') in *Barlow Clowes International Ltd (in liq) v Vaughan* [1992] 4 All ER 22, 35 per Woolf LJ.
108 *Ibid*. This is also the conclusion reached by Briggs J in *Re Lehman Brothers* (above n 84).
109 'Terms of Service' (*OKEx Support*, 26 October 2018), art 2 <https://support.okex.com/hc/en-us/articles/360018829231> accessed 20 April 2020.

to a particular customer to claim that the shortfall should be passed to other particular customers by applying the traditional rules of equitable tracing, especially when the shortfall is significant, and attributable to a specific investor's transaction.[110] The possible coexistence of the two regimes for dealing with a shortfall has received academic support in relation to intermediated securities,[111] although following the Lehman's collapse it has also attracted strong criticisms as an unworkable approach in practice.[112] Greater clarity on the consequences of a shortfall is desirable, possibly along the lines of a recent statutory intervention[113] that ensured the application of the *pari passu* principle in cases involving distribution of client assets where there is a shortfall and the account provider is an 'investment bank'.[114]

3.4.3 *Negotiability*

In contrast to few common law exceptions to the *nemo dat* rule, equity has a general defence against the claims of a beneficial owner over trust assets in the hands of a third party. This is the well-established defence, which protects a good faith purchaser of legal title for value without notice of prior equitable rights.[115] In the words of Millett J in *Macmillan Inc v Bishopsgate Investment Trust plc (No 3)*, an 'equity's darling' is a bona fide purchaser for value 'who obtains the legal estate at the time of his purchase without actual or constructive notice of prior equitable rights and who is entitled to priority in equity as well as at law ... But he must have obtained the legal estate, and the question of notice is normally tested at the time he obtained it'.[116] The most convincing explanation for this exception to the *nemo dat* rule has a very pragmatic rationale. In creating a trust, the property, by the nature of the device, may present to the world a possibly misleading factual situation. The settlor who has privately established to create a trust is exposed to the risk that the trustee who will deal with it may be incompetent or a rogue.[117] However, unlike the case of directly held cryptocurrencies where the common law exception to the *nemo dat* rule always applies if cryptocurrencies qualify as money, the bona fide purchaser defence is of limited help for the innocent purchaser of indirectly held cryptocurrencies.

The explanation is simple. If cryptocurrencies are purchased directly from the crypto exchange, the scenario is substantially identical to the case relating to the acquisition of

---

110 Roy Goode (chair), 'Issue 3 – Property Interests in Investment Securities' (2004) Financial Markets Law Committee (FMLC) Working Paper, 11 <http://fmlc.org/wp-content/uploads/2018/02/Issue-3-Property-Interests-in-Investment-Securities.pdf> accessed 20 April 2020.

111 McFarlane and Stevens (n 101) 43–44.

112 Moss (n 106) 67, drawing from a number of controversial cases (eg, *Re CA Pacific Finance Ltd* (n 100), where thousands of investors had individual trust rights and where the tracing process could have taken many years). See also Jennifer Marshall and Nick Herrod, 'Lehman Brothers Insolvency – Client Assets' (2009) 3 LFMR 145.

113 Investment Bank Special Administration Regulations SI 2011/245, reg 12(2).

114 On this specific issue, see Dermot Turing, *Clearing and Settlement in Europe* (Bloomsbury Professional 2012) 225.

115 The defence is well established in the history of English Law. See *Pilcher v Rawlins* (1872) LR 7 Ch App 259, 268 (James LJ); *Joseph v Lyons* (1884) 15 QBD 280 and *Hallas v Robinson* (1885) 15 QBD 288, 292.

116 *Macmillan Inc v Bishopsgate Investment Trust plc (No 3)* [1995] 1 WLR 978 (Ch D), 1000.

117 See Lionel Smith, 'Unjust Enrichment, Property and the Structure of Trusts' (2000) 116 LQR 412, 431.

directly held cryptocurrencies. The 'equity's darling' defence would be relevant only if cryptocurrencies would not qualify as money at common law. However, the bona fide purchaser defence is not available if the purchaser acquires an equitable interest from the indirect holder of cryptocurrencies: the innocent purchaser of indirectly held cryptocurrencies does not acquire a legal estate, but merely an equitable interest in cryptocurrencies. As between two equitable interests, the general rule, similar, in substance to the *nemo dat* principle, is *qui prior est in tempore potior in iure*.[118] When the bona fide purchaser defence is not available, there are no alternative methods to protect an innocent purchaser of indirectly held cryptocurrencies under English law.[119]

This distinction between sales from the exchange and sales from indirect holders of cryptocurrencies does not seem to have a logical rationale and it is discriminatory among innocent purchasers. The historical explanation according to which in the case of acquisition of a legal estate the court of equity has no jurisdiction to recognise that a transferee is under a duty to the beneficiary is difficult to defend.[120] It creates inconsistencies in the property law system and, above all, may cause unwanted obstacles in the circulation of indirectly held cryptocurrencies.

3.4.4 *Internal soundness and cross-border compatibility*

In order to enhance an intermediated holding system's viability, increase confidence in the ownership and settlement of intermediated cryptoassets and reduce legal risk, it is important that in addition to sound domestic rules, predictable outcomes are also available where the laws of another legal system apply. A domestic legal system may possibly not recognise an investor's ability to hold cryptoassets and effectively exercise rights in them through an intermediary, imposing the need to employ sub-custodians.[121] An alternative is to ban crypto-intermediaries altogether, as has been the case in China since 2017.[122] In this light, competition among exchanges positioned offshore represents a great element of risk for investors in cryptoassets, as more often than not, 'the system – just like in the card-playing

---

118 He who is first in time is better in law. The rule is explained in *Phillips v Phillips* (1861) 4 De GF & J 208, 215, (1861) 45 ER 1164 (Lord Westbury LC).

119 The doctrine of the *tabula in naufragio*, in particular, cannot be successfully invoked in this context. This doctrine is based on the struggle between competing equitable interests for the legal estate when the subordinated holder of equitable interest has a clear incentive in incurring the expense of acquiring the legal estate (and rank ahead of other existing equitable interests). (See *Harpham v Shacklock* (1881) 19 ChD 207 (CA) 214 (Jessel MR); *Taylor v Russell* [1892] AC 244 (HL); *Bailey v Barnes* [1894] 1 Ch 25 (CA).) The defence of 'change of position' is also not available. In *Foskett v McKeown* (n 94), Lord Millett clarified the issue, pointing out that equitable proprietary claims are not concerned with unjust enrichment but with the vindication of the claimant's property rights over assets or its traceable proceeds.

120 See *Pilcher* (n 115) 268 (James LJ).

121 This is for example the case of the Malta-based OKEx exchange, where art 1 (Eligibility and Prohibition of Using Our Services) of the 'Terms of Service' (*OKEx Support*, 26 October 2018) <www.okex.com/support/hc/en-us/articles/360021813691-Terms-of-Service> accessed 20 April 2020.

122 Gabriel Wildau, 'Beijing Set to Shut Bitcoin Exchanges to Ensure Price Stability' (*Financial Times*, 12 September 2017) <www.ft.com/content/b2f1d198-96df-11e7-a652-cde3f882dd7b> accessed 20 April 2020; Kelvin F K Low and Wu Ying-Chieh, 'The Characterization of Cryptocurrencies in East Asia' in David Fox and Sarah Green (eds), *Cryptocurrencies in Public and Private Law* (Oxford University Press 2019) 199, 201.

saloons of the Wild West – is stacked against them, because the tables are controlled from the outset by the sector's greatest rogues and regulatory outlaws'.[123]

Finally, and in addition to complex challenges presented by cryptocurrencies for the conflict of laws,[124] it is difficult to establish what system of laws applies to cross-border transactions regarding the sale, perfection and enforcement of intermediated cryptoassets. The traditional approach adopted to determine the law applicable to proprietary issues (ie, the *lex rei sitae*) is highly unsatisfactory in relation to indirect-holding systems. It may lead to practical impossibilities given the complexities involved in materially locating intermediated cryptocurrencies. In an intermediated system, the location of private keys, the custodian's records and jurisdiction of incorporation of the custodian are not sufficient to identify the holder of intermediated cryptoassets.[125] Various possible solutions can be suggested to address the choice of law problems arising from transactions in intermediated cryptoassets. Among the most promising is the approach that considers the location where the intermediary holds the account to which the cryptoassets are credited in order to determine the proprietary aspects of collateral transactions. Alternatively, it could be the law agreed by the account holder and the intermediary or, where no such choice has been made, the law adopted to govern the account agreement, provided in both cases that the intermediary maintaining the account has some factual links with the jurisdiction whose law is chosen. This would de facto allow for party autonomy on proprietary issues.

4 Conclusions

This chapter highlighted the existing gap between the conventional perception of DLT and the reality of market practice. The idea of a distributed system of trust, based on a transaction ledger which is cryptographically verified and jointly maintained by cryptoassets' users has been particularly attractive to libertarians (as well as drug dealers and speculators), but it has also proved to be unwieldy and technically ineffective. Today, traders, dealers, wallet and crypto payments services get around transaction settlement simply by netting 'off the blockchain' using often-unregulated institutions that effectively play the role of banks in the cryptocurrency world. This market trend has now reached the point where the majority of small-scale payments are not processed on the blockchain at all.

As investors in cryptoassets struggle to understand the consequences of their investment choices in off-chain transactions, there is a fundamental problem of legal and financial education to be addressed. Understanding how cryptoassets are held and transferred by exchanges and specialised custodians on behalf of investors has been the concern of this chapter. While Part II examined the developments in market practice and their rationale, Part III, in the light of the existing regulation in the UK, critically tackled some of most relevant issues of legal uncertainty related to the ownership and transfer of indirectly held cryptocurrencies.

---

123 Kaminska, 'Don't Bet on' (n 60).
124 See Andrew Dickinson, 'Cryptocurrencies and the Conflict of Laws' in David Fox and Sarah Green (eds), *Cryptocurrencies in Public and Private Law* (Oxford University Press 2019) 93–137.
125 See James S Rogers, 'Of Normalcy and Anomaly: Thoughts on Choice of Law for Indirect Holding System' (1998) 9 JIBFL 47 (special supplement).

For the sake of completeness, it should perhaps also be mentioned that this picture is only a partial representation of the changing market practice. A new unsettling trend is now becoming prominent. This is the rise in 'over-the-counter' (OTC) cryptocurrency transactions that are able to cope with the lack of liquidity on major exchanges, while remaining not formally audited and almost invisible on the blockchain (where only net changes are recorded).[126] The trend is particularly relevant, especially considering the volume of the transactions, but well outside the scope of this inquiry on custody arrangements and DLT.

Bibliography

R Anderson and others, 'Bitcoin Redux' (*WEIS 2018*, 28 May 2018) Cambridge University Computer Laboratory <https://weis2018.econinfosec.org/wp-content/uploads/sites/5/2018/05/WEIS_2018_paper_38.pdf> accessed 20 April 2020.

R Armstrong, 'Cryptocurrency Exchange Boss's Death Locks Away $150m in Digital Assets' (*Financial Times*, 5 February 2019) <www.ft.com/content/538b8ece-296e-11e9-a5ab-ff8ef2b976c7> accessed 20 April 2020.

M Arnold, 'European Banks to Launch Blockchain Trade Finance Platform' (*Financial Times*, 27 June 2017) <www.ft.com/content/6bb4f678-5a8c-11e7-b553-e2df1b0c3220> accessed 20 April 2020.

R Auer, 'Beyond the Doomsday Economics of 'Proof-of-Work' in Cryptocurrencies' (2019) BIS Working Papers No 765 <www.bis.org/publ/work765.pdf> accessed 20 April 2020.

A Back, 'Hashcash – A Denial of Service Counter-Measure' (*Hashcash*, 1 August 2002) <http://www.hashcash.org/papers/hashcash.pdf> accessed 20 April 2020.

P Baran, 'On Distributed Communications Networks' (1964) 12 IEEE Transactions of the Professional Technical Groups on Communications Systems 1.

J Benjamin and L Gullifer, 'Stewardship and Collateral: The Advantages and Disadvantages of the No Look Through System' in L Gullifer and J Payne (eds), *Intermediation and Beyond* (Hart Publishing 2019) 215.

Binance Research 'Institutional Market Insights – 2nd edition' (*Binance Research*, 22 November 2019) <https://research.binance.com/analysis/institutional-insights-2nd-edition> accessed 20 April 2020.

M Bridge, 'Security Financial Collateral Transfers and Prime Broker Insolvency' (2010) 4 LFMR 189.

M Bridge, 'Certainty, Identification and Intention in Personal Property Law' in P Davies and J Penner (eds), *Equity, Trusts and Commerce* (Hart Publishing 2017) 87.

British Retail Consortium, 'Payments Survey 2016' (*BRC*, 2016) <https://brc.org.uk/media/179489/payment-survey-2016_final.pdf> accessed 20 April 2020.

M Casey and others, *The Impact of Blockchain Technology on Finance: A Catalyst for Change* (Vol 21 of Geneva Reports on the World Economy, Centre for Economic Policy Research 2018).

M Casey and P Vigna, *The Truth Machine: The Blockchain and the Future of Everything* (St Martin's Press 2018).

---

[126] The bitcoin over-the-counter (OTC) market is approximately three times larger than the exchange market. See Hannah Murphy, '"Bitcoin whales" Control Third of Market with $37.5bn Holdings' (*Financial Times*, 9 June 2018) <https://www.ft.com/content/c4b68aec-6b26-11e8-8cf3-0c230fa67aec> accessed 20 April 2020; and Aaron Stanley, 'Uncharted Bitcoin OTC Markets Gear Up For Institutional Inflows' (*Forbes*, 23 October 2018) <www.forbes.com/sites/astanley/2018/10/23/uncharted-bitcoin-otc-markets-gear-up-for-institutional-inflows/ - 1ecbd4f57bac> accessed 20 April 2020.

L Cermak, 'Up to 86% of Total Reported Cryptocurrency Trading Volume Is Likely Fake, According to Analysis of Exchange Website Visits' (*The Block*, 28 May 2019) <www.theblockcrypto.com/genesis/24878/up-to-86-of-total-reported-cryptocurrency-trading-volume-is-likely-fake-according-to-analysis-of-exchange-website-visits> accessed 15 March 2020.

(Chainalysis) <www.chainalysis.com> accessed 20 April 2020.

L Chambers, 'The Keepers of the Keys: Remedies and Legal Obligations Following Misappropriations of Cryptocurrency' (2016) 11 JIBFL 673.

(*Coinbase | Wallet*) <https://wallet.coinbase.com/> accessed 20 April 2020.

CoinMarketCap 'Top 100 Cryptocurrencies by Market Capitalization' (*CoinMarketCap*) <https://coinmarketcap.com/> accessed 20 April 2020.

F Coppola, 'The Fat Controller of the Lightning Network' (*Coppola Comment*, 17 January 2018) <www.coppolacomment.com/2018/01/lightning-and-fat-controller.html> accessed 20 April 2020.

C Cornish, 'Growing Number of Cryptocurrencies Spark Concerns' (*Financial Times*, 10 January 2018) <www.ft.com/content/a6b90a8c-f4b7-11e7-8715-e94187b3017e> accessed 20 April 2020.

P Daian and others, 'Flash Boys 2.0: Frontrunning, Transaction Reordering, and Consensus Instability in Decentralised Exchanges' (*Cornell University arXiv:1904.05234 [cs.CR]*, 10 April 2019) <https://arxiv.org/abs/1904.05234> accessed 20 April 2020.

D Davies, 'A Brief History of Cryptography' (1977) 2 Inf Secur Tech Rep 14.

P De Filippi and A Wright, *Blockchain and the Law: The Rule of Code* (Harvard University Press 2018).

T Demeester, 'Bitcoin: Digital Gold or Digital Cash? Both' (*Medium*, 15 January 2017) <https://medium.com/@tuurdemeester/bitcoin-digital-gold-or-digital-cash-both-382a346e6c79> accessed 20 April 2020.

(*DEX Watch*) <https://dex.watch/> accessed 20 April 2020.

A Dickinson, 'Cryptocurrencies and the Conflict of Laws' in D Fox and S Green (eds), *Cryptocurrencies in Public and Private Law* (Oxford University Press 2019) 93.

W Diffie and M Hellman, 'New Directions in Cryptography' (1976) 22 IEEE Trans Inf Theory 644.

N Dodd, 'The Social Life of Bitcoin' (2018) 35 Theory, Culture & Society 35.

D Donald, 'The Rise and Effects of the Indirect Holding Systems – How Corporate America Ceded its Shareholders to Intermediaries' (2007) Institute for Law and Finance Working Paper Series No 68.

Financial Conduct Authority, 'Principles for Businesses' (PRIN Handbook, 21 April 2016) <www.handbook.fca.org.uk/handbook/PRIN.pdf> accessed 20 April 2020.

Financial Conduct Authority, 'Business Standards' (CASS Handbook, 3 January 2018) <www.handbook.fca.org.uk/handbook/CASS/6/1.html> accessed 20 April 2020.

Financial Conduct Authority, 'FCA statement on the requirement for firms offering cryptocurrency derivatives to be authorised' (FCA Statement, 6 April 2018) <www.fca.org.uk/news/statements/cryptocurrency-derivatives> accessed 20 April 2020.

Financial Conduct Authority, 'CP19/3: Guidance on Cryptoassets' (January 2019) <https://europeanchamberofdigitalcommerce.com/wp-content/uploads/2019/06/Guidance-on-Cryptoassets-Consultation-Paper.pdf> accessed 20 April 2020.

Financial Conduct Authority, *The Perimeter Guidance Manual* (PERG Handbook, March 2020) <www.handbook.fca.org.uk/handbook/PERG.pdf> accessed 20 April 2020.

Financial Markets Law Committee, 'Issue 3 – Property Interests in Investment Securities' (2004) Financial Markets Law Committee (FMLC) Working Paper, 11 <http://fmlc.org/wp-content/uploads/2018/02/Issue-3-Property-Interests-in-Investment-Securities.pdf> accessed 20 April 2020.

H Finney, 'Bitcoin Bank' (*Bitcoin Forum*, 30 December 2010) <https://bitcointalk.org/index.php?topic=2500.msg34211#msg34211> accessed 30 March 2020.

D Fox, 'Cryptocurrencies in the Common Law of Property' in D Fox and S Green (eds), *Cryptocurrencies in Public and Private Law* (Oxford University Press 2019) 139.

D Fox and S Green (eds), *Cryptocurrencies in Public and Private Law* (Oxford University Press 2019).

T Geron, 'Companies Compete to Be Cryptocurrency Custodians' (*The Wall Street Journal*, 17 September 2019) <www.wsj.com/articles/companies-compete-to-be-cryptocurrency-custodians-11568772060> accessed 20 April 2020.

R Goode, 'Are Intangible Assets Fungible?' in A Pretto and P Birks (eds), *Themes in Comparative Law* (Oxford University Press 2002) 102.

A Green, 'Will Blockchain Accelerate Trade Flows?' (*Financial Times*, 10 November 2017) <www.ft.com/content/a36399fa-a927-11e7-ab66-21cc87a2edde> accessed 20 April 2020.

S Green and J Randall, *The Tort of Conversion* (Hart Publishing 2009).

S Green and F Snagg, 'Intermediated Securities and Distributed Ledger Technology' in L Gullifer and J Payne (eds), *Intermediation and Beyond* (Hart Publishing 2019) 337.

S Haber and W S Stornetta, 'How to Time-Stamp a Digital Document' (1991) 3 J Cryptol 99.

R Harding, 'Bitpoint Exchange Says Hackers Stole $32m in Cryptocurrency' (*Financial Times*, 12 July 2019) <www.ft.com/content/c23930d4-a474-11e9-974c-ad1c6ab5efd1> accessed 20 April 2020.

C Hare, 'Cryptocurrencies and Banking Law: Are There Lessons to Learn?' in D Fox and S Green (eds), *Cryptocurrencies in Public and Private Law* (Oxford University Press 2019) 229.

D Hayton, 'Uncertainty of Subject-Matter of Trusts' (1994) 110 LQR 335.

M Hougan, H Kim and M Lerner, 'Economic and Non-Economic Trading in Bitcoin: Exploring the Real Spot Market for the World's First Digital Commodity' (24 May 2019) Bitwise Asset Management <www.sec.gov/comments/sr-nysearca-2019-01/srnysearca201901-5574233-185408.pdf> accessed 15 March 2020.

K James-Lubin, 'Blockchain Scalability: A look at the Stumbling Blocks to Blockchain Scalability and Some High-Level Technical Solutions' (*O'Reilly Media*, 22 January 2015) <www.oreilly.com/ideas/blockchain-scalability> accessed 20 April 2020.

I Kaminska, 'Blockchain and the Holy Real-Time Settlement Grail' (*Financial Times*, 27 February 2016) <https://ftalphaville.ft.com/2016/02/26/2154510/blockchain-and-the-holy-real-time-settlement-grail/> accessed 20 April 2020.

I Kaminska, 'Bitcoin Bitfinex Exchange Hacked: the Unanswered Questions' (*Financial Times*, 4 August 2016) <https://www.ft.com/content/1ea8baf8-5a11-11e6-8d05-4eaa66292c32> accessed 20 April 2020.

I Kaminska, 'Legal Tussle Looms for Bitcoin Holders in Hacked Bitfinex' (*Financial Times*, 5 August 2016) <www.ft.com/content/c3b9f89c-5b18-11e6-9f70-badea1b336d4> accessed 20 April 2020.

I Kaminska, 'But, But … I Thought Bitcoin Was Supposed to Be Cheap?' (*Financial Times*, 17 March 2017) <https://ftalphaville.ft.com/2017/03/17/2186161/but-but-i-thought-bitcoin-was-supposed-to-be-cheap/> accessed 20 April 2020.

I Kaminska, 'Bitcoin's Fake News Problem' (*Financial Times*, 21 March 2017) <https://ftalphaville.ft.com/2017/03/21/2186260/bitcoins-fake-news-problem/> accessed 20 April 2020.

I Kaminska, 'The Currency of the Future Has a Settlement Problem' (*Financial Times*, 18 May 2017) <www.ftalphaville.ft.com/2017/05/17/2188961/the-currency-of-the-future-has-a-settlement-problem> accessed 20 April 2020.

I Kaminska, 'Don't Bet on Decentralised Exchanges Becoming the New Crypto Frontier …' (*Financial Times*, 11 September 2019) <https://ftalphaville.ft.com/2019/09/11/1568182095000/Don-t-bet-on-decentralised-exchanges-becoming-the-new-crypto-frontier—/> accessed 20 April 2020.

I Kaminska, 'By Jove! Crypto Has Discovered Netting' (*Financial Times*, 5 December 2019) <https://ftalphaville.ft.com/2019/12/04/1575457459000/By-Jove–Crypto-has-discovered-netting/> accessed 20 April 2020.

Y Kim and J Jo, 'Binary Blockchain: Solving the Mining Congestion Problem by Dynamically Adjusting the Mining Capacity' in R Lee (ed), *Applied Computing & Information Technology* (Springer International Publishing 2018) 29.

(*Lightning Network*), <https://lightning.network> accessed 20 April 2020.

K F K Low and E G S Teo, 'Bitcoins and Other Cryptocurrencies as Property?' (2017) 9 Law Innov Technol 235.

K F K Low and W Ying-Chieh, 'The Characterization of Cryptocurrencies in East Asia' in D Fox and S Green (eds), *Cryptocurrencies in Public and Private Law* (Oxford University Press 2019) 199.

J Marshall and N Herrod, 'Lehman Brothers Insolvency – Client Assets' (2009) 3 LFMR 145.

D Martin, 'Demystifying Hash Searches' (2018) 70 SLR 691.

B McFarlane, *The Structure of Property Law* (Hart Publishing 2008).

B McFarlane and R Stevens, 'Interest in Securities: Practical Problems and Conceptual Solutions' in L Gullifer and J Payne (eds), *Intermediated Securities: Legal Problems and Practical Issues* (Hart Publishing 2010) 40.

B McLannahan, 'Bitcoin Exchange Mt Gox Files for Bankruptcy Protection' (*Financial Times*, 1 March 2014) <www.ft.com/content/6636e0e8-a06e-11e3-a72c-00144feab7de> accessed 20 April 2020.

E Micheler and von der Heyde, 'Holding, Clearing and Settling Securities Through Blockchain/ Distributed Ledger Technology: Creating an Efficient System by Empowering Investors' (2016) 31 JIBFL 652.

P J Millett, 'Equity's Place in the Law of Commerce' (1998) 114 LQR 214.

G Moss, 'Intermediated Securities: Issues Arising from Insolvency' in L Gullifer and J Payne (eds), *Intermediated Securities: Legal Problems and Practical Issues* (Hart Publishing 2010) 62.

H Murphy, '"Bitcoin Whales" Control Third of Market with $37.5bn Holdings' (*Financial Times*, 9 June 2018) <https://www.ft.com/content/c4b68aec-6b26-11e8-8cf3-0c230fa67aec> accessed 20 April 2020.

H Murphy, 'Lost Your Bitcoin Password? Call in the Crypto-Hunters' (*Financial Times*, 18 July 2018) <www.ft.com/content/f1b12970-8959-11e8-b18d-0181731a0340> accessed 30 March 2020.

S Nakamoto, 'Bitcoin: A Peer-To-Peer Electronic Cash System' (2008) White Paper <bitcoin.org/bitcoin.pdf> accessed 20 April 2020.

A Narayanan, *Bitcoin and Cryptocurrency Technologies* (Princeton University Press 2016).

W Norris, 'Uncertainty and Informality: Hunter v Moss' (1995) 1 Private Client Business 43.

M Ockelton, 'Share and Share Alike?' (1994) CLJ 448.

P Paech, 'Securities, Intermediation and the Blockchain: An Inevitable Choice between Liquidity and Legal Certainty? (2016) 21 Unif Law Rev 612.

J Poon and T Dryja, 'The Bitcoin Lightning Network: Scalable Off-Chain Instant Payments' (Draft Version 0.5.9.2, 14 January 2016) <https://lightning.network/lightning-network-paper.pdf>.

N Popper, *Digital Gold: Bitcoin and the Inside Story of the Misfits and Millionaires Trying to Reinvent Money* (HarperCollins 2015) 51.

N Popper, 'How China Took Center Stage in Bitcoin's Civil War' (*The New York Times*, 29 June 2016) <www.nytimes.com/2016/07/03/business/dealbook/bitcoin-china.html> accessed 20 April 2020.

N Popper, 'Identity Thieves Hijack Cellphone Accounts to Go after Virtual Currency' (*The New York Times*, 21 August 2017) <www.nytimes.com/2017/08/21/business/dealbook/phone-hack-bitcoin-virtual-currency.html> accessed 20 April 2020.

D Quest, 'Taking Security Over Bitcoins and Other Virtual Currency' (2015) 7 JIBFL 401.

Reuters 'Bitcoin bank Flexcoin shuts down after theft' (*Reuters*, 5 March 2014) <www.reuters.com/article/us-bitcoin-flexcoin/bitcoin-bank-flexcoin-shuts-down-after-theft-idUSBREA2329B20140304> accessed 20 April 2020.

G Richardson, 'Lehman Brothers: Traditional Trusts Principles and 21st Century International Bank Failures' (2011) 17 Trusts & Trustees 226.

J S Rogers, 'Of Normalcy and Anomaly: Thoughts on Choice of Law for Indirect Holding System' (1998) 9 JIBFL 47 (special supplement).

N Roubini, 'The Big Blockchain Lie' (*Project Syndicate*, 15 October 2018) <www.project-syndicate.org/commentary/blockchain-big-lie-by-nouriel-roubini-2018-10?barrier=accesspaylog> accessed 20 April 2020.

R P Salgado, 'Fourth Amendment Search and the Power of the Hash' (2006) 119 Harv Law Rev 38.

Securities Investment Board, 'Custody of Investments under the Financial Services Act 1986' (Guidance Release 5/97, June 1997).

R Smith, 'A Piece of Paper Revisited' (1971) 25 Bus Lawyer 1769.

L Smith, 'Unjust Enrichment, Property and the Structure of Trusts' (2000) 116 LQR 412.

J Smyth, 'ASX Chooses Blockchain for Equities Clearing' (*Financial Times*, 7 December 2017) <www.ft.com/content/c9b86e8e-dae4-11e7-a039-c64b1c09b482> accessed 20 April 2020.

M Solinas, 'Investors' Rights in (Crypto) Custodial Holdings: *Ruscoe v Cryptopia Ltd (in Liquidation)*' (2021) 84 Modern Law Review 155.

A Stanley, 'Uncharted Bitcoin OTC Markets Gear Up For Institutional Inflows' (*Forbes*, 23 October 2018) <www.forbes.com/sites/astanley/2018/10/23/uncharted-bitcoin-otc-markets-gear-up-for-institutional-inflows/-1ecbd4f57bac> accessed 20 April 2020.

A Sulleyman, 'Man who "Threw Away" Bitcoin Haul Now Worth over 80M Wants to Dig Up Landfill Site' (*The Independent*, 4 December 2017) <www.independent.co.uk/life-style/gadgets-and-tech/news/bitcoin-value-james-howells-newport-landfill-hard-drive-campbell-simpson-laszlo-hanyecz-a8091371.html> accessed 20 April 2020.

M Summerville, 'Crypto Trading: Platforms Target Institutional Market' (*TABB Group*, 5 April 2018) <https://research.tabbgroup.com/report/v16-013-crypto-trading-platforms-target-institutional-market/> accessed 20 April 2020.

D Turing, *Clearing and Settlement in Europe* (Bloomsbury Professional 2012).

C Twemlow, 'Why Are Securities Held in Intermediated Form?' in L Gullifer and J Payne (eds), *Intermediation and Beyond* (Hart Publishing 2019) 85.

UK Jurisdiction Taskforce 'Legal Statement on Cryptoassets and Smart Contracts' (*The Law Tech Delivery Panel*, November 2019) <https://35z8e83m1ih83drye280o9d1-wpengine.netdna-ssl.com/wp-content/uploads/2019/11/6.6056_JO_Cryptocurrencies_Statement_FINAL_WEB_111119-1.pdf> accessed 20 April 2020.

J Vermeulen, 'Bitcoin and Ethereum vs Visa and PayPal – Transactions Per Second' (*Mybroadband*, 22 April 2017) <https://mybroadband.co.za/news/banking/206742-bitcoin-and-ethereum-vs-visa-and-paypal-transactions-per-second.html> accessed 20 April 2020.

P Vigna, 'Most Bitcoin Trading Faked by Unregulated Exchanges, Study Finds' (*The Wall Street Journal*, 22 March 2019) <www.wsj.com/articles/most-bitcoin-trading-faked-by-unregulated-exchanges-study-finds-11553259600> accessed 20 April 2020.

K Werbach, *The Blockchain and the New Architecture of Trust* (The MIT Press 2018).

G Wildau, 'Beijing Set to Shut Bitcoin Exchanges to Ensure Price Stability' (*Financial Times*, 12 September 2017) <www.ft.com/content/b2f1d198-96df-11e7-a652-cde3f882dd7b> accessed 20 April 2020.

M Wolf, 'The Libertarian Fantasies of Cryptocurrencies' (*Financial Times*, 13 February 2019) <www.ft.com/content/eeeacd7c-2e0e-11e9-ba00-0251022932c8> accessed 20 April 2020.

R Wolfson, 'Purchasing Property Online: The Revolutionary Way Ukraine Uses Blockchain For Real Estate' (*Huffington Post*, 15 October 2017) <www.huffpost.com/entry/purchasing-property-online-the-revolutionary-way-ukraine_b_59933fe7e4b0afd94eb3f565> accessed 20 April 2020.

M Yates and G Montagu, *The Law of Global Custody* (4th edn, Bloomsbury Professional 2013).

Part VIII
Regtech and Suptech

23 'Computer says no'– benefits and challenges of RegTech

Veerle Colaert

1 Introduction

In the aftermath of the 2008 crisis, the financial sector has been confronted with an unprecedented avalanche of new regulation aimed at restoring financial stability, market integrity and customer protection. This has led to ballooning compliance costs[1] and has exacerbated the challenge for financial institutions to ensure compliance with the vast and ever-expanding regulatory framework.[2]

Today, financial institutions are increasingly deploying technological solutions to facilitate compliance with regulatory requirements and supervisors are seeking to improve and upscale the performance of their supervisory tasks with the aid of technological tools. This in turn explains the growing demand for machine-readable regulation. Both scholars and supervisors have devoted increasing attention to these phenomena[3] under the broad banner of 'RegTech',[4] and the EU legislator has been urged to support the use of RegTech by developing and implementing a comprehensive policy agenda.[5]

In this contribution, we will start by delineating the RegTech concept (Section 2). Section 3 will discuss the main advantages and opportunities of RegTech. In Section 4, we will critically analyse the risks and challenges of the large-scale use of RegTech solutions. The changing role of the financial supervisor in a RegTech era is the topic of the fifth section. We will then conclude.

---

1 Institute of International Finance (IIF), 'RegTech: Exploring solutions for Regulatory challenges' (Oct 2015) 1 https://www.iif.com/Publications/ID/4229/Regtech-Exploring-Solutions-for-Regulatory-Challenges (Call-off date for all hyperlinks, unless stated otherwise: 15 May 2020); Douglas W Arner, Janos Barberis and Ross P Buckley, 'FinTech, RegTech and the Reconceptualization of Financial Regulation' (2017) 37 Nw J Int'l L & Bus 371, 374; Tom Butler and Leanna O'Brien, 'Understanding RegTech for Digital Regulatory Compliance' in T Lynn (ed), *Disrupting Finance* (Palgrave 2019) 85, 87–88; E Schizas and others, 'The Global RegTech Industry Benchmark Report' (Cambridge Centre for Alternative Finance, 30 June 2019) 19–20.
2 Arner and others (n 1) 377; Veerle Colaert, 'RegTech as a Response to Regulatory Expansion in the Financial Sector' (2018) 3 International Journal for Financial Services 56, 56.
3 Bamberger wrote the first extensive contribution on 'technologies of compliance', even before the term 'RegTech' was introduced (Kenneth A Bamberger, 'Technologies of Compliance: Risk and Regulation in a Digital Age' [2010] 88 Texas Law Review 669). See also V Colaert, *Normvlucht en systeemdwang in de financiële sector. Wetsnaleving in tijden van normatieve expansie* (Intersentia 2015).
4 To our knowledge, the term was first used by the UK's Financial Conduct Authority (FCA), 'Call for Input: Supporting the development and adoption of RegTech' (November 2015).
5 Expert Group on Regulatory Obstacles to Financial Innovation, '30 Recommendations on Regulation, Innovation and Finance – Final Report to the European Commission' (December 2019) 17, recommendation 9.

2 'RegTech'

In order to be able to cope with the wide array of financial regulation, compliance with legal rules is increasingly built into a technological solution. A series of data is fed into an IT system, which then automatically produces a compliant result. Although the use of IT in a compliance environment is not new,[6] it has grown exponentially over the last decade, and has become increasingly sophisticated through the integration of new technologies such as artificial intelligence, distributed ledger technology (DLT), machine learning and cloud technologies. Scholarly and supervisory attention for the phenomenon, known as 'RegTech', has risen in tandem. Even though this notion is closely related to 'FinTech' – technology used to support or enable services in the financial sector – most scholars agree that RegTech cannot be seen as a subset of FinTech, since RegTech solutions are also being developed in other sectors than the financial industry.[7]

Like many other buzzwords, the term 'RegTech' has been used to describe a range of different techniques, ideas, systems and even companies. Most commonly however, the term 'RegTech' is used to cover 'the adoption of new technologies to facilitate *compliance* with regulatory requirements'.[8] Certain authors explicitly include technologies which facilitate *supervisory monitoring* in their definition of RegTech,[9] while Micheler and Whaley focus their definition of 'regulatory technology' on the technological solutions that facilitate financial *regulation*.[10]

Arner and others have described RegTech in respect of three different market sectors and groups of participants: (i) the financial industry, which is increasingly applying technology to meet the demands of regulators; (ii) regulators faced with the need to use technology to address the challenges of monitoring and enforcing regulatory requirements; and (iii) policymakers and regulators aiming to build the necessary technological infrastructure to support their regulation.[11] Enriques has defined RegTech as 'the use of IT in compliance and supervision/regulation'. He subsequently distinguishes between 'Operations RegTech', 'ComplianceTech', 'OversightTech' and 'PolicymakingTech'.[12] In our view, however, the use of technology to facilitate the daily operation of a financial institution ('Operations

---

6 See for a historic overview of the development of RegTech: Arner and others (n 1) 385ff. These authors make a distinction between RegTech 1.0 (with risk management since the 1980s increasingly using financial technology and regulators becoming overly confident in the ability of quantitative IT frameworks to manage risks) and RegTech 2.0 (with, since the 2008 financial crisis, an increasingly complex, fragmented and ever-evolving global financial regulatory regime and massive compliance and supervision costs).
7 Arner and others (n 1) 381 and 383; Colaert (n 2) 58; Butler and O'Brien (n 1) 99; Schizas and others (n 1) 18.
8 FCA, Call for input 2015 (n 4) 3. IIF 2015 (n 1) 2; Institute of International Finance (IIF): 'RegTech in Financial Services: Technology solutions for compliance and reporting' (March 2016) 2; European Commission (EC), 'Consultation document. Fintech: a More Competitive and Innovative European Financial Sector' (23 March 2017) 10.
9 Colaert (n 2) 59; Lawrence G Baxter, 'Adaptive Financial Regulation and RegTech: A Concept Article of Realistic Protection for Victims of Bank Failures' (2018) 66 Duke L J 567, 600; Schizas and others (n 1) 18.
10 Eva Micheler and Anna Whaley, 'Regulatory Technology: Replacing Law with Computer Code' (2020) 21 EBOR 349, 350.
11 Arner and others (n 1) 384 and 412.
12 Luca Enriques 'Financial Supervisors and RegTech: Four Roles and Four Challenges' (2017) 4 Revue Trimestrielle de Droit Financier 53, 53.

RegTech') can, as such, not be considered 'RegTech'. The latter can only be considered RegTech if it is (at least in part) aimed specifically at ensuring compliance with certain regulatory requirements by automatically excluding options which are deemed unlawful (it would then qualify as 'ComplianceTech'). [13]

All of the above-mentioned definitions and distinctions have their merits. For the purpose of this contribution, we define RegTech as 'all technological solutions that facilitate compliance with and monitoring of regulatory requirements'. In order to allow for a nuanced analysis of RegTech's benefits and risks, we distinguish the following three subcategories based on the party taking the initiative for its development: (i) technological solutions deployed by financial institutions to facilitate compliance with regulatory requirements ('Compliance RegTech'); (ii) technological solutions deployed by supervisors to facilitate reporting and supervisory monitoring ('Supervisory RegTech', sometimes also referred to as 'SupTech')[14]; and (iii) technological solutions used by regulators to code the law directly into machine-readable and/or machine-executable language ('Regulatory RegTech').[15]

Compliance RegTech has already been used for years in certain areas, such as automated transaction monitoring for anti-money-laundering compliance purposes[16] – and is very rapidly becoming mainstream in many other areas,[17] such as the automated assessment of the suitability of investment products for a particular client,[18] which in its most extreme form culminates in robo-advice.[19]

Supervisory RegTech plays a prominent role in all kinds of reporting requirements,[20] and data collection and data analytics by the supervisor.[21] It may take the form of the

---

13 Enriques (n 12) 53 indeed indicates that when it comes to using software to set legal boundaries to operations for the purposes of better ensuring compliance, Operation RegTech and ComplianceTech should be integrated into one single software
14 D Broeders and J Prenio, 'Innovative Technology in Financial Supervision (Supervisory RegTech) – the Experience of Early Users' (BIS – FSI Insights on policy implementation No 9, July 2018) 3; Schizas and others (n 1) 19.
15 The distinction roughly corresponds with the distinction made by Arner and others, but while they focus the third type on the shift from a know-your-customer to a know-your-data approach, we consider the third type in a slightly different manner, more in line with the definition of Micheler and Whaley.
16 Arner and others (n 1) 391–393; Butler and O'Brien (n 1) 96.
17 The Financial Conduct Authority gives the following examples of areas where RegTech has the potential to improve operational efficiency and effectiveness: trade surveillance, financial crime risk monitoring, anti-money laundering, customer profiling and conduct risk monitoring. See FCA, Call for Input 2015 (n 4) 4.
18 Art. 25 of MiFID II Directive 2014/65/EU. See Colaert (n 2) 59–60 and 74.
19 On robo-advice: FCA, Call for Input 2015 (n 4) 4; Verena Ross, 'Regulatory and Supervisory Developments, the Challenges Ahead – a European Perspective' (Finanstilsynet 30th Anniversary International Conference Oslo, ESMA/2016/1497, 20 October 2016) 5; ESMA, 'Guidelines on certain aspects of the MiFID suitability guidelines' (ESMA 35-43-869, 28 May 2018) 5.
20 RP Buckley and others, 'The Road to RegTech: the (Astonishing) Example of the European Union' (2020) 21 Journal of Banking Regulation 26, 28–29.
21 FCA, Call for Input 2015 (n 4) 4; Arner and others (n 1) 393–395; Broeders and Prenio (n 14) 3 and 5–6, giving an overview of supervisors who are already using Supervisory RegTech, which technology they are using and the areas of supervision in which Supervisory RegTech is used, including reporting, data management, market surveillance, misconduct analysis, and macro- and micro-prudential supervision.

supervisor extracting data directly from supervised institutions' IT systems.[22] The use of DLT could take Supervisory RegTech to the next level: instead of financial institutions reporting to the supervisor, supervisors would require financial institutions to record their reportable transactions in one distributed ledger, with cryptography ensuring confidentiality.[23] In the UK, the FCA and the Bank of England have run extensive tests in this regard.[24] At the EU level, the European Commission has announced that it is working on a comprehensive strategy on DLT and blockchain, addressing all sectors of the economy, including FinTech and RegTech applications in the EU.[25]

Regulatory RegTech takes a further step: legal requirements are no longer formulated in legal language, but written in computer code, or at least machine-readable and machine-executable language.[26] The tests by the FCA and the Bank of England, mentioned above, include the translation of regulatory (reporting) requirements into computer code,[27] while the Expert Group on Regulatory Obstacles to Financial Innovation recommends that the European Commission, in cooperation with the European Supervisory Authorities, adopts a strategy on how reporting and compliance processes may become both machine- and human-readable.[28]

In the next sections we will discuss the benefits and challenges of RegTech in general. Where necessary, we will distinguish between Compliance, Supervisory and Regulatory RegTech.

3 Benefits of RegTech

3.1 *Faster and more effective*

In general, RegTech replaces formerly manual processes and thereby considerably speeds up the compliance process.[29]

Moreover, RegTech allows for the integration of Big Data into an improved compliance system.[30] RegTech tools can, for instance, easily detect any deviations from benchmarks, enabling compliance officers or supervisors to spot even minor anomalies which might otherwise go unnoticed, but may be the best risk indicators.[31]

---

22 Broeders and Prenio (n 14) 6 refers to the National Bank of Rwanda using such a data pull approach.
23 Micheler and Whaley (n 10) 355.
24 Micheler and Whaley (n 10) 355. Butler and O'Brien (n 1) 90–96 extensively describe this experiment, 'the RegTech Sprint'.
25 It has announced, more in particular, that it will consult on further digitalisation of regulated information about EU listed companies, including the possible implementation of a European Financial Transparency Gateway based on distributed ledger technology (European Commission, 'FinTech Action Plan: For a more competitive and innovative European Financial Sector' (COM (2018 109 final, 8 March 2018) 14).
26 Schizas and others (n 1) 19.
27 Micheler and Whaley (n 10) 355 and Broeders and Prenio (n 14) 9, para 21, refer to experiments by the FCA and the Bank of England in this respect.
28 ROFIEG (n 5) 15, recommendation 11.
29 FCA, Call for input 2015 (n 4) at 4: 'innovation and advances in compliance and risk technologies have the potential to improve operational efficiency and effectiveness within financial services firms'. See for examples: Colaert (n 2) 59–60.
30 Arner and others (n 1) 383 and 405 note that our financial system moves 'from one based on Know-Your-Customer principles to one based on a Know-Your-Data approach'.
31 Bamberger (n 3) 700–701 gives many examples and further references. Colaert (n 2) 61–62 refers to the use of Big Data and customer relationship management to improve compliance with the MiFID suitability test.

If the supervisor imposes the use of a single RegTech tool for the entire sector (Supervisory RegTech), then data-consolidation may be even more beneficial. Supervisory RegTech tools for data collection and analytics indeed make 'the humanly impossible' possible.[32] In the areas of transaction reporting, market surveillance and anti-money laundering, Supervisory RegTech tools offer supervisors a real-time picture of a wealth of data.[33] The use of such 'Big Data', analysed with artificial intelligence, may improve the quality of supervision, allowing supervisors to identify patterns and spot potential problems – even of a macro-prudential nature[34] – early on.[35] A triage process may then determine prioritisation and trigger in-depth investigations where appropriate.[36]

3.2 *Reduced risk of individual errors*

RegTech greatly reduces the chance of non-compliance resulting from individual human errors, negligence or fraud.[37] For financial institutions, improved compliance evidently also reduces the risk of administrative or criminal sanctions and liability claims.[38]

However, if an error is built into the system this may cause a new type of major compliance risk, which can give rise to problems on a much larger scale (see Sections 4.2 and 4.3).

3.3 *Reduction of compliance costs?*

One of the main drivers for developing RegTech has been to reduce compliance costs.[39] RegTech has the potential to reduce the need for human intervention, decrease the risk of administrative fines and civil liability, allow for streamlining enterprise-wide risk management compliance and improve the alignment of the compliance function with business operations.[40]

Although these potential efficiency gains are clear, developing and running efficient RegTech tools do not come cheap (see Section 4.1).[41] Moreover, an error in a RegTech tool may cause automated non-compliance entailing a new type of compliance risk, which may result in large fines, liability claims and even criminal sanctions (see Section 4.2).

---

32 Broeders and Prenio (n 14) 16, para 44 and 17, paras 46–47.
33 Broeders and Prenio (n 14) 7, para 14 and 10, paras 23 and 25–26.
34 Micheler and Whaley (n 10) 359; Broeders and Prenio (n 14) 8, para 16.
35 Arner and others (n 1) 382; Micheler and Whaley (n 10) 358.
36 Broeders and Prenio (n 14) 7–8, para 14.
37 Bamberger (n 3) 687; Colaert (n 2) 61; Buckley and others (n 20) 33.
38 Arner and others (n 1) 376 and 384; Colaert (n 2) 61; EC, FinTech Consultation 2017 (n 8) 10.
39 See Arner and others (n 1) 376 and 382; Douglas W Arner, Dirk A Zetzsche, Robert P Buckley and Janis B Barberis, 'FinTech and RegTech. Enabling Innovation while Preserving Financial Stability' (2017) 18 Geo J Int'l Aff 47, 52; EC, FinTech Consultation 2017 (n 8) 10.
40 Bamberger (n 3) 686–687; Colaert (n 2) 62.
41 A 2018 survey found that '55 percent of directors … of U.S. banks above $250 million in assets say that the introduction of technology to improve the compliance function has increased the bank's compliance costs, forcing them to budget for higher expenses. Just 5 percent say that technology has decreased the compliance budget'. See BankDirector, '2018 Risk Survey' 3 https://www.bankdirector.com/files/4515/1982/3582/2018_Risk_Survey_Report.pdf; D Krishna, 'BankThink. Cost savings from regtech won't come overnight' *American Banker* 26 January 2018 https://www.americanbanker.com/opinion/cost-savings-from-regtech-wont-come-overnight.

If a supervisor develops a RegTech tool (Supervisory RegTech), or if a regulator introduces machine-readable regulation (Regulatory RegTech), development and maintenance costs for individual financial institutions can be heavily reduced.[42] The development cost of Supervisory RegTech tools is substantial, but less prohibitive, since the costs are (indirectly) shared by the entire financial industry. Moreover, individual financial institutions cannot be held liable for errors in Supervisory RegTech tools or mistakes in the Regulatory RegTech code. Instead, either the supervisor/regulator will be liable (if national law does not exclude such liability) or society will have to bear the costs of defective Supervisory RegTech/Regulatory RegTech and resulting compliance deficiencies, which may lead to a less stable or fair financial industry.

It can therefore not be stated unequivocally that RegTech reduces the overall cost of compliance for the financial sector and for society as a whole. Nevertheless, cost-saving resulting from Supervisory RegTech and Regulatory RegTech can be assumed to be more pronounced than cost-saving from Compliance RegTech (see also Section 4.1).

3.4 *Additional advantage of Supervisory RegTech and Regulatory RegTech – updating regulation*

Supervisory RegTech enables supervisors to directly monitor data and, with the help of artificial intelligence, detect patterns and potential problems. They can therefore update regulatory requirements much more quickly and accurately, and incorporate emerging new risks in their monitoring activity and Supervisory RegTech tools.[43] If Supervisory RegTech and Regulatory RegTech were combined, adapting to regulatory change could 'become as simple as installing a software update'.[44]

3.5 *Additional advantage of Supervisory RegTech and Regulatory RegTech – regulation is more precise*

If the regulator were to write rules in machine-readable language (Regulatory RegTech) or prescribe the use of certain software developed by the supervisor (Supervisory RegTech), this would free financial institutions from the risks associated with interpreting those rules and from potential negative consequences of erroneous interpretations.[45]

Because of this, however, we believe that SupTech and Regulatory RegTech can only be used in specific circumstances. In many cases the regulator deliberately uses vague or abstract terms, either to avoid a box-ticking mentality, or to allow for the development of various business practices. In our view, Supervisory and Regulatory RegTech can be important tools for facilitating compliance and supervision, but only in respect of certain regulatory requirements, such as reporting obligations, where box-ticking is precisely what is in order.

---

42 Broeders and Prenio (n 14) 2; 17, para 46; 19, para 59.
43 Micheler and Whaley (n 10) 358; Broeders and Prenio (n 14) 3, para 5.
44 Micheler and Whaley (n 10) 357.
45 Micheler and Whaley (n 10) 357–358.

4 Risks and challenges

Even though RegTech may bring about considerable advantages, it is important to note the following risks and challenges associated with RegTech.

4.1 *Costs*

Developing RegTech tools and keeping them up to date naturally comes at a cost,[46] which may be especially problematic for smaller financial institutions.[47] There are several options for a more cost-efficient approach to Compliance RegTech than in-house development. All of them have certain drawbacks, however.[48]

An obvious first option is to acquire the RegTech tool from a third-party vendor.[49] However, (i) RegTech companies often offer regulation-specific tools, instead of a single integrated compliance solution[50]; (ii) certain tools need firm-specific modifications[51]; and (iii) financial institutions also need to bear the costs of maintenance and updates. Moreover, if the acquired RegTech tool turns out not to be fully reliable,[52] the liability risk still lies with the individual firms using it.[53] Financial institutions would therefore also need to make substantial investments in order to allow for a proper evaluation of the available tools. Supervisory certification of RegTech solutions[54] would be helpful in this respect, but could shift liability risks for erroneous solutions to the regulator. Hence, it is unlikely that supervisors will engage in such certification.[55]

A second alternative to in-house development of Compliance RegTech tools would entail the development of open-source RegTech tools by industry organisations.[56] This could definitely reduce costs for each individual financial institution. As of yet, however, the market does not seem ready to take up this challenge.[57] There is also no doubt that if an open-source RegTech tool were to contain errors, the liability risk would still lie with the individual firms using it.[58]

---

46 See footnote 41.
47 Colaert (n 2) 68.
48 Colaert (n 2) 68–72.
49 See for three case studies of RegTech solutions: E Johansson and others, 'RegTech – A Necessary Tool to Keep up with Compliance and Regulatory Challenges? (2019) 8 ACRN Journal of Finance and Risk Perspectives 71, 76–79.
50 Colaert (n 2) 68–69; Butler and O'Brien (n 1) 97 mention that large financial institutions do not want multiple RegTech solutions from multiple vendors as this adds to the proliferation of applications across their institutions.
51 Bamberger (n 3) 672–673 for instance refers to risk regulation: 'Risk is contextual and manifests itself differently across heterogeneous firms'. Recent regulation is therefore 'process-based' or 'management-based' and requires firms to develop individualised risk-management processes.
52 It should be noted in this respect that RegTech firms' business interests are not necessarily aligned with the public interest. Bamberger (n 3) 669–670; Micheler and Whaley (n 10) 360–361.
53 Colaert (n 2) 69; Butler and O'Brien (n 1) 86.
54 Bamberger (n 3) 736; Financial Conduct Authority (FCA), 'Feedback Statement – Call for Input on Supporting the Development and Adopters of RegTech' (FS16/4, July 2016) 10.
55 Colaert (n 2) 69.
56 IIF 2015 (n 1) 2; Colaert (n 2) 69; Butler and O'Brien (n 1) 97.
57 See Micheler and Whaley (n 10) 360, referring to blockchain firm R3 running out of money.
58 Colaert (n 2) 69.

Third, Supervisory RegTech, that is, RegTech solutions developed by the supervisor, would considerably reduce the financial industry's compliance costs. Even if the supervisor were to charge a fee for the use of these tools, the costs could reasonably be assumed to be inferior to those of a proprietary development. However, as mentioned above, developing Supervisory RegTech might entail liability risks which supervisors are not very likely to be willing to take on,[59] unless perhaps when dealing with very straightforward, tick-the-box style regulations.

The last two solutions, moreover, result in a high degree of standardisation, which creates its own risks (see Section 4.3).

4.2 *Inaccurate RegTech solutions lead to systematic errors*

The use of automated systems may lead to a false sense of security.[60] The most important weakness of RegTech is, indeed, that they only achieve the intended compliance outcome to the extent that they function correctly.

The causes of inaccurate or erroneous RegTech tools are manifold, ranging from straightforward software coding mistakes to the use of incomplete or biased datasets.[61] Moreover, RegTech developers have to take discretionary decisions in the process of developing such tools. The issues to decide on range from the choice of data to use and the criteria for assessing a certain outcome as non-compliant, to the interpretation of the legal provisions compliance with which the tool should facilitate. Individual and social biases may distort such decisions.[62] The technology itself also has limitations, as complex legal texts are to be translated into binary rule-based technological idioms, without leaving room for discretion.[63]

An inaccurate or erroneous RegTech tool automates errors and therefore creates problems on a much wider scale than an individual human error in the absence of a RegTech system.[64] In other words, the use of RegTech tools involves an enormous operational risk.[65] Reputational concerns may moreover delay the correction of errors or lead to corrections for the future only, without also correcting past flawed RegTech outcomes.[66] This problem is acute for all types of RegTech: Compliance RegTech, Supervisory RegTech and Regulatory RegTech.

It is therefore crucial that any RegTech system is as correct and nuanced as possible. It should take into account a sufficiently broad range of relevant data and should be tailored to

---

59   Bamberger (n 3) 705.
60   Bamberger (n 3) 706; Micheler and Whaley (n 10) 359; Broeders and Prenio (n 14) 17, para 50.
61   Micheler and Whaley (n 10) 359–360; Broeders and Prenio (n 14) 3, para 6; 8, para 15; and 17, para 51.
62   Bamberger (n 3) 706 with reference to Friedman and Nissenbaum.
63   Bamberger (n 3) 373, 374; 702–703 and especially 706–710.
64   Bamberger (n 3) 717–722 discusses the role of technology failures in the 2007 financial crisis. Colaert (n 2) 63 gives examples regarding rating agencies, capital requirements for banks, anti-money laundering, and the MiFID suitability test. Micheler and Whaley (n 10) 359 point to the limitations of data-based analysis. See also Butler and O'Brien (n 1) 97.
65   'Operational risk is defined as the risk of loss resulting from inadequate or failed internal processes, people and systems or from external events'. (Basel Committee on Banking Supervision, 'International Convergence of Capital Measurement and Capital Standards: A Revised Framework – Comprehensive Version' (30 June 2006) 144, nr. 644).
66   Colaert (n 2) 63–64 refers to such delayed and incomplete reactions by rating agencies in regard to the detection of errors in their rating models during the crisis.

the needs and particularities of the specific financial institutions or the supervisors intending to use the system. An encompassing, effective 'RegTech auditing scheme' – beyond the general internal risk control measures[67] and the more specific risk-management principles for the use of IT systems[68] – would include the following elements.[69]

First, an intense interdisciplinary cooperation between compliance, legal and IT-experts, and – in certain cases – also economic and behavioural experts, is key for the development and monitoring of sound RegTech systems.[70] Compliance officers should, moreover, have a general understanding of the use of algorithms in RegTech tools.[71]

Second, data validation checks should be built into any RegTech system, including data correctness, plausibility and consistency tests, which immediately red flag any discrepancies in the system's output, or between the data and output of the system and the data and output of other databases or systems.[72]

Third, periodic system tests should ensure continuous fine-tuning of the RegTech tool to take account of market evolutions, regulatory developments or new insights. A periodic assessment – for instance annually – should be combined with *ad hoc* checks allowing adjustments when errors or discrepancies are discovered, amendments are made to the relevant legal requirements or new technologies make it possible to further fine-tune or improve the system.[73] Therefore, RegTech tools should be flexible and easily adaptable to new circumstances and new rules.[74]

Fourth, a human individual should critically evaluate the outcome provided by the system in order to (i) detect evident output errors resulting from either flaws in the system or exceptional circumstances, which the system does not take into account, or (ii) decide on

---

67 That is, the 'three lines of defense' against the risks of operating a financial institution: (1) operational management (front office, any client facing activity), which is responsible for the identification, assessment and mitigation of risks; (2) the risk management function, which facilitates and monitors the implementation of effective risk-management practices by operational management – with the compliance function being an important component to limit the specific risk of non-compliance with laws and regulations and (3) the internal audit function, which provides an independent assurance to the board of directors and senior management of the quality and effectiveness of a bank's internal control, risk management and governance systems and processes. See Basel Committee on Banking Supervision (BCBS), 'Guidelines – Corporate Governance Principles for Banks' (July 2015) 5, para 13.

68 See Basel Committee on Banking Supervision, 'Framework for Internal Control Systems in Banking Organisations' (September 1998) 18, principle 8; Basel Committee on Banking Supervision (BCBS), 'Principles for the Sound Management of Operational Risk' (June 2011) 15, nr. 51.

69 Colaert (n 2) 64–68.

70 Colaert (n 2) 65–66; see also Micheler and Whaley (n 10) 359–360 on both computer scientists' and lawyers' limited knowledge about, respectively, the law and the characteristics and limits of computer software.

71 Iain Sheridan, 'MiFID II in the context of Financial Technology and Regulatory Technology' (2017) 12 Capital Markets Law Journal 417, 421.

72 See Colaert (n 2) 65 who refers to the use of online questionnaires and risk profiling software for purposes of the MiFID suitability test as an example where intra-system consistency tests are already required, and to the link between internal systems and external databases (such as ESMA's European Rating Platform, national credit risk databases, or databases with lists of politically exposed persons for anti-money laundering purposes). See also Broeders and Prenio (n 14) 8, para 15.

73 Colaert (n 2) 65.

74 Colaert (n 2) 68. Bamberger (n 3) 710–711 and Sheridan (n 71) 419 point to legacy issues with older technology systems, meaning that any change creates enormous costs, and efficiency challenges and risks.

whether further compliance action – or in case of Supervisory RegTech, enforcement or a change in supervisory policy or regulation – is necessary.[75]

Fifth, the effectiveness and robustness of Compliance RegTech tools should also be subject to control by the competent supervisory authority, which should, on the basis of knowledge and experience acquired through assessments of other financial institutions' solutions, endeavour to improve a financial institution's use of RegTech solutions.[76]

Sixth, RegTech systems should be made fully transparent,[77] both for the institutions using them and for the competent supervisory authority, in order to ensure that everyone working with the tool is well aware of its limitations, the premises on which it is built, and any factors which have not been taken into account when designing the RegTech tool.[78] Intellectual Property Law may pose limits to such transparency, however.[79]

4.3 *Risks of standardisation*

Certain RegTech solutions are or may in the future be widely used in the market – where successful RegTech companies gain a considerable market share, where open-source solutions are developed and widely used, or where supervisors impose a Supervisory RegTech solution. The widespread use of the same tool, however, creates additional risks. Standardisation hampers innovation and means that less expertise is put to work, as there is no or less competition for the optimal RegTech tool.[80] In addition, errors or inaccuracies in such widely used RegTech solutions might affect the entire market and thereby even create systemic risk.[81]

4.4 *Privacy, data-protection and cybersecurity risks*

The use of data mining techniques and cloud-based technology in RegTech solutions raises important privacy, data-protection and cybersecurity issues.[82] Technically, the

---

75 Colaert (n 2) 65–66 with reference to D Kahneman, Thinking, fast and slow (Farrar, Straus and Giroux 2011) 224–225 and 231–232. Colaert gives examples in the field of automated credit-scoring mechanisms for consumer credit, and in the field of the capital requirements for banks. Bamberger (n 3) 711–712 refers to the problem of 'automation bias', a tendency to disregard or not search for contradictory information in light of a computer-generated solution. See also Bamberger (n 3) 727–728 and 736c. Broeders and Prenio (n 14) 3, para 5, point out that currently Supervisory RegTech applications do not replace human judgement, but serve as input for supervisors. Enriques (n 12) 56 points out that Supervisory RegTech is also used to filter trivial violations from violations which require enforcement. It will, however, often be hard for supervisors to tell whether a scant catch is due to high compliance, market participants' ability to play around badly designed rules, or badly engineered software filters.

76 Colaert (n 2) 66–67, with reference to the Supervisory Review Process in the field of the capital requirements for banks.

77 On the problems of the lack of transparency of algorithms written in code that few can understand, see Bamberger (n 3) 727, 729 and 730–734; Sheridan (n 71) 420.

78 Colaert (n 2) 67–68; Butler and O'Brien (n 1) 97.

79 Bamberger (n 3) 729; Sheridan (n 71) 420–421.

80 Colaert (n 2) 70; Buckley and others (n 20) 33.

81 Colaert (n 2) 70–71 refers, by way of example, to the 'standardized' approach in the Basel II capital requirements, and the risk and performance indicators which are used in the PRIIPs KID. See also Micheler and Whaley (n 10) 359; Buckley and others (n 20) 33.

82 Colaert (n 2) 72; Broeders and Prenio (n 14) 18, para 52–53; Buckley and others (n 20) 34.

collection of data and the use of cloud-based systems require the industry as well as supervisors to take robust safety measures against hacking and unauthorised data access (cybersecurity).[83] From a legal perspective, privacy and data protection in the EU is to a large extent addressed by the General Data Protection Regulation. Buckley and others argue that the EU's advanced data protection system has indeed been key to the development of RegTech in the EU.[84]

4.5 *Computing power and data capacity*

The limitations of computing power and data capacity have long hindered RegTech, and especially Supervisory RegTech, from reaching its full potential.[85] As technology – including cloud computing – evolves, these problems will diminish.[86]

4.6 *Dehumanisation*

RegTech goes hand in hand with a reduced reliance on human intervention to ensure compliance. This can have undesirable side effects: employees may feel less involved, which in turn may result in diminished motivation and professional commitment.[87] It can even lead to a box-ticking mentality: if compliance with the law is perceived as a matter of RegTech, individual employees may no longer be ingrained with the fundamental principles of due care towards customers or lose their critical mindset. In view of the limitations of automated RegTech tools, these values are however of the utmost importance. A careful 'human' approach increases the likelihood that the people working in a RegTech context spot discrepancies and errors in RegTech tools in a timely manner and decreases the risk that they would exploit the limitations of RegTech tools in a harmful way.[88]

It is therefore necessary for the introduction of RegTech tools to go hand-in-hand with proper training of the people involved in their use. They have to fully understand how a RegTech tool works, what its limitations are, how anomalies can be detected and – more generally – what the ultimate goals of the regulation are.[89] In addition, any RegTech compliance system should be embedded in a broader corporate culture committed to 'good

---

83 Enriques (n 12) 55. See also ROFIEG (n 5) 15, recommendation 4. Certain EU directives regarding financial services also make this a legal requirement (eg, art. 13 (5) MiFID I, art. 18 AIFMD).

84 Buckley and others (n 20) 29–30 and 34.

85 Bamberger (n 3) 708.

86 Broeders and Prenio (n 14) 3, para 4, 9, paras 18 and 17, para 49.

87 Compare to Kahneman's findings regarding an/his attempt to rationalise an interviewing process for the recruitment of new candidate-soldiers: D Kahneman (n 75) 231: 'These bright young people were displeased to be ordered … to switch off their intuition and focus entirely on boring factual questions'.

88 Colaert (n 2) 73–74 gives examples regarding the MiFID suitability test. See also Bamberger (n 3) 714; Micheler and Whaley (n 10) 327; Broeders and Prenio (n 14) 19, para 60.

89 Colaert (n 2) 73; Buckley and others (n 20) 33.

compliance, not mere compliance'.[90] Corporate culture can in turn be supported by RegTech systems to detect non-compliance risk.[91]

4.7 *Regulatory RegTech: additional problems of democratic legitimacy and regulatory accountability*

With regard to Regulatory RegTech, Micheler and Whaley point to the additional problem of democratic legitimacy and regulatory accountability. Regulators who want to issue or endorse regulation in machine-readable language or in computer code need to either hire computer experts to work closely together with policymakers and/or lawyers or outsource the translation of regulation into machine-readable language or computer code to technology providers. The latter approach might appear more efficient, but would affect democratic legitimacy and regulatory accountability, especially in cases where the regulators allow private providers to exercise discretion when translating natural language, which often leaves room for interpretation, into computer code, which is much more precise.[92]

5 The role of supervisors

In a previous contribution, we have argued that the creed of financial supervisors seems to be evolving from '*comply* with financial regulation' to '*be organized so as to ensure compliance* with financial regulation'.[93] The RegTech evolution matches this emphasis on structural compliance measures. Supervisors should therefore play a prominent role in supporting, encouraging and developing RegTech.

The role of supervisors in the realm of Supervisory RegTech and Regulatory RegTech appears to be rather clear-cut: they impose the use of a certain RegTech tool to facilitate compliance, supervision and/or enforcement (Supervisory RegTech), or provide machine-readable and/or machine-executable regulation (Regulatory RegTech). However, supervisors also have an important role to play in regard of Compliance RegTech. They can do so in many different ways.

First, since the development of RegTech solutions takes time, supervisors should provide for adequate implementation deadlines for new or amended rules.[94] Current implementation

---

90 Title of the contribution of Daniel K Tarullo, 'Good Compliance, Not Mere Compliance' (Federal Reserve Bank of New York Conference 'Reforming Culture and Behavior in the Financial Services Industry', New York, 20 October 2014) http://www.federalreserve.gov/newsevents/speech/tartullo20141020a.pdf. See in this respect also BCBS, Operational Risk 2011 (n 68) 7, para 21; BCBS, Corporate Governance Principles 2015 (n 67) 9–10, nrs 29–32. Since 2010, the Dutch prudential supervisor (De Nederlandsche Bank) has explicitly included 'behaviour and culture of financial organisations' as one of its focus areas of supervision. See for a comprehensive report: De Nederlandsche Bank, 'Supervision of Behaviour and Culture. Foundations, Practices and Future Developments' (DNB 2015), https://www.dnb.nl/binaries/Supervision%20of%20Behaviour%20 and%20Culture_tcm46-334417.pdf. Several other supervisors have followed suit.

91 Tarullo (n 90) 6; IIF 2015 (n 1) 3, last paragraph, referring to Starling as a venture exploring such applications; BCBS, Operational Risk 2011 (n 68) 7, para 21; Basel Committee on Banking Supervision, 'Compliance and the Compliance Function in Banks' (April 2005) 14, para 38.

92 Micheler and Whaley (n 10) 161–162.

93 Colaert (n 2) 75.

94 IIF 2016 (n 8) 4; see also FCA, Feedback Statement 2016 (n 54) 11; Colaert (n 2) 75–76; Buckley and others (n 20) 28.

periods are often simply too short to allow the industry to develop adequate Compliance RegTech solutions.

Second, the availability and willingness of supervisors to rapidly respond to interpretation problems and to give detailed guidance on what a particular piece of legislation requires from financial institutions in practice, is paramount to the timely development of adequate Compliance RegTech solutions.[95] Currently, important Level 3 guidance on the interpretation of new legislation is at times published only weeks before or even after the new legislation's entry into force. This can obviously have important (and expensive) consequences for the RegTech tools developed to ensure compliance with such legislation.[96]

Third, supervisors should welcome Compliance RegTech solutions[97] and allow experimentation in a safe environment, a so-called 'sandbox'.[98] Many supervisors have already established such sandboxes,[99] which has sparked demands for harmonisation in this area at EU level.[100]

Fourth, supervisors need to adapt their supervisory practice to the use of Compliance RegTech solutions by financial institutions and/or develop Supervisory RegTech solutions.[101] This requires significant investment in technology and top engineers, which may be a challenge, however, in view of the limited resources of many supervisors.[102]

Fifth, the question has been raised whether the supervisors should provide certification of Compliance RegTech that meets relevant criteria.[103] This could indeed enhance credibility of the certified RegTech tools and eliminate uncertainty for financial institutions. Nevertheless, we do not consider supervisory certification a viable option for most Compliance RegTech solutions in view of the liability risks for the supervisor issuing the certification (see Section 4.1). Instead, supervisors could consider introducing a certification or licensing regime for RegTech companies[104] and/or publishing guidance and best practices in respect of RegTech on the basis of supervisory experiences.[105]

95 See also FCA, Feedback Statement 2016 (n 54) 10.
96 Colaert (n 2) 76.
97 FCA, Feedback Statement 2016 (n 54) 11; Arner and others, 'FinTech and RegTech' (n 39) 54.
98 See Arner and others (n 1) 408–411.
99 See Banking Stakeholder Group (BSG), 'Regulatory Sandboxes. A Proposal to EBA by the Banking Stakeholders Group' (July 2017) 9–10, discussing the different approaches taken by those regulators.
100 The Banking Stakeholder Group recommends that the European Banking Authority adopt an EU-wide sandbox, to avoid a fragmented ecosystem of national sandboxes with different regimes (BSG (n 99) 13). The European Banking Federation requests that coordination challenges between different sandbox initiatives be remedied by a common position in the European space (European Financial Services Roundtable, 'Paper on Regulatory Sandboxes' (September 2016) http://www.efr.be/documents/news/99.2.%20EFR%20paper%20on%20regulatory%20sandboxes%2029.09.2016.pdf. The Expert Group on Regulatory Obstacles to Financial Innovation recommends that the European Commission and the ESAs further assess the need to establish an EU-level 'regulatory sandbox', or similar scheme (ROFIEG (n 5) 15, recommendation 14).
101 FCA, Feedback Statement 2016 (n 54) 5; Arner and others (n 1) 398, point to the gap between IT-enabled systems in the industry and the lack of IT-enabled solutions among regulators.
102 Bamberger (n 3) 734–735; Enriques (n 12) 54–55; Broeders and Prenio (n 14) 3, para 7; 14, para 39; and 18, para 55. See also ROFIEG (n 5) 15, recommendation 3.
103 FCA, Feedback Statement 2016 (n 54) 10.
104 ROFIEG (n 5) 15, recommendation 5, last bullet.
105 Bamberger (n 3) 736; Colaert (n 2) 76.

Sixth, supervisory awareness of the limits of Compliance RegTech tools should lead to increased supervisory precaution, 'taking into account that unforeseen failures will occur with relative certainty', despite improved compliance.[106]

In sum, the role of supervisors is paramount in the RegTech era. In the complex maze of today's financial regulation, supervisors increasingly take up the role of intermediaries between the legislator and financial institutions, between rules and compliance. RegTech indeed accelerates the evolution towards a cooperative supervisory model, in which supervisors guide financial institutions in their search for adequate and correct compliance and in which financial institutions in turn deliver essential input to supervisors for the development of efficient guidelines, best practices and RegTech solutions.[107]

6 Conclusion

Complying with the exponentially growing body of financial regulation is one of the most pressing challenges facing the financial sector today. Part of the solution appears to be programming compliance into RegTech: technological solutions that facilitate compliance with and monitoring of regulatory requirements.

In this contribution, we have distinguished three types of RegTech based on the party taking the initiative for its development: (i) Compliance RegTech, where financial institutions develop or acquire RegTech tools to facilitate compliance; (ii) Supervisory RegTech, where a supervisor imposes the use of a certain RegTech tool to facilitate compliance, supervision and/or enforcement; and (iii) Regulatory RegTech, where the regulator provides machine-readable and/or machine-executable regulation.

RegTech in general has some undeniable benefits. Because of the use of the newest technology, including Big Data collection and analytics, compliance can be ensured much more quickly and efficiently. Supervisory RegTech and Regulatory RegTech moreover allow supervisors and regulators to quickly act upon new risks with updated supervisory policies and regulation. Automating compliance and reducing human intervention also diminishes the risk of administrative fines and liability risks resulting from individual human errors. Many have claimed that RegTech also reduces compliance costs, while we tend to take a more nuanced stance in this respect, in view of the high costs of development or acquisition of RegTech tools, and because of the emergence of new types of compliance risks.

RegTech indeed also entails important new risks and challenges. When a RegTech solution contains an error (even a small one), this leads to liability risks at a far larger scale than when an individual employee makes an individual mistake. If the same RegTech (including Supervisory RegTech) solution is widely used in the market, an error in the system may even cause systemic compliance failures and create systemic risk. In addition, building watertight systems has a high price tag, which may be prohibitive especially for smaller players. Privacy, data protection and cybersecurity, as well as the dehumanisation that results from RegTech solutions also raise new challenges.

Those risks and challenges, however, do not apply in the same degree to the different types of RegTech. If a supervisor develops a Supervisory RegTech tool which is to be used by an entire industry, or asks a RegTech firm to do so, or if the regulator

---

106 Bamberger (n 3) 738d.
107 Colaert (n 2) 76. See also Bamberger (n 3) 735; Sheridan (n 71) 427.

codes the law into software, this results in massive cost-savings, even if the industry could be asked a fee for using the tool. On the other hand, the use of a single tool by the entire industry also increases the risk of systemic failures, as well as underperforming systems due to a lack of competition in the development phase. Moreover, the use of Supervisory RegTech systems and Regulatory RegTech shifts the liability risk for compliance errors from the industry to the supervisor/regulator and ultimately to the taxpayer.

In the end, circumstances will determine which type of RegTech is the most appropriate to improve compliance in a certain area of financial regulation. Supervisory RegTech and Regulatory RegTech seem to be good solutions for straightforward reporting and other tick-the-box-obligations. It is clear, however, that many other compliance challenges cannot be solved with Supervisory or Regulatory RegTech. In many areas the regulator deliberately chooses vague or abstract terms, in order to avoid a box-ticking mentality, or because they want to allow various business practices to develop. In those instances, the legislator has chosen to entrust financial institutions with the responsibility to interpret the rules, including open-ended principles, and to decide what compliance means in their specific situation. Even in the age of RegTech, it falls upon financial institutions to properly manage their Compliance RegTech solutions to facilitate and ensure 'good' compliance in those areas.

Bibliography

D W Arner, J N Barberis and R P Buckley, 'FinTech, RegTech and the Reconceptualization of Financial Regulation' (2017) 37 Nw J Int'l L & Bus 371.

D W Arner, J N Barberis and R P Buckley, 'FinTech and RegTech in a Nutshell, and the Future in a Sandbox' (Research Foundation Briefs July 2017 Volume 3 Issue 4).

D W Arner, D A Zetzsche, R P Buckley and J N Barberis, 'FinTech and RegTech. Enabling Innovation While Preserving Financial Stability' (2017) 18 Geo J Int'l Aff 47.

K Bamberger, 'Technologies of Compliance: Risk and Regulation in a Digital Age' (2010) 88 Tex L Rev 669.

J Barberis, D W Arner and R P Buckley (eds), *The RegTech Book* (Wiley 2019).

Basel Committee on Banking Supervision, 'Guidelines – Corporate governance principles for banks' (July 2015).

L G Baxter, 'Adaptive Financial Regulation and RegTech: A Concept Article of Realistic Protection for Victims of Bank Failures' (2018) 66 Duke LJ 567.

D Broeders and J Prenio, 'Innovative Technology in Financial Supervision (SupTech) – The Experience of Early Users' (BIS – FSI Insights on policy implementation No 9, July 2018) <https://www.bis.org/fsi/publ/insights9.pdf>.

C Brummer and Y Yadav, 'FinTech and the Innovation Trilemma' (2019) 107 Geo LJ 235.

R P Buckley, D W Arner, D A Zetzsche and R Weber, 'The Road to RegTech: The (Astonishing) Example of the European Union' (2020) 21 J Bank Regul 26.

T Butler and L O'Brien, 'Understanding RegTech for Digital Regulatory Compliance' in T Lynn (ed), *Disrupting Finance* (Palgrave 2019) 85.

V Colaert, *Normvlucht en systeemdwang in de financiële sector. Wetsnaleving in tijden van normatieve expansie* (Intersentia 2015).

V Colaert, 'RegTech as a Response to Regulatory Expansion in the Financial Sector' (2018) 3 Int J Financial Serv 56.

Deloitte, 'RegTech Is The New FinTech' (2016).

L Enriques, 'Financial Supervisors and RegTech: Four Roles and Four Challenges' (2017) 4 *Revue Trimestrielle de Droit Financier* 53.

European Commission, 'Consultation document. Fintech: A More Competitive and Innovative European Financial Sector' (23 March 2017) <https://ec.europa.eu/info/sites/info/files/2017-fintech-consultation-document_en_0.pdf>.

European Commission, 'FinTech Action Plan: For A More Competitive and Innovative European Financial Sector' (COM(2018 109 final, 8 March 2018).

European Financial Services Roundtable, 'Paper on Regulatory Sandboxes' (September 2016) <https://www.efr.be/media/txylyp1j/99-2-efr-paper-on-regulatory-sandboxes-29-09-2016.pdf>.

Expert Group on Regulatory Obstacles to Financial Innovation, '30 Recommendations on Regulation, Innovation and Finance – Final Report to the European Commission' (December 2019) <https://ec.europa.eu/info/sites/info/files/business_economy_euro/banking_and_finance/documents/191113-report-expert-group-regulatory-obstacles-financial-innovation_en.pdf>.

Financial Conduct Authority (FCA), 'Call for Input: Supporting the Development and Adoption of RegTech' (November 2015) <https://www.fca.org.uk/publication/call-for-input/regtech-call-for-input.pdf>.

Financial Conduct Authority (FCA), 'Feedback Statement – Call for Input on Supporting the Development and Adopters of RegTech' (FS16/4, July 2016) <https://www.fca.org.uk/publication/feedback/fs-16-04.pdf>.

Institute of International Finance, 'RegTech: Exploring Solutions for Regulatory Challenges' (October 2015) <https://www.iif.com/Publications/ID/4229/Regtech-Exploring-Solutions-for-Regulatory-Challenges>.

Institute of International Finance, 'RegTech in Financial Services: Technology Solutions for Compliance and Reporting' (March 2016) <https://www.iif.com/Portals/0/Files/private/iif-regtech_in_financial_services_-_solutions_for_compliance_and_reporting.pdf?ver=2019-01-04-142943-690>.

E Johansson K Sutinen, J Lassila, V Lang, M Martikainen and O Mlehner, 'RegTech – A Necessary Tool to Keep up with Compliance and Regulatory Challenges?' (2019) 8 ACRN Journal of Finance and Risk Perspectives 71.

D Kahneman, *Thinking, Fast and Slow* (Farrar, Straus and Giroux 2011).

D Krishna, 'BankThink. Cost Savings from RegTech Won't Come Overnight' *American Banker* 26 January 2018 <https://www.americanbanker.com/opinion/cost-savings-from-regtech-wont-come-overnight>.

E Micheler and A Whaley, 'Regulatory Technology: Replacing Law with Computer Code' (2020) 21 EBOR 349.

I Sheridan, 'MiFID II in the Context of Financial Technology and Regulatory Technology' (2017) 12 Cap Mark Law J 417.

E Schizas, G McKain, B Zhang, A Ganbold, P Kumar, H Hussain, K J Garvey, E Huang, A Huang, S Wang and N Yerolem, *The Global RegTech Industry Benchmark Report* (Cambridge Centre for Alternative Finance, 30 June 2019).

24 FinTech, RegTech and SupTech

Institutional challenges to the supervisory architecture of the financial markets

Paola Chirulli

1 Introduction

Technology has had a dramatic impact on the whole financial sector at a national, European and global level. Not only has it led to a rapid transformation in banking and financial business models, services and products,[1] but it has also had a profound effect on regulation and supervision[2] by changing the way financial institutions comply with regulatory requirements, and how authorities perform their supervisory tasks. FinTech and its subsets – RegTech and SupTech – can be defined as the response of the financial industry, regulation and supervision[3] to the disruptive challenge of innovative technology.[4] Although the boundaries between these areas are sometimes blurred and overlapping – due also to the lack of a common taxonomy and terminology[5] – they have acquired distinctive features and are evolving at a different pace. The Covid-19 pandemic has accelerated the development of FinTech, increasing its opportunities but also its challenges[6].

---

1 We refer to the definition of FinTech given by the Financial Stability Board (FSB), 'Financial Stability Implications from Fintech. Supervisory and Regulatory Issues that merit Authorities' Attention' (27 June 2017) <https://www.fsb.org/wp-content/uploads/R270617.pdf> accessed 15 March 2020: 'technology enabled innovation in financial services that could result in new business models, applications, processes or products with an associated material effect on the provision of financial services'.

2 For an overview of the benefits and related risks of Fintech from a regulatory point of view, see Eugenia Macchiavello, 'FinTech Regulation from a Cross-Sectoral Perspective' in Veerle Colaert, Danny Busch and Thomas Incalza (eds) *European Financial Regulation: Levelling the Cross-Sectoral Playing Field* (Hart 2019) 63, 68.

3 Regulation, through hard-law and soft-law measures, sets the rules and standards with which financial institutions are required to comply, while supervision focuses on the monitoring of the activities of financial institutions and on the enforcement of regulatory requirements. The two functions are sometimes integrated within the same authority but sometimes are assigned to different authorities (in financial markets, national authorities are entrusted with supervision, whereas regulation is mainly done at a EU level; regulation and supervision responsibilities may be divided along industry lines).

4 Iris H Y Chiu, 'FinTech and Disruptive Business Models in Financial Products, Intermediation and Markets - Policy Implications for Financial Regulators' (2017) 21 J Tech L & Pol'y 168.

5 The absence of a 'common language' in the financial industry, and the existence of heterogeneous terms and concepts to describe similar business objects, processes and products has been highlighted in the Expert Group on Regulatory Obstacles on Financial Innovation (ROFIEG) 'Thirty Recommendations on Regulation, Innovation and Finance, Report to the European Commission' (December 2019) <https://ec.europa.eu/info/publications/191113-report-expert-group-regulatory-obstacles-financial-innovation_en> accessed March 2020.

6 On the impact of Covid-19 on Fintech challenges and opportunities, see World Bank and Cambridge Centre for Alternative Finance, 'The Global Covid-19 Fintech Regulatory Rapid Assessment Study' (2020).

While a regulatory framework is gradually emerging for FinTech, RegTech and SupTech have so far mainly spread through practice. Yet the developments in both areas are closely linked and deserve to be considered as part of an overall dynamics. The chapter is structured as follows. After this introduction Section 2 gives an overview of the emerging trends in FinTech regulation across the EU and their impact on the role of regulatory activities. Section 3 explores the current state of play in SupTech, examining its strengths and weaknesses. Section 4 concludes by outlining future challenges and possible developments.

2 Regulatory trends and approaches in the FinTech sector

As financial markets have always been a highly regulated field at national, international and European level – especially in the post-2007/2008 crisis era, the impact of FinTech on legislation, regulation and supervision is magnified. The use of technologies in banking and financial services poses further challenges to investor and consumer protection, financial integrity and stability, cybersecurity and the protection of personal data.[7]

Regulation has a wider reach, since it is aimed not only at addressing failures and stability issues, but also at promoting financial inclusion and the creation of a level playing field for financial institutions.[8] A delicate balance must be found in order to exploit the opportunities offered by the new models, which may promote financial inclusiveness, but also to satisfy the need for a clear assessment of the risks that arise and the call for greater regulatory certainty. Some scholars have pointed out that regulators and supervisors are facing a trilemma, since they have to pursue the conflicting goals of providing clear rules and maintaining market integrity, while at the same time encouraging innovation, arguing that, at most, only two of the three goals are attainable.[9]

In such a rapidly evolving scenario, where the need to have separate regulations for banking, securities, insurance and supervision is currently being questioned,[10] some regulatory tendencies and approaches can be observed which set the scene for the parallel development of RegTech and SupTech.

2.1 *FinTech: an evolving regulatory framework*

The regulatory framework is becoming increasingly more complex and fragmented: while some countries outside the EU have adopted comprehensive FinTech legislation,[11] in the

---

7 For an assessment of expected benefits and risks connected to the spread of decentralised technologies, see FSB, 'Decentralised Financial Technologies. Financial Stability, Regulatory and Governance implications' (6 June 2019) <https://www.fsb.org/wp-content/uploads/P060619.pdf> accessed 15 March 2020.

8 On the impact of innovation on regulation and its scope, also from an equality and justice perspective, see Cristie Ford, *Innovation and the State* (CUP 2017).

9 Chris Brummer and Yesha Yadav, 'Fintech and the Innovation Trilemma' (2019) 107 Geo LJ 235, 278. According to these authors, the trilemma is not a new phenomenon, but one which FinTech has exacerbated, since its three key features (Big Data, artificial intelligence and disintermediation) create new risks and make regulatory choices extremely challenging.

10 The case for adopting a twin-peak architecture, and reforming the current EU supervisory framework, is highly debated in the literature: Wolf-Georg Ringe, Luis Morais and David Ramos, 'A Holistic Approach to the Institutional Architecture of Financial Supervision and Regulation in the EU' in Colaert et al (n 2) 405.

11 Like Mexico with its Fintech Law – Ley para regular las Instituciones de Tecnologia Financiera of 9.3.2018.

EU and in its Member States legislation mostly covers specific sectors and activities. There is uncertainty about the regulatory perimeters and this is coupled with the fact that each national competent authority is moving at a different pace, following their own individual approach towards FinTech regulation.[12]

In particular, while in the financial sector the EU has produced an extensive range of legislative and regulatory measures and, with the reform of the European Supervisory Authorities (ESAs),[13] which strengthened their regulatory and supervisory powers, has come closer to the realisation of the Capital Markets Union,[14] it has initially followed a more cautious and light-touch approach towards FinTech.[15]

Until recently, the EU has been monitoring the trends and developments closely, and has planned future actions.[16] Thematic reports have been published[17] alongside roadmaps and action plans,[18] with the intention to keep the regulatory perimeter relatively open in the short term, while promoting best practices, cooperation and supervisory convergence, in the view of a possible further harmonisation of the legislation.[19]

The EU has recently changed its approach. In specific fields, such as crowdfunding, new legislation has been introduced.[20] Prior to this, the revised Payment Service Directive

---

12 Dirk A Zetzsche, Ross P Buckley, Janos N Barberis and Douglas W Arner, 'Regulating a Revolution: From Regulatory Sandboxes to Smart Regulation' (2017) 23 Fordham J Corp & Fin L 31, have categorised four possible approaches: doing nothing (Zen approach), cautious permissiveness, restricted experimentation and regulatory development.

13 Regulation (EU) 2019/2175 of the European Parliament and of the Council of 18 December 2019 [2019] L 334/1.

14 Franklin Allen, Ester Faia, Michael Haliassos and Katja Langenbucher, *Capital Markets Union and Beyond* (MIT Press 2019). Recently, see European Commission, Communication to the European Parliament, the Council, the European Economic and Social Committee and the Committee of the Regions, 'Capital Markets Union for People and Businesses – New Action Plan' COM (2020) 590 final (24 September 2020).

15 At times European authorities have limited their role to the publication of warnings, as with virtual currencies: ESMA, EBA and EIOPA warn consumers of the risks of Virtual Currencies <https://www.esma.europa.eu/sites/default/files/library/esma50-164-1284_joint_esas_warning_on_virtual_curriesl.pdf> accessed 10 March 2020.

16 For example, see EBA, 'Discussion Paper on the EBA's Approach to Financial Technology (FinTech)' EBA/DP/2017/02 (4 August 2017), which showed that many Fintech firms operated outside any regulatory regime.

17 See EBA, 'The Impact of Fintech on Payment Institutions' and E-Money Institutions' Business Models' (July 2019) and 'Big Data and Advanced Analytics' EBA/REP/2020/01 (January 2020).

18 See EBA, 'EBA Fintech Roadmap' (15 March 2018); European Commission, Communication to the European Parliament, the Council, the European Central Bank, the European Economic and Social Committee and the Committee of the Regions, 'Fintech Action Plan: For A More Competitive and Innovative European Financial Sector' COM (2018) 109 final (8 March 2018).

19 See the European Commission consultation document, 'A New Digital Finance Strategy for Europe/ Fintech Action Plan' (3 April 2020).

20 Regulation (EU) 2020/1503 on European crowdfunding service providers for business, and amending Regulation (EU) 2017/1129 [2020] OJ L 347/1. For a critical insight into the difficulties in agreeing on a final text, given the different approaches followed by the European co-legislators, see Eugenia Macchiavello '"What To Expect When You Are Expecting" A European Crowdfunding Regulation: The Current "Bermuda Triangle" and Future Scenarios for Marketplace Lending and Investing in Europe', EBI Working Paper Series 2019 No 55 <https://ssrn.com/abstract=3493688> accessed 01 December 2020.

(PSD2)[21] required financial institutions to adopt specific technology (Application Programming Interface [API]) in order to meet regulatory requirements relating to the sharing and interoperability of consumer data.

A more comprehensive and ambitious legislative plan is now taking shape. In September 2020, a Commission Communication announced a new digital finance package containing several legislative proposals[22] and a new Digital Finance Strategy for the EU, which further develops the 2018 FinTech action plan.[23]

At national level, there is still little legislative activity covering innovative FinTech business models, products and services.[24] Some countries have introduced specific provisions within the existing legislation and regulation,[25] or have attempted to define new legal categories. However, at times this results in the introduction of overly detailed and burdensome regulatory requirements, which may hinder the development of new products and businesses rather than encourage them.[26] Many activities fall only partially within the current sectoral legislation, which provides for different regimes for banks, investment firms and insurance operators, or for single activities.[27] Whether an activity, service or product is recognised as a financial product or service and is subject to authorisation, registration or other requirements still largely depends on the choices of national legislators. This leaves the regulatory perimeter of FinTech uneven and uncertain, and, at EU level, sees the ESAs mainly entrusted with the task of monitoring ongoing trends, promoting knowledge and experience sharing, facilitating the exchange of information and providing practical guidance to regulators and supervisors. A redefinition of the regulatory and supervisory perimeter is therefore needed, also considering that many FinTech operators outsource cloud computing and data services to third parties, which currently are not covered by regulatory requirements.

The uncertainty of the regulatory perimeter and the gaps in regulatory parameters clearly affect the reach of supervision, which in Europe is currently only partially centralised, and rests mainly with National Competent Authorities (NCAs). For this reason, the recent EU strategy and legislative proposals – albeit aimed at introducing a number of sectoral rather than comprehensive regulations – intend to remove fragmentation and represent an important step towards greater regulatory uniformity.

---

21 Directive (EU) 2015/2366 of the European Parliament and of the Council of 25 November 2015 on payment services in the internal market, amending Directives 2002/65/EC and 2013/36/EU and Regulation (EU) No 1093/2010, and repealing Directive 2007/64/EC [2015] OJ L 337/35.

22 European Commission, which includes the proposal for a new Regulation on Markets in Crypto-Assets (MiCA), a proposal for a Regulation on a Pilot Regime for Market Infrastructures based on Distributed Ledger Technology (DLT Infrastructure Regulation), and a proposal for a regulation on digital operational resilience for the financial sector.

23 European Commission, Communication to the European Parliament, the Council, the European Economic and Social Committee and the Committee of the Regions 'Digital Finance Strategy for the EU' COM (2020) 591 final (24 September 2020).

24 See the EBA report (n 17). Malta has adopted a Virtual Financial Asset Act.

25 For example, in Italy new provisions were inserted into the general financial market legislation (Article 50-*quater*t.u.f.), or individual provisions were stipulated, as with Article 8-ter d.l. no. 135/2018 on distributed ledger technologies and smart contracts.

26 See the Consob Regulation on crowdfunding No 18592 of 26 June 2013 as amended by Decision No 21259 of 6 February 2020.

27 See Macchiavello (n 2).

2.2 *'Structured experimentalism': innovation hubs and sandboxes*

In this scenario, an evolving trend is to provide a flexible and supportive regulatory environment, with the purpose of encouraging the development of FinTech, eliminating obstacles and disseminating good practice, in addition to experimenting with new models before introducing stable regulations.

For this reason, an increasing number of countries have introduced innovation facilitators, through the establishment of regulatory sandboxes[28] or innovation hubs,[29] pilot programs and incubators or innovation offices. At EU level, the European Forum for Innovation Facilitators and the EBA's FinTech Knowledge Hub were set up with the aim of promoting a common understanding of new technologies and their application. Innovation hubs provide firms with non-binding guidance on the conformity of their proposed business models with regulatory requirements, including any regulatory perimeter and authorisation requirements. Most EU Member States have established innovation hubs, while others have so far introduced regulatory sandboxes.[30] The latter are more complex instruments and may require the prior adoption of *ad hoc* legislation and/or regulation.[31] Their key feature is the mutual engagement of financial institutions and supervisory authorities in experiments which allow for the development of innovative business models which can be tested in a controlled environment which takes into account both consumer and data protection issues.[32] The proactive and collaborative quality of the relationship between the regulated entities and the regulators helps the former to understand and comply with

---

28 See the Joint Committee of the ESAs 'Joint Report on FinTech: Regulatory Sandboxes and Innovation Hubs' JC 2018 74 (7 January 2019), whereby regulatory sandboxes are defined as schemes to enable firms to test, pursuant to a specific testing plan agreed and monitored by a dedicated function of the competent authority, innovative financial products, financial services or business models while innovation hubs establish a dedicated point of contact for firms to raise enquiries with competent authorities on FinTech-related issues and to seek non-binding guidance on regulatory and supervisory expectations, including licensing requirements.

29 This is done by providing firms with a contact point for asking questions and initiating dialogue with competent authorities regarding the application of regulatory and supervisory requirements to innovative business models, financial products, services and delivery mechanisms: see the Bank of Italy FinTech Channel or the Project Innovate put in place by the Financial Conduct Authority in the UK.

30 The first and most sophisticated sandbox system is that provided for in the UK since 2016 by the FCA; the USA have a patchy and fragmented picture, since each state has its own regime. The need for a uniform legislation and a federal regulatory sandbox was advocated by Michael M Piri, 'The Changing Landscapes of Fintech and Regtech: Why the United States Should Create a Federal Regulatory Sandbox' (2019) 2 Business and Financial L Rev 233. ROFIEG (n 5), in Recommendation No 14, has advocated the establishment of an EU-level 'regulatory sandbox', taking account of the experience acquired in the context of European Forum for Innovation Facilitators.

31 In Italy a recent statute has provided that a ministerial regulation will set out the requirements for regulatory sandboxes: Article 36, ss 2-bis ff, of l no 58/2019, delegates the Minister of Economy and Finance, after consulting with the Bank of Italy, Consob and IVASS, to adopt a regulation establishing the requirements of regulatory sandboxes in the FinTech sector (the regulation requires currently still approval). The same provision establishes the FinTech Committee, composed of the Ministers of Economy and Finance, Economic development, European Affairs, Bank of Italy, Consob, IVASS, the Competition Authority (AGCM), the Data Protection Authority, the Digital Italy Authority and the Revenue Agency. A similar provision is due to be introduced in Spain through the Draft Law on Measures for the Digital Transformation of the Financial System, currently under approval.

32 Though providing for a more adaptive environment, sandboxes cannot be used to circumvent the application of existing EU and national legislative requirements, nor can they allow regulators to lower the threshold for authorisations and licences.

regulatory requirements and the latter to gain expertise and learn how to focus regulation on the right issues, so as not to hinder the progress of financial innovation and to prevent regulation from becoming a barrier to the entry of new players. One idea behind this is that an adaptive, principles-based regulation[33] could precede the adoption of rules-based regulation, in an environment of structured experimentalism.[34] This approach, in turn, could influence how supervision works in the future. A uniform approach at EU level, through the adoption of a common sandbox model, may prevent regulatory arbitrage and promote a level playing field among operators.[35]

2.3 *Facing new risks*

One of the key issues that recurs frequently is the growing need to assess and mitigate risks appropriately. Increasing operational risks are rightly considered a major concern, with specific regard to cybersecurity and cloud computing. The growing use of technology is likely to result in a greater threat of cyber-attacks. At the same time, the wider use of cloud computing is worsening the risk of excessive concentration of power in the supply of outsourced services across the sector. For this reason, the EU is currently considering the introduction of new rules, which reinforce requirements on incident reporting and Information and Communication Technology (ICT) risk management in order to strengthen cyber resilience.[36] The recently adopted Digital Finance package contains a proposal for a new EU framework for strengthening digital operational resilience.

Big Data and Artificial Intelligence (AI) are used by both financial institutions and regulators to better predict and tackle not only operational, but also more systemic risks, allowing them to adjust micro-and macroprudential regulation and supervision.[37] Even within a technology-neutral approach to regulation, the assessment of licence applications should take into consideration specific FinTech-related risks.[38] Risks are even greater in the so-called alternative finance area of FinTech,[39] where capital loss for investors, fraud, money laundering, exposure of investors to poor-quality financial products and misuse of customer data may represent a threat to financial integrity and consumer protection.

---

33 Which, however, does not come without risks, as argued by Hilary J Allen, 'Regulatory Sandboxes' (2019) 87 Geo Wash L Rev 579, 592, who suggests that principles-based regulation could precede the adoption of rules-based regulation, and that sandboxes should be characterised by rather strict eligibility criteria. On principles-based regulation Julia Black, Martin Hopper and Christa Band, 'Making a Success of Principles-based Regulation' (2007) L and Fin Markets Rev 191.
34 Cemal Karakas and Carla Stamegna, 'Defining an EU Framework for Financial Technology (FinTech): Economic Perspectives and Regulatory Challenges' (2018) 7 Law and Economics Yearly Rev 106, 124.
35 See ROFIEG (n 5), Recommendation No 14.
36 Joint Committee of the ESAs, 'Joint Advice to the European Commission on the Need for Legislative Improvement Relating to ICT Risk Management Requirements in the EU Financial Sector' JC 2019 26 (10 April 2019).
37 The Bank of Italy is using Twitter data as an indicator capable of capturing informational spillover effects across banks and measure the level of trust among depositors: see Matteo Accornero and Mirko Moscatelli, 'Listening to The Buzz: Social Media Sentiment and Retail Depositors' Trust', Bank of Italy Working Paper No 1165 (February 2018).
38 ECB, 'Guide to Assessments of FinTech Credit Institution Licence Applications' (2018).
39 According to the World Bank and CCAF, 'Regulating Alternative Finance: Results from a Global Regulator Survey' (2019), alternative finance refers to financial products that are developing outside the traditional regulated banking and capital market sectors via innovative and predominantly online channels, such as peer-to-peer lending, equity crowdfunding and initial coin offerings.

Data protection issues are arising ever more frequently, due to the increase in data sharing between financial institutions and third-party services providers, as well as to the use of AI tools. Higher standards will be needed to guarantee cybersecurity and adequately protect consumer data.

2.4 *Towards more cooperation, coordination and collaboration*

A crosscutting feature of the evolving scenario is an increasing need for cooperation, coordination and knowledge sharing between regulatory and supervisory authorities.[40]

The absence of a harmonised regulation and the uneven existing framework may give rise to issues related to the cross-border nature of many activities and require a common approach among regulators as well as supranational coordination. Likewise, a balance between a subject-based and an activity-based regulation[41] will need to be found in order to address possible regulatory gaps and arbitrage and this will call for ever closer institutional collaboration and a shared regulatory framework.[42]

Coordination and collaboration are important not only among European supervisory authorities, but also among international and global standard setting bodies, such as the Financial Stability Board, IOSCO, the Basel Committee on Banking Supervision or the Global Financial Innovation Network.[43]

A further important trend is the growing importance of a collaborative approach between supervisors and financial institutions, through either informal dialogues or formal consultations.[44]

Collaboration and forms of partnership between financial institutions and third parties, such as service providers, as well as the creation of industry consortia are also emerging phenomena.[45] Such forms of collaboration develop not only within jurisdictions but also

40 For example, following the ESAs Joint Committee report on Innovations hubs, a European Forum for Innovation Facilitators (EFIF) was established in order to allow supervisors to share experiences, technological expertise and to reach common views.

41 So far an entity-based regulation has been predominant, but jurisdictions often use a combination of the two approaches and a complementary use of both kinds of regulation is often advocated since each of them addresses different risks. The ROFIEG report (n 5), Recommendation No 13, has suggested the adoption of an activity and risk-based regulation, without distinctions between different regulatory standards based on the type of financial institution involved, but rather concentrating on the activity and on the related risks. According to the report, a common regulatory framework should be built on the principle that activities that create the same risks be governed by the same rules. The 'same activities, same risks, same rules' approach has been recently endorsed by the European Commission in the EU Digital Finance Strategy (n 23).

42 International Monetary Fund (IMF), 'Institutional Arrangements for FinTech Regulation and Supervision', FinTech Notes 19/02 (December 2019).

43 See IOSCO, 'Research Report on Financial Technologies (FinTech)' (February 2017) <https://www.iosco.org/library/pubdocs/pdf/IOSCOPD554.pdf> and 'Issues, Risks and Regulatory Considerations relating to Crypto Asset Trading Platforms' (February 2020) <https://www.iosco.org/library/pubdocs/pdf/IOSCOPD649.pdf> accessed 10 March 2020.

44 For example, the consultation conducted by Consob in the preparation of the forthcoming ICO regulation. See also the SSM supervision-industry dialogue at ECB.

45 Chen-Yun Tsang, 'From Industry Sandbox to Supervisory Control Box: Rethinking the Role of Regulators in the Era of FinTech' (2019) U Ill J L Tech & Pol'y 355 has identified four collaboration models: third-party service relationships, like outsourcing arrangements, data sharing arrangements, regulatory experiments and industry consortia.

cross border between different jurisdictions, potentially involving the regulators in a much wider form of cooperation than is common with regulatory sandboxes.

2.5 *The evolution of RegTech*

The growing digitalisation of the financial industry, alongside the increasing proliferation of regulatory requirements has prompted the rise or revamping of RegTech,[46] which has developed as a response of financial institutions to the so-called compliance challenge.[47] RegTech solutions, which are used also in different sectors,[48] allow financial institutions to replace previously manually performed compliance activities with technology-enabled tools and to better tackle risk management issues. It may also play an important role in helping firms to adapt to regulation rather than side-step it.

RegTech is not simply a tool aimed at helping financial institutions to comply with regulations in a less costly and more efficient manner, but it can also allow for the possibility of real-time reporting and thus enable supervisory authorities to better monitor regulated activities and identify abusive conduct earlier.[49] In other words, RegTech has an impact on supervision.

Legal scholars have discussed both the opportunities and the risks associated with RegTech solutions and have also identified possible remedies to the latter.[50] Some of these remedies engage both supervisors and regulators, potentially giving rise to new forms of collaborative partnerships.[51] The cooperative model is already widespread among financial institutions and operators, who have established several independent associations, but it may soon evolve to include regulators.[52] This might result in a shift from an industry-limited phenomenon to a new supervisory approach and to a paradigm shift in the relationship between regulated institutions and supervisors: supervisors could act more as enablers than as mere gatekeepers.

---

46 Douglas W Arner, Janos Barberis and Ross P Buckley, 'FinTech, RegTech and the Reconceptualization of Financial Regulation' (2017) 37 Northwestern J of Intl L and Bus 371, show that RegTech is not a new phenomenon.

47 This is the expression used by Veerle Colaert, 'RegTech as a Response to Regulatory Expansion in the Financial Sector' <https://ssrn.com/abstract=2677116> accessed 10 March 2020.

48 For an overview of the many different areas where RegTech might be deployed, from policing to legal research, see Vicky Wayne 'Regtech: a New Frontier in Legal Scholarship' (2019) 40 Adel L Rev 363.

49 According to Luca Enriques, 'Financial Supervisors and RegTech: Four Roles and Four Challenges' (2017) Revue Trimestrielle de Droit Financier 53, RegTech instruments encompass all the technology which together allows for the aggregation and effective use of amounts of information that flesh-and-blood compliance officers and supervisors could never muster and master.

50 A comprehensive account of the main benefits but also of the risks, which span from systematic errors to excessive standardisation and loss of innovation, to systemic risks, to cybersecurity and data protection, can be found in Colaert (n 47). The author suggests remedies, which in most cases involve the supervisor's role and require a change of attitude towards more cooperation with financial institutions.

51 See the contribution of Yueh-Ping Yang and Cheng-Yun Tsang, 'RegTech and the New Era of Financial Regulators: Envisaging more Public-Private-Partnership Models of Financial Regulators' (2018) 18 U Pa J Bus L 354.

52 For example, the RegTech Council, the RegTech Association, and the International RegTech Association (IRTA). EBA, in the response to the European Commission consultation on the Digital Finance Strategy/Action Plan (June 2020) has suggested the establishment of an industry sponsored RegTech platform.

3 The development of SupTech

In parallel, and partly as a response to the growing phenomena of FinTech and RegTech, supervisors are developing technology-enabled methodologies, which are commonly known as SupTech.[53] RegTech and SupTech are closely connected[54] and hence it is no coincidence that the two expressions are often used interchangeably.[55]

As an umbrella term, SupTech can refer either to the users or to the types of technology used, as well as to the various supervisory activities. In the case of the former, SupTech is currently deployed not only by financial supervisory authorities, but also by non-supervisory authorities.[56] The second refers to the application of Big Data, AI, Machine Learning (ML) and Natural Language Processing (NLP). As for supervisory activities, SupTech has a wide range of possible applications: it can be used in licensing and registering procedures, report monitoring, predictive behavioural and conduct analysis and enforcement, but also in more experimental areas such as sandboxes and blockchain technologies.

So far, however, neither EU nor national law of the Member States has addressed SupTech. Given the absence of specific legislation and of a common taxonomy,[57] SupTech is developing on an experimental basis and at a different pace depending not only on the existing regulatory and supervisory perimeters and parameters, but also on the different level of technological capabilities of supervisory agencies. In many cases, supervisory authorities are still in the process of developing prototypes.

Although SupTech is still at an early stage of development and use, the number of supervisory authorities that are experimenting with it is increasing.[58] Hence four generations of SupTech have been identified in the literature.[59]

---

53 The use of innovative technology by supervisory agencies to support supervision: this broad definition is given by Dirk Broeders and Jermy Prenio, 'Innovative Technology in Financial Supervision (SupTech) – the experience of early users', FSI Insights on policy implementation No 9 (July 2018).

54 The deployment of RegTech mechanisms calls for the use of the same tools and language by the supervisory authorities (RegTech for supervisors). Patrick Armstrong and Alexander Harris, 'RegTech and SupTech-Change for Markets and Authorities' in ESMA 'Report on Trends, Risks and Vulnerabilities' No 1 (2019) 42, draw a distinction between demand drivers, which prompt either financial institutions and supervisory authorities to turn to new technologies, and supply drivers, which stem from the advances in technology and offer new instruments.

55 The ROFIEG recommendations (n 5) refer to RegTech and SupTech without differentiating, and recommend the adoption of standard-based common RegTech and SupTech solutions; in the literature, among many, see Cheng-Yung Tsang, 'A Tentative Analytical Framework and Developing Roadmap for Suptech' (2018) 37 Management Rev 105. In the literature, RegTech refers both to technologies that may be applied in regulation and to technologies that may facilitate the delivery of regulatory requirements.

56 As pinpointed by Simone di Castri, Stefan Hohl, Arend Kulenkampff and Jermy Prenio, 'The Suptech generations', FSI Insights on policy implementation No 19 (October 2019), in respect of financial intelligence units or authorities in charge of monetary or macroeconomic policies.

57 See ROFIEG, Recommendation No 10 (n 5).

58 See ROFIEG, Recommendation No 10 (n 5), for some figures about the degree of deployment of SupTech among financial authorities.

59 According to di Castri et al (n 56), the first generation involves data collection and analysis which require manual work, the second covers the digitisation and automation of paper-based and manual processes, the third engages with big data and a wider automation of data storage and computation, whereas the fourth generation takes automation one step further by using AI in order to manage and analyse data but also to inform the actions of the authority.

So far, the main areas of application of SupTech are that of data collection and data analytics, where it is used not only to monitor compliance but also to identify potential misconduct and market abuse more quickly than in the past.[60] In this area, SupTech complements RegTech by reducing administrative burdens. It also improves supervisory capacity and efficiency by allowing supervisory authorities to collect and analyse greater amounts of granular data faster and to monitor the market in real time. The previously prevalent template-based reporting, based on lengthy and repetitive manual procedures, is replaced by automated reporting systems. The automated data collection mechanisms follow either a data-push (where data are automatically channelled through a central platform) or a data-pull (where the data are extracted directly from the supervised institutions) approach.[61] In addition, it is likely that the reporting activity could soon be supported by the introduction of machine-readable regulations.[62] It has been argued that whereas regulation should remain technology-neutral, supervision should use technology by embracing real-time supervision through the automatic implementation of supervisory measures or even through the participation of supervisors in blockchain technology.[63]

Licence application processing can also benefit from SupTech solutions, which can skim data and flag issues that deserve to be carefully analysed. Data analytics, however, play a major role in conduct analysis, since technologies can provide supervisors with instruments for market surveillance[64] and misconduct assessment, as well as microprudential and macroprudential supervision, thereby influencing the very core of their functions.

In addition, AI, ML and NLP can enhance enforcement capabilities by allowing for a faster analysis of complaints, preparing and/or limiting on-site inspections and better targeting the exercise of sanctioning powers, by reducing false positives.

Concluding from the above, SupTech can be used to oversee financial institutions from market access to conduct supervision, information requirements, prudential supervision and institutional governance.[65] This may entail a certain degree of automation of decisions (so-called algo-supervision).

The overall benefits of SupTech solutions are obvious. They can enhance efficiency and reduce time-consuming repetitive activities, allowing supervisors to focus on matters requiring their human judgment.[66]

---

60 See Armstrong and Harris (n 54) 44.
61 See Toronto Centre, 'FinTech, RegTech and SupTech: What They Mean for Financial Supervision' (August 2017); id, 'SupTech: Leveraging Technology for Better Supervision' (July 2018).
62 The ROFIEG (n 5) (Recommendations Nos 11 and 12) has suggested the adoption of a strategy on how reporting and compliance processes may become both machine-and human-readable but also computable, and, in a longer term, the establishment of a centralised regulatory clearing house, so that compliance and reporting data may be provided back to the supervisors via digital channels.
63 See Raphael Auer, 'Embedded Supervision: How to Build Regulation into Blockchain Finance', BIS Working Papers No 811 (September 2019), who has made a case for the participation of supervisors in the DLT-based market, so that compliance would be automatically monitored by reading the market's ledger.
64 For example, the German Federal Supervisory Authority (BaFin) has put in place an automatic alarm and market monitoring System (ALMA), which performs a variety of pattern recognition functions and allows for the automatic identification of irregularities.
65 Tsang (n 45) 113.
66 Technology can assist through data mining in examining transaction data in order to detect anomalies in the behaviour of market participants, but the assessment of those data and the choice of the right measure will require human supervisors.

These opportunities, however, do not come without operational, institutional and legal risks and challenges.

From an operational point of view, the main risks are:

1 possible errors: the efficacy and accuracy of outcomes depend on the quality of underlying data. Also, algorithms may fail and affect the effectiveness of the final outcome.
2 cybersecurity threats.
3 gaming behaviour of supervised entities, who may try to circumvent supervision.

The most serious challenge for supervisory authorities and their institutional architecture, which is likely to affect the way SupTech is effectively deployed across jurisdictions, lies in the lack of IT skills of the staff and inadequate digital infrastructures.[67] Such development might involve costly investments in resources that in the short run might well outweigh the incoming benefits. In any case, the implementation of SupTech raises issues of institutional design and requires policy decisions and complex procurement procedures[68]. For this reason, collaboration among supervisory authorities should be encouraged and further developed, also through the creation of networks, like the Informal SupTech Network at the Financial Stability Institute, or dedicated platforms, like the SupTech Hub or the SupTech Virtual Lab established at the ECB[69].

With regard to the main legal issues, one major concern is related to the use of data, since the most important application of AI involves the management of structured and unstructured data, which are the common core of every SupTech application, together with the use of algorithms and AI tools.[70]

Another key issue relates to a potential weakening of the rule of law guarantees as a result of automated or quasi-automated decision making. Although the use of technological solutions will not entirely replace human supervisors with machines, it will

---

67 According to Broeders and Prenio (n 53), a tech-oriented rather than a purely finance-legal oriented approach is required. Enriques (n 49) has identified four challenges for supervisors: the human resources challenge (good engineers vs good lawyers and economists); the governance challenge, the cybersecurity challenge and prioritisation and enforcement selection challenge.
68 On this aspect, and other challenges/risks in developing SupTech applications, see FSI, 'The Use of Supervisory and Regulatory Technology by Authorities and Regulated Institutions: market developments and financial stability implications' (9 October 2020). The Commission's Digital Finance Strategy (n 23) mentions the possibility to design targeted assistance programmes with national authorities, that could be done through the Structural Reform Support Programme, that provides tailor-made support to all EU countries for their institutional, administrative and growth-enhancing reforms.
69 The importance of collaboration among supervisors has been recently stressed by the FSI (n 68) 34.
70 At EU level, the ROFIEG (n 5), in Recommendation No 26, has urged a regulatory dialogue between the European Data Protection Board, the European Forum for Innovation Facilitators, national data protection authorities, national and EU competition authorities, national and EU financial regulators and financial supervisors and firms with a view to sharing experiences and promoting a common approach to the regulatory and supervisory choices in the practical application of relevant EU legislation concerning the processing of data. This suggestion has been further developed by the Commission's Digital Finance Strategy, especially in light of the proposed EU digital finance platform (n 23).

prepare and support the human supervisor's judgments.[71] Automated processes will allow the reconstruction of behavioural patterns and data read-across that the human mind would not be able to elaborate at the same speed and with the same presumed accuracy.[72] Technology-enabled activities may also shorten bureaucratic procedures by avoiding burdensome and repetitive manual work in view of the subsequent adoption of human-made decisions, but also carry out some preparatory analysis which could influence the final decisions. On the other side of the spectrum, one might hypothesise that algorithms be used in order to draw up regulation or even to complete the legal provision that defines misconducts for enforcement purposes.[73] Furthermore, there is a risk that AI solutions may allocate risks and misconduct wrongly, resulting in the opacity of decisions and undetectable errors. This would lead to the defying of the rule of law, the principles of legal certainty and the protection of legitimate expectations and human rights,[74] which especially in sanctioning procedures deserve the highest protection.

Procedural, as well as substantial accountability might also be hindered. Compliance with the duty to give reasons could be weakened by black-box effects,[75] which might in turn disguise biases, threatening the requirement of impartiality and transparency. Algorithms, if not properly fed and controlled, could produce decisions which are incomprehensible to the supervisors themselves. Administrative law requires not just public decisions to be correct, but the entire decision-making process to be traceable and accountable.[76] The right to know and understand the reasons behind a decision must also be guaranteed. To this end, 'pure' transparency, that is, simple information may not be sufficient, since 'knowing' is required, not just 'seeing', in other words getting 'meaningful information'.[77] Unless

---

71 For example, see Pentti Hakkarainen, of the Supervisory Board of ECB, 'Supervision in a Digital World: How Modern Technology Is Driving Change', speech at the EBI conference 'Banking in Europe: A Political, a Monetary and a Supervisory Perspective' (14 November 2019) <https://www.bankingsupervision.europa.eu/press/speeches/date/2019/html/ssm.sp191114~766b8e8af0.en.html> accessed 10 March 2020.

72 As Karen Yeung and Martin Lodge, 'Algorithmic Regulation: an Introduction' in Karen Yeung and Martin Lodge (eds), *Algorithmic Regulation* (OUP 2019) underline, algorithmic techniques, applied to large unstructured data sets, are capable of identifying hidden patterns and correlations in the data which would be beyond the capacity of human cognition, or even ordinary computing techniques.

73 On algorithms and regulation see Mireille Hildebrandt, 'Algorithmic Regulation and the Rule of Law' (2018) Phil Trans R S 376.

74 See Council of Europe, 'Algorithms and Human Rights, Study on the Human Rights Dimensions of Automated Data Processing Techniques and Possible Regulatory Implications' DGI (2017)12 (March 2018).

75 This risk has been flagged by Giorgio Gasparri, 'Risks and Opportunities of RegTech and SupTech Developments' (2019) 2 Front Artif Intell 14.

76 Carol Harlow and Richard Rawlings, 'Proceduralism and Automation: Challenges to the Values of Administrative Law' in Elisabeth Fisher Jeff King and Alison Young (eds), *The Foundations and Future of Public Law (Essays in Honour of Paul Craig)* (OUP 2020) 275, argue that 'The speed of decision-making in digital systems will tend to require the diversion of legal control and judicial review away from the individual decision towards the coding of the systems and their overall design'.

77 Cary Coglianese and David Lehr, 'Transparency and Algorithmic Governance' (2019) 71 Administrative L Rev 1, who point out that both 'fishbowl transparency' and 'reasoned transparency' deserve being assured in order to comply with the rule of law and the principle of due process. Even disclosing the source code of a system might not give the data-driven decision rule and therefore would not make automated decisions more accountable.

adequate accountability standards are put in place, the automation of decision-making might even be seen as an unlawful delegation of power.

At the same time, the procedural rights of defence of the affected parties, and the right to an effective remedy, both of which are of utmost importance in sanctioning proceedings, could be endangered.[78] Totally or partially automated processes could prevent the defendant from discovering the facts and evidence on which the final decision was based, making judicial review difficult and unpredictable.[79] A lack of technical expertise in the digital field might also prevent the courts from thoroughly scrutinising the decision-making process, unless supported by experts.

So far, at a legislative level, the problem of automated decision-making and its explainability has been addressed by the EU legislator in the General Data Protection Regulation (GDPR), which in any case concerns the private sector.[80] The issue has recently been lively debated in the legal literature.[81] Some scholars argue that algorithmic accountability is almost impossible to achieve. Others suggest a means by which, with or without opening the black box and trying to account for the internal decision-making process, the addressee of a decision can be given an explanation and grounds for possible subsequent challenges.[82] Some guarantees could be of a more structural kind and would derive from assimilating algorithms to rules, thereby providing a legal framework for participated decision-making, impact assessment procedures and previous publication of proposed regulation.[83] Another possibility would be to ensure that the use of algorithms is oriented by guidelines and standards.

---

78 The need to protect the right of defence and guarantee a fair trial in enforcement and sanctioning decisions has been stressed by the European Court of Human Rights, which requires the exercise of a full jurisdiction involving a thorough scrutiny of both law and fact; eg, cases *Le Compte, Van Leuven and De Meyere v Belgium* (1982) 4 EHRR 1 and *Menarini Diagnostics SRL v Italy* App no 43509/08 (ECtHR, 27 September 2011).

79 In a number of recent cases, the Italian Council of State (judgments No 881/2020 and 2270/2020) established that an algorithm is an essential part of automated decisions and therefore it quashed an administrative decision for breach of the duty to give reasons and of the principle of non-discrimination, since it had not disclosed the algorithm which had been used to decide the place of employment of certain public officials.

80 Regulation (EU) 2016/679 of the European Parliament and of the Council of 27 April 2016 on the protection of natural persons with regard to the processing of personal data and on the free movement of such data, and repealing Directive 95/46/EC [2016] OJ L 119/1 (General Data Protection Regulation) art 22, stating the right of a data subject not to be subject to a decision based solely on automated processing. On automated decision-making, see also European Commission, White Paper on 'Artificial Intelligence. A European Approach to excellence and trust' of 19 February 2020 COM (2020) 65 final, and European Parliament, 'Resolution on automated decision-making processes: ensuring consumer protection and full movement of goods and services' (2019/2015 (RSP)) (10 February 2020). See Celine Castets-Renard, 'Accountability of Algorithms in the GDPR and Beyond: A European Legal Framework on Automated Decision-Making' (2019) 30 Fordham Intell Prop Media & Ent LJ 91, according to whom the goal of algorithmic transparency is not yet successfully ensured in the EU. Margot E Kaminski, 'The Right to Explanation, Explained' (2019) 34 Berkeley Tech LJ 189.

81 Danielle Keats Citron, 'Technological Due Process' (2008) 85 Wash U L Rev 1249.

82 See Sandra Wachter, Brent Mittelstadt and Chris Russell, 'Counterfactual Explanations without Opening the Black Box: Automated Decisions and the GDPR' (2018) 31 Harv J L & Tech 841.

83 Yet the transparency of a rule is not a substitute for individualised review of particular decisions, as argued by Joshua A Kroll, Solon Barocas, Edward W Felten. Joel R Reidenberg and David G Robinson and Harlan Yu, 'Accountable Algorithms' (2017) 165 U Pa L Rev 633, 657.

In conclusion, since it is highly likely that the digitalisation of administrative processes and decisions will advance still further in financial supervision, the search for accountability should be a primary effort, especially considering the strong powers entrusted to national and EU supervisory authorities.

4 Concluding remarks

The rapidly evolving scenario, which has been outlined above, does not allow for definitive conclusions. Instead, some trends and perspectives can be highlighted.

The distinction between regulation and supervision is becoming increasingly blurred: supervision takes place at an earlier stage in the form of corrective action and in the future may even be embedded in regulated activities. Collaborative and cooperative action is gradually replacing reactive and top-down supervision. Through dynamic, real-time and even pre-emptive or predictive supervision, authorities could act not just as gatekeepers, but also as enablers.[84] Enforcement will still be needed, but it might become a last resort supervisory tool.[85]

The increase in the public interests involved in the supervision of financial markets will widen the scope for collaboration not only between sectoral supervisors, but also with other agencies (competition, data protection, etc.). Some provisions are already in place, namely those concerning cooperation and coordination between prudential and Anti-Money Laundering (AML) supervision,[86] but with the expansion of SupTech these may become indispensable. Although some authorities are developing a SupTech strategy,[87] convergence towards a common approach might be desirable.[88] The adoption and the future implementation of the Commission's digital finance package could be an important step towards this goal.

Further developments of SupTech solutions could lead to a gradual shift from the use of technology to support decision-making to the substitution – at least to a certain extent – of human intervention. This may require a new trade-off between efficiency, effectiveness and accountability. To this end, systemic accountability measures, such as expert commissions or *ad hoc* regulators could be provided for, or audits and oversight boards could be established. Such measures ought to be complemented by ex-ante technical requirements and specific procedural provisions aimed to reinforcing individual due process rights.[89] A

---

84 Johannes Ehrentraud, Denise Garcia Ocampo, Lorena Garzoni, Mateo Piccolo, 'Policy responses to fintech: a cross-country overview', FSI Insights on policy implementation No 23 (January 2020) depict Fintech as a tree, whose policy enablers are the roots, enabling technologies are the trunk and Fintech activities are the treetop.

85 See Colaert (n 47) 31.

86 See Basel Committee on Banking Supervision, 'Consultative Document on the Introduction of Guidelines on Interaction and Cooperation between Prudential and AML/CFT Supervision' (November 2019). Regular exchange of information and peer learning between authorities is advocated also by Rogrigo Coelho, Marco De Simoni and Jermy Prenio, 'Suptech applications for anti-money laundering', FSI Insights on policy implementation No 18 (August 2019).

87 In the InsurTech sector, see EIOPA, 'Supervisory Technology Strategy' (February 2020).

88 EBA, in its response to the Commission consultation document on the digital finance strategy (n 19) suggested the creation of the European Strategy for the Supervisory Technology (SupTech).

89 For the distinction and its implications, with a view to the need for both kinds of instruments, see Margot E Kaminski, 'Binary Governance: Lessons from the GDPR's Approach to Algorithmic Accountability' (2019) 92 S Cal L Rev 1529.

further possibility would be to use computational methods to provide procedural account-ability of the automated decision-making. To this aim, closer collaboration between computer and data scientists, policymakers, regulators and supervisors will be crucial, as well as coordination with data and consumer protection authorities. From a legal and institutional point of view, although currently still underdeveloped, this represents a highly sensitive area and deserves the biggest collaborative effort, since it will evolve differently in national jurisdictions, and will potentially pose a serious challenge to the legitimacy and consistency of the overall supervisory architecture.

Bibliography

M Accornero and M Moscatelli, 'Listening to The Buzz: Social Media Sentiment and Retail Depositors' Trust', Bank of Italy's Working Paper No 1165 (February 2018) <https://www.bancaditalia.it/pubblicazioni/temi-discussione/2018/2018-1165/en_tema_1165.pdf?language_id=1> accessed 01 December 2020.

H J Allen, 'Regulatory Sandboxes' (2019) 87 Geo Wash L Rev 579–645.

F Allen, E Faia, M Haliassos and K Langenbucher, *Capital Markets Union and Beyond* (MIT Press 2019).

P Armstrong and A Harris, 'RegTech and Suptech – Change For Markets and Authorities', in ESMA 'Report on Trends, Risks and Vulnerabilities' No 1 (2019) <https://www.esma.europa.eu/sites/default/files/library/esma50-report_on_trends_risks_and_vulnerabilities_no1_2019.pdf > accessed 01 December 2020.

D W Arner, J Barberis and R P Buckley, 'FinTech, RegTech and the Reconceptualization of Financial Regulation' (2017) 37 Northwestern J of Intl L and Bus 371–413.

R Auer, 'Embedded Supervision: How to Build Regulation into Blockchain Finance', BIS Working Papers No 811 (September 2019) <https://www.bis.org/publ/work811.pdf> accessed 01 December 2020.

Bank for International Settlements, Basel Committee on Banking Supervision, 'Consultative Document on the Introduction of Guidelines on Interaction and Cooperation between Prudential and AML/CFT Supervision' (November 2019) <https://www.bis.org/bcbs/publ/d483.pdf> accessed 01 December 2020.

J Black, M Hopper and C Band, 'Making a Success of Principles-Based Regulation' (2007) Law and Financial Markets Rev 191–206.

D Broeders and J Prenio, 'Innovative Technology in Financial Supervision (Suptech) – The Experience of Early Users', Financial Stability Institute (FSI) Insights on Policy Implementation No 9 (July 2018) <https://www.bis.org/fsi/publ/insights9.pdf> accessed 01 December 2020.

C Brummer and Y Yadav, 'Fintech and the Innovation Trilemma' (2019) 107 Geo LJ 235–308.

C Castets-Renard, 'Accountability of Algorithms in the GDPR and Beyond: A European Legal Framework on Automated Decision-Making' (2019) 30 Fordham Intell Prop Media & Ent LJ 91–138.

I H-Y Chiu, 'FinTech and Disruptive Business Models in Financial Products, Intermediation and Markets - Policy Implications for Financial Regulators' (2017) 21 J Tech L & Pol'y 168–223.

D K Citron, 'Technological Due Process' (2008) 85 Wash U L Rev 1249–1314.

R Coelho, M De Simoni and J Prenio, 'Suptech Applications for Anti-Money Laundering', Financial Stability Institute, FSI Insights on Policy Implementation No 18 (August 2019) <https://www.bis.org/fsi/publ/insights18.pdf> accessed 01 December 2020.

C Coglianese and D Lehr, 'Transparency and Algorithmic Governance' (2019) 71 Administrative L Rev 1–51.

V Colaert, 'RegTech as a Response to Regulatory Expansion in the Financial Sector' <https://ssrn.com/abstract=2677116> accessed 10 March 2020.

Council of Europe, 'Algorithms and Human Rights, Study on The Human Rights Dimensions of Automated Data Processing Techniques and Possible Regulatory Implications' DGI (2017) 12 (March 2018).

S di Castri, S Hohl, A Kulenkampff and J Prenio, 'The Suptech Generations', Financial Stability Institute, FSI Insights on Policy Implementation No 19 (July 2019) <https://www.bis.org/fsi/publ/insights19.pdf > accessed 01 December 2020.

EBA, 'Discussion paper on the EBA's approach to Financial Technology (FinTech)' EBA/DP/2017/02 (4 August 2017).

EBA, 'EBA Fintech Roadmap' (15 March 2018) <https://eba.europa.eu/sites/default/documents/files/documents/10180/1919160/79d2cbc6-ce28-482a-9291-34cfba8e0c02/EBA%20FinTech%20Roadmap.pdf> accessed 01 December 2020.

EBA, 'Report on Regulatory Perimeter, Regulatory Status and Authorization Approaches in Relation to FinTech Activities' (18 July 2019).

EBA, 'The Impact of Fintech on Payment Institutions' and E-Money Institutions' Business Models' (July 2019).

EBA, 'Big Data and Advanced Analytics' EBA/REP/2020/01 (January 2020).

EBA, 'Response to the European Commission Consultation on the Digital Finance Strategy/Action Plan' (June 2020).

ECB, 'Guide to Assessments of Fintech Credit Institution Licence Applications' (2018).

J Ehrentraud, D Garcia Ocampo, L Garzoni and M Piccolo, 'Policy Responses to Fintech: A Cross-Country Overview', Financial Stability Institute, FSI Insights on Policy Implementation No 23 (January 2020) <https://www.bis.org/fsi/publ/insights23.pdf> accessed 01 December 2020.

EIOPA, 'Supervisory Technology Strategy' (February 2020) <https://www.eiopa.europa.eu/content/supervisory-technology-strategy_en> accessed 01 December 2020.

European Commission, Communication to the European Parliament, the Council, the European Central Bank, the European Economic and Social Committee and the Committee of the Regions, 'Fintech Action Plan: For a more Competitive and Innovative European Financial Sector' COM (2018) 109 final (8 March 2018).

European Commission, Communication to the European Parliament, the Council, the European Central Bank, the European Economic and Social Committee and the Committee of the Regions, White Paper on 'Artificial Intelligence. A European Approach to excellence and trust' COM (2020) 65 final (19 February 2020).

European Commission, Communication to the European Parliament, the Council, the European Central Bank, the European Economic and Social Committee and the Committee of the Regions, Consultation document, 'A new digital Finance Strategy for Europe/Fintech Action Plan' (3 April 2020).

European Commission, Communication to the European Parliament, the Council, the European Economic and Social Committee and the Committee of the Regions, 'Capital Markets Union for People and Businesses - New Action Plan' COM (2020) 590 final (24 September 2020).

European Commission, Communication to the European Parliament, the Council, the European Economic and Social Committee and the Committee of the Regions, 'Digital Finance Strategy for the EU' COM (2020) 591 final (24 September 2020).

European Parliament, 'Resolution on Automated Decision-Making Processes: Ensuring Consumer Protection and Full Movement of Goods and Services' (2019/2015 (RSP)) (10 February 2020).

Expert Group on Regulatory Obstacles on Financial Innovation (ROFIEG), 'Thirty Recommendations on Regulation, Innovation and Finance', Report to the European Commission (December 2019).

Financial Stability Board, 'Financial Stability Implications from Fintech. Supervisory and Regulatory Issues That Merit Authorities' Attention' (27 June 2017).

Financial Stability Board, 'Decentralised Financial Technologies. Financial Stability, Regulatory and Governance Implications' (6 June 2019).

Financial Stability Board, 'The Use of Supervisory and Regulatory Technology by Authorities and Regulated Institutions: market developments and financial stability implications' (9 October 2020).

C Ford, *Innovation and the State* (CUP 2017).

G Gasparri, 'Risks and Opportunities of RegTech and SupTech Developments' (2019) 2 Front Artif Intell 14.

P Hakkarainen, 'Supervision in a Digital World: How Modern Technology is Driving Change', Speech at the EBI Conference 'Banking in Europe: A Political, a Monetary and a Supervisory Perspective' (14 November 2019).

C Harlow and R Rawlings, 'Proceduralism and Automation: Challenges to the Values of Administrative Law' in E Fisher, J King and A Young (eds), *The Foundations and Future of Public Law (Essays in Honour of Paul Craig)* (OUP 2020) 275.

M Hildebrandt, 'Algorithmic Regulation and the Rule of Law' (2018) Phil Trans R S 376.

International Monetary Fund (IMF), 'Institutional Arrangements for FinTech Regulation and Supervision', FinTech Notes 19/02 (December 2019).

IOSCO, 'Research Report on Financial Technologies (FinTech)' (February 2017).

IOSCO, 'Issues, Risks and Regulatory Considerations Relating to Crypto Asset Trading Platforms' (February 2020).

Joint Committee of the ESAs, 'Joint Report on FinTech: Regulatory Sandboxes and Innovation Hubs' JC 2018 74 (7 January 2019).

Joint Committee of the ESAs, 'Joint Advice to the European Commission on the Need for Legislative Improvement Relating to ICT Risk Management Requirements in the EU Financial Sector' JC 2019 26 (10 April 2019).

M E Kaminski, 'The Right to Explanation, Explained' (2019) 34 Berkeley Tech LJ 189–218.

M E Kaminski, 'Binary Governance: Lessons from the GDPR's Approach to Algorithmic Accountability' (2019) 92 S Cal L Rev 1529–1616.

C Karakas and C Stamegna, 'Defining an EU Framework for Financial Technology (Fintech): Economic Perspectives and Regulatory Challenges' (2018) 7 Law and Economics Yearly Rev 106–129.

J A Kroll, S Barocas, E W Felten, J R Reidenberg, D G Robinson and H Yu, 'Accountable Algorithms' (2017) 165 U Pa L Rev 633–706.

E Macchiavello, '"What to Expect When You Are Expecting" a European Crowdfunding Regulation: The Current "Bermuda Triangle" and Future Scenarios for Marketplace Lending and Investing in Europe', EBI Working Paper Series 2019 No 55 <https://ssrn.com/abstract=3493688> accessed 01 December 2020.

E Macchiavello, 'FinTech Regulation from a Cross-Sectoral Perspective' in V Colaert, D Busch and T Incalza (eds), *European Financial Regulation: Levelling the Cross-Sectoral Playing Field* (Hart 2019) 63–85.

M M Piri, 'The Changing Landscapes of FinTech and RegTech: Why the United States Should Create a Federal Regulatory Sandbox' (2019) 2 Business and Financial L Rev 233–255.

W-G Ringe, L Morais and D Ramos, 'A Holistic Approach to the Institutional Architecture of Financial Supervision and Regulation in the EU' in V Colaert et al (eds), *European Financial Regulation: Levelling the Cross-Sectoral Playing Field* (Hart 2019) 405–429.

Toronto Centre, 'FinTech, RegTech and SupTech: What They Mean for Financial Supervision' (August 2017).

Toronto Centre, 'SupTech: Leveraging Technology for Better Supervision' (July 2018).

C-Y Tsang, 'A Tentative Analytical Framework and Developing Roadmap for Suptech' (2018) 37 Management Rev 105–120.

C-Y Tsang, 'From Industry Sandbox to Supervisory Control Box: Rethinking the Role of Regulators in the Era of FinTech' (2019) U Ill J L Tech & Pol'y 355–404.

S Wachter, B Mittelstadt and C Russell, 'Counterfactual Explanations without Opening the Black Box: Automated Decisions and the GDPR' (2018) 31 Harv J L & Tech 841–888.

V Wayne, 'Regtech: A New Frontier in Legal Scholarship' (2019) 40 Adel L Rev 363–386.

World Bank and Cambridge Center for Alternative Finance, 'Regulating Alternative Finance: Results from a Global Regulator Survey' (2019) <https://www.jbs.cam.ac.uk/wp-content/uploads/2020/08/2019-11-ccaf-regulating-alternative-finance-report.pdf> accessed 01 December 2020.

World Bank and Cambridge Centre for Alternative Finance, 'The Global Covid-19 Fintech Regulatory Rapid Assessment Study' (2020) <https://www.jbs.cam.ac.uk/faculty-research/centres/alternative-finance/publications/2020-global-covid-19-fintech-regulatory-rapid-assessment-study> accessed 01 December 2020.

Y-P Yang and C-Y Tsang, 'RegTech and the New Era of Financial Regulators: Envisaging More Public-Private-Partnership Models of Financial Regulators' (2018) 18 U Pa J Bus L 354–404.

K Yeung and M Lodge, 'Algorithmic Regulation: An Introduction' in Karen Yeung and Martin Lodge (eds), *Algorithmic Regulation* (OUP 2019).

D A Zetzsche, R P Buckley, J N Barberis and D W Arner, 'Regulating a Revolution: From Regulatory Sandboxes to Smart Regulation' (2017) 23 Fordham J Corp & Fin L 31–104.

Index

For Product Safety Concerns and Information please contact our EU
representative GPSR@taylorandfrancis.com Taylor & Francis Verlag GmbH,
Kaufingerstraße 24, 80331 München, Germany

Printed and bound by CPI Group (UK) Ltd, Croydon, CR0 4YY
27/03/2025
01837504-0001